ENGLISH TRANSLATION OF THE MESSAGE OF

THE QURAN

Translated By:
Professor (Dr.) Syed Vickar Ahamed

Delivering THE MESSAGE of THE QURAN to you

Your Source of Authentic Islamic Literature

1) TO ORDER COPIES OF THIS TRANSLATION
2) TO REQUEST ADDITIONAL INFORMATION AND LITERATURE ON
QURAN, ISLAM AND MUSLIMS
3) TO HAVE YOUR QUESTIONS ANSWERED
Contact us at:
1-888-BSF-2754
Quran@bookofsigns.org
http://www.bookofsigns.org

Published By:
Book of Signs Foundation
Delivering THE MESSAGE of THE QURAN to you™
Your Source of Authentic Islamic Literature
444 E. Roosevelt Rd, Suite 173, Lombard, IL 60148, USA
Tel: (888)-BSF-2754 (888-273-2754)
Email: Quran@bookofsigns.org - Web: http://www.bookofsigns.org

Translation Approval
This translation of the Message of The Quran has been approved by:

AL-AZHAR
ISLAMIC RESEARCH ACADEMY
GENERAL DEPARTMENT FOR
RESEARCH, WRITING & TRANSLATION
Cairo, Egypt
&
PUSAT ISLAM (CENTER FOR ISLAM)
Kuala Lumpur Malaysia

A copy of the certificates of approval are available upon request

Translated By:
Syed Vickar Ahamed
www.ahamed.org

ISBN 0-9773009-0-0
ISBN 978-0-9773009-0-7

Printed in USA

Foreword

Please Note: The Quran sometimes written as Koran; is the Sacred Book of the Muslims. Muslims believe that God revealed His word and message to humanity through out the ages. For example, we believe that Moses was given the Torah, David was given the Pslams, and Jesus was given the Gospel. In the same way we believe Muhammad was given the Quran. Due to this belief, Muslims treat the books of other faiths with great care and respect. For instance we do not read these books in bathrooms or even place them on the floor, or handle them unless we are in a state of personal cleanliness. It is our request that you also treat this book with the same respect and handle it as you would your own scripture.

The aim of The Book of Signs Foundation is to bring the message of the Quran to you, free of the political agendas and religious anti-Islam propagandas that have dominated the airwaves and print media. Our goal is to provide direct-to-you a source of authentic information that brings to light the message of the Quran in order that you may judge for yourself the Quranic message. A message that is the principle source of guidance for over 1.2 billion people all over the world that call themselves Muslims.

Sources portraying themselves as honest brokers of information like the news media often take liberties when presenting verses from the Quran without any thought to the context of the verse. Now that you have a copy of this English translation of the Quran we humbly request you to do the following:

When you hear someone say something about what is mentioned in the Quran;

1) Ask for an exact reference in the form of Surah (chapter) and verse number
2) Try to approach the Quran with an open mind – Don't just rely on the so called "expert" opinions you may have heard. Form your own opinion
3) Read a few verses before and after the specific verse so as to get an idea of the context of what is being said and why
4) If you are not sure of the meaning, ask someone who knows – we will be glad to answer any questions. Just as you would go to a Christian to ask questions about Christianity or a Jew to ask about Judaism or a Pandit to ask about Hinduism, why not do the same when it comes to the Quran, Islam or Muslims? Call or email us

What you have here in your possession is the *translation of the Message* of the Glorious and Noble Quran. It is the best effort of an individual to explain, as closely as possible, the meaning from the Arabic language. It is however *NOT* THE QURAN. The Quran was, is, and forever shall be, in ARABIC only[1]. To truly understand the meaning of the Quran one must learn Arabic. The power and impact that the original verses carry, cannot be duplicated in any other language. This

---

[1] The emphasis in not on the language of Arabic, but that the original Quran is in Arabic and so the emphasis is on its preservation. Muslims pride themselves on the fact that they have a holy book still in its pure and original form. It may well be said that it is the fountain-head of the Muslim faith

translation is an attempt to bring the Glory of the Message to those who speak and know only the English language.

It surprises readers to know that the Quran as revealed to Prophet Muhammad (pbuh) 1400 years ago is word-for-word preserved in the Arabic language without an iota of change. This can easily be verified by picking up copies of the Quran in Arabic anywhere in the world and comparing them. Not only is the written text not changed, but MILLIONS of Muslims around the world have committed the entire Arabic text to memory from cover to cover, whether they speak Arabic or not. This mechanism has been in place since its revelation 1400 years ago to ensure that the Quran is free from any tampering and manipulation.

In handling this translation of the Quran we humbly request the following guidelines to be followed:

1) Please remember this is a religious scripture and handle it as you would your own religious scripture
2) Please handle this copy with respect and in a state of personal cleanliness
3) If you do not want this copy, please do not throw it away. You may give to any Muslim you know or your nearest Islamic Center. You may also call us at 1-888-BSF-2754 and we will arrange to pick it up

One who is new to the Quran will find that this copy may not conform to his/her concept of a book. Unlike conventional books, the Quran does not contain information and ideas arranged in literary order. Nor is it a historical account as one may be accustomed to in other scriptures. The Quran presents a complete way of life, a moral code that governs all aspects of life. It defines the creed, expounds moral instruction, admonishes believers and non-believers, invites people to explore, question and validate truths, gives glad tidings of the after life, lays down laws and draws lessons from historical events. With such a vastness of topics covered a reader will find that topics are woven together in an intricate web of subjects that may at times seem confusing. It therefore is a recognized fact that reading this book in a traditional sequence is not essential to understanding the message. A reader may search for familiar words like Jesus (Isa) or Mary or Joseph in the index as a start.

We hope that whether you believe this to be a revealed book or not you will find important guidance from this divine book, and remove previously conceived biases against the Quran, Islam[2] and Muslims[3]. We pray that God Almighty guide us all to His straight path and ultimate salvation.

Sh. Abdur Rahman Khan
Scholar in Residence
Islamic Foundation, Villa Park, Illinois, USA

---

[2] Islam is a lifestyle with a specific moral and legal code of conduct. Islam means submission, submission to God.
[3] Those who profess to follow the Islamic lifestyle are called Muslims. The word Muslim mean the one who has submitted.

Preface

By: Dr. Zakir Naik
President, Islamic Research Foundation

Islam is an Arabic word. It comes from the word '*Salm*' which means peace and from the word '*Silm*', which means submitting your will to Allah – Almighty God. Thus, Islam means peace acquired by submitting your will to Allah (swt[4]). A Muslim is a person who submits his/her will to Allah – the Almighty God.

Many people have a misconception that Islam is a new religion that was formulated about 1400 years ago, and that Prophet Muhammad (pbuh[5]) was the founder of Islam. However, Islam is not the name of some unique religion presented for the first time by Prophet Muhammad (pbuh). Prophet Muhammad (pbuh) was not the founder of Islam but he was the last and final messenger of Allah (swt) sent to earth. Almighty God revived through him the same genuine faith, which had been conveyed by all His previous Prophets.

The Quran states that Islam – the complete submission of man before his only Unique Creator – is the only faith and way of life consistently revealed by God to humankind from the very beginning. Noah, Abraham, Isaac, David, Solomon, Moses, and Jesus – prophets (peace be on them all) who appeared at different times and places - all propagated the same faith and conveyed the same message of *Tawheed* (Oneness of God), *Risaalat* (Prophet hood) and *Aakhirah* (the Hereafter). These prophets of God were not founders of different religions to be named after them. They were each reiterating the message and faith of their predecessors.

Islam thus makes it an article of faith to believe in all the earlier prophets, starting with Adam, and continuing with Noah, Abraham, Ishmael, Isaac, Jacob, Moses, David and Jesus amongst many others (may peace be on them all).

However, Muhammad (pbuh) was the last Prophet of God conveying the same message as all earlier Prophets. This original message had been corrupted and it split into various religions by people of different ages, who indulged in interpolations and admixture. God eliminated these alien elements, and Islam – in its pure and original form – was transmitted to humankind through Prophet Muhammad (pbuh). Hence, Islam is the culmination of the same Divine religion of God to humankind since the advent of humanity, purged and purified, from all human adulterations and restored to its original purity.

Since there was to be no messenger after Prophet Muhammad (pbuh), the Book revealed to him (i.e. the Glorious Quran) was preserved word for word so that it should be the same source of guidance for all times.

Thus the religion of all the prophets was 'total submission to God's will' and one word for that in the Arabic language is 'Islam'. Abraham and Jesus (peace be upon them) too were Muslims, as Allah testifies in the Quran 3:67 and 3:52 respectively.

---

[4] Out of reverence to Almighty God, the suffix (swt) is added to affirm His Purity and His Uniqueness

[5] Out of appreciation and respect for Prophet Muhammad (or any of the prophets), the suffix (pbuh) is added to pray to Allah to bestow peace upon him (or any of the other prophets)

It is mentioned in the Quran, "Surely, We have sent you with the truth, as a bearer of happy news, and as a Warner: And there were never any people, without a Warner who did not live among them (in the past)" [35.24]

At the same time, the Quran says, "And the messengers We have already told you before, and others We have not (told you)." [4.164]

It means that some of the Prophets have been mentioned by name in the Quran while of the others there is no mention. Twenty-five messengers are specifically mentioned in the Quran. One of the followers of the Prophet (pbuh) named Abu Dhar asked: 'O Messenger of Allah, altogether how many messengers were sent?' The Prophet (pbuh) said, 'One hundred and twenty four thousand'." [Mishkat-Ul-Masabih, authenticated by Shaikh Nasiruddun Albani, Vol. 3, Pg. No. 1599, Hadith No. 5737]

However, all the messengers that came before the last and final messenger Prophet Muhammad (pbuh) came with a message that was meant only for a particular period of time[6].

For example, the Quran says, "And (We appointed Jesus) a messenger to the Children of Israel:" [3.49]

Jesus (pbuh) came as a messenger only to the children of Israel. A similar message is given in the Bible where Jesus (pbuh) says, "I am not sent but unto the lost sheep of the house of Israel." [Gospel of Matthew 15:24]

Jesus (pbuh) further says in the Bible. "Go not into the way of the Gentiles, and into any city of the Samaritans enter ye not: but go rather to the lost sheep of the house of Israel." [Gospel of Matthew 10:5-6]. So Jesus (pbuh) was sent only for the Jews and not for the whole of humanity.

However, Prophet Muhammad (pbuh) was not sent only for the Muslims or only for the Arabs, but for the entire humankind. The Quran says, "And We did not send you (O Prophet), except as a mercy to all worlds." [21.107]

"And We have not sent you (O Muhammad) except as one to give them good news, and to warn them (of the punishment; As a messenger and a guide to mankind), but most men do not understand." [34.28]. The religion of all the prophets was 'total submission to God's Will' and the one word for that in the Arabic language is 'Islam'; and the person who does that is a 'Muslim'.

Allah (swt) says in the Quran that Abraham (pbuh) was a Muslim. "Ibrahim (Abraham) was neither a Jew nor even a Christian; But he was true in Faith, and surrendered his will to Allah's, (like a Muslim) and He did not join gods with Allah." [3.67]

It is mentioned in the Quran that Jesus (pbuh) was a Muslim [3.52]. Jesus (pbuh) also says in the Bible. "I seek not my own will, but the will of the Father which hath sent me." [Gospel of John 5:30]. And anybody who seeks the Will of God is referred to as a Muslim.

Islam is the first religion and the only religion, which is acceptable in the sight of God. Therefore Allah (swt) says: "If anyone desires a religion other than Islam (submission to Allah), it will never be accepted from him; In the Hereafter, he will

---

[6] There are three exceptions to this, Adam (pbuh), Abraham (pbuh), and Prophet Muhammad (pbuh)

be with those who have lost (all spiritual reward)." [3.85]

Allah (swt) has sent a revelation in every age. Allah (swt) says in the Quran, "Allah permitted (or ordered, for) each period is a Book (revealed)." [13.38]

There are several revelations sent by Allah (swt) in different ages for the guidance of human beings of the respective ages. Only four revelations are mentioned by name in the Quran. These are the Torah, Zabur, Injeel and the Quran.

Torah is the revelation that was revealed to Prophet Moses (pbuh). Zabur is the revelation that was revealed to Prophet David (pbuh). Injeel is the revelation which was revealed to Prophet Jesus (pbuh) and the Quran is the last and the final revelation, that was revealed to the Last and Final Messenger Prophet Muhammad (pbuh).

The Arabic word 'Quran' comes from the root word '_qara'a_' or '_qa- ra-a_', which means to read, to recite, and to proclaim. The Quran is a collection to be read or to be recited.

Since there was to be no messenger after Muhammad (pbuh), the book revealed to him (i.e., the Quran) was preserved word for word so that it should be a source of Divine Guidance for all times. Each of the revelations, prior to the revelation of the Quran, was meant only for a particular period and for a particular group of people.

As the Quran was the last and final revelation of Almighty Allah, it was revealed not just for Muslims or Arabs but it was revealed for the whole of Humankind. Further, the Quran was not revealed only for the era of the Prophet but it was revealed for all of Humankind until the Last Day.

Allah (swt) says in the Quran, "...A Book (the Quran) which We have revealed to you, (O Prophet!) so that you may lead mankind from the depths of darkness into Light- By the permission of their Lord- To the Path (towards Him), the Exalted in Power, the (One) Worthy of all Praise" [14.1]

"The month of Ramadan is the (month) in which was sent down the Quran as a guide to mankind, also Clear (Signs for) guidance and judgment (between right and wrong)" [2.185].

ISLAM AND UNIVERSAL BROTHERHOOD

There are various types of brotherhoods - brotherhood based on blood relations, brotherhood based on regional affiliations, or brotherhood on the basis of race, caste, creed, ideology, etc. But all these types of brotherhood are limited in their scope, coverage and benefits.

Islam, on the other hand, prescribes Universal Brotherhood. It rejects the thought that human beings have been created in castes or in different levels. In Surah The Inner Apartments (of the Prophet) _Al-Hujurat_ [49:13], Allah (SWT) describes the Islamic concept of Universal Brotherhood.

"O mankind! We have created you from a single (pair) of male and female, and made you into nations and tribes, that you may know one another (not that you may hate each other). Surely, the most honorable of you, in the Sight of Allah is (he, who is) the most righteous of you. Verily, Allah is All Knowing and is Well-Aware (of all things)."

This verse of the Quran indicates that the entire human race originated from a single pair of male and female. All humans have common great-grandparents and ancestors.

Further, Allah (swt) says that he has made nations and tribes, so that humans can recognize each other, and not so that they may despise each other and fight amongst themselves.

This verse also clarifies that the criteria for judgment in the sight of Allah (swt) does not depend on caste, color, creed, gender or wealth, but on *Taqwa* i.e. God's consciousness, piety and righteousness. Anyone who is righteous, pious and God-conscious is honored in the sight of Allah (swt).

Further it is stated in Surah The Romans - *Ar-Rum* [30.22], that, "And among His Signs is the creation of the heavens and the earth, and the difference in your languages, and your colors. Surely, there are signs in this for those who know."

These variations in color and language are not for the purpose of creating animosity or differences between groups of humans. Every language on earth has its own beauty and significance. A foreign language may sound strange and funny to you, but it sounds sweet to those who speak it.

Allah says in Surah The Night Journey - *Al-Isra* [17.70], "We have honored the children of Adam." Allah has not honored only Arabs or Americans or any particular race uniquely. He states that He has honored all the children of Adam, irrespective of race, caste, color, creed or gender.

While there are some religions that believe that humankind originated from a single pair - Adam and Eve (peace be upon them), there are some faiths that say, that it is because of the sin of the woman (Eve -may Allah be pleased with her) that the humans are born in sin. They blame only the woman, who is Eve, for the downfall of human beings. The Quran speaks about the story of Adam and Eve (peace be upon them) in several Surahs, but in all the places, the blame is placed equally on both - Adam and Eve (peace be upon them). According to Surah The Heights - *Al-A'raf* [7.19-27], both of them disobeyed Allah (swt), both of them repented, and both were forgiven.

Both are equally blamed for the mistake. There is not a single verse in the Quran, which puts the blame only on Eve (may Allah be pleased with her). In Surah Ta Ha (Quranic Letters) *Taha* [20.121], it is stated that Adam (pbuh) disobeyed Allah (swt). Certain faiths, on the other hand state that because Eve disobeyed God, she is responsible for the 'sin of humankind'. Hence, God cursed the woman, and said that she will bear labor pains. This implies that pregnancy is a curse.

Islam of course does not support this unjust perspective. In Surah The Women – *An-Nisa* [4.1], Allah states, "And revere (and respect) the wombs (that bore you):" In Islam, pregnancy does not degrade a woman. On the contrary, it elevates the status of a woman. In Surah The Wise (or the person Luqman) - *Luqman* [31.14], it is stated that, "And We have commanded man (to be good) to his parents: In weakness and hardship his mother bore him, and in two years (after) was his weaning:"

The Quran says in Surah The Winding Sand Tracts - *Al-Ahqaf* [46.15], " And We have commanded that it is essential for man to be kind to his parents: In pain did his mother bear him, and in pain did she give him birth."

Islam states that men and women are created equal. The foundation of an Islamic society is justice and equity. Allah has created men and women as equal, but with different capabilities and different responsibilities. Men and women are different, physiologically and psychologically. Their roles and responsibilities are different. Men and women are equal in Islam, but not identical.

According to a Hadith mentioned in Sahih Bukhari, Vol.No. 8, in the Book of Adab, Chapter 2, Hadith No. 2.

"A person came to Prophet Mohammed (saw), and asked him, 'Who is the person who deserves the maximum love and companionship in this world?'

The Prophet replied, 'Your mother.'

The man asked, 'Who next?'

The Prophet said, 'Your mother.'

The man asked, 'After that who?'

The Prophet repeated for the third time, 'Your mother.'

The man asked, 'After that who?'

Then the Prophet said, 'Your father.'"

So, 75% or 3/4 of the love and companionship of the children are due to the mother and only 25% or 1/4 of the love and companionship goes to the father. In other words, the mother gets the gold medal, she gets the silver medal, as well as the bronze medal. The father has to be satisfied with a mere consolation prize.

Amongst the teachings of Islam, it is stated that men and women are equal - but being equal does not mean that both are identical. There are many misconceptions about the status of women in Islam. Such misconceptions can be removed if one studies the authentic sources of knowledge of Islam and their teachings - the Quran and the Sahih Hadith. Let's take an example. In a class, two students - student 'A' and 'B' get the highest marks in a subject, say - 80 out of 100. The question paper consisted of 10 questions, each of 10 marks. In the first answer student 'A' gets 9 out of 10, student 'B' gets 7 out of 10. So in question 1 student 'A' has a degree of advantage than student 'B'. In question 2, student 'B' gets 9 out of 10, and student 'A' gets 7 out of 10. So in question 2, student 'B' has a degree of advantage, than student 'A'. In the remaining 8 questions, both get 8 out of 10, and if you total the marks of both students, both get 80 out of 100. So if you analyze, both student 'A' and 'B' have got over all equal marks. But in answers to some questions, student 'A' has a degree of advantage and in answers to some other questions, student 'B' has a degree of advantage - but in terms of overall marks, both are equal. Similarly, in Islam, men and women are equal.

As another example, if a robber enters my house, I will not say, 'I believe in women's rights, and I believe in women's liberation and therefore my sister, my wife or my mother, should go and fight the robber.'

Allah says in Surah The Women – _An-Nisa_ [4.34], "Allah has given the one more (strength) than the other." Normally, men have more strength than the women. So where strength is concerned, men have a degree of advantage. Since they have been given more strength, it is their duty to protect women.

Where love and companionship from children is concerned, the mother gets three times more love and companionship than the father. Here women have a degree of advantage.

Brotherhood in Islam does not only mean that the same sexes are equal. 'Universal Brotherhood' in Islam means, that besides race, caste, and creed, even the sexes are overall equal. Men and women are equal in Islam, but in some aspects, men have a degree of advantage while in some other aspects, women have a degree of advantage - but overall both are equal.

THE MIRACLE OF PROPHET MUHAMMAD (PBUH)

QURAN, IS FOR ALL TIMES

The miracles performed by the previous prophets such as parting of sea by Prophet Moses (pbuh), giving life to the dead by Prophet Jesus (pbuh), etc. convinced the people of that time but these miracles cannot be analyzed and verified by us today.

Prophet Muhammad (pbuh) is the last and final Messenger of God, sent for the whole of humankind and the message he delivered is for eternity.

Therefore, the miracle of the last and final Messenger should also be everlasting, examinable and verifiable by people of all ages. While Prophet Muhammad (pbuh) performed several miracles as are mentioned in the Hadith (recorded traditions, sayings and actions of the Prophet), he never emphasized them. Though we Muslims believe in these miracles we only boast of the ultimate miracle given to him by Almighty God, which is the Quran.

The Quran is the miracle of all times which proved itself to be a miracle 1400 years ago and which can be reconfirmed today and forever. In short, it is the Miracle of Miracles.

LOGICAL CONCEPT OF GOD

The first question to the atheist is: "What is the definition of God?" For a person to say there is no God, he should know what the meaning of God is. Suppose I hold a book and say 'this is a pen'. The opposite person should know the definition of a pen for him to refute and say that it is not a pen. In a similar manner, for an atheist to say 'there is no god', he should at least know the concept of God. His concept of God is derived from the surroundings in which he lives or has been brought up. The deity that people worship has human qualities and hence he does not believe in such a god. Similarly, a Muslim too does not believe in such false gods.

CONCEPT OF GOD ACCORDING TO SURAH THE PURITY OF FAITH – Al-IKHLAS

The best definition, of Almighty God, that you can find in the Quran is in the four verses of Surah The Purity of Faith - *Al-Ikhlaas*, [112]

112.1. "Say: He is Allah, The One (*Ahad,* and Only One)."

112.2. "Allah the Eternal (*Samad,* the Ever Enduring),

The Absolute (and Alone);"

112.3. "He begets not (has no descendents, no children, none),

Nor was He (ever) begotten;"

112.4. "And there is none like (or comparable) unto Him."

This is a four-line statement about Almighty Allah according to Quran. If any candidate claims to be God and satisfies this definition, Muslims have no objection in accepting such a candidate as god. This Surah The purity of Faith - *Al-Ikhlaas* is the acid test – it is the *'Furqaan'* or the criteria to judge between the One True God and the false claimants to divinity. Whichever deity that any human being on the face of this earth worships – if that deity fulfils these four criteria then such a deity is none else than the one true God.

a. *It is the touchstone of Theology*

Surah The Purity of Faith - *Al-Ikhlaas* [112] is the touchstone of Theology. 'Theo' in Greek means God and 'logy' means study. Thus 'Theology' means 'study of God' and Surah The Purity of Faith - *Al-Ikhlaas* is the touchstone of the study of God.

If you want to purchase or sell your gold jewelry, you would first evaluate it. A goldsmith with the help of a touchstone does such an evaluation of gold jewelry. He rubs the gold jewelry on the touchstone and compares its color with rubbing samples of gold. If it matches with 24 Karat gold, he will say that your jewelry is 24 Karat pure gold. If it is not high quality pure Gold, he will tell you its value - whether it is 22 Karats, 18 Karats or it may not be gold at all. It may be fake because everything that glitters is not gold.

Similarly Surah The Purity of Faith - *Al-Ikhlaas* [112] is the touchstone of theology, which can verify whether the deity that you worship is a true God or a false God. If any one claims to be, or is believed to be Almighty God, and satisfies this four-line definition, then not only will Muslims readily accept that deity as God but this deity is worthy of all worship and is the One True God.

For example, if some one says that Bhagwaan Rajneesh or 'Osho' is Almighty God, lets apply the test.

b. *Is Rajneesh God?*

Let us put this candidate Rajneesh to the test of Divinity as prescribed by Surah The Purity of Faith - *Al-Ikhlaas* [112], the touchstone of Divinity.

(i) The First Criterion is "Say, 'He is Allah One and Only'". Is Rajneesh One and Only? We know several such fake god-men and claimants of divinity amongst humans. Rajneesh is surely not the one and only. However, some disciples of Rajneesh may still state that Rajneesh is unique and that he is the one and only.

(ii) Let us analyze the second criterion "Allah the Absolute and Eternal." Is Rajneesh absolute and eternal? We know from his biography that he suffered from diabetes, asthma, and chronic backache. He alleged that the U.S.A. government gave him slow poison while he was in their jail. Imagine! Almighty God being poisoned! Moreover, all are aware that Rajneesh died and was cremated / buried. So Rajneesh was neither eternal, nor absolute

(iii) The third Criteria is "He begets not, nor is begotten". However, Rajneesh was begotten. He was born in Jabalpur in India. Like all humans, he too had a mother and a father. Later on they chose to become his disciples.

Rajneesh was a very intelligent person. In May 1981 he went to U.S.A. He established a town in Oregon and named it 'Rajneeshpuram'. It seems that he took America for a ride since the U.S. government arrested him and later deported him out of America in 1985. So Rajneesh returned to India and started a 'Rajneesh

Neosanyas commune in Pune in India which was later renamed the 'Osho commune'.

If you visit this 'Osho commune' in Pune you will find it written on his tombstone, "Osho - never born, never died, only visited the planet earth between 11 Dec. 1931 to 19 Jan 1990". They conveniently forget to mention on this tombstone that Rajneesh was not given a visa for 21 different countries of the world. Imagine Almighty God visiting the earth and requiring a visa! The Arch Bishop of Greece had said that if Rajneesh was not deported they would burn his house and those of his disciples.

(iv) The fourth test is so stringent that none besides the One True God, Allah (swt), can pass it. "There is none like Him." The moment you can imagine or compare the candidate or claimant to godhood to anything, this candidate is not god. Neither can you have a mental picture of God. We know that Rajneesh was a human being. He had one head, two hands, two feet, and a white flowing beard. The moment you can think or imagine what the claimant to godhood is, he or she is not god.

THE NAME ALLAH PREFERRED TO THE WORD 'GOD'

The Muslims prefer calling Allah (swt) with His Name Allah, instead of the English word 'God'. The Arabic word Allah is pure and unique, unlike the English word God that can be manipulated. If you add 's' to God, it becomes 'gods' that is plural of God. Allah is one and singular, there is no plural of Allah. If you add 'dess' to God, it becomes 'goddess' that is a female God. There is nothing like male Allah or female Allah. Allah has no gender. If you add father to God, it becomes 'godfather'. "He is my Godfather," means, "he is my guardian". There is nothing like 'Allah *Abba*' or 'Allah father' in Islam. If you add mother to God it becomes 'godmother', there is nothing like 'Allah *Ammi*' or 'Allah Mother' in Islam. If you put tin before God, it becomes tin-god i.e. a fake God, there is nothing like 'tin Allah' or 'fake Allah' in Islam. Allah is a unique word, which does not conjure up any mental picture nor can it be played around with. Hence, the Muslims prefer the name Allah when referring to the Almighty Creator. However, sometimes while speaking to non-Muslims we may have to use the inappropriate word God for Allah as has been used in this preface.

QURAN AND MODERN SCIENCE

These methods of proving the existence of God to an atheist may satisfy some but not all. Many atheists demand a scientific proof for the existence of God. We agree that today is the age of science and technology. Let us use scientific knowledge to prove the existence of God and simultaneously also prove that the Quran is a revelation of God.

SOME SCIENTIFIC FACTS MENTIONED IN THE QURAN

1. *Creation of the universe. 'The Big Bang'*

Astrophysicists in a widely accepted phenomenon, popularly known as the 'Big Bang', explain the creation of the universe. It is supported by observational and experimental data gathered by astronomers and astrophysicists for decades. According to the 'Big Bang', the whole universe was initially one big mass (Primary Nebula). Then there was a 'Big Bang' (Secondary Separation), which resulted in the formation of Galaxies. These then divided to form stars, planets, the sun, the moon, etc. The origin of the universe was unique and the probability of it occurring by 'chance' is zero. The Quran contains the following verse, regarding the origin of the universe. "Do the disbelievers not see that the heavens and the earth were joined together (as one), before We tore them apart?" [21.30]

The striking congruence between the Quranic verse and the 'Big Bang' is inescapable! How could a book, which first appeared in the deserts of Arabia 1400 years ago, contain this profound scientific truth?

2. *Shape of the earth*

In early times, people believed that the earth is flat. For centuries, men were afraid to venture out too far, lest they should fall off the edge. Sir Francis Drake was the first person who proved that the earth is spherical when he sailed around it in 1577.

Consider the following Quranic verse regarding the alternation of day and night. "Do you not see that Allah blends the night into day and He blends the day into night?" [31.29]

Merging here means that the night slowly and gradually changes to day and vice versa. This phenomenon can only take place if the earth is spherical. If the earth were flat, there would have been a sudden change from night to day and from day to night. The earth is not exactly round like a ball, but geo-spherical i.e. it is flattened at the poles. The following verse contains a description of the earth's shape.

"And more, He has extended the earth (far and wide or also in the shape of an egg)" [79.30].

The Arabic word for egg here is *'dahaha'*, which means an ostrich-egg. The shape of an ostrich-egg resembles the geo-spherical shape of the earth. Thus, the Quran correctly describes the shape of the earth, though the prevalent notion when the Quran was revealed was that the earth is flat.

3. *The light of the moon is reflected light*

It was believed by earlier civilizations that the moon emanates its own light. Science now tells us that the light of the moon is reflected light. However, this fact was mentioned in the Quran, 1400 years ago in the following verse:

"He is the blessed (One) Who made groups of stars in the skies, and placed a Lamp in there and a Moon giving light;" [25.61]

The Arabic word for the sun in the Quran is *shams*. It is referred to as *siraaj*, which means a 'torch', or as *wahhaaj*, which means a 'blazing lamp', or as *diya*, which means a 'shining glory'. All three descriptions are appropriate to the sun, since it generates intense heat and light by its internal combustion. The Arabic word for the moon is *'qamar'* and it is described in the Quran as 'muneer', which is a body that gives *'nur'* i.e. light. Again, the Quranic description matches perfectly with the true nature of the moon, which does not give off light itself and is an inert body that reflects the light of the sun. Not once in the Quran, is the moon mentioned as *'siraaj',* *'wahhaaj'* or *'diya'* or the sun as *'nur'* or *'muneer'*. This implies that the Quran recognizes the difference between the nature of sunlight and moonlight.

4. *The sun rotates*

In 1609, the German scientist Yohannus Keppler published the 'Astronomia Nova'. In this he concluded that not only do the planets move in elliptical orbits around the sun, they also rotate upon their axes at irregular speeds. With this knowledge, it became possible for European scientists to explain correctly many of the mechanisms of the solar system including the sequence of night and day. After these discoveries, it was thought that the Sun was stationary and did not rotate about its axis like the Earth.

Consider the following Quranic verse: "And it is He Who created the night and the day, and the sun and the moon: All (the heavenly bodies) go along, each in its rounded path." [21.33]

The Arabic word used in the above verse is *yasbahûn* . The word *yasbahûn* is derived from the word *sabaha*. It carries with it the idea of motion that comes from any moving body. If you use the word for a man on the ground, it would not mean that he is rolling but would mean he is walking or running. If you use the word for a man in water, it would not mean that he is floating but would mean that he is swimming. Similarly, if you use the word *yasbah* for a celestial body such as the sun it would not mean that it is only flying through space but would mean that it is also rotating as it goes through space. Most of the school textbooks have incorporated the fact that the sun rotates about its axis. The rotation of the sun about its own axis can be proved with the help of an equipment that projects the image of the sun on the table top so that one can examine the image of the sun without being blinded. It is noticed that the sun has spots, which complete a circular motion once every 25 days i.e. the sun takes approximately 25 days to rotate around its axis.

In fact, the sun travels through space at roughly 150 miles per second, and takes about 200 million years to complete one revolution around the center of our Milky Way Galaxy. One cannot help but be amazed at the scientific accuracy of the Quranic verses. Should we not ponder over the question. "What was the source of knowledge contained in the Quran?"

5. *Every living thing is made of water*

Consider the following Quranic verse. "We made every living thing from water. Then, will they not believe?" [21.30].

Only after the advancement of science, do we now know that cytoplasm, the basic substance of the cell is made up of 80% water. Modern research has also revealed that most organisms consist of 50% to 90% water and that every living entity requires water for its existence.

Was it possible 14 centuries ago for any human being to guess that every living being was made of water? Moreover, would such a guess be conceivable by a human being in the deserts of Arabia where there has always been a scarcity of water?

6. *Everything made in pairs*

Allah (swt) says in the Quran, "Glory to Allah, Who created all the things in pairs that the earth produces, and also their own kind (also created in pairs) and (other) things about whom they do not know." [36.36]

The Quran here says that everything is created in pairs, including things that the humans do not know at present and may discover later.

7. *Man is created from Alaq – A leech-like substance*

A few years ago a group of Arabs collected all information concerning embryology from the Quran, and presented to Prof. (Dr.) Keith Moore, who was the Professor of

Embryology and Chairman of the Department of Anatomy at the University of Toronto, in Canada. At present, he is one of the highest authorities in the field of Embryology.

Dr. Moore said that most of the information concerning embryology mentioned in the Quran is in perfect conformity with modern discoveries in the field of embryology and does not conflict with them in any way. He added that there were however a few verses, on whose scientific accuracy he could not comment. He could not say whether the statements were true or false, since he himself was not aware of the information contained therein. There was also no mention of this information in modern writings and studies on embryology.

One such verse is: "Proclaim! (And read aloud!) in the Name of the Lord and Cherisher, Who created. Created man, out of a (mere) clot of thickened blood" [96.1-2]

The word *alaq* besides meaning a congealed clot of blood also means something that clings, a leech-like substance. Dr. Keith Moore had no knowledge whether an embryo in the initial stages appears like a leech. To check this out he studied the initial stage of the embryo under a very powerful microscope in his laboratory and compared what he observed with a diagram of a leech and he was astonished at the striking resemblance between the two!

Dr. Keith Moore had earlier authored the book, 'The Developing Human'. After acquiring new knowledge from the Quran, he wrote, in 1982, the 3rd edition of the same book, 'The Developing Human'. The book was the recipient of an award for the best medical book written by a single author. This book has been translated into several major languages of the world and is used as a textbook of embryology in the first year of medical studies.

In 1981, during the Seventh Medical Conference in Dammam, Saudi Arabia, Dr. Moore said, "It has been a great pleasure for me to help clarify statements in the Quran about human development. It is clear to me that these statements must have come to Muhammad from God or Allah, because almost all of this knowledge was not discovered until many centuries later. This proves to me that Muhammad must have been a messenger of God or Allah."

8. *Fingerprints*

"Does man think that We cannot assemble his bones together? Yes! We are able to put together the very tips of his fingers perfectly."[75.3-4].

The disbelievers argue regarding resurrection taking place after bones of dead people have disintegrated in the earth and how each individual would be identified on the Day of Judgment. Almighty Allah answers that He can not only assemble our bones but can also reconstruct perfectly our very fingertips.

Why does the Quran, while speaking about determination of the identity of the individual, speak specifically about fingertips? In 1880, fingerprinting became the scientific method of identification, after research done by Sir Francis Golt. No two persons in the world can ever have exactly the same fingerprint pattern. That is the reason why police forces worldwide use fingerprints to identify the criminal.

1400 years ago, who could have known the uniqueness of each human's fingerprint? Surely it could have been none other than the Creator Himself!

9. *Pain receptors present in the skin*

It was thought that the sense of feeling and pain was only dependent on the brain. Recent discoveries prove that there are pain receptors present in the skin without which a person would not be able to feel pain. When a doctor examines a patient suffering from burn injuries, he verifies the degree of burns by a pinprick. If the patient feels pain, the doctor is happy, because it indicates that the burns are superficial and the pain receptors are intact. On the other hand if the patient does not feel any pain, it indicates that it is a deep burn and the pain receptors have been destroyed.

The Quran gives an indication of the existence of pain receptors in the following verse. "Surely, those who reject Our Signs, We shall soon throw (them) into the Fire: As often as their skins are roasted through, We shall change them for fresh skins, that they may taste the Penalty: Truly, Allah is Almighty, All Wise." [4.56]

Prof. Tagatat Tejasen, Chairman of the Department of Anatomy at Chiang Mai University in Thailand, has spent a great amount of time on research of pain receptors. Initially he could not believe that the Quran mentioned this scientific fact 1,400 years ago. He later verified the translation of this particular Quranic verse. Prof. Tejasen was so impressed by the scientific accuracy of the Quranic verse that at the 8th Saudi Medical Conference held in Riyadh on the Scientific Signs of Quran and Sunnah he proclaimed in public. "There is no God but Allah and Muhammad (pbuh) is His Messenger."

THEORY OF MATHEMATICAL PROBABILITY.

In mathematics, there is a theory known as 'Theory of Probability'. If you have two options, out of which one is right, and one is wrong, the chances that you will choose the right one is half i.e. one out of the two will be correct. You have 50% chances of being correct, similarly if you toss a coin the chances that your guess will be correct is 50% (1 out of 2) i.e. ½. If you toss a coin the second time, the chances that you will be correct in the second toss is again 50% i.e. ½. But the chances that you will be correct in both the tosses are half x half (½ x ½), which is equal to ¼. i.e. 50% of 50% i.e. equal to 25%. If you toss a coin the third time, chances that you will be correct all three times is (½ x ½ x ½) that is 1/8 or 50% of 50% of 50% that is 12.5%.

A dice has got six sides. If you throw a dice and guess any number between 1 and 6, the chances that your guess will be correct are 1/6. If you throw the dice the second time, the chances that your guess will be correct in both the throws is (1/6 x 1/6) which is equal to 1/36. If you throw the dice the third time, the chances that all your three guesses are correct is (1/6 x 1/6 x 1/6) is equal to 1/216 that is less than ½ a percent.

Let us apply this theory of probability to the Quran, and assume that a person has guessed all the information that is mentioned in the Quran, which was unknown at that time. Let us discuss the probability of all the guesses being correct.

At the time when the Quran was revealed, people thought the world was flat. There are several other options for the shape of the earth. It could be triangular; it could be quadrangular, pentagonal, hexagonal, heptagonal, octagonal, spherical, etc. Let's assume there are about 30 different options for the shape of the earth. The Quran rightly says it is spherical, if it was a guess the chances of the guess being correct is 1/30.

The light of the moon can be its own light or a reflected light. The Quran rightly says it is a reflected light. If it was a guess, the chances that it will be correct is ½ and the probability that both the guesses i.e. the earth is spherical and the light of the moon is reflected light is 1/30 x ½ = 1/60.

Further, the Quran also mentions every living thing is made up of water. The options are say about 10,000. Every living thing can be made up of either wood, stone, copper, aluminum, steel, silver, gold, oxygen, nitrogen, hydrogen, oil, water, cement, concrete etc. The Quran rightly says that every living thing is made up of water. Therefore if it's a guess, the chances that it will be correct is 1/10,000 and the probability of all the three guesses i.e. earth is spherical, light of moon is reflected, every living thing is created from water being correct is 1/30 x ½ x 1/10,000 = 1/600,000 which is equal to about .00017%.

The Quran speaks about hundreds of things that were not known at that time. Only in three options, the result is .00017%. We leave it up to you the intellectual readers to work out the probability if all the hundreds of the unknown facts were guesses, the chances of all the guesses being correct and not a single wrong. It is beyond human capacity to have all the guesses correct without a single mistake, which in itself is sufficient to prove to a logical person that the origin of the Quran is divine.

QURAN IS A BOOK OF SIGNS AND NOT SCIENCE

Let us be reminded that Quran is not a book of Science, 'S.C.I.E.N.C.E.' but a book of 'signs' – S.I.G.N.S. i.e. a book of ayaats. The Quran contains more than 6000 ayaats that is 'signs' out of which more than a thousand speak about science. For Muslims, the Quran is the *'Furqaan'* i.e. the criteria to judge right from wrong and it is the ultimate yard stick which is more superior to scientific knowledge. But for an educated man who is an atheist, scientific knowledge is the ultimate test, which he believes in. Using the ultimate yardstick of the atheist, we try to prove to him that the Quran is the word of God and while it was revealed 1400 ago, it contains the scientific knowledge that was discovered recently. Therefore, at the end of the discussion, we both come to the same conclusion that God, though superior to science, does not conflict with it.

THE CREATOR IS THE SOURCE OF THE QURAN

The only logical answer to the question, who could have mentioned all these scientific facts 1400 years ago before they were discovered, is exactly the same answer that would be given by the atheist or any person, to the question "who is the first person who will be able to tell the mechanism of the unknown object?" It is the 'CREATOR,' the Producer, the Manufacturer of that object. Another name in the English Language for this Creator, Producer, Manufacturer of the whole universe and its contents, is 'God' or more appropriately in the Arabic Language is 'Allah'.

SCIENCE IS ELIMINATING MODELS OF GOD
BUT NOT GOD.

Francis Bacon, the famous philosopher, has rightly said that a little knowledge of science makes you an atheist, but an in-depth study of science makes you a believer in God. Scientists today are eliminating models of god, but they are not eliminating God.

If you translate this act – of rejecting false models and wrong notions of God – into Arabic, it is *'La ilaaha illal lah'* which means "there is no god, but God". "There is no god (god with a small 'g' that is fake deities), but God (with a capital 'G')

Prof. Tejasen accepted Islam on the strength of just one scientific 'sign' mentioned in the Quran. Some people may require ten signs while some may require hundred signs to be convinced about the Divine Origin of the Quran. Some would be unwilling to accept the Truth even after being shown a thousand signs. The Quran condemns such a closed mentality in the verse, "They are deaf, dumb, and blind, so they will not return (to the right path)." [2.18]

The Quran contains a complete code of life for the individual and society. *Alhamdulillah* (Praise be to Allah), the Quranic way of life is far superior to the 'isms' that modern man has invented out of sheer ignorance. Who can give better guidance than the Creator Himself?

In Surah The Detailed Explanation - *Al-Fussilat* [41]: "Soon We will show them Our Signs in the (very far) regions (of the earth, and also deep) in their own souls, till it becomes clear to them that this is the Truth. Is it not enough that your Lord Who Witnesses all things?" [41.53].

And Our Final Call is – All praises are for the One and Only God and Creator Allah, Who Alone is worthy of devotion, complete submission and worship. I declare that there is no other deity or god besides Allah. I also declare that Prophet Muhammad is the Last and Final Messenger of Allah.

Dr. Zakir Naik

Islamic Research Foundation,

Mumbai, India.

For additional information on various topics associated with Islam, please visit us online at http://www.bookofsigns.org. Here you will find detailed explanations of topics that may be of additional interest to you, such as, what is Jihad? What is the position of women in Islam? What does Islam say about terrorism? What does Islam say about Jesus (pbuh) or Mary (pbuh)? Also you can ask questions on any other topic that we may not have covered. You may also email your questions to Quran@bookofsigns.org or call us at 1-888-BSF-2754

Prophet Muhammad's Last Sermon

The following is an English translation of the last sermon which Muhammad (Peace Be Upon Him) – the Last and Final Prophet and Messenger of God, delivered at Mt. Arafat on his last pilgrimage to Mecca (Saudi Arabia) a few months before he passed away. This famous sermon laid down the foundations of human rights, dignity and freedom. Sermon was delivered around 632 A.D.

"All praise is for God, the Lord of the Universe. We seek His Help and we seek His Forgiveness for all our sins and we submit our regret and repentance before Him. We seek His protection from the malice of our hearts and from all evils that we have committed. Those who are guided by God to the right path, none can lead them astray; and those who are denied guidance by God, no one can guide them to the path of truth."

"O People! Listen to me. I do not think that after this year, you and I shall ever meet in this place. Therefore listen to what I am saying to you very carefully and take these words to those who could not be present here today. Remember, there is none worthy of being worshipped except God; He is one, He has no partner, all sovereignty belongs to Him. All praise is due unto Him, He is the giver of life and death, and has power over all things."

"O People! Just as you regard this month, this day, and this city as sacred, so regard the life and property of every Muslim as a sacred trust. Return the goods entrusted to you to their rightful owners. Treat others justly so that no one would be unjust to you. Remember that you will indeed meet your Lord, and that He will indeed question you about your deeds. God has forbidden you to take interest/usury *(riba)*, therefore all *interest* obligation shall henceforth be waived. Your capital, however, is yours to keep. You will neither inflict nor suffer inequity. It has been ordained by God that all usury is forbidden. To start with I give up the usury that is due to my relations. And all interest by debtors to 'Abbas, my uncle, son of 'Abd al-Muttalib is given up."

"Compensation for bloodshed committed during the pre-Islamic days of ignorance is canceled. On my part, I give up my claim for compensation for the life of Rabia Bin Harith."

"O People! Beware of Satan, (the evil one), for the safety of your religion. He has lost all hope that he will ever be able to lead you astray in big things so beware of following him in small things."

"O Men! The unbelievers indulge in tampering with the calendar in order to make permissible that which God forbade, and to prohibit which God has made permissible. With God the months are twelve in number. Four of them are holy, three of these are successive and one occurs singly between the months of Jumad-al-thani and Shaban (months of the Islamic Lunar calendar)

"O People! It is true that you have certain rights over your women, but they also have rights over you. Remember that you have taken them as your wives only under God's trust and with His permission. If they abide by your rights then to them belongs the right to be fed and clothed in kindness. Treat your women well and be kind to them, for they are your partners and committed helpers. It is your right that they do not make friends with anyone of whom you do not approve, as well as never be unchaste."

"O People, listen to me in earnest, worship God (The One Creator of the Universe), perform your five daily prayers (*Salah*), fast during the month of Ramadan, and give your financial obligation (zakah) on your wealth. Perform Hajj if you can afford to."

"All mankind is from Adam and Eve. An Arab has no superiority over a non-Arab and a non-Arab has no superiority over an Arab; also a white has no superiority over a black and a black has no superiority over white except by piety and good action. Learn that every Muslim is a brother to every other Muslim and that the Muslims constitute one brotherhood. Nothing shall be legitimate to a Muslim, which belongs to a fellow Muslim unless it was given freely and willingly. Do not, therefore, do injustice to yourselves."

"Remember, one day you will appear before God (The Creator) and you will answer for your deeds. So beware, do not stray from the path of righteousness after I am gone."

"O People! No prophet or messenger will come after me and no new faith will be born. Reason well, therefore, O People, and understand the words, which I convey to you. I am leaving you with the Book of God (the QURAN) and my SUNNAH (the life style and behavior of the Prophet), if you follow them you will never go astray."

"All those who listen to me, pass on my words to others and those to others again; and may the last ones understand my words better than those who listen to me directly. Be my witness O God, that I have conveyed your message to your people."

The following verse was revealed at the end of this sermon:

"...This day have I perfected your religion for you, completed My Favor upon you, and have chosen Islam as your religion..." [5:3].

For more information on Muhammad (pbuh), the last and final Prophet of God, please visit us online at http://www.bookofsigns.org/Muhammad.

BOOK OF SIGNS FOUNDATION

Delivering THE MESSAGE of THE QURAN to you

PRESENTS

ENGLISH TRANSLATION OF THE MESSAGE OF

THE QURAN

Translated By:
Professor (Dr.) Syed Vickar Ahamed

Book of Signs Foundation
Delivering THE MESSAGE of THE QURAN to you™

Your Source of Authentic Islamic Literature

1) TO ORDER COPIES OF THIS TRANSLATION
2) TO REQUEST ADDITIONAL INFORMATION AND LITERATURE ON
QURAN, ISLAM AND MUSLIMS
3) TO HAVE YOUR QUESTIONS ANSWERED
Contact us at:
1-888-BSF-2754
Quran@bookofsigns.org
http://www.bookofsigns.org

English Translation of THE MESSAGE of THE QURAN
Table of Contents

Sura 1. Al-Fatiha,
(The opening chapter): (Makkah, 7 Verses)

**1.1. In the Name of Allah, the All Merciful,
the Ever Merciful;**

**1.2. Praise be to Allah, the Lord
(Cherisher and Sustainer) of the worlds;**

1.3. The All Merciful, the Ever Merciful;

1.4. The Possessor of the Day of Judgment;

**1.5. You (only) we worship and (only)
Your help we seek.**

1.6. Guide us to the Straight Path;

**1.7. The Path of those on whom
You have bestowed Your Mercy,
Not of those against whom You have sent (Your)
wrath,
Nor of (those) who have erred and become lost.**

Sura 2. Al-Baqara,
(The heifer or the calf): (Medinah, 286 Verses)

In the Name of Allah, the Most Gracious, the Most Merciful.

2.1.. Alif Lám Mim:

2.2. This is the Book: In it is guidance, without doubt, for those who fear Allah;

2.3. (For those) who believe in the Unseen, who are steadfast in prayer, who spend out of what We have given them;

2.4. And (for those) who believe in the Revelations sent to you and sent before your time, and (for those, who in their hearts) have the assurance of the Hereafter.

2.5. They are on (true) guidance, from their Lord, and it is these (people) who will prosper.

2.6.. As to those (people) who reject Faith, it is the same to them whether you warn them or do not warn them; They will not believe.

2.7. Allah has set a seal on their hearts and on their hearing, and on their eyes is a veil; Great is the penalty they (have to face).

2.8.. And of the people there are some who say: "We believe in Allah and the Last Day;" But they do not (really) believe.

2.9. Surely! They try to deceive Allah and those who believe, but they only deceive themselves, But do not realize!

2.10. In their hearts is a disease and Allah has increased their disease: And painful is the penalty they (will face), because they are false to themselves.

2.11. When it is said to them: "Do not make mischief on the earth," they say: "Why, we only want to make peace!"

2.12. Surely, they are the ones who make mischief, but they do not realize it.

2.13. When it is said to them: "Believe as the (other) men believe:" They say: "Shall we believe as the fools have believed?" On the contrary, they are the fools, but they do not know.

2.14. When they meet those who believe, they say: "We believe;" But when they are alone with their evil companions, they say: "We are really with you; We (were) only mocking!"

2.15. Allah will throw back their mockery at them, and give them rope in their trespasses; So they will wander like blind ones (back and forth)!

2.16. These are they who have exchanged guidance for error: But their trade is profitless, and they have lost true (right) direction!

2.17.. Their similitude is that of a man who started a fire; When it shed light all around him Allah took away their light and left them in total darkness, so they could not see.

2.18. They are deaf, dumb, and blind, so they will not return (to the right path).

2.19. Or (another similitude) is that of a stormy rain cloud from the sky: In it are zones of darkness, and thunder and lightning. They press their fingers in their ears to keep out the stunning thunder, the while they are in terror of death. But Allah is all around those who reject Faith!

2.20. The lightning almost snatches away their sight, every time the light (helps) them, they walk in there, and when the darkness covers them, they stand still. And if Allah willed, He could take away their hearing and their sight; Because Allah has power over all things.

2.21.. O you people! Worship (and pray to) your Guardian-Lord, Who created you, and those who came before you, that you might have the chance to learn righteousness;

2.22. Who has made the earth a place of rest for you, and the sky your canopy; And sent down rain from the sky; And brought forth from there fruits for your sustenance; Then do not set up rivals to Allah when you know (the truth).

2.23. And if you are in doubt about what We have revealed (from time to time) to Our servant (the Prophet), then produce a Sura like the one here (in the Quran); And call your witness (or helpers if there are any) besides Allah, if you are truthful.

2.24. But if you cannot- And surely you cannot- Then fear the Fire whose fuel is Men and Stones- Which is prepared for those who reject Faith.

2.25. And give glad tidings to those who believe and who act fairly and justly, that their reward is Gardens, beneath which rivers flow. Every time they are fed with fruits from there, they say: "This is what we were fed with before," for they are given similar things; And in there, they have pure (and holy) companions and in there, they live (for ever).

2.26.. Indeed, Allah is not ashamed to use the similitude of things, even as low as the mosquito as well as the highest.

Those who believe know that it is truth from their Lord;

But those who reject Faith will say:

"What does Allah mean by this similitude?" But He does not cause (people) to lose (their path) except those who give (themselves) up.

2.27. (And) those who break Allah's Promise after it is accepted, and who tear apart what Allah has ordered to be joined, and who make mischief on earth; These cause loss (only) to themselves.

2.28. How can you reject the Faith in Allah? Seeing that you were without life, and He gave you life: Then He will cause you to die and (He) will again bring you to life; And again to Him you will return.

2.29. It is He Who has created all things for you that are on earth; In addition, His plans called for the heavens, and He gave Order and Perfection to the seven skies: And of all things He is All Knowing.

2.30.. And (remember) when your Lord said to the angels; "I will create a vicegerent on earth." They said: "Will You place in there, one who will make mischief and shed blood in there? While we (indeed) celebrate Your Praises and glorify Your Holy (Name)?" He said: "I do know what you do not know."

2.31. And He taught Adam the names of all things: Then He placed them before the angels and said: "Tell Me the names of these (things) if you are right."

2.32. They said: "Glory to You: We have no knowledge, except what You have taught us: Verily, in truth it is You Who are Perfect in knowledge and wisdom."

2.33. He said: "O Adam! Tell them their names." When he had told them their names, Allah said: "Did I not tell you that I know the (unseen) secrets of heavens and earth, and I know what you reveal and what you conceal?"

2.34. And (remember) when We said to the angels: "Bow down to Adam:" And they bowed down: Except Satan, he refused and was haughty he was of those who reject Faith.

2.35.. And We said: "O Adam! You and your wife live in the Garden; And eat of the plentiful things in there (wherever and whenever) you want; But do not approach this tree, or you will run into harm and transgression."

2.36. Then Satan did make them slip from the (Garden), and get them out of the state (of joy) which they had been. We said: "Get down, you all (people), with hostility between yourselves, on the earth; (that) will be your living-place and your means of livelihood - For a time."

2.37. Then Adam received the words of inspiration, from his Lord, and his Lord forgave him; For He is One Who accepts Repentance, Most Merciful.

2.38. We said: "Get you all down from here; And if, surely, there comes Guidance to you from Me; Those who follow My guidance, for them there shall be no fear, and they shall not suffer.

2.39. "But those who reject Faith and falsify Our Signs, they shall be companions of the Fire; They shall abide in there."

2.40.. O Children of Israel! Call to mind the (special) favor, which I bestowed upon you, and fulfill (then) your Promise to Me as I fulfill My Promise to you, and fear none but Me.

2.41. And believe in what I reveal, confirming the revelation, which is with you, and do not be the first to reject Faith in there, and do not sell My Signs for a small price: But fear Me, and Me alone.

2.42. And do not cover Truth with falsehood, and do not hide the Truth when you know (it).

2.43. And be steadfast in prayer: Practice regular charity: And bow down your heads with those who bow down (in worship).

2.44. Do you enforce right conduct on the people, and forget (to practice it) yourselves, and yet you study the Scripture? Will you not understand?

2.45. But no! Seek (Allah's) help with patient perseverance and prayer: It is truly difficult except for those who bring a humble spirit-

2.46. Those who bear in mind the Certainty, that they are to meet their Lord, and that they are to return to Him.

2.47.. O Children of Israel! Remember My (special) favor which I bestowed upon you, and that I preferred you to other (nations for My Message).

2.48. Then guard yourself against a Day when one soul shall be of no use to another nor shall intervention be accepted for her, nor shall any compensation be taken from her nor shall anyone be helped (from outside).

2.49.. And (remember) when, We delivered you from the people of Firon (Pharaoh): They set hard tasks and punishments for you, slaughtered your sons and let your women live; In there was a harsh trial from your Lord.

2.50.. And (remember) when, We divided the ocean for you and saved you and drowned Firon's (Pharaoh's) people within your very sight.

2.51. And (remember) when, We appointed forty nights for Musa (Moses), and in his absence you took the calf (the Name of this Sura) (for worship), and you made a terrible mistake.

2.52. Even then We did forgive you; There was a chance for you to be grateful.

2.53.. And (remember), We gave Musa (Moses) the Scripture and the Criterion (right from wrong): There was a chance for you to be rightfully guided.

2.54.. And (remember) when, Musa (Moses) said to his people: "O my people! You have indeed wronged yourselves by your worship of the calf: So turn in repentance to your Creator, and kill yourselves (the wrongdoers); That will be better for you in the sight of your Creator." For He is the One Who Accepts Repentance, the Most Merciful.

2.55. And (remember) when, you said: "O Musa (Moses)! We shall never believe in you until we see Allah openly," but you were dazed with thunder and lightning while you looked on.

2.56. Then We raised you up after your death: So that you had the chance to be grateful.

2.57. And We gave you the shade of clouds and sent down to you manna and quails, (food and birds) saying: "Eat of the good things We have provided for you." [See Note 2.1 about the food and birds as Musa (Moses) fled the armies of Firon (Pharaoh).] (But they rebelled) and, to Us they did no harm, but they harmed their own souls.

2.58.. And (remember) when, We said: "Enter this town, and eat from the plentiful in there as you wish; But enter the gate with humility, in (your) way and in (your) words, and We shall forgive you for your faults and increase (the portion of) those who do good."

2.59. But those who transgressed, changed the words from those (words) that were given to them; So We sent on those who transgressed a plague from heaven, because they disobeyed (Our command) repeatedly.

2.60. And (remember) when, Musa (Moses) prayed for water for his people; We said: "Strike the rock with your staff." Then gushed forth from there twelve springs. Each group knew its own place for water. So eat and drink from the sustenance provided by Allah, and do not practice evil or mischief on the (face of the) earth.

2.61.. And (remember) when, you said: "O Musa (Moses)! We cannot endure one kind of food (always); So pray to your Lord for us to produce for us of what the earth grows- Its pot-herb(s), and cucumber(s), its garlic, lentils, and onions." He said: "Will you exchange the better for the worse? You go down to Misr (any town), and you shall find what you want!" They were covered with humiliation and misery; They drew the anger of Allah on themselves. That was because they kept rejecting the Signs of Allah and killing His Messengers without just cause. That was because they rebelled and went on transgressing.

2.62.. Indeed, those who believe (in the Quran), and those who are Jews, and the Christians and the Sabians, - Any who believe in Allah and the Last Day, and work righteousness, shall have their reward with their Lord; On them there shall be no fear, and they shall not grieve.

2.63.. And (remember) when, We took your Promise and We raised above you (the towering height of) Mount (Sinai) (saying): "Hold firmly to what We have given you and always remember what is in there: That you may fear Allah."

2.64. But you turned back after that: Had it not been for the Grace and Mercy of Allah to you, you surely had been among the lost.

2.65. And you knew well those among you who transgressed in the matter of the (Sacred) day (of Sabbath): We said to them: "Be you (like) monkeys, despised and rejected."

2.66. So We made it an example to (others in) their own time and to their generations, and a lesson to those who fear Allah.

2.67.. And (remember) when, Musa (Moses) said to his people: "Allah commands that you sacrifice a calf." They said: "Are you going to make a laughing-stock of us?" He said: "I seek refuge from Allah that I am among the ignorant (people)!"

2.68. They said: "Pray to your Lord on our behalf to explain to us what (calf) it is!" He said: "He says: The calf should be neither too old, nor too young, but of middling age: Now do what you are commanded!"

2.69. They said: "Pray to your Lord on our behalf to explain to us her color."

He said: "He says: A fawn-colored calf (heifer, also name of this Sura), pure and rich in shade, admired by (its) seers!"

2.70. They said: "Pray to your Lord on our behalf to explain to us what it is: To us all calves (heifers) are alike: We truly want guidance, if Allah wills."

2.71. He said: "He says: A calf not trained to till the soil or water the fields; Healthy and without defects. They said: Now you have brought the truth." Then they offered it (the calf) in sacrifice, but not in good will.

2.72.. And (remember, Musa) when you killed a man (also see verse 20.40 for another reference), and disagreed among yourselves about the crime: But Allah was to bring forth what you did hide.

2.73. So We said: "Strike the (body) with a piece of the calf." Thus Allah brings the dead to life: And shows you His Signs, so that you may understand.

2.74.. From then your hearts hardened: And they became like a rock and even worse in hardness. Even among rocks, there are some from which rivers gush out: Others bring out water, when they are split: And others which sink because of the fear of Allah. And Allah is not unaware of what you do.

2.75. Can you (O men of Faith), hope that they will believe in you? Seeing that a party of them heard the Word of Allah, and altered it knowingly after they understood it.

2.76. And when they meet the men of Faith, they say: "We believe;" But when they meet each other in private, they say: "Shall you tell them what Allah has revealed to you, that they may argue about it before your Lord?" Do you not understand (their aim)?

2.77. Do they not know that Allah knows what they conceal and what they reveal?

2.78. And there are among them who cannot read and who do not know the Book, but (in it they see their own) desires, and they imagine without any basis.

2.79. Then woe to those who write the Book with their own hands, and then say: "This is from Allah." To gain from it for a lowly price! Woe to them for what they write, and for the gain they make from it.

2.80.. And they say: "The Fire shall not touch us but for a few numbered days:" Say: "Have you taken a promise from Allah, because He never breaks His promise? Or you say about Allah what you do not know?"

2.81. Yes! Those who search for gain in evil, and are held round by their sins, they are companions of the Fire: They shall live in there (for ever).

2.82. And those who have faith and work the right deeds they are companions of the Garden: They shall live in there (for ever).

2.83.. And (remember) when, We took a Promise from the Children Of Israel, (that you will) worship no one but Allah, treat with kindness your parents and relatives, and orphans and those in need; Speak kindly and justly to the people; Be regular in prayer; And practice regular charity. Then you turned back, except a few among you, and you go back (on the Promise even now).

2.84. And (remember) when, We took your Promise (that you will) shed no blood among yourselves, and not turn out your own people from your homes: And to this you truly agreed, and to this you (yourselves) can bear witness.

2.85. After (all of) this, you are the same people, who kill among yourselves, and banish a party of your people from their homes; Help (their enemies) against them, in guilt and hate; And if they come to you as captives, you ransom them though it was not right for you to remove them (from their homes). Is it only a part of the Book that you believe in? And do you reject the rest? But what is the reward for those among you who behave like this except disgrace in this life? And on the Day of Judgment they shall receive the most painful penalty. And Allah is aware of what you do.

2.86. These are the people who buy the life of this world at the price of the Hereafter: Their penalty shall not be reduced and they shall not be helped.

2.87.. And indeed, We gave Musa (Moses) the Book and followed him up with other messengers; And We gave Isa (Jesus), the son of Maryam (Mary) Clear (Signs) and strengthened him with the Holy Spirit. Is it that whenever there comes to you a messenger with what you yourselves do not want, you become proud- Some you disbelieved! And some you killed!

2.88. They say, "Our hearts are screened: (we do not want more.)" But no! Allah curses them for their lies: They believe in little.

2.89. And when there comes to them a Book from Allah, confirming what is with them- Although from the past they had prayed for victory against those without Faith- When there comes to them that which they (should) have recognized, they refuse to believe in it. But the curse of Allah is on those without Faith.

2.90. How bad is the price for which they have sold their souls, because they reject (the teachings) with hate; Which Allah has sent down; Allah by His Grace sends it (the teachings) to any of His servants He pleases. Thus they have drawn on themselves Anger upon Anger. And humiliating is the punishment for those who reject Faith.

2.91. And when it is said to them, "Believe in what Allah has sent down," they say, "We believe in what was sent down to us:" Yet they reject everything that which came after it, while it be Truth confirming what is with them. Say, (O Prophet): "Why then have you killed the prophets of Allah in earlier times, if you did truly believe."

2.92. And, indeed Musa (Moses) came to you with clear (Signs); Yet you still worshipped the calf after he left, and you did act wrongfully.

2.93. And (remember) when, We took your Promise and We raised above you Mount (Sinai, saying): "Hold firmly to what We have given you, and obey:" They said: "We hear, and we disobey:" And they had to take into their hearts the worship of the calf because they have no Faith. Say: "The commands of your Faith are truly not enough - If you have any faith!"

2.94. Say (to them, O Prophet): "If the last Home with Allah is only for you, and not for anyone else, then pray for death if you are true."

2.95. But they will never seek for death, because of the (sins) which their hands have sent on before them. And Allah is well aware of those who do wrong.

2.96. And indeed, you will truly find them, from all people, most wanting to live (on), even more than the idolaters: Each one of them wishes he could be given a life of a thousand years: But giving such a life will not save him from the punishment. Because Allah sees well all that they do.

2.97.. Say: "Whoever is an enemy to Gabriel, because he brings down the (teachings) to your heart, by Allah's Will, a confirmation of what went before, and guidance and glad news for those who believe,

2.98. "Whoever is an enemy to Allah and His angels and messengers, to Gabriel and Michael-- Beware! Allah is an enemy to those who reject Faith."

2.99. We have sent down to you clear Signs (verses); And no one rejects them except those who are evil.

2.100. Is it not (the case) that every time they make a promise, some party among them throws it aside? But most of them are faithless.

2.101. And when there came to them a messenger from Allah, confirming what was with them: A party of the People of the Book threw away the Book of Allah behind their backs, as if they did not know!

2.102. They followed what the Satans falsified against the belief of Sulaiman (Solomon); But the Satans disbelieved, teaching men magic, and such things as came down at *Babel* (Babylon), to the angels, *Harut* and *Marut*. (These are two idolized men from the ancient times.) But neither of these two (angels) taught anyone (such things) without warning: "We are only for trial; So do not disbelieve or curse." They learnt from them [Satans] the means to cause separation between man and wife. But they could not harm anyone except by Allah's permission. And they learnt that which harms them and helps them not and they knew that the buyers of (such magic) would have no share in the happiness of the Hereafter. And low was the price for which they sold their souls, if they only knew!

2.103. And if they had kept their faith and guarded themselves from evil, and their duty to Allah far better had been the reward from their Lord, if they only knew!

2.104.. O you who believe! Do not say ambiguous words like *Ráina* (an insult in Hebrew, to the Prophet); But (say) clearly words of respect like Unzurna; (Make us understand), and listen carefully (to him); For those without Faith, there is a painful punishment.

2.105. It is never the wish of those without Faith, among the people of the Book or (the wish) of the pagans, that anything good should come down to you from your Lord. But Allah will choose for His special Mercy whoever He will (choose)-And Allah is Lord of extreme grace.

2.106. None of Our revelations do We change or cause to be forgotten, but We substitute something better or similar; Do you not know that Allah has power over all things?

2.107. Do you (also) not know that to Allah belongs the kingdom of the heavens and of the earth? And except Him, you have neither a friend nor a helper.

2.108.. Or would you question your Prophet (Muhammad) as Musa (Moses) was questioned in the old (days)? And whoever changes from Faith to disbelief, indeed, has strayed without doubt from the right way.

2.109. Many from the People of the Book wish they could turn you (believers) back to disbelief after you have believed, From selfish envy, (even) after the Truth has become clear to them: But forgive and overlook till Allah completes His purpose; Indeed, Allah has power over all things.

2.110. And be regular in prayer, and regular in charity: And whatever good you send forth for your souls before you (from this life), you shall find it with Allah: Surely, Allah sees well all that you do.

2.111. And they say: "None shall enter Paradise unless he is a Jew or a Christian." Those are (only) their vain or empty wishes. Say to them: "Bring your proof if you are truthful."

2.112. But no! Whoever submits his whole self to Allah and does good- He will get his reward with his Lord: For such people, there shall be no fear and they shall not be in pain.

2.113.. The Jews say: "The Christians have nothing firm to stand upon;" And the Christians say: "The Jews have nothing firm to stand upon." Yet they (both say that they) read the (same) Book. Like the words they say they do not know what they say; But Allah will judge between them in their dispute on the Day of Judgment.

2.114. And who are more unjust than those who forbid that in places for the worship of Allah, Allah's name should be celebrated? Whose object is (in fact) to ruin them? It was not right that those (who believe), should themselves enter those (places) except only in fear. For those (who forbid the Praise of Allah's Name) there is nothing but disgrace in this world, and a severe suffering in the world to come.

2.115. And to Allah belong the East and the West: Wherever you turn, there is the Face (the Divine Countenance and Presence) of Allah. For Allah is All Pervading, All Knowing .

2.116. And they say: "Allah has begotten a son:" Glory be to Him- To Him belongs all that is in the heavens and on earth: Everything renders worship to Him.

2.117. To Him is due the very origin of the heavens and the earth: When He decides on anything and He says to it: "Be." And so it becomes.

2.118. Those without knowledge say: "Why does Allah not speak to us? Or why does a Sign not come to us?" The people before them said words of similar nature; Their hearts are alike. We have indeed made clear the Signs to any people who hold firmly to Faith (in their hearts).

2.119. Surely, We have sent you in truth (Islam) as a bearer of glad news and a Warner but to you no question shall be asked about the (disbelievers and) the companions of the blazing Fire.

2.120. The Jews or the Christians will never be satisfied with you (O Prophet,) unless you follow their religion. Say: "The Guidance of Allah- That is the (only) Guidance." And if you to follow their desires after the knowledge that has reached you, then you would find neither protector nor helper against Allah.

2.121. Those to whom We have sent the Book, study it as it should be studied: They are the ones who believe in it: And for those who reject faith in it, the loss is their own.

2.122.. O Children of Israel! Remember the special favor which I bestowed upon you, and that I preferred you to all others (for My Message).

2.123. Then guard yourselves against a Day when one soul shall not be of any use to another, nor shall compensation be accepted from her, nor shall representation profit her, nor shall anyone be helped (from outside).

2.124.. And (remember) when, Ibrahim (Abraham) was tried by his Lord with certain Commands; these he fulfilled. He (his Lord) said: "I will make you an Imam (guide or example) to the Nations." He Ibrahim (Abraham) pleaded: "And also (Imams) from my off-spring!" He (his Lord) answered: "But My Promise is not within the reach of evildoers."

2.125. And (remember) when We made the House (Ka'bah) a Place of assembly for men and a place of safety; And you take the House of Ibrahim (Abraham) as a place of prayer; And We took the Promise from Ibrahim (Abraham) and Ismail (Ishmael), that they should cleanse (and purify) My House for those who circle it round, or use it as a retreat, or bow, or prostrate themselves (in there in prayer).

2.126. And (remember) when Ibrahim (Abraham) said: "My Lord, make this a City of Peace, and feed its People with fruits, - Such of those who believe in Allah and the Last Day." He (his Lord) said: "(Yes), and for such as those who reject Faith- I grant them their pleasure for a while, but will soon drive them to the punishment of Fire- An evil destination (indeed)!"

2.127. And (remember) when Ibrahim (Abraham) and Ismail (Ishmael) raised the foundation of the House (with this prayer): "Our Lord! Accept (this service) from us; Truly, You are the All Hearing, the All Knowing."

2.128. Our Lord! Make of us Muslims, bowing to Your (Will); And of our children a Muslim People, bowing to Your (Will); And show us our places for the celebration of (due) rites; And turn to us (in Mercy); Verily, You are the One Who Accepts repentance, the Most Merciful.

2.129. "Our Lord! Send among them a messenger of their own, who shall rehearse Your Signs to them and instruct them in Scripture and Wisdom, (cleanse) and provide relief for them: Truly, For You are the Almighty, the All Wise."

2.130.. And who turns away from the religion of Ibrahim (Abraham), except those who injure their souls with folly? Him (Abraham)! We chose and rendered pure in this world: And in the Hereafter, he will be in the ranks of the righteous.

2.131. Listen! His Lord said to him: "Bow (your will to Me):" He (Ibrahim) said: "I bow (my will) to the Lord and Cherisher of the Universe."

2.132. And this was the story that Ibrahim (Abraham) left to his sons, and so did Yàqoub (Jacob); "Oh my sons! Allah has chosen the Faith for you:

Then do not die except in the Faith of Islam."

2.133. Or, were you witness when death appeared before Yàqoub (Jacob)? "Look", he said to his sons: "What will you worship after me?" They said: "We shall worship your Allah and the Allah of your fathers- Of Ibrahim (Abraham), Ismail (Ishmael), and Isháq (Isaac), the One (True) Allah: To Him we bow (in Islam)."

2.134. Those were a people that have passed away. They shall reap the fruit of what they did, and you of what you do! About their merits, there is no question in your case!

2.135.. And they said: "Become Jews or Christians, if you would be guided (to salvation)." You say (to them): "No! (I would rather follow) the Religion of Ibrahim (Abraham), the true, and he joined not gods with Allah."

2.136. You say (to them): "We believe in Allah, and the revelation given to us, and to Ibrahim (Abraham), Ismail (Ishmael), Isháq (Isaac), Yàqoub (Jacob), and the Tribes, and that given to Musa (Moses) and Isa (Jesus), and that given to (all) prophets from their Lord: We make no difference between one and another of them and we bow to Allah (in Islam)."

2.137. So if they believe as you believe, they are indeed on the right path; But if they turn back, it is they who are in (different) faction; But Allah will suffice you against them, and He is All Hearing, All Knowing .

2.138. (Our religion is) the purification from Allah: And who can purify better than Allah? And it is He Whom we worship.

2.139.. Say (to them): "Will you dispute with us about Allah, (after) seeing that He is our Lord and your Lord; That we are responsible for our doings and you for yours; And that we are sincere (in our faith) to Him?

2.140. "Or do you say that Ibrahim (Abraham), Ismail (Ishmael), Isháq (Isaac), Yàqoub (Jacob), and the Tribes, were Jews or Christians?" Say (to them): "Do you know better than Allah?" Oh! Who is more unjust than those who hide the evidence they have from Allah? But Allah is not unaware of what you do!

2.141. Those were a people that have passed away. They shall reap the fruit of what they did, and you of what you do! About their merits, there is no question in your case!

2.142. The foolish ones among the men, will say: "What has turned them (the believers) away from their Qibla (the direction of prayer) that they were used to praying?" Say: "To Allah belong both the East and West: He guides whom He will to the Straight Path."

2.143. Thus have We made of you (believers) a nation of Muslims (followers of faith) justly balanced, that you may be witnesses over the nations, and the Prophet (Muhammad), a witness over yourselves; And We had appointed Qibla (the direction of prayer) to which you were used, only to test those who followed the Prophet (Muhammad) from those who would turn on their heels (from the Faith). indeed it was (a change) momentous, except to those guided by Allah. And Allah would never make your faith ineffective. Most surely, Allah is for the mankind Full of Kindness, Most Merciful.

2.144. (O Prophet!), We see your face turning to the heaven: (for guidance). Now shall We turn you to the Qibla, (the direction of prayer), that shall please you. Turn then your face in the direction of the Sacred Mosque (in

Makkah): And wherever you are, turn your faces in that direction. The people of the Book know well that this is the truth from their Lord. And Allah is not unmindful of what they do.

2.145. And even if you were to bring to the people of the Book all the Signs of Allah (together), they would not follow your Qibla (the direction of prayer); Nor are you going to follow their Qibla; Nor indeed will they follow each others Qibla; And after the knowledge has reached you, if you were to follow their (vain) desires- Then you would be clearly among the wrongdoers.

2.146. The people of the Book know Muhammad this as they know their own sons; But some of them hide the truth that they themselves know.

2.147. The Truth is from your Lord; So do not be one of those who doubt.

2.148.. For each one is a direction to which they turn (in prayer); Then strive together (as in a race) towards all that is good. Wherever you are, Allah will bring you together; Truly, Allah has power over all things.

2.149. And, from where ever you start forth, turn your face in the direction of the Sacred Mosque (in Makkah); That is indeed the truth from your Lord. And Allah is not unmindful of what you do.

2.150. So from where ever you start forth, turn your face in the direction of the Sacred Mosque; And where ever you are, turn your faces towards it (as you pray): So that there be no reason for dispute against you among the people, except those of them who are the wrongdoers; So do not fear them, but fear Me; And that I may complete My favors on you, and you may (be willing to) be guided;

2.151. A similar (favor have you already received) in that We have sent among you a messenger (the Prophet) of your own, reciting to you Our Signs, and purifying you, and instructing you in Scripture and Wisdom, and in new Knowledge

2.152. Then do remember Me; I will remember you. And be grateful to Me and do not reject Faith.

2.153.. O you who believe! Seek (Allah's) help with Patience, Perseverance and Prayer: For Allah is with those who patiently persevere.

2.154. And do not say about those (people) who are killed in the sake of Allah: "They are dead." No! They are living, even though you do not perceive it.

2.155. And be sure We shall test you with some fear and hunger, some loss in goods, or lives, or the fruits (of your hard work), but give glad news to those who patiently persevere-

2.156. (And to those) when afflicted with calamity say: "To Allah we belong, and truly, to Him is our return:"-

2.157. They are those on whom (descends the) blessing from Allah, and (His) Mercy, and they are the ones who receive guidance.

2.158.. Look! (The two mountains named) Safa and Marwa are among the Symbols of Allah. So if those who visit the (Sacred) House in the season (of Pilgrimage) or at other times, should go around them, it is no sin in them. And if anyone follows his own wish to do good- Be sure that Allah is He Who recognizes all, All Knowing .

2.159. Indeed, those who conceal the Clear (Signs) that We have sent down, and the Guidance and Evidence- For (all) the mankind. On them shall be

Allah's curse, and the curse of those entitled to the curse-

2.160. Except those who repent and make amends and openly declare (the Truth); To them I turn in forgiveness: And I am the One Who accepts Repentance , Most Merciful .

2.161. Indeed, those who reject Faith, and die rejecting- On them is Allah's curse, and the curse of angels, and the curse of all mankind.

2.162. They will live in there (for ever): Their penalty will not be lightened, nor will forgiveness be for them.

2.163. And your God is One (Allah): There is no god but He, The Most Gracious - The Most Merciful .

2.164.. Surely, in the creation of the heavens and the earth; In the alteration of the night and the day; In the sailing of the ships through the oceans for the benefit of mankind; In the rain which Allah sends down from the sky, and the life which He gives forth with it to an earth that is dead; In the beasts of all kinds, that He scatters through the earth; And in the change of the winds, and the clouds which they trail like the slaves between the sky and the earth; (Here) indeed are Signs for a people who are wise (and who are) understanding.

2.165. And yet there are men who take (for worship) others besides Allah as equal (with Allah): They love them as they should love Allah. But those of Faith are overflowing in their love for Allah. If only the unrighteous could see; Look! Then they would see the Penalty: That to Allah belongs all power, and Allah will strongly enforce the Penalty.

2.166. Then would those who are followed clear themselves from those who follow (them): They would see the Penalty, and all relations between them would be cut off.

2.167. And those who followed would say: "If only we had one more chance, to return to the worldly life, we would clear ourselves from them, as they have cleared themselves from us." Thus would Allah show them (the fruits of) their deeds as (nothing but) regrets. And there will be no way for them out of the Fire.

2.168.. O mankind! Eat what is lawful and good that is on earth; And do not follow the footsteps of the Satan. Surely, he is to you an avowed enemy.

2.169. For he (Satan, the Evil one) commands you (to do) what is evil, and shameful, and that you should say of Allah that of which you have no knowledge.

2.170. When it is said to them: "Follow what Allah has revealed:" They say: "No! We shall follow the ways of our fathers." What! Even though their fathers did not have the wisdom and guidance?

2.171. And the parable of those who reject Faith is similar to the one (shouting) like a shepherd who loudly shouts to things (cattle) that listen to nothing except calls and cries: Deaf, dumb, and blind, they do not have the wisdom!

2.172. O you who believe! Eat of the good things that We have provided for you, and be grateful to Allah if it is indeed He Whom you worship.

2.173. He has only forbidden you dead meat, and blood, and the flesh of swine and that on which any other name has been invoked besides that of Allah. But if one is forced by necessity, without willful disobedience (of Allah's Word), and without transgressing due limits- Then he is guiltless. Verily, Allah is Often Forgiving, Most Merciful .

2.174.. Surely, those who hide Allah's revelation in the Book, and purchase for them a miserable profit- They swallow into themselves nothing but Fire; Allah will not address them on the Day of Judgment, and will not purify them: Their Penalty will be painful.

2.175. They are the ones who buy error in place of Guidance and torment in place of Forgiveness: Oh! What boldness (they show) for Fire!

2.176. (Their doom is) because Allah sent down the Book in truth but those who search the reasons of disputes in the Book are in a section far (from the purpose of truth).

2.177.. It is not rightful conduct that you turn your faces towards East or West; But it is righteousness- To believe in Allah, and the Last Day, and the Angels, and the Book, and the messengers; To spend from your (own) wealth, in spite of your love for it, for your kin, for orphans, for the needy, for the wayfarer, for those who ask, and for the ransom of slaves; to be steadfast in prayer, and practice regular charity; To fulfill the contracts which you have made; And to be firm and patient, in pain (or suffering), and adversity, and throughout the periods of panic. Such are the people of truth, those who fear Allah.

2.178.. O you who believe! The Law of Equality is to be followed by you, in cases of murder: The free for the free, the slave for the slave, the woman for the woman. But if any remission is made by the brother of the slain, then grant any reasonable demand, and compensate him with handsome gratitude. This is a concession and a Mercy from your Lord. After this whoever exceeds the limits shall be in grave penalty.

2.179. And in the Law of Equality there is (saving of) life to you, (and less bloodshed among you), O you men of understanding; That you may restrain yourselves.

2.180.. It is prescribed for you when death approaches any of you, if he leaves any goods, that he make a will to (give to the) parents and next of kin, according to reasonable usage: (This is) due from those who fear Allah.

2.181.. If anyone changes the will after hearing it, the guilt shall be on those who make the change, for Allah hears and knows (all things)..

2.182. But if anyone fears partiality or wrongdoing on the part of the trustee and makes peace between (the parties concerned), there is no wrong in him: Truly, Allah is Often Forgiving, Most Merciful .

2.183.. O you who believe! Fasting is prescribed to you: As it was prescribed to those before you that you may (learn) self-control.-

2.184. (Fasting) for a fixed number of days; But if any of you is ill, or on a journey, the prescribed number (should be made up) from days later. For those who can fast but with hardship, is a ransom; The feeding of one who is in need. But he who will give more, by his own free will, it is better for him. And it is better for you that you fast, if you only knew.

2.185. The month of Ramadan is the (month) in which was sent down the Quran as a guide to mankind, also Clear (Signs for) guidance and judgment (between right and wrong); So every one of you who is present (at his home) during that month should spend it in fasting. But, if any one is ill or on a journey, the prescribed period (should be made up) by days later. Allah intends every facility for you; He does not want to put you to difficulties. (He wants you) to complete the prescribed period. And to glorify Him because He has guided you; And for this reason, you should be grateful to Him.

2.186. When My servants ask you concerning Me, I am indeed close to them: I listen to the prayer of every (humble) caller when he calls Me: Let them also, listen to My call and believe in Me, that they may be led to the right way.

2.187. Permitted to you, on the night of the fasts, is the approach to your wives. They are your garments and you are their garments. Allah knows what you secretly did among yourselves; But He turned to you and forgave you; So now associate with them (your wives), and seek what Allah has made lawful to you and eat and drink until the white thread (light) of dawn appears to you distinct from its black thread (darkness); Then complete your fast till the night appears but do not associate with your wives while you are in retreat in the mosques. These are limits (set by) Allah; Approach them not in its neighborhood. Thus does (He) make clear His Signs to men: That they may learn self-control.

2.188. And do not eat up one another's property among yourselves for show or pettiness, and do not use it as bribe for the judges, with intent that you may eat up wrongfully and knowingly (even) a little of (other) peoples property.

2.189.. They (the people) ask you (the Prophet) concerning the new moons. Say: "They are only Signs to mark fixed periods of time in (the affairs of) men, and for Pilgrimage." It is no virtue if you enter your houses from the back: It is virtue if you fear Allah enter houses through the proper doors: And fear Allah that you may prosper.

2.190.. And fight in the cause of Allah those who fight you, but do not transgress limits: For Allah does not love those who exceed their rightful limits.

2.191. And slay them (who fight against Allah's cause) wherever you catch them, and turn them out from where they have turned you out; For persecution and injustice are worse than killing. But do not fight them at the Sacred Mosque, unless they (first) fight you there; But if they fight you slay them. Such is the reward of those who block Faith.

2.192. But if they cease, then Allah is Often Forgiving, Most Merciful .

2.193.. And keep fighting them until there is no more persecution and injustice. And justice and faith in Allah continues; But if they cease, let there be no hostile acts except against those who (always) practice (hostilities and) injustice.

2.194. The prohibited month (see Note 2.2):- For the prohibited month- And likewise for all things prohibited- The Law of Equality applies. If then anyone violates the prohibition against you, (then) you transgress likewise against him. But fear Allah, and know that Allah is with those who restrain themselves.

2.195. And from your (own) wealth, spend in the cause of Allah, and make not your own hands contribute to (your) destruction; But do good: Because

Allah loves those who do good.

2.196. And complete the Pilgrimage or Umrah (a pious visit to the Sacred Mosque) in the service of Allah. But if you are prevented (from completing it), send an offering for sacrifice, what you may find (and afford): And do not shave your heads until the offering reaches the place of sacrifice. And if any of you is ill, or has an ailment in his scalp, (requiring to shave, he should) in compensation either fast, or feed the poor, or offer sacrifice; And when you are in peaceful conditions (again), if anyone wishes to continue the Umrah on to Pilgrimage (Hajj), he must make an offering, what he can afford, but if he cannot afford it, he should fast three days during the Hajj and seven days on his return, making ten days in all. This is for those whose household is not in (the immediate closeness to) the Sacred Mosque. And fear Allah, and know that Allah is strict in punishment.

2.197.. For the Pilgrimage, the months are well known. If anyone undertakes that duty, let there be no sign of offense, no wickedness, nor disputes during the Pilgrimage (Hajj). and whatever good you do, Allah knows it. And take a provision (with you) for the journey, but the best of provisions is right conduct. So fear Me, O! You, (people) who are wise.

2.198. It is no sin for you if you seek the bounty of your Lord (during pilgrimage).

Then when you come down from (Mount) Arafat, celebrate the Praises of Allah at the Sacred Mountain, and celebrate His Praise as He has directed you, even though, before this, you went astray.

2.199. Then move on at a quick pace from the place whence it is usual for the people to do so, and ask for Allah's forgiveness. Verily, Allah is Often Forgiving, Most Merciful .

2.200. So when you have finished your (prescribed) duties of Hajj, (see Note 2.2 at the end of the Sura), celebrate the Praises of Allah, as you used to celebrate the praises of your fathers- Yes, with much more (feelings), heart and soul. Some men who say: "Our Lord! Give us (Your bounties) in this world!" But they will have no portion in the Hereafter.

2.201. And there are some men who say: "Our Lord! Give us good in this world and good in the Hereafter, and protect us from the severe pain of the Fire!"

2.202. To these (men) will be allotted what they have earned and Allah is quick in account.

2.203. And celebrate the Praises of Allah during the appointed days. (see Note 2.3 for details of the appointed days after Hajj.) But if anyone has to leave in two days, there is no sin on him, and if anyone stays on, there is no sin on him (either), if his aim is to do right. Then fear Allah, and know that you will surely be brought before Him.

2.204.. There is the type of man whose talks about this world's life may dazzle you, and he calls Allah to witness about what is in his heart; Yet he is the most severe of enemies.

2.205. When he turns his back, his aim is to spread mischief everywhere through the earth and destroy crops and cattle. But Allah does not love mischief.

2.206. And when it is said to him, "Fear Allah." He is led by false pride towards (even more) sin. Enough for him is Hell- An evil bed indeed (to lie on)

2.207. And there is the type of man who gives his life to earn the Pleasure of Allah; And Allah is full of kindness to (such) devotees.

2.208.. O you who believe! Enter into Islam whole-heartedly; And follow not the footsteps of the Satan; For he is to you an avowed enemy.

2.209. Then, if you go back after the Clear (Signs) have come to you, then know that Allah is Exalted in Power, Wise.

2.210. Will they (the non believers) wait until Allah comes to them in canopies of clouds, with angels (in His train) and the question is thus settled? But to Allah all the questions go back (for decision.)

2.211.. Ask the Children of Israel! How many Clear (Signs) We have sent to them, but if anyone substitutes (something else), after Allah's favor has come to him, Allah is strict in punishment.

2.212. The life of this world attracts those who reject faith, and they make fun of those who believe. But the righteous will be above them on the Day of Gathering (Resurrection); For Allah grants His abundance without measure on anyone He wills.

2.213. Mankind was a single nation, and Allah sent messengers with glad tidings and warning; And with them He sent down the Book in Truth to judge between people in matters where they (the people) differed: but the People of the Book, after the clear Signs came to them, did not differ among themselves, except those with selfishness and rejection. Allah by His Grace guided the believers to the Truth concerning that in what they differed. And Allah guides whom He wills to a Straight Path.

2.214. Or do you (people) think that you shall enter the Garden (Paradise) without the many (trials) as (they) came to those who passed away before you? They faced suffering and grief, and were so shaken in spirit that even the Prophet (Muhammad) and those of faith who were with him cried: "When (will come) the help of Allah?" Oh! Surely, the help of Allah is (always) near!

2.215.. They ask you (O Prophet), what they should spend (in charity). Say: "Whatever you spend is good, (it) must be for parents and relatives, and orphans, and those in want, and for the wayfarers. And whatever you do (for them) that is good, Allah knows it well."

2.216. Fighting is prescribed for you, and you dislike it. But you may dislike a thing that is good for you and that you may love a thing that is bad for you. But Allah knows and you know not.

2.217.. They ask you (O Prophet), concerning fighting in the Sacred Months (Muharam, Rajab, Zul-Quadah and Zul-Hajjah – months in the Islamic Lunar Calendar): Say: "Fighting in there is a serious (offense): But in the sight of Allah it is more serious to prevent access to the Path of Allah, to deny Him, to prevent access to the Sacred Mosque, and to drive out its Members." Persecution and injustice are worse than killing. And they will not stop fighting you until they turn you back from your faith, if they can. And if any of you turn away from their Faith and die in unbelief, their works will bear no fruit in this life and the Hereafter; They will be companions of Fire and will abide in there.

2.218. Indeed, those who believed and those who suffered exile and fought in the Path of Allah- They have the hope of the Mercy of Allah: And Allah is Often Forgiving, Most Merciful .

2.219.. They ask you (O Prophet) concerning drinking and gambling: Say: "In them is great sin, and some profit, for men; But the sin is greater than the profit." (And) they ask how much they are to spend (in charity), Say: "What is beyond your needs." Thus Allah makes clear to you His Signs: In order that you may think-

2.220. (About their bearings) on this life and the Hereafter. They ask you (O Prophet) concerning orphans: Say: "The best thing to do is what is for their good; If you mix their affair with yours, they are your brethren; But Allah knows (the man) who means mischief from (the man) who means good. And if Allah had wished, He could have put you into difficulties: He is indeed Exalted in Power, Wise."

2.221.. And do not marry unbelieving women (idolaters), until they believe; And indeed, a slave woman who believes is better than an unbelieving woman, even though she (may) allure you. And do not marry (your girls) to non-believers until they believe: A slave man who believes is better than an unbeliever, even though he (may) allure you. non believers (only) call you to the Fire. But Allah calls (you) by His Grace to the Garden (of Joy) and Forgiveness, and makes His Signs clear to mankind that they may celebrate His Praise.

2.222.. They ask you (O Prophet), concerning women's (menstrual) courses: Say: "They are a hurt and a pollution: So keep away from women in their courses, and do not approach them until they are clean. But when they have purified themselves, you may approach them in any manner, time or place, ordained for you by Allah." Because Allah loves those who turn to Him constantly and He loves those who keep themselves pure and clean.

2.223. Your wives are like a tilth for you; Approach your tilth when or how you will; But do some good acts for your souls beforehand: And fear Allah, and know that you are to meet Him (in the Hereafter); And give the good news to those who believe.

2.224.. And do not make Allah's (Name) an excuse in your oaths against doing good and acting rightly, and making peace between persons; And Allah is All Hearing , All Knowing .

2.225. Allah will not call you to account for thoughtlessness in your oaths, but for the intention earned in your hearts; And Allah is Often Forgiving, Most Forbearing.

2.226. For those who take an oath of abstention from their wives, a waiting for four months is approved; If then they return, surely, Allah is Often Forgiving, Most Merciful .

2.227. But if their intention is firm for divorce, Allah is All Hearing, All Knowing .

2.228.. And divorced women shall wait concerning themselves for three monthly (menstrual) periods. It is not lawful for them to hide what Allah has created in their wombs, if they have faith in Allah and the Last Day. And their husbands have the better right to take them back in that period, if they wish to resolve the differences. And women shall have rights similar to the rights against them, according to what is equitable; But men have a degree (of advantage) over them. And Allah is Almighty, All Wise.

2.229. A divorce is only permitted two times: After that the parties should either stay together on just terms, or separate with kindness. It is not lawful for you, (men) to take back any of your gifts (from your wives). Except when both parties fear that would be unable to keep the limits set forth by Allah. If you (judges) do fear that they would be unable to keep the limits set forth by Allah, then there is no blame on either of them if she gives something for her freedom. These are the limits set by Allah- So do not break them; If any (person) does step beyond the limits set forth by Allah, such persons wrong (themselves as well as others).

2.230. And if a husband divorces his wife (a third time), then he cannot, after that, re-marry her until after she has married another husband and he has divorced her. In that case there is no blame on either of them if they re-unite, provided they feel that they can keep the limits set forth by Allah. Such are the limits set by Allah, which He makes plain to those who understand.

2.231. And when you divorce women, and they fulfill the term of their waiting period (of three monthly courses), either take them back on just and fair terms or set them free on just and fair terms; But do not take them back to hurt them, (or) to take undue advantage (of them); If anyone does that, he wrongs his own soul. Do not treat Allah's Signs lightly- But sincerely recite Allah's favors on you, and the fact that He sent down to you the Book and Wisdom, for your instruction. And fear Allah and know that Allah is All Knowing of all things.

2.232.. And when you divorce women, and they fulfill the term (a waiting period of three monthly courses,) do not prevent them from marrying their former husbands, if they both agree on fair terms. This (instruction) is for all among you, who believe in Allah and the Last Day. That is (the path towards) greatest virtue and purity among you. And Allah knows, and you know not.

2.233.. The mothers should nurse their offspring for two whole years, if the father desires to complete their term. But he shall bear the cost of the mother's food and clothing with fairness and justice. No soul shall have a burden laid on it greater than it can bear. No mother shall be treated unfairly on account of her child. Nor father on account of his child, an heir shall be accountable in the same way. If they both decide on weaning by the agreement of both; After due consultation, there is no blame on them if you decide on a foster mother for your baby, there is no blame on you, provided you pay (the mother) what you offered, with fairness and justice. But fear Allah and know that Allah is All Seeing of all that you do.

2.234.. If any of you die and leave widows behind, they shall wait concerning themselves four months and ten days: When they have fulfilled their term, there is no blame on you if they do as they see fit with themselves in a just and reasonable manner and Allah is well Aware of all that you do.

2.235. And there is no blame on you if you make an offer (a hint) of marriage or hold it in your hearts. Allah knows that you admire them in your hearts: But do not make a secret contract with them except in honorable terms, and do not decide on the tie of marriage till the term prescribed is fulfilled. And know that Allah knows what is in your hearts, and so be fearful Allah; And know that Allah is Often Forgiving, Most Forbearing.

2.236.. There is no sin for you if you divorce women before the marital relationship or the fixation of their dower (or dowry); But offer and give them (a suitable gift), the wealthy according to his means, and the poor according to his means; A gift of a reasonable amount is due from those who wish to do the right thing.

2.237. And if you divorce them (the women) before the marital relation but after fixing a dower for them, then the half of the dower (is due to them), unless they remit it or (the man's half) is remitted by him in whose hands is the marriage tie; And the remission (of the man's half) is the closest to the right conduct. And do not forge to be generous between yourselves because Allah is All Seeing of all that you do.

2.238.. Guard strictly (the habit of) your prayers, especially the Middle (late afternoon) Prayer; And stand before Allah in a pious (frame of mind).

2.239. And if you fear (an enemy), pray on foot, or riding, but when you are in security, celebrate Allah's Praises in the manner He has taught you, which you did not know (before).

2.240.. Those of you who die and leave widows should provide for the widows a years maintenance and residence; Without turning them out, but if they leave (the residence), there is no blame on you for what they may do with themselves, provided it is reasonable, and Allah is Almighty, All Wise.

2.241. For the divorced women the maintenance (should be provided) on a reasonable (scale). This is a duty of the righteous.

2.242. Like this Allah makes His Signs clear to you: So that you may understand.

2.243.. Did you not turn your vision to those who abandoned their homes. Though they were thousands (in number), for fear of death? Allah said to them: "Die." Then He restored them to life. Truly, Allah is full of kindness to mankind, but most of them are ungrateful.

2.244. Then fight in the cause of Allah, and know that Allah hears and knows all things.

2.245. Who is he who will loan to Allah a beautiful loan, which Allah will double to his credit and multiply many times? It is Allah Who gives (you) want or plenty, and to Him shall be your return.

2.246.. Have you not turned your vision to the groups of the Children of Israel after (the time of) Musa (Moses)? They said to a prophet (who was) among them (Samuel): "Appoint a king for us, that we may fight in the cause of Allah." He said: "Is it not possible that, if you were commanded to fight, you may not fight?" They said: "How could we refuse to fight in the Cause of Allah after seeing that we were turned out of our homes and our families?" But when they were commanded to fight, they turned back, except for a small band among them. But Allah has full knowledge of those who do wrong.

2.247. And their prophet said to them: "Indeed, Allah has appointed Tálút as king over you." They said: "How can he exercise authority over us when we are better fitted than he to exercise authority, and he is not even gifted with wealth in abundance?" He said: "Indeed, Allah has chosen him above you and has gifted him abundantly with knowledge and bodily strength over all: And Allah grants His authority to whom He pleases. And Allah is Enough for all, All Knowing ."

2.248. And (further) their prophet said to them: "Verily a Sign of His authority is that there shall come to you the Chest of the Covenant, (see Note 2.4), with (an assurance) of security from your Lord, and the relics left by the family of Musa (Moses), and the family of Haroon (Aaron), carried by angels, in this is a Symbol for you if you really have faith."

2.249.. When Tálút started with the armies, he said: "Verily, Allah will test you at the stream: If any (of you) drinks from its water, He will not go with my army: Only those who do not taste from it (the stream) will go with me: A mere sip out of the hand is excused." But they all drank of it, except a few; When they- He and the faithful ones with him- Crossed the river, they said: "This day we cannot fight Goliath and his forces." But those who were convinced that they must (eventually) meet Allah, said: "How often, by Allah's Will, has a small force overcome a big one (force)?" Allah is with those who constantly work (towards the good).

2.250. And when they advanced to meet Goliath and his forces, they prayed: "Our Lord! Grant us constancy and make our steps firm: Help us against those who reject faith."

2.251. By Allah's Will, they defeated them (Goliath and his forces); And Dawood (David) slew Goliath; And Allah gave him (David) power and wisdom and taught him whatever He willed. And if Allah did not check one set of people by another (set of people), the earth would indeed be full of mischief: But Allah is full of bounty to all the worlds.

2.252. These are the Signs of Allah: We teach them to you in truth; Surely, you (O Prophet!) are one of the (many) messengers.

2.253.. Those messengers: We preferred some of them, some above the others: To some of them (Moses), Allah spoke directly; Others (David), He raised to degrees (of honor); To Isa (Jesus), the son of Maryam (Mary), We gave Clear (Signs), and strengthened him with the Holy Spirit (Gabriel). If Allah had so willed, the following generations would not have fought among each other, after Clear (Signs) had come to them, but they (chose) to differ, some believing and others rejecting. If Allah had so willed, they would not have fought each other; But Allah fulfills His plan.

2.254.. O you who believe! Spend from (the gifts) We have given to you, before the Day comes when no bargaining, no friendship, no praise (or intercession will be useful). And those who reject Faith- They are the wrongdoers.

2.255.. Allah!
There is no god but He-
The Living,-
The Self-Sufficient,-
The Infinitely Enduring,-
Slumber or sleep never reaches Him. All things are His, in the heavens and on the earth. Who is there who can plead in His presence except as He permits? He knows what (appears to His creatures), before or after or behind them. They shall not understand the smallest fragment of His knowledge except as He wills. His Throne extends over the heavens and over the earth, and He does not tire in guarding and preserving them; And He is the Most High, the Supreme (in Glory). [This Holy Verse glorifying Allah is known as Ayât-ul-Kursi.]

2.256.. Let there be no force (or compulsion) in religion: Surely- Truth stands out clear from error: Whoever rejects evil and believes in Allah has held the most trustworthy hand-hold that never breaks. And Allah is All Hearing, All Knowing .

2.257. Allah is the Protector of those who have faith: From the depths of darkness (from where) He will lead them into light. Of those who reject faith their friends are the false gods (and their false 'friends') from light they will lead them into the depth of darkness. They will be companions of the Fire, to dwell in there (for ever).]

2.258.. Have you not turned your eyes at the one who disputed with Ibrahim (Abraham) about his Lord, because Allah had granted him power? When Ibrahim (Abraham) said: "My Lord is He Who gives life and death." He said: "I give life and death." Ibrahim (Abraham) said: "But it is Allah that causes the sun to rise from the East can you then cause it (the sun) to rise from the West." Thus the one who rejected faith was abashed. Allah does not give guidance to a people unjust.

2.259. Or (take) the example of one who passed by a little township, all in ruins up to its roofs. He said: "Oh! How shall Allah bring it (ever) to life, after its death?" Then Allah caused him to die for a hundred years, after which He raised him up (again) from death. Allah said: "How long did you remain (waiting so far)?" He said: "Perhaps a day or part of a day." He (Allah) said: "No, you have waited like this for a hundred years: But look at your food and your drink; They show no signs of age: And look at your donkey: And that We may make for you a Sign for the people look further at the bones, how We bring them together and put flesh on them." When this was shown clearly to him, he said: "I know that Allah is Able to do all things." (For a similar case of the Sleepers of Ephesus, see *Ayât* 18.9-18.22 and Note 2.5)

2.260. And (remember) when Ibrahim (Abraham) said: "My Lord! Show me how You give life to the dead:" He (Allah) said: "Do you not believe then?" He (Ibrahim) said: "Yes! But to satisfy my own understanding." He (Allah) said: "Take four birds; Tame them to turn (fly) to you; (Slaughter them into pieces and) put a portion of them (the birds) on every hill, and (then) call to them they will come to you (flying) with speed. Then know that Allah is Highest in Power, Wise."

2.261.. The parable of those who spend what they own in the way of Allah is that of a grain of corn: It grows seven ears, and each ear has a hundred grains. Allah gives increase many times over to whom He pleases; And Allah is Enough , All Knowing .

2.262. Those who spend what they own in the cause of Allah, and do not follow up their gifts with reminders of their generosity, or with injury- For those their reward is with their Lord: On them shall be no fear, and they shall not be in grieve.

2.263. Kind words and the overlooking of faults are better than charity followed by injury. Allah is Free of all wants, (and He is) Most Forbearing.

2.264. O you who believe! Cancel not your charity by reminders of your generosity, or by injury- Like those who spend what they own to be seen of men, but believe neither in Allah nor in the Last Day. They are in the parable like a hard, barren rock, on which is a little soil; On it falls heavy rain which leaves it (just) a bare stone. They will be able to do nothing with the little they have earned. And Allah does not guide those who reject faith.

2.265. And the likeness of those who spend what they own seeking to please Allah and to strengthen their souls, is that of a garden, high and fertile: Heavy rain falls on it but make it produce a double increase of harvest, and if it does not receive heavy rain, even light moisture will be enough for it. And Allah All Seeing of all that you do.

2.266. Does anyone of you wish that he should have a garden with date-palms and vine with streams flowing under, and (with) all kinds of fruit, while he is stricken with old age, and his children are not strong (enough to look after themselves)- That it should be caught in a whirlwind, with fire in there, and be burned up? Thus does Allah make clear to you (His) Signs; That you may consider.

2.267. O you who believe! Give from the good things which you have (honorably) earned, and of the fruits of the earth which We have produced for you, and do not even receive anything bad (or dishonorable), in order that you may give away a part of it; Something, when you yourselves would not receive it except with closed eyes. And know that Allah is Free of all wants, and Worthy of all Praise.

2.268. The Satan causes you to fear poverty and makes you act in a selfish way. Allah promises you His forgiveness and (His) bounties. And Allah is Enough , All Knowing .

2.269. He grants wisdom to whom He pleases; And he to whom wisdom is granted, (he) receives abundant rewards; But none will grasp the Message except men of understanding.

2.270. And whatever you spend in charity or in love, be sure Allah knows it all. But the wrongdoers have no helpers.

2.271. You may mention the (acts of) charity, however, it is better, if you do not talk about them, and make them reach those (who are really) in need: That is best for you; It will remove from you some of your (stains of) evil. And Allah is well Informed of what you do.

2.272. It is not required for you (O Prophet!), to set them on the right path, but Allah sets on the right path anyone He pleases. Whatever good you give benefits your own souls, and you shall only do so hoping for the (Divine) Face of Allah. Whatever good you give, shall be brought back to you and you shall not be dealt with unjustly.

2.273. (Charity is) for those in need, those in Allah's cause are restricted (from travel), and cannot move about in the land, searching (for work). The ones may without knowing think, Because of their modesty that they are free from want. You shall know them by their (constant) habit: They do not beg openly from all and everyone. And whatever good you give, be sure Allah knows it well.

2.274.. Those (who in charity) spend of their goods by night and day, in secret and in public, have their reward with their Lord: On them shall there be no fear, and they shall not grieve.

2.275. Those who eat from (items including moneys that they receive as) interest, will not stand except as stands one whom The Satan by his touch has driven to madness. That is because they say: "Trade is like usury," But Allah has permitted trade and forbidden usury. Those who after receiving the direction from their Lord, do not receive (usury), shall be forgiven for the past; Their case is for Allah (to judge) but those who repeat (receiving usury) are companions of the Fire: They will live in there (for ever).

2.276. Allah will remove all blessing from usury but will give increase for deeds of charity: For He does not love creatures that are ungrateful and wicked.

2.277. Truly, those who believe and do righteous deeds and establish regular prayers and regular charity, (they) will have their reward with their Lord: On them shall be no fear, and they shall not grieve.

2.278.. O you who believe! Fear Allah and give up what remains of your demand for usury, if you are true believers.

2.279. If you do not do it, (then), take notice of war from Allah and His Prophet (Muhammad): But if you turn back (in repentance), you shall have your capital sums: Do not deal unjustly, and you shall not be dealt with unjustly.

2.280. And if the debtor is in difficulty, give him time till it is easy for him to repay. But if you forgive it (the debt) by the way of charity, that is best for you, if you only knew.

2.281. And fear the Day when you shall be brought back to Allah then shall every soul be paid for what it has earned, and none shall be dealt with unjustly.

2.282. O you who believe! When you deal with each other, in transaction involving future obligations in a fixed period of time, reduce them to writing. Let a scribe (writer) write down faithfully as (a responsible person) between the parties: Let not the scribe refuse to write: As Allah has taught him, so let him write. Let him who incurs the liability dictate, (to the writer), but let him (who dictates) fear his Lord Allah and not reduce even a little of what he owes. If the party (who is) liable lacks mental capacity or (he is) weak, or unable himself to dictate, let his guardian dictate faithfully. And get two witnesses out of your own men, and if two men are not there then a man and two women, such as you choose for witnesses, so that if one makes a mistake, the other can remind her. The witnesses should not refuse when they are called on (for evidence). Do not object to reduce to writing (your contract) of the future period, whether it be small or big: It is more just in the sight of Allah, more suitable as evidence, and more convenient to prevent doubts among yourselves. But if it be a transaction that you carry out on the spot among yourselves, there is no blame on you if you do not reduce it to writing but take witnesses whenever you make a commercial contract; And let neither the writer nor the witness suffer harm. If you do (such harm), it would be wickedness in you. So fear Allah; For it is Allah Who teaches you. And Allah is All Knowing of all things.

2.283. If you are on a journey, and cannot find a scribe, a pledge with possession (that may serve the purpose) and if one of you deposits a thing on trust with another, let the trustee (faithfully) discharge his trust, and let him fear his Lord. Do not conceal testimony; For whoever conceals it- His heart is stained with sin. And Allah Knows well all that you do.

2.284.. To Allah belongs all that is in heavens and on earth. Whether you show what is in your minds or hide it, Allah calls you to account for it. He forgives whom He wills, and punishes whom He wills. Because, Allah is Able to do all things.

2.285. The Messenger (Muhammad) believes in what has revealed to him from His Lord, as do the men of faith. Each one (of them) believes in Allah, His angels, His books, and His messengers. (They say:) "We make no distinction between one and another of His messengers." And they say, "We hear, and we obey: (We seek) Your forgiveness, our Lord, and to You is the end of all journeys."

2.286. On no soul does Allah place a burden greater than it can bear. It enjoys every good that it earns, and it suffers every ill it earns. (Pray:) "Our Lord! Forgive us if we forget or make mistakes (on our part.)" (Pray:) "Our Lord! Place not on us a burden like that which You placed on those before us; Our Lord! Place not on us a burden greater than we have the strength to bear. Wipe out our sins, and grant us forgiveness. Have mercy on us. You are our Protector (Benefactor): Help us against those who stand against Faith."

Sura 2 Notes

Note 2.1. This is the reference to the food (manna) and quail (a species of birds) miraculously sent for Musa and his people as they were fleeing the persecution and armies of Firon (Pharaoh). See *Ayâh* 20.80 for additional reference to the special favor of Allah to the early Jewish people.

Note 2.2. The month of Pilgrimage or Zul-Hajj was the sacred month when no wars were allowed. Later on the earlier month or Zul-qad and the following month or Muharram have also been considered sacred. Earlier the month of Rajab was also a prohibited month. But the enemies of Islam broke this custom and fought with the early followers of Islam. Also some areas of Makkah were considered sacred where no wars were allowed. In this verse 2.194, the reference is to all the sacred months, places and areas. Also see verse 2.217.

Note 2.3. A three-day period after the tenth. During these days the Pilgrims stay in the Mina valley to celebrate the Praise of Allah and to say prayer. This was an ancient custom of the Arabs carried into Islam

Note 2.4. This is the reference to the small wooden chest from the days of Musa and Haroon. In this chest the security from the Lord or the Ten Commandments engraved on the stone were kept. It is to signify peace and security that is associated with this chest and the Ten Commandments.

Note 2.5. The reference is to the three, five or even seven youths who spent a long time in a forgotten cave near Ephesus. Also see 18.13 to 18.22 about the youths and their dog who woke up after spending a long confinement in a mountain cave. The story of (seven) youths in the cave is also recognized in the writings pertaining to the final years of the Fall of the Roman Empire. The youths are acknowledged as Christian boys fleeing the persecution by the Roman soldiers. The city of Ephesus is believed to be on the west coast of Asia Minor about fifty miles from Smyrna. Some of the early writers suggest a time frame of 250 (After Christ) when they went to sleep and woke up after some years.

****

Sura 3. Al-'Imran,

(The family of Imran): (Medinah, 200 Verses)

In the Name of Allah, the Most Gracious, the Most Merciful.

3.1.. **Alif Lám Mim:**

3.2.. Allah! There is no god but He,- The Living, the Self-Sustaining, Eternal .

3.3. It is He Who has sent down to you the Book (in stages) in truth, confirming what went before it; And He has sent down the Torah (to Moses) and the Bible (to Jesus).

3.4. Before this (Quran, as the guide to Mankind) He (Allah) sent down the basis (of judgment between right and wrong) then those who reject Faith in the Sign of Allah will suffer the severest penalty, and Allah is Supreme in Might , Lord of due Penalties (and Rewards).

3.5. Surely, from Allah, nothing is hidden on earth or in heavens.

3.6. He it is Who shapes you in the wombs as He pleases; There is no god but He, the Supreme in might , the All Wise .

3.7.. He it is Who has sent down to you the Book: In it are verses basic or fundamental (of established clear meaning); They are the foundation of the Book: Others are those that have abstractions. But those in whose hearts is evil follow the part within it that is abstract seeking disharmony, in searching for hidden meanings; But no one knows its hidden meanings except Allah: And those who are firmly grounded in knowledge say: "We believe in the Book: The whole of it is from our Lord:" And none will grasp the Message except men of understanding.

3.8. (They say:) "Our Lord! Do not let our hearts stray away now after You have guided us, but grant us mercy from Your Own Presence; Truly, You are the Giver of endless bounties.

3.9. "Our Lord! You are He Who will gather Mankind together on a Day (of Judgment) about which there is no doubt; Verily, Allah never fails in His Promise."

3.10.. Those who reject Faith- Neither their possessions nor their (many) offspring will be of any help to them against Allah: They themselves only (become) fuel for the Fire.

3.11. (Their fate will be) no better than that of the people of Firon (Pharaoh), and the earlier people: They denied Our Signs, and Allah punished them for their sins. And Allah is strict in punishment.

3.12. Say to those who reject Faith: "Soon will you be overcome and gathered together into Hell- An evil bed indeed (to lie on)!

3.13. "There has already been for you a Sign in the two armies that met (in battle): One was fighting in the Cause of Allah, and another resisting Allah; Whom they saw with their own eyes as twice their number. But Allah does support with His help whom He pleases. Surely, in this is a warning for those who have eyes to see."

3.14.. Fair in the eyes of men is the love of things they desire: Women and children; Piles of gold and silver, heaped up; Horses branded (for their excellence); And (wealth of) cattle and well-tilled land. Such are the possessions of this world's life; But in the closeness of Allah is the best of the goals (to return to).

3.15. Say (to them): "Shall I give you glad news of things far better than that? For the righteous are Gardens with their Lord, with rivers flowing beneath: In there is their eternal home; With Companions pure (and holy); And the good pleasure of Allah. For in Allah's sight are (all) His servants."-

3.16. Those who say: "Our Lord! We have indeed believed: So forgive us, for our sins, and save us from the punishment of the Fire;"-

3.17. Those who show patience, firmness and self control; Who are true (in word and deed); Who pray with sincerity (and obedience); Who spend (in the way of Allah): And who pray for forgiveness in the early hours of the morning.

3.18. By the Witness of Allah; There is no god but He: (That is the witness of) His angels, and those gifted with knowledge, standing firm on justice, there is no god but He, the Almighty , the All Wise .

3.19. The (true) Religion with Allah is Islam (submission to His Will), the People of the Book did not differ, except by the envy of each other, after knowledge had come to them. But if any deny the Signs of Allah, Allah is quick in calling to account.

3.20. So if they disagree with you, say: "I have submitted my whole self to Allah, and so have those who follow me." And say to the People of the Book and to those who have not yet learned: "Do you (also) submit yourselves?" If they do, they are in right guidance, but if they turn away, your duty (O Prophet) is to convey the Message; And Allah is All Seeing, for all His servants.

3.21.. Verily, those who deny the Signs of Allah, and without (any justice or) right kill prophets, and kill those who teach just dealing with Mankind, tell them about a grievous penalty.

3.22. They are those whose works will bear no fruit in this world and in the Hereafter, nor will they have anyone to help.

3.23. Have you not turned your sight to those who have been given a portion of the Book? They are invited to the Book of Allah, to settle their disagreement, but a party of them turned back and declined.

3.24. This is because they say: "The Fire shall not touch us but for a few numbered days:" For their (own) lies, (they) deceive them(selves) about their own religion.

3.25. But how (will they do) when We gather them together on a Day (the Day of Judgment) about which there is no doubt, and each soul will be paid in full just what it has earned, without (favor or) injustice?

3.26.. Say: "O Allah! Lord of Power (and Order), You give power to whom You please, and You take away power from whom You please: You bless with honor whom You please, and You bring down whom You please: In Your hand is all Good. Surely, You are Able to do all things.

3.27. "You cause the Night to enter the Day, and You cause the Day come into the Night; You bring the Living out from the Dead, and You bring the Dead out from the Living; And You give means (to live) without measure to whom You please."

3.28.. Let the believers not take for friends or helpers unbelievers rather than believers: If any do that, in nothing will there be help from Allah: Except by way of precaution, that you may guard yourself from them. But Allah cautions you Himself; Because the final goal is to Allah.

3.29. Say: "Whether you hide what is in your (breasts) hearts or say it openly, Allah knows it all: And, He knows what is in the heavens, a and what is in the earth. And Allah is Able to do all things.

3.30. On the Day when every soul will be faced with all the good it has done, and all the evil it has done, it will wish there were a large distance between it and its evil. But Allah cautions you Himself. And Allah is full of kindness for His servants

3.31.. (O Prophet) say: "If you love Allah, follow me: Allah will love you and forgive you for your sins: And Allah is Often Forgiving, Most Merciful"

3.32. Say: "Obey Allah and His Messenger (Muhammad):" But if they turn away, then Allah does not love those who reject Faith.

3.33. Allah did choose Adam and Nuh (Noah), the family of Ibrahim (Abraham), and the family of Imran above the (nations of) people-

3.34. Offspring, one of the other: And Allah is All Hearing and All Knowing .

3.35.. (Remember) when a woman of Imran [the mother of Maryam (Mary) said: "O my Lord! I do dedicate to You (Allah) what is in my womb for Your special services: So accept this from me: Surely, You are the All Hearing , the All Knowing ."

3.36. When she (the wife of Imran) was delivered, she said: "O my Lord! I have delivered a female child- And Allah knew best what she brought forth- And in no way is the male like the female. I have named her Maryam (Mary), and I bring her and her offspring to Your protection from the Satan, the Rejected."

3.37. Rightly (and) kindly did her Lord accept her: He made her grow with good manners, purity and beauty: To the care of Zakariyya (Zachariah) was she assigned. Every time he entered (her) chamber to see her he found her supplied with items of food. He said: "O Maryam (Mary)! From where does this (come) to you?" She said: "This is from Allah: For Allah provides sustenance to whom He pleases, without measure."

3.38.. Then did Zakariyya (Zachariah) pray to his Lord, saying: "O my Lord! Grant to me from You, a generation that is pure: (For) You are He Who hears the (call and) prayer!" (see Note 3.1)

3.39. The angels called to him while he was standing in prayer in the chamber "Allah does give you the good news of Yahya (Baptist John), verifying the truth of a Word from Allah, and (of one) noble, chaste, and a prophet- From the noble company of the righteous."

3.40. He said: "O my Lord! How shall I have a son seeing I am very old, and my wife is barren?", "Still", was the answer, "Allah does accomplish what He wills."

3.41. He said: "O my Lord! Give me a Sign!"; "Your Sign," was the answer, "Shall be that you shall speak to no man for three days except with signs (and gestures). Therefore celebrate the Praises of your Lord again and again, and glorify Him in the evening and in the morning."

3.42.. And (remember) when the angels said: "O Maryam (Mary)! Allah has chosen you and purified you- Chosen you above the women of all nations.

3.43. "O Maryam (Mary)! Pray to your Lord sincerely: And prostrate yourself, and bow down (in prayer) with those who bow down."

3.44. This is part of the news about the things unseen, which We reveal to you (O Prophet!) by revelation: You were not with them when they cast lots with arrows, (and when they decided), about which of them should take care of Maryam (Mary): Nor were you with them when they disagreed (about it).

3.45. (Remember) when the angels said: "O Maryam (Mary)! Verily, Allah gives you good news of a Word from Him: Son of Maryam (Mary), his name will be Messiah, Isa (Christ, Jesus), held in honor in this world and the Hereafter and of (the company of) those nearest (to Allah);

3.46. "He shall speak to the people in childhood and in manhood, and he shall be one of the righteous."

3.47. She said: "O my Lord! How shall I have a son when no man has touched me?" He said: "Even so: Allah creates what He wills: When He has decreed a Plan, He only says to it,

'Be'. And it is!

3.48. "And Allah will teach him the Book and Wisdom, the Torah (the Torah) and Bible (the Gospel),

3.49. "And (appoint him) a messenger to the Children of Israel, (with the message): 'I have come to you with a Sign from your Lord, in that I make for you out of clay, (as it were) the figure of a bird, and breathe into it, and by Allah's leave: It becomes a bird; And I heal those born blind, and the lepers, and I wake up the dead, by Allah's leave: And I declare to you what you eat, and what you store in your houses. Surely, in there is a Sign for you, if you only believe:

3.50. " 'And (I have come to you), confirming Torah which was before me. And to make lawful to you part of what was (before) forbidden to you; And I have come to you with proof from your Lord, so fear Allah, and obey me.

3.51. " 'It is Allah Who is my Lord and your Lord; So worship Him Alone. This is the Straight Path.' "

3.52.. When Isa (Jesus) found disbelief on their part, he said: "Who will be my helpers to (the work of) Allah?" The disciples said: "We are Allah's helpers: We believe in Allah, and do you bear witness that we are Muslims.

3.53. "Our Lord! We believe in what you have revealed, and we follow the messenger (Isa); So write us down with those who bear witness."

3.54. And (the unbelievers) plotted and planned, and Allah also planned, and Allah is the best of planners.

3.55.. And (remember) when Allah said: "O Isa, (Jesus)! I will take you and raise you to Myself and clear you (of the lies) of those who blaspheme; And I will make those who follow you above those who reject faith, to the Day of Judgment: Then shall you all return to me, and I will judge between you of the matters in which you dispute.

3.56. "For those who reject faith and disbelieve, I will punish them with terrible pain in this world and in the Hereafter, and they will not have anyone to help.

3.57. "And for those who believe and work righteousness, Allah will pay them their reward in full; But Allah does not love those who do wrong.

3.58. "This is what We (repeatedly) recite to you about the Verses and the Message of Wisdom."

3.59. Truly, before Allah, the similitude of Isa (Jesus) is like that of Adam; He (Allah) created him from dust, then said to him: "Be", and he became.

3.60. This is Truth (that comes) from Allah Alone; So be not of those who doubt.

3.61. If anyone disputes in this matter with you now after (full) knowledge has come to you, say: "Come! Let us gather together- Our sons and your sons, our women and your women, ourselves and yourselves: Then let us earnestly pray, and invoke the curse of Allah on those who lie!"

3.62. Verily, this is the true account: There is no god except Allah; And indeed Allah- (He is) Almighty , the All Wise .

3.63. But if they turn away, Allah has full knowledge of those who do mischief.

3.64.. Say: "O People of the Book! Come to agreement between us and you; That we worship none other than Allah; And that we do not place partners with Him; And that we do not take from among ourselves, lords and patrons other than Allah". If then they turn their back, you say: "Be it known (to you) and you bear witness that we are Muslims (surrendering to Allah's Will)".

3.65. You People of the Book! Why do you dispute about Ibrahim (Abraham), when the Torah and Bible (the Gospel) were not disclosed till after him? Do you have no understanding?

3.66. Surely! You are those who fell into disagreements in matters about which you had some knowledge! But why do you dispute in matters about which you have no knowledge? It is Allah Who knows and you who do not know!

3.67. Ibrahim (Abraham) was neither a Jew nor even a Christian; But he was true in Faith, and surrendered his will to Allah's, (like a Muslim) and He did not join gods with Allah.

3.68. Verily, without doubt among men, the nearest of kin to Ibrahim (Abraham), are those who follow him and) this prophet and those who believe: And Allah is the Protector of those who have faith.

3.69. It is the wish of a party of the People of the Book to lead you astray. But they shall lead astray only themselves, and they do not understand!

3.70. You People of the Book! Why do you reject the Signs of Allah, to which you are (yourselves) witness?

3.71. You People of the Book! Why do you cover truth with falsehood, and hide the Truth, when you have knowledge?

3.72.. And a party of the People of the Book say: "Believe in the morning in what is revealed to the believers, and reject it at the end of the day; That by chance they may (themselves) turn back;

3.73. "And believe no one except the one who follows your religion." Say: "The True guidance is the Guidance of Allah: (Be sure) that a revelation may be sent to someone (else) like that which was sent to you: Or that those (receiving such revelation) should argue with you before your Lord?" Say: "All bounties are in the hands of Allah: He grants them to whom He pleases: And Allah is Enough , All Knowing ."

3.74. For His Mercy, He specially chooses whom He pleases; For Allah is the Bestower of greatest bounties.

3.75. And among the People of the Book are some who, if entrusted with a large amounts of gold, will readily pay it back; Others, who, if entrusted with a single silver coin, will not repay it unless you constantly stand demanding, because, they say, "There is no duty on us (to keep faith) with these ignorant (pagans)." But they tell a lie against Allah, and they know it well.

3.76. Yes! Those who keep their true faith and act right- Surely, Allah loves those who act righteously.

3.77. Verily, those who sell their faith for a small price, they owe to Allah and their own true word; They shall have no portion in the Hereafter: And Allah will not (find it worthy to) speak to them nor to look at them on the Day of Judgment, nor will He clean them (of sin): They shall have a painful Penalty.

3.78. And surely, there is among them a section who change the Book with their tongues (as they read): You would think it is a part of the Book, but it is not a part of the Book; And they say: "That is from Allah", but it is not from Allah: It is they who tell a lie against Allah, and they know it well!

3.79. It is not (possible) that a man, to whom is given the Book, and Wisdom, and the position of a prophet, can say to people; "Be you my worshippers rather than Allah's:" On the contrary (he would say): "Be you the worshippers of Him, Who is truly the Cherisher of all: For you have been taught the Book and you have studied it truthfully."

3.80. Nor, he would not instruct you to take angels and prophets for lords and patrons. What! Would he invite you to disbelief after you have surrendered your will (to Allah in Islam).

3.81.. And (remember), Allah took the (holy) promise from the prophets, saying: "I give you a Book and Wisdom; Then comes to you a Prophet (Muhammad), confirming what is with you; Do you believe in him and render him help." Allah said: "Do you agree, and take this My Promise as binding on you?" They said: "We agree." He said: "Then bear witness, and I am with you among the witnesses."

3.82. If any turn away after this, they are perverted transgressors.

3.83. Do they search (for a religion) other than the Religion of Allah? When all creatures in the heavens and on earth have willingly and unwillingly, surrendered to Him (and accepted Islam), and to Him shall they all be brought back.

3.84. Say: "We believe in Allah, and in what has been sent down to us and what was sent down to Ibrahim (Abraham), Ismail (Ishmael), Isháq (Isaac), Yàqoub (Jacob), and the tribes, and in (the Books) given to Musa (Moses), Isa (Jesus), and the prophets, from their Lord: We make no distinction between one and another of them, and to Allah do we surrender our will (in Islam)."

3.85. If anyone desires a religion other than Islam (submission to Allah), it will never be accepted from him; In the Hereafter, he will be with those who have lost (all spiritual reward).

3.86. How shall Allah guide those who reject Faith after they accepted it and stood witness that the Prophet (Muhammad) was true and that Clear Signs had come to them (the prophets)? But Allah does not guide those (unjust) people

3.87. For such (people) the reward is that on them (rests) the curse of Allah, of His angels, and of all Mankind-

3.88. In that they will dwell; Their penalty will not be lightened, relief will not be their (share)-

3.89. Except for those who repent and after that, make changes (in their actions); Surely, Allah is Often Forgiving, Most Merciful .

3.90. Verily, those who reject Faith after they accepted it, and then go on adding to their defiance of Faith- Their repentance will never be accepted; Because they are those who have (willfully) gone astray.

3.91. Verily, about those who reject Faith, and die rejecting- Never would be accepted from any such (persons) all the gold that the earth contains, even though they should offer it (only) to ransom themselves. For such (people) is a painful penalty, and they will find no helpers.

3.92.. By no means shall you reach righteousness unless you give (freely) of that which you love; And whatever you give, truly, Allah knows it well.

3.93.. All food was lawful to the Children of Israel except what Israel made unlawful to itself (its people), before the Torah (to Musa) was revealed. Say: "You bring the Torah, and read it, if you are men of truth,"

3.94. Then after that, if any (people) invent a lie, and say it is from Allah, they are indeed unjust wrongdoers.

3.95. Say: "Allah speaks the Truth: Follow the religion of Ibrahim (Abraham), the (one) truthful in faith; He was not of the pagans (or the idolaters)."

3.96.. Verily, the first House (of worship) appointed for men was that (one) at Bakkah (Makkah): Full of blessing, and of guidance for all beings;

3.97. In it are clear Signs; The Station of Ibrahim (Abraham); Whoever enters it attains security; Pilgrimage to it is a duty that men owe to Allah- Those who can afford the journey; But if any deny faith, Allah does not need help from any of His creatures.

3.98.. Say: "O People of the Book! Why do you reject the Signs of Allah, when Allah is Himself witness to all you do?"

3.99. Say: "O you People of the Book! Why do you obstruct those who believe, from the Path of Allah trying to make it crooked, when you were yourselves witness (to Allah's Promise)? But Allah is not unmindful of all that you do."

3.100. O you who believe! If you listen to a group from the People of the Book, they would render you dissidents after you have believed!

3.101. And how can you reject Faith when the Signs of Allah are rehearsed to you and among you lives the Messenger (Muhammad)? Whoever holds firmly to Allah will be shown the Straight Path.

3.102.. O you who believe! Fear Allah as He should be feared, and do not die except in a state of Islam (submission to Allah).

3.103. And hold fast, all of you together by the Rope which Allah (stretches out for you), and do not be divided among yourselves (being Muslims); And remember with thanks Allah's favor on you; For you were enemies and He joined your hearts together in love, so that by His Grace you became brethren; And you were on the brink to the Pit of Fire, and He saved you from it. Thus does Allah make His Signs clear to you: That you may be guided.

3.104. Let there arise from among you a group of people inviting to all that is good, bringing together what is right, and forbidding what is wrong: They are the ones to reach ultimate felicity.

3.105. Do not be like those who are divided among themselves and fall into disputes after receiving clear Signs: For them is a dreadful Penalty-

3.106. On the Day when some faces will be (bright with joy) white and some faces will be (in gloom of) black: To those whose faces will be black, (will be said): "Did you reject Faith after accepting it? Taste then the Penalty for rejecting Faith."

3.107. And those whose faces that will be (bright with joy) white, - They will be in (the light of) Allah's Mercy: To live in there (forever).

3.108.. These are the Signs of Allah: We recite them to you in Truth: And Allah does not mean injustice to any of His creatures.

3.109. To Allah belongs all that is in the heavens and on the earth: To Him do all matters go back (for the final decision).

3.110.. You are the best of Peoples ever, evolved from (Mankind and) for Mankind enjoining what is right, preventing what is wrong, and believing in Allah; And if only the People of the Book had faith, it would be best for them: Among them are some who have faith, but most of them are those who exceed the bound with evil in their minds.

3.111. They will not do you any serious harm, but a little trouble; If they come out to fight you, they will turn back, and they shall not get any help.

3.112. Shame is thrown over them (like a tent) wherever they are found, except when (they are) under a promise (of protection) from Allah and from men; They draw on themselves anger from Allah and upon them is thrown severe poverty. This is because they rejected the Signs (verses) of Allah, and killed the prophets without right; And because they rebelled and crossed the bounds.

3.113. Not all of them are alike: From the People of the Book are a portion that stand up (for right); They read (and declare) the Signs (verses) of Allah all night long, and they prostrate themselves in devotion (to Allah).

3.114. They believe in Allah and the Last Day; They join in what is right, and forbid what is wrong: And they hasten (to carry on all the) good works: They are in the ranks of the righteous.

3.115. From the good that they do, nothing will be rejected from them; For Allah knows well those that do right (and act righteously).

3.116. Surely, those who reject Faith- Neither their possessions nor their (numerous) descendants will be of any use against Allah: They will be companions of the Fire- Living in there (forever).

3.117. What they spend in the life from this (material) world may be compared to a wind that brings nipping frost: It strikes and destroys the crops of men who have wronged their own souls: It is not Allah who has wronged them, but they (continue to) wrong themselves.

3.118.. O you who believe! Do not take into your closeness those (who are) outside your (own) circles: They (those outside your own circles) will not fail to spoil you. They only desire your ruin: Hatred of ranks (and people within your circles) has already appeared from their mouths: What their hearts hide is far worse (than what they have said). Indeed, We have made plain to you the Signs, if you have understanding (and wisdom).

3.119. Oh! You are those who love them, but they do not love you- Though you believe in the whole of the Book. When they meet you, they say: "We believe:" But when they are alone, they bite off the very tips of their fingers in their rage at you. Say: "Perish in your rage; Allah knows well all the secrets of the hearts."

3.120. If a little bit of good comes to you, it saddens them; And if some misfortune comes to you, they become happy at it. But if you are constant and do right, not the least harm will their cunning do to you; Because Allah compasses around about all that they do.

3.121.. And (remember) that morning, when you left your household (early) to leave the faithful (ones) at their stations for battle (of Uhud): And Allah hears and knows all things:

3.122. Remember two of your parties took to cowardice; But Allah was their protector, and in Allah should the Faithful keep their trust.

3.123. And Allah had granted victory to you at (the battle of) Badr, when you were a tiny and weak (little) force; Then fear Allah; Thus you may show your thanks.

3.124. (Remember) when you said to the Faithful: "Is it not enough for you that your Lord should help you with three thousand angels (specially) sent down?

3.125. "Yes- If you remain firm, and act right, even if the enemy should rush here on you to corner (you), your Lord would help you with five thousand angels making a terrific fight back."

3.126. Allah made it only a message of hope for you, and an assurance to your hearts: And there is no victory except from Allah, the Almighty , the All Wise :

3.127. That He may cut off a fraction of the Unbelievers or expose them to shame, and they should then be turned back, frustrated from their purpose.

3.128. Not for you, (but for Allah), is the decision: Whether He turns in mercy to them, or punishes them; For they are indeed wrongdoers.

3.129. And to Allah belongs all that is in heavens and all that is in the earth. He forgives whom He pleases, and punishes whom He pleases; And Allah is Often Forgiving, Most Merciful .

3.130.. O you who believe! Do not take usury, doubled and multiplied; But fear Allah; That you may (really) prosper.

3.131. Fear the Fire, prepared for those who reject Faith:

3.132. And obey Allah and the Messenger (Muhammad) that you may obtain mercy.

3.133. Be quick in the race for forgiveness from your Lord, and for a Garden whose width is that (of the whole) of the heavens and of the earth, prepared for the righteous and those firm in their faith.-

3.134. Those who spend (freely in the cause of Allah), whether there is plenty, or there is little; Who control anger, and pardon (all) men:- Verily, Allah loves those who do good-

3.135. And those who, after having done something to be ashamed of, or (after having) wronged their own souls, earnestly bring Allah to conscience, and ask for forgiveness for their sins- And who can forgive sins except Allah? And are never obstinate in persisting in (the wrong that) they have done, after they know;

3.136. For such (people) the reward is forgiveness from their Lord, and Gardens with rivers flowing underneath- An eternal home: How excellent a reward for those who work (and strive)!

3.137.. There were many Ways of Life that have passed away before you: Travel through the earth, and see what was the end of those who rejected Truth.

3.138. Here is a plain statement to men, a guidance and instruction to those who fear Allah!

3.139. So do not become weak (lose heart) and do not fall into sadness and you must gain mastery, if you are true in Faith.

3.140. If a wound (pain and sorrow) has touched you, be sure a similar wound has touched others; And such days (of varying fortunes) We give to men by turns: That Allah may know those who believe, and that He may take as martyrs (close to Himself) from the people those who see and sacrifice (for the sake of truth). And Allah loves not those who do wrong.

3.141. And Allah's object also is to purify those who are true in Faith and destroy those who reject Faith.

3.142. Did you think that you would enter Heaven without Allah's testing those of you who fought hard and remained committed (to His cause)?

3.143. You did indeed wish for death before you met it: Now you have seen it (in battles) with your own two eyes, (and you draw back!)

3.144.. Muhammad is no more than a messenger: And many earlier messengers passed away before him. If he dies or (if he) is killed, then will you turn back on your heels? (And go back from Islam?) If any(one) did turn back on his heels, he will not do the least harm to Allah, but (on the other hand) Allah will swiftly reward those who (serve him) with gratitude.

3.145. No soul can die except by Allah's permission, the term (of life) being fixed as in writing. If any do desire a reward in this life, We shall give it to him; And if any do desire a reward in the Hereafter, We shall give it to him. And swiftly shall We reward those who (serve Us with) gratitude.

3.146. How many a prophet fought (in Allah's cause), and with him (fought) large groups of men with Belief? But if they met with disaster in Allah's cause, they did not weaken (in will) nor (did they) give in. And Allah loves those who are firm and strive patiently.

3.147. All that they said was: "Our Lord! Forgive us our sins and anything we may have done to fail in our duty: Establish our steps firmly, and give us victory against those who resist Faith."

3.148. And Allah gave them the reward in this world, and the excellent reward of the Hereafter. And Allah loves those who do good (as the virtuous).

3.149.. O you who believe! If you listen to the Unbelievers, they will drive you back on your heels, and you will turn back (from Faith) to your own loss (as the losers).

3.150. No! (Instead, remember that indeed,) Allah is your Protector, and He is the best of helpers.

3.151. Soon shall We put fear (and anxiety) into the hearts of the Unbelievers, because they joined companions with Allah in worship, for which He had sent no authority: Their home will be the Fire: And the home of the wrongdoers is evil!

3.152. And Allah did indeed fulfill His promise to you, when you, with His permission were about to destroy your enemy- Until you hesitated and fell to disputing about the order, and disobeyed it after He brought you in sight (of the things won over in the war) which you love. Among you are some who desire this world and some that desire the Hereafter. He diverted you from your enemies in order to test you. Yet surely, He forgave you: And Allah is full of Grace to those who believe.

3.153. And (remember) when you were climbing up the high ground, without even taking a side look at anyone, and from behind, the Messenger (the Prophet) from the rear was calling you back. There did Allah give you one sorrow after another as a repayment to teach you (how) not to feel sad about (the things won in war) that you had not received; And for (the ill) that had come upon you. For Allah is All Aware of all that you do.

3.154. Then after the distress (and unhappiness), He sent down calm on a group of you overcome with sleep, while another group became anxious by their own feelings, moved by wrong suspicions of Allah- Suspicions due to ignorance. They said: "What affair is this of ours?" You say (to them): "Indeed, this affair is wholly Allah's." They hide in their minds what they dare not say to you. They say (to themselves): "If we had anything to do with this affair, none of us should have been in the slaughter here." Say: "Even if you had remained in your homes, for those whom death had to come, would certainly have gone forth to the place of their death;" But (all of this was) because Allah might test what is in your chests; And purify what is in your hearts. And Allah is All Knowing the secrets of your breasts (hearts).

3.155. Those of you who turned back on the day the two armies met-, it was Satan who caused them to fail, because of some (evil) they had done. But Allah has removed (their evil deed): For Allah is Often Forgiving, Most Forbearing.

3.156.. O you who believe! Do not be like the Unbelievers, and who say of their brothers, when they are traveling through the earth or engaged in fighting: "If they had stayed with us, they would not have died, or have been killed." (This is) because Allah may make it a cause of sighs and regrets in their hearts. It is Allah Who gives Life and Death, and Allah is All Seeing all that you do.

3.157. And if you are killed or die, in the cause of Allah, forgiveness and mercy from Allah are far better than all (the wealth) they can cumulate.

3.158. And whether you die, or are killed indeed! It is before Allah that you are brought together.

3.159.. It is (in part) by the mercy of Allah that you dealt gently with them. If you were severe or harsh-hearted, they would have broken away from about you: So overlook (their faults by pardoning them), and ask for (Allah's) Forgiveness for them; And consult them in affairs (of moment). Then, when you have taken a decision, put your trust in Allah. For Allah loves those who put their trust (in Him).

3.160. If Allah helps you, none can overcome you; And if He forsakes you, who is there after Him who can help you, (after that)? In Allah, then, let believers put their trust.

3.161.. It is not for a prophet to be (ever) false to his trust in the matters of the booty (of the war). If any person is so false, on the Day of Judgment, he shall restore what he falsified; Then every soul shall receive its due- Whatever it earned- And none shall be dealt with unjustly.

3.162. Is the man who follows the good pleasure of Allah like the man who draws on himself the anger of Allah, and whose home is in Hell? And a woeful place (to live)!

3.163. They are in varying grades in the sight of Allah, and Allah is All Seeing all that they do.

3.164. Indeed, Allah did grant a great favor on the believers, when He sent among them a messenger from among themselves, reciting to them the Signs of Allah, and purifying them, and instructing them, in (the Holy) Book and in Wisdom, while before that, they had been in manifest error.

3.165.. What! When a single misfortune strikes you, although you have struck (your enemies) with one twice as great, you say? "From where is this (come to us)?" Say (to them): "It is from yourselves: For Allah is Able to do all things."

3.166. And, whatever (loss) you suffered on the day (when) the two armies met, was with the permission of Allah, in order that He might test the believers-

3.167. And that He may test the hypocrites also, they were told: "Come, fight in the cause of Allah, or (at least) drive (the enemy from the city) and defend yourselves." They said: "If we had known how to fight, we should certainly have followed you." On that day they were nearer to disbelief than to Faith, saying with their lips what was not in their hearts. And Allah has full knowledge of all they hide (in their hearts).

3.168. (They are) the ones who said, (about the killed men) while they themselves sat (at ease): "If only they had listened to us, they would not have been killed." Say: "Hold back death from your own selves, if you speak the truth."

3.169.. Think not of those who are killed in Allah's cause as dead. No! They live by finding their means (to live) in the Presence of their Lord;

3.170. They are happy in the many gifts given (to them) by Allah: And with regard to those left behind, who have not yet joined them (in their peace and happiness), the (true believers) are happy because on them is no fear, nor have they (cause to) be sad.

3.171. They are happy in the Grace and the plenty of good things from Allah, and in the fact that Allah does not cause the reward of the faithful to be lost (in the least).

3.172.. Of those who answered to (the call of) Allah and the Messenger (the Prophet), even after being wounded, those who do right and refrain from wrong have a great reward-

3.173. Men told them: "A great army is gathering against you:" And frightened them: But it (only) increased their Faith: And they said: "For us Allah is enough, and He is the Best One to take care of affairs."

3.174. And they returned with grace and plenty from Allah: No harm even touched them: Because they followed the good pleasure of Allah: And Allah is the Owner of the greatest bounty.

3.175.. It is only the Satan who suggests to you the fear of his own friends (and limitations): You do not be afraid of them, but fear Me, if you have Faith.

3.176. And let not those (people) who rush into unbelief, make you sad: Not the least harm will they do to Allah: Allah's Plan is that He will give them no portion in the Hereafter, except a severe punishment.

3.177. Truly, those who purchase unbelief at the price of faith- Not the least harm will they do to Allah. But they will have a grievous punishment.

3.178. And let not the Unbelievers think that Our delay (in punishment) to them is good for themselves: We grant them the delay that they may grow in their injustice, but they will have a shameful punishment.

3.179.. Allah will not leave the believers in the state that which you are now, until He separates what is evil from what is good. Nor will Allah disclose to you the secrets of the Unseen. But Allah chooses as His messengers (for the purpose of revealing) whom He pleases. So believe in Allah and His messengers: And if you believe and be pious to Allah, you have a great reward (without measure).

3.180. And let not those who greedily hold back the gifts which Allah has given to them from His Grace, think that it is good for them (to hold back): No, it will be worse for them: Soon shall the things which they greedily withheld will be tied to their necks like a twisted collar, on the Day of Judgment. And to Allah belongs the heritage of the heavens and the earth; And Allah is well-Acquainted with all that you do.

3.181.. Truly, Allah has heard the (unkind) remarks of those who say: "Truly, Allah is poor (in need) and we are rich!"- We shall certainly record their word and (their act) of killing the prophets by defying of right, and We shall say: "You taste the Penalty of the burning Fire!

3.182. "This is because of the (evil deeds) which your hands sent on before you: For Allah never harms those who serve Him."

3.183. They (also) said: "Allah took our promise not to believe in a messenger (of Allah) unless he showed us a sacrifice (as a sign) consumed by fire (from heaven)." Say: "There came to you messengers before me, with Clear Signs and (also with) even with what you ask for, why did you then kill them, if you speak the truth?"

3.184. Then if they reject you (O Prophet), other messengers were rejected before you, who came with clear Signs, Books of Scripture (and dark prophecies), and the Book of Enlightenment.

3.185.. Every soul shall have a taste of death: And only on the Day of Judgment shall you be paid your full due wages (for what you have earned). Only he who is saved far from the Fire and admitted to the Garden will have attained the object (of life): Because the life of this world is only goods and passing objects (based upon) deception.

3.186. You shall certainly be tried and tested in your possessions and in your personal selves; And you shall certainly hear much that will cause pain for you, from those who received the Book before you and from those who worship many gods. But if you work hard (persistently and) patiently, and guard against evil- Then that will be a determining factor in all affairs.

3.187. And (remember) Allah took holy Promise from the People of the Book, to make it known and clear to Mankind, and not to hide it; But they threw it away behind their backs, and purchased with it some miserable gain! And false was the bargain that they made (by it)!

3.188. Think not that those (people) who take (extreme) joy in what they have brought about, and love to be praised for what they have not done- Think not that they can escape the Penalty for them (such people) is a Penalty painful indeed.

3.189. And to Allah belongs the dominion of the heavens and the earth; And Allah has power over all things.

3.190.. Truly, in the creation of the heavens and the earth, and in the alternation of the night and the day- There are indeed Signs for men of understanding,

3.191. Men who remember (celebrate) the Praises of Allah, standing, sitting and lying down on their sides and contemplate the (wonders of) creation in the heaven and the earth, (with the prayer): "Our Lord! Not for nothing have You created (all) this! Glory to You! Give us relief from the Penalty of the Fire.

3.192. "Our Lord! Any whom You do admit to the Fire, truly You cover (them) with shame, and never will wrongdoers find any helpers!

3.193. "Our Lord! We have heard the call of the one calling (us) to Faith; 'Believe you in the Lord', and we have believed. Our Lord! Forgive us our sins, remove from us (the stains of) our evil deeds (which we may have done), and take to Yourself as we die, our souls in the company of the righteous.

3.194. "Our Lord! Grant us what You did promise to us through Your messengers, and save us from shame on the Day of Judgment: Because You never break Your promise."

3.195. And their Lord has accepted from them, (and answered them:) "Never will I cause the work of any of you to be lost, whether male or female: You are (members), one of another: Those who have left their homes, and been driven out from there, and suffered harm in My Cause, and fought and been slain- Truly, I will remove from them their (stains of) injustices, and admit them into Gardens with rivers flowing beneath- A reward from the Presence of Allah, and from Allah is the best of rewards."

3.196.. Let not the idle talk of the Unbelievers through the land deceive you:

3.197. Little is it for enjoyment: Their final home is Hell: What an evil bed (to lie on)!

3.198. On the other hand, for those who fear their Lord, are Gardens, with rivers flowing beneath; In there are they to live (for ever)- A gift from Allah; And that which is with Allah is the best (of happiness) for the righteous.

3.199. And there are, certainly, among the People of the Book, those who believe in Allah, in what has been revealed to you, and in what has been revealed to them, bowing in humility (love and obedience) to Allah: They will not sell the Verses of Allah for a low price (miserable gain)! For them is a reward with their Lord, surely, Allah is swift in account.

3.200. O you who believe! Endure and be more patient (struggle on with patience and constancy;) complete in such struggles; - Strengthen each other; And fear Allah; That you may prosper.

Sura 3 Note

Note 3.1: It is implied that Zakariyya (Zachariah) being much older had considered adoption: Perhaps of Maryam (Mary), herself. In any case, his prayers were answered (see 19.7) and he was blessed with a son Yahya (John, the Baptist) late in his life. Allah bestowed high honors on Yahya (Baptist John) and is considered in high esteem with other messengers (Zakariyya, Isa, and Ilyas) of Allah. (see 6.85).

****

Sura 4. An-Nisa',

(The women): (Medinah, 176 Verses)

In the Name of Allah, the Most Gracious, the Most Merciful.

4.1.. O Mankind! Fear (and respect) your (Guardian) Lord, Who created you, from a single person (Adam), and from him, He (Allah) created his mate of similar nature, and from both (the two of them) spread (like seeds) countless men and women- And fear Allah, through Whom you demand your mutual (rights), and revere (and respect) the wombs (that bore you): For Allah always watches over you.

4.2.. To orphans give back their property (when they reach their age); Do not substitute (your) worthless things for (their) good ones; And do not consume their sustenance (by mixing it up) with your own. Because this is truly a great sin.

4.3.. If you fear that you shall not be able to act justly with the orphan (girls), then marry (other) women of your choice, two, or three, or four; But if you fear that you will not be able to deal justly (with them), then marry one, or (a captive) that your right hands possess. That will be more suitable, to prevent you from doing injustice.

4.4. And give the women (in marriage) their dowry as a free gift; But if they, with their own good pleasure, give back any part of it to you, take it and enjoy it with right good cheer.

4.5.. Do not give away the property, which Allah has made as a means of support for (all of) you, to those weak of understanding (and the unwise), but feed and clothe them with it, and speak to them words of kindness and justice.

4.6.. Test (make a trial of) the orphans until they reach the age of marriage; If then you find them of sound judgment, release their property to them; But do not consume it wastefully nor in haste, before their growing up. If the guardian is well-off, let him not receive payment, but if he is poor, let him have for himself what is just and reasonable. And when you release their property to them, take witnesses in their presence: And Allah is All Sufficient in taking account.

4.7.. There is a share for men and a share for women, from what is left by parents and those nearest related; Whether the property be small or large- A determined share.

4.8. But if at the time of division other relatives, or orphans, or poor, are present, feed them out of the (property) and speak to them words of kindness and justice.

4.9. Let those (disposing of an estate) have the same fear in their minds as they would have for their own if they had left a helpless family behind: So let them fear Allah, and speak words of appropriate (comfort).

4.10. Verily, those who unjustly eat up the property of orphans, they eat up only fire into their own bodies: And they will soon be enduring a blazing Fire!

4.11.. Allah commands you regarding (the inheritance for) your children: To the male, a portion equal to that of two females: If only daughters, two or more, their share is two-thirds of the inheritance; If only one, her share is a half... For parents, a sixth share of the inheritance to each, if the deceased left children; If no children, and the parents are the (only) heirs, the mother has a third; If the deceased left brothers (or sisters), the mother has a sixth. (The distributions in all cases is) after the payment of legacies or debts. You know not, which of them, whether your parents or your children are nearest to you in benefit. These are portions settled by Allah; And Allah is ever All Knowing , All Wise.

4.12.. In that which your wives leave, your share is a half, if they leave no child; But if they leave a child, you get a fourth of what they leave; After payment of legacies or debts. In that which you leave, their share is a fourth, if you leave no child; If you leave a child, they get an eighth; After payment of legacies and debts.

..If the man or woman whose inheritance is in question, has left neither parents nor children, but has left a brother or a sister, each one of the two gets a sixth; But if more than two, they share in a third; After payments of legacies or debts; So that no loss is caused (to anyone). It is thus ordained by Allah; And Allah is Always All Knowing , Most Forbearing.

4.13.. Those are limits set by Allah: Whosoever obey Allah and His Messenger (Muhammad) will be admitted to Gardens with rivers flowing beneath, to live in there (for ever) and that will be the Supreme achievement.

4.14. And whosoever disobeys Allah and His Messenger (Muhammad) and exceed His limits, he will be admitted to a Fire, to live in there: And they shall have a humiliating punishment.

4.15.. And if any of your women are guilty of being illicit in (sexual) conduct, take the evidence of four witnesses from your (own) people against them; And if they testify, confine them to the house until they die or Allah decides some (other) way for them.

4.16. And the two persons among you are guilty of lewdness, punish them both; And if they repent and improve, leave them alone; Surely, Allah Forgives and Accepts repentance, Most Merciful .

4.17. Allah accepts only the repentance of those who do evil in ignorance and (their) foolishness and repent soon afterwards; To them will Allah turn in mercy: For Allah is full of knowledge and wisdom.

4.18. And the repentance of those who continue to do evil deeds is of no effect, until death faces one of them, and he says, "Now have I repented indeed," nor of those who die rejecting Faith: For them We have prepared a punishment most painful.

4.19.. O you who believe! You are forbidden to inherit women against their will nor should you treat them with harshness, that you may take away part of the dowry you have given to them- Except where they have been guilty of open illicit sexual deeds (lustfulness); On the contrary live with them on a basis of kindness and justice. If you take a dislike to them it may be that you dislike a thing, and Allah brings about through it a great deal of good.

4.20. But if you decide to take one wife in place of another, even if you had given the latter a whole treasure for dowry, do not take back the least bit of it: Would you take it by slander and a clear wrong?

4.21.. And how could you take it (back) when you have gone in unto each other, and they have taken from you a holy promise?

4.22.. And marry not women whom your fathers married- Except what is past: It was shameful and offensive- A very unpleasant custom indeed.

4.23.. Prohibited to you (for marriage) are-

Your mothers, your daughters, your sisters;

Your father's sisters, your mother's sisters;

Your brother's daughters, your sister's daughters;

Your foster mothers (who breast fed you), your foster sisters; Mothers of your wives;

Your stepdaughters under your guardianship, born of your wives unto whom you have gone in-

(Those who have been) wives of your sons whom you have fathered;

And two sisters in wedlock at one and the same time,

Except for what is past; Verily, Allah is ever Often Forgiving, Most Merciful ;

4.24. Also (prohibited are) women already married, except those whom your right hand possess (as captives in the wars); Allah has thus set limits (prohibitions) against you: Except for these, all others are lawful, provided you seek (them in marriage) with gifts from your property desiring chastity, not lust (nor illicit sexual conduct) seeing that you derive benefit from them, give them their dowry (at least) as prescribed; But if, after a dowry is decided, both of you agree (to change it), then there is no blame on you, and Allah is Always All Knowing , All Wise.

4.25. If any of you do not have the means with which to wed free believing women, they may wed believing (captive or slave) girls from among those whom your right hand possess: And Allah has full knowledge about your Faith; You being one (individual different) from another. In every case, you are to wed them with the permission of their owners (guardians), and give them their dowries, according to what is reasonable: They should be chaste, not lustful (nor sinful), nor taking (illicit) partners; And when they are taken in wedlock, if they fall into shame, their punishment is half that of free women. This (permission) is for those among you who fear sin; But it is better for you that you practice self-control. And Allah is Often Forgiving, Most Merciful .

4.26.. Allah does wish to make clear to you and to show you the faults (ways) of those before you; And (He does wish to) turn to you (in Mercy): And Allah is All Knowing , All Wise.

4.27. Allah does wish to turn to you but the wish of those who follow their lusts is that you should turn away (from Him)- Far, far away.

4.28. Allah does wish to lighten your (difficulties): And man was created weak.

4.29. O you who believe! Do not eat up your property among yourselves in (worthless) deception: But let there be among you exchange and trade by mutual good-will: And do not kill (or destroy) from yourselves: Surely, to you Allah has been Most Merciful !

4.30. And if any does that in hate and injustice- Soon shall We throw him into the Fire: And it is easy for Allah (to do).

4.31. If you (only) avoid the most (excessively) evil of the things that you are forbidden to do, We shall expel out of you all the evil in you, and admit you to a Gate of Great Honor (the Paradise).

4.32. And it is not wise to seek out those things in which Allah has bestowed His gifts more freely on some of you than on others: To men is reward for what they earn, to women (also) is reward for what they earn: And ask Allah of His bounty. Surely, Allah is All Knowing of all things.

4.33. To (benefit) everyone, We have appointed sharers and heirs to property left by parents and relatives. To those also, to whom your right hand pledged, give their due portion. Truly Allah is Total Witness to all things.

4.34.. Men are the protectors and maintainers of women, because Allah has given the one more (strength) than the other, and because they support them from their means. Therefore the righteous women are devoutly obedient, and guard in (the husbands) absence what Allah would have them guard. As to those women on whose part you fear disloyalty and ill-conduct, caution (and warn) them (against the specific faults, at first), refuse to share their beds (next), beat them (lightly, at the very last); But if they return to obedience, seek not against them means (of angering them): Truly, Allah is Most High, Most Great.

4.35. If you fear a break up between the two of them, appoint (two) individuals (to settle their differences), one from his family, and the other from hers (her family); If they wish for peace, Allah will cause their reconciliation: Verily, Allah is All Knowing , and is Well Acquainted with all things.

4.36.. Serve Allah, and do not join any partners with Him; And do good- To parents, (relatives) kinfolk, orphans, those in need, neighbors who are near to you in kin, neighbors who are strangers, the companion by your side, the way-farer (you meet), and what your right hand possess: For Allah does not love the arrogant, the boasters-

4.37. (Nor) those who are miserly (and stingy) or invoke stinginess on others, and hide the bounties which Allah has bestowed on them; And We have prepared, for those who resist Faith, a punishment that pushes them in contempt-

4.38. Nor those who spend of their substance, to be seen of men, but have no faith in Allah and the Last Day: If any take the Satan for their close friend, what a dreadful friend he is!

4.39. And what is the burden on them if they had Faith in Allah and in the Last Day, and they spend out of what Allah has given to them for living? For Allah is All Knowing of them.

4.40. Surely, Allah is never unjust in the least degree: If there is any good (done), He doubles it, and gives from His own Presence a great reward.

4.41. What if We brought from each people a witness, and We brought you (O Muhammad) as a witness against these people!

4.42. On that Day, those who reject Faith and disobey the messenger (Muhammad) will wish that they were buried in the earth: But never will they hide a single fact from Allah!

4.43.. O you who believe! Do not approach prayers (in a murky mind) intoxicated, until you can understand all that you say- Nor in a state of ceremonial impurity except when traveling on the road, until after washing your whole body; And if you are ill, or on a journey, or one of you comes from offices of nature, or you have been in contact with women, and you find no water, then take for yourselves clean sand or earth and rub with it your faces and hands. Truly, Allah is Ever-Pardoning and All Forgiving (again and again).

4.44.. Have you not taken a look at those who were given a portion of the Book? They deal in error, and wish that you should lose the right path.

4.45. And Allah has full knowledge of your enemies: Allah is enough for a Protector and Allah is enough for a Helper.

4.46. Among the Jews there are some who displace words from (their) right places, and say: "We hear your word and we disobey;" And "Hear what is not heard;" And (spoken as) Rá'ina; With a twist of their tongues (meaning; 'the bad one'), and a slander to Faith. If only they had said: "We hear and we obey;" And "Do make us understand (spoken as Unzurna):" It would have been better for them, and more proper: But Allah has cursed them for their disbelief; And only a few of them will believe.

4.47.. O you People of the Book! Believe in what We have (now) revealed, reassuring what was (already) with you, before We change the faces and fame of some (of you) beyond all recognition, and turn them backwards, or curse them as We cursed the Sabbath-breakers, for the decision of Allah must be carried out.

4.48. Indeed, Allah forgives not that partners should be set up with Him; But He forgives anything else, to whom He pleases; And he who sets up 'partners' with Allah has devised a sin most wicked.

4.49.. Have you not taken a look at those who claim holiness for themselves? No! But Allah gives holiness (and purity) to whom He pleases. And they will not fail to receive justice in the least little thing.

4.50. Look! How they invent a lie against Allah! But that by itself is clearly a sin!

4.51.. Have you not taken a look at those who were given a portion of the Book? They believe in magic and evil, and say to the disbelievers that they are better guided in the (right) way than the believers!

4.52. They are those whom Allah has cursed: And he whom Allah has cursed, you will not find, any helper for him.

4.53. Or have they a share in dominion (or power)? Look! They do not give anything of value to their fellow men?

4.54. Or do they envy Mankind for what Allah has given them of His bounty? Then We had already given to the family of Ibrahim (Abraham) the Book and Wisdom, and conferred upon them a great kingdom.

4.55. Some of them believed in it, and some of them turned their faces from it: And enough is Hell for burning them.

4.56. Surely, those who reject Our Signs, We shall soon throw (them) into the Fire: As often as their skins are roasted through, We shall change them for fresh skins, that they may taste the Penalty: Truly, Allah is Almighty, All Wise.

4.57. But those who believe and act righteously, We shall soon admit to Gardens, with rivers flowing beneath- Their eternal home: In there shall they have pure and holy companions: We shall admit them to shades, cool and ever deepening.

4.58.. Allah commands you to fulfill your trusts to those to whom they (your trusts) are due; And when you judge between man and man, that you judge with justice. Surely how excellent is the teaching that He (Allah) gives you! Surely, Allah is All Hearing , All Seeing.

4.59. O you who believe! Obey Allah, and obey the Messenger (Muhammad), and those charged with authority among you. If you differ about anything within yourselves, refer it to Allah and His Prophet (Muhammad), if you believe in Allah and the Last Day: That is best and most suitable for final determination.

4.60.. Have you not seen those (hypocrites) who declare that they believe in the Revelations that have come to you and to those before you? Their (real) wish is to resort together for judgment (in their disputes) to the false judges (and the Satan), though they were ordered to reject them (and him). But Satan's wish is to lead them far astray (from the right).

4.61. And when it is said to them: "Come to what Allah has revealed, and to the Messenger (Muhammad):" You see the hypocrites turn their faces from you in disgust.

4.62. How then, when they are seized by misfortune, because of the deeds which are the acts of their own hands? Then they come to you, swearing by Allah: "We only meant good-will and conciliation!"

4.63. Those men- (the hypocrites) are the ones whom Allah knows what is in their hearts; So keep away from them, but warn them, and speak to them a word that reaches their very souls.

4.64. We did not send a messenger, but only to be obeyed, in accordance with the Will of Allah. If they had only come to you when they were unjust to themselves, and asked for Allah's forgiveness, and the messenger had asked for forgiveness for them, (then) they would have found Allah is Forgiving and accepts repentance, Most Merciful .

4.65. But no! By your Lord, they can have no (real) Faith, unless they make you judge in all disputes between them, and find no objections in their souls against your decisions, but accept them with the fullest conviction.

4.66. And if We had ordered (them) to sacrifice their lives or to leave their homes, very few of them would have done it: But if they had done what they were (actually) told, it would have been the best for them, and would have gone farthest to strengthen their (Faith);

4.67. And indeed, We would then have given them from Our Presence a great reward;

4.68. And indeed, We would have shown them the Straight Path.

4.69.. All who obey Allah and the Messenger (Muhammad) are in the company of those on whom is the Grace of Allah- Of the prophets (who teach), of the Sincere (who are true) of the Martyrs (who are killed in

Allah's cause), and of the Righteous (who do good): Oh! What a beautiful Companionship!

4.70. Thus is the Bounty from Allah: And it is sufficient that Allah knows all.

4.71.. O you who believe! Take your precautions, and either go forward in parties or go forward all together.

4.72. There are certainly among you men, he who would fall behind: If a misfortune befalls you, he says: "Allah did favor me because I was not present with them."

4.73. But if good fortune comes to you from Allah, he would be sure to say- As if there were no affection between you and him- "Oh! I wish I had been with them; A fine thing should I then have made of it!"

4.74.. Let those (people) fight in the cause of Allah, (those) who sell the life of this world for the Hereafter. To him who fights in the cause of Allah- Whether he is slain or gets victory- Soon We shall give him a reward that is Great.

4.75. And what is wrong with you (believers) not to fight in the cause of Allah, those (believers) who, are weak, the ill-treated (and oppressed)? Men, women, and children, the cry is: "Our Lord! Rescue us from this town, whose people are oppressors; And from You give us a guardian who will protect; And from You give us one who will help!

4.76. Those who believe, fight in the cause of Allah and those who reject Faith (and) fight in the cause of Evil: So you fight against the friends of Satan: Weak indeed is the cunning of Satan.

4.77.. Have you not looked at those who were told to hold back their hands (from fight) but establish regular prayers and spend in regular Charity? When (at last) the order to fight was issued to them, look! A section of them feared men as- Or even more than- They would have feared Allah: They said: "Our Lord! Why have You ordered us to fight? Would You not grant us the delay (of death) to our (natural) term, near (enough)?"- Say: "Short is the enjoyment of this world: The Hereafter is the best for those who do right: Never will you be dealt with unjustly in the very least!

4.78. "Wherever you are, death will find you out, even if you are in towers built up strong and high!"

..If some good happens to them, they say, "This is from Allah;" But if evil (happens, to them), they say, "This is from you (O Prophet)." Say: "All things are from Allah." But what has come to these people, that they do not understand a single word?

4.79. Whatever good, (O man!) happens to you, is from Allah; But whatever evil happens to you, it is from your (own) soul. And We have sent to you a messenger to (instruct) Mankind, and Allah is enough for a witness.

4.80. He who obeys the Messenger (Muhammad), obeys Allah: But if any turn away, We have not sent you (O Prophet) to watch over their (evil deeds).

4.81. They have "Obedience" on their lips; But when they leave you, some of them think all night about things quite different from what you tell them. But Allah records their nightly (plots): So keep away from them, and put your trust in Allah, and enough is Allah as a Disposer of affairs.

4.82. Do they not consider the Quran (with care)? If it was from (any) other than Allah, they would surely have found in there lot of discrepancy (and contradictions).

4.83. When there comes to them some matter about (public) safety or fear, they make it be known. If they had only referred it to the Messenger (Muhammad), or to those charged with authority among them, the proper investigators would have verified it (directly) from them. If it were not for the grace and mercy of Allah to you, all but a few of you would have fallen into the (evil) hands of Satan.

4.84.. Then fight in Allah's cause- You are held responsible only for yourself- And stir up the believers (to fight with you). It may be that Allah will hold back the fury of the unbelievers; And Allah is the Strongest in might and punishment.

4.85. Whoever supports and helps a good cause, will have a reward for it: And whoever supports and helps an evil cause, shares in its burden: And Allah has power over all things.

4.86.. When a (courteous) greeting is offered you, follow it with an even more courteous greeting, or (at least) of equal courtesy. Allah takes careful account of all things.

4.87. Allah! There is no god but He, (and no one deserves to be worshipped except Him:) Surely, He will gather you together in the Day of Judgment about which there is no doubt. And whose word can be truer than Allah's?

4.88.. Why should you (O believers), be divided into two parties about the liars (and pretenders)? Allah has defeated them for their (evil) deeds. Would you guide those whom Allah has thrown out of the (Straight) Way? For he whom Allah has thrown out of the Way, you shall never find the Way for him.

4.89. They only wish that you should reject Faith, as they do, and therefore become like them: But do not take friends from their groups until they flee, to the way of Allah (away from what is forbidden). But if they become those who deny (Faith), catch them (by force) and kill them wherever you find them; And do not take friends or helpers from their groups-

4.90. Except those who join a group that has an understanding (of peace) with you, or those who approach you with their hearts not willing to fight you and also not willing to fight their own people. If Allah had pleased, He could have given them power over you, and they would have fought you therefore if they withdraw from you, but fight you not, and (they also) send you (assurances of) peace, then Allah has opened no way for you (to war against them).

4.91. Others you will find, they wish to gain your confidence as well as that of their people: Every time they are sent back, they give in (and yield) to temptation: If they do not pull back from you and do not give you (assurances) of peace besides withholding their hands (from fight), catch them (by force) and kill them wherever you find them: In their favor, We have provided you with a clear argument against them.

4.92.. And a believer should never kill a believer; But (if it so happens) by mistake, (compensation is due): If one kills a believer (by mistake) it is necessary that he (the killer) should free a believing slave, and pay compensation (known as blood-money known as Diya) to the dead persons family, unless they remit it freely. If the dead person belonged to a people at war with you, and he was a believer, the freeing of a believing slave (is enough). If he belonged to a people with whom you had a treaty of mutual understanding, then the   compensation (or Diya) should be paid to his family, and a believing slave be freed. For those who find this beyond their means, he must fast of two months running (without breaks): By way of repentance to Allah: And Allah is All Knowing , All Wise.

4.93. If a man kills a believer intentionally, his penalty is Hell, to remain in there (for ever): And the anger and curse of Allah are upon him, and a dreadful penalty is prepared for him.

4.94.. O you who believe! When you go abroad in the cause of Allah, find out (everything) carefully, and do not say to anyone who offers you a greeting: "You are not a believer!" While wanting the perishable goods of the worldly life. With Allah are plenty of profits and spoils. Even though, you were yourselves (like this) before, till Allah conferred on you His favors: Therefore carefully find out everything (and detail). Verily, Allah is All Aware of all that you do.

4.95.. Believers who sit (at home), except the disabled; And receive no hurt (of fight), are not equal to those who struggle and fight in the cause of Allah with their goods and their person. Allah has granted a position higher to those who struggle and fight with their goods and persons than to those who sit (at home). To each Allah has promised good (reward): But Allah has given a (special) position to those who struggle and fight above those who sit (at home) with a great reward-

4.96. Positions specially given by Him- (And also) Forgiveness and Mercy. And Allah is Often Forgiving, Most Merciful .

4.97.. Verily, as for those, when angels take the souls of those who die in sin against their souls, they (angels) say: "What (condition) were you in?" They reply: "We were weak and oppressed in the earth." They say: "Was the earth of Allah not spacious enough for you to move yourselves away (from evil)?" Such men will find their home in Hell- What an evil refuge!

4.98. Except those who are (really) weak and oppressed- Among men, women, and children- Who have no means in their power, nor (a guide post) to direct their way.

4.99. For these (weak and oppressed), Allah may forgive: And Allah is Often-Pardoning, Often Forgiving.

4.100. He who leaves his home in the cause of Allah, finds on the earth, many places (of rest), (which are) wide and spacious: Should he who has left home, die as a person away from home for (the sake of) Allah and His Messenger (Muhammad), his reward becomes due and certain with Allah: And Allah is Often Forgiving, Most Merciful .

4.101.. And when you travel through the earth, there is no blame on you if you shorten your prayers, for fear the disbelievers may put you in trial (attack you): Surely, the disbelievers are open enemies to you.

4.102. When you (O Prophet) are with them, and stand to lead them in prayer, let one party from them stand up (in prayer) with you, taking their arms with them: When they finish their prostration's, let them take their position in the rear. And let the (believers of) other party come up which have not yet prayed- And let them pray with you, taking all precautions, and bearing arms: Those who disbelieve wish, if you were careless of your arms and your baggage, to attack you in a single attack (or rush). But there is no blame on you if you put away your arms because of the inconvenience of rain or because you are ill; But take every precaution for yourselves. Allah has prepared a humiliating punishment for the disbelievers.

4.103. When you pass (congregational) prayers, celebrate Allah's Praises, standing, sitting down, or lying down on your sides; But when you are free from danger, set up regular prayers: Verily, prayers are enjoined on the believers at stated times.

4.104. And do not slow down in following up the enemy: If you are suffering difficulties, they are suffering similar difficulties; But you have hope from Allah, (for the Reward from Him), while they have none. And Allah is All Knowing , All Wise.

4.105.. Surely, We have sent down to you (O Muhammad) the Book in truth that you might judge between men, as guided by Allah: So be not (used) as a representative by those who betray their trust;

4.106. And ask the forgiveness of Allah; Certainly, Allah is Often Forgiving, Most Merciful .

4.107. And do not speak up on behalf of such as (those who) betray their own souls; For Allah loves not one given to betrayal of faith and crime;

4.108. They may hide (their crimes) from men but they cannot hide (them) from Allah, seeing that He is in their middle when they plot by night in words that He cannot approve: And Allah does compass round all that they do.

4.109. Oh! These are the sort of men on whose behalf you may speak up in this world; But who will speak with Allah on their behalf on the Day of Judgment, or who will defend them?

4.110. If anyone does evil or wrongs his own soul but afterwards asks for Allah's forgiveness, he will find Allah Often Forgiving, Most Merciful .

4.111. And, if anyone earns sin, he (the sinner) earns it against his own soul: And Allah is full of knowledge and wisdom.

4.112. But if anyone earns a fault or a sin and blames it on to one who is innocent, he (the sinner) carries (on himself both) a falsehood and an open sin.

4.113.. If it was not by the Grace of Allah and His Mercy upon you, a party of them would have truly plotted to lead you astray. But (in reality) they will only lead their own souls astray, and to you they can do no harm in the least. Allah has sent down to you the Book and Wisdom and He taught you what you did not know (before): And the Grace of Allah is great for you.

4.114. There is no good in most of their secret talks: Except if one thinks of a deed of charity, or of justice, or of bringing men together: To (the person) who does this for the good pleasure of Allah, We shall soon give him a reward of the highest (value).

4.115. If anyone opposes (and contradicts) the Messenger (Muhammad) after guidance has been plainly given to him, and follows a path that is different from the one for the men of Faith, We shall leave him in the path he has chosen and put him in Hell, what an evil refuge!

4.116.. Verily, Allah does not forgive (the sin of) joining other gods with

Him; But He forgives (those) Whom He pleases sins other than this (sin): The one who joins other gods with Allah, has strayed far, far away (from the Right).

4.117. (The pagans), leaving Him (Allah), seek out female goddesses: And they only seek out only Satan, the persistent rebel!

4.118. Allah did curse him (Satan), and he said: "I will take from Your servants a portion marked off;

4.119. "Verily, I will mislead them, and surely, I will create in them false desires; And certainly, I will order them to slit the ears of cattle, and surely, I will order them to spoil the (fair) nature created by Allah." Whoever, by rejecting Allah, takes Satan for a friend, instead of (taking) Allah, (he) has surely suffered a clear loss.

4.120. He (Satan), makes promises to them, and creates in them false desires; And Satan's promises are nothing but deception (and falsehood).

4.121. They (friends of Satan) will have their homes in Hell, and from it they will find no way of escape from it.

4.122. But those who believe and do good deeds of righteousness- We shall soon admit them to Gardens, with rivers flowing beneath- To live in there forever. Allah's promise is the truth, and whose words can be truer than those of Allah.

4.123.. Neither your desires, nor those of the People of the Book (can last): Whoever works evil, will be paid back accordingly. Nor will he find any protector or helper besides Allah.

4.124. If anyone (or a group) acts righteously- Be they male or female- And (they) have faith, they will enter Paradise and not the least injustice, even to the size of (small) spot on the seed, will be done to them.

4.125. And who can be better in religion than the one who submits his whole self to Allah, the doer of good deeds; And follows the way of Ibrahim (Abraham), the (one) true in faith? And Allah did take Ibrahim (Abraham) for a true friend; (Ibrahim is addressed as a true friend of Allah).

4.126. And to Allah belong all things in the heaven and on earth: And it is Allah Who encompasses all things.

4.127. They ask your legal instruction concerning the women; Say: "Allah does instruct you about them: And (remember) what has been stated to you in the Book, concerning the orphans girls to whom you give not the portions prescribed; And yet whom you desire to marry, and also concerning the children who are weak and oppressed: Yet you stand firm for justice to orphans. There is not a good deed which you do, Allah is Well Acquainted with it."

4.128.. And if a woman fears cruelty or desertion on her husband's part, there is no blame on both of them if they arrange all agreeable settlement between themselves; And such settlement is best; even though men's souls are swayed by greed. But if you do good and practice self-restraint, Allah is Well Acquainted with all that you do.

4.129. You are never able to be (totally) fair and just between women, even if it is your true (and sincere) wish: So do not turn away (from a woman) altogether, so as to leave her hanging (without support). If you come to a friendly understanding, and practice self-restraint, then Allah is Often Forgiving, Most Merciful .

4.130. But if they disagree (and must part by divorce), Allah will provide abundance for all from His all-reaching bounty: And Allah is sufficient for all , All Wise.

4.131.. And to Allah belong all things in the heavens and on earth. And surely, We have directed the People of the Book before you, and you (O Muslims!) to fear Allah. But if you deny Him, (then) listen! To Allah belong all things in the heavens and on earth, and Allah is Free of all wants, worthy of all Praise.

4.132. Yes, to Allah belong all things in the heavens and on earth, and Allah is Enough to complete all affairs.

4.133. If He (so) wills, He could destroy you, O Mankind, and create another race; And Allah has the Power to do this.

4.134. If anyone desires a reward in this life, then with Allah is the reward of this life and of the Hereafter: And Allah is All Hearing , All Seeing.

4.135.. O you who believe! Stand out firmly for justice, as witness to Allah, even against yourselves, or your parents, or your kin, and whether it be (against) rich or poor: Allah protects you both (much) better. So follow not the desires (of your hearts), because you may swerve, and if you distort justice, or decline to do justice; Surely, Allah is Well Acquainted with all that you do.

4.136. O you who believe! Believe in Allah and His Messenger (Muhammad), and the Book (the Quran) that He has sent down to His Messenger (Muhammad) and the Scripture (the Message) that He sent down to those before (him). Any (person) who denies Allah, His angels, His Books, His messengers, and the Day of Judgment, then indeed he has gone far, far astray.

4.137.. Verily, those who believe, then (later) disbelieve, then believe (again) and (again) disbelieve, and go on increasing in disbelief- Allah will not forgive them, nor guide them on the (righteous) Way.

4.138. To the hypocrites give the news that there is for them a painful Penalty-

4.139. To those who take for friends' disbelievers rather than believers: Is it honor they seek among them? Surely, then all the honor is with Allah.

4.140. Already He has sent you the Word in the Book, that when you hear the Signs of Allah held in defiance and disrespect, You are not to sit with them (the disbelievers) unless they turn to different conversation: If you did, you would be like them. For Allah will collect the hypocrites and those who defy Faith- All in Hell-

4.141. (The hypocrites are) the ones who sit and watch about you: If you do gain a victory from Allah, they say: "Were we not with you?"- But if the disbelievers gain a success, they say (to them): "Did we not gain an advantage over you, and did we not guard you from the believers?" But Allah will judge between you on the Day Of Judgment. And never will Allah grant to the disbelievers a way (to win) over the believers.

4.142.. Surely, they, the hypocrites, search ways of deceiving Allah, but it is He Who will deceive (and reach over) them: When they stand up to prayer, they stand without sincerity, to be seen of men, but little do they hold Allah in remembrance;

4.143. (They are distracted in mind) swaying between this and that being (sincere) to neither one group nor to the another (group). (He) whom Allah leaves straying- Never will you find for him the Way.

4.144. O you who believe! Do not take for friends' disbelievers rather than believers: Do you wish to give Allah a manifest proof against yourselves?

4.145. Verily, the hypocrites will be in the lowest depths of the Fire: You will not find a helper for them-

4.146. Except for those who repent, do righteous and good deeds, mend (their life), hold fast to Allah, and purify their religion as in Allah's sight: If so they will be (included) with the believers. And soon will Allah grant to the believers a reward of great value.

4.147. What can Allah gain by your punishment, when you are grateful and you believe? No! It is Allah Who is Appreciative (of all the good), All Knowing .

4.148.. Allah does not love that evil should be talked (and spread in any form) in (any) place, in public speech, except by one against whom injustice has been done; For Allah is All Hearing , All Knowing .

4.149. Whether you declare a good deed, or hide it or cover evil with pardon, surely Allah is Often Pardoning, All Powerful.

4.150. Verily, those who deny Allah and His messengers, and (those who) wish to separate out Allah from His messengers by saying: "We believe in some but reject others:" And (those who) wish to take a course in between-

4.151. They are, in truth disbelievers. And We have prepared for Unbelievers a humiliating Punishment.

4.152. To those who believe in Allah and His messengers and make no distinction between any of them, We shall soon give their (due) rewards: For Allah is Often Forgiving, Most Merciful .

4.153.. The People of the Book ask you to make a book to come down to them from heaven: Indeed, they asked Musa (Moses) for an even greater (miracle), because they said: "Show us Allah in public," but they were overpowered by what they had asked for, with thunder and lightning because of their wrongdoing. Then they worshipped the calf even after clear proofs had come to them; (Even) then We forgave them; And We gave Musa (Moses) clear proofs of authority.

4.154. And for their holy promise We raised over them (the towering height) of Mount (Sinai); And (on another occasion), We said: "Enter the gate prostrating (bowing) with humility ;" And (once again) We commanded them: "Do not transgress in the matter of the Sabbath." And We took from them a truly holy promise.

4.155. (They have earned displeasure of Allah): Because they broke their holy promise; And they rejected the Signs of Allah; And they killed the prophets in defiance of the right; And they said, "Our hearts are the covers (which preserve Allah's Word; We need no more);" - No! Allah has set the seal on their hearts for their blasphemy, and it is little that they believe-

4.156. And because they rejected Faith; And they talked against Maryam (Mary) a seriously false charge;

4.157. And because they said (in boast): "We killed the Messiah, Isa (Christ, Jesus) the son of Maryam (Mary), the messenger of Allah;" - But they did not kill him, nor crucified him, but so it was made to appear to them, and those who differ in this (matter) are full of doubts, with no (certain) knowledge; They follow nothing but idle talk, for sure they did not kill him:-

4.158. But! Allah raised him up to Himself, and Allah is Exalted in Power, All Wise-

4.159. And there is nobody from the People of the Book, but must believe in him (Christ), before his (Christ's) death; And on the Day of Judgment he (Christ, himself) will be a witness against them-

4.160. For the injustice of the Jews, We made unlawful for them certain good and wholesome (foods) which had been lawful for them (earlier)- (And) because they hindered many from Allah's Way-

4.161. And they took interest (usury), though they were forbidden to take it; And that they consumed men's belongings wrongfully- We have prepared for the disbelievers among them who reject Faith a painful punishment.

4.162.. But those among them who are well-founded in knowledge and the believers, believe in what has been revealed to you and what was revealed before you: And (especially) those who establish regular prayers and practice regular charity and believe in Allah and in the Last Day: To them shall We soon give a great reward.

4.163.. Surely, We have sent to you the revelation, like We had sent it to Nuh (Noah) and the prophets after him: We sent revelation to Ibrahim (Abraham), Ismail (Ishmael), Isháq (Isaac), Yàqoub (Jacob) and the Tribes, (the generations of the twelve sons of Yàqoub), to Isa (Jesus), Ayub (Job), Yunus (Jonah), Haroon (Aaron), and Sulaiman (Solomon), and to Dawood (David), We gave the Zabur (Psalms).

4.164. And the messengers We have already told you before, and others We have not (told you)- And Allah spoke directly to Musa (Moses)-

4.165. The messengers gave good news as well as warning, that after (the coming) of the messengers, Mankind should have no (reason to) complain against Allah: Because Allah is Almighty, All Wise.

4.166.. But Allah bears witness that which He has sent to you, He has sent from His (Own) Knowledge, and the angels bear witness: And Enough is Allah for a Witness.

4.167. Surely, those who reject Faith and prevent (men) from the Way of Allah, have surely strayed far, far away from the (right) Path.

4.168. Surely, those who reject Faith and do wrong- Allah will not forgive them nor guide them to any way-

4.169. Except the way of Hell, to live in there forever, and for Allah this is easy.

4.170. O Mankind! Surely, the Messenger (Muhammad) has come to you in truth from your Lord: Believe in him: It is best for you (to believe in him). But if you reject Faith, to Allah belong all things in the heavens and on earth: And Allah is forever All Knowing , All Wise.

4.171. O People of the Book! Do not commit excesses in your religion: Nor say anything except the truth about Allah. Messiah Isa (Christ Jesus), the son of Maryam (Mary) was (no more than) a messenger of Allah, and His

Word, which He sent down to Maryam (Mary), and a Spirit created by Him: So believe in Allah and His messengers. Do not say 'Trinity': Stop (saying so): It will be better for you: Because Allah is One Allah: Glory be to Him: (Far Supreme and Glorious is He) above having a son. To Him belong all things in the heavens and on earth. And, Enough is Allah as a Disposer of affairs.

4.172.. Messiah (Christ) does not find it unworthy to serve and worship Allah, nor do the angels (find it unworthy), those (angels) nearest (to Allah): Those who find His (Allah's) worship unworthy and (those who) are arrogant- He will collect them all together to Himself (to answer for their actions).

4.173. But to those who believe and do deeds of righteousness, He will give their (due) rewards- And more, out of His bounty: But those who are the rejecters and (those who are) arrogant He will punish with a painful penalty. And they will not find, besides Allah, anyone to protect or help them.

4.174. O Mankind! Surely, there has come to you a clear proof from your Lord: And We have sent to you a light (that is) clear.

4.175. Then those who believe in Allah, and hold fast to (and depend upon) Him- Soon will He admit them to mercy and grace from Himself, and guide them to Himself by the Straight Path.

4.176.. They ask you for a legal decision: Say: "Allah directs (thus) about those who leave no descendants or ascendants (i.e., nobody from later or early generations) as inheritor (of belongings). If it is a man who dies, leaving a sister but no child, she shall have half the inheritance: If (such a deceased was) a woman, who left no child, her brother takes her inheritance: If there are two sisters, they shall have two-thirds (between them): If there are brothers and sisters, (they share) the male having twice the share of the female. Like this does Allah make clear to you (His law), in case you make a mistake and Allah has knowledge of all things."

****

Sura 5. Al-Ma'ida,
(The table spread): (Medinah, 120 Verses)
In the Name of Allah, the Most Gracious, the Most Merciful.

5.1.. O you who believe! Fulfill (all your) obligations. Lawful to you are all the beasts of cattle (animals, for food), except those named (below); Unlawful is the game (animals and creatures that you may chase to catch) when you are wearing the I'hram, (the special garments for Pilgrimage or Umrah): Surely, Allah commands what He wills.

5.2. O you who believe! Do not change the holiness of the (sacred) Symbols of Allah, nor of the sacred Month of Ramadan, nor of the animals brought for sacrifice, nor of the garlands (for such animals or of the people), nor of the people coming to the Sacred House (in Makkah) seeking the bounty and the good pleasure of their Lord. But when you are away from the Sacred Grounds and (out) of the pilgrim clothes (I'hram), you may hunt: And let not the hate of some people who (earlier) shut you out of the Sacred Mosque (in Makkah) lead you to overstepping your (own) limits (and bitterness on your part). You help one another in righteousness and in good deeds, but do not help one another in sin and evil: Fear Allah: Because Allah is strict in punishment.

5.3. Forbidden to you (for food) are: Dead meat, blood, the flesh of swine, and that on which has been pronounced the name of (any) other than Allah; And that which has been killed by choking or by a violent blow, or by a headlong fall, or by being (repeatedly) stabbed to death; And that which has been (partly) eaten by a wild animal; Unless you are able to slaughter it (in due form); And that which is sacrificed on stone (alters); (Forbidden) also is the division (of meats) by tearing apart with arrows (for luck): That is impiety. This day, those who reject Faith have given up all hope of (taking you away from) your religion: Yet do not fear them but fear Me. This day have I perfected your religion for you, completed My Favor upon you, and have chosen Islam as your religion for you. But if any (one) is forced by hunger, without any wish to disobey, Allah is truly Often Forgiving, Most Merciful .

5.4. They ask you what is lawful to them (for food), say: "Lawful for you are all good and pure things: And what you have taught your trained hunting animals (to catch) in the manner you have been directed by Allah: So eat what they catch for you, but pronounce the Name of Allah over it: And fear Allah; For Allah is Swift in taking account.

5.5. "This day (all) good and pure things are made lawful for you. The food of the People of the Book is lawful for you and yours is lawful for them. (Lawful for you in marriage) are (not only) chaste women who are believers, but also chaste women among the People of the Book (that was) sent down before your time- Provided you give them their due dowers, and wish purity, not (illicit or lustful) desire, nor secret (and illegal) relations, nor as "women friends." If anyone rejects Faith, then his work is useless, and in the Hereafter he will be among the ranks of the losers (of all spiritual reward).

5.6.. O you who believe! When you get ready for prayer, then wash your faces, and your hands (and arms) up to the elbows; Rub your head (with water); And wash your feet up to the ankles. If you are in a state of bodily impurity, (resulting from sexual contact,) bathe your whole body. But if you are ill, or on a journey, or one of you have come from the offices of nature (i.e., toilet), or you have been in contact with women and you do not find water- Then take for yourself clean sand or earth, and rub your faces and hands with it. Allah does not wish to place you in difficulty, but to make you clean, and to complete His favor on you, that you may be thankful.

5.7. And remember the Favor of Allah on you, and His Promise, which He confirmed with you, when you said: "We hear and we obey:" And fear Allah, because Allah is All Knowing of the secrets of your breasts (hearts).

5.8. O you who believe! Stand out firmly for Allah, as just witness for just (and fair) dealing, and do not let the hatred of others to make you lean towards wrong and go away from Justice. Be just: That is next to Piety: And fear Allah, because Allah is Well-Acquainted with all that you do.

5.9. Allah has promised to those who believe and act rightfully, forgiveness and a great reward.

5.10. And those who reject Faith and deny Our Signs (they) will be companions of Hell-fire.

5.11. O you who believe! Bring into your mind (by remembering) the Favor of Allah on you when certain men made the design to stretch out their hands against you, but (Allah) held back their hands from you: So fear Allah. And upon Allah let believers put all their trust.

5.12.. Indeed, Allah took a Promise from the Children of Israel, and We appointed twelve leaders among them. And Allah said: "I am with you if you (only) establish regular Prayers, practice regular Charity believe in My messengers, honor and help them, and (offer a) loan to Allah a beautiful loan; Surely I will take away your evils from you, and admit you to the Gardens with rivers flowing below; But after this if any of you, stands against (and opposes) faith, he has truly gone away from the path of justice (and honesty)."

5.13. But because of their break of their (own) Promise, We cursed them, and made their hearts grow hard: They change the words from their (right) places and gave up a good part of the Message that was sent to them, also you will not stop finding them- Except a few of them- Always bent on (telling new) lies: But forgive them, and overlook (their wrong doings): For Allah loves those who do good deeds.

5.14. Also from those (people), who call themselves Christians, We did take a Promise, but they (also) gave up a good part of the Message that was sent to them: So We moved them (from love and favor), towards opposition and hatred between the one and the other, till the Day of Judgment, and soon will Allah show them what it is that they have done.

5.15. O People of the Book! Our Messenger (Muhammad) has come to you (now), making it known to you much what you used to hide in the Book, and bypassing much (that is now not necessary): There has come to you a (new) Light from Allah and a (very) clear Book (the Quran)-

5.16. With (this Book) Allah guides all (those) who seek his good pleasure towards the ways of peace and safety, and (He) leads them out of darkness, by His Will to Light- And (He) guides them to the Straight Path.

5.17.. Truly, in blasphemy are those who say that Allah is Messiah (Christ), the son of Maryam (Mary); Say (to them): "Who then has (even) the least power against Allah, if His Will was to destroy Messiah (Christ), the son of Maryam (Mary), his mother, and all- Every one, that is on the earth? And to Allah belongs the kingdom of the heavens and the earth, and all that is between. He (Allah) creates whatever He pleases. For Allah is Able to do all things."

5.18.. (Both) the Jews and the Christians say: "We are sons of God, and His beloved." Say: "Why then does He punish you for your sins? No, you are only men (mere human beings)- Of the (other) men He has created: He forgives whom He pleases, and He punishes whom He pleases: And to Allah belongs the kingdom of the heavens and the earth, and all that is between: And to Him is the final goal (of all)."

5.19. O People of the Book! Now has come to you, making (things) clear for you, Our Messenger (Muhammad), after the break in (many of) Our messengers, in case you should say: "There came to us no bringer of glad tidings and no Warner (from evil):" But now has come to you a bringer of glad tidings and a Warner (from evil). And Allah is Able to do all things.

5.20. Remember Musa (Moses) when said to his people: "O my people! Remember the favor of Allah to you, when He made prophets (from those) among you, made you kings, and gave you what He had not given to any other (peoples and creations) of the worlds.

5.21. "O my people! Enter the holy land which Allah has granted to you and do not turn back as if you do not know, because then you will returned as losers."

5.22. They said: "O Musa (Moses)! In this land, there are a people of great strength: And we shall never enter it until they leave it: If (once) they leave, then we shall enter."

5.23. (But) among (their) men who feared Allah were two on whom Allah had granted His grace: They said: "Attack them at the (proper) gate: When once you are in, victory will be yours: And put your trust on Allah, if you have Faith."

5.24. They said: "O Musa (Moses)! While they remain there, never shall we be able to enter to the end of time. You go, and your Lord, and you two fight, while we sit here (and watch)."

5.25. He said: "O my Lord! I have power only over myself and my brother: So separate us from this defiant people!"

5.26. Allah said: "For this reason the land will be out of their reach for forty years: They will wander aimlessly through the land: But you do not feel sorry over of these defiant people."

5.27.. Read to them the truth of the story of the two sons of Adam. When each presented a sacrifice (to Allah): It was accepted from one, but not from the other. Said the latter: "Be sure, I will kill you." Surely, said the former, "Allah does accept the sacrifice from those who are righteous.

5.28. "If you do stretch your hand against me, to kill me, (then) it is not for me to stretch my hand against you to kill you: Because I do fear Allah, the Cherisher of the Worlds.

5.29. "As for me, I intend to let you take upon yourself my sin as well as yours, for you will be among the Companions of the Fire, and that is the reward of those who do wrong."

5.30. The (selfish) soul of the other (brother) led him to the murder of his brother: (For) he murdered him, and became (himself) one of the lost ones.

5.31. Then Allah sent a raven (a black crow) that scratched the ground, to show him how to hide the dead body of his brother, "Shame (and curse) on me!" Said he: "Was I not even able to be like this crow, and (be able) to hide the dead body of my brother?" Then he became full of sorrow (for his actions)-

5.32. On that basis: We ordained for the Children of Israel that if anyone killed a person- Unless it be for murder or for spreading mischief in the land- It would be as if he killed all mankind (the people): And if anyone saved a life, it would be as if he saved the life of all mankind (the people). Then although there came to them Our messengers with Clear Signs, yet even after that, many of them continued to commit excesses (and do injustices) in the land.

5.33.. The punishment for those who wage a war against Allah and His Messenger (Muhammad), and work hard with strength and taste for mischief through the land, is: Execution, or crucifixion, or the cutting off of hands and feet from opposite sides, or exile from the land: That is their disgrace in this world, and their punishment is heavy in the Hereafter;

5.34. Except for those who repent before they fall into your power: In that case, know that Allah is Often Forgiving, Most Merciful .

5.35.. O you who believe! Do your duty towards Allah, find the ways to come close to Him, and work hard with (all your) strength and will in His cause: That you may prosper.

5.36. Surely, those who reject Faith- If they had everything on earth, and twice again, to offer to save them, from the penalty of the Day of Judgment, it would never be accepted from them. Theirs would be a painful Penalty.

5.37. Their wish will be to come out of the Fire, but they will never come out from there: Their Penalty will be one that continues (on and on).

5.38.. And for the thief, male or female, cut off his or her hands: As a repayment or what they committed a punishment from Allah to be seen for their crime: And Allah is Highest in Power, All Wise.

5.39. But if the thief repents after his crime, and changes his attitude by doing righteous deeds, Allah turns to him in forgiveness; Because Allah is Often Forgiving, Most Merciful .

5.40. Do you not know that to Allah (Alone) belongs the kingdom of the heavens and of the earth? He punishes whom He pleases, and He forgives whom He pleases: And Allah is Able over all things.

5.41. O Messenger (Muhammad)! Do not let those (people) make you sad, (those) who go faster than the others towards disbelief: (Whether it be) among those who say, "We believe", with their lips but whose hearts have no faith; Or it be among the Jews- Men who will listen to any lie- (Men who) will listen even to others who have never even come to you. They change words from their right times and (from their right) places: They say, "If you are given this, take it, but if not, be aware!" If anyone's trial is intended by Allah, you (O Prophet!) have no authority in the least over him to protect from Allah. For such (people) - It is not Allah's Will to purify their hearts. For them there is disgrace in this world, and a severe punishment in the Hereafter.

5.42. (They are fond of) listening to lies, (and) of consuming anything (that is) forbidden. If they come to you, either judge between them, or refuse to interfere. If you refuse, they cannot harm you in the least. If you judge, judge with justice between them. Surely, Allah loves those who judge with justice.

5.43. But why do they come to you for decision, when they have (their own) Torah before them? In there is the plain Command of Allah; Yet even after that, they would turn away. For, they are not (really the) people of Faith.

5.44.. Verily, it was We Who sent down the Torah (to Moses): There was guidance and light in it. By its teachings, the Jews have been judged by the prophets who bowed to Allah's Will- (in submission), by the Rabbis, and by the Doctors of (Judaic) Law: Because the protection of Allah's Book was given to them and they were witness to it: Therefore do not fear men, but fear Me, and do not sell My Signs for a low price. If any do fail to judge by (the light of) what Allah has made clear, they are (no better than) disbelievers.

5.45. And We ordained in there for them: Life for life, eye for eye, nose for nose, ear for ear, tooth for tooth, and wounds equal for equal. But if anyone forgives the revenge by way of charity, it is an act of peace for himself. And if any fail to judge by (the light of) what Allah has made clear, they are (no better than) wrongdoers.

5.46.. And in their footsteps (as if to follow them) We sent Isa (Jesus), the son of Maryam (Mary), restating the Torah that had come before him: We sent the Bible, the Gospel to him: There was guidance and light in it, and confirmation of Torah that had come before him: A guidance and a warning to those who fear Allah.

5.47. Let the people of Bible (Gospel), the Christians judge by what Allah has made clear in there. If any do fail to judge by (the light of) what Allah has made clear, they are (no better than) those who rebel.

5.48.. To you (O Prophet!) We sent the Book (the Quran) in truth confirming the Scripture that came before it, and guarding it in safety: So judge between them (those who come to you) by what Allah has revealed, and do not follow their useless wishes, going away from the Truth that has come to you. To each (of the prophets) among you We have prescribed a law (as in Torah and Gospel) and an Open Way. If Allah had so willed, He would have made you (all) a single People, but (His plan is) to test you in what He has given you: So work hard as if (you are) in a race in all the good deeds. The goal for all of you is Allah: It is He Who will show you the truth of the matters in which you disagree.

5.49. And this (He) commands that: You judge between them by what Allah has made clear, and follow not their useless wishes, but be aware of them in case they misguide you from any of that (teaching) which Allah has sent down to you. And if they turn away, be sure that for some of their crimes, it is Allah's purpose to punish them. And truly, most men are rebellious.

5.50. Do they then try to find a judgment based upon (the days of) Ignorance? For a people whose Faith is assured, who but Allah can give better judgment?

5.51.. O you who believe! Do not take the Jews and the Christians as (friends and) protectors: They are only (friends and) protectors to each other. And he from yourselves who turns to them (for friendship) is (one) of them. Surely Allah does not guide unjust people.

5.52. (And) those (people) in whose hearts is a disease- Do you see how eagerly they run about among themselves, saying: "We do fear that a change of fortune will bring us ruin." Oh! Perhaps Allah will give you victory, or a decision according to His Will, then they will feel sorry for the thoughts that they secretly kept in their hearts.

5.53. And, those who believe will say: "Are these, the (very) men who made their strongest promises by Allah, that they were with you?" All that they do will be useless, and they will fall into (nothing) but ruin.

5.54.. O you who believe! (In case) any from among you turns back from his Faith (in Islam, be sure that), soon Allah will produce a people whom He will love as they will love Him- (People who are) humble with the believers, strong against the Rejecters (of Faith) fighting in the Way (the Cause) of Allah, and never afraid of the (unpleasant) words from those who find fault. That is the Grace of Allah, which He will bestow on whom He pleases. And Allah is All Encompassing and Sufficient, All Knowing.

5.55. Your (real) protector (and helper) is Allah, His Prophet (Muhammad), and the (company of) believers- Those who perform regular prayer and (give) regular charity and they bow down humbly (in prayer to Allah).

5.56. As to those who turn (for friendship) to Allah, His Messenger (Muhammad), and the (company of) believers for protection- It is the party of Allah that must certainly be victorious (over everything).

5.57.. O you who believe! Do not take for (friends and) protectors those who take your religion as a joke or (take it) lightly- Whether (they are) among those who have received the Scripture before you, or among those who reject Faith; But you (who believe) fear Allah, if you (really) have Faith.

5.58. And when you recite your call to prayer they take it as a joke without (any) seriousness that is because they are a people without understanding.

5.59. (To such people) say: "O People of the Book! Do you disapprove of us for no reason other than that we believe in Allah, and the Message that has come to us and that which has come before (us), and (perhaps) because most of you rebel and disobey?"

5.60. Say (to them): "Shall I point out something to you much worse than this, (judging) by the treatment it received from Allah? Those who received the curse from Allah and His anger, those (are the people) of whom some He transformed into apes and swine, those who worshipped Evil and false gods- These are (much) worse in rank, and far more astray from the even Path!"

5.61.. When they come to you, they say: "We believe:" But in reality they enter with a mind (set) against Faith, and they go out with the same (mind). But Allah knows completely all that they hide.

5.62. Many of them you do see, competing with each other in sin and hate, and eating from things forbidden. Indeed! Evil are the things that they do.

5.63. Why do not the Rabbis and the Doctors of (Judaic) Law prevent them (such people) from their (habit of) saying sinful words and eating things forbidden? Evil indeed are their works.

5.64.. The Jews say: "Allah's hand is tied up." Be (it is) their hands (that are) tied up and (let) them be cursed for the (lies) they say (against Allah!). No! Both His hands are widely stretched out: He gives and spends as He pleases. Surely, the Message that comes to you from Allah increases in many of them, their rebellion and disbelief (against Allah). Among them We have placed opposition and hatred till the Day of Judgment. Every time they light a fire for war, Allah extinguishes it: But they (always) work hard in doing mischief on earth. And Allah does not love those who do mischief.

5.65. If the people of the Book had only believed and been righteous, We should indeed have removed their sin and admitted them to Gardens of Happiness.

5.66. If they had only truthfully followed the Torah and the Gospel, and all the revelation that was sent to them from their Lord, they would have enjoyed happiness and satisfaction from all direction. From among them, there is a party on the right path: But many of them follow a path that is evil.

5.67.. O Messenger (Muhammad)! Proclaim (the Message) which has been sent to you from your Lord: If you did not, you would not have conveyed and made clear His Message. And Allah will defend you from men (who intend to harm you). Allah does not (help and) guide those who reject Faith.

5.68. Say: "O People of the Book! You have no ground to stand on unless you truly stand by the Torah, the Gospel, and all of the Message that has come to you from your Lord." It is the (same) Message that comes to you from your Lord, that increases in most of them their long lasting revolt and lies (meant against Allah). But you do not feel sorry for these people without Faith.

5.69. Surely, those who believe (in the Quran), and those who follow the Judaic (Jewish) scriptures and the Sabians and the Christians- Any who believe in Allah and the Last Day, and (people who) work towards righteousness- Upon them there shall be no fear, and they shall not be in pain.

5.70. We took the Promise from the Children of Israel and sent them messengers. Every time, a messenger came to them with what they themselves did not want- Some (of these messengers) they called liars (only acting as messengers), and some they (would even) kill.

5.71. They thought there would be no trial (Or punishment for their actions) so they became blind and deaf; (not to see or to hear about their own actions.) yet Allah (in Mercy) turned to them; even after that, many of them became blind and deaf. But Allah sees well all that they do.

5.72.. They surely lie (against Allah, those) who say, "Allah is Messiah (Christ), the son of Maryam (Mary)." But Messiah (Christ himself) said: "O Children of Israel! Worship Allah, my Lord and your Lord." Verily, whoever joins other gods with Allah, Allah will forbid him the Garden, and the Fire will be his home. For the wrongdoers there will be no one to help.

5.73. They surely lie (against Allah, those) who say, "Allah is one of three in a Trinity:" There is no god except One Allah. If they do not stop (themselves) from their word (of lies), a painful penalty will surely fall upon the liars among them.

5.74. Why do they not turn to Allah, and seek His forgiveness? For Allah is Often Forgiving, Most Merciful .

5.75. Messiah (Christ), the son of Maryam (Mary) was no more than a messenger; (And there were) many messengers that have passed away before him. His mother was a woman of truth. They both had to eat their (daily) food. See how Allah does make His Signs clear to them; Yet see in what ways they are misguided far from the truth!

5.76. Say: "Will you worship, besides Allah, something which has no power to either harm (you) or to help you? But Allah- He is the All Hearing , the All Knowing ."

5.77. Say: "O People of the Book! Do not exceed the limits in your religion (of what is proper by) going beyond the truth, and do not follow the useless desires of people who went wrong in old times- (Those) who misled many, and wandered (themselves away) from the even path."

5.78.. Curses were said by the tongues of Dawood (David) and of Isa (Jesus), the son of Maryam (Mary): On those among the Children of Israel who rejected Faith; Because they disobeyed and continued to be excessive.

5.79. Also (because) they did not (often) prevent one another from the iniquities that they committed: The deeds that they did were indeed evil.

5.80. You see many of them turning in friendship to the disbelievers. Evil indeed are (the works) which their souls have sent forward before them (as a result), that Allah's anger is on them, and in extreme pain will they live.

5.81. If they had only believed in Allah, in the Prophet, and in what has been sent down to him, they (the believers) would have never taken them (the disbelievers) for friends and protectors, but most of them are rebellious, wrongdoers.

5.82. Verily, you will find the Jews and polytheists among the strongest men in opposition to the Believers; And you will find nearest in love to the believers those who say, "We are Christians:" Because among these (people) are men devoted to learning and men who have given up the world, and they are not haughty.

5.83. And when they listen to the Message received by the Messenger (Muhammad), you will see their eyes overflowing with tears, because they recognize (and see) the truth: They pray: "Our Lord! We believe; Write us down among the witnesses.

5.84. "What cause can we have not to believe in Allah and the truth which has come to us, seeing that we lovingly want for our Lord to admit us to the company of the righteous?"

5.85. And for this (and) their prayer, Allah has rewarded them with Gardens, with rivers flowing below- Their lasting Home. Such is the reward of those who do good.

5.86. But those who reject Faith and make lies about Our Signs- They shall be Companions of Hell-fire.

5.87.. O you who believe! Do not make unlawful the good things that Allah has made lawful for you, but do not overdo (anything or be excessive): For Allah does not love those who overdo (as a habit).

5.88. Eat from the lawful and good things that Allah has provided for you, but fear Allah, in Whom you believe.

5.89. Allah will not ask you to account for what is unintentional in your oath; But He will ask you to account for your deliberate oath: To make up (in such cases), feed ten needy persons, on a scale of the average food of your families; Or clothe them; Or give a slave his freedom. If that is beyond your means, fast for three days. That is to make up (or compensate) for the oath you have sworn. But keep to your oath, like this Allah does make clear to you His Signs, that you may be thankful.

5.90.. O you who believe! Intoxicants and gambling, stones (for sacrifice or for idyllic gestures), and (divination by) arrows, are (all most) undesirable- Of Satan's tricks (and his works) avoid such (undesirable things), so that you may prosper.

5.91. Satan's plan is (only) to cause opposition and hatred between you, with intoxicants and gambling, and hinders you from remembering Allah, and from (your) prayer (to Him): Will you then avoid (and keep away from them)?

5.92. Obey Allah, and obey the Messenger (Muhammad), and be aware (of evil) if you do turn back, (you) know that it is the duty of Our Messenger (Muhammad) to speak out (the Message) clearly.

5.93. On those who believe and do righteous deeds; There is no blame for what they ate (as food in the past) when they guard themselves from evil, and believe, and do righteous deeds- (Once) again! Guard themselves from evil and believe- (Once) again! Guard themselves from evil and do good. For Allah loves those who do good.

5.94.. O you who believe! Allah does make a trial for you in a little matter of game well within reach of your hands and your means, so that He may test who (really) fear Him Unseen: Any who exceed (their limits) afterwards, will have a painful penalty.

5.95. O you who believe! Kill not game (for sport or for food) while in the

Sacred Grounds (of the Holy Mosque) or (while being) in pilgrim clothes
(or I'hram). If any of you does so knowingly, the compensation is an
Offering, brought to the *Ka'bah*, of a domestic animal equivalent to the one
he killed, as decided by two just men from yourselves; Or by way of
making up (the peace), the feeding of the needy, or its equivalent in fasts;
That he may taste the penalty of his deed. Allah forgives what is past: For
repeating (such acts) Allah will take from him the penalty. And Allah is
Almighty, and Lord of Retribution.

5.96. Lawful to you is the pursuit of water-game and its use for food- For
the benefit of yourselves and those who travel; But forbidden is (the
pursuit) of land-game; As long as you are in the state of I'hram (or in
pilgrim clothes). And fear Allah, to Whom you shall be gathered back.

5.97. Allah made the Ka'bah, the Sacred House, a place of security and
benefit for men, as also (He made) the Sacred Months, and the animals for
offerings, and the garlands, that mark them: That you may know that Allah
has knowledge of all what is in the heavens and in the earth and that Allah
is All Knowing of all things.

5.98. Know that Allah is strict in punishment; And that Allah is Often
Forgiving, Most Merciful .

5.99. The duty of the Messenger (Muhammad) is only to proclaim the
Message but Allah knows what you reveal and what you conceal.

5.100. Say: "Things that are bad and things that are good, are not equal,
even though the plenty (and extent) of the bad may surprise (and even
attract) you; So fear Allah, O you who understand; So that you may
prosper."

5.101. O you who believe! Do not ask questions about things which, if (they
are) made clear to you, may bring about trouble to you. But if you ask about
things when the Quran is being recited (and made clear to you), then they
will be made plain to you, Allah will forgive those (questions): And Allah is
Often Forgiving, Most Forbearing.

5.102. Some people before you asked such questions, and for that reason
(they) lost their faith.

5.103. It was not Allah, who began (false beliefs like those of) a slit-ear
female camel, and a female camel let loose for free grazing, and idol
sacrifices for twin-births in animals, and stallion-camels freed from work: It
is the blasphemers who invent a lie against Allah: But most of them
(simply) lack wisdom.

5.104. When it is said to them: "Come to what Allah has revealed, and come
to the Messenger (Muhammad):" They say: "The ways we found our fathers
following are enough for us." What! Even though their fathers did not have
the knowledge and guidance?

5.105. O you who believe! Guard your own souls: If you follow (right)
guidance, no pain (or sorrow) can come to you from those who have lost
their way. The return for all of you is Allah: It is He Who will show you the
truth of all that you do.

5.106. O you who believe! When death comes near any of you, (take)
witnesses among yourselves when making (legal or last time) changes-
Entrust two just men from your own (community) or others from outside, if

you are traveling through the earth (world), and the chance of death comes to you (thus). If you doubt (their truthfulness) make them both stay after prayer, and let them both swear by Allah: "We do not wish for any worldly gain in this (matter) even though the (beneficiary) be our near relation: We shall not hide the evidence before Allah if we did, then look! The sin (will) be upon us!"

5.107. But if it gets known that these two were guilty of the sin (of lying after their promise), let two others stand forth in their places- Nearest of kin from among those, who claim a lawful right: Let them swear by Allah: "We affirm that our witness is truer than that of those two, and that we have not altered (the truth) or gone beyond (the bounds of duty) if we did, then look! The wrong (will) be upon us!"

5.108. That is most suitable: That they may give evidence in its true nature and shape, (and in its true meaning) or else they would fear that other statements would be taken after their statements. And fear Allah, and listen (with sincerity to His Word): For Allah does not guide people who are rebellious.

5.109.. On the Day, when Allah will gather the messengers together, and asks them: "What was the response you received (from men to your teaching)?" They will say: "We have no knowledge: (It is) only You are All Knowing of all that is Hidden."

5.110. Then will Allah say (on the Day of Judgment): "O Isa (Jesus) the son of Maryam (Mary)! Remember My favor to you and to your mother; Look! I strengthened you with the Holy Spirit (Gabriel) so that you did speak to the people in childhood and in maturity. Look! I taught you the Book and Wisdom, the Torah and the Gospel, and when you made out of clay, as it were, the figure of a bird, by My leave, and you breathed into it, and it became a bird, by My leave, and you healed those (who were) born blind, and the lepers, by My leave. And when you brought forth the dead, by My leave; And when I did restrain the Children of Israel from (harming) you; When you did show them the Clear Signs, and the disbelievers among them said: 'This is nothing but clear magic.'

5.111. "And look! I inspired the disciples to have faith in Me and My messenger: They said: 'We have faith, and do you (also) bear witness that we bow to Allah as Muslims.' "

5.112.. Remember! The disciples said: "O Isa (Jesus) the son of Maryam (Mary)! Can your Lord send down to us a Table set (spread with food) from heaven?" (For which) Isa (Jesus) said: "Fear Allah, if you have faith."

5.113. They said: "We only wish to eat from there and satisfy our hearts, and to know that you have indeed told us the truth: And that we ourselves may be witness to the miracle."

5.114. Isa (Jesus), the son of Maryam (Mary), said: "O Allah, our Lord! Send us from heaven a Table set (with meats and food), that there may be for us- For the first and the last of us- A true and holy feast and a Sign from You; And provide for us the means to live, for You are the Best Provider (of our needs)."

5.115. Allah said: "I will send it (the Table) down to you: But if any of you does not accept faith after that, I will punish him with a penalty like that I have not inflicted on anyone from among all the peoples."

5.116.. And remember! Allah will say (on the Day of Judgment): "O Isa

(Jesus) the son of Maryam (Mary)! Did you say to men, 'Worship me and my mother as gods in derogation of Allah'?" He (Isa) will say: "Glory be to You! It was not for me to say what I had no right to say. If I had said such a thing, You would indeed have known it. You know what is in my heart, even though I do not know what is in Yours. Truly, You fully know all that is hidden and unseen.

5.117. "Never did I say to them anything except what You did command me to say, which is, worship Allah, my Lord and your Lord: And I was a witness over them while I lived among them; When You did take me up, You were the Watcher over them, and You are a Witness to all things.

5.118. "If You do punish them, they are Your servants: If You do forgive them; Surely, You are the Almighty , the All Wise ."

5.119. Allah will say: "This is a day on which the truthful will profit from their truth: Theirs are Gardens, with rivers flowing below- Their eternal Home: Allah well-pleased with them, and they with Allah: That is the great Joy (and Peace, the fulfillment of all desires)."

5.120. To Allah belongs the kingdom of the heavens and the earth, and all that is in there, and it is He Who is Able to do all things.

****

Sura 6. Al-An'am,
(The cattle): (Makkah, 165 Verses)
In the Name of Allah, the Most Gracious, the Most Merciful.

6.1. All the Praises (and thanks) be to Allah Who created the heavens and the earth, and made the darkness and the light. Yet those who disbelieve hold others as equal with their Guardian-Lord!

6.2. He it is Who created you from clay, and then granted (you) a span of time (to live). And in His Presence, there is (still) another determined length of time; Yet, you doubt within yourselves!

6.3. And He is Allah in the heavens and on earth. He knows, what you conceal, and what you reveal, and He knows (what) you earn (for your deeds).

6.4.. But never did even one Sign (verse) from the (many) Signs (verses) of their Lord reach those (who reject Faith), but they turned away from them (the Signs of their Lord).

6.5. Indeed, they reject the truth when it reaches them: But soon shall they learn the reality of what they used to make fun about.

6.6. Do they not know how many of those (who reject faith) before them We did destroy?

Generations We had established on the earth, in strength which We have not given to you- For whom We poured out rain from the skies in abundance, and gave streams (for water and for tilling the lands) flowing beneath (their) feet: Yet because of their sins We destroyed them, and raised new generations in their place.

6.7.. If We had sent a (message) to you written on a (sheep's) skin, so that they could touch it with their hands, the unbeliever would have been sure to say: "This is nothing but sheer magic!"

6.8. And they say: "Why is an angel not sent down to him?" If We did send down an angel, the matter would be settled at once, and no relief (from pain) would be granted to them.

6.9. And indeed, if We had made an angel as it (the Sign), We should have sent him as a man, and (then) We would certainly have caused confusion for them in a matter in which they are already full of confusion.

6.10. Messengers before you were mocked; But the mockers were surrounded and circled by the (same) thing that they mocked.

6.11.. Say: "Travel through the earth and see what was the end of those who rejected Truth."

6.12. Say: "To whom belongs all that is in the heavens and on the earth?" Say: "To Allah. He has inscribed for Himself (the rule of) Mercy; (and that) He will gather you together for the Day of Judgment, there is no doubt whatever. It is they who have lost their own souls that (they) will not believe.

6.13. "And to Him belongs all that lives (or hides away) in the night and the day. And He is the All Hearing and All Knowing ."

6.14. Say: "Shall I take as protector to myself anyone other than Allah, the Maker of the heavens and the earth? And it is He Who feeds but is not fed." Say: "Surely not! For I am commanded to be the first of those who bow to Allah (in submission), and you be not of the company of those who join gods with Allah."

6.15. Say: "If I disobeyed my Lord, indeed, I would have fear of the penalty of a dreadful Day.

6.16. "On that Day, if the penalty is kept away from anyone, it is because of Allah's Mercy: And this is the great manifest success, the true fulfillment of all desire.

6.17. "If Allah touches you with pain (and sorrow), no one can remove it, except He; And if He touches you with good, He is Able to do all things.

6.18. "He is the One Who cannot be resisted, (watching) from above over His servants; And He is the All Wise , the All Aware of all things."

6.19. Say: "What thing is great as witness?" Say: "Allah is Witness between me and you; And this Quran has been made known to me by revelation, so that I may warn you and all (those to) whom it reaches. Do you really bear witness that besides Allah there are other gods with God?" Say: "No! I cannot bear witness!" Say: "But, in truth He is One God (Allah), and I am truly free from (the falsehood of) joining others with Him."

6.20. Those to whom We have given the Book (Scripture) know this as they know their own sons. Those who have lost their own souls (and they) therefore refuse to believe.

6.21.. And who does more evil than he who invents a lie against Allah or rejects His Sign? But truly the evildoers shall never prosper.

6.22. And one Day We shall gather them all together: We shall say to those who joined partners (to Us): "Where are the partners whom you talked about?"

6.23. Then there will be (left) no escape for them except to say: "By Allah, our Lord, we were not those who joined in worship other gods with Allah."

6.24. Watch! How they lie against themselves! But, the (lie) which they forged will leave them defenseless.

6.25. And among them there are some who (pretend) to listen to you; But We have thrown veils over their hearts, so they do not understand it, and deafness in their ears; And even if they saw any of the Signs, they will not believe in it; However, when they come to you, they will only dispute with you; The disbelievers say: "These are nothing but (fairy) tales from the ancient ones."

6.26. And they forbid others from him (the Prophet), and they themselves they keep away from him (the Prophet); But they only destroy themselves, and they do not realize it.

6.27. If you could only see when they are faced with the Fire! They will say: "If only we were sent back! Then we would not reject the Signs of our Lord, but would be among those who believe!"

6.28. No! In their own (eyes) it will become clear what they used to hide before. But if they were returned, they would surely fall back to the things they were forbidden. And they truly are liars.

6.29. And they say: "There is nothing but our present life on this earth, and we shall never be raised up again."

6.30. If you could only see when they are faced by their Lord! He will say: "Is not this the truth?" They will say: "Yes indeed! By our Lord!" He will say: "Then you taste the penalty, because you rejected Faith."

6.31.. Lost indeed are those who treat it as a lie that they must meet Allah- Until all of a sudden the hour (sign of death) comes to, and they say: "Oh! Sorrow upon us that we did not give any thought to it;" For they bear their burdens on their backs. And truly how evil are the burdens that they bear!

6.32. And what is the life of this world except play and amusement? But best is the Home in the Hereafter for those who are righteous. Will they not understand?

6.33.. We, truly know the sorrow that their words bring to you: It is not you (whom) they reject: But it is the Signs of Allah, which the evildoers deny.

6.34. Surely, (many) messengers before you were (also) rejected: (But) with patience and constancy they withstood their rejection and their harmful deeds until Our help did reach them: There is no one who can alter the Words of Allah. Surely, you have already received some tidings of those messengers (before you).

6.35. If their (the disbeliever's) rejection (of the Message) is hard on your mind, and even if you were able to find a tunnel in the ground or a ladder to the sky and bring them a Sign- (What will be the good?). If it was Allah's Will, He could gather them together to (His) true guidance: So you (O Prophet,) do not be among the ignorant!

6.36. Be sure that those who (really) hear, will (in fact) accept: As for the dead, Allah will raise them up; Then they will be returned to Him.

6.37.. And they say: "Why is a Sign not sent down to him (the Prophet) from his Lord?" Say: "Allah certainly has the Power to send down a Sign: But most of them do not understand."

6.38. There is not a creature (that lives) on the earth, nor a being that flies with its wings, that is not (a member of) nations (and groups) like unto yourselves. Nothing have We omitted from the Book, and they (all) shall be gathered to their Lord in the end.

6.39. Those who reject Our Signs are deaf and dumb- Dwelling in the middle of entire darkness: Whomsoever Allah wills, He leaves to wander: Whomsoever He wills, He places on a Straight Path.

6.40. Say: "Think you to yourselves, if there come upon you the chastisement of Allah, or the Hour (that you fear), will you then call to anyone other than Allah? (Reply) if you are truthful!

6.41. "No! You will (only) call to Him, and if it be His Will, He will remove (the suffering) which made you call upon Him, and you would forget (the false gods) which you join with Him!"

6.42.. Indeed, We sent (messengers) to many nations before you, and We gave the nations suffering and poverty that they may learn to be humble.

6.43. When the punishment reached them from Us, why did they not learn to be humble? (But) instead, their hearts became hard, and Satan made their (sinful) actions seem likable to them.

6.44. But (even) when they forgot the warning that they had received, We opened unto them the gates of all (good) things to them, until, in the middle of their enjoyment of Our gifts, all of a sudden, We called them to account, when see! They were fell into sorrow (and suffering)!

6.45. Of the wrongdoers the last remaining one was cut off. And all the Praises (and thanks) be to Allah, the Cherisher of the Worlds .

6.46.. Say: "Do you think that if Allah took away your hearing or your sight, and sealed up your hearts, who - Any god other than Allah - Could give them back to you?" See how We explain the Signs (verses) in many (ways); (But) yet they turn away.

6.47. Say: "Do you think that if the punishment of Allah comes upon you, whether suddenly or openly, will any be destroyed except those who do wrong?"

6.48. We send the messengers only to give good news and to warn: So that those who believe and become better (in their lives), upon them there shall be no fear, nor shall they grieve.

6.49. But those who reject Our Signs- Upon them shall the Punishment visit, because of their ungodly actions.

6.50. Say: "I do not tell you that the treasures of Allah are with me, and I do not know the unseen, also I do not tell you that I am an angel. I only follow what is revealed to me." Say: "Can the blind be held equal to the seeing man? Will you then not consider?"

6.51.. Deliver this warning to those in whose (hearts) is the fear that they will be brought (to Judgment) before their Lord: Apart from the Lord they will have no protector nor anyone to ask for mercy (on their behalf): So that they may guard (against evil now).

6.52. Do not send away those who call upon their Lord in morning and evening, seeking His (Divine) Face. You are not responsible for them in the least bit of their account, and they are not responsible for you, in the least bit of your account, in case that you may turn them away, and then (you) be (one) of the unjust.

6.53. It is like this We have tried some of them by others, in case they may say: "Is it because Allah has favored these ones from among us?" Does Allah not know best those who are grateful?

6.54. When those who believe in Our Signs (verses), come to you, say: "Peace be on you: Your Lord has prescribed for Himself Mercy: Surely, in case you did evil in ignorance, there after you repent, and amend (your conduct), then truly He is Often Forgiving, Most Merciful .

6.55. Like this do We explain the Signs (verses) in detail: That the way of the sinners may be manifest.

6.56.. Say: "I am forbidden to worship those- Other than Allah- Whom you call upon." Say: "I will not follow your idle wishes: If I did, I would wander away from the Path, and (then I will) not be of the company of those who receive (true) guidance."

6.57. Say: "For me, I (work) on a clear Sign from my Lord, but if you reject it, what (punishment) you would see hastened, is not in my power. The Command rests with none but Allah: He declares the Truth and He is the Best of judges."

6.58. Say: "If what you see hastened was in my power, the matter would be settled at once between you and me. But Allah knows best those who do wrong."

6.59. And with Him are the keys of the Unseen, the treasures that no one knows but He. He knows whatever is in land and in sea. Not a leaf falls without His knowledge: There is not a grain in the darkness (or depths) of the earth, nor anything fresh or dry, except what is (written) in a clear record.

6.60. It is He, Who takes your souls by the night and (He) has knowledge of all that you have done by day: By day He raises you up again; That a term appointed will be fulfilled; In the end to Him will be your return; Then He will show you the truth of all that you did.

6.61.. He is the Irresistible, (Watchful) from above over His servants, and He sets guardians over you. At the end, when death approaches one of you, Our angels take his soul, and they never fail in performing their duty.

6.62. Then (all) men are returned to Allah, their Truest Protector, the (only) Reality: Is not His the (total) Command? And He is the Swiftest in taking account.

6.63. Say: "Who is it that delivers you from the dark corners of land and sea, when you call upon him in humility and in silent terror: 'If only He delivers us from these (dangers, we promise) we shall truly show our gratitude'?"

6.64. Say: "It is Allah Who delivers you from these and all (other) sorrows: And yet you worship false gods!"

6.65. Say: "He has the power to send serious harm to you from above you or from under your feet, or to cover you with confusion within the sects, (or conflict), giving you a taste of mutual evil to suffer one from the other." See how We explain the Signs by various (symbols); That you may understand.

6.66. But your people reject this (the Quran, the Message), even though it is the Truth. Say: "The responsibility is not mine for managing your affairs;

6.67. "For every Message there is a limit of time, and soon you shall know it."

6.68.. And when you see men engaged in useless talk about Our Signs, turn away from them unless they turn to a different talk. Or if Satan ever makes you forget, then after remembering it, you do not sit in the company of those who do wrong.

6.69. On their account no responsibility falls on the righteous, but (it) is to remind them that they may (learn to) fear Allah.

6.70. And leave (them) alone, those who take their religion to be mere play and joke, and (those who) are deceived by the life of this world. But remind (them) thereby: That every soul takes itself to ruin by its own actions: It will find for itself no protector or benefactor (or intercessor) except Allah: If it offered every ransom, (or gift), none will be accepted: Such is (the end of) those who take themselves to ruin by their own acts: They will have (only) boiling water to drink, and for punishment, one most painful because they continued to disbelieve.

6.71. Say: "Shall we indeed call on others besides Allah- (Such) things that can do us neither good nor harm- And turn (back) on our heels after receiving Guidance from Allah? Like one whom the Satans' have made into a fool, wandering bewildered through the earth, (with) his friends calling 'Come to us', (vainly) guiding him to the Path." Say: "Allah's guidance is the (only) guidance and we have been asked to submit ourselves to the Lord of the worlds-

6.72. "To establish regular prayers and to fear Allah: For it is to Him that we shall be gathered together."

6.73. It is He Who created the heavens and the earth in true (proportions): The day He says, "Be!", Look! It is. His Word is the Truth. His will be the Dominion the day (when) the Trumpet will be blown. He knows the unseen and that which is open. For He is the All Wise , All Aware (with all things).

6.74.. And (remember), Ibrahim (Abraham) said to his father Azar: "Will you take idols as gods? Indeed, I see you and your people in open error."

6.75. So also did We show Ibrahim (Abraham) the power and the laws of the heavens and the earth, that he might have (both) the Faith and certainty (with understanding).

6.76. When the night covered over him, he saw a star, he said: "This is my Lord." But when it set, he said: "I love not those that set."

6.77. When he saw the moon rising in splendor, he said: "This is my Lord." But when the moon set, he said: "Unless my Lord guides me, I shall surely be among those who go astray."

6.78. When he saw the sun rising in splendor, he said, "This is my Lord; This is the greatest (of all)." But when the sun set, he said: "O my people! I am indeed free from all that you enjoin as partners (giving false gods for worship instead of Allah).

6.79. "Surely, for me, I have set my face, firmly and truly, towards Him Who created the heavens and the earth, and never shall I give partners to Allah."

6.80. His people disputed with him. He said: "Do you (come to) dispute with me, about Allah, when He (Himself) has guided me? I do not fear (the beings) that you associate with Allah; Unless my Lord wills, (nothing can happen). My Lord masters all things in His knowledge. Will you not remember?

6.81. "And how should I fear (the beings) you associate with Allah, when you do not fear giving partners to Allah without any reason having been given to you? Which of (us) two parties has more right to security? (Tell me) if you know.

6.82. "It is those who believe and do not confuse their beliefs with wrong- Who are (truly) in security, for they are on (right) guidance."

6.83.. And that was the reasoning about Us, which We gave to Ibrahim (Abraham to use) against his people: We raise whom We will, little by little: Truly, your Lord is All Wise, All Knowing .

6.84. We gave him, (and his sons) Isháq (Isaac) and Yàqoub (Jacob): All (three) We guided: And before him, We guided Nuh (Noah), and among his descendants Dawood (David), Sulaiman (Solomon), Ayub (Job), Yusuf (Joseph), Musa (Moses), and Haroon (Aaron): Thus We do reward those who do good:

6.85. And Zakariyya (Zachariah) and Yahya (John, the Baptist), and Isa (Jesus) and Ilyas (Elias): All in the company of the righteous:

6.86. And Ismail (Ishmael) and Al-Yasa (Elisha), and Yunus (Jonah) and Lut (Lot): And to each one We gave favor above the nations:

6.87. (To them) and to their fathers, and the descendants and brothers: We chose them, and We guided them to the Straight Path.

6.88. This is the Guidance of Allah: He gives that Guidance to whom He pleases, from His worshippers. If they were to join other gods with Him, all that they do will be useless for them.

6.89. These were the men to whom We gave the Book, authority, and prophet hood: If these (their descendants) reject them, look! We shall entrust their charge to a new People who do not reject them (the Book, and authority, and prophet hood).

6.90. These were the (prophets) who received the guidance from Allah: Copy the guidance they received; Say: "I do not ask from you any reward for this: This is not less than a Message for (all the creations of) the worlds."

6.91.. They do not make the right measure of the Power of Allah when they say: "Allah sends nothing down to man (as revelation):" Say: "Who then sent down the Book (Torah) that Musa (Moses) brought? (It is) a light and a guidance to man: But you make it into (separate) sheets for show, while you hide much (of its contents): In there, you were taught that which you did not know- Neither you nor your fathers." Say: "Allah (sent it down):" Then leave them to sink into idle talk and meaningless remarks.

6.92. And this is a Book which We have sent down, bringing blessings, and confirming (the Revelations) which came before it: That you may warn the (people living in the) mother of Cities (Makkah) and all around her; Those who believe in the Hereafter believe in this (Book) and those who constantly guard over their Prayers.

6.93.. And who can be more wicked than one who invents a lie against Allah, or says: "I have received revelation," when he has received nothing, or (again the one) who says, "I can reveal the like of what Allah has revealed." And if you could only see how the wicked (are) in the flood of agonies at death! The angels stretch forth their hands, (as they say), "Give up your souls: This day shall you receive your reward- A penalty of shame, because you used to tell lies against Allah, and scornfully reject His Signs (verses)!

6.94. "And look! You (man) come to us bare and alone as We created you for the first time: You have left behind all what We conferred on you: We do not see with you your intercessors whom you thought to be partners in your affairs: So now all relations between you have been cut off, and your (false) hopes have left you in a bind!"

6.95.. Surely, it is Allah Who causes seed-grain and date-stone to split and send out leaves (as it germinates into a plant). He causes the living to come from the dead, and He is the One to cause the dead to come from the living. That is Allah: Then how is it that you are far away from the truth?

6.96. He it is that opens the day-break (from the dark), He makes the night for rest and peace, and the sun and moon for the measure (of time): Such is the Judgment and the Order from (Him), the Exalted in Power (Almighty), the All Knowing and the Omniscient.

6.97. It is He Who makes the stars (as lights) for you, so that you may find your way with their help, through the dark spaces of land and sea: We detail Our Signs for (those) people who know.

6.98. It is He Who has produced you from a single person (Adam)! Here (this world) is a place of stop-over and (also) a place of departure: We present Our Signs for people who understand.

6.99. It is He Who sends down rain from the sky: And with it We produce plants of all kinds: From some We produce green (crops), out of which We produce grain, heaped up (at harvest time); Out of the date-palm and its sheaths (or spathes) (come) clusters of dates hanging low and near: And (then there are) gardens of grapes, and olives, and pomegranates, each similar (in kind) yet different (in variety): When they begin to bear fruit and they become ripe later. Look! In these things there are the Signs for people who believe.

6.100.. Yet they make the jinns' (the Evil ones as) equals with Allah! Even though Allah created the jinns'; And they falsely, having no knowledge, give to Him sons and daughters. Praise and Glory be to Him! (for He is) above whatever they have described!

6.101.. He is the Originator of the heavens and the earth: How can He have children when He has no one as female companion? He created all things and He is All Knowing of all things.

6.102. That is Allah, your Lord! There is no god but He: The Creator of all things: So you worship Him Alone: And He is the Trustee and Disposer of all affairs.

6.103. No vision can hold Him but His grasp is over all (the) vision: He is the Subtle beyond any understanding yet He is All Aware of all things.

6.104.. "Surely, now the proofs have come to you, from your Lord, (to open your eyes): If any (one of you) will see, it will be for (the good of) his own soul; If any (one) will be blind, it will be to his own (harm): I am not (here) to watch over your doings."

6.105. Like this We explain the Signs by various (symbols): That they may say: "You have taught (us) properly", and so We may make the matter clear for those who know and understand.

6.106. You follow what (you) are taught by revelation from your Lord: There is no god but He: And turn away from those who join gods with Allah.

6.107. If it was Allah's Will, they would not have taken false gods: But We did not make you the one to watch over what they do, nor are you set over them to take care of their affairs.

6.108.. Do not be abusive towards those whom they call upon besides Allah, lest out of anger, they may be abusive towards Allah, in their ignorance. So have We made attractive to each people its own doings. In the end, they will return to their Lord, and We shall then tell them the truth of all that they did.

6.109.. They make their strongest oaths by Allah, that if a (special) Sign came to them, (then) by it, they would believe. Say: "(All) Signs are certainly, in the Power of Allah: But what will make you (believers) realize that (even) if (special) Signs came, they will not believe?"

6.110. We (too) shall give their hearts and their eyes (confusion), because they refused to believe in this (Sign) in the first place: We shall leave them to exceed their limits (and) to wander in (confusion and) distraction.

6.111.. And even if We did send angels to them, and the dead did speak to them, and We gathered together all things before their very eyes, they are not the ones to believe, unless it is in Allah's Will. But most of them are ignorant (towards the Message).

6.112. In this way, for every messenger, We did make an enemy- Satans' among men and jinns', confusing each other with flowery talk, with lies that mislead. If your Lord had so willed, they would not have done it: So leave them and their inventions alone.

6.113. To such (an evil way), let the hearts of those be turned, (those) who have no faith in the Hereafter: Let them become happy in it, and let them earn from it what they may.

6.114.. Say: "Shall I try to find a judge (anyone) other than Allah? When He it is Who has sent to you the Book, (and) explained in detail." They know fully well to whom We have given the Book, that it has been sent down from your Lord in truth. Then, never be of those (people) who doubt.

6.115. The Word of your Lord always finds its fulfillment in truth and in justice: No one can change His Words: For He is the All Hearing , the All Knowing .

6.116. And if you obey the most part of those on earth, they will lead you astray from the Way of Allah. They (the people) follow only (sheer) imagination: They do nothing but are merely conjecturing.

6.117. Surely, your Lord knows well who wanders away from His Way: He (also) knows well those who receive His guidance.

6.118.. So eat the (meats) on which Allah's Name has been said, if you have faith in His Signs (verses).

6.119. And why should you not eat the (meats) on which Allah's Name has been mentioned? When He has explained to you in detail what is not allowed for you- Except under compulsion of necessity; And indeed, many do mislead (men) by their caprices without any knowledge. For sure, Your Lord knows best those who transgress.

6.120. Keep away from all sin, open or secret: Surely, those who commit sin will get their due recompense for what they committed.

6.121. Do not eat from the (meats) on which Allah's Name has not been mentioned: For sure, this is sin and disobedience. But the Satans' always inspire their friends to argue with (create doubt in) you, if you were to obey them, you would truly be pagans.

6.122.. Can he who was dead, and to whom We gave life, and a light by which he can walk among men, be like him who is in the depths of darkness, from which he can never come out? Therefore, to those who are without Faith, their own actions seem pleasing.

6.123. And thus have We placed chief leaders in every town, its wicked men, who plot (evil and place themselves in there: But they only plot against their own souls, and they do not understand it.

6.124. And when a Sign (from Allah) comes to them, they say: "We shall not believe until we receive one (exactly) like that received by messengers of Allah." Allah knows best where (and how) to carry out His Mission. Soon will the wicked be overtaken by humiliation before Allah, and a severe punishment, for all their plots.

6.125. Those to whom Allah (in His Plan) wills to guide- He opens his breast (heart) to Islam; Those whom He wills to leave wandering- He makes his breast (heart) narrow and tight, as if he had to climb up to the sky (through his own heart): Thus does Allah (place) the penalty on those who refuse to believe.

6.126. And, this is the Way of your Lord, leading (you) Straight: We have explained the Signs for those who receive the warning.

6.127. For them will be a Home of Peace in the Presence of their Lord: He will be their (close) Protector, because they practiced (righteousness).

6.128. And on the Day, when He will gather all of them, (the jinns',) together (and say): "O you assembly of jinns'! Many of you did mislead from the men." Their friends among men will say: "Our Lord! We profited from each other: But, we have reached (the end of) our term- Which You did appoint for us." He will say: "The Fire will be your dwelling place: You will live in there for ever, except as Allah wills. For your Lord is All Wise, All Knowing ."

6.129. And thus, We make the wrongdoers turn to each other, because of what they have earned.

6.130. "O you assembly of jinns' and men! Did the messengers not come to you from among you, telling you of My Signs and warning you of the facing of this Day?" They will say: "We bear witness against ourselves." It was the present life that deceived them. And they will bear witness against themselves that they rejected Faith (as disbelievers).

6.131. (The messengers were sent), because your Lord would not destroy the townships of men for their wrong-doing while the people (of the townships) were not warned.

6.132. For all (men, there) are degrees (or ranks) set by their deeds: And your Lord is not unmindful of anything that they do.

6.133. And your Lord is Self-Sufficient, Full of Mercy: If He (so) wills, He can destroy you, and in your place appoint whom He wills as your successors, (or) even as He had raised you up as the descendants of other people.

6.134. Surely, all that has been promised to you will come out as true: Nor can you stop it (in the least bit).

6.135. Say: "O my people! Do whatever you can: I will do (my part): Soon will you know who they are whose end will be (the best) in the Hereafter: It is certain that the wrongdoers will not succeed."

6.136. And out of what Allah has produced in plenty as crops and as cattle, they assigned Him a share: And they say, according to their wish: "This is for Allah, and this- For Our 'partners'!" But the share of their 'partners' does not reach Allah, whereas, the share of Allah reaches their 'partners'!

Evil (and unjust) is how they judge!

6.137. Even so, in the eyes of most of the (unbelieving) pagans, their 'partners' made the killing of their (own) children look nice, in order to lead them to their own destruction, and cause confusion in their religion. If Allah had willed, they would not have done so: But leave them and their inventions alone.

6.138. By their claim, they say that such and such cattle and crops, are not for general use, and none should eat from them except those whom- They say- We wish; Further, there are cattle forbidden to yoke (around their necks for work) or for burden, and (there are) cattle on which, (at the time of slaughter), the Name of Allah is not pronounced; - Inventions against Allah's Name: Soon He will punish them for their own inventions.

6.139. And they say: "What is in the wombs of such and such cattle is specially reserved (for food) of our men, and forbidden to our women; But if it is born without life, then all have shares in it." For their falsehoods (of superstitions to Allah), He will soon punish them: Surely, He is All Wise, All Knowing.

6.140. Indeed, lost are those who kill their children, with evil (and), without knowledge, and forbid food that Allah has made for them, inventing lies against Allah. They have truly gone astray and have not heeded for the guidance.

6.141.. And it is He, Who produces gardens, with trellises and without (trellises), and date-palms, and crops with produce of all kinds, and olives and pomegranates, similar (in kind) and different (in variety): Eat from their fruit in their season, but give the dues (in charity) that are proper on the day that the harvest is gathered. But do not waste by the way of excess: Verily, Allah does not love the wasters.

6.142. And from the cattle (are some) for (carrying) burden and (some) for meat: Eat from what Allah has provided for you, and do not follow the footsteps of Satan: For he is a well-known enemy to you.

6.143. Eight pairs (of cattle), two (male and female): Of sheep, a pair; And two of goats, a pair; Say: "Has He forbidden the two males, or the two females, or (the young) which the wombs of the two females hold? Tell me with knowledge, if you are truthful:"

6.144. And of the camels a pair, and of oxen a pair; Say: "Has He forbidden the two males, or the two females, or (the young) which the wombs of the two females hold? or were you present when Allah ordered you such a thing?" Then who does more wrong than one who invents a lie against Allah, to lead astray the Mankind without knowledge? For Allah does not guide people who do wrong.

6.145.. Say: "I do not find in the message that it was revealed to me any (meat) forbidden to be eaten by one who wishes to eat it, unless it is a dead meat, or blood poured forth, or the flesh of swine- Because it is disgusting (an abomination) or, what is impious, (meat) on which a name has been invoked, other than Allah's (Name)." But (even then), if a person is forced by necessity, without willingly disobeying, nor going against proper limits- Your Lord is Often Forgiving, Most Merciful .

6.146. And for those who followed the Judaic (Jewish) Law, We did not permit (animals) with undivided hoof, and We did not permit them the fat of the ox and the sheep, except what adheres to their backs or their insides (intestines), or is mixed with bone: This is to adjust for their willful disobedience: For We are True (in Our laws).

6.147. If they accuse you of falsehood, say: "Your Lord is full of Mercy, All Embracing; But His anger will never be turned back from guilty people."

6.148.. Those who give partners (to Allah) will say: "If Allah had wished, we should not have given partners to Him, nor would our fathers; Nor should we have had any (of such) conducts." So did their ancestors argue falsely, until they tasted Our might. Say: "Have you any (certain) knowledge (or proof)? If so produce it before us. Surely, you follow nothing but (unsupported) thought: You do nothing but lie."

6.149. Say: "With Allah is the argument that reaches the end: If it had been His Will, He could have really guided you all."

6.150. Say: "Bring forward your witnesses to prove that Allah did forbid such and such." Even if they bring such witnesses, you do not be among them, nor you follow their vain desires, desires of those who treat Our Signs as lies, and of those who do not believe in Hereafter: And they hold others as equal with their guardian-Lord.

6.151.. Say: "Come, I will say (again) what Allah has (really) forbidden you from: Do not join anything as equal with Him; Be good to your parents; Do not kill your children on an excuse of want- We provide sustenance for you and for them- Do not come near to any such shameful sins, whether openly or in secret; Do not take life, which Allah has made sacred, except by way of justice and law:" Thus does He command you, that you may learn wisdom.

6.152. And do not come near to the orphans property except to improve it (or to make it better), till he (or she) attains the age of full strength; Give full measure and full weight with (total) justice- No burden do We place on any soul, except that what it can bear- And whenever you speak, speak justly, even if a near relative is concerned; And fulfill the duty (and promise) to Allah: Thus does He command you, that you may remember.

6.153. And surely, this is My Way, leading (you) Straight: Follow it: (And) follow not (other) paths: They will scatter you from His (straight) Path: Thus He commands you, that you may be Righteous.

6.154.. Then, We gave Musa (Moses) the Book (Torah), completing (Our favor) to those who would do right, and explaining all things in detail- And a guide and a blessing, that they might believe in the meeting with their Lord.

6.155.. And this is a blessed Book (the Quran) that We have revealed as a blessing: So follow it and be righteous, that you may (also) receive mercy:

6.156. In case that you should say: "The Book was sent down to two sects before us, and for our part, we remained unaware with all that they learned by serious study;"

6.157. Or in case that you should say: "If the Book had only been sent down to us, we should have followed its guidance better than they (did)." Now then, has come to you a clear (proof, this Quran) from your Lord, and a guide and a mercy: Then who could be more wrong than one who rejects Allah's Signs, and turns away from it? In good time We shall punish those who turn away from Our Signs (verses), with terrifying penalty, for their turning away.

6.158.. Are they waiting to see if angels come to them or your Lord (Himself), or certain of the Signs of your Lord! The day that certain of the Signs of your Lord do come, it will not do good to a soul to believe in them then, if it did not believe before nor earned righteousness through its Faith. Say: "You wait: We are also waiting."

6.159. Verily, as for those who divide their religion and break it up into sects, you have no part in them in the least: Their affair is with Allah: He will tell them the Truth in the end of all that they did.

6.160. He who does good shall have ten times as much to his credit: He that does evil shall be given back according to his evil: No wrong shall be done to (any of) them.

6.161.. Say: "Surely, my Lord has guided me to a Way that is Straight- A religion of right- The Path (walked) by Ibrahim (Abraham) the true in faith, and he (certainly) did not join gods with Allah."

6.162. Say: "Truly, my prayer and my service of sacrifice, my life and my death, are (all) for Allah, the Lord (and Cherisher) of the Worlds:

6.163. "He has no partners: This am I commanded, and I am the first of those who bow to His Will."

6.164.. Say: "Shall I seek for (my) Lord other than Allah when He is the Lord of all things? Every soul draws the reward of its acts on none but itself: No bearer of burdens can bear the burden of another. Your goal in the end is towards Allah: He will tell you the Truth of the things about which you disputed."

6.165. And it is He Who has made you generations, (and) inheritors replacing each other on the earth,: He has raised you in ranks, some above others: That He may try you by the gifts that He has given to you: Surely, your Lord is quick in punishment: And indeed, He is Often Forgiving, Most Merciful .

****

Sura 7. Al-A'raf,
(The heights): (Makkah, 206 Verses)
In the Name of Allah, the Most Gracious, the Most Merciful.

7.1.. Alif Lám Mim Sád:

7.2.. (This is) a Book (the Quran) sent down unto you- (O Prophet,) so do not let your heart be held back by any difficulty because of it- And with it, you may warn (the disbelievers), and teach the believers:

7.3. (O people!) follow the revealed teachings given to you from your Lord and do not follow (any) other than Him, as (your) friends or protectors; You remember little of the warning (given to you).

7.4.. And how many towns have We destroyed (for the sins of their people)? Our punishment took them all of a sudden by night or during their sleep for their afternoon rest.

7.5. When Our punishment got them, they did not say anything except this: Truly, we did wrong!

7.6.. Then surely, shall We ask those to whom Our Message was sent and those (messengers) by whom We sent it.

7.7. Then surely, We shall bring up (their whole story) with (full) knowledge, for We were never absent (at any time or place).

7.8. And the (weighing) balance on that Day will be true: Those whose scale (of good deeds) will be heavy, shall prosper (by entering into the Paradise):

7.9. And for those whose scale (of good) will be light, will find their souls in contempt (and danger), because they mistreated Our Signs.

7.10. And surely, it is We Who have placed you (O men!) with authority on earth, and given you there the means to fulfill your life: Small are the thanks that you give!

7.11.. It is We Who created you and gave you shape; Then We asked the angels to bow down to Adam, and they bowed down, except Satan, he refused to be of those (angels) who bowed down.

7.12. (Allah) said: "What prevented you (O Satan) from bowing down when I Commanded you?" He (Satan) said: "I am better than he (Adam): You created me from Fire, and him (Adam) from clay."

7.13. (Allah) said: "Get yourself down of it (Paradise): It is not for you to be arrogant here: Get out because you are of the disgraced and shameful."

7.14. He (Satan) said: "Give me respite (rest) till the Day (of Resurrection when) they are raised up."

7.15. (Allah) said: "You be among those who have a rest."

7.16. He (Satan) said: "Because you have thrown me out of the Way: Look! I will lie in wait against them on Your Straight Path:

7.17. "Then I will attack them, from before them and behind them, from their right and their left: And You will not find most of them to be thankful (for Your Mercies)."

7.18. (Allah) said: "Get out from it, disgraced and expelled. If any of them follow you- Then, surely, I will fill the Hell with all of you.

7.19.. "And, O Adam! You and your wife live in the Paradise, and enjoy (the good things) as you like (them): But do not go near this tree, or you will be unjust and wrongdoers (in sin)."

7.20. Then Satan began to whisper doubts to both them, bringing openly to their minds all their shame that was hidden from them: He said: "Your Lord asked you not to come near this tree, lest you should become angels or such beings as (those who) live forever."

7.21. And he (Satan) swore to both of them: "I am one of the sincere well wishers to both of you."

7.22. So by lying (and deception) he brought about their Fall: When they tasted (the fruit) from the tree, their shame became clear to them, and they began to sew together the leaves of the Garden over their bodies. And their Lord called to them: "Did I not ask you to keep away from that tree, and tell you that Satan was an avowed enemy to you?"

7.23. They said: "Our Lord! We have wronged our own souls: If You will not forgive us and grant from your Mercy upon us, We shall certainly be losers."

7.24. (Allah) said: "Get yourselves down with enmity between yourselves. On earth shall be your place to live and your means of livelihood- For a time."

7.25. He said: "You shall live there, and there you shall die; But you shall be taken out of it (the earth)."

7.26.. O you Children of Adam! We have given you clothing to cover yourselves (and private parts), and also for decoration for you. But the clothing of righteousness- That is the best. These are among the Signs of

Allah, that they may receive the warning (and advice).

7.27. O you Children of Adam! Let not the Satan misguide you, in the same way that he got your parents out of the Garden, taking away from them their clothing, to expose their shameful (private) parts: Surely, he and his tribe (other jinns') watch you from a position that you cannot see them; Truly, we have made the Satans' as friends (only) of those without Faith.

7.28.. And when they do a little that is shameful, they say: "We found our fathers doing the same;" And, "Allah commands us like this (or that):" Say: "No! Allah never commands what is shameful: Do you speak about Allah what you do not know?"

7.29. Say: "My Lord has ordered Justice; And that you give your entire selves (to Him) at every time and place of prayer, and call upon Him, making your prayers true (and sincere) as it would be in His Sight: Like He created you in the beginning, like that you shall return."

7.30. Some (people,) He has guided: Others (by their own doing) have earned the loss of their Way; By doing that, they took the Satans', by (their own) choice over Allah, as their friends and their protectors, and think that they receive guidance.

7.31. O Children of Adam! Put on your beautiful clothing at every time and place of prayer: Eat and drink, but waste not by excess: For Allah does not like the wasters.

7.32.. Say: "Who has forbidden the beautiful (gifts) of Allah, which He has made for His servants, and (those) clean and pure things He provided, for living?" Say: "In the life of this world, they are for those who believe, (and only) purely for them on the Day of Judgment: Thus We explain the Signs in detail for those who understand."

7.33. Say: "The things that my Lord has truly forbidden are: Shameful deeds, in open or in secret; Sins and lies against truth or reason; Assigning partners to Allah, for which He has given no authority; And saying things about Allah, which you do not know."

7.34.. To every People is a time period fixed: When their time ends, they cannot delay an hour, and not (an hour) can they advance (the end).

7.35. O Children of Adam! Whenever there come to you messengers from among you, reciting my Signs to you- Those who are righteous and correct (themselves)- For them there shall be no fear and they will not be sad.

7.36. But those who deny Our Signs and treat them with displeasure and false pride- They are Companions of the Fire, to live in there (for ever).

7.37. Who is more unjust than the one who makes up a lie against Allah or rejects His Signs? For such (people), their punishment given must come to them from the Book (of Judgment): Until, when Our messengers (of death) come and take their souls, they say: "Where are the things that you used to call other than Allah?" They will reply: "They have left us in a difficult position," and they will speak against themselves, that they had rejected Allah.

7.38. He (Allah) will say: "You enter the company of the peoples who passed away before you- Men and jinns'- Into the Fire." Every time a new (group of) people enters, it curses its peoples of related place (and time before) until they follow each other, all into the Fire. Say the last (group) about the first (group): "Our Lord! It is these (people) who misled us: So give them a double the penalty of the Fire." He will say: "Doubled for all:" But this you do not understand.

7.39. Then the first (group) will say to the last (one): "Now you see! You have no advantage over us; So you taste the penalty for all that you did!"

7.40.. Verily, for those (people) who deny Our Signs and treat them with displeasure and false pride, there will be no opening of the gates of heavens, and they will not enter the Garden, until the camel can pass through the eye of the needle: Our reward is like this for those in sin.

7.41. For them there is Hell, as a seat (to hold them from below) and folds and folds (of Fire) for covering above: Our repayment is like this for those who do wrong.

7.42.. But for those who believe and do righteousness- We place no burden on any soul, except that which it can bear- They will be Companions of the Garden, to live in there (for ever).

7.43. And We shall remove from their hearts any left over sense of hurt- Beneath them will be rivers flowing- And they shall say: "Praises (and thanks) be to Allah, Who has guided us to this (happiness): We could never have found guidance, if it was not for the Guidance of Allah: Indeed it was the truth that the messengers of our Lord brought to us," and they shall hear the cry: "Look! The Gardens before you! You have been made to take them over, because of your acts (of righteousness)."

7.44. The Companions of the Garden will call out to the companions of the Fire: "We have truly found the promise of our Lord to us to be true: Have you also found your lords promises true?" They shall say: "Yes;" But a crier shall speak out between them: "The curse of Allah is on the wrongdoers-

7.45. Those who would make it difficult for (men) to come to the Path of Allah, and would seek in it something crooked: And they were those who denied the Hereafter."

7.46. Between them shall be a veil, and on the heights (of honor) will be men who would know everyone by his marks: They will call out to the companions of the Garden, "Peace upon you:" And at that time they will not have gone in (the Garden), but they will be assured (of their entry).

7.47. When their eyes shall be turned towards the companions of the Fire, they will say: "Our Lord! Do not send us to the company of the wrongdoers."

7.48.. The men on the heights (of honor) will call certain (others) whom they will know by their marks, saying: "What profit to you were your heaps (of wealth) and your haughty (and unpleasant) habits?

7.49. "Look! Are these not the men whom you swore that Allah with His Mercy will never bless?" It has been said to them: "You enter the Garden: There shall be no fear on you, and you shall not be sorrowful."

7.50. The companions of the Fire will call to the companions of the Garden: "Pour down to us water or anything of that Allah does provide for your living." (In reply) they will say: "Both (water and provisions), Allah has forbidden for those who rejected Him-

7.51. "Those who took their religion only as amusement and play, and were deceived by the present life-" On that day We shall forget them like they forgot their meeting on this day, and like they used to reject Our Signs.

7.52. And, We had certainly sent a Book to them, based on knowledge, which We explained in detail- As a guide and a mercy to all who believe.

7.53. Do they just wait for the final completion of the event? On the day that the event is finally completed, those who disregarded it before will say: "Surely, the messengers of our Lord in fact brought true (news). Have we nobody to speak for us now (and) to intercede on our behalf? Or could we be sent back? Then we will do (good) deeds other than our evil actions." In fact, they will have lost their souls, and the things they invented will leave them in the lurch (and without help).

7.54.. Indeed, your Guardian-Lord is Allah, Who created the heavens and the earth in six days, and then He rose over on the Throne (of authority): He draws the night as a veil over the day, each (day and night) searching the other in rapid sequence: And He created the sun, the moon, and the stars, (all) governed by laws of His (divine) Order. Surely, is it not His to create and to govern? Blessed is Allah, the Lord (and the Cherisher) of all the Worlds!

7.55. Call on your Lord (in prayer) while being humble and in private: Because Allah does not love those who exceed (their) bounds.

7.56. And do not do mischief in the land, after it has been put in order, but call to Him with fear and (longing) in hope (for Him): Because the Mercy of Allah is close to those who do good.

7.57. It is He Who sends the winds like giver of happy news, coming (to you) before His Mercy (the rains): When they have carried the heavily loaded clouds (with water), We drive them to a land that is dead, make rain to fall on it; Then We produce every kind of crop with it: Like this We shall raise up the dead: In case you may remember or take the warning.

7.58. From the land that is clean and good, (and) by the Will of its Cherisher, comes up a crop (rich) after its kind: But from the land that is bad, comes up nothing except that which is meager: Thus We explain the Signs in many (ways) to those who are grateful.

7.59.. Indeed, We sent Nuh (Noah) to his people, he said: "O my people! Worship Allah! You have no other god except Him. Truly, I fear for you the punishment of an awful Day!"

7.60. The leaders of his people said: "Verily, We see you clearly in error."

7.61. He said: "O my people! There is no wandering in my (mind): Quite the opposite, I am a messenger from the Lord (and Cherisher) of the Worlds!

7.62. "I only do (my) duties for you from the Will of my Lord: My advice is sincere to you. And I know from Allah something that you do not know.

7.63. "Do you wonder that a message from your Lord has come to you, through a man of your own people, to warn you- So that you may fear Allah and by chance receive His Mercy?"

7.64. But they rejected him (Nuh) and We delivered him, and those with him, in the Ark: But We overcame (and drowned) in the Flood those (of his people) who rejected Our Signs (verses). They were truly a blind people!

7.65.. To the 'Ad people, (We sent) Hud, one of their (own) brothers: He said: "O my people! Worship Allah! You have no other god but Him. Will you not fear (Allah)?"

7.66. The leaders of disbelievers from his people said: "Verily, we see you are a fool, and verily, we think you are among the liars."

7.67. He said: "O my people! I am not a fool, but (I am) a messenger from the Lord (and Cherisher) of the Worlds!

7.68. "I (only) convey unto you the Message of my Lord: To you, I am a sincere and trustworthy advisor.

7.69. "Do you wonder that a message from your Lord has come to you, through a man of your own people, to warn you- And remember that He made you successors after the people of Nuh (Noah), and gave you a position high among the nations. So remember the benefits (to you) from Allah: So that you may prosper."

7.70. They said: "Do you come to us (saying), that we may worship Allah alone, and give up the way (for worship) of our fathers? So bring us what you threaten us with, if you are (really) telling the truth!"

7.71. He said: "Punishment and anger have already come to you from your Lord: Do you (still) argue with me over names which you have made up-, you and your fathers- Without authority from Allah? Then wait, I am with you among those who are waiting."

7.72. We saved him and those who stayed close to him, by Our Mercy, and We cut off the roots of those who rejected Our Signs and did not believe.

7.73.. To the Samood (Thamud people, We sent) Sálih, one of their own brothers: He said: "O my people! Worship Allah; You have no other god but Him. Now a clear (Sign) has come to you from your Lord! This female camel (she-camel) of Allah is a Sign to you: So let her graze in Allah's earth, and do not harm her, or you shall be caught up in a painful punishment.

7.74. "And remember how He made you to take after the 'Ad people, and gave you places to live in the land: You built for yourselves palaces and castles in (open) plains, and carve out homes in the mountains; So remember the benefits (to you) from Allah, and keep away from evil and mischief on the earth."

7.75. The leaders of the proud ones from among his people said to those who were known to be powerless- Those among them who believed: "Do you know that Sálih is truly a messenger from his Lord?" They said: "We do indeed believe in the Revelation which has been sent through him."

7.76. The proud ones said: "As our part, we reject what you believe in."

7.77. Then they crippled (by cutting the hamstrings of) the she-camel, and proudly opposed the order of their Lord, saying: "O Sálih! Bring on your threats, if you are truly a messenger (of Allah)!"

7.78. So the earthquake overtook them while they were not aware, and they lay on their face down in their homes in the morning!

7.79. He (Sálih) left them, saying: "O my people! I did truly bring to you the Message for which I was sent by my Lord: I gave you good advice, but you did not love good advisors!"

7.80.. We also (sent) Lut (Lot): He said to his people: "Do you practice indecent acts that no people in creation (ever) did before you?

7.81. "Because you practice your (sexual) desires on men in preference to women: You are truly a people going beyond bounds,"

7.82. And his people did not answer except this: They said: "Drive them out of your city: These are men who want to be clean and pure from sins!"

7.83. But We saved him and his family, except his wife: She was of those who lagged behind,

7.84. And We rained on them a shower (of brimstone): See then, what was the end of those who practiced sin and crime!

7.85.. To the Madyan people, We sent Shu'aib, one of their own brothers: He said: "O my people! Worship Allah; You have no other god except Him. Surely, a clear (Sign) has come to you from your Lord! Give just (and proper) measure and weight, and do not keep away from the people the things that are their due; And do not do mischief in the land after it has been put in order: That will be best for you, if you have Faith.

7.86. "And do not sit on every road, saying threats, blocking from the Path of Allah those who believe in Him and searching for something crooked in it; Remember how you were a few and He gave you increase. And hold in you mind's eye what was the end of those who did mischief.

7.87. "And if there is a group (of people) from you who believes in the Message with which I have been sent, and a group which does not believe, keep yourselves in patience till Allah decides between us: For He is the best to decide."

7.88. The leaders, the proud group from among his people said: "O Shu'aib! We shall really drive you out of our city- (You) and those who believe with you; Or else you (both) will have to return to our ways and religion." He said: "What! Even though we (strongly) dislike (them)?

7.89. "We should really make up a lie against Allah, if we returned to your religion after Allah has saved us from them; And we could not return to it by any way or means, unless it is in the Will and Plan of Allah, Our Lord. Our Lord can reach out to the deepest corners of things by His knowledge. In Allah Alone is our trust. Our Lord! You decide between us and our people in truth, because You are the Best to judge."

7.90. The leaders of the disbelievers from his people, said to their people: "If you follow Shu'aib, be sure then you will be the losers!"

7.91. But the earthquake took them without warning, and they lay on their face in their homes before the morning!

7.92. The men who rejected Shu'aib became as if they had never been in the homes where the had grown up (in joy and happiness): The men who rejected Shu'aib- Were ruined!

7.93. (So Shu'aib) left them, saying: "O my people! I really brought the Message to you for which I was sent by my Lord: I gave you good advice, but how shall I feel sad for people who refuse to believe!"

7.94.. And whenever We sent a prophet to a town (and they rejected him,) We helped its people in suffering and misfortune, so that they might learn humility.

7.95. Then We changed their suffering into success and joy, until they grew and multiplied, and began to say: "Our fathers (too) had suffering and success"- Look! We called them to account all of a sudden, when they were not aware (of the situation).

7.96. And if the people of the towns had only believed and feared Allah, certainly We should indeed have opened out to them blessings from heavens and earth; But they rejected (the truth), and We brought them to account for their wrong doings.

7.97. Did the people of the towns feel safe against the coming of Our anger (on them) during the night while they slept?

7.98. Or else did they feel safe against the coming of Our Punishment, in open (broad) daylight while they played about?

7.99. Did they then feel safe against the Plan of Allah? But no one can feel safe from the Plan of Allah, except those (falling) into (his own) ruin!]

7.100.. To those (people) who take over the earth after its (previous) owners, is it not a guiding (lesson) that, if We so wanted, We could (also) punish them for their sins, and close their hearts so that they could not hear?

7.101. Such were the towns whose story We bring to you (like this): Truly, there came to them their messengers with clear (Signs): But they would not believe what they had rejected before, thus does Allah close the hearts of those who reject Faith.

7.102. We did not find most of them, those men (true) to their promise: But We found most of them rebellious and disobedient.

7.103. Then after them We sent Musa (Moses) with Our Signs to Firon (Pharaoh) and his chiefs, but they wrongfully rejected them: So (then) see what was the end of those who caused mischief.

7.104. Musa (Moses) said: "O Firon (Pharaoh)! I am a messenger from the Lord of the Worlds-

7.105. "One for whom, it is right to say nothing but the truth about Allah! Now I have come to you (People), from your Lord, with a clear (Sign): So let the Children of Israel depart with me."

7.106. (Firon) said: "If you have truly come with a Sign, show it forth- If you tell the truth."

7.107. Then (Musa) threw his (wooden) stick (his rod), and look! It simply was a (huge) snake!

7.108. And, he drew out his hand, and look! It was white (lit up) to all those seeing!

7.109.. Said the Chiefs of the people of Firon (Pharaoh): "This is truly a (very) well-versed magician.

7.110. "His plan is to get you out of your land: So then what do you advise?"

7.111. They said: "Keep him and his brother wondering (for a while); And send (out) callers to the cities to find-

7.112. "And bring up to you all (our very) good magicians."

7.113.. And so there came the magicians to Firon (Pharaoh): They said: "Of course, we want a (suitable) reward if we win!"

7.114. He (Firon) said: "Yes, (and more)- And in that case (you win), you shall be (given positions) closest (to me)."

7.115. They said: "O Musa (Moses), will you throw (first), or shall we have the (first) throw?"

7.116. Said Musa (Moses): "You throw (first)." So when they threw, they surprised the eyes of the people, and struck fear in them: Because they showed a great (act of) magic.

7.117. And We revealed to Musa (Moses): "(Now) throw your (wooden) stick:" And look! It swallowed up at once all the lies that they made up!

7.118. Like this the truth was proved. And all that they did, had no effect.

7.119. So the (great ones) were put to shame there and then, and were made to look small.

7.120.. But the magicians fell down on their face (praying) in praise and appreciation (of Allah).

7.121. Saying: "We believe in the Lord of the Worlds,

7.122. "The Lord of Musa (Moses) and Haroon (Aaron)."

7.123. Firon (Pharaoh) said: "You have believed in him (Moses) before I give you permission? Surely, this is a trick that you had planned in the City to drive out its people: But soon you will know (what will happen).

7.124. "Be sure I will cut off your hands and your feet on opposite sides, then and I will make all die on the cross."

7.125. They said: "For us, we are only sent back to our Lord:

7.126. "And you do take out your revenge on us simply because we believed in the Signs of our Lord when they reached us! Our Lord! Pour out on us patience and constancy, and take our souls as Muslims to You."

7.127.. Said the chiefs of Firon (Pharaoh)s people: "Will you leave Musa (Moses) and his people, to spread mischief in the land, and to give up you and your gods?" He (Firon) said: "We will kill their male children; (Only) their females will we save alive; And we have over them (power) supreme."

7.128. Said Musa (Moses) to his people: "Pray for help from Allah, and (wait) in patience and constancy: Because the earth is Allah's, to give as a gift to such of His servants whom He pleases; And the end will be (best) for the righteous."

7.129. They said: "We have had (only) trouble, both before and after you came to us." He said: "It may be that your Lord will destroy your enemy and make you the inheritors in the earth; That so He may try you by your actions."

7.130.. And indeed, We punished the people of Firon (Pharaoh) with years (of drought) and shortness of crops; That they might listen to guidance.

7.131. But when good (times) came, they said: "This is due to us;" When overcome by hardship, they made the reason for it to evil omens connected with Musa (Moses) and those with him! Look! In truth the omens of the evil are theirs, in Allah's sight, but most of them do not understand!

7.132. They said (to Musa): "Whatever are the Signs that you will bring, to work your magic on us with them, we will never believe in you."

7.133. So We sent (misfortunes) on them: Typhoons, locusts, lice, frogs, and blood: Signs openly self-explained: But they remained (unjustly) proud- A people given to sin.

7.134. And when the punishment fell upon them, they said: "O Musa (Moses)! Call to your Lord with virtue on behalf of His promise to you: If you will remove the punishment from us, we will truly believe in you, and we will send away the Children of Israel with you."

7.135. But every time We removed the punishment from them lasting for a fixed time, which they had to undergo- Look! They broke their word!

7.136. So We took the toll (penalty) from them: We drowned them in the sea, because they rejected Our Signs, and failed to take the warning from them.

7.137. And We (still) made a people, who were thought as being rather weak, the inheritors of lands in both East and West- Those lands in which,

We sent Our blessings. The holy promise of your Lord was fulfilled for the Children of Israel, because they had patience and constancy, and We brought down to the ground the great works and fine buildings that Firon (Pharaoh) and his people had erected (in their pride).

7.138.. And We took the Children of Israel (safely) to the other side of the sea. And (here) they found a people who were completely devoted to some idols that they had (worshipped) they said: "O Musa (Moses)! Put together for us a god like the gods that they have." He said: "Surely, you are a people without Knowledge.

7.139. "Surely, these people (from here)- Will be destroyed for what they practice (idol worship): And the (worship) that they do is useless."

7.140. He (Musa) said: "Shall I find a god for you other than the (True and Only) Allah, when He has given you the gift above the creations (of men and jinns)?"

7.141. And (remember when) We saved you from Firon's (Pharaohs) people, who punished you with the harshest of penalties, who killed your male children and kept alive your females. And in that was a great trial from your Lord.

7.142.. And We set out thirty nights for Musa (Moses), and completed (the period) with ten (more): Thus the term of (holy fellowship) with his Lord, was completed in forty nights. And Musa (Moses) had instructed his brother (Haroon, before he went upon the mountain): "(Take over and) act for me among my people: Do right, and do not follow the way of those who do mischief."

7.143. And When Musa (Moses) came to the place set by Us, and his Lord called to him, he (Musa) said: "O my Lord! Show (Yourself) to me, that I may look at You." Allah said: "By no means can you see Me (directly); But look upon the mountain; If it still there in its place, then you shall see Me." When his Lord showed His Glory to the Mountain, He made it like dust, and Musa (Moses) fell down (being) unconscious. When he came back to his senses he said: "Glory be to You! To You, I come in repentance, and I am the first (one) to believe."

7.144. (Allah) said: "O Musa (Moses)! I have chosen you over (other) men, by my message that I (have given to you) and by my words I (have spoken to you): Take then the (revelation) that I give to you, and be of those who give thanks."

7.145. And We put together laws for him (written) in tablets (of stone), regarding all matters, both by commanding and by explaining all things, (and said to him): "Take and hold these (laws) with firmness, and instruct your people to firmly follow by the best in the standards (of conduct): Soon I will show you the homes of the rebellious- (How they will be destroyed)."

7.146. I will turn them away from My Signs (verses), those who behave with pride on the earth opposing the right- And even if they see all the Signs (verses), they will not believe in them; And if they see the way to right conduct, they will not follow it as the Way; But if they see the way to wrong, that is the way they will follow. (They do this) because they rejected Our Signs (verses), and have not taken the warning from them.

7.147. Those who reject Our Signs (these verses of Quran), and the Meeting in the Hereafter, their actions are useless: Can they expect to be given (anything) other than what they have worked for?

7.148.. During his absence, the People of Musa (Moses), from their (own) ornaments made, the image of a calf, (for worship): It seemed so low (and improper): (That also, it had a low pitch sound when struck) did they not see that it could not speak to them, nor show them the Way? They took it (for worship) and they did wrong.

7.149. When they felt sorry (and regretted), and saw that they had made a mistake, they said: "If our Lord does not have mercy upon us and forgive us, we shall be truly of those who perish."

7.150. When Musa (Moses) came back to his people, angry and sad, said: "It is evil, what you have done in my place (and) in my absence: Did you make haste to bring on (yourselves) the judgment (and anger) of your Lord?" He threw the Tablets, held his brother (Haroon) by (the hair of) his head, and dragged him to himself. Haroon (Aaron) said: "Son of my mother! Indeed, the people truly treated me as nothing and came near to killing me! So do not make the enemies rejoice over my misfortune, and you do not count me with the people in sin."

7.151. Musa (Moses) prayed: "O my Lord! Forgive me, and my brother! And admit us into Your mercy because You are the Most Merciful of those who show mercy!"

7.152.. Certainly, those who took the calf (for worship) will truly be overcome by the anger of their Lord, and with shame in this life: Thus do We recompense those who make up (lies).

7.153. But those who do wrong and repent afterwards and (truly) believe- Surely, your Lord is afterwards Often Forgiving, Most Merciful .

7.154. And when the anger of Musa (Moses) was calmed he took up the Tablets (of stone), with the writing upon them; (And) it was the guidance and Mercy for those who fear their Lord.

7.155. And Musa (Moses) chose from his people, seventy of his (best) men for Our place of meeting: When they were caught in severe earthquake, he prayed: "O my Lord! If it was Your Will, you could have destroyed, much before, both them and me: Would You destroy us for the actions of the foolish ones among us? This is no more than Your trial: By it You make whom You will to lose the path, and You lead whom You will to the right path. You are our Protector:- So forgive us and give us Your mercy; For You are the Best of those who forgive.

7.156. "And grant for us that which is good, in this life and in the Hereafter: Because we have (repented and) returned to You." He (Allah) said: "With My Punishment, I visit whom I will; But My Mercy extends to all things. That I shall grant for those who do right, and practice regular charity, and for those who believe in Our Signs;"-

7.157. Those who follow the Messenger, Prophet (Muhammad), the unlettered who can neither read nor write, whom they find mentioned in their own (books)- In the Torah and the Gospel)- For he (the Prophet) commands them what is just and forbids them what is evil; He allows them as lawful what is good (and pure) and prohibits them from what is bad (and impure); He releases them from their heavy burdens and from the heavy yokes that are upon them. So it is those who believe in him, honor him, help him, and follow the light sent down with him- It is they who will prosper."

7.158.. (O Prophet!) say: "O Mankind! I am sent to you all, as the Messenger of Allah, to Whom belongs the kingdom of the heavens and the earth: There is no god but He: It is He Who gives both life and death. So believe in Allah and His Messenger, the unlettered prophet, who believes in Allah and His Words: Follow him that you may be guided."

7.159. And from the people of Musa (Moses) there is a community who guide and do justice in the light of truth.

7.160. We divided them into twelve Tribes or nations. We directed Musa (Moses) by inspiration, when his (thirsty) people asked him for water: "Strike the rock with your (wooden) staff:" Out of it gushed out twelve springs: Each group knew its own place for water. We gave them the shade of the clouds, and sent down to them (the gifts of) manna (something sweet like honey) and quails (small birds for their food), (saying): "Eat from the good things We have given to you:" (But they rebelled); To Us they did no harm, but they hurt their own themselves.

7.161. And (remember) when it was said to them: "Live in this town and eat from there as you wish, but say the word of modesty (without pride) and enter the gate in a state of being humble: We shall forgive you for your faults; We shall increase (the portion of) those who do good."

7.162. But those who exceeded the limits among them changed the word from what was given to them; So We sent on them a misery from heavens-For that they exceeded their limits many times.

7.163.. Ask them about the town standing close to the sea. Look! They transgressed about the Sabbath. Because on the day of their Sabbath their fish did come to them, openly holding up their heads; But on the day they had no Sabbath, they did not come: Thus did We make a trial for them, because they were used to transgression.

7.164. When some of them said: "Why do you teach to a people whom Allah will destroy or come down with a terrible punishment?"- Said the teachers: "To fulfill our duty to your Lord, so that they may fear Him."

7.165. When they had rejected the warnings that were given to them, We saved those who prevented evil; But We came down upon the wrongdoers with a painful punishment, because they were given to transgression.

7.166. When in their haughtiness, they exceeded (all) that was prevented, We said to them: "You be (like) monkeys, disliked and rejected."

7.167.. And (remember), your Lord did (clearly) state that He would send against them, till the Day of Judgment, those who would hurt them with grievous penalty. Your Lord is quick in retribution (getting back), but (He) is also Often Forgiving, Most Merciful.

7.168. And We broke them up in sections on this earth. There are among them some who are the righteous, and some who are the opposite. And We have tried them with plenty and little (prosperity and adversity): So that they might turn (to Us).

7.169. After them succeeded an (evil) generation: They took over the (holy) Book, but they chose the showy things of this world, saying (for excuse): "(Everything) will be forgiven for us." (Even then), when similar things came their way, they would (once again) grab them. Was the sacred Promise of the Book not taken from them, that they would not say about Allah anything but the truth? And that they would study what is in the Book? And best for the righteous is the home in the Hereafter. Will you not understand?

7.170. And to those who hold fast to the Book and establish regular Prayer-

Certainly, We shall never let the reward of the righteous to perish.

7.171. And (remember), when We shook the mount over them, as if it had been a cloud, and they thought it was going to fall on them (We said): "Hold firmly to what We have given to you, and (always) remember what is in there, so that you fear Allah and obey Him."

7.172.. And (remember) when your Lord took from the Children of Adam- From their loins- Their descendants, and made them speak out about themselves: "Am I not your Lord?" - They said: "Yes! We testify for sure." (This is so), just in case you may say on the Day of Judgment: "We were never aware of this:"

7.173. Or in case you may say: "Our fathers before us may have taken false gods, but we are (their) descendants: Then will You destroy us because of the deeds of men who were useless?"

7.174. Like this We explain the Signs in detail; And so that they may come back (to Us).

7.175.. Tell them the story of the man to whom We sent Our Signs, but he let them pass: So Satan kept after him, and he went astray.

7.176. And if it had been Our Will, We should have raised him with Our Signs; But he was tempted (down) to the earth, and followed his own useless desires. So the similarity is that of a dog: If you attack him, he puts out his tongue (and pants), or if you leave him alone, he (still) hangs out his tongue (and pants). That is the similarity of those who reject Our Signs; So relate the stories; So that they may think.

7.177. Evil is the example of people who reject Our Signs and (they) used to wrong themselves.

7.178. And surely, whomsoever Allah guides, he is on the right path; Whom He rejects from His guidance- Such are the persons who perish.

7.179. We have made many jinns' and men for Hell: They have hearts with which they do not understand, they have eyes with which they do not see, and they have ears with which they do not hear (the truth). They are like cattle- No (even) more lost: Because they are careless (of warning).

7.180.. The Most Beautiful Names belong to Allah: So call on Him by them; And keep away from such men who use vulgarity (blasphemy) in His names: For what they do, they will be soon punished.

7.181.. And of those people, We have created are such (people) who help (others) with truth. And give out justice with it.

7.182.. For those who reject Our Signs, We shall slowly come down with punishment, in ways that they are not (even) aware;

7.183. And I will grant (some) relief to them: For My plan is Mighty (and never failing).

7.184. Do they not think (deeply)? Their companion (the Prophet) is not taken by madness: He is only a clear (and an unmistakable) Warner.

7.185. Do they see nothing in the dominion of the heavens and the earth and all things that Allah has created? (Do they not see) that it may really be that their time is nearly coming to an end? In what Message after this will they believe?

7.186. For those whom Allah rejects from His guidance, there can be no guide: And He will leave them exceeding their limits, wandering aimlessly (without going anywhere).

7.187.. They ask you about the (final) Hour, (Resurrection)- When is its appointed time? Say: "Its knowledge is with my Lord (alone): No one except He can say when it will happen. Its burden was heavy through the heavens and the earth. Only, all of a sudden it will come to you." They ask you as if you were eager in search of it: Say: "Its knowledge is with Allah (alone), but most men do not know."

7.188. Say: "I have no power over any good or harm to myself except as Allah wills. If I had knowledge of the unseen, I should have multiplied all good, and no evil could have touched me: I am only a Warner, and a bringer of glad tidings to those who have Faith (in Allah)."

7.189.. It is He Who created you from a single person (Adam), and made his mate (Eve) of similar nature, that he might live with her (in peace and love). When they are close together, she bears a light burden (and responsibility) and carries it about (well and easily). When she grows heavy, they both pray to Allah their Lord, (saying): "If You give us a good child, we promise we shall be grateful."

7.190. But when He does give them a good child, they give to others a share (of thanks) for the gift that they have received: But Allah is supremely High above the partners they ascribe to Him.

7.191. Do they truly give to Him as partners' things that can create nothing, but are themselves created (by Him)?

7.192. No help can they (the partners) give to them, nor can they help themselves!

7.193. If you call them to guidance, they follow you not: For you it is the same whether you call them or you hold your peace!

7.194.. Surely, those whom you (people) call upon besides Allah are (mere) servants like you: Call to them, and let them hear your prayer, if you are (really) truthful!

7.195. Do they have feet to walk with? Or hands to hold with? Or eyes to see with? Or ears to hear with? Say: "Call your 'god-partners', plan (the worst) against me, and give me no relief!

7.196. "Surely, my Protector is Allah, Who revealed the Book (the Quran), and He protects the righteous.

7.197. "But those you call upon besides Him (Allah) are not able to help you, and indeed (even) to help themselves."

7.198. If you call them to guidance- They will not hear, you will see them looking at you, yet they do not see.

7.199.. Show forgiveness (on your part); Instruct what is right; But turn away from those who are foolish.

7.200. If a suggestion from Satan attacks your (mind), find (your) shelter with Allah; Verily, He hears and knows (all things).

7.201. Verily, those who fear Allah- When an evil thought from Satan attacks them, bring Allah to mind (by remembering Him), indeed, they see (alright again)!

7.202.. But their brothers (the Satans' among them) get them deeper into error, and never let go.

7.203. And if you do not bring them a miracle, they say: "Why have you not put it together?" Say: "I only follow what is revealed to me from my Lord: This is (only) Light, (the Quran) from your Lord, and Guidance and Mercy for any who have Faith."

7.204.. So when the Quran is read, listen to it with attention, and hold your peace: That you may receive (your Lord's) Mercy.

7.205. And you (also, O reader!) bring your Lord into yourselves [by remembering Him, in your (very) soul], with modesty and in respect, without loud words, in mornings and evenings; And you do not be of those who do not listen (to warning).

7.206. Indeed, those who are with your Lord (the angels), do not stop (or hesitate) to worship Him: They recite His Praises, and bow down before Him.

{A Muslim generally prostrates to Allah after reciting this verse}
****

Sura 8. Al-Anfal,
(The spoils of war): (Medinah, 75 Verses)
In the Name of Allah, the Most Gracious, the Most Merciful.

8.1.. They ask you (O Muhammad) about (things taken as) spoils of war. Say: "(Such) spoils (of war) are for Allah and the Messenger (Muhammad): So fear Allah, and settle the differences between yourselves (with fairness): Obey Allah and His Messenger (Muhammad), if you do believe."

8.2. Those only are the believers who feel a tremor (and thrill) in their hearts when (the Name of) Allah is mentioned, and when they hear His Signs rehearsed, find their faith becoming strong, and place (all) their trust in their Lord;

8.3. Who establish regular prayer and spend (freely) from the gifts We have given to them for (their) living:

8.4. Like this are the true believers: They have grades of dignity with their Lord, and forgiveness, and generous sustenance:

8.5. Just like your Lord commands you to go away from your house in (the way of) truth, and surely, some of the believers disliked it,

8.6. Debating with you about the truth after it was made clear, as if they were pushed towards death and they (actually) saw it.

8.7. And (remember), Allah had promised you that one of the two (enemy) parties should be yours: You wished that the one unarmed should be yours, but Allah had willed to prove the Truth according to His words, and to cut off the roots of the disbelievers-

8.8. That He might prove the Truth and prove what is false that amounts to nothing, even though it may be unpleasant to the guilty (criminal) .

8.9. (Remember that), you humbly prayed for help from your Lord, and He answered you (by saying): "I will help you with a thousand of the angels, (coming down) ranks on ranks."

8.10. Allah made it only a message of good news, and an assurance to your hearts: And, there is no help except from Allah: Verily, Allah is Exalted in Power, All Wise:

8.11.. (Remember when) He brought a sense of sleep over you to give you calm from Himself, and He made the rain to fall on you from the sky, to clean you with it, and to remove from you the spot of Satan, and to give strength to your hearts, and to hold your feet firmly in the sandy place with it.

8.12. (Remember when) your Lord revealed (the Message) to the angels: "Verily, I am with you: Give strength to the believers: I will bring about terror into the hearts of the disbelievers: So you strike above their necks and hit hard over all of their finger-tips and toes."

8.13. This is because they stood against Allah and His Messenger (Muhammad): And if any stand against Allah and His Messenger (Muhammad), Allah is strict in punishment.

8.14. Like this (it will be said to them): "Then you taste it (the punishment): For those who resist Allah, the penalty is the Fire."

8.15.. O you who believe! When you meet the disbelievers in battle fields (and wars), do not turn your backs to them.

8.16. And if anyone turns his back on them on such a day, unless it is a plan of the war, or to come back to (his own) army- He has indeed drawn on himself the Anger of Allah, and his home is Hell, an evil refuge to be!

8.17. It is not you who killed them: It was Allah Who killed them; And when you threw (a handful of dust), it was not your act, but Allah's (act): So that He might test the believers by a kind trail from Himself: Surely, Allah is All Hearing , All Knowing .

8.18. That (is so), and also because Allah is He Who makes the plans and strategies of the disbelievers weak and shaky.

8.19. (O disbelievers!) If you had asked for victory and judgment (during the war), now the judgment has come to you: If you stop (the wrong you do), it will be best for you, and if you return (to the war), so shall We return, and your forces will not be of the least good to you even if they were many times over: And surely, Allah is with those who believe!

8.20.. O you who believe! Obey Allah and His Messenger (Muhammad) and do not turn away from him when you hear (him speaking to you).

8.21. And do not be like those who say: "We hear", but they do not hear:

8.22. Verily, in the sight of Allah, the worst of the animals are the deaf and dumb, those who do not understand, (the disbelievers).

8.23. If Allah had found any good in them, he would truly have made them listen: And even if He made them listen, they would have only gone back and rejected (faith).

8.24. O you who believe! Give your answer to Allah and His Messenger (Muhammad) when He calls you to that which will give you life; And know that, Allah comes in between a man and his heart, and that, it is He to Whom you shall (all) be gathered.

8.25. And fear the affliction (and retribution), which affects not only those of you in particular, who do wrong: (But also the innocent and weak), and know that Allah is strict in punishment.

8.26. And remember when you were few (a small group), not well liked through out the land, and afraid that men might rob and take you away (by force); But He provided a place of safety for you, strengthened you with His help, and gave you good things for living; That you may be thankful.

8.27.. O you who believe! Do not betray to the trust of Allah and the Messenger (Muhammad), and do not steal (or cheat) knowingly from the things given to you in trust.

8.28. And you know that the things you own, and your children (descendants) are only a trial; And that it is Allah with Whom is your highest reward.

8.29.. O you who believe! If you fear Allah, He will give you a basis (to judge between right and wrong), (He will) remove from you the evil (that may be close to) you, and forgive you: And Allah is the Lord of unlimited grace.

8.30.. And (remember) how the disbelievers planned against you, to put you in prison, or to kill you, or get you out (of your home, Makkah). They plotted and planned, and Allah also plotted but the best of planners is Allah.

8.31.. When Our verses are read to them, they say: "We have heard this (before): If we wanted, we could say (words) like these: These are nothing but old stories."

8.32. And (remember) when how they said: "O Allah! If this is indeed the Truth from You, then rain down on us a shower of stones from the sky, or send us a painful penalty."

8.33. And Allah was not going to send them a penalty while you (O Muhammad) were with them; And He was not going to punish them when they could ask for pardon.

8.34. But what plea do they have that Allah should not punish them, when they keep out (men) from the Sacred Mosque- And they are not its guardians (or keepers)? No men can be its keepers except the righteous; But most of them do not understand.

8.35. Their prayer at the House (of Allah) is only whistling and clapping of hands: (And its only answer can be), "You taste the Penalty because you lied."

8.36.. The disbelievers spend their wealth to keep (men) away from the Path of Allah, and so will they keep on spending; But in the end they will have regrets and sighs; At the end they will be defeated: And the disbelievers will be brought together to Hell-

8.37. In order that Allah may separate the wicked from the good, (and the impure from the pure), put the impure, one over another, heap them together, and throw them into Hell. They will be the ones to have lost.

8.38.. Say to the disbelievers, if they stop themselves (from disbelief), their past (actions) would be forgiven to them; But if they continue, the punishment of those before them is already (before them as a warning).

8.39. And keep on fighting them till there is no more unrest (commotion) or injustice (cruelty), and there exists justice and faith in Allah altogether and everywhere; But if they stop, surely, Allah sees all that they do.

8.40. And if they refuse, be sure that Allah is your Protector- The Best (One) to protect and the Best to help.

8.41. And know that out of all the things (won in war and) those that you may collect (during the war) verily, a fifth share is to be set aside for Allah's cause- And for the Messenger (Muhammad), and for near relatives, the orphans, the needy, and the traveler far from home- If you believe in Allah and in the teachings We sent down to Our Servant (the Prophet) on the day of Test, (the battle of Badr)- The day of the meeting of the two forces, and Allah is Able to do all things.

8.42.. (And remember) when you (the army of the believers) were on the near side of the valley, and they were on the far side (of the valley), and the caravan (of Quraish) on lower ground than you. Even if you had made a mutual time to meet (for war), you would certainly have failed at that time: But (again you met) for Allah to complete an act already decided; So that those who died would die after a clear Sign (of Allah), and those who lived would live after a clear Sign (of Allah). And surely Allah is All Seeing and All Knowing (of all things).

8.43. (And remember) in your dream Allah showed them (the enemy) to you as few (men) if He had shown them to you as many (men); you would surely have lost your courage and you would surely have argued (your) decision. But Allah saved (you): Surely, He knows well the (secrets) of (all) hearts.

8.44. And (remember) when you met (in war), he showed them (the enemy) to you as a few (men) in your eyes, and He made you appear as few (and worthless) in their eyes: For Allah to complete an act already decided; For all questions go back to Allah (for decision).

8.45.. O you who believe! When you meet an enemy, be firm; And stand up against them, and recall Allah in remembrance much so that you may prosper:

8.46. And obey Allah and His Messenger (Muhammad); And do not get into disputes (among yourselves), lest you lose heart and lose your power; And be patient and persevering (dedicated): Surely, Allah is with those who patiently persevere:

8.47. And do not be like those who started (for war) from their homes haughtily and to be seen by men, and to want to stop (men) from the Path of Allah: For Allah controls all about all that they do.

8.48. And (remember) when Satan made their (sinful) acts appear attractive to them, and said: "No one from among men can defeat you this day, while I am near to you": But when the two armies came to oppose each other, he ran away and said: "Surely! I have nothing to do with you; Verily, I see what you do not see; For sure, I fear Allah, for Allah is strict in punishment."

8.49.. When those hypocrites (who hide the truth), and those in whose hearts is a disease, say: "These people (the believers)- Their religion had misled them." But if any of those who trust in Allah, then surely, Allah is Supreme in Strength, All Wise.

8.50. And if you could see, when the angels take the souls of the disbelievers (at the time of their death), that they smite their faces and (strike) their backs, (saying): "Taste the Penalty of the burning Fire-

8.51. "This is because of what your hands sent forward: Verily, Allah is never unjust to His servants:

8.52. "(Deeds) like those of the People of Firon (Pharaoh) and those before them: They rejected the Signs of Allah, and Allah punished them for their evil acts: For Allah is Strong, and Strict in punishment:

8.53. "Because Allah will never change the grace which He has given to a people until they change what is in their (own) souls: And surely Allah is All Hearing , All Knowing

8.54. "(Deeds) like those of the People of Firon (Pharaoh) and those before them": They treated the Signs from their Lord as false: So We destroyed them for their evil acts, and We drowned the People of Firon (Pharaoh): For they were all unjust (cruel) and wrongdoers.

8.55.. Verily, in the sight of Allah, the worst of animals are those who reject Him: (And) they will not believe.

8.56. They (the disbelievers) are those with whom you made a promise, but they break their promise every time, and they do not have the fear (of Allah).

8.57. So if you win victory over them in war deal with them, and scatter them (and) those who follow them, that they may remember.

8.58. If you fear disloyalty (or break of trust) from any group, remind (their promise) to them, (so as to be) on equal terms: For sure, Allah does not love the disloyal.

8.59.. And do not let the disbelievers think that they can gain (over and escape the punishment): They will never be able to save themselves.

8.60. Against them make ready all your strength to the utmost of your power, including the (strong) horses of war, to cause fear in the enemies of Allah and your enemies, and others besides (them), whom you may not know but whom Allah does (indeed) know. And whatever you spend in the Cause of Allah, (it) shall be repaid back to you; You shall not be treated unjustly.

8.61.. But if the enemy shows willingness towards peace, you (also) show willingness towards peace, and trust in Allah: Verily, He is All Hearing , All Knowing .

8.62. And if they want to deceive you- Surely Allah is sufficient for you: He it is Who has made you strong with His help and with the believers;

8.63. And (in addition), He has placed unity between their (believer's) hearts: Even if you had spent all that is in the earth, you could not have produced that unity (and love); But Allah has so united them, surely, He is Supreme in Strength, All Wise.

8.64. O Prophet! Allah is sufficient for you- And for those who follow you among the believers.

8.65. O Prophet! Make ready the believers to the fight. If there are twenty from you, (who are) steadfast (patient and persevering) persons, they will defeat two hundred: If there be a hundred steadfast persons from you, they will defeat a thousand of the disbelievers: Because these are the people without understanding.

8.66. Now Allah has made your (task) easy, for He knows that there is a weakness in you: But (even then), if there are a hundred of you, steadfast (patient and persevering) persons, they will defeat two hundred of the disbelievers and if a thousand of you, they will defeat two thousand, of the disbelievers, with the approval of Allah: And Allah is with those who patiently persevere.

8.67.. It is not appropriate for a prophet that he should take prisoners of war (for ransom monies) until he has fought and completely won over the land. You may wish for the material gains of this world; But Allah desires the Hereafter (for you): And Allah is Supreme in Strength, All Wise.

8.68. If it was not for a previous command from Allah, a severe penalty would have come over you for the (repayment) that you took.

8.69. But (now) enjoy what you have as booty in the war, (as far as it is) lawful and good: But fear Allah: Certainly, Allah is Often Forgiving, Most Merciful .

8.70.. O Prophet! Say to those who are prisoners in your hands: "If Allah finds any good in your hearts, He will give you something better than what has been taken from you, and He will forgive you: And Allah is Often Forgiving, Most Merciful ."

8.71. But if they have evil plans against you, (O Prophet! Know that), they have already been in treason against Allah, and so He has given (you) the power over them. And Allah is All Knowing , All Wise.

8.72.. Verily, those who believed, and who left their homes (in the time of Hijrah), and who fought for the Faith with their property and their persons, in the Cause of Allah, and those who gave (them) shelter and help- These are (all) friends and protectors, of one another. And as to those who believed but did not leave their homes (or emigrate in Hijrah), you have no duty to protect them, until they do emigrate (and come into your protection); But if they ask for your help in religion, it is your duty to help them, except against a people with whom you have a treaty of mutual alliance (agreement or friendship). And (remember) Allah sees all that you do.

8.73. And the disbelievers are one another's protectors: Unless you (Muslims, also) do this, (by protecting each other), there will be unrest (commotion) and injustice (cruelty), on earth, and great mischief.

8.74. And those who believe, and adopt exile (by emigrating or leaving their homes), and fight for Faith in the Cause of Allah, as well as those who give (them) protection and help, these are (all) very truly the believers: For them is the forgiveness of sins and things (of rewards) most generous.

8.75. And those who accept Faith later on, and adopt exile and emigrate (by leaving their homes), and fight for Faith alongside with you, they are (also the people) from you. But children by blood are nearer to one another (and have earlier rights regarding the inheritance) in the Book of Allah. Surely, Allah is All Knowing of all things.

****

Sura 9. At-Tauba,

(Repentance), Also known as Baráatun (Immunity): (Medinah, 129 Verses)

9.1.. An (offer) of agreement from Allah and His Messenger (Muhammad), to those of the pagans (idolaters) with whom you have a treaty (obligations of mutual alliances):

9.2. Then, you (the pagans) go for four months, backwards and forwards, all through the land, but you know that you cannot frustrate Allah but (it is) Allah, Who will cover with shame those who reject Him.

9.3. And an announcement from Allah and His Messenger (Muhammad), to the people (gathered) on, the day of the great pilgrimage, (the Tenth of the month of Zul-Hajjah)- That Allah (and His Messenger Muhammad) give up (the treaty and the) obligations with the (distrusted) pagans. If then, you repent, (and join the believers) it will be best for you; But if you turn away, you know that you cannot frustrate Allah. And declare a painful penalty to those who reject Faith.

9.4. (But the treaties of mutual friendship are) not given up with those (trusted) pagans with whom you have entered into alliance (of friendship), and who have not later on (broken them and) failed you (believers) even a little bit, nor helped anyone (of the enemies) against you. So complete your agreements with them to the end of their time: Because Allah loves the righteous.

9.5.. But when the forbidden (four) months are over then fight and kill the (distrusted) pagans wherever you find them, and catch them, attack them, and stay waiting for them in every stage (of war); But if they repent, and establish regular prayers and practice regular charity, then make it easy for them: Verily, Allah is Often Forgiving, Most Merciful .

9.6. If one of the pagans asks you for place of safety give it to him, so that he may hear the Word of Allah (the Quran); And then take him to where he can be safe. That is because they are men without knowledge.

9.7.. How can there be a treaty before Allah and His Messenger (Muhammad), with the pagans, except those with whom you made a treaty near the Sacred Mosque? As long as these (pagans) remain true to you, you remain true to them: Verily Allah does love the righteous.

9.8. How (can there be such a gathering), seeing that if they get an advantage over you, they do not respect for you the ties either of friendship or of promise (and treaty)? With (words from) their mouths they invite you, but their hearts are against you; And most of them are rebellious and wicked.

9.9. They have sold the Signs of Allah for a small price, and (many) have stopped others entering His Way: Truly, evil are the acts that they have done.

9.10. They do not respect the ties of friendship or of promise, in a believer. It is they who have exceeded all limits.

9.11.. But if they repent, perform regular prayers, and give regular charity- They are your brothers in Faith: (Like this) We explain the Signs in detail, for those who understand.

9.12. But if they break their word after their promise, and make fun of you for your Faith- (Then) you fight the leaders of disbelief: Their words (of promise) are nothing to them: Like this they may be restrained.

9.13.. Will you (believers) not fight the people who have broken their promises, plotted to drive away the Messenger (Muhammad, from Makkah) and became aggressive by being the first ones (to injure) you? Do you fear them? No! It is Allah Whom you should more truly fear, if you believe!

9.14. Fight against them! And Allah will punish them with your hands, cover them with shame, help you (to win) over them, heal the chests of believers,

9.15. And bring down the anger of their hearts. For Allah will turn (in mercy) to whom He will; And Allah is All Knowing , All Wise.

9.16. Or do you think that you will be left alone, as if Allah did not know those from you who work with (their physical) strength, and take no one for friends and protectors except Allah, His Messenger (Muhammad), and the believers? But Allah is Well-Acquainted with what you do.

9.17. It is not for those who join gods with Allah, to visit maintain the mosques of Allah while they witness against their own souls as faithless. The works of such (people) have no reward: And in fire they shall live.

9.18. The Mosques of Allah shall be visited and maintained by such (people) who believe in Allah and the Last Day, establish regular prayers, and practice regular charity, and fear none except Allah. They are the ones on true guidance.

9.19. Do you make the giving of drink to pilgrims, or the maintenance of The Sacred Mosque, equal to (the pious service of) those who believe in Allah and the Last Day, and work hard with their physical strength in the cause of Allah: In the sight of Allah, they are not the same: And Allah does not guide those who do wrong.

9.20. Those who believe, and leave their homes, work hard with their strength, in Allah's cause, with their goods and their person, hold the highest position in the Sight of Allah: They are the people who will achieve salvation.

9.21. Their Lord gives them the happy news of mercy from Himself, of His good pleasure, and of Gardens for them, where there are joys that will last (forever):

9.22. They will live in there forever. Surely, in Allah's Presence is reward, the greatest (reward of all).

9.23.. O you who believe! Do not have for protectors (and helpers) your fathers and your brothers if they choose Disbelief above Faith: If any of you do so, they do wrong.

9.24. Say: "If your fathers, your sons, your brothers, your mates, or your children; The wealth that you have gained; The trade that you fear will go down: Or the house in which you have joy (and peace)- Are dearer to you than Allah, or His Messenger (Muhammad), or the hard work in His cause- Then wait till Allah brings out His decision: And Allah does not guide the rebellious."

9.25.. Surely Allah did help you in many battle grounds and on the day of (battle at the town of) Hunayn: Look! Your large numbers made you very happy, but they did not help you a little bit: The land, being that it is wide, blocked you, and you turned back to withdraw (from war).

9.26. But Allah did pour His peace on the Messenger (Muhammad) and on the believers, and sent down forces (angels) which you did not see: He punished the disbelievers: Like this He rewards those without Faith.

9.27. Allah will again, (even) after this, turn (in mercy) to whoever He wills. and Allah is Often Forgiving, Most Merciful .

9.28.. O you who believe! Truly, the pagans are unclean (people); So after this year of theirs, do not let them come to the Sacred Mosque.

And if you fear poverty (due to reduced trade), Allah will soon make you rich, if He wills, from His bounty; Indeed, Allah is All Knowing , All Wise.

9.29. Fight those who do not believe in Allah nor the Last Day, nor hold that forbidden which has been forbidden by Allah and His Messenger (Muhammad), nor accept (as true) the Religion of Truth, (even if they are) of the People of the Book- Until they pay the dues (the payment for protection by the Islamic regime) with satisfaction and willing submission, and feel themselves subdued.

9.30.. And the Jews say Uzair (Ezra) is a son of God, and the Christians say Messiah (Christ) is the son of God. That is a saying from their mouth; (In this) they tell what the disbelievers of the old (days) used to say. Let Allah's curse be on them: How they are deceived, away from the Truth!

9.31. They hold their priests and their monks to be their lords besides Allah, and (they hold as Lord), Messiah (Christ) the son of Maryam (Mary); Yet they were ordered to worship only One Allah: There is no god but He. Praise and Glory to Him: (Far is He) from having the partners they associate (with Him).

9.32. They want to put out Allah's Light with their mouths (by the lies they say), but Allah will not allow (it); except that His Light should be perfected, even though the disbelievers may hate (it).

9.33. It is He, Who has sent His Messenger (Muhammad) with guidance and the Religion of Truth, to declare it over all religions, even though the pagans may hate (it).

9.34. O you who believe! Truly, there are many of the priests and monks, who in (their) lies eat up the sustenance of men and block (them) from the Way of Allah. And there are those who bury gold and silver and do not spend it in the Way of Allah: Declare to them a most painful penalty-

9.35. On the Day when heat will be produced from that (very wealth) in the fire of Hell, and with it will be burned on their foreheads, their flanks, and their backs.- "This is the (wealth) which you buried for yourselves then you taste, the (wealth) you buried!"

9.36.. Verily, in the sight of Allah, the number of months (in a year) is twelve - So decided by Him, the day when he created the heavens and the earth; Of them (the twelve months) four are sacred: That is the proper religion. So do not go wrong yourselves about it: And fight the pagans (idolaters and polytheists) all together as they fight you all together. But know that Allah is with those who are pious (and hold themselves back from evil).

9.37. Surely, the delaying (of the sacred months) adds to the disbelief: The disbelievers are led to wrong by it: Because they make it a lawful (month) one year, and a forbidden (month) another year, in order to adjust (against) the number of months forbidden by Allah and make such forbidden ones lawful. The evil of their actions seems pleasing to them. But Allah does not guide those who reject Faith.

9.38.. O you who believe! What is the matter with you, that, when you are asked to go out in the Cause of Allah, you stay on (tied) tightly to the earth? Do you prefer the life of this world to the Hereafter? But the comfort of this life is very small, compared with (the comfort of) the Hereafter.

9.39. If you do not go forth, He will punish you with a painful penalty, and put others in your place (as believers); And to Him you would not (cause any) harm in the least. For Allah is Able to do all things.

9.40. If you do not help (the Prophet, it is unimportant): Because Allah truly did help him, when the disbelievers drove him out (from Makkah): He (the Prophet) had only one companion (Abu Bakr): The two of them were in the Cave (of Thaur), and he said to his companion, "Do not fear, because Allah is with us:" Then Allah sent down His peace (and calm) upon him, and strengthened him with forces that you did not see, and made the word (to take the Prophet's life) of the disbelievers completely false. But Allah's Word is glorified to the highest: And Allah is Exalted in Strength, All Wise.

9.41. Go forth, with light or heavy (means), and work hard and struggle, with your goods and yourselves, in the Cause of Allah. That is best for you, if you (only) knew.

9.42. If there was (something) to be gained right away, and the journey was easy, they would (all) have followed you without doubt but, the distance (from Medinah to Tabuk) was long for them. They would truly swear by Allah, "If we only could, we would surely have come out with you:" They destroy their own souls (by lying); And Allah does know that they are only lying.

9.43.. May Allah forgive you, (and give you grace)! Why did you grant them exemption (from fighting the holy war) until those who told the truth could be clearly seen by you, and you had (also) known the liars?

9.44. Those who believe in Allah and the Last Day do not ask you for exemption from fighting with their goods and lives. And Allah knows well those who are pious (and those who fear Him).

9.45. It is only those who do not believe in Allah and the Last Day ask you for exemption and in whose hearts is doubt, so that they are thrown from one side to another in their doubt.

9.46. If they had wanted to come out, then truly they would have made some preparation for it; But Allah was against their being sent forth; So He made them fall behind, and they were told, "Sit among those who sit (inactive at home)."

9.47. If they had come out with you, they would not have added to your (strength) but only (have created) disorder, going here and there in your middle and causing rebellion among you, and there would be some from you who would listen to them. But Allah knows well those who do wrong.

9.48. Verily, indeed they had planned rebellion before, and caused problems for you, till the Truth came, and the Order of Allah became clear, much to their dislike.

9.49.. And among them is (many) a man who says: "Grant me exemption and do not bring me into trial." Surely, are they not in trial already? And truly Hell is (all) around the disbelievers.

9.50. If good comes to you, it saddens them; But if a misfortune comes to you, they say, "We really took our precautions beforehand," and they go away being happy.

9.51. Say: "Nothing will happen to us except what Allah has decreed for us: He is our Protector:" And in Allah put their trust as believers.

9.52. Say: "Can you expect for us (anything) other than one of two best things while we wait for you, that Allah will give to us? (Death as a martyr or victory)? But we can expect for you that either Allah will send His punishment from Himself, or by our hands. So wait, we will also wait with you."

9.53. Say; "Spend (in Allah's Cause), willingly or unwillingly: It will not be accepted from you: Verily, you are a people rebellious and wicked."

9.54. And the (only) reasons why their offerings (and contributions) are not accepted are: That they reject Allah and His Messenger (Muhammad); That they come to prayer in laziness; And that they make (their) offerings unwillingly.

9.55. So let not their wealth, nor their sons amaze you: In reality, Allah's Plan is to punish them with these things in this life, and that their souls may die as disbelievers.

9.56. They swear by Allah that they are truly of you; While (in reality) they are not of you: But they are people (hypocrites) afraid (that you may kill them).

9.57. If they could find a place of refuge, or caves, or a place of hiding, they would run there at once, in great hurry.

9.58. And among them are men who speak ill of you in the matter of (the distribution of) charity: If they are given part of it, then they are happy, but if not, look! They are angry (and indignant)!

9.59. If only they had been pleased with what Allah and His Messenger (Muhammad) gave them, and had said, "Allah is sufficient for us! Allah will give us from His bounty, and His Messenger (from the charity): To Allah do we turn our hopes!" (That would have been right).

9.60.. Alms (goods and money given in charity) are for the poor and the needy, and those employed to manage the (funds); For those whose hearts have turned (to truth and belief recently); For those in slavery (and for the freedom of captives) and in debt; And for (fighters in) the cause of Allah; And for the wayfarer: (It is so) ordered by Allah, and Allah is All Knowing , All Wise.

9.61. Among them are men who annoy (and bother) the Prophet and say, "He is all ears (listens to everyone)." Say, "He listens to what is best for you: He believes in Allah, has faith in the believers, and is a Mercy to those of you who believe." But those who annoy the Messenger will have a painful punishment.

9.62. To you (who believe), they swear by Allah, only to please you: But it is more correct that they should please Allah and His Messenger (Muhammad), if they (also) are believers.

9.63. Do they not know that for those who oppose Allah and His Messenger (Muhammad, there is) certainly the Fire of Hell? They will live in there. That is the lowest disgrace.

9.64.. The hypocrites (liars) are afraid that a Sura should be sent down (just) about them, showing them what is in their hearts. Say (to them): "(Go ahead with the mockery and) mock ! But surely Allah will bring to light all that you are afraid (will get revealed)."

9.65. If you question them, they say (with force): "We were only talking simply and in joke." Say: "Was it at Allah, and His Signs, and His Messenger (Muhammad), about whom you were mocking?

9.66. "You do not make excuses: You have rejected Faith after you had accepted it. If We pardon some of you, We will punish others among you:" (This is) because they were in sin.

9.67.. The hypocrites (liars), men and women, (understand) each other: They enjoin evil with force, and prevent what is good (and just), and (they) withhold (charity) with their hands. They have forgotten Allah; So He has forgotten them. Surely, the hypocrites are rebellious and wrongful.

9.68. Allah has promised the hypocrites, men and women and the disbelievers, the Fire of Hell: They shall live in there: That is enough for them: The curse of Allah is for them, and this is their lasting Punishment-

9.69. Like the case of those before you, they were stronger than you (the hypocrites and disbelievers) in power, and richer in wealth and children. They had their enjoyment of their portion:
And you have of yours, like those before you;
And you get into idle talk as they did. They, their works are useless (both) in this world and in the Hereafter, and they will lose (everything good).

9.70. Has the story of those before them not reached them? The people of Nuh (Noah), and Ad, and Samood (Thamud); The people of Ibrahim

(Abraham), the men of Madyan (Midian), and the Cities (all) defeated. Their messengers came to them with Clear Signs. It is not Allah Who does wrong to them, but (it is) they who do wrong to their own souls.

9.71.. The believers, men and women, are protectors, are supporters one of another: They enjoin what is just, and prevent what is evil: They perform regular prayers, practice regular charity, and obey Allah and His Messenger (Muhammad). On them Allah will spread His Mercy: Truly, Allah is Supreme in Power, All Wise.

9.72. Allah has promised to believers, men and women, Gardens under which rivers flow, to live in there forever, and beautiful (and large) homes in gardens (the Paradise) of eternal joy. But the greatest joy is the Good Pleasure of Allah: That is the supreme happiness.

9.73.. O Prophet! Struggle hard against the disbelievers and the hypocrites, and be firm against them. Their home is Hell- Truly an evil place (to hide).

9.74. They swear by Allah that they said nothing (evil), but truly they have told lies (and falsehood), and they did this after accepting Islam; And they plotted a scheme (against the Prophet) which they could not carry out: This evil action of theirs was the only return for the bounty with which Allah and His Messenger (Muhammad) had made them rich! If they repent, that will be the best for them; But if they go back (to their old ways), Allah will punish them with a painful penalty (both) in this life and in the Hereafter: They shall have no one on the earth to protect or help them.

9.75. And among them are men who made a promise with Allah, that if He granted to them from His bounty, they would give (substantially) in charity, and be truly from those who are righteous.

9.76. Then, when He gave them of His bounty, they became greedy, and turned back opposed. (As if to break their promise with Allah).

9.77. So He punished them with hypocrisy in their hearts, till the Day when they shall meet Him: Because they broke their promise with Allah, (and) what they had promised to Him and because they lied (again and again).

9.78. Do they not know that Allah knows their secret (thoughts) and their secret counsels, and that Allah knows well all the unseen things?

9.79.. Those who tell lies and false stories about the believers who give themselves freely to (deeds of) charity, and who can find nothing to give but the fruits of their (hard) work- So they (the disbelievers) mock at them (the believers)- Allah will throw back their mockery on them: And they shall have a painful penalty.

9.80. Whether you (O Muhammad) ask forgiveness for them (the hypocrites) or not, (their sin will not be forgiven): Even if you ask forgiveness for them seventy times for their forgiveness, Allah will (still) not forgive them: Because they have rejected Allah and His Messenger (Muhammad): And Allah does not guide those who are wrongfully rebellious.

9.81.. Those who stayed behind (from the Tabuk expedition) were happy not doing anything behind the back of the Messenger (Muhammad) of Allah: And they hated to struggle and fight, with their goods and themselves, in the Cause of Allah: And they said, "Do not go out in the heat." Say, "The Fire of Hell is hotter in heat." If they could only understand!

9.82. So let them laugh a little: And (they will) weep a lot: A repayment for the (evil) that they do.

9.83. If, after this, Allah brings you back to any of them, and they ask for your permission to go out (with you to fight) say: "You shall never come out with me, nor fight an enemy with me: Because you liked to sit without doing anything in the first place: Then you sit (now) with those who stay behind."

9.84. Nor do you ever pray (the funeral prayer) for any of them who dies, nor stand at his grave. Certainly, they (the hypocrites) rejected Allah and His Messenger (Muhammad), and died in a state of wrongful revolt.

9.85. Do not let their wealth, nor their sons (to follow them) overwhelm you: Allah's plan is to punish them with these things in this world; And that their souls may die by their (very) denial of Allah.

9.86.. And when a Sura comes down, (strongly) guiding them to believe in Allah and to work and fight along with His Messenger (Muhammad), those with wealth and power (over others) from them ask you to excuse (them), and say: "Leave us (behind): We will be with those who sit (at home)."

9.87. They like to be with those, who remain behind: Their hearts are closed, and so they do not understand.

9.88. But the Messenger (Muhammad), and those who believed with him, worked hard and fought with their wealth and themselves (their lives): (All) the good things are for them: And it is they who will succeed.

9.89. Allah has prepared for them Gardens under which Rivers flow, to live in there forever: That is the utmost happiness.

9.90.. And among the desert Arabs, there were men who made excuses and came to ask for exemption (from fighting) and those who lie to Allah and His Messenger (Muhammad and they only) sat at home. Soon, a painful penalty will get the disbelievers among them.

9.91. There is no blame on those who are weak or ill or (those) who find nothing to spend, if they are sincere (in duty) to Allah and His Messenger (Muhammad) no reason (for blame) can there be against such as (those) act right: And Allah is Often Forgiving, Most Merciful .

9.92. There is no (blame is there) on those who came to you to be given the mounts (for riding horses for war), and when you said, "I can find no mounts for you," they turned back, their eyes pouring with tears of sorrow that they had nothing with which the expenses could be met.

9.93. The reason (for blame) is against those who want exemption being that they are rich. They prefer to stay with those who remain behind: Allah has sealed their hearts; So they do not know.

9.94.. They (the hypocrites) will give their excuses to you when you return to them. (Then) you say: "Do not give excuses: We shall not believe you: Allah has already informed us of the true condition of things about you: Allah and His Messenger (Muhammad) will watch your actions: In the end, you will be brought back to Him Who knows what is hidden and what is open: Then He will show you the truth of all you did."

9.95. When you return to them (the hypocrites), they will swear to you by Allah, that you may leave them alone. So leave them alone: Surely, they are intensely disliked (by Him), and their living-place is Hell- A suitable repayment for the (evil) they did.

9.96. They (the hypocrites) will swear to you, that you may be pleased with them; But (even) if you are pleased with them, certainly Allah is not pleased with those who (rebel and) disobey.

9.97.. The Arabs of the desert are the worst in the lack of belief and in hypocrisy, and most likely to be unaware of the command which Allah has sent down to His Messenger (Muhammad): And Allah is All Knowing , All Wise.

9.98. And some of the desert Arabs consider their payments (of charity) as a fine, and wait for disasters for you: Upon them be the disaster of Evil: And Allah is He Who hears and knows (all things).

9.99. But some of the desert Arabs (do) believe in Allah and the Last Day, and look on their payments as gifts that bring them nearer to Allah and get the prayers of the Messenger (Muhammad). Yes, truly they will bring them nearer (to Allah): Allah will bring them in His Mercy: Surely, Allah is Often Forgiving, Most Merciful .

9.100.. The foremost leaders (of Islam)- The first of those who left (their homes) and of those who gave them help, and (also) those who followed them in good deeds- Allah is very pleased with them, as are they (are also pleased) with Him: He has prepared for them (the Paradise) Gardens under which rivers flow, to live in there forever: That is the utmost happiness.

9.101.. And among some of the desert Arabs around you are hypocrites, as well as (desert Arabs) from the Medinah folk: They are firm in (their) hypocrisy: You do not know them: (But) We know them: We shall punish them twice: And also they shall be sent to a painful Penalty.

9.102. And (some) others have agreed to their wrong doings: They have mixed a good deed with another that was evil. Perhaps Allah will turn to them (in forgiveness): Surely, Allah is Often Forgiving, Most Merciful .

9.103. From their goods (you) take charity, like this you might purify and cleanse them holy; And pray for them. Surely your prayers bring peace to them: And Allah is All Hearing , All Knowing .

9.104.. Do they not know that Allah does accept repentance from His (true) worshipers and receives their gifts of charity, and that surely, Allah is He, the forgiving Who accepts repentance, Most Merciful .

9.105. And say: "Work (righteousness): Soon will Allah look at your work, and His Prophet (Muhammad), and the believers: Soon you will be brought back to the All Knower of what is hidden and what is open: Then He will show you the truth of all that you did."

9.106. And there are (also) others, kept in suspense about the Command of Allah, whether He will punish them, or turn in forgiveness to them: And Allah is All Knowing , All Wise.

9.107.. And there are those who built a mosque by the way of mischief and without (true) faith- To divide the believers- And in preparation for one who fought against Allah and His Messenger (Muhammad) before. Truly, they will swear that their intention is nothing but good; But Allah declares that they are surely liars.

9.108. You do not ever stand forth in there. Indeed, there is a mosque whose foundation was laid from the first day on devotion (to Allah); It is more worthy of your standing forth (for prayer) in there. In it are men who love to be purified and cleansed; And Allah loves those who become pure and clean.

9.109. Then, who is best? He (the one) who lays the foundation of his building (home) on devotion to Allah and His Good Pleasure? or he who lays the foundation of his building on a weak sand-hill ready to break to pieces? And it (the mosque) does break to pieces with him, into the fire of Hell. And Allah does not guide people who do wrong.

9.110. The foundation of those who build like this is never free from doubt and shakiness in their hearts, until their hearts are cut to pieces. And Allah is All Knowing , All Wise.

9.111.. Verily, Allah bought from the believers their persons and their goods for (the price) that for them (as a return) shall be the Garden (of Paradise): They fight in His cause, so they kill and are killed: A promise binding upon Him in truth; It is in the Torah [of Musa (Moses)], the Gospel [of Isa (Jesus)], and the Quran (revealed to the Prophet Muhammad). And who is truer to his promise than Allah? Then feel happy in the bargain that you have ended: That is the greatest success.

9.112. Those who turn (to Allah) with repentance; Who worship Him, and (who) praise Him; Who wander in love for the cause of Allah; Who bow down, prostrate themselves in prayer; Who reinforce good and prevent evil; And who stay within the limits set by Allah- (These are the happiest people). So proclaim the glad news to the believers.

9.113.. It is not (proper), for the Prophet and those who believe, that they should pray for forgiveness for polytheists (pagans), even though they are of kin, after it is clear to them that they are dwellers of the Fire (having died as disbelievers).

9.114. And Ibrahim (Abraham) prayed for his fathers' forgiveness only because of a promise he (Ibrahim) had made to him (his father). But when it became clear to him (Ibrahim) that he (his father) was an enemy of Allah, he (Ibrahim) broke ties from him (his father): Surely, Ibrahim (Abraham) was most kind, forgiving.

9.115. And Allah will not lead astray a people after He has guided them, so that He may make clear to them what to fear (and to avoid)- Surely, Allah is All Knowing of all things.

9.116.. Indeed, to Allah belongs the kingdom of the heavens and the earth. He gives life and He causes death. Except for Him you have no protector nor helper.

9.117. Allah turned with forgiveness to the Prophet, the Mahajirs (leaving Makkah with the Prophet), and the Ansar (hosting the Prophet in Medinah)- Who followed him in a time of difficulty (to Tabuk), afterwards the hearts of some of them nearly turned away (from duty); But He turned to them (also with forgiveness): Certainly, He is to them Most Kind, Most Merciful.

9.118. And (Allah also turned with forgiveness to) the three (Ka'b bin Malik, Hilal bin Umayyah and Murarah bin Ar-Rabi; All from the Ansar people) who stayed behind (from the *Tabuk* expedition); (They felt guilty) so much that the earth seemed small to them, in spite of all its space, and their (very) souls seemed narrow to them- And they felt that there was no running from Allah (and no home or shelter) except to Himself. Then He forgave them, that they might repent: Verily, Allah is He Who accepts repentance, Most Merciful .

9.119.. O you who believe! Fear Allah and be with those who are true; (In their words and their deeds).

9.120. It was not befitting for the people of Medinah and the Bedouin Arabs from around (Medinah) to refuse to follow Allah's Messenger (Muhammad), nor to prefer their own lives to his life: Because nothing could they suffer or do, except that it would be (added) to their credit as an act of righteousness- Whether they felt thirst, or (felt) tired, or hunger, in Allah's Cause, or taken to the road to cause anger to the disbelievers, or taken any (tiny) injury from an enemy: Surely, Allah does not let the reward to be lost by those who do good-

9.121. Nor do they spend anything (for Allah's Cause) small or large (in contribution), nor cut across a valley (in courage) that the action is written to their credit; So that Allah may repay for the best (reward) of their actions that they used to do.

9.122.. And it is improper for (all) the believers to go away together (for Jihad). A (small) section from every expedition should remain behind, so they could devote themselves to studies in religion, and warn the people when they returned to them- That, thus they may guard themselves (against evil).

9.123.. O you who believe! Fight such of the disbelievers who are close to you, and let them find strength in you: And know that Allah is with those who fear Him.

9.124. And whenever a Sura comes down, some of them say: "Which of you had his faith increased by it?" Yes, those who believe- Their faith is increased, and they become happy.

9.125. But those in whose hearts is a sickness- It will (only) add doubt to their doubt, and they will die in a state of unbelief.

9.126. Do they not see that they are tried every year once or twice? Yet they do not turn in repentance, and they do not pay attention (to what they do).

9.127. And whenever a Sura (or Chapter in the Quran) comes down, they (the hypocrites) see each other, (saying), "Does anyone see you?" (And) then they turn away: Allah has turned their hearts (away from Light) because they are a people who do not understand.

9.128.. Now a messenger (the Prophet) has come to you from yourselves: It grieves him that you should suffer or be injured: He is extremely thoughtful (eager and caring) for you: For the believers, he is kind, merciful and full of pity.

9.129. But (yet) if they turn away, say: "Allah is enough for me: There is no god but He: I put my trust in Him- And He is the Lord of the Mighty (and Supreme) Throne!"

****

Sura 10. Yunus,

(Jonah): (Makkah, 109 Verses)

In the Name of Allah, the Most Gracious, the Most Merciful.

10.1.. Alif Lám Ra: These are the *Ayât*, (Verses) from the Book of Wisdom (the Quran).

10.2. Is it a matter of wonder for men that We have sent Our revelation to a man (who is) from themselves? (Declaring) that he should warn Mankind (of the danger), and give the good news to the believers that they have before their Lord the highest Rank of Truth. (But) the disbelievers say: "This (man, the Prophet) is clearly a magician!"

10.3. Surely, your Lord is Allah, Who created the heavens and the earth in six Days- And then rose over the Throne (of power), regulating and governing all things. No intercessor (or pleader can request from Him) except after His permission (is given to him). This is Allah your Lord; Therefore Him, you worship: Will you not remember (to take the guidance)?

10.4. To Him will be your return- All of you. The Promise of Allah is true and sure. It is He Who begins the process of creation, and repeats it, that He may reward with justice those who believe and work righteousness; But those who reject (and disbelieved) him will have streams of boiling liquids (to drink), and a painful penalty because they rejected Him.

10.5. It is He Who made the sun to be a shining glory and the moon to be a light (of beauty), and set out the phases for it; So that you may know the number of years and count (the time). Allah did not create this except in truth and righteousness. (Like this) He explains His Signs in detail, for people(s) who have knowledge.

10.6. Surely, in the changing of the night and day, and in all that Allah has created, in the heavens and the earth, (there) are Signs for those who fear Him.

10.7. Verily, those who do not keep their hope on their meeting with Us, but are happy and content with the life of the world (and present), and those who do not pay attention to Our Signs-

10.8. (For those), their home is the Fire, because of the (evil) they have earned.

10.9. Verily, those who believe, and work righteousness- Their Lord will guide them through their Faith: Beneath them will flow rivers in Gardens (the Paradise) of delight.

10.10. In there, their cry will be: "Glory to You, O Allah!" And "Peace" will be their greeting in there! And the close (echo) of their voice will be: "Praise be to Allah, the Cherisher and Sustainer of the Worlds,!"

10.11. And if Allah were to bring forward for men the bad (that they have earned) as they would happily hasten on the good- Then their period of rest will be settled at once. But We leave those who do not keep their hope on their meeting with Us, in their sins, wandering about being lost.

10.12. And when trouble touches a man, he cries to Us (in many ways)- Lying down on his side, or sitting, or standing. But when We have solved his trouble, he goes on his way as if he never cried to Us for the trouble that had touched him! Thus the actions of who exceed their limits look all right in their (own) eyes!

10.13.. And indeed, generations before you We have destroyed when they did wrong: Their messengers came to them with Clear Signs, but they would not believe! Like this We repay the sinners (and criminals)!

10.14. Then after them, We made you the successors generations after generations to take over the land, to see how you will behave!

10.15. And when Our Clear Signs (*Ayât*) are rehearsed on them, those who do not keep their hope on their meeting with Us, say: "Bring to us a Quran other than this, or change this," say: "It is not for me, to change it by myself: I follow nothing except what is made known to me: If I was to disobey my Lord, I should fear the penalty of a Great Day."

10.16. Say: "If Allah had so willed, I should not have delivered it to you, nor would He have made it known to you. Surely, a whole life-time before now, I have been with you: Then will you not understand?

10.17.. Who do more wrong than those who make up a lie against Allah, or deny His Signs? But those who sin will never prosper.

10.18. Besides Allah, they worship things that do not hurt them, nor help them, and they say: "These are our intercessors (helpers) with Allah." Say: "Do you really tell Allah something that He does not know, in the heavens or on earth? Glory to Him! And High is He above the partners they ascribe (to Him)!"

10.19. Mankind was only one nation, but differed later. If it was not because of a Word from your Lord that came before their differences would have been settled between them.

10.20. And they say: "Why is a Sign not sent down to them from their Lord?" Say: "The Unseen is only for Allah (to know). Then you wait: I will also wait with you."

10.21.. And then We make Mankind taste of some mercy after pain (and sorrow) has touched them, they start to plot against Our Signs! Say: "Allah! Is swifter to plan." Surely, Our messengers write down all the plots that you make!

10.22. It is He, Who enables you to travel by land and sea; So that when you get into ships- They (the ships) sail with them by the right wind, and they become happy with it; Then comes a stormy wind and the waves come to them from every side, and they think they are being overcome: Then they cry to Allah, truly offering (their) duty to Him, saying, "If You save us from this, we shall truly show our thanks!"

10.23. But when He saves them, behold! They exceed all limits proudly on earth against the right! O Mankind! Your insolence is against your own souls, an enjoyment of the life of the present! To Us is your return, in the end; And We shall show you the truth of all that you did.

10.24.. Verily, the life of the present is like the rain which We send down from the skies: With its occurrence come the crops of the earth- Which provide food for men and animals: (They grow) till the earth wears its golden ornament and is strung out (in beauty): The people to whom it belongs think they have all the control over it (the earth): (However) by night or by day, Our Command reaches it and We make it like a harvest (crop) cleanly cut, as if it had not flourished the day before! Like this We explain in detail Our Signs for those who meditate.

10.25. But Allah does call (you) to the Home of Peace: He does guide whom He pleases to the Straight Path.

10.26. To those who do right is a good (reward)- Yes, more (than that), no darkness, no dust, nor shame shall be over their faces! They are the companions of the Garden; In there they will live (for ever)!

10.27. But those who have earned evil deeds will have a repayment of like evil: And (humiliating) shame and dishonor will cover their (faces): None will they have to save from (the anger of) Allah: Their faces will be covered, so to say, with pieces of the deep darkness of Night: They are the companions of the Fire: In there they will live forever!

10.28. And one Day, We shall gather them all together- Then We shall say to those who joined gods (with Us): "(Go) to your place! You and those you joined as 'partners'." Then We shall separate them, and their 'partners' shall say: "It was not us that you used to worship!

10.29. "Allah is enough as a witness between us and you: Truly we did not know anything of your worship of us!"

10.30. In there, every soul will know (the fruits of) the deeds it sent before: They will be brought back to Allah their rightful Lord, and their lies (the 'partners' that they) invented will leave them without (help or) support.

10.31.. Say: "Who is it that provides you (for life) from the sky and from the earth? Or who is it that has power over hearing and sight? And who is it that brings out the living from the dead, and the dead from the living and who is it that rules and controls all affairs?" They will soon say, "Allah!" Say: "Then will you not show piety (to Him)?"

10.32. Such is Allah, your true Cherisher and Sustainer: Apart from Truth, what (remains) but wrong? Then why are you turned away?

10.33. It is (indeed) the Word of the Lord (always) proved true against those who rebel: Surely they will not believe.

10.34. Say: "Of your 'partners' can anyone originate creation and repeat it?" Say: "It is Allah Who begins creation and repeats it: Then why are you deceived away (from the truth)?"

10.35. Say: "From your 'partners', is there any that can give any guidance towards Truth?" Say: "It is Allah Who gives guidance towards Truth. Then, is He Who gives guidance to truth more worthy to be followed, or he who does not find guidance (for himself) unless he is guided? What then is the matter with you? How do you judge?"

10.36. And most of them follow nothing but (their) wishes: Truly, wishes can be of no use against Truth. Surely, Allah is well aware of all that they do.

10.37. And this Quran is not like anything that can be produced by (anyone) other than Allah; But (for sure), it confirms the (revelations) that went before it, and a more complete explanation of the Book- In which there is no doubt- From the Lord of the Worlds.

10.38. Or do they (the disbelievers) say, "He made it up?" Say: "Bring then a Sura of its like, and call (for your help) anyone you can, besides Allah, if it is that you speak the truth!"

10.39. No! They say it is false that whose knowledge they cannot understand, even before its proof has reached them: Like this did those before them accuse as false: But see what was the end of those who did wrong!

10.40. And of them there are some who believe in it, and (there are) some who do not (believe): And your Lord knows best those who are there to make mischief.

10.41. If they accuse you with lies, say (to them): "My work is for me, and yours is for you! You are free from responsibility about what I do, and I (am free from responsibility) about what you do!"

10.42. And among them are some who (show as if they) listen to you: But can you make the deaf to hear- Even though they do not understand?

10.43. And among them are some who look at you: But can you guide the blind- Even though they will not see?

10.44. Surely, Allah will not deal unjustly with (any) man in the least bit: It is man who does wrong to his own soul.

10.45. And on the Day, when He will gather them together: (It will be) as if they had not stayed except by an hour of a day: They will recognize each other: Surely, those will be lost who denied the meeting with Allah and refused to receive Guidance.

10.46. Whether We show you (in this life) some part of what We promise them (that is the punishment)- Or We take (back your) soul- (to Our Mercy before that) in any case, their return is to Us: In the end, Allah is witness to all that they used to do.

10.47.. And for every nation a messenger was sent when their messenger has come (and told them), the matter will be decided between them justly, and they will not be wronged.

10.48. And they say: "When will this promise come true- If you (really) tell the truth?"

10.49. Say: "I have no power over any harm or gain to myself except as Allah wills. A term is fixed for every people: When their term is come, they can not postpone it by an hour, nor can they advance (it by an hour)."

10.50. Say: "Do you see- If the punishment from Him should come to you by night or by day- Which part of it (punishment) would the sinners want to hasten?

10.51. "At last, would you then believe in it, when it actually comes true?" (It will then be said:) "Well now? And you wanted to hasten it on!"

10.52. In the end, (it) will be said to them, the wrongdoers: "You taste the lasting punishment! You get only the repayment of what you earned!"

10.53. And they would like to be told by you: "Is that true?" Say: "Yes! By my Lord! It is the very truth! And you cannot escape from it!"

10.54. And every soul that has sinned, if it had all (the treasure) that is on earth; It would gladly give it (the treasure) in ransom: (But it will not be accepted, such souls), they would declare (their) repentance when they see the Penalty: But the judgment between them will be just, and no wrong will be done to them.

10.55. Is it not that to Allah belongs whatever that is in the heavens and on the earth? Is it not that Allah's promise is definitely true? But most of them do not understand.

10.56. It is He Who gives life and Who causes death, and to Him, all of you shall be brought back.

10.57.. O Mankind! There has come good advice (and guidance) to you from your Lord and a cure for (what is) in your breasts (hearts)- And for those who believe, a Guidance and a Mercy.

10.58. Say: "In the Bounty of Allah and in His Mercy- In that let them find joy (and happiness):" That is better than (the wealth) they (greedily) save.

10.59. Say: "Do you see what provision Allah has sent down to you for your living? And you make (some) unlawful (from the provision) and (you make some things) lawful." Say: "Has Allah really permitted you, or do you make up (things) to attribute to Allah?"

10.60. And what do those who make up lies against Allah, think of the Day of Judgment? Surely, Allah is full of Bounty to mankind, but most of them are ungrateful.

10.61.. Whatever business you may be in- Whatever part of the Quran you may be saying- And whatever act you may be doing- Still, We are witnesses to them (all); When you are deep in thought about them. And there is nothing (as little as) the weight of an atom that is hidden from your Lord on the earth or in the heaven. And not the least, and not the greatest of these things happen except what are recorded in a clear Record.

10.62. Look! Surely upon the friends and allies of Allah, no fear shall befall upon them; Nor they shall grieve;

10.63. (They are) those who believe and guard against evil: - And fear Allah

10.64. For them is happy news, in the present life and in the Hereafter: There can be no change in the Words of Allah. This is truly the supreme (and greatest) happiness.

10.65. Do not let their (disbelievers) talk make you sad: Because all the power and honor belongs to Allah: He is All Hearing , All Knowing .

10.66. Look! Surely to Allah belong all creatures in the heavens and on the earth. And those (disbelievers) who worship others beside Allah, do not indeed, follow the 'partners'; They follow nothing but (false) thoughts, and they (say) nothing but lies.

10.67. It is He Who has made the night for you so that you may rest in it, and the day to make things to be seen (by you). Surely in this are (His) Signs for those who listen (to His Message).

10.68. They say, "Allah has fathered a son!"- Glory be to Him! He (Allah) is Self-Sufficient! His are all things in the heavens and on earth! No reason do you have for this (lie about Allah)! Do you say about Allah what you do not know?

10.69. Say: "Verily, Those who make up a lie against Allah will never succeed."

10.70. (A little) enjoyment in this world! And then, their return will be to Us. Then We shall make them taste the harshest penalty for their lies (and falsehood about Allah).

10.71.. And recite to them the story of Nuh (Noah). When he said to his people: "O my people! If it is difficult for your (minds) that I should stay (with you) and tell (you) the Signs of Allah- Still I put my trust in Allah, then you get an agreement about your plan and among your 'partners', so that your plan for you is not dark and dubious. Then pass your judgment about me, and give me no (special) consideration or relief.

10.72. "But if you can not do this, (then remember): I have asked no reward from you: My reward is to come only from Allah, and I have been ordered to be from those (people) who bow (down) to Allah's Will (in Islam)."

10.73. They rejected him, but We saved him, and those with him in the Ark, and We made them take over (the earth), generation replacing one after another while We overpowered in the Flood those who rejected Our Signs (*Ayât*). Then, see what was the end of those who were warned. (But did not pay attention)!

10.74.. Then after him, We sent messengers to their people: They (messengers) brought them clear proofs (of Allah), but they would not believe what they had already rejected before. Like this, We do close the hearts of those who transgress their limits.

10.75. Then after them We sent Musa (Moses) and Haroon (Aaron) to Firon (Pharaoh) and his chiefs with Our Signs (*Ayât*), but they were proud: They were people in sin (and crime).

10.76. So when the Truth did come to them from Us, they said: "This is really clear magic!"

10.77. Musa (Moses) said: "Do you say (this) about Truth when it has (actually) come to you? Is this (like) magic? But magicians will not prosper."

10.78. They said: "Have you come to us to turn us away from the way (that) we found our fathers following- So that you two, (Musa) and your brother (Haroon) may have fame in the land? But we shall not believe in you!"

10.79. And said Firon (Pharaoh): "Bring me every magician who is very good (in magic)."

10.80. And when the magicians came, Musa (Moses) said to them: "You throw whatever you (want) to throw!"

10.81. When they finished their throw, Musa (Moses) said: "What you have brought is magic: Surely, Allah will make it have no effect: Verily, Allah does not grant success to the work of those who do evil and mischief."

10.82. And by His Words, Allah proves and establishes His Truth, however much the sinners may dislike it!

10.83.. But no one believed in Musa (Moses) except some offspring of his people, because of the fear of men, Firon (Pharaoh) and his chiefs, in case they should punish them; And Firon (Pharaoh) was really arrogant and cruel on the earth and one who exceeded all limits.

10.84. Musa (Moses) said: "O my People! If you (really) believe in Allah, then put your trust in Him (and) you bow (to His Will) if you are Muslims."

10.85. They said: "We do put our trust in Allah. Our Lord! Do not make us a trial for those who act in cruelty and who are the wrongdoers;

10.86. "And with Your Mercy, save us from those who reject (You)."

10.87.. And We inspired Musa (Moses) and his brother with this message: "Make homes for your people in Egypt, make your homes into places of worship, and practice regular prayers: And give the happy news to those who believe!"

10.88. Musa (Moses) prayed: "Our Lord! You have truly granted to Firon (Pharaoh) and his Chiefs fame and wealth in the life of the present, and so our Lord, they mislead (others) from Your Path. Our Lord! Destroy the power of their wealth, and send hardness (and suffering) to their hearts, so much so they will not believe till they have seen the great penalty."

10.89. Allah said: "Your prayer is accepted (O Musa and Haroon)! So you stand straight, and do not follow the path of those who do not know."

10.90.. And We took the Children of Israel across the sea: Firon (Pharaoh) and his armies followed them with pride and anger. At the end, when overpowered with flood, he said: "I believe that there is no god except He in Whom the Children of Israel believe: I am of those who bow (to Allah in Islam)."

10.91. (It was said to him:) Oh now! But just a little while before, you were in (angry) revolt! And you did mischief (and violence)!

10.92. This day We shall save you in (your dead) body, so that you may be a sign to those who come after you! But surely, many from the mankind are careless of Our Signs!

10.93.. We made home for the Children of Israel in a beautiful place to live, and gave to them sustenance of the best (kind): It was after wisdom had been given to them, that they divided into (various) groups. Surely, Allah will judge among them about their groups, on the Day of Judgment.

10.94. If you were in doubt about what We have revealed to you, then ask those who have been reading the Book from before you: Verily, the Truth has really come to you from your Lord: So do not be in any way of those in doubt.

10.95. And do not be of those who reject the Signs (*Ayât*) of Allah, or you shall be of those who will perish.

10.96.. Truly, those against whom the Word of the Lord has been proved, (also) would not believe-

10.97. Even if every Sign was brought to them- Until they (themselves) see the great penalty.

10.98. Was there not a single township of people (among those We warned), which believed- So that its faith should have helped it- Except the people of Yunus (Jonah)? When they believed, We removed from them the penalty of dishonor in the present life, and let them to enjoy (their lives) for a while.

10.99.. If it had been your Lords Will all of them would have believed- All who are on earth! (But) will you then compel mankind, against their will, to believe?

10.100. No soul can believe, except by the Will of Allah, and He will place (basic) doubt on those who will not understand.

10.101. Say: "Behold! All that is in the heavens and on the earth;" But neither Sign nor warners can help those who do not believe.

10.102. Then do they expect (anything) different from (what happened in) the days of men who passed away before them? Say: "Then you wait: Because I, also, will wait with you among those who wait."

10.103. In the end We save Our messengers and those who believe: Thus it is right on Our part that We should save those who believe!

10.104.. Say (O Muhammad): "O you men! If you are in doubt about my religion, (look!) I do not worship what you worship, other than Allah! But I worship Allah Who will take back your souls: I am ordered to be among the believers,

10.105. "And further (that): 'Set your face to religion with true (and complete) devotion, and never in any way be of the idolaters (disbelievers);

10.106. " 'And do not pray to any other than Allah- Such (others) will neither help you nor hurt you: If you do, look! You shall truly be from those who do wrong.' "

10.107. And if Allah touches you with harm, there is no one who can remove it except He: And if He plans some benefit for you, then there is no one who can keep back His mercy: He makes it reach whoever of His servants that He pleases. And He is the Often Forgiving, the Most Merciful .

10.108. Say: "O you men! Now the Truth has reached you from your Lord! Those who receive guidance, will do so for the good of their own souls; Those who wander, do so to their own loss: And I am not (sent) over you to fix your affairs (for you)."

10.109. And, you (O Muhammad!) follow the revelation sent to you, and be patient and constant, till Allah will decide: And He is the Best of (all) the judges.

****

Sura 11. Hud,
(The prophet Hud): (Makkah, 123 Verses)
In the Name of Allah, the Most Gracious, the Most Merciful.

11.1. **Alif Lám Ra:** (This is) a Book, with true Verses (and firm meaning), explained in more detail, from One Who is All Wise, Well-Acquainted: (With all things)

11.2. (It teaches) you should worship none but Allah. (Say:) "Surely, I am (sent) to you from Him to warn and to bring good news:

11.3. "(And it also teaches you like this), 'You ask for the forgiveness of your Lord, and come back to Him in repentance; So that He may let you have the good (and true) enjoyment, for a time given (fixed for you), and grant His plentiful Grace on all who deserve merit! But if you turn away, then I fear for you the penalty of a great Day:

11.4. " ' To Allah is your return, and He is able to do all things (and everything)'. "

11.5. Without doubt! They (the disbelievers) close their hearts that they may stay hiding from Him! Surely! Even when they cover themselves with their clothes, He knows what they hide, and what they reveal: Verily, He knows well the (deepest secrets) of the hearts.

11.6.. And there is no moving creature on earth whose sustenance does not depend on Allah: And He knows the time and place of its firm home and its temporary stay: All is (recorded) in a clear Book.

11.7. And it is He Who created the heavens and the earth in six Days- And His Throne was over the Waters, that He might try you, which of you is the best in deeds (and conduct). But if you were to say to them, "You shall truly be raised up after death;" The disbeliever will surely say; "This is nothing but clear (and open) magic!"

11.8. If We postpone the penalty for them for a fixed time, they are sure to say, "What keeps it back?" Verily! On the day when it reaches them, nothing will turn it away from them, and they will completely fall into what they used to joke about!

11.9.. And if We give man a taste of mercy from Us, and then take it away from him, surely! He is in sadness and turns ungrateful (to Us).

11.10. But if We give him a taste of (Our) kindness after sorrow (and hardship) has come upon him, he is sure to say, "All evil has gone away from me:" Surely! He falls into (victorious) joy and pride.

11.11. Except those who show patience and constancy do not act thus, and (they) work righteousness; (For) those, theirs will be forgiveness and a great reward (Paradise).

11.12.. If by chance you may (feel the desire) to give up a part of what is revealed to you, and your heart feels heavy (sad) for it, because they say, "Why is not a treasure sent down to him, or why does not an angel come down with him?" But you are only a Warner (to them)! Allah is Guardian (Who arranges) all things!

11.13. Or they say, "He has forged it (made it up himself)." Say: "Then you bring ten Suras made up, similar to it, and call anyone you can (to help), other than Allah! If you speak the truth!

11.14. "If then they (your false gods) do not answer your (call for help), you will know that this (Book of) Revelation is sent down with (full) knowledge of Allah, and that there is no god except He! Even then, will you submit (to Islam)?"

11.15.. Those who want the life of the world and its (showy) brightness- We shall pay them (for) their deeds in there- And they will have no reduction (in their penalty).

11.16. They are those for whom there is nothing in the Hereafter but the Fire: Useless are the deeds they did there in (the world), and of no effect are the acts that they did!

11.17. Can they be (like) those (Muslims) who accept a Clear (Message, the Quran) from their Lord, and whom a witness (Gabriel) from (Allah) Him(self) recites (and follows) it, like the Book of Musa (Moses) before it- A Guide and a Mercy? They believe in it; But those of the Sects that reject it- The Fire will be their promised meeting-place. So do not be in doubt about it: Verily, it is the Truth from your Lord: But many among men do not believe!

11.18.. And who does more wrong than he who invents (makes up) a lie against Allah? They will be sent back to the Presence of their Lord, and the witnesses will say, "These are the ones who lied against their Lord! No doubt! The Curse of Allah is on those who do wrong!

11.19. "Those who would (try to) block (others) from the path of Allah and search for something crooked in it: These were they who denied the Hereafter!"

11.20. In no way, will they escape (His design) on earth, and they have no protectors besides Allah! Their penalty will be doubled! They lost the power to hear, and they did not see (the truth)!

11.21. They are the ones who have lost their own souls: And the (things) they invented have left them in the (most) difficult position!

11.22. No doubt, they are the greatest losers in the Hereafter!

11.23. Surely, those who believe and act the good deeds, and humble themselves before their Lord- They will be companions of the Garden, to live in there forever!

11.24. The likeness two types (of men) may be compared to the blind and deaf, and those who can see and hear well. Are they equal when compared? Will you not then take the warning?

11.25.. And indeed, We sent Nuh (Noah) to his people (with a message, and he said): "I have come to you with a clear Warning:

11.26. "So that you worship none except Allah: Surely, I do fear for you the penalty of a painful Day."

11.27.. But the chiefs of the disbelievers from his people said: "We see (in) you only a man like ourselves: Nor do we see that any follow you except the lowest from us, (those who are) immature in judgment: Nor do we see in (all of) you any merit above us: In fact, we think you are all liars!"

11.28. He (Nuh, Noah) said: "O my people! Tell me, if (it is that), I have a Clear Sign from my Lord, and that He has sent (His) Mercy to me from His own Presence, and that (the Mercy) is hidden from your sight? Shall we compel you to accept it when you do not like it?

11.29. "And O my people! I do not ask you for wealth in return: My reward is from no one except Allah: But I will not drive (send) away those who believe: Surely, they are going to meet their Lord, and I see that you are the ignorant ones!

11.30. "And O my people! Who would help me against Allah if I drove (sent) them away? Then will you not take the warning?

11.31. "And, I do not tell you that the treasures of Allah are with me, nor do I know what is hidden, nor do I claim to be an angel, nor do I say, that of those whom you look down in contempt that Allah will not grant them what is good: Allah knows best what is in their souls: I should, if I did (drive them away), truly be a wrong-doer."

11.32. They said: O Nuh (Noah)! "You have disputed with us, and you have prolonged the dispute with us: Now bring upon us what you threaten us with, if you speak the truth!"

11.33. He said: "Truly, Allah will bring it (the punishment) on you if He wills- And then, you will not be able to escape (or stop it)!

11.34. "And, my advice will be of no benefit for you, even though I would like much to give you good advice, if it be Allah Who wills to leave you astray: He is your Lord! And to Him will you return!"

11.35.. Or do they (the pagans) say, "He has forged it?" Say (then): "If I had forged it, my sin is upon me! But I am free of the sins of which you are guilty!"

11.36.. And it was revealed to Nuh (Noah): "None of your people will believe except those who have already believed! So do not be sad because of what they are used to do.

11.37. "And build an Ark under Our eyes and Our Inspiration, and address Me, not (any more) on behalf of those who are in sin: For they are about to be drowned (in the Flood)."

11.38. Right away he (Nuh) started building the Ark: Every time that the Chiefs of his people passed by him, they mocked him. He said: "If you ridicule us now, we can (also) look down on you with similar ridicule!

11.39. "And soon you will know who it is on whom a penalty will fall that will cover him with shame- On whom will be open a Penalty lasting:"

11.40.. At the end, look! There came Our Command, and the fountains (of water from the earth) gushed out! We said: "Climb in there, two of each kind, male and female, and your family- Except those against whom the word has gone forth, and the believers." And only a few believed with him.

11.41. And he said: "Climb in to the Ark, in the Name of Allah will be its moving (path) or (its place of) rest! Surely, my Lord is Often Forgiving, Most Merciful !"

11.42. So the Ark floated with them on the waves (high) as the mountains, and Nuh (Noah) called out to his son, who had separated himself (from the rest of the believers): "O my son! Climb in with us, and do not be with the disbelievers!"

11.43. The son replied: "I will take myself to some Mountain: It will save me from the water." Nuh (Noah) said: "This day nothing can save from the Order of Allah, except those on whom He has Mercy!" - And the waves came between them, so (the son) was among those drowned in the Flood.

11.44.. Then the Word (from Allah) was said: "O earth! Swallow up your water, and O sky! Hold back (your rain)! And the water lowered, and the matter was ended." The Ark rested on Mount Judi, and the Word (from Allah) was said: "Away with those who are wrongdoers!"

11.45.. And Nuh (Noah) called to his Lord, and said: "O my Lord! Surely my son is of my family! And Your promise is true, and You are the Most Just (and Truest) of judges!"

11.46. He (Allah) said: "O Nuh (Noah)! He (your son) is not of your family: Surely, his conduct is not righteous. So do not ask from Me, that about which you have no knowledge! I give you advice, in case you act like one who does not know!"

11.47. Nuh (Noah) said: "O my Lord! I seek refuge with You, in case I ask You for that about which I have no knowledge. And until You forgive me and have Mercy on me, I will truly be lost!"

11.48. The Word (from Allah) came: "O Nuh (Noah)! Come down (from the Ark) with Peace from Us, and blessing on you and on some of the peoples (to come) from those with you: But (there will be other) peoples to whom We shall grant their (worldly) pleasures, but in the end, a painful Penalty will reach them from Us."

11.49.. Some of the news of the Unseen are like this, which We have made known to you: Neither you nor your people knew them till now. So remain firm (on right) and (work) patiently: Because the End is for those who are righteous.

11.50.. To the 'Ad (people, We sent) Hud, one of their own brothers. He said: "O my people! Worship Allah! You have no other god except Him. Certainly, you do nothing but invent lies!

11.51. "O my people! I ask no reward for it (for this Message). My reward is from Him, He Who created me: Then will you not understand?

11.52. "And O my people! Ask forgiveness from your Lord and turn to Him (in repentance): He will send you the (clouds in the) skies pouring plentiful rain and add strength to your (own) strength: So you do not turn back (from Him) as criminals!"

11.53. They (his people) said: "O Hud! No clear (proof) have you brought to us, and we are not the ones to give up our gods (based only) upon your word! And we shall not believe in you!

11.54. "We say nothing except that some of our gods may (possibly) have trapped you in stupidity." He said: "I call Allah to witness, and (also) you to witness, that I am free from the sin of joining (others) with Him.

11.55. "Other gods as 'partners'! So, all of you, plan (what you wish) against me, and give me no relief (or favors).

11.56. "I put my trust in Allah, my Lord and your Lord, there is not a moving creature, whom He does not (firmly) grasp by its hair in front (of the head). Surely, it is my Lord Who is on (and along) a the Straight Path (The Ultimate Path of Truth).

11.57. "So, if you (my people) turn away- Still I have (at least) given the Message (to you) with which I was sent to you. My Lord will make another People to come after you, and you will not, in the least harm Him. Surely, my Lord is the Protector over all things."

11.58.. And when Our Commandment came forth, We saved Hud and those who believed with him, by (special) grace from Us (Allah): And We saved them from a severe Penalty.

11.59. The 'Ad people were like this: They rejected the Signs of their Lord and Cherisher; Disobeyed His messengers; And followed the orders of every powerful, difficult (and harsh) outlaw (and ruler who acted beyond his limits).

11.60. And they were followed by a curse in this world- (through and till) the Day of Judgment. Surely! Because the 'Ad (people) rejected their Lord (and Cherisher)! So 'Ad, the people of Hud were removed (and banished from sight)!

11.61.. And to the Samood (Thamud people, We sent) Sálih, one of their brothers. He said: "O my people! Worship Allah: You have no other god but Him. It is He Who has created you from the earth and settled you in there: Ask then forgiveness from Him, and turn to Him (in repentance): Certainly, my Lord is Near, Responsive."

11.62. They said: "O Sálih! You have been among us, as a figure and focus of our hopes, so far do you (now) stop us from the worship of what our fathers worshipped? But we are really in suspicious doubt about that to which you invite us (to worship)."

11.63. He said: "O my people! Tell me- If I have a Clear (Sign) from my Lord and He has sent mercy to me from Him- Who then can help me against Allah if I were to disobey Him? Then what could you add to my (portion) except a bad curse?

11.64. "And O my people! This she-camel from Allah is a Symbol to you: Let her (freely) feed on Allah's earth, and cause no harm to her, or a swift penalty will seize you!"

11.65. But they slaughtered her (by cutting her tendons). So he said: "Enjoy yourselves for three days in your homes: (Then there will be your ruin): (Look!) There is a promise not to be false!"

11.66. So when Our Commandment came forth, We saved Sálih and those who believed with him, by (special) Grace from Us (Allah)- And from the shame (and dishonor) of that day. Verily, your Lord- He is All Strong (in every sense), and All Mighty .

11.67. And the (mighty) explosion (an awful cry) came over the wrong doers, and they lay in their homes dead, before the morning,

11.68. As if they had never lived and grown up happily there. Verily! Because the Samood (Thamud) rejected their Lord and Cherisher! The Samood (Thamud) were removed (and banished from sight)!

11.69.. And surely, there came Our messengers to Ibrahim (Abraham) with good news. They said, "*Salaam* (Peace)!" He answered, "Peace!" And he hastened to welcome and feast them with a roasted calf.

11.70. But when he saw their hands did not go to (the food), he felt a little distrust towards them, and became fearful of them. They said: "Do not fear:

We have been sent against the people of Lut (Lot)."

11.71. And his wife was standing there, and she laughed: But We gave her the good news of Isaac, and after him, of (a grandson) Yàqoub (Jacob).

11.72. She said: "Alas for me! Shall I bear a child seeing that I am an old woman, and my husband here is (also) an old man? Verily! That would indeed be a strange thing!"

11.73. They said: "Do you wonder at Allah's Command? The Grace of Allah and His blessings be on you, O you people of the house! For He is truly worthy of all Praise, full of all Glory!"

11.74.. When the fear had left (the mind of) Ibrahim (Abraham) and the good news had reached him, He began to plead with Us for the good of Luts' (Lots') people.

11.75. Surely, Ibrahim (Abraham) was truly forgiving, and used to pray in humility (to Allah, Ibrahim) was repentant.

11.76. "O Ibrahim (Abraham)! Do not ask for this. Indeed, the order of your Lord is out: For them (Luts' people), there will come a penalty that cannot be turned back!

11.77.. And when Our messengers came to Lut (Lot), he was saddened for them (his people) and felt himself helpless (to protect) them. He said: "This is a distressful day."

11.78. And his people came forward towards him, and for long they were used to practice of hateful and loathsome things (of alleged homosexuality). He said: "O my people! Here are my daughters: They are purer for you (if you marry)! Now fear Allah, and do not cover me with shame about my guests! Is there not one single right-minded man among you?"

11.79. They said: "Surely, you know well that we do not need your daughters: Indeed, you know very well what we want!"

11.80. He said: "Should that I had strength to over power you or that I could take myself to some powerful support."

11.81. They (the messengers) said: "O Lut (Lot)! Verily we are messengers from your Lord in no way can they reach you! Now travel with your family in a (remaining) part of the night and let not any of you look back: But your wife (will remain behind): The punishment for the people will (also) be upon her; Indeed, their appointed time is the morning: Is the morning not near?"

11.82. So when Our Commandment came forth, We turned (their cities) upside down, and sent down upon them rains of stones: hard as baked clay, spread, layer upon layer-

11.83. As if marked from your Lord, they (the stones and their cities) are not at all far apart: From those who do wrong!

11.84.. And to the Madyan people, (We sent) Shu'aib, their brother: He said: "O my people! Worship Allah: You have no other god but Him. And do not give short in measure or in weight: I see you in prosperity, and verily, I fear for you the penalty of a Day that will circle (you) all round.

11.85. "And O my people! Give full measure and weight, in (total) justice and do not keep away from the people the things that are due to them: Do not do evil making mischief in the land causing corruption.

11.86. "What is left for you by Allah is good for you, if you believe (in Him)! But I am not placed over you to keep watch!"

11.87. They said: "O Shu'aib! Does your prayer order you that we stop the worship our fathers practiced, or that we stop doing what we like with our property? Truly, you are the one who forgives (our) faults, and are right-minded!"

11.88. He said: "O my people! Tell me if I have a clear (proof) from my Lord, and He has given me good (and pure) livelihood from Himself, (shall I corrupt it with unjust money?), I do not wish to do what I forbid you to do. I only wish for (your) betterment to the best of my power (and ability); And my guidance can only come from Allah. In Him I trust, and to Him I look in repentance.

11.89. "And O my people! Let not my differing (with you) cause you, to suffer a fate similar to that of the people of Nuh (Noah), or of Hud, or of Sálih, and the people of Lut (Lot) are not far off from you!

11.90. "Then ask forgiveness from your Lord, and turn to Him in repentance: Verily, my Lord is Most Merciful , Lovingly Kind."

11.91. They said: "O Shu'aib! We do not understand much of what you say: In fact, some of us see that you are (indeed) weak, if it was not for your family, we would really have stoned you! Because with us, you have no great position!"

11.92. He said: "O my people! Then, does my family have more consideration with you than Allah? And you have thrown Him away behind your backs (with disregard). But surely my Lord encompasses all you do from all sides!

11.93. "And O my people! Do what you are able to do, (but) I will do (my part): And soon you will know on whom comes down the penalty of shame (and dishonor), and who is a liar! And you watch; Verily, I am also watching with you!"

11.94. When Our Order came forth, We saved Shu'aib and those who believed with him, by (special) mercy from Us: But the explosion (an awful cry) caught the wrongdoers, and they lay (dead) in their homes bent down,

11.95. As if they had never lived and grown happily there. So the Madyan were removed (from sight), just like the Samood (Thamud) were removed!

11.96.. And indeed, We sent Musa (Moses), with Our Clear (Signs) and open authority,

11.97. To Firon (Pharaoh) and his chiefs, but they followed the order of Firon (Pharaoh), and the order of Firon (Pharaoh) was not the right guide.

11.98. He (Pharaoh) will go ahead of his people on the Day of Judgment, and lead them into the Fire: And truly terrible is the place to which they are led!

11.99. And they are followed by a curse in this (life) and (also) on the Day of Judgment: Terrible is the gift to be given (to them).

11.100.. Those are some of the stories of the (peoples of) town that We tell you: Some of them are (still) standing (here) and some have been ripped down (by time).

11.101. We did not wrong them: But they wronged their own souls: The (unholy) objects, other than Allah, whom they called upon did not help them (even) a little when the Order of your Lord was issued: And they added little but suffering!

11.102. Such is the punishment of your Lord: When He punishes peoples in the midst of their wrong; Truly painful and severe is His punishment.

11.103. Indeed, in that is a definite lesson for those who fear the Punishment in the Hereafter: That is a Day for which mankind will be brought together: And that will be the Day when all will be present (for testimony).

11.104. And We delay it only for an (already) fixed term.

11.105.. On the Day when it arrives, no person shall speak except by His Permission: From those (brought up) some will be miserable and (some will be) blessed.

11.106. As for those who are miserable shall be in Fire: For them there will be (only) a lot of sighs and sobs in there:

11.107. They will live there for all the time that the heavens and the earth can bear, except as what your Lord wills: Verily, your Lord is (truly the) Accomplisher of what He plans.

11.108. And those who are blessed shall be in the Garden: They will live there for all the time that the heavens and the earth can bear, except as what your Lord wills: An (eternal) gift without an end.

11.109. Then do not be in doubt as to what these men worship. They worship only what their fathers worshipped before: And surely We shall pay them back their portion without the least (bit of) decrease in it.

11.110.. Indeed, We really gave the Book to Musa (Moses), but differences came about in it: And if it was not for a Word from your Lord that was out before, the matter would have been decided between them: And indeed, they are in suspicious doubt about it (the Quran).

11.111. And, surely, your Lord will pay back (in full) for their deeds: For He is Well-Acquainted with all that they do.

11.112. So hold firmly (to the Straight Path) as you are commanded- You and those who repent with you and turn (to Allah); And do not transgress away (from the Straight Path): Verily, He is All Seeing of all that you do.

11.113. And do not lean (or move) towards those who do wrong, or the Fire will catch (up to) you; And you have no protectors other than Allah, then you shall not be helped.

11.114. And perform prayers regularly at the two ends of the day and at the approaches of the night: Surely those things that are good (for you) remove those that are evil: Let that be the word to remember (the Lord) for those who remember:

11.115. And be steady (and consistent) in patience; Surely Allah will not let the reward of the righteous to be lost.

11.116.. Why were there not, from generations before you, persons with balanced wisdom (and good sense), who prohibited (men) from mischief in the earth- Except a few of them whom We saved (from harm)? But the wrongdoers chased the enjoyment of the good things of life that were given to them and continued in sin (as criminals).

11.117. And your Lord would not be the One to destroy towns for a single wrong-doing, while the members were likely to become better.

11.118. And if your Lord had so willed, He could have made (all) mankind one People, but (even then) they will not stop disagreeing,

11.119. Except those on whom your Lord has granted His Mercy: And for this did He create them: And the Word of your Lord (is that); "I will fill

Hell with jinns' and men all together," has been (already) fulfilled:

11.120.. All that We reveal to you (O Muhammad) from the stories of the messengers- With it We strengthen (and affirm) your heart: And in them comes to you the Truth, with a strong warning and a message to remember for those who believe.

11.121. And say to those who do not believe: "Act according to your ability: We (too) are acting (in our own way)";

11.122. "And you wait! We will also wait."

11.123. And to Allah belong the unseen (secrets) of the heavens and the earth, and to Him goes back every affair (for decision): So worship Him, and put your trust in Him: And your Lord is not unaware in the least of what you do.

****

Sura 12. Yusuf,

[The prophet Yusuf (Joseph)]: (Makkah, 111 Verses)

In the Name of Allah, the Most Gracious, the Most Merciful.

12.1.. Alif Lám Ra: These are the Signs (Verses) of the Book that is (pure and) clear.

12.2. Verily, We have sent it down as Arabic Quran, in order for you to (learn and) understand .

12.3. We relate to you the most beautiful of stories; From these (stories) We make it known to you this (part of) Quran: And before this, you were also from those who did not know it.

12.4. Remember, when Yusuf (Joseph) said to his father: "O my father! For sure, I saw (in my dream) eleven stars and the sun and the moon: I saw them prostrate themselves to me!"

12.5. (His father) said: "O my son! Do not tell your dream (vision) to your brothers in case, they make up a plot against you: Verily, Satan is an avowed enemy to man!

12.6. "This way your Lord will choose you and teach you the interpretations of stories (and events) and complete His blessing to you and to (all) the children of Yàqoub (Jacob)- Like He had completed it (His blessing) to your fathers Ibrahim (Abraham) and Isaac before! Verily your Lord is All Knowing , All Wise."

12.7.. Surely, in Yusuf (Joseph) and his brothers are Signs for those who ask (and search for Truth).

12.8.. When they (his older half-brothers) said: "Truly Yusuf, (Joseph) and his (full) brother are loved more by our father than we are: But we have a strong group! True our father is clearly swaying (in his mind)!

12.9. "You kill Yusuf (Joseph) or throw him (away) into some (unknown) land, so that your father's favor (love) will be given to you alone: After that, you become righteous!"

12.10. One of them (his half brothers said): "Do not kill Yusuf (Joseph) but if you must do something, throw him down to the bottom of a well: He will be taken by some group of travelers."

12.11.. They said: "O our father! Why don't you trust us with Yusuf (Joseph)- Seeing we are truly his sincere well wishers?

12.12. "Send him with us tomorrow to enjoy himself and play, and surely we shall take every care of him."

12.13. Yàqoub (Jacob) said: "Really it makes me sad that you should take him away: I am afraid that the wolf may eat him when you are not attending to him."

12.14. They said: "If the wolf were to eat him when we are (so large) a party, then truly we should be the losers!"

12.15.. So when they did take him away, and they all agreed to throw him down to the bottom of the well: And We put into his heart (the foretelling): "Surely, you will tell them (one day) the truth of this their affair while they do not know (you)."

12.16.. And they came crying to their father in the early part of the night.

12.17. They said: "O our father! We went racing with one another, and left Yusuf (Joseph) with our things; And the wolf ate (devoured) him... But you will never believe us even though we tell the truth."

12.18. And they brought his shirt stained with false blood. He said: "No, only (you) yourselves have made up a story (that may sound alright) for you. (As for me) patience is most suitable: And against (the lie) what you keep saying, it is Allah Whose help can be prayed for..."

12.19.. And there came a group of travelers: They sent their water-bearer (for water), and he let down his bucket (in the well)... He (the bearer) said: "Oh there! Good news! Here is a (handsome) boy!" So they kept him hidden like a treasure! But Allah knew well all that they did!

12.20. And the (travelers) sold him for a low price- For a few dirhams (that were) counted out: They were those who held him in such a low value!

12.21.. And he (the man) in Egypt who bought him, said to his wife: "Make his stay (respectful and) honorable: Maybe he will bring us a lot of good, or we shall make him an adopted-son." Like this We made a place for Yusuf (Joseph) in the land, so that We might teach him the interpretations (the true meaning) of the stories (and events). And Allah has full power and control on His affairs; But most of mankind do not know it.

12.22. And when he [Yusuf, (Joseph)] reached his full manhood, We gave him power and knowledge: Like this We reward those who do right.

12.23.. But she (the wife) in whose house he was, wanted to (wrongfully mislead and) seduce him from his (noble and true) self: She closed the doors, and said: "Come on (to me), O you (dear one)!" He said: "I seek Allah's help: (Allah forbid)! Truly he (your husband) is my lord! He made my stay (with you) comfortable! Truly, nothing good comes to those who do wrong!"

12.24. And she wanted to have him (very much), and he would have fallen to her (desire), but that he clearly saw the Presence of his Lord: Like this (We planned) that We turn away from him (all) evil and shameful acts: Surely, he was one of Our servants, sincere and purified.

12.25.. So they both outran each other to the door, and she tore his shirt from the back: They both found her lord (the husband) by the door. She said: "What is the (suitable) punishment for one who has made an evil plan against your wife, except prison or a severe punishment?"

12.26. He (Yusuf) said: "It was she who tried to seduce me- From my (true) self." And one of (the members of) her household saw and told what happened, (like this):- "If it is that his shirt is torn from the front, then what she says is true, and he is the liar!

12.27. "But if it is that his shirt is torn from the back, then is she the liar, and he is telling the truth!"

12.28. So when he (the husband) saw his (Yusuf's) shirt- That it was torn at the back- (Her husband) said: "Surely! It is a plot of you women! Truly, your plot is strong (and large)!

12.29. "O Yusuf (Joseph), forget this event! (O wife! Now you), ask forgiveness for your sin; Verily, you have been at fault!"

12.30.. And the (other) ladies from the city, said: "The wife of the (great lord) 'Aziz is trying to seduce her young man (the slave) from his (true and noble) self: Truly he must have aroused strong love in her: Surely, we see clearly that she is going astray."

12.31. So when she heard of their harmful talk, she invited them and invited them for a banquet (and held a gathering) for them: She gave each of them a knife (for the fruits): And she said (to Yusuf), "Come out before them." When they saw him, they praised him much (for his looks and beauty), and (in their amazement, they had) cut their hands: They said, "Allah is Perfect! This is not a mortal (man)! This is no one except a noble angel!"

12.32. She said: "Before you, there is the man about whom you blamed me! I wanted to seduce him from his (true) self but he refused (himself by being guiltless)! And now, if he does not act by my command, he will certainly be thrown into prison, and (he will) be from the lowliest!"

12.33. He said: "O my Lord (Allah)! The prison is more to my liking than to what they invite me: Unless You (Almighty Allah) turn away their plot from me, I may (in my youth) feel inclined towards them and be of those people who do not know (ignorant)."

12.34.. So his Lord listened to him (in his prayer), and turned away their plot from him: Surely, He is the Listener and Knower (of all things).

12.35.. Then it came to the minds of the men, after they had seen all the proof (of his innocence), (that they should) send him to the prison for a while.

12.36.. And there two (other) young men (also) came with him into the prison. One of them said: "I see me (in a dream) pressing (grapes for) wine." The other one said: "I see me (in a dream) carrying bread on my head, and birds are eating from it." (They both said): "Tell us the truth and meaning of it (all): Verily, we see that you are the one who does good (for everyone)."

12.37. He (Yusuf) said: "Before any food comes (in due course) to feed either of you, I will reveal to you the truth and meaning of this before it (actually) happens to you: That is part of the (things) that my Lord has taught me. (I assure you that,) I have given up the way of a people who do not believe in Allah and who deny the Hereafter.

12.38. "And I follow the religion of my fathers- Ibrahim (Abraham), Isháq (Isaac), and Yàqoub (Jacob); And we could never attribute any partners to Allah: Those (ways that come because) of the Grace of Allah to us and to mankind: Still most men are not grateful.

12.39. "O, the two companions of prison! Are many different lords (gods, who differ among themselves) better or Allah, the One Supreme and Irresistible?

12.40. "You do not worship besides Him, except (those false) names that you have named- You and your fathers- For which Allah has not sent down any authority: The Command is for none but Allah: He has commanded that you worship none but Him: That is the right religion, but most men do not understand.

12.41. "O the two companions of prison! As to one of you, he will pour out the wine for his lord (the king) to drink: As for the other, he will be hung (crucified) on the cross, and the birds will eat from off his head. (So) has been ordered regarding matter about which the two of you ask"...

12.42.. And of the two, to the one whom he considered ready to be saved, he (Yusuf) said: "Tell your lord (the king) about me." But Satan made him forget to talk about him (Yusuf) to his lord (the king): And (Yusuf) stayed in prison for a few years.

12.43.. And the king (of Egypt) said: "Verily, I saw (a dream in which) seven fat cows, whom seven lean ones eat up- And seven green ears of corn, and seven (others) dried up. O you chiefs! Explain to me my dream if you can tell the meanings of dreams."

12.44. They (the chiefs) said: "A confused mixture of false dreams: And we are not skilled in interpreting the meaning of dreams."

12.45.. Then one of the two (men from the prison) who was set free, and who now thought of him (Yusuf) after a long time, said: "I will tell you the truth of its meaning: So you send me."

12.46. (The man from the prison said:) "O Yusuf (Joseph)! O man of truth! Explain to us (the dream) of seven fat cows whom seven lean ones eat up, and of seven green ears of corn and others dry: That I may go back to the people, and that they may know (and understand the meaning of the dream)."

12.47. (Yusuf) said: "For seven consecutive years you shall carefully sow (and grow) as you are used to (doing): And the crops that you reap, you will leave them in the ear- Except a little, from which you will eat.

12.48. Then after that will come (a period of) seven terrible (and hard years), which will eat (away) what you will have saved before for them- (All) except a little which you will have saved (specially for seed).

12.49. "Then after that will come a year in which the people will have plenty of water, and in this (year) they will press (wine and oil)."

12.50.. And the king said: "You bring him (Yusuf) to me," but when the messenger came to him, (Yusuf) said: "You go back to your king and ask him, 'What is the state of mind of the ladies who cut their hands?', For my Lord (Allah) is Well-Aware of their plot.'"

12.51. (The king) said (to the ladies): "What was your affair when you wanted to seduce Yusuf (Joseph) from his (true) self?" The ladies said: "Allah save us! We know of no evil against him! The 'Aziz's wife said: "Now the truth is clear (to all): It was I who wanted to seduce him from his (true) self: He is surely from those who are (always) true (and noble).

12.52. "(I say) this, so that he may know that I have never been false to him in his absence, and that Allah will never help the plots set by the false ones. (see Note 1 at the end of the Sura.)

12.53. "And I will not forgive my own self (of the sin): True, the soul is likely to fall into evil, unless my Lord grants His Mercy: But surely my Lord is Often Forgiving, Most Merciful ."

12.54.. And the king said: "Bring him (Yusuf) to me; That I will take him only to serve around me personally." Therefore when he (the king) had spoken to him, he (the king) said: "Be sure that in our presence today you are, firmly placed with position (and honor) and truthfulness fully proved!"

12.55. (Yusuf) said: "Place me to (care for) the store-houses of the land: I will truly guard like one who knows (their importance)."

12.56.. This way We gave full authority to Yusuf (Joseph) in the land, to take possession in there as, when, or where he wanted. We give from Our Mercy to whom We please, and We make not the reward of those who do good to be lost.

12.57. And surely, the reward of the hereafter is the best for those who believe, and are constant in (their) righteousness.

12.58.. And Yusuf (Joseph)'s brothers came: They entered his presence, and he knew them but they did not know him.

12.59. And when he had given them the supplies for them, he said: "Bring to me a brother that you have from the same father as yourselves, (but a different mother): Do you not see that I give out full measure and that I give the best hospitality (for you)?

12.60. "But if you do not bring him to me, you will have no measure (of supplies) from me, and you cannot (even) come near me."

12.61. They said: "We will really try our wish to get him from his father: Indeed we will do it."

12.62.. And (Yusuf) told his servants to put their money used to trade (for the supplies) into their saddle bags, so that they would know it only after they returned to their people, (and) so that they might come back (again).

12.63.. So when they returned to their father, they said: "O our father! We will not get any more measure of grain (unless we take our brother): So send our brother with us, that we may get our measure; And we will really take every care of him."

12.64. He (Jacob) said: "Shall I trust you with him with any result different from when I trusted you with his brother before? But Allah is the best to take care (of him), and He is the Most Merciful of those who show mercy!"

12.65.. Then when they opened their baggage, they found their money (used to trade for grain) had been returned to them. They said: "O our Father! What (more) could we want? This, the money (used to our trade) has been returned to us: So we will get (more) food for our family; We will take care of our brother; And add a full camel's load (of grain of food). This is a small quantity (for the king to give to us)."

12.66. (Yàqoub, (Jacob), their father) said: "I will never send him with you until you swear a sincere promise to me, in the Name of Allah, that you will be sure to bring him back to me unless you are yourselves surrounded (and powerless)." And when they had sworn their truest promise, he said: "To all that we say, let Allah be the Witness and Guardian!"

12.67. And he said: "O my sons! All of you do not enter by one gate: (But) you enter by different gates. (It is) not that I can help you by the least against (the Will of) Allah: Verily, no one can command except Allah: On Him do I have my trust: And let all who trust have their trust in Him."

12.68. And when they entered in the way their father had told, it did not help them in the least against (the Plan of) Allah: It was only a need for Yàqoub's (Jacob's) soul, which he had fulfilled. Because by Our instruction, he was full of knowledge (and wisdom): But most men know not.

12.69.. And when they came in Yusuf's (Joseph's) presence, he invited his (full) brother (Benjamin) to stay with him. He (Yusuf) said (to his brother): "Verily! I am your (own) brother: So do not feel sad because of their doing."

12.70. At the end, after he gave them the provisions (suitable) for them, he put the drinking cup into his brother's saddle-bag. Then (one of) the announcers shouted: "O you (in) the Caravan! Surely! Without doubt, you are thieves!"

12.71. They (the brothers) said, turning towards them: "What is it that you miss?"

12.72. They said: "We miss the great drinking cup of the king; For him who produces it, is (the reward of) a camel load (of grain); I will be bound by it."

12.73. (The brothers) said: "By Allah! Indeed you know well that we did not come to make mischief in the land, and we are not thieves!"

12.74. (The Egyptians) said: "Then what will be the penalty for this, if you are (shown) to have lied?"

12.75. They said: "The penalty should be that he in whose saddle-bag it (the drinking cup) is found, should be held to make up for the (crime). It is like this that we punish the wrongdoers!"

12.76.. So he (Yusuf) began (the search) through their bags, before (he came to) the bag of his (full) brother: At the end, he brought it out of his (full) brother's bag. Thus did We plan for Yusuf (Joseph). He could not take his brother by the law of the king except that Allah willed it (so). We raise to (different) levels (of wisdom) whom We please: But above all blessed with knowledge is One, the All Knowing .

12.77. They (the brothers) said: "If he steals, there was a brother of his who did steal before (him)." But Yusuf (Joseph) kept these things locked in his heart, without telling the secrets to them. He said (to himself): "You are in worse position; And Allah knows best the truth of whatever you say!"

12.78.. They said (to the king): "O high one! Verily! He has an old and respected father, (who will feel very sad without him); So take (and keep) one of us in his place; Indeed, we see that you are (kind) in doing good."

12.79. He (Yusuf) said: "Allah forbid that we take other than him with whom we found our property: Truly (by that), we should be acting wrongfully."

12.80.. Now when they saw (that there was) no hope of his (keeping one of them), they met together in private. The eldest among them said: "Do you not know that your father took an oath from you in Allah's Name, and (also) before this, how you had failed in your duty with Yusuf (Joseph)? Therefore I will not leave this land (Egypt) until my father permits me, or Allah decides for me; And He is the best of all the judges.

12.81. "You return back to your father, and say, 'O our father! Verily! Your son has stolen, and we only bear witness to (and say) what we know, and we could not protect against the unseen!

12.82. " 'Ask (those from the town) where we have been and the caravan in which we returned, and surely, (you know) we are really telling the truth.' "

12.83.. He [Yàqoub (Jacob)] said: "Nay! But you have yourselves made up a story (good) for you. So patience is most suited (for me). May be, Allah will bring them (again) all to me. For He is indeed full of Knowledge and Wisdom."

12.84. And he turned away from them, and said: "How great is my sadness for Yusuf (Joseph)!" And his eyes became white with sorrow, and he lost his sight overcome by unspoken sorrow.

12.85. They said: "By Allah! (Never) will you stop to remember Yusuf (Joseph), until you reach the final end of illness, or until you die!"

12.86. He said: "I only complain of my (extreme) sorrow and pain to Allah, and I know from Allah that which you do not know.

12.87. "O my sons! You go and inquire about Yusuf (Joseph) and his brother, and never give up hope of Allah's (gift of) Mercy: Truly, no one feels sad for Allah's (gift of) Mercy, except those who have no faith."

12.88. Then when they came into (Yusuf's) presence, they said: "O mighty one! (Extreme) suffering has come upon us and our family: And we have (now) brought only little capital: So do give us full measure (of grain, we request you) and treat it as charity to us: Truly, Allah does reward the charitable."

12.89. He (Yusuf) said: "Do you know how you dealt with Yusuf (Joseph), and his brother, while you were ignorant?"

12.90. They said: "Are you truly Yusuf (Joseph)?" He said: "I am Yusuf (Joseph), and this is my brother (Benjamin): Allah has truly been Gracious to us (all). He who is righteous and patient- Then surely, Allah will never make the reward to be lost, for those who do right."

12.91. They said: "By Allah! Truly, Allah has chosen you over us, and we certainly have been guilty of sin!"

12.92. He (Yusuf) said: "This day let there be no blame on you: May Allah forgive you, and He is the Most Merciful of those who show mercy!

12.93. "(Now you) go with this, my shirt; And put it over the face of my father: He will start to see (clearly again). Then you come (back here) to me together with your entire family."

12.94.. And when the caravan left (Egypt to come to Jacob), their father said: "I truly scent the presence of Yusuf (Joseph): Do not think me as a feeble (old man)."

12.95. They said: "By Allah! Truly, you are in your old wandering mind."

12.96. Then when the bearer of the good news came, he put (the shirt) over his (Jacobs) face, and he right away regained clear sight. He said: "Did I not tell you, 'I know from Allah what you do not know?'"

12.97. They said: "O our father! Ask for us forgiveness (from Allah) for our sins, indeed, we were truly at fault."

12.98. He said: "Soon I will ask my Lord for forgiveness for you: Truly! He, Only He is Often Forgiving, Most Merciful ."

12.99.. Then when they (all) came in the presence of Yusuf (Joseph), he gave a home for his parents with himself, and said: "May you (all) enter Egypt, if Allah wills, in security (and safety)."

12.100. And he placed his parents high on the throne (of dignity) where he sat, and they fell down in prostration before him. And he said: "O my father! This is the completion of my old dream! Allah has made it come true! He was indeed good to me when He took me out of prison and brought you (here) out of the desert, (even) after Satan had caused (big) hate between me and my brothers. Surely, my Lord is the Most Gentle and Kind to those whom He chooses. Surely, He (and Only He,) is All Knowing and All Wise.

12.101. "My Lord! You have truly given me some power, and taught me some of the meanings of dreams and events- You! The Creator of the heavens and the earth! You are my Protector in this world and in the Hereafter. You (Almighty!) take my soul (at death) as (one who bows down to Your Will) as a Muslim and join me with the righteous."

12.102.. That is one of the stories of what happened unseen, which We make it known to you (O Prophet,) by revelation: And you were not with them when they made up their plans together and while coming up with their plots.

12.103. Still the larger part of mankind will not have any Faith: However much you may like it (for them).

12.104. And you ask no reward from them for this: It (the Quran) is nothing less than a (Clear) reminder for all creatures (and a Message to all the jinns' and men).

12.105.. And how many (of Our) Signs in the heavens and the earth do they pass by? Yet they turn (themselves) away from them!

12.106. And most of them do not believe in Allah without associating (others) with Him!

12.107. Do they then feel safe from the approach against them of the covering curtain of the Anger of Allah- Or from the approach against them of the Final Hour- Suddenly, while they are not (even) aware?

12.108.. Say (to them): "This is my way: I invite to Allah- On evidence clear as the sight of one's eyes- I and those who follow me (invite you), and Glorified and Supreme is Allah! And never will I join gods with Allah!"

12.109. And before you, We did not send any except men (as messengers, men) whom We inspired- Living in human homes (and groups). Do they not travel through the earth, and see what was the end of those before them? And verily, the home of the Hereafter is the best, for those who do right. Then, will you not understand?

12.110. (Time will be given to them) until, when the messengers (of Allah) give up hope and think that they were treated as liars, then Our help reaches them and those whom We want are taken into safety. And Our punishment is never taken away from those who are in sin.

12.111. Indeed, in their stories, there is guidance for men blessed with understanding. It (the Quran) is not a story made up, but a affirmation of what went on before it- And a detailed statement of all things, and a Guide and a Mercy for any of those who believe.

Sura 12 Notes

The interpretation of the two *Ayât* 12.52 and 12.53, differs slightly in the various translations. In this Quran, we have interpreted that these words are from the wife of the king Aziz and she had turned to the righteousness after Yusuf was sent to prison (see *Ayâh* 12.35) and she says the words of Praise to Allah. Whereas the interpretation that is presented appears most logical, it could also be interpreted that prophet Yusuf was saying the words of *Ayâh* 12.52 and *Ayâh* 12.53. In this sense, if these are the words of Yusuf rather the words of the wife of the king Aziz, then it signifies that he (Yusuf) was restating his innocence to the king even during the king's absence in spite of the advances of the king's wife while Yusuf was in the household of the king. This interpretation may also be attested by what is said in *Ayâh* 12.54.

****

Sura 13. Ar-Ra'd,

(Thunder): (Medinah, 43 Verses)

In the Name of Allah, the Most Gracious, the Most Merciful.

13.1. Alif Lám Mim Ra: These are the Signs (or Verses) of the Book (the Quran): And what has been revealed to you (O Muhammad) from your Lord, is the Truth; But most men do not believe.

13.2. Allah is He, Who raised the heavens without any pillars that you can see; And (He) is firmly placed on the Throne [of Power]; He has forced the sun and the moon (to His law)! Each one runs its (path) for a fixed time. He controls all things, explaining (to you) the Signs in detail, so that you may surely believe in the meeting with your Lord.

13.3. And it is He Who spread out the earth, and placed upon it mountains standing firm, and rivers (flowing): And fruits of every kind He made in pairs, two and two: He draws the Night as a cover over the Day. Verily, surely in these things there are Signs for those who think and reflect.

13.4. And in the earth are adjoining regions (which differ even though they are) next to each other, and gardens of plants (of flexible stems) and fields planted with corn, and (many) palm trees- Growing out from single roots or otherwise: Watered by the same water, yet some of them We make much better than others to eat. (Look,) surely in these things there are Signs for those who understand!

13.5.. If you wonder (at their faith), then (equally) surprising is their saying: "After we are dust, then shall we be truly remade in a new creation?" They are those who disbelieve in their Lord! They will be of those with their hands tied to their necks with iron chains (and vices mounted for submission): They will be companions of the Fire, to live in there!

13.6. They ask you to bring the evil sooner than the good: Yet before them, (many) severe punishments have come true! But surely your Lord is full of forgiveness for mankind in spite of their evil actions, and surely, your Lord is (also) strict in punishment.

13.7. And the disbelievers say: "Why is a Sign not sent down to him (the Prophet) from his Lord?"- You are truly a Warner, and to every people there is a guide.

13.8.. Allah knows what every female (womb) bears, and by how much the wombs fall short or exceed (their time or numbers). Everything is in (proper) proportion before His Sight.

13.9. He knows the Unseen and the seen: (He is) the Most Great, the Most High.

13.10. It is the same (to Him) whether any of you hides his (the human) speech or says it openly: Whether he lies hidden by night or walks out freely by the day.

13.11. For each one (human), there are (angels) one following the other, before and behind him: They guard him by the command of Allah. Surely Allah will not change the condition of a people until they change it themselves. But when Allah wills a punishment for a people, there is no holding it back; Nor will they find, anyone other than Him, to protect them.

13.12. It is He Who shows you the lightning, both as fear and as hope: And it is He Who raises up the clouds, heavy with rain!

13.13. And more, the thunder repeats His Praises, and glorifies Him, like the angels do, with respect and fear: He throws the loud resounding thunder-bolts, and with it He strikes whomsoever He wills- Even then they (the disbelievers) dispute about Allah, and He is Mighty in strength and severe in punishment.

13.14.. The True prayer is for Him (and only for Him): Any other (things) that they call to besides Him do not hear them any more than the one who stretches out his hands for water to reach his mouths but it does not reach him: Because the prayer of those without faith is nothing but (useless) misguidance.

13.15. And whatever beings there are in the heavens and the earth prostrate themselves to Allah (in respect and fear)- Willingly or unwillingly (with good will or in spite of themselves): Like their shadows do, in the mornings and the evenings.

{A Muslim generally prostrates to Allah after reciting this verse}

13.16.. Say: "Who is the Lord and Sustainer of the heavens and the earth?" Say: "It is Allah." ... Say: "Then do you take (for worship) protectors other than Him, such as (those who) have no power, for good or for harm to themselves?" Say: "Is the blind and the one who sees equal? Or the depths of darkness and Light equal?" Or do they assign to Allah 'partners' who have created like His Creation, so that the creation seemed similar to them? Say: "Allah is the Creator of all things: And He is The One, the Supreme and Irresistible."

13.17. He sends down water (rain) from the sky, and the channels flow (with water), each by its measure: But the flood carries away (to clean) the foam that comes up to the surface. And like this, from the (ore) which they heat (to melt) in the fire, to make ornaments or pots (and pans) from it, also there is a scum (or foam). Thus Allah clearly shows forth truth and vanity for the scum disappears when it is thrown out; Whereas what remains is for the good of mankind on the earth. Thus Allah does set forth examples (parables).

13.18. For those who respond to their Lord, there are (all) the good things. But those who do not respond to Him- Even if they had all that there is in the heavens and on earth, and as much more, (for no use) would they offer it to save themselves. For them the penalty will be huge and painful their home will be Hell, and worst indeed is that place for rest!

13.19.. Then is the one who knows what has been made clear to you from your Lord is the Truth, the same as the one who is blind? It is those who are blessed with understanding that receive advice-

13.20. Those who fulfill the Promise to Allah and do not fail in their word;

13.21. And those who combine the things which Allah has ordered to be joined, (truth with virtue, prayer with charity, and patience with perseverance) hold their Lord in respect and fear, and fear terrible penalty (if they do wrong);

13.22. And those who patiently persevere, seeking the (Divine) Face of their

Lord; establish regular prayers; Spend from what We have blessed for their life, secretly and openly; And block evil with good: For them there is the final reach of the (eternal) Home-

13.23. Gardens that hold unending joy: They will enter there, like the righteous ones from their fathers, their spouses, and their children: And angels will enter unto them from every gate.

13.24. (With the welcome and praise): "Peace be upon you because you persevered (and worked hard) with patience! Now how wonderful is the final Home!"

13.25.. And those who break the promise to Allah, after giving their word to it, and cut out those (relations and) things that Allah has ordered to be joined, and cause mischief in the land- Upon them is curse: (And a unhappy) evil home (and Hell) is for them.

13.26.. Allah gives more, or restricts to (the right) measure, the provision (and support) to whomsoever He pleases and they are happy in the joy in the life of this world: But the (very) life of this world is only of short enjoyment compare to the (joy in the) Hereafter.

13.27.. The disbelievers say (about the Prophet): "Why is not a Sign sent down to him from his Lord?" Say: "Truly Allah leaves to wander whom He wills; But He guides to Himself those who turn to Him in patience (and repentance)-

13.28. "Those who believe, and whose hearts find satisfaction in remembering Allah: Verily, in remembering Allah do hearts find (real) satisfaction.

13.29. "For those who believe and work righteousness, is (every) blessing and a beautiful place for (the final) Return."

13.30.. Thus have We sent you (O Prophet!) within a people before whom (other) peoples have (gone and) passed away; So that you may repeat to them what We send down to you by inspiration; Yet they reject (Him), the Most Gracious! Say: "He is my Lord! There is no god but He, my trust is upon Him and (only) to Him I turn!"

13.31. And if there was a Quran with which mountains were moved, or the earth was split open, or the dead were to speak, (this Quran would be that Book!) but, truly, the command for all things is with Allah! Do the believers not know, that if Allah willed, He could have guided all mankind (to the Right)? But for the disbelievers- Disaster will never stop to grab them for their (ill) deeds, or fall close to their homes, until the promise of Allah has come true, because truly, Allah will not fail in His promise.

13.32.. And indeed (many) messengers (of Allah) were mocked before you: But I (Allah) gave (a short) relief to the disbelievers, and finally I (Allah) punished them: Them how (terrible) was My (Allah's) punishment!

13.33. Then, is He Who stands over every soul (and knows) all that it does, (same as others)? And yet they ascribe partners to Allah. Say: "But name them! Is it that you will tell Him of something He does not know on earth, or is it (just) a show of words?" And moreover! To those who do not believe, their action seems pleasing, but they are kept away (with it) from the Path. And those whom Allah leaves to wander, no one can guide.

13.34. For them is a penalty in the life of this world, and certainly, harder is the Penalty of the Hereafter. And they have no defender (protector) against Allah.

13.35. The setting (description) of the Garden that the righteous are promised! Beneath it flow rivers: Unending is the enjoyment and the shade in there: The end of the righteous is like this; And the end of the disbelievers is the Fire.

13.36.. Those to whom We (Allah) have given the Book find joy in what has been revealed to you: But in the tribes there are (some of) those who reject a part of it. Say: "I am ordered to worship Allah, and not to join partners with Him. (Only) unto Him I call, and to Him is my return."

13.37. And like this We have made it (the Quran) known to be a Judgment of Authority in Arabic. If you were to follow their (worthless) desires after the knowledge that has reached you, then you will find neither protector nor defender against Allah.

13.38.. And indeed, We (Allah) did send messengers before you, and gave them wives and children: And it was never the duty of a messenger to bring a Sign except as Allah permitted (or ordered, for) each period is a Book (revealed).

13.39. Allah removes and confirms what He pleases: The Mother of the Book is with Him.

13.40.. Whether We shall show you (in your life) a part of what We promised them or take your soul to Ourselves (before)- Your duty is to make (the Message) reach them: It is Our part to call them to account.

13.41. Do they not see that We slowly reduce the land (for them) from its outer (borders) regions? (When) Allah judges, there is no one to undo His Judgment: And He is Swift in calling to Account.

13.42. And verily, those before them (also) made plots; But in all things the master-planning is by Allah. He knows the doing of every soul: And soon the disbelievers will know who gets (the better) home in the last Destination.

13.43. And the disbelievers say: "You (O Muhammad!) are not a messenger." Say: "Between you and me, Allah is enough as a witness, and those who have knowledge of the Book ."

****

Sura 14. Ibrahim,

(Abraham): (Makkah, 52 Verses)

In the Name of Allah, the Most Gracious, the Most Merciful.

14.1. Alif Lám Ra: A Book (the Quran) which We have revealed to you, (O Prophet!) so that you may lead mankind from the depths of darkness into Light- By the permission of their Lord- To the Path (towards Him), the Exalted in Power , the (One) Worthy of all Praise!

14.2. Allah, to Whom belong all things in the heavens and on earth! But grief to the disbelievers for a terrible Penalty (for their lack of Faith)-

14.3. Those who love the life of this world more than the Hereafter, and who try to stop (men) from the Path of Allah and try to find in there something crooked: They are out (of the Path) by a long distance.

14.4.. We did not send a messenger except (to teach) in the language of his (own) people, so as to make (things) clear to them. Then Allah leaves wandering those whom He pleases: And guides whomsoever He wills: And He is the Exalted in Power , the Full of Wisdom .

14.5. And indeed, We sent Musa (Moses) with Our Signs (and Command, saying): "Bring out your people from the depths of darkness into Light, and teach them to remember the Days of (special Mercy from) Allah." Surely, in this there are Signs for such as (those who) are truly patient and constant- Grateful and thankful.

14.6. And remember! Musa (Moses) said to his people: "Think of the gift from Allah to you when He saved you from the people of Firon (Pharaoh): They set you to hard work and punishments, killed your sons, and let your women live: And in there was a huge trial from your Lord."

14.7.. And (also) remember! Your Lord has (openly) proclaimed: "If you are thankful, I will add more (gifts) for you; But if you show thanklessness, verily, My (reference to Allah's) punishment is really terrible."

14.8. And Musa (Moses) said: "If you disbelieve (and show thanklessness), you and all on earth together- Then verily Allah is Free of all Wants, Worthy of all Praise.

14.9.. Has the story of those before you not reached you? Of the people of Nuh (Noah), and 'Ad and Samood (Thamud) and of those who were after them? No one knows them but Allah. The messengers (from Allah) came to them with Clear (Signs): But they put their hands to their mouths, and said: "Verily, we reject (the very purpose) for which you have been sent, and we are really in distrustful (uneasy) doubt about that to which you invite us."

14.10. Their messengers (from Allah) said: "Is there a doubt about Allah, the Creator of the heavens and the earth? It is He, Who invites you, so that He may forgive you for your sins and give you relief for a fixed time!" They said: "Oh! You are not any more than a human (being), like ourselves! You want to turn us away from the (gods) our fathers worshipped: Then bring us some clear authority."

14.11. Their messengers (from Allah) said to them: "(It is) true, we are human like yourselves, but Allah grants His grace (mercy) to some of His servants whom He pleases. It is not for us to bring you an authority except when Allah permits. And in Allah, let all men of faith have their trust.

14.12. "And we have no reason why we should not put our trust on Allah, since He has indeed, truly guided us to the Ways that we (follow). We shall certainly bear with patience all the pain you may bring to us. For those who put their trust should (indeed) put their trust in Allah."

14.13.. And the disbelievers said to their messengers: "Be sure that we will drive you out of our land, or you will (have to) return to our religion." But their Lord revealed (this message to) them: "Surely, We will destroy the wrongdoers!

14.14. "And surely We shall make you remain in the land, and take over after them. This is for such (people) who fear the time when they will stand before My court- Such as (those people) who fear the punishment set for them."

14.15. And they wanted to win and (wanted) the decision, and failure (and defeat) was the fate of every powerful (and) willful transgressor.

14.16. In front of such a (person) is Hell, and for drinking he is given boiling foul smelling water.

14.17. He will drink it unwillingly, by the mouthful, but he will never be near to swallowing it down his throat: And death will come to him from every direction, yet, he will not die: And for him will be an unending punishment.

14.18.. The parable of those who reject their Lord is that their works are like ashes, on which the wind blows strongly on a windy day: They have no power over (even the) little bit of what they have earned: That is the wandering far, far (from the goal).

14.19. Do you not see that Allah has created the heavens and the earth with (Candor and) Truth? If He wants, He can remove you and put a new Creation (in your place)?

14.20. For Allah, that is not any great matter.

14.21. They all will be gathered before Allah together: Then the weak say to those who were proud, "For us, we only followed you; then, can you be of any use to us against the Punishment of Allah?" They will reply, "If we had received the Guidance of Allah, we should have given it to you: It makes no difference to us (now) whether we are angry, or bear (the pain) with patience: For ourselves there is no way of escape."

14.22.. And when the matter is settled Satan will say: "Verily, Allah Who promised with (and in) Truth: I had also promised you, but I failed you in my promise. I did not have any authority over you except to tempt you (to the wrong), but you responded to (and followed) me: Do not blame me, but blame your own selves. I cannot help you, and you cannot help me. I reject your earlier act of associating me as a partner with Allah. For wrongdoers there must be a painful Penalty."

14.23.. But those who believe and act righteously, will be admitted to Gardens beneath which rivers flow- (In the Paradise) to live in there for ever, with the permission of their Lord. Their greeting in there will be "*Salaam*- (Peace)!"

14.24.. Do you not see how Allah sets forth a parable? A good Word (from Allah is) like a good tree, whose root is firmly fixed, and its branches (reach) to the sky-

14.25. It brings out its fruits at all times, by the permission of its Lord. And Allah sets forth stories for men, so that they may remember and receive guidance.

14.26. And the parable of an evil word is like that of an evil tree: It is pulled up by the root (see 15.34) from the surface of the earth; It cannot be stable (alive).

14.27. Allah establishes those who believe with strength with the Word (from Allah) that stands firm, (both) in this world and in the Hereafter, and Allah will let those who do wrong to go astray: And Allah does what He wills.

14.28.. Have you not looked at to those who have changed the kindness of Allah to false words (by falsifying the teaching of the Prophet) and caused their people to come down to the house (Hell) of eternal punishment?

14.29. Into Hell? They will burn in there- An evil place to be in!

14.30. And they set up (others) as equal to Allah, to mislead (men) from the (right) Path! Say: "Enjoy (for a while)! But surely you are making (your) way straight for Hell!"

14.31. Talk to My servants who have believed, that they may establish regular prayers, and spend (in charity) out of the goods that We have given them; Secretly and openly, before the arrival of a Day in which there will be neither mutual give and take nor making any friends.

14.32.. It is Allah Who has created the heavens and the earth and sends down the rain from the sky, and with it (He) brings out fruits to feed you; It is He Who has made ships to serve you, that they may sail through the sea to His Command; And He has made the rivers as well, to serve you.

14.33. And He has made the sun and the moon to serve you, both truly following their courses (orbits): And He has made the Night and the Day (also) to serve you.

14.34. And He gives you from what you ask for. But if you count the mercies of Allah, you will never be able to number them. Truly, man is used to being unjust and ungrateful.

14.35.. And (remember) Ibrahim (Abraham) said: "O my Lord! Make this city (Makkah), one with Peace and security: And save me and my sons from praying to idols.

14.36. "O my Lord! They (the idols) have truly led many among mankind astray; Then he who follows my (ways), surely he is of me, and he who disobeys me (is going astray)- But You are truly Often Forgiving, Most Merciful .

14.37. "O our Lord! I have made some of my children to live in the valley without (any) cultivation to (be near) Your Sacred House (*Ka'bah*); So that, O our Lord, they may establish regular Prayer: So fill the hearts of some from among men with love towards them, and feed them with fruits: So that they may offer thanks (to You).

14.38. "O our Lord! You truly know what we hide and what we reveal: For there is nothing that is hidden from Allah, either on earth or in heaven.

14.39. "All the Praises (and thanks) be to Allah, Who has granted me in old age Ismail (Ishmael) and Isháq (Isaac): Verily, my Lord is indeed the Hearer of prayer!

14.40. "O my Lord! Make me one who establishes regular prayer, and (also make me raise such) from my children: O our Lord! And accept my prayer (and pleading).

14.41. "O our Lord! (Bestow us with Your) Forgiveness for- Me, my parents, and (all) believers, on the Day that the counting (of good and evil) will happen!"

14.42.. Do not think that Allah does not care for the actions of the wrongdoers. But He (Allah) only gives them (a short time of) relief against a Day when the eyes will constantly stare in fear (of the punishment)-

14.43. (They will be) running forward with necks hung out, their heads torn away, their looks not coming back towards them, and their hearts a (large open) hole!

14.44.. And warn mankind of the Day when the Anger (and Punishment) will reach them: Then the wrongdoers will say: "O Lord! Grant some relief to us (even) for a little while: We will come back to Your Call, and follow (Your) messengers!" (The reply will be:) "What! Were you not used to swearing before that you will not leave (this world for the Hereafter).

14.45. "And you lived in the houses of men who harmed their own souls;

And it was clear how We dealt with them; And We set out (many) parables to properly warn!"

14.46. Truly powerful were the plans they made, and their plans were plainly visible to Allah, though they were not (even) plotting to remove the mountains from their places!

14.47. Do not think that Allah will fail in His promise to His messengers: For Allah is Supreme in Power totally Able to inflict punishment (for the wrongdoers).

14.48.. On the Day the earth will be changed to a different earth and also (there) will be the heavens, and (all creatures) will be brought out, before Allah, the (Single) One, the Irresistible;

14.49. And on that Day, you will see the criminals (and sinners) tied together in chains (and shackles)-

14.50. Their clothes of liquid (pitch black) tar, and their faces covered with fire;

14.51. That Allah may pay back each soul according to what it has earned; Surely Allah is Swift in taking account.

14.52. This (Quran) is a Message for all mankind, let them (the men) take warning from it, and let them know that He is One God (Allah): Let men of understanding pay attention!

****

Sura 15. Al-Hijr,

(The rocky path): (Makkah, 99 Verses)

In the Name of Allah, the Most Gracious, the Most Merciful.

15.1. Alif Lám Ra: These are the Signs (*Ayât*, Verses) of the Book- And the Quran that makes things clear.

15.2.. Again and again, those who disbelieve, will wish that they bowed (to Allah) in Islam.

15.3. Leave them alone to eat and enjoy (this life) and to please themselves: Let (their false) hope amuse them: Soon knowledge (and truth) will (wake them).

15.4. And We never destroyed a population that did not have a term already decided (written) and allocated.

15.5. And not any people can foresee its term, nor can they delay it.

15.6. And they say: "O you to whom the Message is being revealed! You are truly mad (or possessed)!

15.7. "Why will you not bring the angels to us if it is that you have the Truth?"

15.8. We do not send down the angels except with truth (for a valid cause): If they came (to the ungodly), look! No chance will they (the disbeliveers) have!

15.9. Without doubt, We have sent down the Message; And We will surely guard it (safely from evil).

15.10. And indeed, We sent (messengers) before you from the religious people of earlier communities:

15.11. And never came to them a messenger whom they (the people) did not mock.

15.12. But, We let it (evil) come into the hearts of the guilty,

15.13. That they should not believe in (the Message, the Quran); But (now) the ways of the old have passed away.

15.14. Even if We opened to them a gate from heaven, and they continued to climb in there,

15.15. They would only say: "Our eyes have been intoxicated: Nay, we have been overpowered by magic."

15.16. And indeed, We have set out the Zodiacal Signs (for planets) in the heavens, and made them seem fair to the onlookers;

15.17. And (also) We have guarded them from every evil spirit that is cursed:

15.18. Except any that may gain a hearing by hiding away, is chased (out) by a flaming fire, bright (to see).

15.19. And We have spread out the earth (flat); Placed mountains (on it) firm and immovable; And in it made all kinds of things in proper balance.

15.20. And in it We have provided the means to live- For you and for those for whom you do not provide (the means to live).

15.21. And there is not a thing whose (unending) treasures are not with Us; And We only send down from there in correct and known measures.

15.22. And We send the (water) bearing winds to fertilize, then We cause the rain to come down from the sky, and then give it (the rain) to you with water to drink, though you are not the keepers of its stores.

15.23. And surely, it is We Who give life, and Who give Death: It is We Who remain Inheritors (at the end).

15.24. And indeed, We know the first generation of you who have past away, and indeed, We know the present generation of you and also those who will come later.

15.25. Surely it is your Lord Who will bring them together: Truly, He is All Wise and All Knowing .

15.26. And indeed, We created man from dried clay (earth) that is capable of making sounds, from mud cast into shapes;

15.27. And (the race of) jinns', which We had created before, from the smokeless flames (of fire).

15.28. And remember! Your Lord said to the angels: "I am going to create man, from dried sounding clay from mud cast into shape;

15.29. "So, when I have fashioned him (Adam, the first man) in the his proper measures and breathed into him (Adam), the soul that I (Allah) created for him, then you (angels) fall down prostrate (in a show of respect) for him."

15.30. So the angels prostrated themselves, all of them together:

15.31. Except *Iblis* [Satan, the chief of the (evil) jinn race], he refused to be amongst who prostrated themselves.

15.32. (Allah) said: "O *Iblis*! What is the reason for not being from those who prostrated themselves?"

15.33. (*Iblis*) said:" I am not one to prostrate myself to man, (a mere human) whom You (Allah) created from sounding clay; From mud cast into shape."

15.34. (Allah) said: "Then you get out from here; For (this) verily, you are an outcaste and cursed.

15.35. "And surely! The curse shall be on you till the Day of Recompense (Judgment)."

15.36. (*Iblis*) said: "O Lord! Give me then relief (and time) till the Day the (dead) are raised."

15.37. (Allah) said: "To you relief is granted-

15.38. "Till the Day of the Time appointed."

15.39. (*Iblis*) said: ""O Lord! Because You have put me in the wrong, I will make (wrong) seem fair to them (the humans) on the Earth, and I will put them all in the wrong-

15.40. "Except Your servants among them, truthful and purified (by You)."

15.41. (Allah) said: "This (truth and purification) is indeed (the Straight Path), a Way that reaches Straight to Me.

15.42. "Certainly, you shall have no power over My servants except those who keep themselves in the wrong by following you."

15.43. And surely, Hell is the promised home for them all!

15.44. To it are seven gates: For each of those gates there is a class (of sinners) assigned.

15.45. Truly, the righteous (ones will be) in the Gardens and fountains.

15.46. (Their greeting will be) : "You enter here in (total) peace and security."

15.47. And from their hearts, We shall remove any left over sense of pain and injury: (Like) brothers (happily) facing each other on thrones (of dignity).

15.48. In there, sense of being tired will not come to them, and they will never be asked to leave.

15.49. Tell My servants that I am indeed the Often Forgiving, the Most Merciful .

15.50. And that My Penalty will (also) be indeed the most painful penalty.

15.51. Tell them about the (angels) guests of Ibrahim (Abraham).

15.52. When they entered his presence and said: "*Salaam* (Peace)!" He said, "Indeed, we feel afraid of you!"

15.53. They said: "Do not fear! We bring the happy news of a son blessed with wisdom."

15.54. He said: "Do you give me the happy news that old age has come over me? Then about what is your good news?"

15.55. They said: "We give you the happy news in truth: Then do not despair!"

15.56. He said: "And who despairs of the Mercy of his Lord, except those who go astray?"

15.57. Ibrahim (Abraham) said: "Then what is the (other) business on which you (have come), O you messengers (of Allah)?"

15.58. They said: "We have been sent to a people in guilt and sin,

15.59. "Excepting the followers of Lut (Lot): We are certainly to save them (from harm), all-

15.60. "Except his wife, who, we have known, will be from those who will remain behind."

15.61. Then the messengers (the angels) came to the family of Lut (Lot),

15.62. He said: "You seem to be unknown (unusual) people."

15.63. They said: "Yes, we have come to you with the penalty to complete that about which they doubt.

15.64. "And we have brought to you the truth (the destruction that is about to take place), and surely we tell the truth.

15.65. "Then (you) travel with your household, when a portion of the night (still remains), and you go behind in the rear: And let no one from you look back, but go on to where you are ordered."

15.66. And We made known this decree (order) to him that the last remaining of those (sinners) should be left behind by the early morning.

15.67. And the people of the city (with its evil ways) rushed over in (perverse and sinful) joy (at news of the young men as the messengers.)

15.68. [Lut, (Lot)] said: "Verily, these are my guests: And so do not shame me:

15.69. "And fear Allah, and do not disgrace me."

15.70. They said (to Lut): "Did we not forbid you to host and entertain any of the righteous (away from us)?"

15.71. (Lut) said: "These are my daughters (to marry), if you must act (so perversely)."

15.72. Surely, by your life (O Prophet), in their wild misled condition (of intoxication), they wander distracted back and forth.

15.73. But the Blast (an explosion) overtook them (the Lut people) before morning,

15.74. And We turned upside down (the cities of Sodom), and rained down on them brimstones (yellow sulfurous stones) hard as baked clay.

15.75. Surely! In this (story of Lut) there are Signs for those who understand by tokens.

15.76. And (the cities were) right on the high-road (between Arabia and Syria).

15.77. Surely! In this (story of the cities) there is a Sign for those who believe!

15.78. And the people of the Woods were also wrongdoers;

15.79. So, We gave their due (punishment) to them. They were both on an open highway, plain to see.

15.80. And verily, the companions of the Rocky Trail also rejected the messengers:

15.81. And We sent them Our Signs, but they continued to turn away from them.

15.82. And they cut out large houses out of the mountains, (trying to become safe and) secure.

15.83. But the blast (explosion) overtook them on, early in the morning,

15.84. And what they had (built with so much care and) done was of no use to them!

15.85. And We did not create the heavens and the earth, and all between them, except for just ends and the (final) Hour is surely coming. So, overlook (their faults) with kind forgiveness.

15.86. Surely! Your Lord is the Master-Creator, All Knowing .

15.87. And We have blessed upon you (O Prophet) the Seven often repeated (verses, the *Ayât* of Sura 1 in *Surath Al-Fatiha*) and Quran, the Great (Book).

15.88. Do not (longingly) look with your eyes at what We have gifted some of their groups, and do not feel sad for them: But lower your arm (in respect and kindness) to the believers.

15.89. And say: "I am indeed he who warns openly and without uncertainty,"-

15.90. (Anger) as We have sent down on those who have divided (the Word of Allah in parts as they please)-

15.91. (Also on those who) have made the Quran into tiny sections (to accept or reject as they please).

15.92. Therefore, by your Lord, surely, We will call them to account,

15.93. For all of what they used to do.

15.94. Therefore explain openly what you are commanded, and turn away from those idolaters (who join false gods with Allah).

15.95. Because We are enough for you against those who show contempt and mock-

15.96. Those who take up another god with Allah, but soon they will come to know (the Truth).

15.97. Indeed, We know how your breast (heart) becomes tight (and feels sad) at what they say.

15.98. So, celebrate the Praise of your Lord, and be of those who prostrate themselves in sincere love (for Allah).

15.99. And worship your Lord till the Hour that is certain (death), comes to you.

****

Sura 16. An-Nahl,
(The bee): (Makkah, 128 Verses)
In the Name of Allah, the Most Gracious, the Most Merciful.

16.1. The Command of Allah (always) comes (true): You, then do not try to make it happen earlier: Glory to Him! And He is far above having (false) partners they ascribe to Him!

16.2. He sends down the angels with Revelations of His Command, to those of His servants, (as and) whom He pleases, (saying): "Warn (men) that there is no god but I: So fear Me (by safeguarding against all evil)."

16.3. He has created the heavens and earth in Truth (For their true cause): He is far above having (any false) partners they ascribe to Him!

16.4. He has created man from a drop of semen (sperm); And look this same (man) becomes an open challenger (about the creation)!

16.5. And He has created the cattle for you: You receive warmth (from the their skin), and many other benefits from them, and you eat from their (meat).

16.6. And you have a sense of pride and beauty in them while you drive them home in the evening, and as you take them out to the grazing land in the morning.

16.7. And they carry your heavy loads to a land where you could not (possibly) go except with considerable pain to (your bodies and) selves: Truly, your Lord is Most Kind , Most Merciful .

16.8. And (He has created) horses, mules, and donkeys, for you to ride and use for show; And He has created other things about which you do not have (any) knowledge.

16.9. And to Allah leads Straight the Way, but there are ways (of the world) that turn away: If Allah had so willed, He could have guided all of you.

16.10. It is He Who sends down water (the rain) from the sky: From it (the rain water) you drink, and out of it (grows) the vegetation with which you feed your cattle.

16.11. With it (the rain), He causes for you the (many) crops to grow, the corn, the olives, the date-palms, the grapes, and every kind of fruit: Surely in this, there is a Sign for those who think.

16.12. And He has made the Night and the Day for you; And (as He has made) the Sun and the Moon; And the Stars that obey His Command: Surely, in this there are Signs for those who understand.

16.13. And on this earth, (are) the things that He has made many, in different colors (and qualities): Surely, there is a Sign in this for those who speak (and say) the Praises of Allah.

16.14. And He, it is Who has made the sea subject (to His Command), so that you may eat the flesh (of the fish) from there that is fresh and tender, and so that you may extract from there ornaments (and pearls) to wear; And you see the ships in there that break the waves, so that you may find the bounty of Allah and that you may be grateful.

16.15. And He has placed the mountains standing firm on the earth, in case it should roll with you; And rivers and roads; So that you may guide yourselves;

16.16. And markers and sign-posts (upon the earth); And by the stars (so that men) guide themselves.

16.17. Is then He Who creates like (the false) one who does not create? Will you not take the warning (and guidance)?

16.18. And if you would try to count the Favors of Allah, you will never be able to number them: Truly, Allah is Often Forgiving, Most Merciful .

16.19. And Allah knows what you conceal (hide away), and (also) what you reveal.

16.20. Those whom they call upon other than Allah create nothing and are themselves created.

16.21. (They are) dead, lifeless: And they do not know when they will be raised up (themselves).

16.22. Your God is One (Allah). As to those who do not believe in the Hereafter, their hearts do not want to know, and they are proud (and haughty).

16.23. Without a doubt Allah knows what they hide, and (also) what they reveal: Surely, He does not love the proud (and haughty).

16.24. And when it is said to them, "What is it that your Lord has revealed?" They say: "Stories of the old!"

16.25. On the Day of Judgment let them fully bear their own burdens, and also some of burdens of those that knew not, whom they misled. Alas, how painful (and heavy are) the burdens they will bear!

16.26. Those before them also plotted (against Allah): But Allah took (away) their structures from their foundation, and the roof fell down upon them (right) from above them; And the punishment caught up with them from directions they did not (even) think.

16.27. Then, on the Day of Judgment (the Resurrection), He (Allah) will cover them with shame, and say: "Where are My 'partners' about whom you used to argue (with the believers)?" Those blessed with knowledge will say: "Truly, this Day, the disbelievers are covered with shame and misery-

16.28. "Those (disbelievers) whose lives the angels take in a state of doing wrong to their own souls." Then, would they offer submission (and say),

"We did no evil (knowingly)." (The angels will reply), "Yes, truly Allah knows all that you did;

16.29. "So enter the gates of Hell, to live in there. And indeed, so really evil is the home of the proud."

16.30. (When) it is said to the righteous, "What is it that your Lord has revealed?" They say: "All that is good;" To those who do good, there is good in this world, and the home of the Hereafter is even better and really wonderful is the home of the righteous,

16.31. Gardens of Eternity that they will enter: Beneath them flow (pleasant) rivers: They will have all that they wish in there: Thus Allah rewards the righteous-

16.32. Those (righteous ones) whose lives the angels take in a state of purity, saying (to them), "Peace be on you; You enter the Garden, because of what you did (in your life)."

16.33. Do the (ungodly) wait until the angels come to them, or there comes the Command from your Lord (for their death)? Like this (also) did those who went before them. And Allah did not wrong them: But! They wronged themselves (and their souls).

16.34. Then the evil results of their actions came upon them, and that very (anger of Allah) at which they had mocked surrounded them.

16.35. The worshippers of false gods say: "If Allah had so willed then we would not have worshipped anybody but Him- Neither we and nor our fathers- Nor would we have forbade anything other than His (things which He forbids)." Like this did those who went before them. But what is the duty of messengers (from Allah) except to teach the Clear Message?

16.36. And We surely sent from every people a messenger (with the Command), "Serve Allah, and avoid evil:" From the people were some whom Allah guided, and some for whom error could not be avoided. So travel through the earth, and see what was the end of those who rejected (the Faith and the Truth).

16.37. If you (O Prophet!) are eager for their guidance, then surely, Allah guides not those whom He leaves to stray (away from the Path), and there will be no one to help them.

16.38. And they swear their strongest promise by Allah, that Allah will not raise up those who die: Yes! (He will raise them and) it is a promise (to be made real) from Him in Truth: But most men do not realize it.

16.39. (They must be raised up) so that He may clarify to them the Truth where they differed, and that the rejecters of Truth may realize that they had really (given in to) falsehood.

16.40. Verily, to anything that We have willed (to be), We only say the word, "Be", and it is.

16.41. And to those who emigrated (and left) their homes in the cause of Allah, after suffering oppression- We will surely give a goodly home in this world; But the reward of the Hereafter will be truly greater, if they only realized!

16.42. Those (are the people) who remain constant with patience, and put their trust on their Lord.

16.43. And also before you the messengers that We sent were only men, to whom We gave (the Message by) revelation: If you do not realize this, ask of those who possess the Message.

16.44. (We also sent them, the earlier messengers) with Clear Signs and Books of strong prophecies and We have sent down to you the Message (the Quran); That you may explain clearly to men what is sent for them, and that they may reflect.

16.45. Then do those who make up evil (plots) feel safe that Allah will not make the earth to swallow them up, or that the Anger (of Allah) will not catch up with them from directions they are not aware of?

16.46. Or that He may not bring them to account in the middle of their coming and going with never a chance of stopping Him?

16.47. Or that He may not bring them to account by a process of slow wasting (of themselves)- For your Lord is truly full of Kindness and Mercy

16.48. Do they not look at Allah's creation, among (all) things- How (even) their shadows turn round, from the right and the left, prostrating themselves to Allah, and that (they do) in the humblest manner?

16.49. And all that is in the heavens and on the earth, prostrate (fall down with fear and respect) to Allah, be they the moving (living) creatures and the angels: Because none is proud (before Allah).

16.50. They all fear their Lord, high above them, and they do all that they are commanded.

{A Muslim generally prostrates to Allah after reciting this verse}

16.51. Allah has said: "Do not take two gods (for worship): Indeed, He is only One Allah: Then fear Me (only)."

16.52. To Him belongs what is in the heavens and on the earth, and always to Him is duty due: Then will you fear (anything) other than Allah?

16.53. And you do not have any blessing or good thing except that it is from Allah: And also, when you are touched by difficulty, you cry to Him with painful sighs;

16.54. Then, when He removes the difficulty from you, look! Some of you turn to other gods to join with their Lord in worship!

16.55. So as show their thanklessness for the favors We have blessed on them! Then enjoy (for a little while); But you will know (your mistake) soon!

16.56. And to things they do not know, they assign a portion out of what We have blessed for their livelihood! By Allah, you shall truly be brought to account for your false stories (you made up).

16.57. And they give daughters for Allah! Glory be to Him! Far above (is He) than what they associate with Him- And for themselves (they give sons-) what they desire!

16.58. And when news of a female (baby's birth) is taken to one of them, his face darkens (with sorrow), and he is filled with sadness inside!

16.59. He hides himself with shame from his people, because of the bad news he has! Will he keep it (the baby) with pain and disgrace, or bury her it in the dust? Oh! What an evil (choice) they decide on?

16.60. For those who do not believe in the Hereafter, is applied the similarity of evil: To Allah is applied the Highest Similitude: He is the Supreme in Power , the All Wise .

16.61. And if Allah was going to punish men for the wrongs (they have) done, He would not spare, on the (earth), even a single living creature: But

He gives them relief for a given time: When their time comes, they cannot delay (it even) by a single hour, just like they cannot advance it (even by a single hour).

16.62. They give to Allah what they dislike (for themselves), and their tongues insist on the lies that all good things are for themselves: Without doubt, the Fire is for them, and they will be the first to be pushed into it!

16.63. By Allah, We sent (messengers) to peoples (and nations) before you; But (to some), Satan makes their actions attractive to them: Also, he is their supporter today, but they shall have a most painful penalty.

16.64. And We sent down the Book (Quran) to you, for the clear purpose that you make clear to them those things about which they do not agree, and that it should be a guide and as a mercy for the believers.

16.65. And Allah sends rain down from the sky, and with it gives life to earth that is dead: Surely there is a Sign in this for those who listen.

16.66. And surely, in cattle, you will find a parable to learn (and to remember). Form their bodies (and from) what is between excretions and blood, We produce milk for you to drink, (milk) that is pure and pleasant for those who drink it.

16.67. And from the fruit of the date-palm and the vine, you get healthy drink and food: Also in this is a Sign for people who are wise.

16.68. And your Lord taught the bee "Make your (beehive) cells in the mountains, in the trees, and in the houses;

16.69. "Then to eat from all the fruits (of the earth), and with find the ways made easy by your Lord": From their bodies comes a drink (honey) of varying colors, wherein is healing for men: Surely in this is a Sign for those who think.

16.70. And (it is) Allah Who creates you and takes your souls at death; And there are some of you who are sent back to a weak (old) age, when they know nothing after having known (much in their young age): For Allah is All Knowing , All Powerful.

16.71. Allah has blessed His gifts of livelihood more freely on some of you than on others: Then those who are more blessed will not (equally) hand over their gifts to those whom their right hands possess, so as to be equal in that respect. Will they then deny the Favors of Allah?

16.72. And Allah has made for you mates (and spouses) of your own nature, and made for you, out of them, sons and daughters and grandchildren, and given to you the best of things to live on will they still believe in vain things, and be thankless for Allah's Favors?

16.73. And they (the idolaters) worship other than Allah- Such as have no power to provide them, anything in heavens or on earth for life, and cannot possibly have any such power?

16.74. So, do not make up similitude for Allah: Truly, Allah knows and you do not know.

16.75. Allah brings forward the case (of two men: One) a slave under the control of another; He (the slave) has no power at all; And (the other) a man upon whom We have granted many good favors from Ourselves, and he spends from them (freely), privately and publicly: Then are the two equal? All the Praises (and thanks) be to Allah. But most of them do not understand.

16.76. And Allah brings forward (another) case of two men: One of them dumb, with no power of any type, he is a tiresome burden on his master; Wherever he (master) directs him (the dumb one), he brings no good: Is such a man equal to one who acts justly, and is on the Straight Path?

16.77. And the Mystery of the heavens and of the earth belongs to Allah. And the Decision of the Hour (of Judgment) is as (quick as) the wink of an eye, or even closer: Truly, Allah is Able to do (and has Power over) all things.

16.78. And it is He Who brought you out from the wombs of your mothers when you did not know anything; And He gave you hearing, sight, and hearts (for understanding and love): So that you may give thanks (to Him).

16.79. Do they not see the birds, held balanced in the middle of the sky? Nothing holds them up except (the Power of) Allah. Surely, in this are Signs (*Ayât*) for those who believe.

16.80. It is Allah Who made your houses, places of rest and peace for you; And out of the skins of the animals, (He) made (tents for) dwellings for you, which you find so light when you travel and when you stop (to rest); And out of their wool, and their soft fibers; And their hair, (He made) valuable things and articles of use (to serve you) for a time.

16.81. And it is Allah Who made out from the things He created, some things to give you shade; From the hills He made some for your shelter; And He made you clothes to protect you from heat, and coats of (metallic) mesh to protect you from your anger (and fights between each other). Like this He completes and perfects His Favors on you that you may bow to His Will (in Islam).

16.82. Then, if they (still) turn away, your duty is only to give the Message in a clear way.

16.83. They (see and) know the Favor of Allah; Then they reject it (by idolizing to false gods): And most of them are disbelievers.

16.84. And on the Day when from all peoples (nations), We shall raise a Witness (their own messenger): Then no excuses will be taken from disbelievers, nor will they be allowed (to return and repent) to ask for the Forgiveness (from Allah).

16.85. And when the wrongdoers see the penalty, then it will not be lightened in any way and then they will not have any delay.

16.86. And when those (men) who gave 'partners' to Allah will see their 'partners', and they (the men) will say: "Our Lord! These are our 'partners', those whom we used to call upon besides You." But they will throw their word back at them: (And say): "Truly, you are liars!"

16.87. And on that Day they will yield in submission to Allah; And all their inventions will leave them in the hardest position.

16.88. Those who reject Allah and try to stop (men) from the Path of Allah-For them We will add penalty to penalty; Because they used to spread mischief.

6.89. On the Day when from all people, and We shall raise a witness (from themselves) against themselves: And We shall bring you (O Prophet!) as a witness against them (your people who reject Allah): And to you, We have sent down the Book (the Quran) explaining everything, a Guide, a Mercy, and Happy News for Muslims.

16.90. Verily, Allah commands Justice, the acts of kindness, and generosity towards relatives, and He forbids all shameful (immoral) deeds, injustice and rebellion: He instructs you, that you may receive guidance.

16.91. And fulfill the Covenant (Commitment of promise) taken in the Name of Allah, when you make it, and do not break your promises after you have agreed to keep them; In reality you have made Allah your Witness; Verily, Allah knows all that you do.

16.92. And do not be like a woman who breaks to untwisted fibers, the thread which she has spun, after it has become strong. And do not make promises to (hide the) acts of dishonesty (and deception) between yourselves, especially when there be more (people) in one party than in the other: Allah will test you by this; And on the Day of Judgment (Resurrection), He will surely make clear to you (the truth about) what you disagree.

16.93. And if Allah had so wanted, He could make you all as one People (one Nation): But He leaves wandering those whom He pleases, and He guides those whom He pleases: But you shall certainly be called to account for all your actions.

16.94. And do not make your promises to (hide the) acts of dishonesty (and deception) between yourselves, with the effect that someone's foot may slip after it was firmly placed, and you may have to taste the evil (penalty) for having blocked (men) from the Path of Allah, and the mighty Anger (of Allah) come upon you.

16.95. And do not use the Oath of Allah for a cheap (worldly) gain: For with Allah is (a reward) much better for you, if you only knew.

16.96. What is with you will go out of existence: What is with Allah will stay behind (for ever). And We will certainly bless upon those, their reward by the best of their actions, for those who patiently remain constant and committed (towards the right),

16.97. Whosoever works right, (be it) man or woman, and has Faith (in Allah), surely, to him will We give a good Life, a life that is good and pure, and We will bless upon those their reward by the best of their actions.

16.98. So when you recite the Quran, ask (and plead) for Allah's protection against Satan, the outcast and cursed one.

16.99. Verily, he (Satan) has no authority on those who believe and put their trust only in their Lord.

16.100. His (Satan's) authority is only over those, who take him as an (evil) guide and follow him and who join (false) 'partners' with Allah.

16.101. When We replace one verse for another- And Allah knows best what He reveals (in stages)- They (the disbelievers) say, "You are only a forger:" But most of them do not understand.

16.102. Say: "The Angel Gabriel (*Jibrael*) has brought the revelation from your Lord in Truth, as to strengthen (all) those who believe and as a guide and as good news to Muslims."

16.103. We also know that they (the disbelievers) say, "It is a man who teaches him (the Prophet)." His (the Prophet's) tongue, that they (wickedly) point to be notably different, whereas this is Arabic, pure and clear.

16.104. Verily, those who do not believe in the Signs and Revelations of Allah- Allah will not guide them, and theirs will be a painful penalty.

16.105. It is those who do not believe in the Signs of Allah- They makeup falsehood and forge lies; It is they who lie!

16.106. Any one who, after accepting the Faith in Allah, says (words of) unbelief- Except under force (from outside, but in) his heart remaining firm in Faith- (Whereas) on such as those who open their chests to unbelief- On them is Anger from Allah, and theirs will be a fearful Penalty.

16.107. This is because they love the life of this world better than the Hereafter: And Allah will not guide those who reject Faith.

16.108. They are those whose hearts, ears and the eyes Allah has sealed up, and they do not take warning.

16.109. No doubt, in the Hereafter, they will be the (painful) losers.

16.110. Then surely, your Lord- For those who emigrated (left their homes) after trials and persecution- And who afterwards work hard and fight for Faith and patiently remain constantly committed- Your Lord, after all this, is Often Forgiving, Most Merciful .

16.111. The Day when every soul will come forward struggling (and praying) for itself, and every soul will be paid back (in full) for all its actions, and no one will be unjustly treated.

16.112. And Allah brings forward a story: A city having (the comfort of) security and peace, well supplied with livelihood from every place: Yet it was still thankless for the gifts of Allah: So Allah made it taste hunger and fear (choking it) like a coat (from every side), because of what (its people) earned.

16.113. And there came to them a messenger from among themselves, but they falsely rejected him; So the Anger (of Allah) caught them even in the middle of their sins.

16.114. So (from the livelihood), eat lawful and good food that Allah has given to you; And be thankful for the Favors of Allah, if it is He Whom you serve.

16.115. He has only forbidden for you, meat from dead (animals), and blood, and the flesh of swine (any type of pig), and any (food) over, which the name of (anyone) other than Allah has been called upon. But if one is forced by (extreme) need, without willful disobedience, and not exceeding the rightful limits- Then, Allah is Often Forgiving, Most Merciful .

16.116. And do not say- For anything that is false that your tongues may put forth- "This is lawful, and this is forbidden," so as to ascribe false things to Allah. Verily, those who ascribe false things to Allah, will never prosper.

16.117. (When such type of lies are spoken, there) is only a very little worthless profit; But they will have a most painful penalty.

16.118. And for the Jews (also), We prohibited such things like what We have told you before: We did not do them any wrong, but they were used to doing wrong to themselves.

16.119. Then surely your Lord- For those who do wrong without knowing, and who afterwards repent and make corrections- Verily your Lord, after all of this, is (still) Often Forgiving, Most Merciful .

16.120. Verily, Ibrahim (Abraham) was a true model, (sincerely and) piously obedient to Allah, true in faith, and he did not join gods with Allah:

16.121. He showed his thanks for the Favors of Allah, Who chose him, and guided him to a Straight Path.

16.122. And We gave him good in this world, and in the Hereafter, he will be together with the Righteous.

16.123. Then, We have taught you (O Prophet!) the inspired (Message), "Follow the ways of Ibrahim (Abraham), the (one) True in Faith, and he did not join gods (with Allah)."

16.124. The Sabbath (the seventh day of the week) was only made (Holy) for those who disagreed (about it); And surely, your Lord will decide between them on the Day of Judgment about their differences.

16.125. Invite (all) to the Way of your Lord with wisdom and holy teaching, and reason with them by ways that are the best (and most gracious): Truly, your Lord knows best, (those) who have strayed from His Path, and (those) who receive guidance.

16.126. And if you punish them, then no worse than that they punish you: But if you show patience that is really the best for those who are patient.

16.127. And be patient because your patience is only from Allah; And do not feel sad over them: And do not be in distress yourself because of their (evil) plots.

16.128. Truly, Allah is with those who guard themselves, and those who do good.

****

Sura 17. Al-Isra',
(The night journey) or Bani Israel (The children of Israel): (Makkah, 111 Verses)
In the Name of Allah, the Most Gracious, the Most Merciful.

17.1.. Glory be to (Allah), Who took His Servant (the Prophet Muhammad) for a Journey during the night from the Sacred Mosque (in Makkah) to the Farthest Mosque at (*Masjid-ul-Aqsa*, Jerusalem) whose Vicinities We blessed, so that We may show him some of Our Signs (*Ayât*): For He is the All Hearer , the All Seer (One Who hears all and sees all).

17.2. And We gave Musa (Moses) the Scripture (*Taurát*), and made it a Guidance to the Children of Israel, (saying to them:): "Do not take (anyone) other than Me to be the Disposer of (your) affairs."

17.3. O (you) descendents who have come from those whom We carried (in the Ark) with Nuh (Noah)! Surely he was a true servant, most grateful.

17.4. And We had decreed (and gave (clear) warning to) the Children of Israel in the Scripture (*Taurát*, Torah), that you would make mischief twice on the earth and become very unjust and turn very arrogant (and that they would be punished twice)!

17.5. So when the first of the warnings came true, We sent against you (Children of Israel) Our servants (the Babylonians, who were) used to ruthless warfare: They entered the deepest parts of your homes; And it was a warning (totally) fulfilled.

17.6. Then We gave you a return (to freedom) against them: And We increased your resources and sons, and made you more numerous for manpower.

17.7. (And We said:) "If you do well, you do well for yourselves; If you do evil, (you do it) against yourselves." So, when the second warnings came true, (We let your enemies) disfigure your faces, and enter your mosque (in

Jerusalem) like they had entered it before, and bring destruction to all that fell into their power.

17.8. It may be that your Lord may (still) show mercy to you; But if you go back (to your sins), We shall go back (to Our punishments): And We have made Hell a prison for disbelievers.

17.9. Surely, this Quran guides to what is just and right and gives the good news to the believers who work deeds of righteousness, that they shall have a great reward (of Paradise);

17.10. And to those who do not believe in the Hereafter, (it warns) that for them We have prepared a painful penalty (of Hell).

17.11.. And man calls to (Allah) in (his) evil as he calls to (Allah) for the good, and man is used to hasty (actions).

17.12. And, We have fixed the night and the day as two Signs: The Sign of the night We have hidden away, whereas the Sign of the day, We have made to give you light; So that you may seek the Bounty from your Lord, and that you may know the number (of days) and count of the years: And all things We have fully explained (in detail).

17.13. And We have tied every man's fate onto his own neck: We shall bring out on the Day of Judgment for him a (register like) document, which He will see laid open (for him).

17.14. (It will be said to him:) "Read your (own record) book: Your soul is enough this day to make out an account against you."

17.15.. Whoever takes the guidance, takes it for his own good: And Whoever goes astray does so to his loss: No bearer of burdens can bear the burden of another: And We will not come down with Our Anger until We had sent a messenger (to warn).

17.16. When We decide to destroy a town (a population) We (first) send a firm order to those from them who are given the good things of this life and still exceed (their) limits; So that the word (of warning) is proved true against them: After this We destroy it to total destruction.

17.17. And how many generations have We destroyed after Nuh (Noah)? And your Lord is sufficient as totally Informed and All Seer of the sins of His servants.

17.18.. If any (of you) wish for the passing things (of this life), We give him readily- Those things as We will, to those persons as We will: In the end, We have (also) made Hell for him: He will burn in there, disgraced and rejected.

17.19. Whosoever wishes for the (reward in) Hereafter, and works hard for it with all his due effort, and keeps (his) Faith- He is the one whose effort is acceptable (by Allah).

17.20. From the (many) gifts of your Lord, We give freely to all- These (people) as well as those (people): The gifts of your Lord are not limited (to any).

17.21. See how We have given more to some than to others; But surely the Hereafter is higher in value and position and greater in excellence.

17.22. Do not take with Allah another god for worship; Or you (O man!) will sit in disgrace and neglect.

17.23.. And your Lord has commanded that you worship none but Him. And that you be kind to your parents. Whether one or both of them reach old age in your life, do not say a word of (hate and) disrespect to them, and do not brush them aside, instead, talk to them with (respect and) honor.

17.24. And, (out of kindness), lower to them the arm of submission by being humble through mercy, and say: "My Lord! Grant to them Your Mercy as they brought me up (dearly) during my childhood."

17.25. Your Lord knows best what is in your hearts and souls: If you do deeds of righteousness, then surely He is Most Forgiving to those who turn to Him again and again (in true repentance).

17.26.. And give the relatives their due rights, and (also) to those in want, and to the wayfarer: But do not waste (your wealth) like a spendthrift (or a wasteful person).

17.27. Surely wasters are brothers of the Satans'; And the Evil one (Satan) is ungrateful to his Lord.

17.28. And even if you have to turn away from them (the deserving) to find from the Mercy from your Lord, which you expect, then speak a word of comfort and kindness to them.

17.29. And do not make your hand tied to your neck, (like a miser), nor push it out to its longest reach, so that you become worthy of blame and being penniless.

17.30. Surely, your Lord gives plenty for livelihood to whom He pleases, but He gives in a right amount (to all). Verily, He knows and regards all His servants.

17.31.. And do not kill your children because of the fear of poverty (or of want): We shall give livelihood to them and also to you. Surely, killing them is a terrible sin.

17.32. And do not come close to adultery: Verily, it is a shameful (deed) and an act evil, opening the road (to many other evils).

17.33. And do not take life- Which Allah has made holy- Except for just (and true) cause. And if anyone is killed wrongfully, We have given his heir the right (to demand justice within due limits or to forgive): But let him not exceed the limits in the matter of taking life; Verily, he (too) is helped (by Islamic law).

17.34.. And do not come near to the orphan's property except to make it better, until he attains the age of full strength; And fulfill (every) promise (and commitment), verily, (every) act will be questioned (on the Day of Judgment).

17.35. And give full measure when you measure, and weigh with a balance that is (correct and) straight. That is the most suitable and most helpful in the final evaluation.

17.36. And do not follow that about which you have no knowledge; Verily, every act of hearing, or of seeing, or of (wandering of) the heart will be questioned (on the Day of Judgment).

17.37. And do not walk on the earth with (injustice and) deceit, arrogance (and rudeness): Verily, you can not rip the earth apart, and cannot reach the mountains in height.

17.38. Of all such things, (it is) evil that is hateful in the sight of your Lord,

17.39. These are among the (words of) wisdom, which your Lord has revealed to you. And do not take, with Allah, another god for worship, lest, you (too) will be thrown into Hell, worthy of blame and rejected (from Allah's Mercy).

17.40.. Then has your Lord, (O disbelievers!) given you sons, and taken for

Himself daughters from the Angels: Indeed! You say a most terrible thing!

17.41.. And surely, We have made clear in many (ways) in this Quran, so that they may be warned and guided, but it only makes them go away (from the Truth)!

17.42. Say (to the disbelievers): If there were (other) gods with Him- As they (the disbelievers) say- Then they would certainly have searched a way to the Lord of the Throne!

17.43. Glory be to Him! He is high above the things they say! Supreme and Great (beyond every measure)!

17.44. The seven heavens and the earth, and all beings in there, speak His Glory: There is not a thing which does not celebrates His Praise; And yet you do not understand how they declare His Glory! Surely, He is Often-Forbearing, Most Forgiving!

17.45.. And when you recite the Quran, We put between you and those who do not believe in the Hereafter, an invisible shade:

17.46. And We put coverings over their hearts (and minds) that they may (even) understand the Quran, and (We put) deafness into their ears: When you say the Praise of your Lord (and Him) Alone, in the Quran; They turn their backs, running away (from Truth).

17.47. We know very well why is it that they listen, when they listen to you; And when they meet in private conference, then the wrongdoers say, "You follow no one except a man bewitched [under a (magical) spell]!"

17.48. See what comparisons they make for you: So they have gone astray, and they can never find a way (to come back).

17.49.. And they say: "What! When we are reduced to bones and torn apart (destroyed as dust), will we really be raised up as a new creation?"

17.50. Say: "You be stones or iron,

17.51. "Or (be any) created matter which to you, is greater (and harder) in your hearts (to be raised up- Still you shall be raised up)!" Then they will (still) say: "Who will cause us to come back (alive)?" Say: "He, Who created you first!" Then they will shake their heads towards you and say, "When will that be?" Say, "May be, it is near!

17.52. "It will be on a Day when He will call you, and you will answer (to His call) with His Praise and servitude, and you will (only) think that you delayed only for a short while!"

17.53. And say to My servants that they should (only) say those words that are best: Verily, Satan brings in disagreements and disharmony between them: Surely, Satan is to man an open enemy.

17.54. It is your Lord Who knows you best: If He pleases, He grants you (His) Mercy, or if He pleases, (His) Punishment: We have not sent you as a guardian of their affairs for them.

17.55. And it is your Lord Who knows best all beings that are in the heavens and on earth: And indeed, We have preferred some prophets over others: And to Dawood (David), We gave the Psalms (*Zabur*),

17.56.. Say: "Call on those, besides Him- Whomsoever you may pretend: They have neither the power to remove the pain from you nor to change it to another person."

17.57. Those whom they call upon want a way to reach their Lord- Even those who are nearest: Hope for His Mercy, and fear His Anger: Because the Anger of your Lord is something to regard.

17.58.. There is not a community that We shall not destroy it before the Day of Judgment or punish it with a terrible penalty: That was indeed written in the (eternal) Record.

17.59. And nothing could stop Us from sending the Signs, except that the men of earlier generations denied them as false: And We sent the she-camel to the Samood (Thamud) to open their eyes (to the truth), but they treated her wrongfully: And We only send the Signs to bring fear in (them and to keep them away from evil).

17.60. And (remember) when We told you that your Lord surrounds mankind around: And We gave the Vision which We showed you, only as a trial for men- As also the cursed tree in the Quran: (Mentioned as *Zaqqum* in verses 37.62-65; 44.43-46; And 55.52.) We put fear (and warning) into them, but it only increases their excessive evil in nothing but their vast disbelief, injustices and disobedience!

17.61.. And (remember) when We said to the angels: "Bow down (prostrate yourselves) to Adam": They bowed down except *Iblis* (Satan): He said, "Shall I bow down to one whom You created (only) from clay?"

17.62. He (*Iblis*) said, "Do You see? This is one whom you have honored above me! If You will only grant me relief till the Day of Judgment, I will surely take his children under my control- And mislead them- All, except a few!"

17.63. (Allah) said: "Go your way; If any of them follow you, surely! Hell will be the repayment for you (all)- And enough (it is) for a repayment.

17.64. "Lead to destruction those whom you can among them, gradually, with your seductive voice (of evil); Make attacks on them with your horsemen and soldiers; Together with them share wealth and children; And make (false) promises to them." But Satan promises them nothing but lies.

17.65. "Verily! About My (loyal and true) servants, you will not have authority over them:" And your Lord is All Sufficient as a Guardian of affairs.

17.66.. Your Lord is He Who makes the ship go smoothly for you through the sea, so that you may seek from His Bounty. Truly, He is Most Merciful to you.

17.67. And when suffering (or distress) gets you at sea, those that you call upon- other than Himself- Leave you in a difficult position! But when He safely brings you back to land, you turn away (from Him). And man is most ungrateful!

17.68. Do you then feel secure that He will not cause a side of the land to swallow you (even when you are on land), or that He will not send a strong storm against you (with shower of stones) so that you will have no one as a guardian for you?

17.69. Or do you feel secure that He will not send you back to sea a second time and send against you a heavy gale to drown you because of your disbelief, then you find no helper against Us in there?

17.70. And indeed, We have honored the children of Adam; And We have provided them with transport on land and sea; And We have provided them with good and pure things for livelihood; And given them Special favors, over and above a great part of Our Creation.

17.71.. The day when We shall call all human beings together with their (leaders) Imams: (With the Books of their scriptures and their own deeds:)

Those who are given their record in their right hand will read it (with joy) and they will not be treated unjustly in the least.

17.72. And those whoever was blind (to the Signs of Allah) in this world, will also be blind in the Hereafter, and most astray from the Path.

17.73.. Verily, their purpose was to tempt you away from what We had revealed to you, (and) to replace in it (the Quran) something quite different against Us: And then, they would certainly have made you a close friend!

17.74.. And if We had not given you strength, you would have certainly listened to them a little.

17.75. If that was so, We would have made you taste twice the part (of punishment) in this life, and twice the part after the death; And in addition, you would have found no one to help you against Us!

17.76. And verily, their purpose was to frighten you so much as to drive you away from the Land; But in that case, they would not have stayed (therein) after you, except for a short time.

17.77. (This was our Sunnah or the) way with the messengers whom We had sent before you: And you will not find any change in Our ways.

17.78.. Establish regular prayers— from the middle of the day, till the darkness of the night, and recite the Quran in the early dawn: Surely, the reading (and *Faj'r* prayer) of the early dawn is witnessed (by special angels).

17.79. And pray during a part of the night (in the small hours of the morning): An additional prayer (or spiritual value) for you: Your Lord will raise you soon, to a place of honor and glory!

17.80. Say: "O my Lord! Let my entry be by the Gate of Truth and Honor, and also (make) my exit by the Gate of Truth and Honor; And grant me from Your Presence an authority to help (me)."

17.81. And say: "Truth has (now) come through and lies are dead: Surely, lies (by their nature) are bound to die."

17.82. And of the Quran, We send down what is a healing and a mercy to those who believe: And to those who are not just, it causes nothing but loss (and grief).

17.83.. And when We grant Our gifts to man, he turns away and becomes far on his (own) side (instead of turning to Us), and when evil touches him, he gives himself up to sorrow!

17.84. Say: "Everyone does (things) depending on his own tendencies: And your Lord knows best who it is that is most guided on the Way."

17.85.. And they ask you about the Spirit; Say: "The Spirit (comes) by the command of my Lord: Of the knowledge, it is only a little that is made known to you,"

17.86. And if it was Our Will, We could take away that which We have sent to you by revelation: Then you will not find anyone to plead your affairs in that matter as against Us-

17.87. Except as a Mercy from your Lord: Verily, His Bounty to you is great.

17.88. Say: "If the entire mankind and jinns' were to get together to produce (something) like this Quran, they could not produce (anything) like it, even if they tried altogether with help and support."

17.89. And in this Quran, We have explained to man, every kind of similitude yet the larger part of them refuse (to be guided) even a little and that with thanklessness!

17.90. And they say: "We shall not believe in you, unless you make a spring (of water) to come up for us from the earth.

17.91. "Or (unless) you have a garden of date-palm (trees), and grape-vines, and make rivers to come up in their midst carrying plenty of water;

17.92. "Or you make the sky to fall in pieces, as you say (it will happen), against us; Or you bring Allah and the angels before (us), face to face;

17.93. "Or you have a house decorated with gold, or you climb a ladder right into the skies; No, we shall not even believe in your ascent unless you send down to us a book that we can read." Say: "Glory be to my Lord! Am I anyone except only a man- A messenger (of Allah)?"

17.94. What kept men away from belief when Guidance came to them, was nothing but this: They said, "Has Allah sent (only) a man to be (His) messenger?"

17.95. Say; "If on the earth, there were placed, angels walking about in peace and (quiet) security, We should certainly have sent them down from the heavens an angel as a messenger."

17.96. Say: "Allah is enough for a witness between me and you: Verily, He is the totally-Informed, the All Seer (Well Acquainted, seeing all things).

17.97.. And he whom Allah guides, he is on true guidance; And he whom He leaves astray- For those you will find no protector besides Him. And on the Day of Judgment, We shall bring them together lying on their faces, blind, dumb, and deaf: Their home will be Hell: Every time it reduces, We shall increase for them the intensity of the Fire.

17.98. That is their recompense (and repayment), because they rejected Our Signs, and said, "When we are reduced to bones and tiny fragments, should we really be raised up (as) a new Creation?"

17.99. Do they not see that Allah, Who created the heavens and the earth, has power to create (others) like them (again)? And only He has ordered a set time; Of this, there is no doubt. But the unjust refuse (to accept) even a little and that with thanklessness!

17.100. Say: "If you had control of the Treasures of the Mercy of my Lord, then you would keep them back, in the fear of spending them: Because man is (always) stingy!"

17.101.. And to Musa (Moses) We did give nine clear Signs (See Note 28.4): Ask the Children of Israel: When he came to them, Firon (Pharaoh) said to him: "O Musa (Moses)! I consider you truly, to have been worked upon by magic!"

17.102. [Musa (Moses)] said: "Verily, you know well that these things have been sent down by no one but the Lord of the heavens and the earth as eye-opening evidence: And I consider you truly, O Firon (Pharaoh), to be one ill-fated to destruction!"

17.103. So he (Firon) decided to remove them from the face of the earth: But We did drown him and all who were with him.

17.104. And after him, We said to the Children of Israel, "Live safely in the land (of promise)": Then as the second of the warnings comes true, (the birth of Messiah, the Christ or the Day of Judgment) We will gather you together in a mingled crowd (of many peoples and nations).

17.105.. And We sent down the (Quran) in Truth and in Truth, it has come down: And We sent you (O Prophet!) only to give the Happy News (to the believer) and to warn (sinners).

17.106. And (it is) a Quran that We have divided (into parts from time to time), so that you may recite it to men at intervals: We have revealed it (to you) by stages.

17.107. Say: "Whether you believe in it (the Quran) or do not believe (in it), verily, it is true that those who were given (its) knowledge earlier, when it is recited to them, fall down on their faces in respectful prostration,

17.108. "And they say: 'Glory to our Lord! Truly the Promise of our Lord has been fulfilled!' "

17.109. They fall down on their faces with tears, and it increases their (truly heartfelt) humility.

{A Muslim generally prostrates to Allah after reciting this verse}

17.110. Say: "Call upon Allah, or call upon the Most Gracious: By whatever Name you call upon Him, (that is fine) because the Most Beautiful Names belong to Him. Offer the prayers, neither speak the words aloud, nor speak them in a low voice, but seek a middle path between."

17.111. Say: "All Praises (and thanks) be to Allah, Who has no son, and has no partner in (His) kingdom: Nor does He (need) anyone to protect from humiliation: And magnify Him for His Greatness and Glory!"

****

Sura 18. Al-Kahf,
(The cave): (Makkah, 110 Verses)
In the Name of Allah, the Most Gracious, the Most Merciful.

18.1.. All Praises (and thanks) are due to Allah, Who has sent down to His Servant (the Prophet) the Book (the Quran), and has permitted no unevenness (or crookedness) in it:

18.2. (He has made it) Straight (and Clear) so that He may warn (the disbelievers) of the terrible punishment from Him, and that He may give the good news to the believers who do righteous deeds, that they will have a (very) suitable reward,

18.3. Where they will remain (in joy) forever:

18.4. Also, that He may warn those who say, "Allah has begotten (fathered) a son (or a child):"

18.5. They have no knowledge of such a thing, nor did their fathers. It is a serious (and painful) thing that comes from their mouths as a saying. What they say is nothing but lies!

18.6.. Perhaps you will only sadden yourself to death, in case (you are) following after them, in grief, if they do not believe in this Message.

18.7. Verily, whatever is on earth, We have made it only as a shining show for the earth. So that We may test them- As to which (ones) of them are best in conduct.

18.8. And surely, whatever is on earth We shall reduce it only to dust and dried soil.

18.9.. Do you think that the companions of the Cave (located near the town of *Aylah*, see Sura Notes 2.5) and of the Writings (on a stone Tablet Sura Notes 2.4) were wonders among Our Signs?

18.10. When the young men took themselves (in hiding) to the Cave: They said, "Our Lord! Grant upon us mercy from Yourself, and take care of things (in our lives) for us in the right way!"

18.11. Therefore We drew (a veil) over their ears, for a number of years, in the Cave, (so that they did not hear):

18.12. Then We woke them, so as to test which of the two groups was better at calculating the number of years they had slept away!

18.13.. We let you know their story in (all) truth: Truly, they were youths who believed in their Lord, and We forwarded them in guidance:

18.14. And We affirmed (the courage in) their hearts: And they stood up and said: "Our Lord is the Lord of the heavens and of the earth: We shall never call upon any god other than Him: If we did, we would have truly said extreme wickedness!

18.15. "These (people,) our people, they have taken gods other than Him for worship: Why do they not show an authority which is clear (and convincing) for what they do? And who do more wrong than those who invent a lie against Allah?

18.16. "And when you turn away from them (the people) and the things they worship other than Allah; Come up yourselves to the Cave: Your Lord will bless His mercy on you and take care of things (in your lives) towards comfort and ease."

18.17. And you would have seen the sun, when it rose, down below to the right (side) from their Cave, and when it set, turning away from them to the left while they lay in the open space in the middle of the Cave (thus keeping them cool). These are from the Signs of Allah: He whom Allah guides is rightly guided; But he whom Allah leaves to wander (aimlessly)- For him will you find no protector (to lead him to the Right Way).

18.18.. And you would have thought they were awake, while they were (actually) sleeping, and We turned them on their right and on their left sides: And their dog spreading out his two front legs at the entrance: If you had (just accidentally) found them, you would have truly turned back from them to run away (in flight), and (you) would truly have been filled with fear of them.

18.19. ☼ Such (being their condition), We woke them up (from their sleep), that they may question each other. One of them said, "How long have you stayed (here)?" They said, "We (might) have stayed a day, or part of a day." (At the end), they (all) said, "Allah (alone) knows best how long you have stayed here... Now then you send one of you with this silver coin of yours to the town: And let him find out which is the best food (to eat) and bring some of that (food) to you, so that (you may) satisfy your hunger with it: And let him act with care and courtesy, and let him not inform anyone about you.

[☼ -Most scholars affirm that the middle of the Quran is in this *Ayâh.*]

18.20. "Because if they should find you, they would stone you to death (for believing in your Lord) and force you to return to their (ways of) worship; And then you will never gain prosperity."

18.21.. Thus We made their story known to the people, that they might know that the Promise of Allah is true, and that there may be no doubt about the Hour of Judgment. (Remember) they argued within about their affair. (Some) said, "Construct a building over them:" Their Lord knows best about them: Then those who were in control over their affair said,

"Surely, let us build a place of worship over them."

18.22. (Some) say they were three (youths), the dog being the fourth among them; And (others) say they were five, the dog being the sixth- Doubtfully guessing the unknown; And (yet others) say they were seven, the dog being the eighth. (O Prophet!) You say (to them): "My Lord knows best their number; It is only a few who know their (real number)." Therefore, do not enter into disputes about them, except about a matter that is clear, nor speak to any of them about (the affair of) the people of the Cave.

18.23.. And do not say about anything, "I shall surely do this and this tomorrow"-

18.24. Without (also saying), "(*Insha-Allah,*) if Allah so wills!" And call your Lord to mind when you forget, and say, "I hope that my Lord will guide me ever closer (even) than this to the right road."

18.25.. And they (the Sleepers) stayed in their Cave three hundred years, adding nine (more).

18.26. (O Prophet!) say: "Allah knows best how long they stayed: With Him is (the knowledge of) the secrets of the heavens and of the earth: How clearly He sees, how finely He hears! They have no protector other than Him; And He does not share His command and His rule with anyone (whomsoever)."

18.27.. And recite (and teach) what has been revealed to you (O Prophet,) from the Book of your Lord: None can change His Words, and you will find none as a protector except Him.

18.28. And keep your soul (O Prophet,) restful with those who call on (pray to) their Lord morning and afternoon, looking for His face; And do not let your eyes go beyond them, looking for the show and shine of this life; And do not listen to any whose heart We have permitted to neglect the remembrance of Us, and one who follows his own wishes, whose case has gone beyond all bounds.

18.29.. And say: "The Truth is from your Lord:" Then let him who will, believe (in it), and let him who will, reject (it): Verily, for the wrongdoers We have prepared a Fire whose (smoke and flames), like the walls and roof of a tent, will close them in: And if they beg for relief they will be given water like molten brass, that will burn their faces. How dreadful is the drink! And how uncomfortable a couch to lie on!

18.30. Surely, for those who believe and work righteousness, certainly, We shall not let the reward die for any who do (even) a (single) righteous deed.

18.31. (For) these! For them will be the Gardens of Eternity; Under which rivers will flow therein: They will be beautified in there with bracelets of gold, and they will wear green clothes of fine silk and heavily decorated cloth; They will lie in there on raised thrones. How good the reward and repayment! How beautiful a couch to lie on!

18.32.. And present to them the example of two men: For one of them We gave two gardens of grape-vines and surrounded them with palm trees; In between the two We placed corn-fields.

18.33. Each of the gardens grew its crops, and did not fail even a little in it (the crops) in the middle of them We caused a river to flow.

18.34. The crops were (large enough) that this man had: He said to his companion (the other man), during a mutual argument: "I am more in wealth and sons (men to follow) than you,"

18.35. He went into his garden in a state (of mind) unfair to his soul: He said, "I do not think that this (garden) will ever wither away,

18.36. "And I do not think that the Hour (of Judgment) will (ever) come: Even if I am brought back to my Lord, I shall surely find (there) something better in exchange than this (what I have)."

18.37. His companion said to him, during the argument with him: "Do you reject Him Who created you from dust, then out of a sperm-drop, then made you into a man?

18.38. "But on for my part, (I believe) that He is Allah, my Lord, and I shall not associate (anyone or anything as a 'partner') with my Lord.

18.39. "It was better for you to say, as you went into your garden: 'Allah's Will (will be done)! There is no power except with Allah!' If you do see me less than you in wealth and sons,

18.40. "It may be that my Lord will give me something better than your garden, and that He will send thunderbolts onto your garden from the sky, (by the way of warning) from heaven, making it slippery sand!

18.41. "Or the water of the garden will run off underground so that you will never be able to find it."

18.42. So his fruit (and joy) were surrounded (by ruin) and he remained twisting and turning his hands over what he had spent for his property, which had (now) fallen to pieces to its very foundations, and he could only say, "Shame upon me! If I had never given partners to my Lord and Cherisher!"

18.43. And he did not have number (of his men) to help him against Allah, and he was not able to save himself.

18.44. There, the (only) protection comes from Allah, the True One. He is the Best to reward, and the Best to give success.

18.45. Present to them the similitude of the life of this world: It is like the rain which We send down from the sky: And the earth's vegetation absorbs it, but soon it becomes fresh and green (but) later it becomes dry and short sticks, which the winds spread about: And it is (only) Allah, Who has the Power and Ability to do all things.

18.46. Wealth and sons are (only) desires and temptations in the life of this world: But the things that last, good deeds with your Lord, are the best as (the basis for all) reward and hopes.

18.47. And (remember), the Day We shall remove the mountains, and you will see the earth as a level field, and We shall gather them, all together, and We shall not leave out even one of them.

18.48. And they will be brought up before your Lord in ranks (Allah will say): "Now you have come to Us as We had created you the first time: Yes, you thought We shall not fulfill the appointment made for you to meet (Us)!"

18.49. And the Book (of deeds) will be placed (before you); And you will see the criminals in great fear because of what is (written) in there; They will say, "Woe (sorrow) to us! What a book this is! It does not leave out anything small or big, but takes account of it (in there)!" And they will find all that they did, present and placed (in writing) before them: And your Lord will not treat even one with injustice.

18.50.. And (remember) when We said to the angels: "Bow down to

Adam:" So they (all) bowed except *Iblis* (Satan). He was one of the (chief) jinns', and he (willfully) disobeyed the command of his Lord. Will you then take him and his progeny (and his klan) as (your) protectors rather than Me? While they (the klan of *Iblis*) are enemies to you! Evil will be the exchange for the evildoers!

18.51. I did not call them to see the creation of the heavens and the earth, nor (even) their own creation: And it is not for Me to take as helpers those who lead (men) astray!

18.52. And (remember) the Day, when He will say, "Call on those whom you thought to be My 'partners', " and (when) they will call on them, but they will not listen, and We shall make for them a (common) place of endless sorrow.

18.53. And the criminals shall see the Fire and know that they have to fall in there: And they will not find any way to turn away from it.

18.54.. And indeed, We have explained in detail in this Quran, for the benefit of mankind, every kind of similarity: But in most things, man is opposing.

18.55. And what is there to keep back men from believing, now that (Allah's) Guidance has come to them, and from praying for forgiveness from their Lord, except that (they like) the ways of the old be repeated with them, or the punishment (of Allah) be brought to them face to face?

18.56. And We only send the messengers to give good news, and to give warnings: But the disbelievers dispute with useless argument, so as to weaken the truth with it, and treat My Signs as a joke, as also the fact that they are warned!

18.57. And who does more wrong than one who is reminded of the Signs of his Lord, but turns away from them, forgetting the (actions) that his hands have sent forth? Surely, We have put veils over their hearts in case they should understand this, and over their ears, deafness. If you call them to guidance, even then they will never accept guidance.

18.58. And your Lord is Most Forgiving, Owner of Mercy. If He were to call them (now) to account for what they have earned, then surely, He would have hastened their punishment: But they have their fixed time, after which they will have no place to hide.

18.59. And such were the peoples, We destroyed when they committed injustices; But We fixed a definite time for their destruction.

18.60.. And (remember) when Musa (Moses) said to his servant-boy: "I will not stop until I reach the Junction of the two seas or (until) I spend years and years in travel."

18.61. But when they reached the Junction of two seas, they forgot their Fish, which made its way through the sea (straight) as if (it was) in a tunnel.

18.62. When they had traveled (some more), he (Musa, Moses) said to his attendant: "Bring us our early meal; Truly, we have suffered much fatigue at this (time in) our journey."

18.63. He replied: "Do you remember (what happened) when we took ourselves to the rock? Truly, I did forget the fish: None but Satan made me forget to tell (you) about it: It made its way through the sea in a marvelous way!"

18.64. [Musa (Moses)] said: "That was what we were searching for:" So they went back on their (own) footsteps, following (the way that they had come).

18.65.. Then they found one (of the wise men) on whom We had bestowed Mercy from Ourselves and whom We had given knowledge from Our Own Presence.

18.66. Musa (Moses) said to him (the wise man, Khidr): "May I follow you, with the intention that you may teach me something of the (greater) Truth which you have been taught (by Allah)?"

18.67. (The wise one) said: "Surely, you will not be able to have patience with me!

18.68. "And how can you have patience about things about which your understanding is not complete?"

18.69. [Musa (Moses)] said: "You will find me (really) patient: If Allah so wishes, and I will not disobey you even a little."

18.70. The other said: "If then you were to follow me, do not ask me any questions about anything until I, myself speak to you about it."

18.71.. So they both proceeded on: Until, when they boarded in the boat, (and) he (Khidr) damaged it.; [Musa (Moses)] said: "Have you damaged it in order to drown those in it? Truly a strange thing have you done!"

18.72. He (Khidr) answered: "Did I not tell you that you will not be able to have patience with me?"

18.73. [Musa (Moses)] said: "Do not be angry with me for forgetting, nor make me sad by causing difficulties on my part."

18.74.. Then they proceeded further: Until, when they met a boy, he (Khidr) killed him. Musa (Moses) said: "Have you killed an innocent person who has killed no one? Truly a wicked thing have you done!"

18.75. He answered: "Did I not tell you that you can have no patience with me?"

18.76. He (Musa) said: "If ever I ask you about anything after this, do not keep me in your company: Then you would have received (full) reason from my side."

18.77.. Then they proceeded further: Until, when they came to the people of a town, they asked them for food, but they refused to have them as guests. Then they found there a wall almost falling down, but he put it up straight. (Musa) said: "If you wanted, surely you could have asked for some repayment (wages) for it!"

18.78. (Khidr) answered: "This is the separation between me and you: Now I tell you the meanings of (those things) over which you were not able to have patience.

18.79.. "As for the boat, it belonged to certain men who were in great need: They used (it) for working the sea: I only wished to make it useless (temporarily), because, after them was a certain king who took over (seized) every boat by force.

18.80. "As for the boy, his parents were believers, and we feared that he would dishearten (and offend) them by (bitter and) prolonged revolt and by disbelief (to Allah).

18.81. "So we wanted that their Lord would give them in exchange (a son) with more purity (of actions) and closer (to them) in (his) affection.

18.82. "And as for the wall, it belonged to two youths, orphans in the Town;

Beneath it, there is a buried treasure, to which they were entitled; Their father had been a righteous man: So your Lord wanted that they should reach their age of full strength and (then) get out their treasure- As a mercy (and gift) from your Lord. And I did not do it of my own accord. This is the meaning of (the things) over which you were not able to hold patience."

18.83. (O Prophet!) They ask you about Zul-Qarnain. Say, "I will recite to you some of his story."

18.84. Surely, We established his power on earth, and We gave him the ability to do everything.

18.85.. One (such) way he followed (to do),

18.86. Until, when he reached the setting place of the sun, he found it set in a pool of murky water: And near it he found a people: We said: "O Zul-Qarnain! You either punish them or treat them with kindness."

18.87. He said: "As to whoever does wrong, (only) him shall we punish; And then he shall be sent back to his Lord; And He will punish him (the wrong-doer) with severe punishment.

18.88. "But as to whoever believes, and work righteousness- He shall have a good reward, and his task we (Zul-Qarnain) order will be easy by our command."

18.89.. Then he followed (another) way,

18.90. Until, when he came to the rising of the sun, he found it rising on a people for whom We (Allah) had provided no protection against the sun.

18.91. (He left them) as they were, (and) We completely understood what was before him.

18.92.. Then he followed (yet another) way,

18.93. Until, when he reached (a valley) between two mountains, he found, beneath them, a (primitive) people who did not understand a word.

18.94. They said: "O Zul-Qarnain! Verily, the *Yajuj* and *Majuj* (Gog and Magog) do great mischief on the earth: Shall we pay you the tribute and honor if you may build a wall between us and them?"

18.95. He said: "(The power) that my Lord has placed in me is better (than honor): So help me with strength (and work): I will build a strong wall between you and them:

18.96. "Bring me blocks of iron;" At length, when he had filled the space between the two steep mountain-sides, he said, "Blow (with your bellows into the fire.)" Then, when he had made them (red) as fire; He said: "Bring me the molten lead, that I may pour over them."

18.97. Thus they (*Yajuj* and *Majuj*) were made helpless to climb it (the wall) or to dig through it.

18.98. He said: "This is a mercy from my Lord: But when the promise of my Lord comes to pass, He will bring it (the wall) into dust on the ground; And the Promise of my Lord is true."

18.99.. And on that Day, We shall leave them (*Yajuj* and *Majuj*) to climb like waves one upon another: And the Trumpet will be blown, and We shall bring them (the creatures) all together.

18.100. And on that Day We shall give Hell for disbelievers to see, all spread out (for them)-

18.101. (To the disbelievers) whose eyes were under a cover from remembering Me, and who had been unable even to hear (the divine call).

18.102.. Do the disbelievers then think that they can take My servants as protectors besides Me? Surely, We have prepared Hell for the disbelievers for (their) entertainment.

18.103. Say: "Shall We tell you of the greatest losers because of their deeds?

18.104. "Those whose actions were wasted in this life, while they thought that they were acquiring good by their works?"

18.105. They are those who reject the Signs of their Lord and the fact of their having to meet Him (in the Hereafter): Useless will be their works, nor shall We, on the Day of Judgment, give them any consideration.

18.106. That is their reward, Hell; Because they rejected Faith, and took My Signs and My messengers as a joke.

18.107.. Verily as to those who believe and do righteous deeds, they have, for their pleasure, the Gardens of Paradise,

18.108. Where they shall live (for ever): They will wish for no change from them.

18.109. Say: "If the ocean were ink (to write with), the words of (Praise for) my Lord, sooner would the ocean be dry than would the words of my Lord would be finished, even if We added another ocean like it, for its help."

18.110. Say: "I am only a man like yourselves, (but) the revelation has come to me that, your God is the One God (Allah): So whoever expects to meet his Lord, let him work righteousness, and associate not in the worship of his Lord, anyone as a 'partner'."

****

Sura 19. Maryam,
(Mary): (Makkah, 98 Verses)
In the Name of Allah, the Most Gracious, the Most Merciful.

19.1. Káf Há Yá A'in Sád:

19.2. (This is) a statement of Mercy from your Lord to His servant Zakariyya (Zachariah).

19.3. When he cried to his Lord in secret,

19.4. (And he) prayed: "My Lord! Indeed my bones are weak, and the hair of my head shine with gray: But never am I not blessed (by You), O my Lord, in my prayer to You!

19.5. "And surely, I am afraid (what) my family (and friends) will do after me: But my wife is barren. So give me an heir as if from Yourself-

19.6. "(Someone) who will inherit (and stand) for me, and stand for the children of Yàqoub (Jacob); And, my Lord! Make him one with whom You are well pleased!"

19.7. (Zakariyya's prayers were answered, and Allah said): "O Zakariyya (Zachariah)! Verily, We (Allah) give you the good news of a son: Whose name shall be Yahya (John): On no one by that name have We given (so much) honor before."

19.8. He (Zakariyya) said: "O my Lord! How shall I have a son, when my wife is barren and I have become quite weak from old age?"

19.9. He (Allah's angel who brought the message) said: "(It will still be) so: Your Lord says, 'That is easy for Me: Certainly, I did really create you before when you were nothing!' "

19.10. (Zakariyya) said: "O my Lord! Give me a Sign." The answer was, "Your Sign shall be that you shall not speak to mankind for three nights, even though you are not dumb."

19.11. Then he [Zakariyya (Zachariah)] came out from his chamber to his people: He told them by Signs to recite Allah's praises in the morning and in the afternoon.

19.12.. (To his son came Allah's command), "O Yahya (John)! Hold on to the Book with strength": And even as (he was) a youth, We gave him Wisdom,

19.13. And pity (for all creatures) as from Us, and purity: He was truly pious,

19.14. And kind to his parents, and he was not overbearing nor rebellious.

19.15. And Peace on him, the day he was born, the day he dies, and the day he will be raised (again) to life!

19.16.. In the Book (Quran), tell (the story of) Maryam (Mary), when she went away from her family (for Prayer) to a place in the East (her chamber).

19.17. She placed a screen (to hide herself) from them; Then We sent to her Our angel, and he appeared before her in the form of a man of respect in every way.

19.18. She said: "Verily, I ask for shelter from you with (Allah) Most Gracious: (Do not come near me) if you guard (yourself) against evil."

19.19. He said: "I am a messenger from your Lord, (only to announce to) you, the gift of a righteous son:

19.20. She said: "How shall I have a son, when no man has touched me, and I am not immodest (or indecent)?"

19.21. He said: "(It will still be) so: Your Lord says: 'That is easy for Me: And (We wish) to appoint him as a Sign to men and a Mercy from Us': It is a matter (already) ordered."

19.22. So she started to carry him (baby Jesus in her womb), and she went (to rest) with him to a far place.

19.23. And the pains of childbirth took her to the trunk of a palm-tree: She cried (in her pain): "Oh! If I had died before this! If I was a thing forgotten and not (even) seen!"

19.24. Then (a voice) cried to her from under (the tree): "Do not feel sad! Because your Lord has made (for you) a stream underneath you;

19.25. "And shake towards yourself the trunk of the palm-tree: It will drop fresh ripe dates (fruits) upon you.

19.26. "So eat and drink and cool (wet your) eye. And if you see any man, say, 'I have promised solemnly to (Allah) the Most Gracious, and this day, I will not enter into talk with any human being.' "

19.27.. At the end she brought the (baby) to her people, carrying him (baby Jesus in her arms). They said: "O Maryam (Mary)! Truly an amazing thing have you brought!

19.28. "O sister of Haroon (Aaron)! Your father was not an evil (adulterous) man, and your mother was not an immoral woman!"

19.29. Then, she pointed to the baby (Jesus). They said: "How can we talk to one who is (only) a child in the cradle?"

19.30. He [the baby Isa (Jesus)] said: "Indeed I am a servant of Allah: He has given me the Scripture [*Injeel* (Gospel)] and made me a prophet;

19.31. "And He (Allah) has made me blessed where ever I be, and has commanded for me prayer and charity as long as I live;

19.32. "[He (Allah)] has made me kind to my mother, and not arrogant or miserable;

19.33. "And Peace is on me the day I was born, the day I die, and the day I will be raised (again) to life!"

19.34.. Isa (Jesus), the son of Maryam (Mary) was like this: (It is) a statement of truth, about which they dispute (without any use).

19.35. It is not suited for (Almighty) Allah that He should father a son. Glory to Him (Allah)! When He determines anything, He only says to it, "Be", and it is.

19.36. [Isa, (Jesus) said:] "And surely Allah is my Lord and your Lord: Him (Alone,) you therefore worship (and serve): This is the Straight Path."

19.37. Then, the groups differed among themselves: so (this is a) warning to the disbelievers because of the Judgment on a great Day!

19.38. How plainly will they see and hear, the Day that they will appear before Us! But today, the unjust are clearly in error!

19.39. But warn them of the Day of regrets and sorrow, when the matter will be determined: For they are negligent and they do not believe!

19.40. Verily, It is We Who will take back the earth, and all living things upon it: And they will all be returned to Us.

19.41.. And in the Book (Quran); Tell (the story of) Ibrahim (Abraham), he was a man of truth (and) a prophet.

19.42. When he said to his father: "O my father! Why worship (something) that does not hear and does not see, and (something that) can be of no profit to you?

19.43. "O my father! Verily, knowledge has come to me which has not come to you: So follow me: I will guide you to a Path that is Even (and Straight).

19.44. "O my father! Do not serve Satan: Surely, Satan is a rebel against (Allah,) the Most Gracious.

19.45. "O my father! Surely, I fear that a penalty fall on you from (Allah) Most Gracious, so that you will become a friend of Satan."

19.46. (The father) replied: "Do you hate my gods, O Ibrahim (Abraham)? If you do not stop, I will really stone you: Now get away from me for a good long time!"

19.47. Ibrahim (Abraham) said: "Peace be on you: I will pray to my Lord for your forgiveness: Verily, He is affectionate towards me.

19.48. "And I will go away from (all of) you and from those whom you call upon besides Allah: And I will call on my Lord: Perhaps, by my prayer to my Lord, I shall be not condemned."

19.49. When he had gone away from them and from those whom they worshipped besides Allah, We bestowed on him Isháq (Isaac) and Yàqoub (Jacob), and each one of them We made a prophet.

19.50. And We blessed them from Our Mercy, and We granted them high honor on the tongue (of truth with praise).

19.51.. And in the Book (Quran), tell (the story of) Musa (Moses), verily, he was specially chosen, and he was a messenger, a prophet.

19.52. And We called him from the right side of Mount (Sinai) and made him come near to Us, for sacred (and holy conversation).

19.53. And from Our Mercy, We gave him his brother Haroon (Aaron), (also) a prophet.

19.54.. And in the Book (Quran), tell (the story of) Ismail (Ishmael), verily he was true to his promise, and he was a messenger, a prophet.

19.55. And he used to bring together his people with prayer (*As-Salat*) and charity (*Zakat*), and he was welcome in the Sight of his Lord.

19.56.. And in the Book (Quran), tell (the story of) Idris, verily, he was a man of truth, (sincerity and) a prophet:

19.57. And We raised him to a high position.

19.58.. Those were some of the prophets on whom Allah blessed His Grace- From the followers of Adam and from those whom We took (in the Ark) with Nuh (Noah), and from the followers of Ibrahim (Abraham) and Israel (Yàqoub or Jacob)- From those whom We guided and chose. When the Signs of (Allah) Most Gracious were told to them, they would fall down face down in prostration (love and worship) and in tears.

{**A Muslim generally prostrates to Allah after reciting this verse**}

19.59. But after them there came descendents who missed prayers and went after (their) desires soon, then, will they come to (their) destruction-

19.60. Except those who repent and believe, and work righteousness: For these will enter the Garden and will not be wronged in the least-

19.61. Gardens of Eternity, those that (Allah) Most Gracious has promised to His servants in the Unseen: Verily, His promise must (always) come true.

19.62. They will not hear within it any useless talk, except only words of Peace: And in there they will have their sustenance, morning and afternoon.

19.63. Like this is the Garden that We give as an inheritance to those of Our servants who keep away from evil.

19.64.. (The angels say:) "We do not come down except by command of your Lord: To Him belongs what is before us and what is behind us, and what is between: And your Lord is never forgetful-

19.65. "Lord of the heavens and the earth, and (Lord) of all that is between them: So worship Him, and be regular and patient in His worship: Do you know of anyone who is similar to Him- (Worthy of the same Name as He)?

19.66. And man says: "What! When I am dead, then shall I be raised up alive?"

19.67. But does not man remember that We created him even while he was nothing?

19.68. So, by your Lord, without doubt, We shall bring them together, and (also) the Evil ones (Satans', with them), then shall We bring them forward on their knees around Hell;

19.69. Then indeed, We shall pull out from every sect all those who were worst in strongest rebellion against (Allah) the Most Gracious.

19.70. Then certainly, We know well those who are most worthy of being burned in there.

19.71. And (there is) not one of you who will not go over it (Fire): That is a Decree with your Lord, which must be completed.

19.72. Then We shall save those who kept away from evil, and We shall leave the wrongdoers in there, (pulled down) on their knees.

19.73.. And when Our Clear Signs are read to them, the disbelievers say to those who believe, "Which of the two sides is better in position? Which makes the better show in public?"

19.74. And how many (countless) generations have We destroyed before them, (those) who were even better in wealth and (looked) brighter to the eye?

19.75. Say: "If any men go towards wrong, (Allah) Most Gracious extends (the rope) to them, until, when they see the warning of Allah (being completed) - either as punishment or as (the coming of) the (final) Hour- At the end, they will see who is worse in position, and (who is) weaker in forces!

19.76. "And Allah advances in guidance those who search for Guidance: And the things that last, good deeds, are best in sight of your Lord, as rewards, and best for (their) final returns."

19.77.. Have you then seen the (sort of) man who rejects Our Signs, yet says: "I will truly be given wealth and children (if I was to be alive again)"?

19.78. Has he gone into the Unseen, or has he taken a promise from (Allah) Most Gracious.

19.79. Nay! We shall record what he says, and We shall keep adding to his punishment.

19.80. And to Us shall return all that he talks about, and he shall come lonesome and alone, before Us.

19.81. And they have taken (for worship) gods other than Allah, that they may give them power and glory!

19.82. Instead, they (their false gods) shall reject their worship, and become enemies against them. [Section 5]

19.83.. Do you not see that We have set the Evil ones (Satan) against the disbelievers, to make them (insane) with evil (and anger)?

19.84. So do not make haste against them, for We only count out for them a (few) number (of days).

19.85. The Day We shall bring the righteous to (Allah) Most Gracious, like a group brought before a king for honors,

19.86. And We shall drive the criminals (and sinners) to Hell, like thirsty cattle driven down to water-

19.87. None shall have the power to plead (for them), except such a one, who has had permission from (Allah) the Most Gracious.

19.88.. And they say: "(Allah,) The Most Gracious has fathered a son!"

19.89. Indeed you (sinners) have brought forward a most horrible thing (and a lie)!

19.90. As if the skies are ready to burst (open), the earth to split apart, and the mountains to fall down in total ruin,

19.91. That they assign (or give) a son for (Allah), the Most Gracious.

19.92. For it is not befitting for the Majesty of (Allah) the Most Gracious that He should father a son.

19.93.. (There is) not (even) one being in the heavens and the earth that will not come to (Allah), the Most Gracious as (His) servant.

19.94. Verily, He (Allah) takes an account of them (all), and has numbered them (all) exactly.

19.95. And everyone of them will come individually to Him on the Day of Judgment.

19.96. On those who believe and do works of Righteousness, (Allah), the Most Gracious will bless (His) Love upon them.

19.97.. So, We (Allah) have made (the Quran) easy in your own tongue, only that with it, you (O Prophet,) may give the good news to the righteous, and warnings to people used to challenge.

19.98. And how many generations before them have We destroyed? Can you (now) find a single one of them, or (even) hear a whisper of them?

****

Sura 20. Ta-Ha,

(Quranic letters T. H.): (Makkah, 135 Verses)

In the Name of Allah, the Most Gracious, the Most Merciful.

20.1. Ta Ha:

20.2. We have not sent down the Quran unto you to (cause) for you (suffering or) sorrow,

20.3. But only as a remainder to those who fear (Allah),

20.4. A Revelation from Him Who created the earth and the high heavens above.

20.5. (Allah) the Most Gracious rose over the Throne (of authority).

20.6. To Him belongs all that is in the heavens and all that is on the earth, and all that is between them, and all that is underneath the soil.

20.7. And if you speak out the Word loudly, (it may not matter much): Then verily and surely, He (Allah) knows what is secret and what is still more hidden.

20.8. Allah! There is no god but He! Unto Him (Allah) belong the Most Beautiful Names.

20.9.. And has the story of Musa (Moses) reached you?

20.10. When he (Musa) saw a fire: He said to his family, "You stay (behind); I see a fire;

2.10. Cont. Perhaps I can bring you something burning from it, or some guidance at the fire."

20.11. And when he came to the fire, a voice was heard: "O Musa (Moses)!

20.12. "Surely I am your Lord! Therefore (in My presence) remove your shoes: You are in the sacred valley Tuwa:

20.13. "And I have chosen you: Listen to the revelation (you will receive).

20.14. "Surely, I am Allah, there is no god but I: So you worship (only) Me, and establish regular prayer by saying My Praise.

20.15. "Surely the Hour (of Judgment) is coming- My plan is to keep it hidden- For every soul to get back its reward by the measure of its actions.

20.16. "Therefore do not let those who do not believe in it and follow their own desires, take you away from it, or you will (also) perish!...

20.17.. "And what is that in your right hand, O Musa (Moses)?"

20.18. He (Musa) said, "It is my rod: I lean on it; With it I beat down corn stalk for my cattle; And in it I find other uses."

20.19. (Allah) said, "Throw it, O Musa (Moses)!"

20.20. He threw it, and look! It was a snake, actively in motion.

20.21. (Allah) said, "Seize it, and do not fear: We shall return it at once to its former state...

20.22. "Now draw your hand close to your side: It shall come out white (and shining), without harm (or stain)- (Yet) as another Sign-

20.23. "That We may show you (two) of Our Greater Signs.

20.24. "You go to Firon (Pharaoh), verily, he has transgressed all limits."

20.25.. Musa (Moses) said: "O my Lord! Open up my chest (and my understanding) for me;

20.26. "Make my work easier for me;

20.27. "And loosen the knot (that came about when baby Musa put a piece of burning fire in his mouth:) from my tongue (to make me speak more freely),

20.28. "So that they (will) understand my speech:

20.29. "And give me an assistant from my family,

20.30. "Haroon (Aaron), my brother;

20.31. "Increase my strength with his (strength),

20.32. "And make him share my task:

20.33. "That we may recite your Praise much,

20.34. "And remember You much:

20.35. "Verily, You (Allah) are He, Who (always) looks over (and sees) us."

20.36. (Allah) said: "Your prayer is granted, O Musa (Moses)!

20.37.. "And indeed, We have truly granted a favor on you another time (before).

20.38. "When We sent by inspiration to your mother, the message

20.39. " 'Put [the child, (baby Musa)] in the chest, and put (the chest) into the river: The river will put him up on the bank, and there he will be taken up by one who is an enemy to Me and is an enemy to him': And I placed love over you (O Musa,) from Me: And (this way) you may be brought up under My eye.

20.40. "When your sister went out and said: 'Shall I show you one who will nurse and bring up the (child)'? So We brought you (Moses) back to your mother, so that her eye might be cooled and she should not be sad. Then you did kill a man, but We saved you (O Musa!) from great suffering, and We tried you in many ways. Then you waited a number of years with the people of Madyan (*Midian*). Then you came here after the term I (Allah) had decided (for you), O Musa (Moses)!

20.41. "And I have prepared you for Myself (for My service)...

20.42.. "Go, you and your brother, with My Signs, and either of you do not become careless, in remembering Me.

20.43. "Go, both of you to Firon (Pharaoh), verily, he has transgressed (and exceeded) all limits;

20.44. "And speak to him mildly; In case he may take the warning or fear (Allah)."

20.45. They (Musa and Haroon) said: "Our Lord! Verily, We fear that he (Pharaoh) act quickly in (anger to cause) harm against us, or that he transgress against us."

20.46. He (Allah) said: "Do not fear, verily, I am with both of you: I hear and see (everything).

20.47. "So you both go to him and say, 'Surely, we are messengers sent by your Lord: Therefore, send out the Children of Israel with us, and do not injure them: Truly, we have come from your Lord with a Sign! And Peace to all, who follow guidance!

20.48. " 'Surely it has been revealed to us that the punishment (of Allah waits for) those who reject and turn away.' "

20.49.. (When this message was delivered Pharaoh) said: "Who, then, O Musa (Moses), is the Lord of you two (Musa and Haroon)?"

20.50. He (Musa) said: "Our Lord is He Who gave to each thing its form and nature, and also gave (it) guidance."

20.51. (Pharaoh) said: "Then what is the status of earlier generations?"

20.52. He replied: "The knowledge of that is with my Lord, (all) properly written out: My Lord never makes mistakes, nor forgets-

20.53. "He Who has made for you the earth like a bed spread out; And (He, Who) has enabled you to go about upon it by all means of roads (canals and every means of transportation): And has sent down water from the sky;" With it have We produced varied pairs of plants each separate from the others.

20.54. Eat (for yourselves) and graze your cattle: Surely, in this there are Signs for men blessed with understanding.

20.55.. We created you from the (earth), and into it We shall return you, and from it shall We bring you out once again.

20.56.. And indeed, We showed Firon (Pharaoh) all Our Signs, but he rejected and refused (them).

20.57. He said: "Have you come to drive us out of our land with your magic, O Musa (Moses)?

20.58. "Surely then, we can produce magic like yours! So make a trial between us and you, which we shall not fail to keep- Neither we nor you- In a open place where we both will be just and equal."

20.59. Musa (Moses) said: "Your trial is (on) the day of the festival, and let the people be gathered when the sun is well up (risen in the fore noon)."

20.60. So Firon (Pharaoh) went away: He came up with his plan, and then came (back).

20.61. Musa (Moses) said to them: "Misery upon you! You do not make up a lie against Allah, else He completely destroy (all of) you (at once) with (severe) punishment: Surely, he who makes up lies (against Allah) fails totally!"

20.62. So they disputed, with one another, over their differences, but they kept their talks secret.

20.63. They (Pharaoh and his people) said: "Surely, these two are truly (top) magicians: Their idea is to drive you out from your land with their magic, and to get rid of your most respected customs.

20.64. "Therefore make up your plot, and then assemble in (ordered) ranks: And today he who gains the upper hand, wins (all)."

20.65.. They said; "O Musa (Moses)! Either you be the one who throws (first) or will we be the first to throw?"

20.66. He said: "No, you throw first!" Then look, their ropes and their rods- So it appeared to him, because of their magic- Began to be in life-like movement!

20.67. So Musa (Moses), in his mind had a (sort of) fear.

20.68. We (Allah) said: "Fear not! Because you truly have the upper hand:

20.69. "And throw that which is in your right hand: quickly it will swallow up what they have faked (and) what they have faked is only a magicians trick: And the magician does not succeed, wherever he may go or whatever skill he may attain."

20.70.. So the magicians were laid down to prostration: They said: "We believe in the Lord of Haroon (Aaron) and Musa (Moses)."

20.71. (Pharaoh) said: "(Will) you believe in Him before I give you permission? Surely, this must be your leader, who has taught you (your) magic! Be sure I will cut off your hands and feet on opposite sides, and I will have you crucified on the trunk of palm-trees: So that you will know for sure (about), which of us can give the more severe and longer lasting punishment!"

20.72. They said: "We will never consider you as more than the Clear Signs that have come to us, or (more) than Him Who created us! So order whatever you want to order: Because you can only order (about things in) the life of this world.

20.73. "Verily, for us, we have believed in our Lord: That He (Allah) may forgive us our mistakes, and the magic which you forced us (to perform): And Allah is Best (One for rewards) and (Allah is) Most Enduring."

20.74. Surely he who comes to his Lord as a criminal (at Judgment), for him is Hell: In there he will neither die nor live.

20.75. But those who come to Him as believers who have worked righteous deeds- For them are supreme ranks-

20.76. Gardens of Eternity, under which flow rivers; They will live in there for ever: Like this is the reward for those who purify themselves (of evil).

20.77.. And indeed, We revealed to Musa (Moses): "Travel during the night with My servants, and keep on a dry path for them through the sea, without fear of being overtaken (by Firon) and without (any other) fear."

20.78. Then Firon (Pharaoh) came after them with his (hosts of) armies, but the (tidal) waters completely came over them (Pharaoh and armies) and covered them up.

20.79. And Firon (Pharaoh) led his people away from right instead of leading them towards right path.

20.80.. O you Children of Israel! We delivered you from your enemy and We made a promise to you on the right side of Mount (Sinai) and We sent down to you manna and quails (see Note, Sura 2.1):

20.81. (By instructing you): "Eat from the good things We have given to you for your living, but do no excesses in there, else My Anger should rightfully come down on you: And those upon whom comes down my Anger, they will be damned.

20.82. "And verily, without doubt, I am (also) He Who forgives again and again, those who repent, believe, and do right- Who, in reality, are ready to receive true guidance."

20.83.. (And when Musa was on the Mount, Allah asked:) "What made you hurry ahead of your people O Musa (Moses)?"

20.84. He replied; "They are close on my footsteps: And I hurried to You, O my Lord, that You may be pleased."

20.85. (Allah) said: "Verily, We have tested your people in your absence: And As-Samiri has led them astray."

20.86. Then Musa (Moses) returned to his people in a state of (slight) anger and sorrow. He said: "O my people! Did your Lord not make a fair (and valuable) Promise to you? Then did the Promise seem long (in coming) to you? Or did you want that Anger to come down from your Lord upon you, and so you broke your (own) promise to me?"

20.87. They said: "We did not break the promise to you, as far as it was within our power: But we were made to carry the weight of the ornaments of (all) the people, and we threw them (into the fire), and that was what the As-Samiri suggested,

20.88. "Then he (As-Samiri) brought out (of the fire) the image of a calf before the (people): It seemed to moo (like a low noise of a cow): So they said: 'This is your god, and the god of Musa (Moses), but he (Musa) has forgotten (his god)!' "

20.89. Could they not see that it could not reply a word to them, and that it had no power either to harm them or to do them (any) good?

20.90.. And before this, Haroon (Aaron) had already said to them: "O my people! You are being tested in this: And surely, your Lord is (Allah) the Most Gracious: So follow me and obey my command."

20.91. They had said (to Haroon): "We will not stop this worship, till Musa (Moses) returns to us."

20.92. [Musa (Moses)] said: "O Haroon (Aaron)! What stopped you, (even) though you saw them going wrong,

20.93. "From following me? Did you then disobey my order?"

20.94. [Haroon (Aaron)] replied: "O son of my mother! Do not grab (me) by my beard, nor by (the hair of) my head! Truly, I feared that you may say; 'You have caused a split in the Children of Israel, and you did not respect my word!' "

20.95. [Musa (Moses)] said: "Then, what is your case, O Samiri?"

20.96. He replied: "I saw what they did not see: So I took a handful (of dust) from the footprint of the messenger, and threw it (into the calf): Thus did my soul tell me."

20.97. [Musa (Moses)] said: "Then, be gone! And surely your (punishment) in this life will be that you will say, 'Do not touch me': And verily (as future punishment), you have a promise (a curse) that will not fail: Now look at your god, of whom you have become a true worshipper: We will surely (melt) it in a (hot) burning fire and throw it far and wide in the sea!"

20.98. But the God for all of you is One Allah: There is no god but He: He understands all things in His Wisdom.

20.99.. Like this do We tell you some stories about what happened before: And indeed, We have sent you (O Prophet!) A Message from Our Own Presence.

20.100. If any (of the people) do turn away from it, surely they will bear the burden on the Day of Judgment;

20.101. They will stay in this (state) and painful will be the burden upon them on that Day of Judgment-

20.102. The Day when the Trumpet will be sounded: That Day, We shall gather the criminals (disbelievers), (their) eyes dim (with fear).

20.103. In whispers will they talk with each other: "You have waited no longer than ten (days);"

20.104. We know very well what they will say: When their leader, the best one in conduct will say: "You have waited no longer than a day!"

20.105.. They ask you about the Mountains: Say, "My Lord will pull them out and throw them like dust;

20.106. "Then He will leave it like smooth and level plains;

20.107. "Nothing bent (crooked) or curved will you see in their place."

20.108. On that Day, the mankind will strictly follow (the voice of Allah's) Caller: No crookedness (can they show) him (the Caller): All sounds shall be quiet in the Presence of (Allah), the Most Gracious: And you shall hear nothing except the hidden voice [or the secret speech - (in the trample of their march)]

20.109. On that Day shall no pleading help except those for whom permission has been granted by (Allah) the Most Gracious and whose word is acceptable to Him.

20.110. He knows what is before (them now), or after or behind them (in the Hereafter): And what they shall not understand it with what they know.

20.111. And (all) faces shall look down before (Him)- The Ever-Living, the Self-Sustaining and the Eternal: Truly hopeless will be the man who carries injustice (on his back).

20.112. And he who works acts of righteousness, and has faith, (he) will have no fear of harm nor of any stopping (of what is due to him).

20.113.. Thus We have sent this down- As the Quran in Arabic- And in there some of the warnings are explained in detail, so that they may fear Allah, or that it may make them remember (Him).

20.114. Then High above all is Allah, the King, (and) the Truth! Do not be in haste with the Quran before its revelation to you is completed, but say, "O my Lord! Enhance me in Knowledge."

20.115. And indeed, before this, We had already taken the promise from Adam, but he forgot: And on his part, We found no firm commitment.

20.116.. And (remember) when We said to the angels: "Prostrate yourselves to Adam," they prostrated themselves, but not *Iblis* (Satan): He refused.

20.117. Then We said: "O Adam! Surely, this (creature of smokeless flame) is an enemy to you and your wife: So let him not get you both out of the Garden, so that you end up in suffering.

20.118. "In there, there are (enough things) for you not to go hungry nor to go naked,

20.119. "And not to suffer from thirst, nor from the suns heat."

20.120.. Then Satan whispered evil to him: And he said: "O Adam! Shall I lead you to the tree of eternity and to a kingdom that never declines (or spoils)?"

20.121. Then, they (Adam and his wife) both ate from the tree, and so their nakedness (private parts) appeared to (could be seen by) them: They began to sew together, for their covering, leaves from the Garden (Paradise): Thus Adam disobeyed His Lord, and allowed himself to be misled (into wrong conduct).

20.122. Then his Lord chose him (again for His Grace): He (Allah) turned to him with forgiveness, and gave him guidance.

20.123. He said: "Get you down, both of you- All together from the Garden (Paradise), with hate (and anger) between one another: Then if, as it is for sure, guidance comes to you from Me, then whosoever follows My guidance, will not lose his way, nor fall (deep) into sorrow.

20.124. "But whosoever turns away from My Message, surely for him is a life narrowed down, and We shall raise him up blind on the Day of Judgment."

20.125. He (the disbeliever) will say: "O my Lord! Why have You raised me up blind whereas I had sight (before)?"

20.126. (Allah) will say: "(You acted) like this, when Our Signs came to you; You disregard them (and acted blind): So will you, this Day, be disregarded."

20.127. And like this, We will repay him who exceeds beyond the limits and does not believe in the Signs of his Lord: And the Penalty of the Hereafter is far more painful and more lasting.

20.128. Is it not a warning to those men (to remember) how many peoples We destroyed before them, in whose shadows they (now) move? Surely, in this are Signs for men blessed with understanding. [

20.129. And if it was not for a Word that came before from your Lord, (the punishment) must necessarily have come: But there is a time appointed (for respite).

20.130. So (O Prophet!) be patient with what they say, and (constantly) say (and recite) the Praises of your Lord, before the raising of the sun, and before its setting; Yes, say (and recite) them for a part of the hours of the night, and at the (two) ends of the day: So that you may have (all the spiritual) joy.

20.131. And do not strain your eyes in the desire of the things We have given for enjoyment to some of those people, the splendor of the life in the world, by which We test them: But the gift from your Lord is better and more lasting.

20.132. And enjoin prayer on your family, and be constant in (insisting upon) it. We ask you not to provide livelihood: We provide it for you. And the (gift of) the Hereafter is for righteous.

20.133.. They say: "Why does he not bring us a sign from His Lord?" Has not a Clear Sign come to them of all that was in the former Books of Revelation?

20.134. And if We had sent a penalty on them before now, surely, they would have said: "Our Lord! If only You had sent us a messenger, we should certainly have followed Your Sign before we were humiliated and put to shame."

20.135. Say: "Each one (of us) is waiting: So you wait too, and you will know who are on the Even (and Straight) Path and those who have let themselves be guided."

****

Sura 21. Al-Anbiyaa,
(The prophets): (Makkah, 112 Verses)
In the Name of Allah, the Most Gracious, the Most Merciful.

21.1.. Nearer and nearer comes to mankind the Accounting of their (actions); Yet they do not listen and they turn away with carelessness.

21.2. Not even (a little) of a new Message comes to them from their Lord, but they (only) listen to it as they play-

21.3. Their hearts playing with petty things, the wrongdoers hide their private talk: "Is this (human, the Prophet) more than a man like yourselves? Will you go into magic while you can see?"

21.4. He (the Prophet) said: "My Lord knows (every) word (spoken) in the heavens and on the earth: And He is All Hearing , All Knowing ."

21.5. They (the disbelievers) say, "No, (they are) confused (songs) of dreams! No, he wrote it (by himself)! No, he is (only) a poet! Let him then bring us a Sign like those that were sent to (prophets) of old!"

21.6. (As to those people) before them, not even one of the peoples whom We destroyed believed: Will these believe?

21.7. Also before you, the messengers we sent were only men, to whom We granted the Revelation: If you do not know this, ask those, the people of the Remainder [of the Scripture, *Taurát* (Torah) and *Injeel* (Gospel)].

21.8. Nor did We give them bodies that did not eat food, nor were they exempt from death,

21.9. In the end, We kept Our promise to them, and We saved them and those whom We pleased, but destroyed those who exceeded (their) limits.

21.10. Indeed, We have made clear for you a Book (the Quran) in which is a Message for you (mankind): Will you not then understand?

21.11.. How many were the populations We have totally destroyed because of their injustices, and set up in their places other peoples?

21.12. Then, when they felt Our Punishment (coming), look, they (tried to) run away from it.

21.13. Do not run away, but come back to the good things of this life given to you, and to your homes, in order that you may be called to account.

21.14. They said: "Oh! Woe unto us! (Misery to us)! Truly, we were wrongdoers!"

21.15. And that cry of theirs did not stop, until We made them like a field to be cut (down) likes ashes silent and put out.

21.16.. And not for play did We create the heavens and earth and all that is between!

21.17. If it had been Our wish to make a game, we should surely have made it from the things nearest to Us, if We would do (such a thing)!

21.18. No, We throw the truth against falsehood, and it (truth) destroys it (the falsehood), and look! Falsehood disappears! Oh! Misery be to you for the (false) things that you ascribe (to Us).

21.19. And to Him belong all (creatures) in the heavens and on earth: And even those who are in His Presence are not too proud to worship Him, nor are they (ever) tired (of His service):

21.20. They celebrate His praises night and day, nor do they ever get tired or slip.

21.21.. Or have they taken (other) gods from the earth who can raise the dead?

21.22. In the heavens and the earth, if there were other gods besides Allah, there would have been ruin to both! But Glory to Allah, the Lord of the Throne: (High is He) above whatever they associate with Him!

21.23. He cannot be questioned for His actions, but they will be questioned (for theirs).

21.24. Or have they taken for worship (other) gods besides Him? Say: "Bring your clear proof: This is the Message of those with me and the Message of those before me." But most of them do not know the Truth, and so they turn away.

21.25. And not (even) one messenger did We send before you without this revelation sent by Us to him that; "There is no god but I (Allah): So worship Me."

21.26.. And they (disbelievers) say: "(Allah), the Most Gracious has begotten a son (child)." Glory to Him! They are (only) servants raised to honor.

21.27. They do not speak before He (Allah) speaks (to them), and they act (only) by His command.

21.28. He knows what is before them, and what is behind them, and they offer no mediation except for those for whom (the intercessions) are accepted, and they stand in fear and respect to His (Glory).

21.29. And if any of them should say: "Verily, I am a god besides Him," such a one We should reward with Hell: Like this We reward those who do wrong.

21.30.. Do the disbelievers not see that the heavens and the earth were joined together (as one), before We tore them apart? We made every living thing from water. Then, will they not believe?

21.31. And on the earth we have set mountains standing firm, in case it should shake with them, and in there We have made wide roads (between mountains) for them to pass through: That they may receive guidance.

21.32. And We have made heavens as (a proof) safe and well-guarded canopy. Still do they turn away from the Signs which these things (point to)?

21.33. And it is He Who created the night and the day, and the sun and the moon: All (the heavenly bodies) go along, each in its rounded path.

21.34.. And we did not give permanent life to any man before you (in the world): Then if you should die, can they live permanently?

21.35. Every soul shall have a taste of death: And We test you with evil and with good by way of trial. To Us you must be returned.

21.36. And when the disbelievers see you, they treat you only with ridicule. "Is this," (they say), "the one who talks of your gods?" And they lie (and slander) at the mention about (Allah,) the Most Gracious!

21.37. Man is a creature of haste: Soon (enough) will I (Allah) show you My Signs: Then you will not ask Me to hasten (them!)

21.38. And they say: "When will this promise become true, if you are telling the truth?"

21.39. If the disbelievers only knew (the time) when they will not be able to keep away the Fire from their faces, nor from their back and (when) no help can reach them!

21.40. No, it may come to them all of a sudden and imprison them: No power will they have then to turn it away, nor will they (then) get relief.

21.41. Indeed, many messengers before you were mocked, but their mockers were closed in by the (very) thing that they mocked:

21.42. Say: "Who can keep you safe by night and by day from (the Anger of Allah,) the Most Gracious?" Yet, they turn away from the remembering of their Lord.

21.43. Or do they have gods who can guard them from Us? They have no power to help themselves, nor can they be protected (from the Anger) from Us.

21.44. No, We gave the good things of this life to these men and their fathers till (their) time grew long for them; Do they not see that We slowly reduce (their) land from its far borders? Then, is it they who will win?

21.45. Say: "I only warn you by the Revelation:" But the deaf will not hear the call, (even) when they are warned!

21.46. And if only a breath of the punishment from your Lord touches them, they will then say: "Misery to us! Truly, we did wrong!"

21.47. And We shall set up scales of justice for the Day of Judgment, so that not a soul will be treated unjustly in the least. And if there is (anything less than) the weight of a mustard seed, We will bring it up (for justice): And We are enough to take account.

21.48.. And indeed, We gave to Musa (Moses) and Haroon (Aaron) the basis (for judgment), and a Light and a Reminder (the Book, *Taurát*) for those who would do right-

21.49. Those who fear their Lord in their (inner) most secret thoughts, and who hold the Hour (of Judgment) in fear.

21.50. And this (Quran) is a blessed Reminder that We have sent down: Then will you reject it?

21.51.. And indeed, We bestowed on Ibrahim (Abraham), his guidance (and the courage of conduct), and We know well all about with him.

21.52. When he said to his father and his people, "What are these images, to which you are (strongly) devoted?"

21.53. They said: "We found our fathers worshipping them."

21.54. He said: "Indeed, you have been clearly in error- You and your fathers."

21.55. They said: "Have you brought us the Truth, or are you one of those who play around?"

21.56. He said: "No, your Lord is the Lord of the heavens and the earth, He Who created them (from nothing): And I am one of the witnesses to this (truth).

21.57. "And by Allah, I have a plan for your idols- After you go away and turn your backs."

21.58.. So he broke them to pieces, (everyone) except the biggest of them, that they might turn (and try asking) it.

21.59. They said: "Who has done this to our gods? Truly, he must be a person of impiety."

21.60. They said: "We heard a young man talking about them: He is called Ibrahim (Abraham)."

21.61. They said: "Then bring him before the eyes of the people, so that they may bear witness,"

21.62. They said: "Are you the one that did this to our gods, O Ibrahim (Abraham)?"

21.63. He said: "No, this was done by- This is the biggest one of them! Ask them, if they can speak sensibly!"

21.64. So they turned amongst themselves and said, "Surely, you are the ones in the wrong!"

21.65. Then they were confused, faced with shame: (They said:) "You know very well that these (idols) do not speak!"

21.66. Ibrahim (Abraham) said: "Then do you worship, besides Allah, things that can neither be of any benefit to you nor do you any harm?

21.67. "Disgust (and shame) upon you, and upon things that you worship besides Allah! Have you no sense?" ...

21.68.. They said: "Burn him and protect your gods, if you do (anything at all)!"

21.69. We (Allah) said: "O Fire! You become cool, and (be a means of) peace for Ibrahim (Abraham)!"

21.70. And then they tried a scheme against him: But We made them the ones who lost most!

21.71. But We saved him and (his nephew) Lut (Lot, and took them) to the land that We have blessed for the nations.

21.72.. And We gave to him Issaq (Isaac) and as an additional gift, (a grandson), Yàqoub (Jacob), and We made righteous men of every one (of them).

21.73. And We made them leaders, leading (men) according to Our Command, and We sent them revelation to do good acts, to establish regular prayers, and to give out regular charity; And they constantly worshiped Us.

21.74.. And (remember) to Lut (Lot), also, We gave judgment and knowledge, and We saved him from the town that did terrible things: Truly, they were a people given to evil, a defying people.

21.75. And We admitted him into Our Mercy: Truly, he was one of the righteous.

21.76.. And (remember) Nuh (Noah), when he cried (to Us) before: We listened to his (prayer) and saved him and his family from great difficulties.

21.77. We helped him against people who rejected Our Signs: Truly, they were a people given to evil: So We drowned them all (in the Flood).

21.78.. And (remember) Dawood (David) and Sulaiman (Solomon), when they judged in the matter of the field into which the sheep of certain people had accidentally entered by night: We did witness their judgment.

21.79. And We made Sulaiman (Solomon) understand of the (complex) matters: And to each (of them) We gave judgment and knowledge; It was Our Power that made the hills and the birds celebrate Our praises with Dawood (David): And it was We Who did (all these things).

21.80. And We Who taught him how to make (metallic) coats with (overlapping) rings for your use, to protect you from each other's attack: Then will you be grateful?

21.81.. And (it was Our Power that made) the stormy wind flow (gently) for Sulaiman (Solomon) to his order, to the land (with rain) that We had blessed because We know all things.

21.82. And from the Satans, there were some who (instantly) obeyed him (Sulaiman, see 27.39) and did other work in addition; And it was We Who guarded them.

21.83.. And (remember) Ayub (Job), when he cried to his Lord, "Truly, (major) distress has caught me, but You are the Most Merciful of those that are merciful."

21.84. So We listened to him, We removed the suffering that was on him, and We gave back his people to him, and doubled their number- As a Grace from Ourselves, and as a lesson to remember, for all who worship Us.

21.85.. And (remember) Ismail (Ishmael), Idris, and Zul-kifl, all (men) of constancy and patience;

21.86. And We admitted them in Our Mercy: Verily, they were from the Righteous ones.

21.87.. And (remember) Zun-nun (Jonah or Yunus, see 7.139), when he left in anger: And he imagined that We had no power to punish him! But he cried through the depths of darkness (after being swallowed by a fish), by saying: "There is no god except You: Glory to You (Pure and Pristine): Truly, I was one of the wrongdoers!"

21.88. So We listened to him: And delivered him from (his) difficulty: And like this We save and rescue those who have faith.

21.89.. And (remember) Zakariyya (Zachariah), when he cried to his Lord: "O my Lord! Do not leave me without children, even though You are the best of inheritors."

21.90. So We listened to him: And We granted him Yahya (Baptist John): We cured his wife's (inability to bear children) for him. Verily, these (three) were quick to learn the good works: And they used to remember Us with love and respect, and to humble themselves before Us.

21.91.. And (remember) her, Maryam (Mary) who safeguarded her chastity: We breathed into her from Our Spirit, and We made her and her son [baby Isa (Jesus)] a Sign for all nations (and peoples).

21.92.. Surely, this brotherhood of yours is a single brotherhood (of prophets) and I am your Lord and Cherisher: Therefore worship Me (and no other).

21.93. But (later people) differed in their religion, one from another: (Yet) they will all return to Us.

21.94.. So whoever does any deed of righteousness and has Faith- Verily, his effort will not be rejected: We shall record it (in the book of deeds) for him.

21.95. And there is a limitation on any population that We have destroyed: (And that is) that they shall not return,

21.96. Until the time, *Yajuj* and *Majuj* (Gog and Magog) are allowed through (their barrier) and they quickly approach and attack from every hill.

21.97. And the true Promise will draw near (to coming true): Then look! The eyes of the disbelievers will (only) constantly look on with fear: "Oh! Misery to us! Truly, we were careless of this; No, truly we did wrong!"

21.98. Surely, you (disbelievers), and the gods whom you worship besides Allah, are fuel for Hell! To it (Hell) you will come!

21.99. If these had been gods, they would not enter there! But each one (of you) will live in there.

21.100. There crying (bitterly) will be their fate, nor will they hear (anything else) there.

21.101.. Verily, about those for whom the good (record) has gone before from Us, (they) will be moved far from there (Hell).

21.102. They will not hear the slightest sound of it (Hell): What their souls wanted, in it they will live.

21.103. The Great Fear will bring them no sorrow: And the angels will meet them (with the greetings) "This is your Day- That you were promised."

21.104. And (remember) the Day when We will roll up the heavens like a (written up) paper rolled up for Books- Even as We made the first Creation, like that We will make a new one: A promise We have taken up: Truly, shall We fulfill it.

21.105.. And indeed, before this (Quran), We wrote in Zabur (Psalms, revealed to David or Dawood), following the Sacred Message (given to Musa): "My righteous servants shall inherit the earth."

21.106. Surely, in this (Quran) is a Message for the people who truly worship Allah.

21.107. And We did not send you (O Prophet), except as mercy to all worlds.

21.108. Say: "What has come to me by Revelation is that your God is One (Allah) : Will you therefore bow to Him (in Islam)?"

21.109. But if they turn back, say (to them): "I have proclaimed the

Message to you all alike and in truth; And I do not know whether what you are promised is near or far.

21.110. "Verily, it is He Who knows what is open in speech and what you hide.

21.111. "And I do not know except that it may be a trial for you, and a gift of (your) livelihood for a time."

21.112. He (the Prophet) said: "O my Lord! Judge You in truth! Our Lord, the Most Gracious is the One Whose help should be found against the lies that you say!"

****

Sura 22. Al-Hajj,
(The pilgrimage): (Medinah, 78 Verses)
In the Name of Allah, the Most Gracious, the Most Merciful.

22.1.. O Mankind! Fear your Lord! Because the (violent) earthquake of the Hour (of Judgment) will be a terrible thing!

22.2. The Day when you will see that every nursing mother (feeding her baby from her breast) will forget her suckling-baby, and every pregnant female will drop her (unformed) load: You will see mankind as (if it is) in a drunken state, even though not drunk: But fearful will be the Anger of Allah.

22.3. And still there are among men who dispute about Allah, without knowledge, and follow each (Satan) of the Satans' (from its evil race) bent upon revolt!

22.4. About him (the Satan), it is ordained that anyone who turns to him for friendship, he (Satan, the Evil one) will lead him astray, and he will lead him to the penalty of the Fire.

22.5.. O Mankind! If you have doubt about being raised (for Judgment, remember that) We created you from dust, then out of semen (see 36.77), then out of a watery clot then out of a part of flesh, partly formed and partly unformed, so that We may make you be aware of (Our Power); And We make whom We wish to stay in the wombs for a fixed time, then We bring you out as (baby) infants, then (make you grow up so) that you may reach your age of full strength; And some of you are picked to die young, and some are picked for the weak old age, so that he does not know much after knowing (a lot), and (also), you see the earth that is empty and lifeless but when We pour rain upon it, it is moved (to life), and it swells, and it puts out every type of beautiful growth (in pairs).

22.6. This is so, because Allah is the Truth (and reality): And it is He Who gives life to the dead, and it is He Who is Able to do all things.

22.7. And the Hour will surely come: There can be no doubt about it, and certainly Allah will raise up all who are in the graves.

22.8. And still there is (one) among the men who disputes about Allah, without knowledge, without guidance, and without a Book of enlightenment from Allah-

22.9. Moving his side, so as to lead (men) astray from the Path of Allah: For him there is dishonor in this life, and on the Day of Judgment We shall make him taste the penalty of burning (Fire).

22.10. (It will be said to him): "This is because of the acts which your hands sent before, for surely, Allah is not unjust to His servants,"

22.11.. Among men, there is (one) who worship Allah, as if like being on the edge (of Faith): If (something) nice comes to him, he is well content with it: But if a trial comes near him, he turns on his face (in sorrow and disbelief): He loses both this world and the Hereafter: That is loss for all to see!

22.12. He (in disbelief) calls on other gods besides Allah, (those) who can neither harm nor help him: Truly, that is going far away (from the right)!

22.13. (Perhaps) he calls on the (Evil) one whose harm is closer than his help: Truly, evil is the helper and evil the companion!

22.14.. Surely, Allah will admit those who believe and work rightful deeds, to Gardens, under which rivers flow: Verily, Allah makes all that He plans happen.

22.15. If any (one) thinks that Allah will not help him (His Prophet) in this world and in the Hereafter, let him pull out a rope to the ceiling and cut (himself) off: Then let him see whether his plan will remove what makes (him) angry!

22.16. Thus, We have sent down Clear Signs like this; And surely, Allah guides (those) whom He wills!

22.17. Verily, those who believe (in the Quran,) those who are the Jews, and the Sabians (a small religious tribe from southern Iraq), Christians, Magians (*Majûs*, and the fire-worshipers from Persia, Madyan (*Midian*) and old Mesopotamian valleys) and Polytheists (worshipers of many gods)- Truly, Allah will judge between them (all) on the Day of Judgment: Verily, Allah is Witness of all things.

22.18.. Do you not see that all things that are in the heavens and on earth, bow down to Allah in worship- And the sun, and the moon, and the stars; And the hills, and the trees, and the animals; And a great number among mankind prostrate themselves to Allah? But there are those in a great number, for whom Punishment is (coming and) justified: And those whom Allah shall disgrace- None can lift (them) to grace: Because Allah fulfills everything that He wills.

{**A Muslim generally prostrates to Allah after reciting this verse**}

22.19. Those two (groups) who are opposed fought with each other about their Lord: But those who reject (their Lord)- For them will be cut out garments of Fire: Boiling water will be poured over their heads.

22.20. What is in their bodies and (their) skins will be burned with it (the boiling water).

22.21. Also there will be (spiked) clubs of iron (to punish) them.

22.22. Every time they like to get away there from, in (the most severe) pain, they will be pushed back therein, and (it will be) said to them: "You taste the Penalty of burning!"

22.23.. Allah will admit those who believe and work righteous deeds, to Gardens below which rivers flow (Paradise): In there, they shall be decorated with (thick) bangles of gold and pearls; And their garments therein will be of silk.

22.24. And they have been guided to the purest of sayings; They have been guided to His Path, Who is Worthy of all Praise.

22.25. Verily, as to those who have rejected (Allah), and have kept back (men) from the Way of Allah, and from the Sacred Mosque (*Masjid Al-Haram in Mecca*), which We have made (open) to (all) men- Equal is the one who lives (near) there and the visitor from the country- And any whose reason in there is not pious but wrong-doing- We will make them taste of a most painful Penalty.

22.26.. And (remember) when We gave the site to Ibrahim (Abraham) for the (Sacred) House, (saying): "Do not associate anything (in worship) with Me; And purify (and cleanse) My House for those who go round it (in *Tawaf*), and those who stand up (for prayer), and those who bow, and those who prostrate themselves (while being in the House).

22.27. "And proclaim (the duties of pilgrimage) among men: They will come to you on foot and on every kind of camel, (turned) lean because of travels through deep and distant mountain roads;

22.28. "That they may see the rewards for themselves, and celebrate the Name of Allah, through the appointed Days over the (sacrifice of the) cattle which He has provided for them: Then (you) eat from there and feed the poor in need.

22.29. "Then let them complete the specific rites stated for them, make their (sacred) vows, and go around (in *Tawaf*) the Ancient House (*Kab'ah*)."

22.30.. Like this (is the pilgrimage): Whoever (respectfully) obeys the sacred duties (rites) of Allah, for him, this is good in the sight of his Lord. Lawful to you (for food during pilgrimage) are cattle, except those mentioned to you (before): But avoid all the (intensely) hateful things about idols, and avoid the word that is not true-

22.31. Being true in faith to Allah and never assigning partners to Him: If (anyone) assigns partners to Allah, it is as if he had fallen from heavens and been snatched up by birds, or (as if) the wind had snatched (him) and thrown him into a faraway place.

22.32. (His condition is) like this: And for he who respects the Symbols of Allah, such (respect) should truly come from the devotion of the heart (to Allah).

22.33. In these (cattle for sacrifice) you have benefits (the meat, hide, etc.) for a fixed time: In the end their place of sacrifice is near the Ancient House.

22.34.. And to every nation (and people) We have appointed rites (of sacrifice), so that they might celebrate the Name of Allah over the food He gave them from animals (fit for sacrifice). But your God is One (Allah); Then submit your will to Him (in Islam): And you give the good news to those who humble themselves (before Allah)-

22.35. (To those) whose hearts are filled with fear, when (the Name of) Allah is mentioned- And who show patient steadfastness over their sorrows, perform regular prayer, and spend (in charity) from what We have given to them.

22.36.. And We have made for you the camels for sacrifice as among of the Symbols from Allah: In them, there is (much) good for you: Then pronounce the Name of Allah over them as they line up (for the sacrifice): Then when they are down on their sides (after the slaughter), you eat there from and feed those who live in contentment (but who do not beg) and those who beg with due humility: Thus We have made animals at your command, so that you may be thankful.

22.37. It is neither their meat nor their blood, that reaches Allah: It is your devotion (to Allah) that reaches Him: He has thus made them at your command, for you may glorify Allah for His guidance to you: And declare the good news to all who do right.

22.38. Surely, Allah protects those who believe: (And) surely, Allah does not love anyone who betrays faith (or shows ingratitude to Allah.)

22.39.. Permission (to fight) is given to those believers against whom war is made, because they (the righteous) have been wronged- And surely, Allah is Most Powerful for their help and (He) grants them the victory;

22.40. Those who have been expelled from their homes (unjustly) in defiance of right- (For no reason) except that they say, "Our Lord is Allah." Did Allah not stop one set of people by means of another, for sure, there have been destroyed, monasteries, churches, synagogues, and mosques, where the Name of Allah is praised most often. Allah will surely help those who support (His) cause- Because truly, Allah is Full of Strength, exalted in Might.

22.41. Those (are the believers) who, if We establish them firmly (in power) in the land, they establish regular prayer and give regular charity, enjoin the right and forbid wrong: And with Allah rests the end of (all) affairs.

22.42.. And if they treat your (cause for Islam) as untrue, like so did the peoples before them (with their prophets)- The People of Nuh (Noah), and 'Ad and Samood (Thamud);

22.43. Those of Ibrahim (Abraham) and Lut (Lot);

22.44. And the companions of the Madyan people; And Musa (Moses) was rejected (like this). But I gave (some) relief to the disbelievers, and (only) after that I did punish them: But how (terrible) was My rejection (of them)!

22.45. And how many townships (or populations) have We destroyed, which were used to doing wrong? They fell down on their tops. And how many wells are lying idle and neglected, and the tall and well-built castles?

22.46. Do they not go through the land, so that their hearts can thus learn wisdom and their ears may thus learn to listen? Truly it is not their eyes that are blind, but their hearts that are in their chests.

22.47. And yet they ask you to quicken the punishment! But Allah will not fail in His promise. Surely, a Day in the sight of your Lord is like a thousand years of your calculation.

22.48. And to how many populations did I (Allah) give relief, those who were used to doing wrong? In the end I (Allah) punished them. To Me is the destination (of all).

22.49.. Say: "O men! I am (sent) to you only to give a clear warning:

22.50. "Those who believe and do righteous deeds, for them is forgiveness and a livelihood most plentiful.

22.51. "But those who work hard against Our Signs, to stop (or block) them- They will be companions of the Fire."

22.52.. We never sent a messenger or a prophet before you, but, when he (the messenger or prophet) alluded a call (towards Allah), Satan threw some (lowliness) into his call: But Allah will hide anything (lowly) that Satan brings in, and Allah will confirm (and clarify) His Signs: For Allah is full of knowledge and wisdom:

22.53. (It is) that He (Allah) causes the thought of Satan, only a trial for those in whose hearts is a disease and who are hardened in heart: Surely, the wrongdoers are removed far (from the Truth):

22.54. And that those to whom knowledge has been granted may learn that (the Quran) is the Truth from your Lord, and that they may believe in it, and their hearts may be made humbly (open) to it: For surely Allah is the Guide to the Straight Path, for those who believe.

22.55. And those who reject Faith will never stop to remain in doubt about (the Revelation) until the Hour (of Judgment) falls suddenly upon them, or the penalty of a Day of disaster comes to them.

22.56. On that Day, the Kingdom will be that of Allah He will be the Judge between them: So those who believe and do the rightful deeds will be in Gardens of delight.

22.57. And for those who reject Faith and refuse Our Signs, there will be a humiliating Punishment.

22.58.. Those who leave their homes in Allah's cause, and are then killed or die- Surely, Allah will grant a large provision upon them: Truly Allah is He Who is the Best of (all) the providers.

22.59. Surely, He will admit them to a place with which they will be very pleased: Verily, Allah indeed is All Knowing , Most Forbearing.

22.60. That is so. And if one retaliates with no greater an (injury) than the injury received, and is again forced to act (in retaliation due to additional injury) inordinately, Allah will help him: Verily, Allah is One Who wipes out (sins) and forgives (again and again).

22.61.. That is because Allah merges night into day, and He merges day into night, and surely, it is Allah Who hears and sees (all things).

22.62. That is because Allah- He is the Truth; And those besides Him whom they invoke- They are only useless lies; Surely, Allah is He, the Most High, the Most Great.

22.63. Do you not see that Allah sends down rain from the sky, and with it the earth becomes covered with green? Verily, Allah is He Who understands the finest mysteries, and is Well Acquainted.

22.64. All that is in the heavens and on earth belongs to Him: Because surely Allah- And verily, He is One free of all wants, Worthy of Praise.

22.65.. Do you not see that Allah has made to serve you all that is on the earth, and the ships that sail through the ocean by His command? He stops the sky from falling on the earth except by His permission: Verily, Allah is, for mankind, Most Kind , Most Merciful .

22.66. It is He Who gave you life, (And He) will cause you to die, and (He) will again give you life: Truly, man is most ungrateful (creature)!

22.67.. To every nation (people) have We set out (their) rites and customs which they must obey: Let them not dispute with you about this matter, but you invite (them) to your Lord: Verily, you are guided onto the straight (way).

22.68. If they argue with you, say, "Allah knows best of what it is, you are doing.

22.69. "Allah will judge between you on the Day of Judgment about the matters in which you differ."

22.70. Do you not know that Allah knows all that is in heavens and on earth? Truly, it is all in a book, truly that is easy for Allah.

22.71. And they worship, besides Allah, things for which no authority has been sent down to them, and about which (things) they have no knowledge: And for those who do wrong there is no helper.

22.72. And when Our Clear Signs are recited to them, you will see a denial on the faces of the disbelievers! They almost attack with force those who recite Our Signs to them. Say, "Shall I tell you of something worse than these Signs? It is the Fire (of Hell)! Allah has promised it to the disbelievers! And evil is that place to go!"

22.73.. O Mankind! Here is a story told (to you)! Listen to it! Verily, those to whom you call, besides Allah, cannot create (even) a fly, if they all get together for the purpose! And if the fly should grab anything from them, they would have no power to regain it from the fly. Weak are those who call and (weak are) those to whom they call!

22.74. They have not made a true estimate of Allah: For Allah is He Who is strong and Almighty (to carry out His Will).

22.75. Allah chooses messengers from angels and from men. Verily, Allah is He Who hears and sees (all things).

22.76. He knows what is before them and what is behind them: And to Allah all questions return (for decision),

22.77. O you who believe! Bow down, prostrate yourselves, {see **Note** at the end of the Sura} and worship your Lord; And do good: That you may prosper.

22.78. And strive in His cause like you should strive, (with devotion and dedication). He has chosen you, and has made no hardships for you in (your) religion; It is the religion of your father Ibrahim (Abraham). It is He Who has named you Muslims, both before and in this (Revelation, the Quran); So that the Messenger (Muhammad) may be a witness for you, and you be a witness for mankind! So perform regular Prayer, give regular Charity, and hold strongly to Allah! He is your Protector- Best to protect, Best to help!

Sura 22 Note
Imam Sháfi suggests a Sajda here.
{A Muslim generally prostrates to Allah after reciting this verse}
****

Sura 23. Al-Mu'minun,
(The believers): (Makkah,118Verses)
In the Name of Allah, the Most Gracious, the Most Merciful.

23.1.. Successful! Indeed must be the believers!

23.2. Those who make themselves humble in their prayer;

23.3. And those who avoid useless talk;

23.4. And those who are give (the due) charity (*Zakat*);

23.5. And those who guard their chastity, (And their private parts from immoral acts of sex);

23.6. Except with those united to them by the bond of marriage, or (those) whom their right hands possess- For them, they are free from blame,

23.7. But those whose desires are beyond such limits- (They) are the transgressors-

23.8. Those who truly keep their trusts and their promises;

23.9. And who (strictly ensure and) guard their prayers-

23.10. These are indeed, the heirs;

23.11. Who will inherit the Paradise: They will live in there forever.

23.12.. And indeed, We created man from purest (of the clay);

23.13. Then We placed him like (a drop of) semen firmly fixed, in a place of (its) rest;

23.14. Then We made the semen into a mass of half-solidified blood; Then from that mass We made an (early embryonic baby-like) lump: Then We made from the lump bones and covered the bones with flesh; Then We developed from it another creature, so blessed be Allah, the Best to create!

23.15. After that, at length, surely you will die.

23.16. Then again, surely, on the Day of Judgment, you will be raised up.

23.17. And above you, We have made seven heavens; And We are never unmindful of (Our) Creation.

23.18.. And We send down water from the sky in (proper) quantity, and We make it sink (deep) in the soil; And truly We are able to drain it off.

23.19. Then with it (the water) We grow gardens of date-palms and vines for you; In them you have plenty of fruits; And from them you eat (and you rejoice)-

23.20. And also a tree that grows from Mount Sinai, which produces oil and relish for those who use it for food.

23.21. And truly, (also) in cattle you have an example to learn from: From inside their bodies We produce (milk) for you to drink: (In addition), from them there are many (other) benefits for you: And you eat from their (meat);

23.22. And on them, as in ships, you ride.

23.23.. (For your guidance, We sent many prophets). And indeed, We sent Nuh (Noah) to his people: (To them) he said: "O my people! Worship Allah! You have no god except Him. Then will you not fear (Him)?"

23.24. The leaders of the disbelievers from his people said: "He is no more than a man like yourselves; His wish is to make his superiority over you: If Allah had wished, He could have sent down angels: We never heard any such thing (like he says), from our forefathers of the old."

23.25. (And some said): "He is only a man in madness: So wait (and be patient) with him for a while."

23.26. He (Nuh) said: "O my Lord! Help me; Because they deny me (and blame me of lying!)"

23.27. So, We revealed to him (this command): "Build the Ark within Our view and under Our guidance: Then when Our command comes (true), and the fountains of the earth open up, you take (into the Ark) pairs of every species, male and female, and your family- Except those of them against whom the word has already gone out: And do not ask Me for favor to the wrongdoers; Surely, they will be drowned (in the flood).

23.28. "And when you have climbed onto the Ark- You and those with you- Then say: 'All the Praises (and thanks) be to Allah, Who has saved us from the people who do wrong.'

23.29. "And say: 'O my Lord! Cause me to land (the Ark) at a blessed place for landing: Because You are the best of those to bring (us back) to land.' "

23.30. Surely, in this, there are Signs (from Us for men to understand: And so) do We try (them).

23.31.. Then, We raised after them another generation.

23.32. And We sent to them a messenger from among themselves, (saying). "Worship Allah! You have no god except Him. Then will you not fear (Him)?"

23.33.. And the leaders of his people, who disbelieved and denied the meeting in the Hereafter, and to whom We had granted the good things of this life, said: "He is no more than a man like yourselves: He eats from that of which you eat, and drinks from what you drink.

23.34. "If you obey a man like yourselves, then verily it is certain that you will be lost.

23.35. "Does he promise you that when you die and become dust and bones, you will be brought up (again)?

23.36. "Far, very far is that which you are promised!

23.37. "There is nothing except our life in this world! We shall die and (now) we live! And we shall never be raised up again!

23.38. "He is only a man who makes up a lie against Allah, but we are not the ones to believe in him!"

23.39. (The prophet) said: "O my Lord! Help me; Because they deny me (and blame me of lying)."

23.40. (Allah) said: "In only a little while, they are sure to be sorry!"

23.41. Then the blast (an awful cry) came to them with justice, and We made them like rubbish of dead leaves so, away with the wrongdoers!

23.42.. Then, after them, We raised other generations.

23.43. No nation can quicken its term, nor can it delay (it).

23.44. Then We sent Our messengers one after another: Every time there came to a people their messenger, they denied him (and blamed him of lying): So, We made them follow each other (with punishment): And We made them like a tale (that is told): So away with the a people who will not believe!

23.45.. Then We sent Musa (Moses) and his brother Haroon (Aaron), with Our Signs and clear authority,

23.46. To Firon (Pharaoh) and his chiefs: But these acted with insolence and disrespect: And they were an arrogant people.

23.47. They said: "Shall we believe in two men like ourselves? And their people are obedient to us in humility!"

23.48. So they denied them both (and accused them of lying), and they became of those who were destroyed.

23.49. And indeed, We gave Musa (Moses) the Book (*Taurát*), that they might receive guidance.

23.50. And We made (Isa or Jesus) son of Maryam (Mary) and his mother like a Sign: And We gave them both protection on high ground, offering rest and security and gave them springs (for water).

23.51.. O you messengers (of Allah)! Eat (all) the good and the pure things, and carry out righteousness: Verily, I am Well Acquainted with what (ever) you do.

23.52. And surely, this Religion (brotherhood of Islam) of yours is One single Religion (Islam), and I am your Lord and Cherisher: Therefore fear Me (Allah, Alone).

23.53. But people have broken their feelings (for Unity), between them, into (different) groups: Each group rejoices in what is with itself.

23.54. So, leave them in their error (unclear and uninformed condition) for a while.

23.55.. Do they think that because We have granted them plenty of wealth and sons,

23.56. We would quicken every good (thing) upon them? No! They do not understand.

23.57.. Surely those who live in reverence for the fear of their Lord;

23.58. And those who believe in the Signs of their Lord;

23.59. And those who do not join partners with their Lord;

23.60. And those who give out their charity with their hearts full of fear, because they will return to their Lord-

23.61. It is these who are quick in every good work, and these who are first among them (who are good).

23.62.. And We place not a burden upon anyone except according to the capacity of the person: And with Us is a record clearly showing the truth: And they will never be wronged.

23.63. But (for some) their hearts are unclear and uninformed about this; And therein lie their (evil) actions, which they will (continue) to do-

23.64. Till (that time), when We grip in Punishment those of them who received the good things of this world, behold! They will groan (in pain and) in hurt!

23.65. (It will be said): "Do not groan in (pain and) hurt today; Certainly, you will not be helped by Us.

23.66. "Indeed, My (Allah's) Signs used to be recited to you, but you used to go back (running) on your heels-

23.67. "In defiance, (while) talking nonsense about (the Quran), like someone is saying (false) stories by night."

23.68.. Do they not think deeply over the Word (of Allah), or has anything (new) come to them (now) that did not already come to their fathers of old?

23.69. Or do they not recognize their Messenger (Muhammad) that they reject him?

23.70. Or do they say: "Is there madness (deep) in him?" No! He has brought them the truth, but most of them hate the truth.

23.71. And if the truth was according to their desires, surely, the heavens and the earth, and all the beings in there will be in confusion and ruin! No! We have sent them their reminder (and guidance), but they turn away from their warning.

23.72. Or is it that you ask them for wages or reward? But the repayment of your Lord is best: He is the Best of those who give livelihood.

23.73. But surely you call them to the Straight Way:

23.74. And certainly, those who do not believe in the Hereafter are wandering away from that Path.

23.75.. And even though We had mercy on them and removed the difficulty that is on them, still they would stubbornly continue to exceed their limits, wandering here and there being diverted.

23.76. And indeed, We seized them with Punishment, still they did not humble themselves to their Lord, and they do not humbly receive (Him)!

23.77. Till We open on them a gate of a harsh Punishment: Then listen! They will be drowned in pain (and sorrow) in there!

23.78.. It is He Who has made for you (the faculties of) hearing, sight, feeling and understanding: (Yet) it is that you give little thanks!

23.79. And He has spread you throughout the earth, and you will be gathered back to Him.

23.80. And it is He Who gives life and causes death, and to Him (is due) the exchange (alternation) of night and day: Then will you not understand?

23.81. To the opposite (effect), they say things similar to what the olden (people) said.

23.82. They said: "What! When we die and become dust and bones, can we really be raised up again?

23.83. "Verily, such things have been promised to us and our fathers before! This is nothing but the stories of the ancient!"

23.84. Say: "To whom belong the earth and all beings in there? (Answer) if you know!"

23.85. They will say: "To Allah!" Say: "Yet will you not take warning (and guidance)?"

23.86. Say: "Who is the Lord of the seven heavens, and the Lord of the Throne Supreme?"

23.87. They will say: "(They belong) to Allah." Say: "Then will you not be filled with fear (and respect)?"

23.88. Say: "Who is it in whose hands is the sovereignty (and order) of all things- Who protects (all), but is not protected: (Answer) if you know."

23.89. They will say: "(It belongs) to Allah." Say: "How, then are you deceived away from truth?"

23.90.. We have sent them the truth: And verily, they practice lies!

23.91. Allah fathered no son, and there is not any god alongside with Him: (If there were many gods), then, each god would have taken away what he had created, and some (of them) would have lorded it over the others! Glory to Allah! (He is free) from the (sort of) things they attribute to Him!

23.92. He knows what is hidden and what is open: Very high above is He for the partners they attribute to Him!

23.93.. Say: "O my Lord! If You will (ever) show me that, with which they are threatened (as the Hellfire) -

23.94. "Then, O my Lord! Do not put me amongst the people who do wrong!"

23.95. And surely, We are able to show you that, with which We have threatened them.

23.96. Put off evil with that which is best: We are very familiar with the things they say.

23.97. And say: "O my Lord! I seek protection with You from the whisperings of the Satans'.

23.98. "And I seek protection with You O my Lord! In case they should come near me."

23.99.. (In lies will they be) till death comes to one of them, he says: "O my Lord! Send me back (again to life)-

23.100. "So that I may work rightfully the things that I neglected." - "By no means! It is only a word that he says." - Before them is a partition till the Day they are raised up.

23.101. Then, when the Trumpet is blown, there will be no relations between them that day, and they will not ask after another!

23.102. Then, those whose balance (of good deeds) is heavy- These, they will be successful:

23.103. And those whose balance (of good) is light, will be those who have lost their souls; They will live in Hell.

23.104. The Fire will burn their faces, and therein they will smile (in ugliness) with their lips displaced.

23.105. "Were My Signs not recited to you, and you only treated them as lies?"

23.106. They will say: "O Lord! Our bad luck overtook us, and we became a people who had lost our way!

23.107. "Our Lord! Bring us out from this: If we ever return (to evil), then truly we shall be wrongdoers!"

23.108. He (Allah) will say: "Remain you in it! (With worst shame)- And you do not speak to Me

23.109. "Verily, there was a party of My servants who used to Pray,
'Our Lord! We believe; Then You do forgive us, and have mercy upon us: For You are the Best of those who show mercy!'

23.110. "But you made fun of them to the extent that (it) made you forget My Message while you were laughing at them!

23.111. "Verily, I (Allah) have gifted them this Day for their patience and constancy: Really, they are the ones who are successful."

23.112. He will say: "How many years did you stay on earth?"

23.113. They will say: "We stayed a day or part of a day: But ask those who keep account."

23.114. He will say: "You stayed only for a little (while)- If you had only known!

23.115. "Then did you think that We had created you for a joke, and that you will not be brought back to Us?"

23.116.. So, Allah be Exalted, the King of Truth: There is no god except He, the Lord of the Throne of Mercy!

23.117. And if anyone calls besides Allah, any other god when he has no authority for it; And his accounting will be only with his Lord! And surely the disbelievers will not win through!

23.118. And say: "O my Lord! You grant forgiveness and mercy! Because You are the Best of those who show mercy!"

****

Sura 24. An-Nur,
(The light): (Medinah, 64 Verses)
In the Name of Allah, the Most Gracious, the Most Merciful.

24.1.. (This is) a Sura (in Quran) which We have sent down and which We have enjoined its laws: And in it have We revealed clear (Ayât) Signs, so that you may remember and receive warning (about the laws so enjoined).

24.2.. The woman and the man guilty of adultery (unlawful sexual relations) severely whip each of them with a hundred stripes: Do not let kindness move you in their case- In a matter that is already decided by Allah, if you (truly) believe in Allah and the Last Day: And let a party of the believers witness their punishment.

24.3. Let not any man guilty of adultery (unlawful sexual relations) marry anybody except a woman similarly guilty, or a disbeliever (woman): Let not any such guilty woman marry anybody except a man similarly guilty or a disbeliever (man): But such a thing (marriage to the guilty or to the disbelievers) is forbidden to the believers (men and women).

24.4.. And those who start a charge against pure women, and do not have four witnesses (in support of the accusation)- Severely whip them with eighty stripes; And do not ever accept their testimony afterwards: Because such men are wicked transgressors -

24.5. Except those who repent afterwards and change and do righteous deeds verily, Allah is Often Forgiving, Most Merciful .

24.6.. And for those who start a case (of adultery) against their wives, and do not have witnesses (in support) except their own (testimony)- (Then, the) only evidence (from such a man is) if he testifies (under oath) four times, by Allah that he is honestly saying the truth;

24.7. And the fifth (oath should be) that he truly bring the curse of Allah upon himself if he is telling a lie.

24.8. But it would save the punishment on the wife, if she testifies (under oath) four times, by Allah, that (her husband) is telling a lie;

24.9. And the fifth (oath should be) that she truly brings the Anger of Allah upon herself if (her husband) is telling the truth.

24.10. If it was not because of Allah's grace and mercy upon you, (a painful penalty would have overtaken you): And Allah forgives and accepts repentance, Full of Wisdom.

24.11.. Verily, those who brought out the slander (lie) are a group from yourselves: Do not think (of the incident) to be an evil for you; No! It is good for you: For every man from them (is the punishment) of the sin that he has earned, and for him who took on himself the lead from them, the penalty (for him) will be great.

24.12. Why then, did not the believers-men and women - When you heard of the incident- Put the best reasons after it in their own minds and say, "This (slander) is an open lie?"

24.13. Why did they (the accusers) not bring four witnesses to prove it (the blame)? When they have not brought the witnesses: In the Sight of Allah, such men (hold) themselves as liars!

24.14. If it was not because of the grace and mercy of Allah on you, in this world and the Hereafter, a painful penalty would have caught you because you so easily spoke about this affair.

24.15. When you move it forward with your tongues, and said from your mouths things of which you had no knowledge; And you thought it to be a light matter, when it was most serious in the Sight of Allah.

24.16. And why did you not, when you heard it, say- "It is not right of us to speak of this: Glory to Allah! This is a most serious lie (against any person)!"

24.17.. Allah does warn and forbids you, that you may never repeat such (actions), if you are true believers.

24.18. And Allah makes the Signs plain (and clear) to you: And Allah is All Knowing, , All Wise.

24.19. Verily, those who love (to see) lies circulated openly among the believers, they will have a painful penalty in this life and in the hereafter: And Allah knows, and you do not know.

24.20. If it was not because of Allah's grace and mercy upon you, and that Allah is full of kindness , Most Merciful ; (You would be truly lost). [Section 2]

24.21.. O you who believe! Do not follow Satan's footsteps: If any will follow the footsteps of Satan's, verily, he will command what is shameful and wrong: And if it was not because of Allah's grace and mercy upon you, not (even) one of you would ever have been pure: But Allah does purify whomsoever He pleases: And Allah is All Hearing , All Knowing .

24.22. And let not those from you who are blessed with grace and abundance of means resolve by oath against helping their relatives, those in want, and poor and those who have left their homes in Allah's cause: Let them forgive and overlook, do you not wish that Allah should forgive you? And Allah is Often Forgiving, Most Merciful .

24.23. Verily, those who spread accusations (about the character of) chaste believing women, who are (truly) pure (in their character)- Are cursed in this life, and in the Hereafter: And for them is a painful penalty-

24.24. On the Day when their tongues, their hands, and their legs will bear witness (and speak out) against them about their actions.

24.25. On that Day, Allah will pay them back (all) their dues in full, and they will realize that Allah is the (Very) Clearest Truth.

24.26. Bad words are for bad people; [Disbelieving (or impure) women for disbelieving (or impure) men], bad people are for bad words; [Disbelieving (or impure) men for disbelieving (or impure) women], good words are for good people; [Also implied is that good women are for good men;] good people are for good words; [Also implied is that good men are for good women;] such are the (truly) innocent of the bad words they say: For them there is forgiveness, and a honored provision.

24.27.. O you who believe! Do not enter houses other than your own, until you have asked for permission (to enter) and greeted those (who are) inside them: That is best for you, so that you may remember.

24.28. And if you find no one in there (the house), still do not enter until permission is given to you: And if you are asked to go back, go back: That makes for greater (piety) purity for yourselves: And Allah is All Knowing of all that you do.

24.29. It is not a fault on your part to enter houses not used for living (or uninhabited), (but) which serve some (other) use for you: And Allah has knowledge of what you say and what you hide.

24.30.. Say to the believing men that they should lower their gaze and guard their shyness (and looks) and protect themselves and their privacy (from illicit sex): That will make for greater purity for them: Verily, Allah is familiar with all that they do.

24.31. And say to the believing women that they should lower their gaze and guard their modesty (and looks) and protect themselves and privacy (from illicit sex): And that they should not display their beauty and jewels except what (may usually) appear; That they should draw cover over their bodies and bosoms, and not display their beauty except to their husbands, or their fathers, or their husband's fathers, or their sons, or their husband's sons, or their brothers or their brother's sons, or their sister's sons, or their (Muslim) women, or the slaves whom their right hands possess, or the male servants without physical (and sexual) needs, or little children who are not aware of the nakedness of women; And that they should not strike their feet in order to draw attention to their hidden ornaments. And O believers! All of you turn together towards Allah (seeking His Forgiveness), so that you may be successful.

24.32.. Marry those among you who are single, and the virtuous ones among your slaves, male servants and maid servants: If they are in poverty, Allah will provide them ways out of His grace: And Allah understands all needs; He knows all things.

24.33. And let those who do not find the (financial) means to marry, keep themselves pure, until Allah provides them means out of His grace. And if any of your slaves ask for a note (of promise) in writing (to enable them to earn their freedom), give them such a note (of promise); If you know any good (ones) from them; And give them something from yourselves out of the wealth that Allah has bestowed upon you. And do not force your maids to prostitution when they like purity (of their moral conduct), so that you may make a gain in things of this life. But if anyone forces (or has forced) them (the maids), still, after such compulsion (or circumstances), Allah is Often Forgiving, Most Merciful (to the maids because of the force or compulsion.)

24.34.. And indeed, We have already sent down to you Signs (*Ayât*, and verses) making things clear, and a clarification from (the lives of) people who have gone before you, and an advise and warning to those who fear (Allah).

24.35.. Allah is the Light of the heavens and the earth. The parable of His Light is as though there is a Niche (opening) and within it is a Lamp: The Lamp is enclosed in glass: The glass as if it was (itself) a bright star: Lit from a blessed Tree, an Olive, neither of the East nor of the West, whose Oil is almost (by itself) bright, even though fire never touched it: Light upon Light! Allah guides whomever He wills to His Light: And Allah sets forth parables for mankind: And Allah knows all things.

24.36. (This Light shines bright) in those houses, that Allah has permitted to be raised to the honor; For the celebration of His Name in them: In them (His Names and the houses), He is glorified mornings and in evenings (of everyday)-

24.37. To (those) men whom neither trade nor business can take away from remembering Allah, and not from (their) regular prayer, and not from the giving of regular charity: Their (only) fear is of the Day when hearts and eyes will be transformed (in a new universe)-

24.38. That Allah may reward them according to the best of their deeds, and add even more for them from His Grace: And Allah provides for those whom He wills, without (any) limits.

24.39.. As for those who disbelieved (in this life)- Their deeds are like a mirage in sandy deserts, which a thirsty one mistakes it to be water; And when he comes up to it, he finds it to be nothing: But (instead) he finds Allah (always) with him, and Allah will pay him his account that is due: And Allah is swift in taking account.

24.40. Or (the disbelievers condition) is like the depths of darkness in a vast deep ocean, overcome by huge waves on top of huge waves, with (darkest) clouds at the top: Depths of darkness, one upon another: If a man opened out his hand, he can barely see it! And for him Allah does not give Light, there is no Light!

24.41.. Do you not see that it is Allah Whose praises all beings in the heavens and on earth celebrate, and the birds with wings spread out? For each one (of the beings), He (Allah) knows its own (way of saying the) prayer and praise. And Allah knows well everything that they do.

24.42. And to Allah belongs the kingdom of the heavens and the earth; And to Allah is the final goal (of all).

24.43. Do you not see that Allah makes the clouds move slowly, then gathers them together, then makes them into a heaps of layers? Then you see the rain come out from their middle. And He sends down from the sky vast volumes (of dark clouds) in which is hail: He hits with it whom He pleases and He turns it away from whom He pleases. The clear (distinct) flash of His lightning that almost blinds the sight.

24.44. It is Allah Who causes the night and the day to succeed (to search and to overtake) each other: Surely, in these things, there is a teaching for those who can see (and search).

24.45. And Allah has made every animal from water: Of them, some slide on their abdomens; And some walk on two legs; And some walk on four (legs). Allah creates what He wills; For surely, Allah is Able to do all things.

24.46. We have indeed sent down clear Signs that make things clear and Allah guides whom He wills to the Straight Path.

24.47.. They say, "We believe in Allah and in the Messenger (Muhammad) and we obey:" But even after (saying) that, some of them turn away: They are not (true) believers.

24.48. And when they are called to Allah and His Messenger (Muhammad), in order that he may judge between them, look! Some of them do not agree (to come).

24.49. But if the right is on their side, they (would) come to him (the Prophet) with all the submission (to listen and accept).

24.50. Is there a disease in their hearts? Or do they doubt, or are they in fear, that Allah and His Messenger (Muhammad) will deal unjustly with them? No, it is they themselves who are the wrongdoers.

24.51.. The answer of the believers, when called to Allah and His Messenger (Muhammad) so that he may judge between them is nothing other than this: They say: "We hear and we obey:" And it is such as these who will be successful.

24.52. It is such (believers) who obey Allah and His Messenger (Muhammad), and fear Allah and work right, who will be successful.

24.53. They gave their strongest oath by Allah that, if you were to only order them, they would (even) leave (their homes). Say: "You do not (just) swear; Obeying is (more) reasonable to hold your oath; Surely, Allah is quite familiar with all that you do."

24.54. Say: "Obey Allah, and obey the Messenger (Muhammad): But if you turn away, he (Prophet, the Messenger) is only responsible for the duty given to him, and you for that (the duty) given to you. If you obey him, you will be on right guidance. The Messenger's (Muhammad's) duty is only to teach the clear (Message)."

24.55.. Allah has promised those among you who believe and work righteous deeds, that He will surely grant them inheritance in the land, as He granted it to those before them; That He will affirm with authority their religion- The one which He has chosen for them; And that He will change (their condition), after the fear in which they lived, to one (condition) of security and peace: "They will worship (only) Me and not join anyone with Me," if any do reject Faith after (accepting) this, they are rebellious and wicked.

24.56. And establish regular prayer and give regular charity; And obey the Messenger (Muhammad); That you may receive mercy.

24.57. You do not ever think that the disbelievers are going to block (Allah's Plan) on earth: Their home is the Fire- And it is truly an evil place (for shelter)!

24.58.. O you who believe! Let those whom your right hands possess, (servants and servant-girls) and the (children) among you who have not come of age (to puberty) ask your permission (before they come in your presence), on three occasions: Before the morning prayer; And the time you take off your clothes for the mid-day (afternoon) heat; And after the late-night prayer: (These) are your (three) times for privacy: At times other than these, it is not wrong for you or for them to move about taking care of each other. Thus Allah makes the Signs clear to you: And Allah is All Knowing and All Wise.

24.59. And when the children from you come to puberty, let them (also) ask for permission, like those older than them do (ask for permission). Thus Allah makes the Signs clear to you: And Allah is All Knowing and All Wise.

24.60. And such older women who are over the possible chances of marriage- There is no blame on them if they put away their (outer) garments, so long as they make not a willful show of their beauty: But it is best for them to be decent. And Allah is All Hearing , All Knowing .

24.61.. There is no (such) restriction for the blind, nor for one born lame, nor for one struck with illness, nor (is there any restriction) for yourselves,

if you eat in your own houses,

or the houses of your fathers,

or the houses your mothers,

or the houses your brothers,

or the houses your sisters,

or your the houses father's brothers,

or the houses your father's sisters,

or the houses your mother's sisters,

or in houses whose keys you have,

or in the houses of a sincere friend of yours:

There is no blame on you, whether you eat in company or alone. But when you enter houses, greet yourselves (and each other)- A greeting of blessing and purity as from Allah. Thus Allah makes the Signs clear to you: That you may understand.

24.62.. Only those are believers, who believe in Allah and His Messenger (Muhammad): And when they are with him about a matter needing joint action, they do not leave until they ask for his permission; Verily, those who ask for your (Prophet's) consent are those who believe in Allah and His Messenger (Muhammad); So when they ask for your permission (to leave), for some matters of theirs, give the permission to those of them whom you will, and ask Allah for their forgiveness: Truly, Allah is Often Forgiving, Most Merciful .

24.63. Do not treat the call of the Messenger within yourselves, like the call of one of you to another: Allah does know those of you who slip away under some excuse; Then let those who listen to the Prophet's order, warn in case some trial befall them, or a painful penalty be handed down over them.

24.64. Be sure that to Allah belongs whatever is in the heavens and on earth. Indeed, He (Allah) knows well what you are up to doing: And one Day they will be brought back to Him, and He will tell them the truth of what they did: And Allah, about all things, is All Knowing .

****

Sura 25. Al-Furqaan,
(The criterion): (Makkah, 77 Verses)
In the Name of Allah, the Most Gracious, the Most Merciful.

25.1.. He is the Blessed (One), Who sent down the Criterion (*Al-Furqaan*) to His servant (the Prophet), so that it may be a warning and guidance to all creations-

25.2. He (is the One) to whom belongs the kingdom of the heavens and the earth: He has fathered no son, nor does He have a partner in His kingdom; It is He Who has created all the things, and made them in proper (proportions) sizes.

25.3. Even then, besides Him, have they taken gods that can make nothing, and are themselves made; That have no control to harm or do good for themselves; And they cannot control death, or life, or Resurrection.

25.4.. But the disbelievers say: "This is nothing but a lie that he (the Prophet) has made up, and others have helped him at (making) it." In reality, it is they who have put forward an injustice and a lie.

25.5. And they say: "Stories of the old times, which he has made to be written: And they are dictated before him morning and afternoon."

25.6. Say: "(The Quran) was sent down by Him Who knows the Secret in the heavens and the earth: Surely, He is Often Forgiving, Most Merciful .

25.7.. And they say: "What sort of a messenger is this, who eats food, and walks in the streets? Why has an angel not been sent down to him to give warning and guidance with him?

25.8. "Or (why) has a treasure not been granted to him, or why has he (not) a garden for enjoyment?" The wicked say: "You follow no one other than a man under spell."

25.9. See what types of comparisons they make for you! But they have gone away from the right, and they will never be able to find a way!

25.10.. He is the blessed (One) Who, if it was His Will, could give you better (things) than those- Gardens under which rivers flow; And He could give you palaces (to live in).

25.11. And for they reject the Hour (of Judgment): And We have made a blazing fire for those who falsify the Hour.

25.12. When it sees them from a far away place, they will hear its fury and its angry roar.

25.13. And when they are thrown in, bounded together, into a tight place in there, they will plead for (their) death.

25.14. "This Day plead not for a single death: Plead for death (that is) repeated many times!"

25.15. Say: "Is that better, or the eternal Garden (Paradise, that is) promised to the righteous? For them, that is a reward and a goal (of joy).

25.16. "For them in there, there will be all that they wish for: And they will live (there) forever: A promise to be prayed for from your Lord."

25.17.. And on the Day He will collect them together and those whom they worship besides Allah, He will ask (those): "Was it you who led My servants away, or did they go away from the Path themselves?"

25.18. Those (whom they worship besides Allah) will say: "Glory to You! Not proper was it for us that we should take for protectors others besides You (Allah): But You (Allah) did give them and their fathers, the comfort and good things (in life), until they forgot the Message: For they were a people (who were) lost."

25.19. (Allah will say): "Now they have made you liars about what you say: So you cannot escape (penalty) or (get) help." And whoever from you does wrong; We shall make him taste a great penalty.

25.20. And the messengers whom We had sent before you, (they) were all (men) who ate food, and walked through the streets: We have made some of you like a trial for others: Will you have patience? And your Lord is All Seeing.

25.21.. And those who do not expect (their) meeting Us said: "Why are the angels not sent down to us, or (why) do we not see our Lord?" Truly, they have a false opinion of themselves with rudeness in their great arrogance!

25.22. On the Day (when) they see the angels- There will be no joy for the sinners that Day: The (angels) will say: "There is a limit totally banned (for you)!"

25.23. And We shall turn to those deeds they did and We shall make such deeds like floating dust thrown around.

25.24. The companions of the Garden (Paradise) will be well that Day, in their Home, and have the most beautiful and the happiest of places for rest.

25.25. And the Day the heaven will be torn apart by clouds, and the angels shall be sent down, descending (in order and in grandeur)-

25.26. That Day, the Sovereignty of right and truth, shall be (only) for the Most Merciful: And it will be a Day of great difficulty for the disbelievers.

25.27.. And the Day when the wrong-doer (of every type) will bite at his hands; He will say: "Oh! If only I had taken a (Straight) path with the Messenger (of Allah)!

25.28. "Oh! I am (now in) misery! If only I had never taken such an (Evil) one as a friend!

25.29. "He led me astray from the Message (of Allah) (even) after it had come to me! And Satan is only a traitor to man!"

25.30. And the Messenger (Muhammad) will say: "O my Lord! Truly, my people (took the Message lightly and) abandoned this Quran."

25.31. Like this We have made for every prophet an enemy from the criminals (and sinners): But your Lord is enough to guide and to help.

25.32.. And those who reject Faith say: "Why is Quran not sent to him all at once?" (It is sent) like this so that We may give strength to your heart with it, and We have made it known to you in slow well-ordered stages, little at a time.

25.33. And no example or parable do they bring to you that We have not made known to you the truth and the best explanation (of the questions).

25.34.. Those who will be gathered to Hell (fallen) on their faces- They will be in evil fate, on a path most astray.

25.35.. And indeed, (before this,) We sent Musa (Moses) the Scripture (*Taurát*), and appointed his brother Haroon (Aaron) with him as minister:

25.36. And We commanded: "Both of you, go to the people who have rejected Our Signs (*Ayât*):" And those (people) We destroyed with total ruin.

25.37. And the people of Nuh (Noah)- When they rejected the messengers, We drowned them, and We made them like a Sign for (all) mankind: And We have prepared a (most) painful penalty for (all) wrongdoers-

25.38. And like (the people of) 'Ad and Samood (Thamud), and the companions of the Rass, and many a generation between them.

25.39. And for each one (of the peoples) We set forth parables and examples; And each one We broke to total ruin (for their sins).

25.40. And truly, the (disbelievers) must have passed by the town on which was rained by a shower of evil: Then did they not see it (with their own eyes)? But they fear not the Resurrection.

25.41.. And when they see you, they treat you no other way than in joke: "Is this the one whom Allah has sent as a messenger?

25.42. "Truly, he would have almost misled us from our gods, if we were not unchanging towards them!" - Soon will they know, when they see the penalty, who it is that is most misled from the (true) path!

25.43. Do you see the one who takes for his god his own desire (or impulse)? Could you be a guardian of affairs for him?

25.44. Or do you think that most of them listen or understand? They are only like cattle- No! They are worse astray in path.

25.45.. Have you not turned your sight (and thoughts) towards your Lord? How He pulls the shadow (longer during the evenings and mornings)! If He willed, He could make it fixed! Then We make the sun its guide (as it lengthens);

25.46. Then We draw it in towards Ourselves- A shortening by easy stages (during the night and noon).

25.47.. And it is He Who makes the night as a (long) cover for you, and sleep as rest, and makes the day (like) a resurrection.

25.48.. And it is He Who sends the winds as messages of glad news (and tidings), that go before His Mercy (of the rain), and We send down pure water from the sky-

25.49. So that We may give life with it to the land that is dead, and quench the thirst of things We have created- Cattle and men in large numbers.

25.50. And indeed, We have distributed the (water) among them, in order that they may recite (Our) praises, but most men are ungrateful and denying.

25.51.. And if it was Our Will, We could have sent a Warner to every town.

25.52. Therefore do not obey the disbelievers, but work hard against them with the greatest strength, (with the Quran by your side).

25.53.. And it is He Who has released the two parts of flowing water; One (that is) drinkable and sweet, and the other (that is) salty and bitter; And He has set a barrier between them, a boundary forbidden to be crossed (by the waters).

25.54.. And it is He Who has made man from water: Then He has set up relationships of family and marriage: And your Lord is ever All Powerful (over all things).

25.55.. And still, do they worship things besides Allah that can neither profit them nor harm them? And the disbeliever is a helper (of Evil), against his own Lord!

25.56. And We only sent you (O Prophet), to give glad tidings and warning.

25.57. Say: "I do not ask any reward from you for it except this: That each one who will (wish to do so), may take a (straight) Path to his Lord."

25.58.. And (you, O Muhammad!) put your trust in Him Who lives but does not die; And recite His Praise, and He is All Aware of the faults of His servants-

25.59. He Who created in six Days, the heavens and the earth and all in between, and rose over on the Throne (of Authority); (Allah,) the Most Gracious! Then ask Him as the All Aware and informed (about all things).

25.60. And when it is said to them, "You adore (Allah) the Most Gracious!"

{A Muslim generally prostrates to Allah after reciting this verse}

They say, "And what is (Allah), the Most Gracious? Shall we adore that which you order us?" And it increases their flight (from the truth).

25.61.. He is the blessed (One) Who made groups of stars in the skies, and placed a Lamp in there and a Moon giving light;

25.62.. And it is He Who made the night and the day to come after each other: For such as (those who) have the will to celebrate His Praise or to show their gratitude (to Allah).

25.63.. And the servants of (Allah), the Most Gracious are those who walk on the earth with humility, and when those who do not know talk to them, they (the servants, gently) say: "*Salaam* (Peace)!"

25.64. Those who spend the night in the devotion to their Lord (either) prostrate and standing;

25.65. And those who say: "Our Lord! Take away from us the torture of Hell, verily, its torture is an eternal severely painful (and a fierce) punishment-

25.66. "Evil indeed, is it as a home, and as a place to rest in;"

25.67. And those who, when they spend are not wasteful and not miserly, but hold a fair (balance) between those (limits);

25.68. And those who do not call, with Allah, any other god, and do not kill the life which Allah has made sacred, except for honest cause, and do not commit adultery- And any who does this (the evil acts) shall get the penalty

25.69. (And even) the penalty on the Day of Judgment will be doubled to him, and he will live in there with dishonor.-

25.70. Unless he repents, believes, and does rightful acts, because Allah will change the evil of such persons into good deeds, and Allah is Often Forgiving, Most Merciful .

25.71. And whoever repents and does good has truly turned to Allah with a (true) change (towards righteousness)-

25.72. Those who do not testify to lies, and if they come by useless (things), they avoid it with honor;

25.73. And those who, when they are warned by the Signs of their Lord, do not sink down (low) at them as if they were deaf or blind;

25.74. And those who pray, "Our Lord! Give to us wives and children who will be the comfort of our eyes, and give us (the grace) to lead the righteous."

25.75. Those are the ones who will be rewarded with the highest place (in Paradise), because of their patient constancy: Therein they will be met with welcome and with words of peace and respect,

25.76. Living in there- How beautiful a home and place of rest!

25.77.. Say (to the disbelievers): "My Lord does not care for you if you do not pray to Him: But you have in fact rejected (Him), and soon will come the inescapable (punishment)!"

****

Sura 26. Ash-Shu'ara',
(The poets): (Makkah, 227 Verses)
In the Name of Allah, the Most Gracious, the Most Merciful.

26.1.. **Ta Sin Mim:**

26.2. These are verses of the Book that clarifies (all the many things).

26.3.. It may be that you upset your soul with sorrow, because they do not become believers.

26.4. If (it) was Our Will, We can send down a Sign from the heaven to them, to which they will bow their necks in humility.

26.5. But to them, there does not come (even) one new revelation from (Allah,) the Most Gracious, but they (already) turn away from it.

26.6. Truly, they have rejected (the Message): So they will soon know the truth about that which they made fun!

26.7. Do they not look at the earth- How many noble things of all types We have produced in there?

26.8. Surely, there is a Sign (*Ayâh*) in this: But most of them do not believe.

26.9. And surely, your Lord is He, (Who is) Exalted in Might, Most Merciful .

26.10.. And (remember) when, your Lord called unto Musa (and said): "Go to the people who are wrongdoers-

26.11. "The people of Firon (Pharaoh): Will they not fear Allah?"

26.12 Said (Musa): "O my Lord! I fear that they may deny me (and accuse me of falsehood):

26.13. "My chest may become strained: And my speech may not go smoothly; So send forth (with me) Haroon (Aaron).

26.14. "And they have a charge of crime (see Note 1 at the end of the Sura) against me; And I fear that they may kill me."

26.15. Said (Allah): "Not at all! Now both of you go with Our Signs; Verily, We are with you, and (We) will listen (to you).

26.16. "So both of you, go forth to Firon (Pharaoh), and say: 'We are the messengers of the Lord (and Cherisher) of the Worlds ; (see Note 2 at the end of the Sura.)

26.17. "'You send with us the Children of Israel (*Bani-Israel*).'"

26.18. (Firon) said (to Musa): "Did we not cherish you as a child with us, (see Note 3 at the end of the Sura,) and did you not stay many years of your life amidst us?

26.19. "And you did an act that which you did (killed an Egyptian, see Note1) and you are a thankless (wretch)!"

26.20. Musa (Moses) said: "I did it then, when I was wrong.

26.21. "So, I ran away from (all of) you, when I feared you; But (after that) my Lord has granted me judgment (and wisdom) and made me one of the messengers.

26.22. "And this is the old favor with which you put me to shame- That you have made the Children of Israel, (your) slaves!"

26.23.. Firon (Pharaoh) said: "And what is the 'Lord and Cherisher of the Worlds '?"

26.24. Said (Musa): "The Lord and Cherisher of the heavens and the earth, and all between- If you want to be quite sure."

26.25. Said (Pharaoh) to those around: "Do you not listen (to what he says)?"

26.26. Musa (Moses) said: "Your Lord and the Lord of your fathers (right) from the beginning!"

26.27. Said (Firon): "Truly, your messenger who has been sent to you is undeniably a madman!"

26.28. Said (Musa): "Lord of the East and the West, and all between! If you only had the sense (to understand)!"

26.29. Said (Firon): "If you bring forward any god other than me, I will really put you in prison!"

26.30. Said (Musa): "Even if I showed you something clear (enough) to make you believe?"

26.31. Said (Firon): "Show it then, if you tell the truth!"

26.32. So (Musa) threw his rod, and look, it was a (huge) snake, clearly (for all to see)!

26.33. And he drew out his hand, and look! It was white (and bright) to the seers!

26.34.. (Firon) said to the chiefs around him: "This is truly a magician of high skill."

26.35. His plan is to get you out of your land by his magic; Then what is it (that you) command?

26.36. They said: "Keep him and his brother in suspense, and send out the callers to the cities to collect-

26.37. "And bring to you all magicians of high skill."

26.38.. So, the magicians were brought together for the event on a well known day,

26.39. And the people were told: "Are you (all now) gathered?

26.40. That we may follow (the religion of) the magicians, if they win?"

26.41. So, when the magicians arrived, they said to Firon (Pharaoh): "Truly- Shall we have a (worthy) reward if we win?"

26.42. Said (Firon): "Yes, (and more)- Because, in that case (if you win), you will be (given positions) near (to me)."

26.43. Said Musa (Moses) to them: "You throw- Whatever you are about to throw!"

26.44. So, they threw their ropes and their rods, and said: "By the might of Firon (Pharaoh), it is we who will really win!"

26.45. Then (Musa) threw his rod, when, look! It right away swallows up all the lies that they make up! (see Note 4 at the end of the Sura.)

26.46.. Then the magicians fell down, prostrate in praise,

26.47. Saying: "We believe in the Lord of the Worlds ,

26.48. "The Lord of Musa (Moses) and Haroon (Aaron)."

26.49. Said (Firon): "Will you believe in Him (Allah) before I give you permission? Surely, he (Musa) is your chief, who has taught you magic! But you will know soon! Be sure I will cut off your hands and your feet on opposite sides, and I will cause you all to die on the cross!"

26.50. They said: "(That) does not matter! About us, we shall only go back to our Lord!

26.51. Verily, our desire is that our Lord will forgive us for our mistakes, that we may become first among the believers!"

26.52. By inspiration We revealed to Musa (Moses): "Go (away from Firon) by night with My servants; Because surely, you will be chased."

26.53. Then Firon (Pharaoh) sent news to (all) the Cities,

26.54. "These (people) are only a small group,

26.55. "And they are very angry against us;

26.56. "But we are a many more with enough warning."

26.57.. So We expelled them from gardens, springs, (see Note 5)

26.58. Treasures, and every kind of honorable position;

26.59. It was like this, that We made the Children of Israel inheritors of these things.

26.60.. So they (Firon) chased them (Musa and the Israelites) at sunrise.

26.61. And when the two groups saw each other, the Musa's (Moses') people said: "We are sure to be overtaken (and overrun)."

26.62. (Musa) said: "Not at all! My Lord is with me! He will soon guide me!"

26.63. Then We told Musa (Moses) by revelation: "Strike the sea with your rod." And so, it (the sea) divided, and each separate part became like the huge, firm part of a mountain.

26.64. And We made the other people come there.

26.65. We saved Musa (Moses) and all who were with him;

26.66. Then We drowned the others.

26.67. Surely, there is a Sign in this: But most of them do not believe.

26.68. And surely your Lord is He (Who is), the Exalted in Might , Most Merciful .

26.69.. And recite to them Ibrahim (Abraham)'s story.

26.70. When he said to his father and his people "What do you worship?"

26.71. They said: "We worship idols, and we remain attending to them always."

26.72. He said: "Do they listen to you when you call unto (them)

26.73. "Or do (they) cause (any) good or harm to you?"

26.74. They said: "No, but we found our fathers doing like this (what we do)."

26.75. He said: "Then do you see what you have been worshipping-

26.76. "You and your fathers before you?

26.77. "Verily, they are enemies to me; except the Lord of the Worlds ;

26.78. "Who created me, and it is He Who guides me;

26.79. "And it is He Who gives me food and gives me drink,

26.80. "And when I am ill, it is He Who cures me;

26.81. "And it is He Who will cause me to die, and then bring me to life (again);

26.82. "And Who, I hope, will forgive me for my mistakes on the Day of Resurrection..

26.83. "O my Lord! Give me wisdom, and join me with the righteous (people);

26.84. "And give me honorable saying on the tongue of truth (see Note 6 at the end of the Sura) of the later (generations) to come;

26.85. "And make me one of the inheritors of the Garden of (Eternal) Joy (the Paradise);

26.86. "And forgive my father, verily, he is among those who go astray;

26.87. "And let me not be in disgrace on the Day when (men) will be raised up;" -

26.88.. The Day when neither wealth nor sons will be of (any) use,

26.89. Except only he who brings to Allah a good heart (will be treated well);

26.90. The Garden will be brought near to the righteous,

26.91. And the Fire will be placed in full sight to those lost in evil;

26.92. And it shall be said to them: "Where are the (gods that) you worshipped-

26.93. "Besides Allah? Can they help you or help themselves?"

26.94. Then they will be cast right into the (Fire)- They and those lost in evil,

26.95. And the whole groups from (the race of) *Iblis* (or Satan) altogether.

26.96. They will say, while they quarrel in there:

26.97. " 'By Allah, truly, we were in a clear error,

26.98. " 'When we held you (*Iblis*) as equal to the Lord of the Worlds ;

26.99. " 'And none has led us astray except those who were criminals, (deeply) soaked in sin;

26.100. " 'Then, we have none to intercede (for us) now,

26.101. " 'Nor a close single friend to feel (sorry for us now).

26.102. "Now if we only had a chance to return, we shall truly be of those who believe!' "

26.103. Surely in this is a Sign but most of them do not believe.

26.104. And surely your Lord is He (Who is) the Almighty , the Most Merciful .

26.105.. The people of Nuh (Noah) denied the messengers.

26.106. When their brother Nuh (Noah, see Note 7) said to them: "Will you not fear and obey (Allah, in total trust or Taq'wa)?

26.107. "I am to you a messenger fit for all trust:

26.108. "So fear Allah, and obey me,

26.109. "I do not ask for any reward for it from you: My reward is only from the Lord of the Worlds:

26.110. "So fear Allah, and obey me."

26.111. They said: "Shall we believe in you when it is the lowliest who follow you?"

26.112. He (Noah) said: "And what do I know about what they do?

26.113. "Their account is only with my Lord, if you can (only) understand.

26.114. "I am not one to drive away those who believe.

26.115. "I am only a plain Warner (to warn you clearly)."

26.116. They said: "O Nuh (Noah)! If you do no stop, you will be stoned (to death)."

26.117. He said: "O my Lord! Truly my people have rejected me.

26.118. Then, You judge between me and them openly, and save me and those of the believers who are with me."

26.119. And We saved him and those with him, in the Ark full of (all of creatures).

26.120. After that We drowned those who remained behind.

26.121. Surely in this is a Sign but most of them do not believe.

26.122. And surely your Lord is He (Who is) the Almighty , the Most Merciful .

26.123.. The 'Ad (people) rejected the messengers.

26.124. When their brother Hud said to them; "Will you not fear (Allah)?

26.125. "Verily, I am to you a messenger fit for all trust:

26.126. "So fear Allah and obey me.

26.127. "I do not ask for any reward for it from you: My reward is only from the Lord of the Worlds :

26.128. "Do you build an important place on every high place to bring joy to yourselves?

26.129. And do you get for yourselves fine buildings with the hope of living in there (for ever)?

26.130. "And when you play your strong hand (with force), do you act like cruel men with absolute power ?

26.131. "Now fear Allah, and obey me.

26.132. "Yes, fear Him Who has given you freely all that you know.

26.133. "He has freely given you cattle and sons-

26.134. "And gardens and springs.

26.135. "Truly, I fear the Penalty of a Great Day for you."

26.136.. They said: "It is the same for us if you preach (warn) us or do not be among (our) warners!

26.137. "This is nothing different from the customary actions of the ancient (people),

26.138. "And we are not the ones to take pains and penalties!"

26.139. So they rejected him, and We destroyed them. Surely there is a Sign in this but most of them do not believe.

26.140. And surely your Lord is He (Who is) the Almighty , the Most Merciful .

26.141.. The Samood (Thamud people) rejected the messengers.

26.142. When their brother Sálih said to them: "Will you not fear (Allah)?

26.143. "I am to you a messenger fit for all trust.

26.144. "So fear Allah, and obey me

26.145. "I do not ask for any reward for it from you: My reward is only from the Lord of the Worlds .

26.146. "Will you be left safe (for ever), in (the enjoyment of) all that you have here?

26.147. "In gardens and springs,

26.148. "And corn-fields and date palms with their (leafy) covers almost breaking (with the weight of fruit)

26.149. "And you dig out houses out of (rocky) mountains with high skill.

26.150. "But fear Allah and obey me;

26.151. "And do not follow the call of those who are wasteful-

26.152. "Who do mischief in the land, and do not correct (their ways)."

26.153.. They said: "You are only one of those under a (magical) spell!

26.154. "You are no more than a human like us:
"Then bring us a Sign, if you tell the truth!"

26.155. He said: "Here is a she-camel: She has a right to (come to the) water, and you have a right to (come to the) water, on a day appointed.

26.156. "And do not touch her with harm, or the penalty of the Great Day seize you."

26.157. But they killed her (by cutting the hamstrings): Then they became full of sorrow.

26.158. But the penalty seized them, surely there is indeed a Sign in this but most of them do not believe.

26.159. And surely your Lord is He (Who is), the Almighty , the Most Merciful .

26.160.. The people of Lut (Lot) rejected the messengers.

26.161. When their brother Lut (Lot) said to them: "Will you not fear (Allah)?

26.162. "Verily, I am to you a messenger fit for all trust.

26.163. "So, fear Allah and obey me.

26.164. "I do not ask for any reward for it from you: My reward is only from the Lord of the Worlds .

26.165. "Will you run after males, of all creation (made) in the worlds,

26.166. "And leave those (the females) whom Allah has made for you to be your wives? No! You are a people exceeding (all moral limits)!"

26.167.. They said: "O Lut (Lot)! If you do not stop, you will surely be one of those driven out!"

26.168. He said: "I am one of those who disapproves your acts (of sodomy) with severe hate and anger.

26.169. "O my Lord! Save me and my family from such things like what they do!"

26.170. So, We saved him and his family- All,

26.171. Except an old woman who kept behind.

26.172. But the rest We destroyed totally.

26.173. And, We rained down on them a shower (of hard clay-stone): And evil was the shower on those who were warned (but did not listen)!

26.174. Surely there is a Sign in this but most of them do not believe.

26.175. And surely your Lord is He (Who is) the Almighty , the Most Merciful .

26.176.. The companions of the Wood rejected the messengers. (see Note 8 at the end of the Sura)

26.177. When Shu'aib said to them: "Will you not fear (Allah)?

26.178. "I am to you a messenger fit for all trust.

26.179. "So fear Allah and obey me.

26.180. "I do not ask for any reward for it from you: My reward is only from the Lord of the Worlds .

26.181. "Give proper measure (to others) and do not make loss (for others by cheating).

26.182. "And weigh with true and upright scales.

26.183. "And do not defraud (hold back) things that are truly due to men, and do no evil in the land, by making mischief.

26.184. "And fear Him Who created you and the generations before (you)."

26.185.. They said: "You are only one of those under a (magical) spell!

26.186. "You are no more than a human like us: And really, we think that you one of the liars!

26.187. "Now make a piece of the sky to fall on us, if you are truthful!"

26.188. He said: "My Lord knows well what you do."

26.189. But they denied him. Then the punishment of a day of great sorrow seized them, indeed that was the penalty of a Great Day.

26.190. Surely, in that, there is a Sign but most of them do not believe.

26.191. And surely your Lord is He (Who is) the Almighty , the Most Merciful .

26.192. And Truly, this is a Revelation from the Lord of the Worlds :

26.193. With this (the Quran), the Spirit [*Jibrael* or (Gabriel)] of truth came down (to bring it)-

26.194. To your heart and (to your) mind that you (O Prophet) may warn and guide

26.195. In clear (and easily understood) Arabic tongue.

26.196. And without doubt it is (from) the mystic Books of the earlier peoples. (see Note 9 at the end of the Sura.)

26.197. Is it not a Sign to them that the learned from the Children of Israel knew it (as true)?

26.198. If We had revealed it to any of the non-Arabs,

26.199. And if he read it to them, they would not have believed in it.

26.200.. Like this We have made it enter the hearts (and minds) of the criminals.

26.201. They will not believe in it until they see the painful penalty;

26.202. But the (penalty) will come to them swiftly, when they are not aware of it;

26.203. Then they will say: Will we be given some relief?

26.204.. Then do they ask them for Our Penalty to be hurried on?

26.205. Do you see? (Even) if We let them enjoy (this life) for a few years,

26.206. And still at the end, there will come to them (the punishment) that they were promised!

26.207. It will not help them that they enjoyed (this life)!

26.208. And We never ruined a population that did not have its warners-

26.209. As a reminder (to mankind); And We never are unjust.

26.210.. And no Satans' (or the Evil ones) have brought down this (Message):

26.211. It would not befit them, and they would not be able (to produce it).

26.212. As a fact, they have been removed far away from even hearing it.

26.213. So do not call on any other god with Allah, or you will be from those under the penalty.

26.214. And advise and warn your nearest relatives.

26.215. And lower you arms (as greetings) to the believers who follow you.

26.216. Even then, if they disobey you, say: I am free (of responsibility) for what you do!

26.217. And place your trust on the Almighty , the Most Merciful .

26.218. Who sees you standing up (in prayer),

26.219. And (sees) your movements among those who prostrate themselves.

26.220. Verily, it is He Who hears and knows all things.

26.221.. (O my people!) Shall I inform you, on whom it is that Satans' (or the Evil ones) come down?

26.222. They come down on every lying, sinful person,

26.223. (In their ears) they fill half-true, worthless things, and most of them are liars.

26.224. As for the poets- Those astray (in evil) who follow them:

26.225. Do you not see that they (anxiously) speak about every subject (of lies and sin) in their poetry?

26.226. And that they say what they do not do?

26.227. Except those who believe and work rightfully, and do much in the remembering of Allah, and (act to) defend themselves only after they are wrongly attacked. And soon will the unjust attackers know what sudden changes their actions will take!

Sura 26 Notes

Note 26.1: As a young man Musa (Moses) was enraged by the angry blow of an Egyptian to an Israelite. Musa in his rage killed the Egyptian and this charge was retained against Musa. In 26.14, the reference is to the charge that was pending against Musa.

Note 26.2: Musa is the only prophet who had the status of being spoken to, by Allah. In the Glorious Quran this capacity of Musa to be spoken by Allah is stressed again and again.

Note 26.3: Musa was born in an Israelite home and set afloat in a small chest on the river by his family to escape the persecution by the Egyptians (see 20.37-40). He was rescued by members of the Firon's (Pharaoh's) own family and reared as a child. But Musa's inner self bore a sympathy for the cause of Israelites suffering at the hands of Firon's army.

Note 26.4: When Musa threw his rod, it became a huge serpent, huge enough to swallow all the other smaller serpents that appeared when the other magicians had thrown their ropes and rods. They appear to move and wiggle around (see 20.66)

Note 26.5: There are two ways of interpreting 26.57-69: First that it was Firon who expelled Israelites from the gardens and second that it was Allah (We, in 26.58), Who expelled Firon's' people from the gardens and springs and truly made the Israelites the (26.60) inheritors of these things. The later interpretation is the more accepted in Quranic circles. In either case, the moral of Fironic (Pharaonic) culture is evident. It was they (i.e., Firon and his people) who lost the conflict against Allah and His prophet Musa.

Note 26.6: These words "tongue of truth" are repeated in 19.50. They indicate prophet Ibrahim's (Abraham's) firm desire to be remembered as an honorable and righteous person for the many generations to come.

Note 26.7: Brother Nuh (Noah) is used to indicate that Nuh (Noah) was much like an elderly and respected figure in the community around his people. He was already well known as a respected person and trusted fully within the community.

Note 26.8: The companions of the Wood are mentioned four times (15.78, here in 26.176-191, 38.13 and 50.14) in the Glorious Quran. It is believed that these people were the People of Madyan to whom Shu'aib was sent as a prophet, or a small group of people living close to Madyan People. These folks are mentioned in the Glorious Quran in 7.83.

Note 26.9: The five Scriptures mentioned in the Glorious Quran are the Book (or *pages*, see 87.19) of Ibrahim, *Taurát* (or the Torah) revealed to Musa (Moses), *Zabur* revealed to Dawood (David), *Injeel* (the Gospel) revealed to Messiah (Christ), and the Glorious Quran revealed to Prophet Muhammad (Peace of Allah be upon him). These five holy books, (the *'pages'* of Ibrahim, *Taurát* (Moses), *Zabur* (David), *Injeel* (Christ), and *Quran)* all carry the same Message directing mankind to the Straight Path towards One Almighty Allah. There is a reference (see 87.19) that prophet Ibrahim (Abraham) also received the *'pages'* of a holy book in his own times. The teachings of other prophets have not been documented and preserved as carefully as the Glorious Quran.

****

Sura 27. An-Naml,
(The ants): (Makkah, 93 Verses)
In the Name of Allah, the Most Gracious, the Most Merciful.

27.1. Ta   Sin: These are the *Ayât* (Verses) of the Quran- A Book that makes (things) clear;

27.2. A Guide; And Glad Tiding (news) to the believers-

27.3. Those who perform prayers regularly and give charity (*Zakah*) regularly, and also have (total) belief in the Hereafter.

27.4. Verily, those who do not believe in the Hereafter, We have made their actions pleasing in their eyes; And so they walk around lost without a focus.

27.5. These are they for whom lies a painful penalty: And their loss will be greatest in the Hereafter.

27.6. And verily, you (O Prophet!), the Quran is granted upon you from the One, All Wise, All Knowing .

27.7.. (Remember) when Musa (Moses) said to his household: "Surely, I see a fire; Soon I will bring you some news from there, or I will bring you a burning piece to light our (own fire) fuel, so that you may warm yourselves."

27.8. But when he came to the (fire), he was called: "Those in the fire and those around are blessed: And Glory to Allah, the Lord of the Worlds.

27.9. "O Musa (Moses)! Surely, I am Allah, the Supreme in Might , the Wise!

27.10. "And now you throw your rod!" But when he saw it moving (by itself) like it was a snake, he was set back wondering, and (he) did not look back on his steps: (Again, the voice said), "O Musa (Moses)! Do not be afraid! Truly, in My Presence, those called as messengers (they) do not have (any) fear-

27.11. "But if any have done wrong and have afterwards replaced good in place of evil, then truly, I am Often Forgiving, Most Merciful .

27.12. "Now put your hand on your chest, and it will come out white without stain: (These are) from the nine Signs (you will take) to Firon (Pharaoh) and his people: Verily, they are unruly people exceeding all limits."

27.13. But when Our Signs came to them that should have (really) opened their eyes, they said: "This is clearly magic!"

27.14. And they denied (rejected) those Signs with injustice and pride, even though their souls were convinced of them: So, see what was the end of those who acted wrongly!

27.15.. And indeed, We gave knowledge to Dawood (David) and to Sulaiman (Solomon): And they both said: "All the Praises (and thanks) be to Allah, Who has chosen us above many of His servants who believe!"

27.16. And Sulaiman (Solomon) was to inherit after Dawood (David). He said: "O you people! We have been taught the language of Birds, and to us is given (a little) of all things: Truly, this is (by Allah's) clear Grace."

27.17. And before Sulaiman (Solomon) were gathered his armies- Of jinns' and men, and birds, and all of them marching forward in order and ranks.

27.18. Till when they came to a valley of the ants, (and) one of the ants said: "O you ants, get into your houses, lest Sulaiman (Solomon) and his armies will crush you (while marching) without knowing it."

27.19. So he (Sulaiman) smiled, amused at her speech; And he said: "O my Lord! Command me that I may be thankful for Your mercies, which You have blessed upon me and upon my parents, and that I may act righteous that will please You: And admit me, by Your Grace, to the ranks of your righteous servants."

27.20.. And he took a troop of the birds, and he said: "Why is it I see not the Hoopoe? (A bird with feathers like a crown on its head) or is he from those absent?

27.21. "I will really punish him with a harsh penalty, or (even) kill him, unless he brings to me a clear reason (for being absent)."

27.22.. But (the Hoopoe) did not stay behind too far: He (approached Sulaiman and) said: "I have traveled (through lands) where you have not gone and I have come to you from Saba (Sheba) with true (and correct) news.

27.23. "I found a woman (*Bilqiz*) ruling (there) over them and made things available for every want; And she has a grand (and beautiful) throne.

27.24. "I found her and her people worshipping the sun besides Allah: Satan has made their actions appear pleasing to their eyes, and (he) has kept them away from the (Straight) Way- So they receive no guidance-

27.25. "(And) so they do not prostrate themselves before Allah, Who brings to light what is hidden in the heavens and the earth, and knows what you hide and what you show.

27.26. "Allah! There is no god but He! Lord of the Throne Supreme!"
{A Muslim generally prostrates to Allah after reciting this verse}

27.27. (Sulaiman) said: "Soon shall we see if you have told the truth or you are one of the liars!

27.28. " Go you with this letter from me, and give it to them: Then get back from them, and (wait to) see what answer they give back." ..

27.29. She (the queen of Saba) said: "You chiefs! Here is a letter delivered to me- A noble letter.

27.30. "It is from Sulaiman (Solomon), and is (written): 'In the Name of Allah, the Most Gracious, the Most Merciful:

27.31. " 'You do not act proudly with me, but come to me as Muslims, in submission (to the Religion of Allah).' "

27.32. She (the queen) said: "You chiefs! Advise me about (this) ordeal of mine: No ordeal have I decided without your presence."

27.33. They said: "We are blessed with great strength, and used to fierce war: But the power is with you; So think about what you will command."

27.34. She said: "Verily, when kings enter a country, ruin it, and make the noblest from its people, its meanest; They act like this.

27.35. "But verily, I am going to send him (Sulaiman) a present, and (wait) to see with what (answer) return (my) ministers."

27.36.. So, when (the ministers) came to Sulaiman (Solomon), he said: "Will you give me a lot of wealth? But what Allah has given me is better than what He has given to you! Really! It is you who take joy in your gift!

27.37. "Go back to them, and be sure we will come to them with strong armies that they will never be able to meet: And we shall remove them from there in disgrace, and they will feel in low position."

27.38. He said (to his own army): "You chiefs! Which of you can bring me her throne before they come to me surrendering as Muslims, in submission?

27.39. Said an Ifrit, from the (race of) jinns': (see Note 1 at the end of the Sura-) "I will bring it to you before you get up from your Court (and gathering now): Truly, I have the full strength for the deed, and (I am) trustworthy for such work (service to you)."

27.40. Said one who had knowledge of the Scripture: (see Note 2 at the end of the Sura-) "I will bring it to you by the blinking of an eye!" then as (Sulaiman) saw it placed firmly before him, he said: "This is by the Grace of my Lord! To test me whether I am thankful or unthankful! And if anyone is thankful, truly, his gratitude is (only for the good) for his own soul; But if anyone is unthankful, truly, My Lord is free of all Needs, All Bountiful (in His generosity)!"

27.41. He said: "Change her throne that it is beyond recognition by her let us see whether she is guided (to Allah) or (she) is one of those who takes no guidance."

27.42.. So when she arrived, she was asked, "Is your throne like this?" She said; "(It is) as if it was just the same;" He said: "Knowledge was bestowed to us before her, and we have submitted to Allah (in Islam)." (see Note 3 at the end of the Sura-)

27.43. And she came away from the worship of others besides Allah: For she was from a people who had no faith.

27.44. She was asked to enter the high palace: (see Note 4 at the end of the Sura-) but when she saw it, she thought it was a pool (lake) of water, and (pulled up her skirts), showing her legs. He (Sulaiman) said: "This is only a palace smoothly covered with sheets of glass." She said: "O my Lord! Truly, I have wronged my soul: And I submit with Sulaiman (Solomon) to Allah and to the Lord of the Worlds ."

27.45.. (Before now), We sent to the Samood (Thamud), their brother Sálih, saying, "Worship (serve) Allah:" But look! They became two groups arguing with each other.

27.46. He said: "O my people! Why do you hurry to evil rather than the good? If you only ask Allah for forgiveness, you can (still) hope to receive (His) mercy."

27.47. They said: "We foresee bad sign from you, and from those who are with you." He said: "Your bad sign is with Allah; Yes, you are a people under trial."

27.48. And in the City, there were Nine men of a family, who made mischief in the land, and would not correct (themselves).

27.49. (Among themselves) they said: "Make a common oath by Allah that we shall make a secret night-attack on him (Sálih) and his household, and that we shall then tell his heirs (when they want to punish us): 'We were not there at the killing of his household, and verily, we are surely telling the truth'. "

27.50. So they plotted and planned but We too planned, even while they were not aware of it.

27.51. Then see what was the end of their plan! (Only) this- That We ruined them and their people, altogether.

27.52. Now their houses were like this- In utter ruin, because they did wrong, surely in this, there is a Sign (*Ayâh*) for people with knowledge.

27.53. And We saved those who believed and did righteousness.

27.54.. (And We also sent) Lut (Lot, as a prophet): When he said to his people, "You do what is shameful (sodomy), even though you see (it is wrong and unjust)?

27.55. "Would you really run after men in your excessive (sexual) desire rather than after women? No! You are a people (totally) ignorant!"

27.56. But his people gave no other answer except this: They said, "Drive out the followers of (Lot) from your City: Truly, these are men who want to be clean and pure!"

27.57. So We saved him and his family, except his wife: We destined her to be of those who remained behind.

27.58. And We rained down on them a rain (of yellow sulfurous stones): And evil was the rain on those who were warned (but did not pay attention)!

27.59.. Say: "Praise (and thanks) be to Allah, and Peace on His servants whom He has chosen. (Who) is better? Allah or the false gods they associate (with Him).

27.60. "Is it not He, Who has created the heavens and the earth, and Who sends down rain for you from the sky? Yes, We cause well planted gardens to grow with it full of beauty and delight: It is not in your power to cause the growth of (such) trees in them. (Is there another) god with Allah? No! They are a people who turn away from justice.

27.61. "Is it not He, Who has made the earth strong to live on; Made rivers in its middle; Set mountains firmly upon it; And made a separating boundary between the two expanses of flowing water? (Is there another) god with Allah?" - No! Most of them do not know.

27.62. "Is it not He, Who listens to the hurting (soul) when it calls on Him, and Who removes its hurt, and makes you (believers) inheritors of the earth? (Is there another) god besides Allah? Little is the attention you give!

27.63. "Is it not He, Who guides you in middle of the depths of darkness on land and sea, and Who sends the winds as (the blowing) Signs of the good news, which come before His Mercy? (Is there another) god with Allah? Allah is High above what they associate with Him!

27.64. "Is it not He, Who originates Creation, then repeats it, and Who gives you the means to live from heaven and earth? (Is there another) god with Allah?"- Say: "Bring up your reasons, if you tell the truth!"

27.65. Say: "No one in the heavens or on earth, except Allah, knows what is the unseen:" Nor can they foresee when they shall be raised up (for Judgment).

27.66. Even less can their knowledge understand the Hereafter: No! They are in doubt and uncertainty about it; No! They are blind to it!

27.67.. The unbelievers' say: "What! When we become dust- We and our fathers- Will we truly be raised (from the dead)?

27.68. "Indeed, we were promised this- We and our fathers before (us): These are nothing but the stories of the old."

27.69. Say to them: "Travel through the earth and see what is the end of the criminals."

27.70. But do not feel sad for them, and do not pain yourself because of their plots.

27.71.. And they say: "When will this promise (be true)? (Speak) if you are truthful."

27.72. Say: "It can be that some of the events that you want hurried can be following (close to) you!"

27.73. But surely, your Lord is full of grace to mankind, still most of them show no gratitude.

27.74. And surely, your Lord knows all that their hearts conceal, and all that they reveal.

27.75. And there is nothing from the unseen, in heaven or earth, which is not (written) in a clear book (a record).

27.76.. Surely, this Quran does explain to the children of Israel most of the things about which they disagree.

27.77. And it certainly is a Guide and a Mercy to those who believe.

27.78. Surely, your Lord will decide between them by His Order: And He is Supreme in Might, All Knowing .

27.79. So, (believers!) put your trust in Allah: Surely, you (O Prophet!) are on (the Path of) clear (and open) Truth.

27.80. Truly, you cannot make the dead to hear, nor can make the deaf to hear the call, especially when they go away in hiding,

27.81. Nor can you lead the blind, from wandering away (from the Path): You will get only those who believe in Our Signs to hear, and those who have submitted (to Allah as Muslims).

27.82. And (remember) when the Word is made true against them, We shall bring out from the earth a beast to (face) them: To speak to them, because mankind did not believe in Our Signs with (due) certainty.

27.83.. And (remember) one Day We shall bring together from every people a group of those who reject Our Signs (*Ayât*), and they shall be kept in (their proper) order-

27.84. Until, when they come (for Judgment, Allah), will say: "Did you reject My Signs, even though you did not understand them with (any) knowledge, or what you were doing?"

27.85. And the Word will be made true against them, because of their doing wrong, and they will not be able to speak (for mercy).

27.86. Do they not see that We have made the night for them to rest and the day to give them light? Surely, in this are Signs for any people who believe!

27.87. And (remember) the Day that the Trumpet will be blown—and all those who are in the heavens and those who are on earth, will be struck with fear; except those as Allah will please (to forgive): And all will come to His (Presence) as the created (ones) aware of their lowliness.

27.88. You see the mountains and think that they are firmly fixed; But they (too) will blow away like the clouds blow away: (Like this is) the doing of Allah, who regulates all things with Perfect Order: Verily, He is very familiar with all that you do.

27.89. If any do good, (their portion of) good will (increase) for them from it; And they will be safe from the terror that Day.

27.90. And if any do evil, their faces will be thrown straight down into the Fire: (It shall be said:) "Do you receive a reward different from what your actions have earned (for you)?"

27.91.. For me, I have been ordered to worship (and serve- See Note 5 at the end of the Sura,) the Lord of this City (Makkah), He Who has cleansed it (as pure and holy) and (He) to Whom belong all things: And I am ordered to be of those who bow in Islam to Allah's Will-

27.92. And to recite (and rehearse) the Quran: And if any accept guidance, they do it for the good of their own souls, and if any wander away, say: I am only a Warner.

27.93. And say: "All the Praise (and thanks) be to Allah, He, Who will soon show you His Signs, and you will recognize them"; And your Lord is not unaware of all that you do.

Sura 27 Notes

Note 27.1: King Sulaiman (Solomon) had his power extended over men, jinns' and birds and gifted with understanding their languages. In his prophesied role, he was able to command and he brought forth to counsel them at his discretion. Ifrit was one of the more powerful jinns'. Jinn's are made of smoke-less flame and their role is different from that of man in this world.

Note 27.2: The power of Ifrit is still held in lower esteem than the one who has understanding of the Book of Allah. This gives a hint to compare power with understanding, and power gets undermined when the role of understanding is brought forth.

Note 27.3: The Queen of Saba (*Bilqiz*, as she was called) understood the implication of this question asked to her. She takes the hint and answers to the proposition that she comes committed to accepting Islam. But there is some doubt left in Sulaiman's (Solomon's) mind regarding her total honesty in accepting Islam. In his wisdom he invites her to enter the high Palace.

Note 27.4: The invitation to enter the high Palace is symbolic. It suggests the Queen of Saba understood the more divine and closer Call towards Allah. This second test was when she mistook the glass to be a lake.

Note 27.5: These are the words uttered by the holy prophet in Makkah about five years before his migration (*Hijrat*) to Medinah. This migration resulted because of the persecution of the people of Makkah and their continued denial of the Prophet and his holy teachings.

****

Sura 28. Al-Qasas,
(The narration): (Makkah, 88 Verses)
In the Name of Allah, the Most Gracious, the Most Merciful.

28.1.. Ta Sin Mim:

28.2. These are the *Ayât* (Verses) of the Book (Quran) that makes (things) clear.

28.3. We recite (and restate) to you with truth a part of the story of Musa (Moses) and Firon (Pharaoh), for people who believe.

28.4.. Truly, Firon (Pharaoh) had raised himself in the land and broken up its people into groups, keeping a small group (Israelites) lowly among them: Their sons, he killed but keep their females alive: Verily, he was truly a mischief-maker.

28.5. And We wished to be kind to those who were kept lowly in the land, to make them leaders and to make them the inheritors,

28.6. To make a firm place for them in the land, and to show Firon (Pharaoh), Haman, and their armies, at their (Israelites) hands, exactly those things which they were careful (to avoid themselves).

28.7.. And We sent this inspiration to Musa's (Moses') mother: "(Breast) feed (baby Musa), but when you have fears for him, put him into the river (in a basket), (see Note 1 at the end of the Sura-) but do not fear or feel sad (for him): Verily, We shall bring him back to you, and We shall make him one of Our messengers."

28.8. Then the household of Firon (Pharaoh) lifted him up (from the river): (It was) that (baby Musa) would be an opponent and a reason of sorrow for them: Verily, Firon (Pharaoh) and Haman and their armies were men of sin.

28.9. And Firon's (Pharaoh's) wife said: "(He is) a comfort (and joy) of the eye for me and for you: Kill him not! It could be that he will be of use to us, or we may adopt him as a son." And they did not foresee (what they were doing)!

28.10. And there come an emptiness in the heart of the mother of Musa (Moses): She was almost going to tell his (story and her loss), if We had not strengthened her heart (with faith), so that she may remain a (true) believer;

28.11. And she said to his (Musa's) sister, "Follow him (floating on the river)," so she (the sister) watched him from a distant place, as a stranger, and they (Egyptians) did not know.

28.12. And We commanded that he refused to (breast) feed at first, until (the sister) said: "Shall I point to you the people of a house who will feed and raise him for you and be truly attached to him?"

28.13. Like this We brought him back to his mother, so that her eye might be comforted, and that she might not feel sad, and that she might know that the Promise of Allah is True: But most of them do not understand.

28.14.. And when he reached full maturity (of manhood), and was well placed (in life), We gifted him with wisdom and knowledge. Like this We reward those who do good

28.15. And at one time he entered the City while its people were not watching: And he found there, two men fighting- One of his own part (religion), and the other, of his enemies (Egyptians). Now the man of his own religion asked for help against his enemy, and Musa (Moses) hit him (the Egyptian) with his fist and (that) killed him. (see Note 2 at the end of the Sura-). (In regret Musa,) he said: "This is a work of Satan verily, he is an enemy who clearly misleads!"

28.16. He prayed: "O my Lord! I have wronged myself! So (I pray You) forgive me!" Then (Allah) forgave him: Verily, He is the Often Forgiving, Most Merciful .

28.17. He said: "O my Lord! For what You have granted Your Grace on me, I will never be a help to those who are criminals!"

28.18. So he saw the morning in the City, (still) looking around in a state of fear, when look! The man who had wanted his help, the previous day, called loudly for his help (again). Musa (Moses) said to him: "Clearly, you are truly a quarrelsome fellow!"

28.19. Then, when he decided to catch the man who was an enemy to both of them, that man said: "O Musa (Moses)! Is it your intention to kill me like you killed a man yesterday? Your intention is nothing except to become a harsh powerful man in the land, and not to be one who sets things right!"

28.20. And (about the same time) there came a man, running from the far end of the City. He said: "O Musa (Moses)! Verily, the Chiefs together are (now) Taking an opinion about you, to kill you: So you go away, truly, I am one of the sincere advisors to you."

28.21. Therefore he got away from there, looking around (still) in a state of fear. He prayed: "O my Lord! Save me from people used to doing wrong."

28.22.. And then, when he turned (went) towards Madyan, (see Note 3 at the end of the Sura-) he said: "I hope that my Lord will show me the smooth and straight Path."

28.23. And when he came to the watering (place) in Madyan, there he found a group of men watering (their herds), and in addition to them, he found two (young) women who were holding back (their herds). He said: "What is the matter with you?" They said: "We cannot water until the shepherds take back (their herds); And our father is a very old man."

28.24. So, he watered (their herds) for them; Then he turned back to the shade, and said: "O my Lord! Truly, I am in need of any good that you will send me!"

28.25.. Afterwards one of the (two young women) came, walking shyly to him. She said: "Verily, my father invites you so that he may reward you for having watered (our herds) for us." So when he came to him and narrated the story, he (the father) said: "You, do not be afraid: You have run away from unjust people."

28.26. And one of the (two women) said: "O my father! Hire him on wages: Truly, the best of men to work for you is the (man) who is strong and trustworthy."

28.27. He (the father) said: "I want to marry one of these (two) daughters of mine to you, provided you serve me for eight years; But if you complete ten years, it will be (kindness) from you. But I do not want to put you under a difficulty: You will truly find me, if Allah wills, one of the righteous."

8.28. He (Musa) said: "Let that be (the agreement) between me and you: Whichever of the two duration's I fulfill, let there be no bad feelings for me. Let Allah be a witness to what we say."

28.29.. When Musa (Moses) had fulfilled the time, and was journeying with his family, he saw a fire in the direction of Mount Túr. He said to his family: "You wait (here); I see a fire; I hope to bring some news from there for you, or (bring) a piece of burning fire, so that you may warm yourselves."

28.30. So when he came to the (fire), a voice was heard from the right side of the valley, from a tree in hallowed ground: "O Musa (Moses)! Surely, I am Allah, the Lord of the Worlds ...

28.31. "Now you throw your rod!" But when he saw it moving (of its own accord) as if it was a snake, he turned back going away, and did not look back (at the past): "O Musa (Moses)!" (The voice said): "Come near, and do not be afraid: Verily, you are of those (people) who are safe.

28.32. "Move your hand towards your chest, and it will come out white without stain (or disease), and take your hand close to your side (to guard) against fear. These are the two Signs from your Lord (see Note 4 at the end of the Sura-) to Firon (Pharaoh) and to his chiefs: Verily, they are a people unruly and rebellious."

28.33. He said: "O my Lord! I have killed one of their men, and I fear that they will kill me.

28.34. "And my brother Haroon (Aaron)- He is more fluent in speech than me: So send him (also) with me as a helper, to support (and strengthen) me: Indeed, I fear that they may accuse me of lying."

28.35. (Allah) said: "We will certainly (strengthen you,) make your arm strong through your brother, and trust you both with power (and authority), so that they will not be able to touch you: With Our Signs (*Ayât*), both of you, and those who follow you- Will be the victorious."

28.36.. Then when Musa (Moses) came to them with Our Clear Signs (*Ayât*), they said: "This is nothing but magic made up (for us): We never heard (anything) like this from our fathers of the past!"

28.37. Musa (Moses) said: "My Lord knows well who comes with guidance from Him and whose end will be the best in the Hereafter: It is sure that the wrongdoers will not prosper."

28.38. And Firon (Pharaoh) said: "O Chiefs! I do not know of any god for you except myself: Therefore, O Haman! Fire up a (large oven to make bricks) from the clay for me, and build me a high palace, so that I may climb up to the God of Musa (Moses): But as far as I know, I think (Musa) is one of the lairs!"

28.39. And he and his armies were arrogant and rude in the land, beyond limit- without (being) right, they thought that they would not have to come back to Us!

28.40. So, We caught him and his armies, and We threw them all into the sea: So see what was the end of the wrongdoers!

28.41. And We made them (only) the leaders inviting (others) to the Fire: And on the Day of Judgment, they will find no help.

28.42. And We made a curse to follow them in this world: And on the Day of Judgment they will be from the hated (and damned).

28.43.. And We gave the Book to Musa (Moses) after We had ruined the earlier generations, (as a) Vision (of Truth, the *Taurát*) to men, and Guidance and Mercy, that they may receive warning (and guidance).

28.44. And you (O Prophet!) were not on the Western side (of the Tawa valley of Mount Túr) when We gave the prophet hood to Musa (Moses) and you did not see (those events).

28.45. But We raised up (new) generations from them, and the ages that passed over them were long; And you were not a resident among the people of Madyan, repeating Our Signs to them; But it was We Who send (them) messengers.

28.46. And you were not at the side of (the Mountain of) Túr, when We called (to Musa). Still (O Prophet! You are sent) as a Mercy from your Lord, to give warning to a people (of Arabia) to whom had come no Warner before you: In order that they may remember and receive the warning.

28.47. And if (We had) not (sent you to the people of Makkah)- (and) if a misfortune came over them for (the actions that) their hands have already done, they might say: "Our Lord! Why did You not send a messenger to us? We should then have followed Your Signs and been from those who believe!"

28.48.. But (now), when the Truth has come to them from Ourselves, they say, "Why are not (Signs of Allah) sent to him, like those (Signs; The rod, the glowing hand) which were sent to Musa (Moses)? Then, did they not reject (the Signs) which were formerly sent earlier to Musa (Moses)? They say: "Two types of magic, one helping the other!", And they say: "For us, We reject all (types of magic)!"

28.49. Say (to such rejecters): (see Note 5 at the end of the Sura-) "Then you bring a Book from Allah, which is a better Guide than earlier of them, that I may follow it! If you are truthful!"

28.50. But if they do not listen to you, (You) know that they only follow their own wishes: And who is more lost than one who follows his own wishes without the guidance from Allah? Verily, Allah does not guide people used to doing wrong.

28.51.. And indeed, We have made the Word (this Quran) reach them, so that they may remember and receive the warning.

28.52. Those to whom We sent the Book before this- They (also) believe in it (the Word of Allah);

28.53. And when it is read out to them, they say: "We believe in it, verily, it is the Truth from our Lord: Truly, we have been Muslims even before this."

28.54. These (people) will be given their reward twice over, because they have persevered, and (in) that they repel evil with good, and that they spend (in charity) from what We have given to them.

28.55. And when they hear evil and vain talk, they turn away from it and say: "To us our deeds, and to you yours; Peace be to you: We do not search out the ignorant."

28.56. It is true that you will not be able to guide everyone whom you love;

But Allah guides those whom He will. And He knows best those who receive guidance.

28.57.. And they say: "If we were to follow the guidance with you, we will be driven away from our land." Have We not built for them a land of safety, to which are brought all types of fruits, as gifts- A stock (of food) from Ourselves? But most of them do not understand.

28.58. And how many a town have We destroyed, (those) that became thankless for the livelihood: Now after them (the people of the towns), their homes lie empty and unlived- All except for a little! And We took over after them!

28.59. And your Lord was never the One to ruin a population until He had sent to its center a messenger, reciting (and rehearsing) to them Our Signs; And We not going to ruin a population unless its members commit injustice.

28.60. And whatever (worldly) things you are given are only the comforts of this life and its show; But what is with Allah is better and more lasting: Then will you not be wise?

28.61.. Can (these two) be the same? One to whom We have made a good promise, and who is going to see its (fulfillment), and (the other) one to whom We have given the good things of this life, but who, on the Day of Judgment, will be from those raised up (for punishment)?

28.62. And the Day when (Allah) will call to them, and say: "Where are My (so called) 'partners'? Whom you thought (to be so)?"

28.63. Those against whom the charge will be proved, will say: "Our Lord! These are the ones whom we led astray: Because we were astray ourselves: We free ourselves (from them) in Your Presence: They did not worship us."

28.64. And it will be said (to them): "Call to your 'partners' (for help):" They will call to them, but they will not listen to them; And they will see the penalty (before them); (They will wish:) "Only if they were open to guidance!"

28.65.. And that Day (Allah) will call to them, and say: "What was the answer you gave to the messengers (of Allah)?"

28.66. Then on that day, the (whole) story will seem dark (and distant) to them and they will not be able to question each other.

28.67.. But any who had repented, believed, and worked righteousness, will hope to be with those who are successful.

28.68.. And your Lord creates and chooses as He pleases: No choice have they (about it): Glory to Allah! And He is far above the 'partners' they give (to Him)!

28.69. And your Lord knows what their breasts (hearts) hide and what they reveal.

28.70. And He is Allah: There is no god but He. To Him be praise, at the first and at the last: For Him is the Command, and to Him you will be returned.

28.71.. Say: "Tell me! If Allah was to make the night last for ever for you till the Day of Judgment, which god is there other than Allah, can give you Light? Then will you not listen?"

28.72. Say: "Tell me! If Allah was to make the day last for ever for you till the Day of Judgment, which god is there other than Allah, can give you a night in which you can rest? Then will you not see?"

28.73. And it is from His Mercy that He has made for you night and day-

That you may rest in it (the night), and that you may seek His Grace (in the day)- And so that you may be thankful.

28.74.. And the Day that when He will call to them, and He will say: "Where are My (so called) 'partners'? Whom you thought (to be of those)?"

28.75. And from each people, We will draw a witness, and We shall say: "Produce your proof:" Then shall they know that the Truth is with Allah (Alone), and the (lies) that they had invented will leave them in the bad situation.

28.76.. Verily, Qârûn (Qaroon) was from the people of Musa (Moses); But he acted rudely towards them: The treasures We had given to him were such that just their very keys would have been a burden to a group of strong men; "Remember", his (Qaroon's) people said to him: "Do not feel overjoyed, because Allah does not love those who are joyful (in their wealth).

28.77. "But search out, with the (wealth) that Allah has given to you, the Home of the Hereafter, and do not forget your lawful (and good) fortune in this world: But you do good, like Allah has been good to you, and do not search (to make) mischief in the land: Verily, Allah loves not those who do mischief."

28.78. He said: "This (wealth) has been given to me only because of a certain knowledge which I have." Did he not know that Allah had ruined, before him, (whole) generations- Which were superior to him in strength andexceeded in the amount (of riches) that they had collected? But the wicked are not called (right away) to account for their sins.

28.79. So he went before his (own showy) people with the (pride of his worldly) show. Those whose goal is the life of this world, said: "Oh! If only we had the (wealth) like what Qârûn (Qaroon) has got! Verily, he is truly a lord of very good fortune!"

28.80. But those who had been given (true) knowledge said: "Sorrow for (woe unto) you! The reward of Allah (in the Hereafter) is best for those who believe and act righteousness: But this no one will get, except those who continuously persevere (in good)."

28.81. So, then We made the earth to swallow him up and his house; And he had not (the smallest) group to help him against Allah, and he could not protect himself.

28.82. And those who wished his position the day before began to say the next day: "Ah! It is truly Allah, Who grows the provision or shrinks it, to any of His servants He pleases! If it was not that Allah was kind to us, he could have caused the earth to swallow us up! Those who disbelieve will never be successful."

28.83.. We will give that Home of the Hereafter to those who do not want arrogance or mischief on earth: And the end is (best) for the righteous.

28.84. If any does good, the reward for him is better than his deed; But if any does evil, the doers of evil are only punished to the extent of their deeds.

28.85. Surely (O Prophet!) He, Who ordained the Quran for you, will bring you back to the Place of Return (*Ma'âd*, Makkah or the Hereafter). Say: "My Lord knows best who brings true guidance, and who is openly in the wrong."

28.86. And you had not expected that the Book would be sent down to you, except as a Mercy from your Lord: Therefore you do not give any support to those who reject (Allah's Message).

28.87. And let nothing keep you away from the Signs of Allah (*Ayât*) after they have been made known to you: And invite (men) to your Lord, and do not be in the company of those who join gods with Allah.

28.88. And call not, besides Allah, to another god. There is no god but He: Everything (that lives) shall die except His Own Face. To Him belongs the Command, and to Him will (all of) you be brought back.

Sura 28 Notes

Note 28.1: This part of Musa's (Moses') story as he was a child also repeats in Sura 20. See 20.38-40 for the details of how Musa was likely to be slain by Egyptian midwives who had orders to kill Israelite boys. The story continues as to how he was saved and raised in the royal palace of Firon (Pharaoh) under the care of his own real mother and his sister who followed the baby Musa in the basket floating on the river Nile, to find out who rescues him.

Note 28.2: This was apparently an accident since Musa was attempting to release the Israelite from the Egyptians. This event caused people to realize that Musa was really an Israelite at heart and had attempted to rescue an Israelite from an Egyptian.

Note 28.3: The Madyan area is South South-East of Egypt. The other areas leading to Sinai and Syria were patrolled by the Egyptians to capture Musa. So Musa headed towards the East and South-East Egypt mostly occupied by nomad Arabs rather than Egyptians.

Note 28.4: Allah had blessed Musa with nine of His Signs. Also see 7.133 and 17.101. In the Glorious Quran, these are listed as (a) his rod: 17.101, (b) his glowing (white) hand: 7.108, (c) the draught years for the Egyptians 7.130, (d) very few crops: 7.130, (e) epidemics and diseases: 7.133, (f) locusts: 7.133, (g) lice: 7.133, (h) frogs: 7.133, and (i) water turning to blood 7.133.

Note 28.5: This is perhaps the strongest challenge to the unbelievers. To be able to produce the Signs (*Ayât*, verses of Truth and Guidance) as they exist in the Glorious Quran. This is simply not human, not feasible by the living or dead magicians. These Signs were blessings to the holy Prophet, (an *ummi* or an illiterate) and only to him.

****

Sura 29. Al-Ankabut,
(The spider): (Makkah, 69 Verses)
In the Name of Allah, the Most Gracious, the Most Merciful.

29.1.. Alif Lám Mim:

29.2.. Does mankind think that by (just) saying, "We believe," they will be left alone and that they will not be tested?

29.3. And We indeed, did test those who were before them, so that Allah will indeed know, those who are true and He will know those who are liars.

29.4. Or do those who act evil think that they will gain over Us (Allah)? Evil is their judgment (if they think so)!

29.5. Whosoever hope (and wish) for meeting with Allah (let them work hard); Because the Time (fixed) by Allah is surely coming: And He is the All Hearing , All Knowing .

29.6. And whosoever strive a(with will and strength), they do so for their own souls: For Allah is Free of all needs from all Creation.

29.7.. Those who believe, and do righteous good deeds- Surely, from them, We shall remove any evil deeds still (left) in them, and We shall truly, reward them according to the best of their deeds.

29.8. And We have enjoined kindness to parents from men: But if they (either one) try hard to make you join (anything) with Me (others for worship) anything about which you have no knowledge, do not obey them. (All of) you have to return to Me (Allah), and I will tell you (the truth) of all that you did.

29.9. And for those who believe and do righteous good deeds- Surely, We shall admit them to the company of righteous.

29.10.. Then there are among men who say, "We believe in Allah;" But if they suffer pain in (the cause of) Allah, they treat men's suffering as if it was the Anger of Allah! And if victory comes (to them) from your Lord, they are sure to say: "Verily, we have (always) been with you!" Does Allah not know best all that is in the breasts (hearts) of all Creation?

29.11. And indeed, Allah most truly knows those who believe, and as truly (He knows) those who are the hypocrites (who hide the truth).

29.12. And those who disbelievers say to those who believe: "Follow our path, and we will bear (the burden) of your faults." Never (and not) in the least will they bear (the burden of) their faults: In fact they are liars!

29.13. And verily, they will bear their own burdens, and the burdens (of others) with their own, and surely, they will be called to account, on the Day of Judgment, for their lies that they made up.

29.14.. And We (once before) sent Nuh (Noah) to his people, and he waited with them for a thousand years less fifty years; But the Flood overtook them while they (kept up their) sin.

29.15. Then We saved him and the companions of the Ark, and We made (the Ark) a Sign for all peoples!

29.16.. And (remember, We also saved Abraham) Ibrahim, when he said to his people, "Worship (and serve) Allah and fear Him: That will be best for you- If you (only) understand!

29.17. "You worship idols besides Allah, and you bring out falsehood. Verily, those whom you worship besides Allah have no power to give you the provision to live: For this reason, you seek your livelihood from Allah, worship (and serve) Him, and be grateful to Him: Your return will be to Him,

29.18. "And if you reject (this Message), many generations before you also did so: And the duty of the messenger is only to preach plainly and openly (and clearly)."

29.19.. Do they not see how Allah originates the creation, (and) then repeats it: Truly that is easy for Allah.

29.20. Say: "Travel through the earth and see how (Allah) originated the creation; Like this Allah will bring forth a later creation (Hereafter): Verily, Allah is Able to do all things.

29.21. "He punishes whom He wills, and He grants mercy to whom He wills, and towards Him will you return.

29.22. "And neither on earth nor in heaven; Will you be able to escape (His Plan), and you have no protector nor helper besides Allah."

29.23.. And those who reject the Signs of Allah and the meeting with Him (in the Hereafter)- They shall suffer without My mercy: And they will (also suffer) a most painful penalty.

29.24.. So nothing was the answer from (Ibrahim's) people except that they said: "Kill him or burn him." Then Allah did save him from the fire. Surely, in this indeed, are Signs for people who believe.

29.25. And he (Ibrahim) said: "For you, you have taken (for worship other) things (idols) besides Allah, out of mutual love and regard between yourselves in this life; But on the Day of Judgment you shall refuse to know each other and curse each other: And your home will be the Fire, and you will have no one to help."

29.26. So, Lut (Lot) had faith in Him (Allah): He said: "I will emigrate (leave my home) for the sake of my Lord: Verily, He is the Supreme in Power , the All Wise ."

29.27. And We gave (Ibrahim), Isháq (Isaac as a son) and Yàqoub (Jacob as a grandson), and We gave to his descendants prophet hood and book, and in this life, We granted him his reward and verily, he was (made) in the Hereafter (to be the company) of the righteous.

29.28.. And (remember) Lut (Lot): When he said to his people: You commit such immoral sins (sodomy), that none (other) in the creation (ever) have done before you.

29.29. "You really approach men (with wicked intent), and you rob the wayfarer? And practice evil (even) in your gatherings?" But his people gave no answers except this: They said: "Bring us the Anger of Allah, if you say the truth."

29.30. He said: "O my Lord! You (Alone) help me against people who do make (serious) crimes and mischief!"

29.31.. And when Our messengers (Allah's angels) came to Ibrahim (Abraham) with the good news, they said: "Truly, we are going to ruin the people of this town: Surely, its people have been the wrongdoers.

29.32. He (Ibrahim) said: "But, Lut (Lot) is also in there." They said: "We know well who is there: We will surely, save him and his family- Except his wife, she is from those who fall behind!"

29.33. And when Our messengers came to Lut (Lot), he was sad because of them (his people), and felt himself without power (to save) them: They (the messengers) said: "Have no fear, nor be sad: We are (here) to save you and your family, except your wife, she is from those who will fall behind.

29.34. "Verily, now we are going to bring upon the people of this township, a punishment from heaven, for their wickedness and rebellion."

29.35. And indeed, there We have left an evident Sign, (In the town under the Dead Sea now in Palestine) for any people who (want to) understand.

29.36.. And to the Madyan (people) We sent their brother Shu'aib. Then he said: "O my people! Worship Allah, and fear the Last Day; And do not do evil on the earth, purposely to do mischief."

29.37. And they rejected him: Then the mighty earthquake seized them, and they lay overcome (face down) in their homes by the morning.

29.38.. And (also remember) the 'Ad and the Samood (Thamud people): From (the remains) of their buildings (their fate) will appear clearly to you: The Satan made their actions look nice to them, and kept them away from the (right) Path, though they were gifted with intelligence and ability.

29.39. And (remember Qaroon), Qârûn, Firon (Pharaoh), and Haman: And indeed, Musa (Moses) came to them with Clear Signs (*Ayât*), but they acted with pride (and arrogance) on the earth; Yet they could not reach beyond Us.

29.40. So We punished each one of them We caught for his crime: Against some of them, We sent a powerful storm (with showers of stones); And some of them were caught by a (mighty) Blast; Some We caused the earth to swallow up; And some We drowned (in the waters): It was not Allah Who wronged (or hurt) them: But they hurt (and injured) their own souls.

29.41.. The story of those who take protectors other than Allah is like that of the Spider, who builds a house (web for itself); But truly, the weakest of the houses is the Spiders house- If they only knew.

29.42. Surely, Allah knows (everything) about whatever they call to (pray) besides Him: And He is the Supreme in Power , the All Wise .

29.43. And stories (with guidance) like these, We bring out for mankind, but only those who have knowledge understand them (the stories).

29.44. Allah created the heavens and the earth in true (matching sizes and proportions): Surely, in that there is a Sign for those who believe.

29.45.. Say (and recite) what is revealed from the Book made known to you (O Prophet!), and perform Prayer regularly: Verily, the prayer holds back shameful and immoral sins; And remembering Allah is without doubt the greatest (of deeds). And Allah knows all (the acts) that you do.

29.46. And you do not argue (or dispute) with the People of the Book, except with better ways (reasons and facts); Unless it is with those of them who cause injustice (or injury): But say (to them), "We believe in the Revelation which has come down to us and in that which came down to you; Our God (Allah) and your God is One; And it is to Him we bow (in Islam)."

29.47. And like this We have sent down the Book to you. So that the People of the Book believe in it, as some of these (pagan Arabs) also believe: And no one but unbelievers reject Our Signs.

29.48. And you were not (able) to say (and recite) a Book before this (Book came), and you are not (able) to write it with your right hand: Truly, if that was the case, the idle talkers would have doubted.

29.49. No! These are the clear and firm Signs that are in the hearts of those gifted with knowledge: And no one but the unjust reject Our Signs.

29.50. And yet they say: "Why are not Signs sent down to him from his Lord?" (O Prophet!) Say: "The Signs are truly with Allah: And I am indeed a clear Warner."

29.51. And is it not enough for them that We have sent down to you the Book that has been told (and given) to them? Surely, in it is Mercy and a Reminder to those who believe.

29.52. Say: "Allah is enough as a witness between me and you: He Knows what is in the heavens and on earth. And those who believe in show and falsehood and reject Allah, it is they who will be the losers."

29.53. And they ask you to hurry the punishment: And if it was not for a fixed time (of relief), the punishment would truly have come upon them: And it will really reach them- All of a sudden, when they are not aware!

29.54. They ask you to hurry the (severe) punishment: But surely, Hell as the surety will hold (all) the rejecters of Faith!

29.55. On the Day when punishment shall cover them from above them (and) from below them, (a Voice) will say: "You taste (the fruits) of your actions!"

29.56.. O My servants who believe! Truly, My Earth has lot of space (and room): Therefore you serve Me- (and none else)!

29.57. Every soul shall have a taste of death: In the end, you shall be brought back to Us.

29.58. And for those who believe and work righteousness, to them We give a home in the Paradise (Heaven)- High (and beautiful) homes under which rivers flow, to live forever in there:- An excellent reward for those who do (good)!

29.59. Those who work and continue with patience and put their trust in their Lord (and Cherisher).

29.60.. And how many creatures do not carry their own food to remain alive? It is Allah Who feeds (both) them and you: And He the All Hearing , the All Knowing .

29.61. And if you truly ask them: "Who has created the heavens and the earth and subjected the sun and the moon (to His law)?" They will certainly reply, "Allah." Then, why are they turned away (from the truth)?

29.62. Allah expands the things to live (which He gives) to whomever of His servants He pleases; And He (also) grants by (true) measure, (as He pleases): Verily, Allah is All Knowing of all things.

29.63. And if you truly ask them: "Who sends down rain from the sky, and gives life with it (rain) to the earth after its death?" They will certainly reply, "Allah." Say: "All the Praises (and thanks) be to Allah!" Nay, most of them understand not.

29.64.. And what is the life of this world but an amusement and a play? But surely, the home in the Hereafter- That is (Eternal) life indeed, if they only knew.

29.65. And when they climb onto a boat, they invoke (to worship) Allah, making their prayers only to Him; Only when He has brought them safely to land, look! They give a share (of their worship with others)!

29.66. Rejecting thanklessly Our gifts, and giving themselves into (short-lived) enjoyment! But soon they will know.

29.67. Then, do they not see that We have made a secure Sacred Place (at Makkah), and that men are being snatched (pulled) away from all around them? Still, do they believe in what is useless, and reject the Graces of Allah?

29.68. And who does more wrong than he who makes up a lie against Allah or rejects the Truth when it reaches him? Is there not a home in Hell for the disbelievers?

29.69. And those who work and struggle (and continue in Our Cause)- We will truly guide them to Our Paths: And surely, Allah is with those who are the righteous.

****

Sura 30. Ar-Rum,
(The Roman empire): (Makkah, 60 Verses)
In the Name of Allah, the Most Gracious, the Most Merciful.

30.1.. Alif Lám Mim:

30.2. The Romans have been defeated-

30.3. In a nearby land: And they, after their defeat will be victorious-

30.4. Within a matter of years. The Decision is with Allah- In the Past and in the Future: And on that Day, the believers shall rejoice-

30.5. With the help of Allah. He helps whomsoever He wills; And He is the Almighty , the Most Merciful .

30.6. (That is) the Promise of Allah, Allah never departs from His Promise: But most men do not understand.

30.7. They know only the appearance (the outer things) of life in this world: But they do not care for the end of (all) things.

30.8.. In their own minds, do they not think (deeply)? That Allah has (indeed) created the heavens and earth and all between only for true cause and for a fixed duration: Yet really, there are many from (these) men who deny the meeting with their Lord (in the end)!

30.9. Do they not travel in (and about) the earth; And see what was the end of those before them? They were superior (and) stronger than these (men): And they tilled the soil and populated it with more (men) than these (men): To them (the earlier people) came their messengers with Clear (Signs), (whom they rejected, to their own destruction): And it was not Allah Who wronged them, but they wronged themselves (their own souls).

30.10. Over a long time terrible evil will be the end of those who do evil; Because they rejected the Signs (*Ayât*) of Allah, and made fun of them.

30.11.. It is Allah Who originates (begins) the creation; Then repeats (He) it; Then you shall be brought back to Him.

30.12. And on the Day when the Hour will be established, the criminals will sink deep in despair.

30.13. From their 'partners' (they have given to Allah) there will be nobody to help them, and they will refuse and reject their 'partners'.

30.14. And on the Day when the Hour will be established, that Day (all men) shall be separated (according to what they have done).

30.15. Then those who have believed and done righteous deeds, such shall be esteemed and made happy in the luxury of Gardens of Delight.

30.16. And those who have rejected Faith and falsely denied Our Signs (*Ayât*) and the meeting of the Hereafter- These shall be brought out for punishment.

30.17.. So (recite) the Glory to Allah when you enter the evening (*'Asr, Maghrib* and *Isha* prayers), and when you enter the morning (*Faj'r* prayer);

30.18. And Praise be to Him, in the heavens and on earth; And (Glorify Him) in the late afternoon (*Zuh'r* prayer), and when the day begins to decline.

30.19. It is He Who brings out the living from the dead, and brings out the dead from the living, and (it is He) Who gives life to the earth after it is dead: And like this you shall be brought out (from the dead).

30.20. And among His Signs (*Ayât*), is this, that He created you from dust; And then (you) see- You are men spread (far and wide)!

30.21. And among His Signs (*Ayât*), is this, that He created (your) mates for you from yourselves, that you may live in joy (and peace) with them, and He has placed love and mercy between your (hearts): Surely, there are Signs in this for those who think.

30.22. And among His Signs (*Ayât*), is the creation of the heavens and the earth, and the difference in your languages and (the difference of) your colors: Surely, there are Signs in this for those who know.

30.23. And among His Signs (*Ayât*), is the sleep that you have by night and by day, and the search that you (make for a living) from His many Gifts (in plenty): Surely, there are Signs in this for those who listen.

30.24. And among His Signs (*Ayât*), He shows the lightning, as both fear and hope, and He sends down the rain from the sky. And with it (He) gives life to the earth after it is dead: Surely, there are Signs in this for those who are wise.

30.25. And among His Signs (*Ayât*) is this that heaven and earth stand by His Order: Then when He call you, by a single call, behold, you shall come up from the earth.

30.26. To Him belongs every creature in the heavens and on earth: All are faithfully obedient to Him.

30.27. And it is He Who originates the creation; Then (He) repeats it; And for Him it is extremely easy. To Him belongs the highest similitude (of Honor) in the heavens and earth: And He is the Almighty , the All Wise .

30.28.. He (Allah) brings out for you a similitude from your own selves (and thinking): Do you have partners from those whom your right hands possess, to be your equals to share in (your) wealth We have given to you? Do you fear them as you fear each other? Like this We explain the Signs in detail to those people who understand.

30.29. No! The wrongdoers follow their (own) desires, lacking enough knowledge (and understanding). Then who will guide those whom Allah leaves them astray (to wander)? And for them there will be no helpers.

30.30.. So, you direct your face (and your sight) calmly, surely and truly towards the Faith: (Act on) Allah's plan according to the Way upon which He has made mankind: (There should be) no change in the deeds for Allah. That is the (only) straight (and stable) Religion: But most of mankind has no knowledge.

30.31. (O Mankind) you turn back in repentance to Him, and fear Him: Perform prayers regularly, and you do not be from those who join gods (with Allah),

30.32. (And you do not be from) those who break up their Religion, and become (divided into) sects- Each sect becoming happy in that which is its own.

30.33.. And when trouble comes to men, they call sincerely to their Lord, turning back to Him in repentance: But when He gives them a taste of Mercy, behold! Some of them do a part of their worship to other gods besides their Lord-

30.34. (As if) to show their thanklessness for the (gifts) We have given to them! Then enjoy (a little while); But soon you will realize (your mistakes).

30.35. Or is it that We have sent down the power (or capacity) to them, which shows them the things to which they do a part of their worship?

30.36. And when We give men a gift of (Our) Mercy, they are very happy (as if in pride) with it: But when some evil comes upon them because of the doings of their (own) hands, behold! They are sorrowful!

30.37. Do they not see that Allah gives the means (to live) in plenty or reduces them to anyone He pleases? Surely, in that are Signs for those who believe.

30.38.. So give what is due to the relatives and the needy, and the wayfarer (away from home) that is best for those who search for Allah's Holy Face (Allah's Divine Countenance), and such are those (who give) that will prosper.

30.39. And that which you put aside in interest (*Riba*, as your own to be spent) to grow by using the property of (other) people, (that) will have no increase with Allah: But that which you give for charity, in search of Allah's Holy Face, that will grow: These (are the people) who will get a reward many times larger.

30.40. It is Allah Who created you: Then He has given you the things to live; Then He will cause you to die; Then He will give you life. Are there any of your (false) 'partners' that can do even a single one of these things? Glory be to Him! And High is He above the 'partners' they attribute (to Him)!

30.41. Mischief has appeared on land and on sea because of what men have earned by their (own) hands, thus (Allah) gives them the taste of some of their actions: This way they can come back (to Him).

30.42. Say: "Travel through the earth and see what was the end of those before (you)! Most of them worshipped others besides Allah."

30.43. But you set your face (and your sight) to the straight (and the right) religion, before there comes the Day from Allah; (And) no chance, is there of turning away (this Day): On the Day men shall be divided (in two groups, one for the Paradise and one for the Fire of Hell).

30.44. Those who reject Faith (now) will be in pain because of that rejection (then): And those who work righteousness will spread their resting place for themselves (in heaven):

30.45. That He may reward from His Grace for those who believe and do righteous deeds. Surely, He does not love those who reject Faith.

30.46.. And among His Signs is this, that He sends the Winds, as the glad tidings (to sail the ships) giving you a taste of His (Gifts and) Mercy- And that the ships may sail by His Order and that you may search (for your livelihood) from His bounty, for you to be thankful (to Him).

30.47. And indeed, before you (O Prophet!), We did send (other) messengers to their (own) peoples, they came to them with (clear) proofs: Then, for those who exceeded their limits, We gave out harsh punishments: And it was due from Us to help those who believed.

30.48.. It is Allah Who sends the winds, and they bring up the clouds: Then He spread them in the sky as He wishes, and then break them into (small) fragments, until you see the drops of rain form within them; (And) then when He has made them reach those of His servants as He wills! Look, they are happy!

30.49. And verily, even though, before they received (the rain)- just before this-they were full of sorrow!

30.50. Then see and think (about it, O man!) the proof of Allah's Mercy! How He gives life to the earth after its death: Surely, the Same (Allah) will give life to men after they are dead: And He is Able to do all things

30.51. And if We (only) send a wind by which they see (their crops) become yellow- Behold! They become disbelievers!

30.52. So surely, you cannot make the dead to hear, and (you) cannot make the deaf to hear, the Call (from Allah), when they show their backs and turn away.

30.53. And you cannot guide (bring back) the blind from wandering (without knowing where he is going): Only those can you make (them) hear, who believe in Our Signs (*Ayât*) and submit (themselves to Allah in Islam).

30.54.. It is Allah Who created you in weakness (as a helpless baby) then gave strength after the weakness, then gave weakness (again with your age) and head with gray (and torn hair) He creates what He wills, and He is the All Knowing , All Powerful.

30.55. And on the Day that the Hour (of Judgment) will be (finally) set, those who exceeded the limits will swear that they idled away no longer an hour like this they were used to being fooled!

30.56. And those who are blessed with knowledge and faith will say: "Indeed you remained within Allah's Decree, to the Day for being raised (again), and this is the Day for being raised but you-you were not aware!"

30.57. So, on that Day no excuse from them will be of use to those who exceeded the limits, and they will not be welcome to (Allah's) pleasure.

30.58.. Surely, for men, We have set forth in this Quran, every kind of story (with a moral in it). But if you take any Sign (of Allah) to them, the unbelievers are sure to say (to the believers): "You say nothing except useless (things)."

30.59. Thus does Allah seal up the hearts of those who do not understand.

30.60. So patiently remain constant (and firm): Surely, the Promise of Allah is true: And do not let those (unbelievers) who have no certainty of faith, move you from your firmness (of your Faith).

****

Sura 31. Luqman,

(The wise): (Makkah, 34 Verses)
In the Name of Allah, the Most Gracious, the Most Merciful.

31.1. Alif Lám Mim:

31.2. These are Verses (*Ayât*) of the Book of Wisdom -

31.3. A Guide and a Mercy to those who do good -

31.4. Those who establish prayer regularly (*Salat*), and give charity regularly (*Zakat*), and have (the truest) belief in the Hereafter.

31.5. These are (the people truly) guided by their Lord; And these are the ones who will prosper.

31.6.. And from mankind, there are, those who buy useless talk, without knowing (the meaning), to mislead (others) from the Path of Allah and to make lowly jokes (about Allah's Path): For them there will be a demeaning penalty.

31.7. And when Our Signs (*Ayât*) are rehearsed to such a one (person), he turns away with (empty) pride, as if he did not hear them, as if there was deafness in both of his ears: So, announce to him of a (very) painful penalty.

31.8. Verily, for those who believe and work righteous deeds, there will be Gardens of Joy,

31.9. To live therein. His, the promise of Allah is true: And He is the Almighty and All Wise .

31.10.. He has created the heaven without any pillars that you can see; And He set mountains standing firmly (on the earth) in case it should shake with you; And upon it He has spread beasts of all kinds. And We send down rain from the sky, and We made on the earth every kind of noble creation to grow therein.

31.11. This is Allah's Creation: So, now show Me what is there that others, besides Him, have created: No! But the transgressors are clearly in error.

31.12.. And indeed, We gave Wisdom to Luqman saying: "Give (your) thanks to Allah." And anyone who is grateful does this to benefit his own soul: And if anyone is ungrateful, surely, Allah is free of all wants, Worthy of all Praise.

31.13. And when Luqman said to his son while he was advising him: "O my son! Do not join (others) with Allah in worship: Verily, joining others in worship (with Allah) is a terrible wrong indeed."

31.14. And We have commanded man (to be good) to his parents: In weakness and hardship his mother bore him, and in two years (after) was his weaning: (So the command of Allah is), "Show thankfulness to Me and to your parents: To Me is (your final) Destination.

31.15. "But if they (the parents) try hard to make you join (others) in worship with Me things about which you have no knowledge, then do not obey them; But stay with them through this life in a just manner (and pay regard for them), and follow the way of those who come back to Me (with love): In the end, the return for all of you is to Me, and I will tell you the truth (and meaning) of everything that you did."

31.16. (Luqman said,) "O my son! Even if there be (only) the weight of a mustard seed and it was (hidden) in a rock, or (anywhere) in the heavens or in the earth, Allah will bring it forth (in the open): Verily, Allah knows (even) the finest mysteries and is Absolutely Informed (of them).

31.17. "O my son! Perform prayer regularly, enjoin (and support) what is good (and just), and stop (and prevent) what is wrong: And be patient and constant with whatever happens to you, verily, these are of the firm commandments.

31.18. "And do not turn your cheek (with pride) from men, and do not walk in (rude) arrogance on the earth; Verily, Allah does not love any arrogant boaster.

31.19. "And be moderate in your walking (and actions) and lower your voice, verily, (without a doubt), the harshest of sounds is the call (braying) of an ass."

31.20.. Do you not see that Allah has subjected to your (use) whatsoever is in the heavens and whatsoever is on earth, and has in a large part, made His gifts come to you (both as being) seen and unseen? Even then, there are from the men those who dispute (and argue) about Allah, without knowledge and without guidance, and without a Book to show the light to them.

31.21. When they are told to follow the (Book) that Allah has sent down, they say: "No, we will only follow the ways that we found our fathers (following)." What! Even if Satan, was calling them (the fathers) to the penalty of the Fire?

31.22.. And whosoever submits his entire face (self) to Allah, and is one who does good, then (he) has truly grasped the most trustworthy hand-hold: And with Allah are the end and the decision of (all) things.

31.23. And if anyone disbelieves (and rejects Faith), let not his rejection make you sad: All of them return to Us, and We shall tell them the truth of their actions: Verily, Allah is All Knowing of what is in their breasts (hearts).

31.24. We give them their pleasure for some time: Then in the end shall We push them into a punishment that is terrible.

31.25.. And if you ask them: "Who created the heaven and the earth." They will certainly say: "Allah." Say: "All Praises (and thanks) be to Allah!" But most of them do not understand (the true meaning behind it.)

31.26. To Allah belongs everything in the heavens and the earth: Surely, He is Allah, Free of all wants, Worthy of all Praise.

31.27. And if all the trees on the earth were pens and the ocean (were ink), with seven (more) oceans behind it to add to it, even so the Words of Allah will not be exhausted (in His Praise): Verily, Allah is All Mighty, All Wise.

31.28. And your being created or being raised up (for Judgment) is only as if it was for a single soul: Verily, Allah is All Hearing , All Seeing.

31.29. Do you not see that Allah blends the night into day and He blends the day into night? And He makes the sun and the moon obey (His Order), each running along its way for a time appointed? And that Allah is All Informed with what you do?

31.30. That is because Allah, He is the Truth, and because that which they invoke besides Him is falsehood; And that Allah- He is the Most High, Most Great.

31.31.. Do you not see that ships sail through the Ocean by the Grace of Allah? That He may show you His Signs? Surely, in this, there are Signs, for all who (constantly) persevere and give thanks.

31.32. And when waves come over them like blankets, they (the men call to and) invoke Allah, giving Him (their) true prayers (and love). But when He has brought them safely to land, there are from them, those who stop midway between (right and wrong). And none deny Our Signs except those who break their promise and who are ungrateful.

31.33. O Mankind! Do your duty to your Lord, and fear the Day when no father can be even the least bit useful for his son, nor a son the least bit useful for his father. Surely, the Promise of Allah is true: Then, do not let this present life deceive you, nor let the Chief Deceiver (Satan) deceive you about Allah.

31.34. Surely, the knowledge of the Hour is (only) with Allah. It is He Who sends down the rain, and He Who knows what is in the wombs. Nor does anyone know what it is that he will earn tomorrow: Nor does anyone know in which land he will die. Surely, Allah is All Knower , All Aware.

****

Sura 32. As-Sajda,
(Adoration): (Makkah, 30 Verses)
In the Name of Allah, the Most Gracious, the Most Merciful.

32.1.. Alif Lám Mim:

32.2.. (This is) the Revelation of the Book in which there is no doubt- From the Lord of the Worlds.

32.3. Or do they (the unbelievers) say: "Has he fabricated it (or made it up)?" No! It is the Truth from your Lord, so that you may warn a people to whom no Warner has come before you, so that they may receive guidance.

32.4.. It is Allah Who has created the heavens and the earth, and all (that is) between them, in six Days, then He is firmly rose over the Throne: Besides Him, you have no one, to protect or come to (your) help: Then, will you not remember and take the warning?

32.5. He (Allah) rules (over all) affairs from the heavens to the earth; Then in the end (all affairs) will go up to Him, in one Day, where the space will be a thousand years of your (worldly) understanding.

32.6. He is like so, the Knower of all things, hidden and open, the Almighty , the Most-Merciful -

32.7. He Who has made everything in which He has created most Good: And He began the creation of man with clay,

32.8. Then He made his (the human race) children (of Adam) from the purest and essential part (of life, namely sperm) with the nature of a fluid held in low regard:

32.9. Then He made him (man) in correct proportions, and breathed into him a little of His (Own) Spirit. And He gave you (the capability of) hearing, and sight and feeling (and understanding): (And yet) you give little thanks!

32.10. And they (the unbelievers) ask: "(What!) When we lie (hidden and) lost in the earth, shall we indeed be made again a (distant) new Creation?" No! But they deny the Meeting with their Lord!

32.11. Say: "The Angel of Death, who is put in charge of you will (really) take your souls (on time): Then you shall be brought back to your Lord."

32.12.. And if you could only see when the criminals will hold their heads low before their Lord (saying:) "Our Lord! We have seen and we have heard: So, now send us back (again to the world): That we will work righteousness, verily, we believe now with (all the) certainty."

32.13. And if We so wanted, surely, We could have brought every soul its true guidance: But the Word from Me will come true, "I will fill Hell with jinns' and mankind all together.

32.14. "Then you taste (the penalty) because you forgot the Meeting of yours on this Day, surely, We too will forget you- You taste the penalty of eternity for your (evil) actions!"

32.15. Only those who believe in Our Signs (*Ayât*), who, when they are read to them, fall down in deepest love and respect (*Sajda*),

   {A Muslim generally prostrates to Allah after reciting this verse}
and celebrate the Praises of their Lord, and they are never haughty with pride.

32.16. Their limbs leave their beds of sleep, during the time that they invoke their Lord, with fear and hope: And they spend (in charity) from of things that We have given them.

32.17. No person really knows those joys of the eye that are kept hidden (and treasured) for them- As a reward for their (good) actions.

32.18.. Is then the man who believes like the man who rebels (and is wicked)? They are not equal.

32.19. As for those who believe and do righteous good deeds, for them are Gardens as inviting homes, because of (their good deeds), what they used to do.

32.20. And for those who are rebels and are wicked, their homes will be the Fire: Every time they want to get away from there, they will be forced into it (the Fire): And it will be said to them: "You taste the Penalty of the Fire, which you used to deny (reject) as a lie."

32.21. And verily, We will truly make them taste the Penalty in this (life even) before the supreme penalty, so that they may (repent and) return.

32.22. And who does more wrong than the one who is reminded of the Signs (*Ayât*) of his Lord and he turns away from them (*Ayât*). Surely, We shall take the price from those evildoers who exceed their limits.

32.23.. And indeed, before We did in truth give the Book [Torah, (_Taurát_)] to Musa (Moses): So, do not be in doubt of meeting with him (in _Mai'raj_: The ascent of the Prophet in Sura 53): And We made it (_Taurát_) a guide to the Children of Israel (_Bani-Israel_).

32.24. And from them, We appointed leaders, giving guidance under Our Command, as long as they struggled with patience and continued to have faith in Our Signs (_Ayât_).

32.25. Surely, your Lord will judge between them on the Day of Judgment, in the matters in which they differed.

32.26. Does it not teach them a lesson (to see), how many generations We have destroyed before them, in whose (ruined) houses they go back and forth? Surely, in that are (Allah's) Signs: Then, do they not listen?

32.27. And do they not see that We drive the rain to the dried soil without plants, and grow crops with it, which give food for their cattle and themselves? Do they have no sight (to see)?

32.28.. They say: "When will the (Day of) Decision (wrath and punishment) be, if you are telling the truth?"

32.29. Say (to them O Prophet!): "On the Day of Decision, it will be of no use to the unbelievers, if they believe then! And they will not be given any relief."

32.30. So turn away from them and wait: Verily, they too are waiting!

****

Sura 33. Al-Ahzâb,
(The allies): (Medinah, 73 Verses)
In the Name of Allah, the Most Gracious, the Most Merciful.

33.1. O Prophet! Fear Allah and do not obey the unbelievers and the hypocrites (those who hide the truth). Surely, Allah is All Knower A, All Wise.

33.2. And follow the (guidance) which comes unto you from your Lord by (inner) Revelation: Verily, Allah knows well everything that you do.

33.3. And put your trust in Allah, and Allah is enough to be a Disposer of affairs.

33.4. Allah has not made for any man, two hearts in his (one) body: Nor, (O people!) has He (Allah) made your wives, whom you declare to be like your mother's backs (and thus divorce them by the evil practice of _Az-Zihar,_ see 58.2-4), your real mothers: Nor has He made your adopted sons your (real) sons. This is (only) your (manner of) speaking by your mouths. But Allah reveals (to you) the Truth, and He shows the (right) Way.

33.5. Call them by (the names of) their fathers: That is more correct in the Sight of Allah. But if you do not know their fathers (names, then call them) your brothers in faith, or your freed helpers. And there is no sin on you if you made a mistake. Except unless your hearts willfully intended: And Allah is Often-Returning, Most Merciful .

33.6. The Prophet is closer to the believers than their own selves, and his wives are (in a holy sense) their mothers. By the Command of Allah, blood-relations among each other have closer personal ties, than (the brotherhood of) believers and those traveling from distant lands: However, you do what is just to your closest friends: Such is the writing in the Command (Book from Allah).

33.7.. And remember that from the prophets, We took their truest Covenant (their Promise) as (We took, O Prophet!) from you: From Nuh (Noah), Ibrahim (Abraham), Musa (Moses), and Isa (Jesus), the son of Maryam (Mary). From them, We took a strong Covenant:

33.8. That (Allah) may question the truthful ones about the Truth they (were to protect). And for the unbelievers, He has prepared a painful penalty.

33.9.. O you who believe! Remember the Grace of Allah upon you, when crowds (of people) came down against you: But We sent a storm and forces to oppose them that you did not see. And, Allah is Ever All Seer all that you do.

33.10. When they came upon you from above you and from below you, and when the eyes became dim, and the hearts came up to the throats, and you had many doubts about Allah!

33.11. There the believers were tried in that event: They were shaken as by a huge shaking.

33.12.. And when the hypocrites (those who hide the truth) and those whose hearts have sickness (even) say: "Allah and His Messenger (Muhammad) promised us nothing but delusions (and false hopes)!"

33.13. And when a party among them said: "You men of Yathrib (the Prophet's old town)! You cannot withstand (the attack), so go back!" And a group of them asked the Prophet to be excused (to go away), saying: "Truly, our houses are bare and in danger," even though they were not in (any) danger: They wanted nothing but to run away (from fighting).

33.14. And if an attack had come upon them from the (sides of the city), and they had been asked to rebel, certainly, they would have quickly made it true, with only a little delay.

33.15. And indeed, they had already made a promise to Allah not to turn their backs (and run away), and a promise to Allah must be kept.

33.16. Say: "Running away will not help you, if you are running away from death or slaughter; And even then (if you do run away), you may be allowed to enjoy no longer than a short time!"

33.17. Say: "Who is it that can save you from Allah; If it is He wishes to give you punishment or (wishes) to give you Mercy?" And, besides Allah, they will not find any protector or helpers for themselves.

33.18. Surely, Allah knows those (people) among you who hold back (others) and those who say to their brothers: "Come along to us," while they do not come to fight except for only a little while:

33.19. Being stingy towards you; Then when the fear comes, you will see them looking to you with their eyes turning like (the eyes of a person) for whom death is near: But when the fear is gone, they will strike at you with their sharp tongues (with the) love of things. Men like this do not have faith, therefore, Allah has made their actions have no effect: And that is easy for Allah (to do).

33.20. They think that the groups (opposing Islam) have not (lost and) withdrawn; And if those groups should come (again), they wish they were in the deserts together with the (wandering) Bedouins, and trying to find news about you (from far); And if they were in among you, they will fight very little.

33.21.. In the Messenger (Muhammad) of Allah, you have a beautiful (pattern of conduct) and example for one whose hope is in Allah and the Final Day, and who Praises Allah much (often and deeply).

33.22. And when the believers saw the Confederates (the armies and groups against Islam), they said; "This is what Allah and His Messenger (Muhammad) had promised us, and Allah and His Messenger (Muhammad) told us what was true." And it only added to their faith and their true cause (for Islam) in obedience.

33.23. Among the believers are men who have been true to their Covenant (Promise) to Allah: Of them, some have completed their promise (fully) and some (still) waiting: But they have not changed (the willingness) even by a little:

33.24. So that Allah may reward the men of truth for their Truth, and punish the hypocrites (who hide the truth), if that was His Will, or accept their repentance and turn to them: Verily, Allah is Often Forgiving, Most Merciful .

33.25.. And Allah drove back the unbelievers in spite of their anger: They did not gain any advantage; And Allah is enough for the believers in fight. And Allah is Full of Strength, All Mighty.

33.26. And those of the people of the Book who helped them- Allah did take them down from their firm places and cast extreme fear into their hearts; Some you killed, and some you took captives.

33.27. And He made you take over their lands, and their houses, and their riches (belongings), and of a land that you had not even visited. And Allah is Able to do all things.

33.28.. O Prophet! Say to your wives (women of purity): "If what you like is the life of this world, and its (false) joys- Then come! I will provide for your enjoyment and set you free in a nice (and wealthy) way.

33.29. "But if you like Allah and His Messenger (Muhammad) and the Home of the Hereafter, then surely, Allah has prepared for the well-doers from you a great (and generous) reward."

33.30. O Wives of the Prophet! If any of you were guilty of open ill-conduct, the punishment will be doubled to her, and that is easy for Allah (to do).

33.31. And if any of you who is true and sincere in the obedience of Allah and His Messenger (Muhammad), and works good deeds of righteousness-We shall give her, her reward twice: And We have prepared for her a noble portion.

33.32. O Wives of the Prophet! You are not like any (other) women: If you fear (Allah), do not be soft in (your) speech (about what is said while you teach Islam), in case a person in whose heart is a sickness should be moved with desire: But you speak honorably (in what is to be said).

33.33. And remain quietly (and peacefully) in your houses, and do not make a display of yourselves, like in the earlier days without (true) guidance, and establish regular Prayer, and give regular Charity; And obey Allah and His Messenger (Muhammad). And Allah only wants to remove all bad from you, you, members of the Family (of the Prophet), and to make you pure and pristine (totally cleansed).

33.34. And remember to repeat (to others) what is recited to you in your homes regarding the Signs of Allah and His Wisdom: Verily, Allah is always informed of every detail (and) Well-Acquainted with all things.

33.35.. Verily, the Muslim men and women- The believing men and women- The (deeply) religious men and women- The true men and women- The men and women who are patient and constant-
The men and women who make themselves humble (before Allah)-
The men and women who give charity- The men and women who fast-
The men and women who guard their chastity-
And the men and women who remember Allah much- With their hearts and (words on) their tongues; For them (such men and women) Allah has prepared forgiveness and great reward.

33.36.. It is not right for a believer, man or woman, when something has been already judged by Allah and His Messenger (Muhammad), to have any choice about the judgment: And whoever disobeys Allah and His Messenger (Muhammad), he is indeed on a clearly wrong path.

33.37. And (remember) when (O Prophet)! You said to the person (Zaid) who had received the gift from Allah and your favor: "You keep (the marriage with) your wife and fear Allah. But you did hide in your heart what Allah was about to make it clear: You did fear the people, but it is better that you fear Allah. So, when Zaid had dissolved (his marriage) with her, after the necessary (steps of divorce), We joined her in marriage with you: So, that there are no questions for the believers (regarding the) marriage with the wives of their adopted sons, after they have dissolved the marriage with the necessary (steps) with them (their ex-wives). And Allah's (Divine) Order must be completed and fulfilled.

33.38. There can be no blame for the Prophet in what Allah has made legal for him. It was done by those in the old and past days (and approved) by Allah; And the Command of Allah is a decision made.

33.39. (And for) those who convey the Messages of Allah, and fear Him and fear no one but Allah. And Allah is enough to bring (men) to account.

33.40. Muhammad (the Prophet) is not the father of any (one) of your men, but (he is) a Messenger of Allah, and the Seal (at the end) of the prophets. And Allah is All Knowing of all things.

33.41. O you who believe! Remember (and Glorify Allah), and do this (deeply and a great) many times;

33.42. And Glorify Him (with Praise), morning and afternoon.

33.43. It is He Who sends blessings upon you like His angels do, so that He may take you out from depths of darkness into Light: And verily, He is Full of Mercy for the believers.

33.44. On the Day when they will meet Him, the greetings (of joy) for them will be: "*Salaam* (Peace!)"; And He has made a great Reward for them.

33.45. O Prophet! Truly, We have sent you as a witness, a bearer of happy news (to the believers), and a Warner (to the disbelievers)-

33.46. And (We have sent you) as one who invites to (the Protection of)

Allah, by His Leave, and as a Lamp spreading Light.

33.47. And give the glad news to the believers, that they shall have large Bounty from Allah.

33.48. And do not obey the unbelievers and the hypocrites (those who hide the truth); Overlook and ignore them, and have trust in Allah, sufficient is Allah as a Trustee.

33.49.. O you who believe! When you marry believing women, and then divorce them before you have touched them, you do not have to wait the ('*Iddat*) period of waiting for them (to complete the divorce): So, give them a present, and set them free in a wholesome (and happy) way.

33.50.. O Prophet! Verily, We have made it lawful for you, your wives to whom you have paid their dowers; And those whom your right hand possesses from the prisoners of war whom Allah has given to you; And the daughters of your uncles and aunts, from your fathers side; And the daughters of your uncles and aunts, from your mothers side; Those who moved with you (from Makkah to Medinah); And any believing woman who gives herself to the Prophet if the Prophet wishes to wed her; This is only for you (O Prophet), as a privilege and not for (all) the believers; Indeed, We know that for them, We have made lawful their wives and those prisoners whom their right hands possess- So that there should be no difficulty on you. And Allah is Often Forgiving, Most Merciful .

33.51. You can postpone (the turn of) any of them (the women) whom you please, and you may receive any whom you please: And there is no blame on you if you invite one whose (turn) you had put aside. This is better for (their peace of mind), the cooling of eyes (in the joy of seeing you), to keep off their sorrow, and for their satisfaction- That all of them (are happy) with what you have to give to them: And Allah knows (all) that is in your hearts: And Allah is All Knowing , Most Forbearing.

33.52. (O Prophet!) It is not lawful for you (to marry more) women after this, or to change them for (other) wives, even though their beauty may attract you, except any (women whom) your right hand should possess (as handmaidens): And Allah is Watchful over all things.

33.53.. O you who believe! Do not enter the Prophet's houses- Unless permission is given to you- (If you go) for a meal, do not be (so early as) to wait for its preparation: But when you are invited, enter (his house); And when you have taken your meal, go away, without trying to get into idle talk. Verily, such (behavior) does not please the Prophet: And he is (too) shy to ask you to leave, but Allah is not shy (to tell you) the truth. And when you ask (his ladies) for anything you may want, ask them with a screen between (them and you): That allows greater purity in your hearts and theirs. And it is not right for you that you may displease Allah's Messenger (Muhammad), nor that you may marry his widows after him (after his death at any time). Truly, in Allah's sight, such a thing is an enormous and evil act.

33.54. Whether you openly say anything or hide it, surely, Allah is All Knowing of all things.

33.55. There is no sin (on the women when they go) before their fathers, or their sons, their brothers, or their brothers' sons, or their sisters' sons, or their (believing) women, or the (female) slaves whom their right hands possess. And, fear Allah: Verily, Allah is Witness for all things.

33.56.. Allah and His angels send blessings on the Prophet: O you who believe! Send your blessings on him (the Prophet), and salute him with all respect.

33.57. Verily, those who displease Allah and His Prophet (Muhammad)- Allah has cursed them in this world and in the Hereafter, and has prepared for them a demeaning punishment:

33.58. And those who annoy (and unjustly displease) believing men and women have (the guilt on themselves of) slander and an evident sin.

33.59.. O Prophet! Tell your wives and your daughters, and the believing women, that they should wear their outer clothes over their bodies (when outside): That is most suitable (and appropriate), so that they should be known (as believing women) and not be annoyed (or attacked). And Allah is Often Forgiving, Most Merciful .

33.60. Truly, if those hypocrites (who lie against Islam) and those in whose hearts is a disease, cause unrest in the City (Medinah), do not stop (their mischief and wickedness), We shall certainly make you stand up against them: Then will they not be able to stay in it (the City) as your neighbors for a long time:

33.61. They have evil (curse around and) upon them: Wherever they are found, they shall be caught and killed.

33.62. Such was the practice (approved) by Allah, among those who lived before: (And) you will find no change in the practice (approved) by Allah.

33.63.. People ask you about the (final) Hour: Say: "Its knowledge is with Allah (Alone):" And what will make you understand? Just in case the Hour is near!

33.64. Surely, Allah has cursed the unbelievers and prepared a blazing Fire for them,

33.65. To live in there for ever: They will not find any protector or any helper.

33.66. The Day when their faces will be turned over in the Fire, they will say: "Sorrow upon us! If only we had obeyed Allah and obeyed the Messenger (Muhammad)!"

33.67. And they will say: "Our Lord! Verily, we obeyed our chiefs and our great ones, and they misled us from the (right) path.

33.68. "Our Lord! Give them double the penalty and send them the curse (torment) of a mighty Curse!"

33.69.. O you who believe! You do not be like those who annoyed and insulted Musa (Moses), but Allah saved him from what (insults) they said, and he (Musa) was honorable in Allah's Sight.

33.70. O you who believe! Fear Allah, and always speak words straight (to the point).

33.71. That He (Allah) may make your actions pure and true and forgive you your sins: And he who obeys Allah and His Messenger (Muhammad), he has already reached the greatest goals.

33.72.. Truly, We did offer the trust, duty and responsibility to the heavens, and the earth, and the mountains; But they refused to undertake it, because they were afraid of it: But man undertook it- Verily, he was being ignorant (and foolish about the responsibility)-

33.73. (And hence) Allah has to punish those hypocrites (who lie and hide the truth), men and women, and the unbelievers, men and women, and Allah will pardon (receive the repentance of) the true believers, both men and women: And Allah is Often Forgiving, Most Merciful .

****

Sura 34. Saba',

[The city of Saba (Sheba)]: (Makkah, 54 Verses)

In the Name of Allah, the Most Gracious, the Most Merciful.

34.1.. All the Praise, (admiration and gratitude) be to Allah, to Whom belong all that is in the heavens and all that is on earth: To Him be Praise in the Hereafter: And He is the All Wise , the All Aware.

34.2. He knows (all) that which goes into the earth, and (all) that which comes out from it; (All) that which comes down from the heaven, and (all) that which rises to it; And He is the Most Merciful , the Often Forgiving.

34.3.. The unbelievers say: "The Hour will never come to us;" Say: "No! By my Lord, but most surely, it will come upon you- By Him Who knows (everything) not (even) seen- From Whom is not hidden the smallest little (indivisible) particle in the heavens or on earth: And there is not a thing less than that, or greater, which is not clearly written in the Clear Book (Record):

34.4. "That He may reward those who believe and work deeds of righteousness: For such (persons there) is forgiveness and most generous ways (and means) to live."

34.5. But those who strive against Our Signs (*Ayât*), to stop them (from success) in every way.- For such (persons there) will be a Penalty- A Punishment that is most humiliating.

34.6.. And those to whom knowledge has come see that the (Revelation) sent down to you (O Prophet, is) from your Lord- That (it) is the Truth, and that it guides to the Path of the (One Allah) Supreme in Strength, Worthy of all Praise.

34.7.. (To mock) the unbelievers say: "Shall we show you a man who will tell you, (that) when you are all thrown about in dust with total disintegration, that you shall (then be raised) in a New Creation?

34.8. "Has he invented a lie against Allah, or has madness (seized) him?"- No, but those who do not believe in the Hereafter, (they) are in (real) penalty, and in greatest error.

34.9. Do they not see what is before them and (what is) behind them, of the heaven and the earth? If We wished, We could make the earth swallow them up, or make a piece of the heaven fall upon them. Surely, in this is a Sign for the (loyal) servant who turns to Allah (in repentance).

34.10.. And indeed, We have bestowed grace on Dawood (David) from Us, by saying: (And by ordering the mountains and birds) "O you Mountains! Glorify the Name of Allah with him! And you birds (also sing back with him)!" And We made the iron soft for him-

34.11. (By saying to him), "You make perfect coats of (metallic) rings and by balancing the rings of chain in the (defensive) clothing, and you work rightful deeds; For be sure, I am All Seeing of all that you do."

34.12.. And (We made) the Wind (obedient) to Sulaiman (Solomon): Its early morning (flow) was a months (journey), and its evening (flow) was a months (journey); And We made a (large) container (made) from molten brass to flow (like water) for him; And by the leave of their Lord, there were jinns' that worked in front of him, and if anyone of them turned away from Our command, We made him taste the penalty of the blazing Fire.

34.13. They (the jinns') worked for him as he wished (making) arches, images, basins (to hold liquids) as large as ponds (of water) and (large cooking vats or) kettles held (firmly in places): "Family of Dawood (David), you work with thanks! But only a few of My servants are thankful!"

34.14.. Then when We ordered the death (for Sulaiman) nothing showed them (the jinns') his death except a little worm from the earth, which (slowly) kept biting away at his stick (staff): So when he (Sulaiman) fell down, the jinns' clearly saw that, if they had known the unseen, they would not have been in the humiliating penalty (of their work for him).

34.15.. (Even) before this time, there was Sign for (the people of the City of) Saba (Sheba, see Sura 27, *Ayâh* 22) in their home-land two (rows of) Gardens to the right and to the left. Eat from the provisions (provided) by your Lord, and be grateful to Him: A fair and happy place (for the) City, and a Lord Often Forgiving!

34.16. But they turned away (from Allah), and against them, We sent a flood from the dams, and We made their two (rows of) Gardens into gardens growing bitter bad fruit, and shrubs and some few lote-trees (thorny bushes).

34.17. That was the repayment We gave them because they thanklessly rejected Faith: And We never give (such) repayment except to those who are thankless disbelievers (of Faith).

34.18. And We had placed for them, between the Towns on which We had granted Our blessings, (other) Cities in important locations, and between them We had fixed stages of journey in due proportion, saying: "Travel in there, safely, by night and by day."

34.19. But they said: "Our Lord! Place longer distances between the stages of our journey." And (so doing), they wronged themselves; So We made them like a story (that is told in the land), and We spread them out all in small groups. Surely, in this are Signs for every (one who is) always patient and grateful.

34.20. And indeed, *Iblis* (Satan) did prove his true purpose to be against them: And they followed him all, except a group who believed.

34.21. And he had no authority over them- Except that We may test the man who believes in the Hereafter, from him who is in doubt about it: And your Lord watches Protectively over all things.

34.22.. (O Prophet!) Say: "Call upon those who you think are your other (gods), besides Allah: (But) they have no power- Not the weight of an atom- In the heavens or on earth: Nor any share do they have in there nor is any of them a helper to Allah.

34.23. "No intercession (or help) can be of use in His Presence except for those to whom He has given permission. So far (is this true) that, when the fear is taken away from their (even the angel's) hearts, they will say: 'What is it that your Lord ordered?' (But then again) they will say: 'That which is true and just; And He is the Highest, the Greatest.' "

34.24. Say: "Who gives you provision (your livelihood), from the heavens and (from) the earth?" Say: "It is Allah; And it is (also) certain that either we or you are in right guidance or in clear error!"

34.25. Say: "You shall not be asked about our sins, and we shall not be asked about what you do."

34.26. Say: "Our Lord will bring (all of) us together and in the end, (He) will judge the matter between us in truth and justice: And He is the One to judge, the All Knowing (of the true status of all affairs)."

34.27. Say: "Show me those whom you have joined with Him as 'partners' (to Him): Nay! But He is Allah, the Almighty , All Wise ."

34.28. And We have not sent you except as one to give them good news, and to warn them (of the punishment; As a messenger and a guide to mankind), but most men do not understand.

34.29. And they say: "When will this promise (come true), if you are (really) telling the truth?"

34.30. Say: "The time (fixed) for you is till a Day, which you cannot delay even by an hour nor make it sooner."

34.31.. And those who disbelieve say: "We shall neither believe in this Quran nor in (any) that (came) before it." But if you could only see when the wrongdoers will be made to stand before their Lord, shifting the word (blaming) one another! Those who had been disliked will say to the proud and arrogant ones: "If it was not for you, we should certainly have been believers!"

34.32. Those who were arrogant will say to those weak ones: "Did we keep you back from Guidance (even) after it reached you? No! Instead, it was you were at fault."

34.33. Those who were the weak ones will say to the arrogant ones: "No! It was a (your) plot by day and by night: When, you (always) ordered us to be thankless to Allah and to find (others) equal with Him!" And they will say (their) repentance when they see the Penalty: And We shall put (stiff) clamps on the necks of the unbelievers: It would only be a repayment for their (ill) deeds.

34.34.. And We never sent a Warner to a (group in) town but the wealthy ones from them said: "We do not believe in the (Message) with which you (the Warner) have been sent with."

34.35. And they said: "We have more in wealth and sons, and we are not going to be punished."

34.36. Say: "Surely, my Lord gives more or less things to whom He pleases, but most men do not understand."

34.37.. And it is not your wealth, nor your children, that will bring you (by the least bit) nearer to Us: But only those who believe and work righteousness- These are the ones for whom there is an increased Reward many times for their deeds, while they are safely placed in (the high home of) Paradise in peaceful bliss.

34.38. And those who work against Our Signs (*Ayât*), to block and impede them, they will be put in punishment.

34.39. Say: "Surely, my Lord gives more or less livelihood to those of His servants as He pleases: And there is nothing of what you spend in the least (for Him) that He does not replace it: And He is the Best of those to give livelihood."

34.40.. And the Day He will gather them all together, and say to the angels, "Was it you that these men used to worship?"

34.41. They (the angels) will say: "Glory to You! - You are (our) Protector, not them. No! But they worshipped the jinns': Most of them (even) believed in them (jinns')."

34.42. So, today (the Day or Judgment), no one can help or harm each other: And We shall say to the wrongdoers, "You taste the Penalty of the Fire; The one which you used to deny!"

34.43.. And when Our Clear Signs (*Ayâh*) are recited to them, they say: "Here is only a man who wishes to get in your way of the (worship) which your fathers practiced." And they say: "This is only a lie that is invented!" And about the Truth, when it comes to them the unbelievers say, "This is nothing but clear magic!"

34.44. And We had not given them the Books (of Scripture) that they could read (and understand), nor sent messengers to them before you as warners.

34.45. And their earlier generations rejected (the Truth): These have not received a tenth (of the Guidance) of what We had granted to those: Yet when they rejected My messengers how (terrible) was My rejection (of them)!

34.46. Say: "I do warn (and advice) you on one point: That you stand up before Allah- (Either) in pairs, or as single (individuals)- And think deeply (within yourselves): Your Companion (the Prophet) is not possessed: He is no less than a Warner to you, (as those) who will face a terrible Penalty."

34.47. Say: "Whatever reward I might have asked from you is yours: My reward is only to come from Allah; And He is a Witness over all things."

34.48. Say: "Surely, my Lord sheds the (brightness of) truth (over some of His servants)- He, Who is All Knowing of what is hidden."

34.49. Say: "The Truth has come (now), and lies neither create anything new, nor bring back anything (hidden)."

34.50. Say: "If I am lost (from the Straight Way), my loss will only harm my own soul: But if I receive guidance, it is because of the inspiration from my Lord to me: Verily, He is All Hearing , the Nearest (to all)."

34.51.. If you can only see when they will tremble with fear; But at that time there will be no escape and they will be grabbed from a place very near.

34.52. And they will say: "We believe (now) in the (Truth);" But how can they receive (Faith) from a place (so) far away-

34.53. Knowing that they rejected Faith before, and that they told lies about the Unseen from a place far off?

34.54. And between them and their desires, a barrier is placed, as was done (and a barrier placed) in the past with the people of their party: Verily, they were truly in a grave doubt.

****

Sura 35. Fátir,
(The Originator of creation) or Malaika, (the Angels): (Makkah, 45 Verses)

In the Name of Allah, the Most Gracious, the Most Merciful.

35.1. All Praises (and thanks) be to Allah, Who is the Originator of the heavens and the earth, Who made the angels (as) messengers with wings-Two, three, or four (Pairs): He adds to (His) Creation as He pleases: Verily, Allah is Able to do all things.

35.2. From His Mercy, whatever Allah gives to human beings, there is no one (who) can withhold it; (And) whatever He does not give, there is no one, other than Himself (who) can give it thereafter: And He is the Almighty , Full of Wisdom .

35.3.. O Mankind! Remember the Grace of Allah to you! Is there a Creator, other than Allah, Who gives you the means to live from heaven or earth? There is no god but He: Then, how are you deceived from the Truth?

35.4. And if they (the unbelievers) deny you, (many earlier) messengers were (also) rejected before you; All affairs go back to Allah for the (final) decision.

35.5. O Mankind! The Promise of Allah is certainly true! Then, do not let the life of the world, deceive you, and do not let the Chief Deceiver (Satan) deceive you about Allah.

35.6. Surely, Satan is an enemy to you: So treat him like an enemy. He only calls to his followers, so that they may (also) be companions of the blazing Fire.

35.7. For those who reject Allah, there is a terrible penalty: But for those who believe and do rightful good deeds, there is Forgiveness, and a great Reward.

35.8.. Is he, then, to whom the evil of what he does, looks to be attractive, (equal as the one who is rightly guided)? Surely, Allah leaves to wander whom He wills, and guides whom He wills, so (O Prophet!) do not let your soul go out in sorrow after them: Truly, Allah is All Knowing of all that they do!

35.9. It is Allah Who sends out the winds, so that they pick up (and move) the clouds, and We drive them towards a land that is dead (barren), and then bring back life to the earth after its death: Like this there (will be) the Resurrection (to bring back the dead for Judgment)!

35.10. In case any want glory and power- (Let it be known to them that) to Allah belong all Glory and Power. To Him go up (and suit all) words of (utmost) Purity: It is He Who glorifies every deed of Righteousness. For those who plot Evil- For them is a terrible penalty; And the plotting of such (Evil) will be of no use.

35.11. And Allah created you from dust (at first); Then from a sperm-ovary drop; Then He made you in pairs. And no female becomes pregnant, or lays down (her baby), except with His knowledge. Also no old man is given more number of days, and no part is taken away from his life; except as it is in a record (with Allah). All this is easy for Allah.

35.12. And the two (seas) kinds of water are not alike (and the same)- One is tasteful, sweet and pleasant to drink, and the other, (tastes of) salt and is bitter. Yet from (both of) them, you eat fresh and tender flesh (fish and foods from the seas); From each (group of water), and you take out ornaments (pearls) to wear; And in there you see the ships that go through the waves, for you to search from the (riches and) bounty of Allah that you may be thankful.

35.13.. He merges the night into day and He merges the day into night, and He has forced the sun and the moon (to His law) each goes on its course for a fixed period of time. Such is Allah! Your Lord: To Him belongs all Kingdom. And those, whom you invoke other than Him do not even own a tiniest skin (of a data-stone) of anything.

35.14. If you invoke them, they will not hear your call, and (even) if they were to hear, they cannot answer to your (prayer). And on the Day of Judgment, they will disown your 'partnership'. And no one, can tell you (the Truth) like Him (One Allah), Who is All Informed of all things.

35.15.. O you mankind! It is you who have the need for Allah: But Allah is the One Free from all wants, (and the One) Worthy of all Praise.

35.16. If He so wanted, He could completely remove you and bring in a New Creation:

35.17. And (even) that is not difficult for Allah.

35.18. And no bearer of burdens shall bear another (person's) burden. And if one (person) carrying a heavy burden should call another to (bear) his load, nothing of it will be lifted (by the other) even though he be near of kin (closely related). (O Prophet!) you can only warn those who fear their Lord, Unseen and establish regular Prayer. And whoever purifies himself (from all kinds of sin) does it to benefit his own soul; And the Return (of all) is to Allah.

35.19.. Not the same are the blind and the seeing;

35.20. Neither are the depths of darkness and the light;

35.21. Neither are the (cool) shade and the (burning) heat of the sun:

35.22. Neither are the same, those who are living and those who are dead. Verily, Allah can make any whom He wills to hear; And you cannot make those who are (buried) in graves to hear.

35.23. You are none except a Warner.

35.24. Surely, We have sent you with the truth, as a bearer of happy news, and as a Warner: And there were never any people, without a Warner who did not live among them (in the past).

35.25. And if they (the people) deny (and reject) you, so, also did (reject) those before them, to whom came their messengers, with Clear Signs, and with Scripture (books of harsh prophecies), and the Book of Enlightenment.

35.26. In the end, I (Allah) did punish those who rejected Faith: And how (terrible) was My rejection (of them)!

35.27.. Do you not see that Allah sends down the rain from the sky? With it We then bring out crops (and farm produce) of various colors. And (there) are streaks (in fruits, rocks and minerals) in the mountains white and red, of many shades of color, and black, deep in (its) coloration.

35.28. And also among men and moving (crawling) creatures and cattle, they are (also) of various colors. Among His (Allah's) Servants, (there are) those who truly fear Allah, are (those) who have knowledge (that) verily, Allah is Almighty, Often Forgiving.

35.29. Verily, those who recite the Book of Allah, and perform regular

Prayer, and spend (in charity), from what We have given to them secretly and openly; The Hope for a sure-trade (the reward) will never fail:

35.30. He (Allah) will pay them their reward in full, He will give them (even) more from His bounty (and His many Rewards): Verily, He is Often Forgiving, Most Appreciative (of good service and deeds).

35.31.. That which We have revealed to you of the Book it is (indeed) the Truth- Confirming what was (already revealed) before it: Verily, regarding His (slaves and) servants, Allah is All Aware, All Seeing.

35.32. Then, We have given the Book to be passed down the generations to only those of Our servants as We have chosen: Then (even) there are among them, some who harm their own souls; And of them, some who take a middle course; And of them, some who are, by Allah's permission, leaders in good deeds; That is truly, the highest grace.

35.33. Gardens of Paradise, they will enter: In there, they will be decorated with bracelets of gold and pearls; And (in) there, their garments will be of silk.

35.34. And they will say: "All the Praise (and thanks) be to Allah, Who has taken away from us (all) misery and sorrow: Verily, our Lord is truly Often Forgiving, Most Appreciative (of good deeds and service):

35.35. "Who, out of His bounty, has placed us in a Home that will last forever: No hard work, nor (any) sensation of being tired shall touch us in here."

35.36.. But those who disbelieve (and reject Allah)- For them (there) will be the Fire of Hell. No length of time shall be given to them, so that they may die, nor shall its penalty be made easy for them. Thus do We reward every ungrateful one!

35.37. Therein, they will cry loudly (for help): "Our Lord! Take us out (of here): We shall work good deeds and righteousness, not the (things) we used to do!"- (Their answer from Allah will be:) "Did We not give you (a) life long enough so that, he who would (have listened), was warned? And (moreover) the Warner came to you. So you taste (the rewards for your deeds): For the wrongdoers there is no helper."

35.38.. Surely, Allah knows (all) hidden things of the heavens and the earth: Surely, He fully knows all that is within (men's) hearts.

35.39. It is He, Who has made you the inheritors (successors from one generation to the next) in the earth: Even then, if any (of you) disbelieve (in Islam), their rejection (works) against themselves: In the sight of their Lord their rejection only adds to the disgrace of the disbelievers: Their rejection only adds to (their own) ruin.

35.40. Say: "Have you seen (these) partners of yours, whom you call upon other than Allah? Show me what is it that they have created in the (whole) earth. Or do they have a part in the heavens? Or have We given them a Book from which they get clear proof from it (the Book)? No, the wrongdoers promise each other nothing but false hopes."

35.41. Verily, it is Allah Who keeps the heavens and the earth in existence, in case they stop (working) and if they fail (in their work), there is none- Not anyone - That can maintain them after that: Surely, He is Most Forbearing, Often Forgiving.

35.42.. And they promised with their strongest words by Allah (Himself, they swore) that if a Warner came to them, they would follow teachings better than any of the (other) peoples: But when a Warner came to them, it has only increased their turning away (from righteousness)-

35.43. (This is) because of their (false) pride in the land and their evil plots. But the plotting of evil will only force the plotters (of the evil) inside it. Then, are they only looking for the way the ancient (peoples) were dealt with? But no change will you find in the way in which Allah (deals): (And) no stopping will you find in the Way Allah (deals).

35.44. Do they not go through the land (the earth), and see (for themselves) what was the end of those (peoples) before them- Though they were stronger than them. Allah is not to be stopped by anything whatsoever in the heavens or on earth: Verily, He is All Knowing , All Powerful (Omnipotent).

35.45. And if Allah was to punish men according to what they have earned (and deserved), He would not leave a single living creature on the back of the (earth): But He gives them relief for a fixed time: And when the time comes to an end, surely, Allah is All Seeing over His servants.

****

Sura 36. Ya-Seen,
meant to address **Mankind (O Insan!) The Leader of Mankind (Prophet Muhammad):** (Makkah, 83 Verses)
In the Name of Allah, the Most Gracious, the Most Merciful.

36.1.. Ya Sin:

36.2. By the Quran, full of Wisdom -

36.3. Truly, (O Prophet!), you are one of the messengers,

36.4. On the Straight Path.

36.5. It is a Revelation (disclosed and) sent down by (Allah), the Supreme in Strength , Most Merciful ;

36.6. In order that you may warn a people, whose fore-fathers did not receive the warning and (those) who therefore remain unaware (of the Signs of Allah).

36.7.. Indeed, the Word (Punishment of Allah) is proved true against the greater part (or most) of them: Still, they do not believe,

36.8. Verily, We have put clamps (tightly) round their necks high up to their chins, so that their heads are forced up (and they cannot see).

36.9. And We have put a barrier in front of them and a barrier behind them, and also, We have covered them up (in their disbelief); So that they cannot see.

36.10. It is the same to them whether you warn them or you do not warn them: They will not believe.

36.11.. You can only warn such (a person) who follows the Reminder (the Warning in the Quran) and fears (Allah) Most Gracious, Unseen: Therefore, give such (a person), good news of Forgiveness and of most kind Reward.

36.12. Surely, We shall give life to the dead, and We record what they send before (Judgment) and that which they leave behind (in life), and We have taken record of all things in a book (of evidence).

36.13.. And put forward to them (and tell them), by way of a story (with a warning), about the companions of the City (which was destroyed). When the messengers (of Allah) have come to it.

36.14. When We sent two (messengers) to them, they rejected them both: So, We strengthened them (the two) with a third: (See Note 1 at the end of the Sura.-) They (the three messengers) said, "Truly, we have been sent as messengers to you."

36.15. The (people) said: "You are only beings like ourselves; And (Allah) the Most Gracious sends nothing to be made known (or disclosed): You do nothing but lie."

36.16. They (the three messengers) said: "Our Lord does know that we have been sent on a mission to you:

36.17. "And our duty is only to tell (you) the clear message."

36.18. The (people) said: "About us, we see an evil sign from you: If you do not stop, we will surely stone you, and a truly painful punishment will be given to you by us."

36.19. They (the prophets) said: "Your evil signs are with yourselves: (Consider this to be an early sign), that you are warned. No, but you are a people exceeding all limits!"

36.20. Then from a far part of the City, came running, a man saying, "O my People! Obey the messengers (of Allah):

36.21. "Obey those who do not ask any reward from you and (those) who have themselves received (Allah's) Guidance.

36.22. "It is not reasonable for me if I did not serve Him Who created me, and to Whom you shall (all) be brought back.

36.23. "Shall I take (other) gods besides Him? If (Allah) Most Gracious should have some misfortune for me, their pleading for me will not be of any use and they cannot set me free.

36.24. "If I do so, truly I will be (making) a clear mistake.

36.25. "For me, I have faith in the Lord of you (all): Then, listen to me!"

36.26. It was said: "You enter the Garden." He said: "O me! If only my people knew (what I know)!

36.27. "That my Lord has given me Forgiveness and has given me (a place) among those held in honor!"

36.28. And We did not send down any army from heaven against his people, after him. And it was not necessary for Us to do that.

36.29. It was not more than a single Mighty Blast (A powerful explosion), and look! They were (like ashes) put out (quiet) and silent.

36.30. Ah! Sorrow on the part (My) servants! There has not come one messenger (of Allah) to them that they have not made fun of him!

36.31. Do they not see how many of the generations before them We have destroyed? Verily, they (messengers) will not return to them:

36.32. But each one of all of them (the generations)- Will be brought before Us (for Judgment).

36.33.. And a Sign for them is (that when) the earth is dead: We give it life, and produce grain from it, from which you do eat.

36.34. And We produce in it gardens with date trees and grapes (in vines that climb), and We cause springs to come from within it:

36.35. That they may eat the fruits of this (gift from Allah) it was not their hands that made this (possible): Then will they not give thanks?

36.36. Glory to Allah, Who created all the things in pairs that the earth produces, and also their own kind (also created in pairs) and (other) things about whom they do not know.

36.37.. And a Sign for them is the night: We withdraw from it the day, and look, they are thrown in darkness;

36.38. And the sun moves along its way for a (length of) time set for him: That is the order of (Allah), the Almighty , the All Knowing .

36.39. And the moon- We have measured for it stages (to travel) till it comes back like the old (and worn out like the) lower part of a (crescent, dried out) date stalk.

36.40. It is not allowed for the sun to overtake the moon, nor can the night overtake the day: Each (can only) stay on in (its own) path (according to the Order of Allah).

36.41.. And a Sign for them is that We held together their race (through the Flood) in the loaded Ark (of Nuh);

36.42. And We created for them similar (ships) on which they ride.

36.43. If it was Our Will, We could drown them: (And) then there would be no helper (for them), nor could they be saved.

36.44. Except as the part of Mercy from Us, and as a part of a few (worldly) things (for them) for a (little) while.

36.45.. And when it is said to them: "You fear that which has happened before you, and that which will come after you, so that you may (also) receive (Allah's) Mercy," (then they do not listen and go away).

36.46. From the many Signs (*Ayât*) of their Lord, there is not (even) one Sign (*Ayâh*) that comes to them from which they do not turn away.

36.47. And when they are told: "You spend from (the many gifts) that Allah has given to you;" The unbelievers say to those who believe: "Shall we really feed those (people) whom, if Allah had so willed, He (Himself) would have fed? You are in nowhere but in clear mistake."

36.48. And they also ask: "When will this promise (be fulfilled), if you are truthful?"

36.49. They will not (have to) wait for anything, except a single Blast (A powerful explosion), it will catch (and grip) them while they are still quarreling among themselves!

36.50. Then they will have no (chance by their own) will to settle (their affairs), and not (even) to return to their own people! [Section 3]

36.51.. And the Trumpet (a very loud instrument) shall be sounded, when (you will) see! From the graves (men) will come quickly forward to their Lord!

36.52. They will say: "Ah! Sorrow to us! Who has raised us up from our place of sleep?" (A voice will say:) "This is what (Allah) the Most Gracious had promised, and the word of the messengers was (really) true?"

36.53. It will be no more than a single Blast, so behold! They will all be brought up before Us!

36.54. Then, on that Day, not (even) one soul will be unfairly treated in the least, and you shall be only given the (just) reward for your past actions.

36.55.. Surely, on that Day, the companions of the Gardens shall be busy and happy in everything that they do;

36.56. They and their wives will be in the (cool) shade of thick trees, resting on thrones (of dignity);

36.57. There will be (every type of) fruit for them; They shall have whatever they want;

36.58. (Their word will be), "*Salaam* (Peace)!" A Word (of greeting) from the Lord, Most Merciful !

36.59.. (To others, the word will be:) "And, you O criminals (the peoples of sin!) You get (yourselves) far away on this Day!

36.60. " Did I not command you? O! Children of Adam! That you should not worship Satan; Verily, he is to you an open enemy.-

36.61. "And that you should worship Me (Allah); For, that is the Straight Path.

36.62. "And he (Satan) did take (you) a large number of you, (away towards evil). Then, did you not understand?

36.63. "This is the Hell of which you were promised (many times)!

36.64. "This Day, you burn (yourself in the Fire) because you rejected (the Truth many times)."

36.65.. This Day, We shall set a seal on the mouths. And their hands will speak to Us, and their legs will bear witness to all that they did.

36.66. If it was Our Will, We could surely have wiped out (blinded) their eyes; So that they would have run about searching for the Path, but (then again) how could they have seen?

36.67. And if it was Our Will, We could have transformed them (just to be) in their places; Then they would not have been able to forward (move about), and they could not have turned back.

36.68.. And if We gave long life to anyone, We would have reversed him in creation (by making him weak after giving him strength) then will they not understand?

36.69.. And We have not taught the (Prophet) poetry, and (poetry) is suited not for him: This is no less than a Message and Quran making things clear:

36.70. (And also) that it may warn anyone (who is alive), and that its Word (Message) may be justified against the disbelievers.

36.71. Do they not see that it is We Who have created from the (many) things that Our hands have fashioned for them- (Is also) cattle, for which they are the owners?

36.72. And We have subdued them (the cattle) for their (use)? Of them some are for riding, and some they eat:

36.73. And they have (other) benefits from them (the cattle), and they get (milk) to drink; Then will they not be thankful?

36.74. And they take besides Allah, other false gods, (thinking) that they might be helped (by the false gods)!

36.75. They (the gods) have not the power to help them: But they (the unbelievers) will be brought forward (for Judgment) as a (whole) group (to be punished).

36.76. So, do not let their (idle) talk, make you sad (O Prophet!). Surely, We know what they hide and what they say.

36.77.. Does man not see that it is We Who created him from (a clot in the) sperm-ovary drop? Yet see! He (makes himself) an open enemy!

36.78. And he puts forth (and invents) comparisons for Us, and forgets his own (true origin of) Creation: (And) he says: "Who can give life to the bones after they have become rotten and turned to dust?"

36.79. Say: "He will give them (the bones) life (the One) Who created them for the first time! And He is All Knowing of every kind of creation!

36.80. "The same (Allah); He, Who produces fire out of the green tree, for you, who see! You may start a fire with it.

36.81. "Is not He Who created the heavens and the earth able to create (another) like them? Yes indeed! (He can recreate them.) He is the Supreme Creator, the All Knowing

36.82. "Surely, when He wants anything, His Command to it is, 'Be', and it is!"

36.83. So Glory be unto Him, in Whose hands is the kingdom of all things, and to Him all of you will be brought back.

Sura 36 Note

Note 36.1 These Ayâh are considered (by some of the commentators) as a reference to the Greek City of Antioch (in Northern Syria), where Messiah (Christ), his disciples and the earlier prophets preached.

****

Sura 37. As-Saffát,

[The rows of people (arranged by their ranks)]:
(Makkah, 182 Verses)
In the Name of Allah, the Most Gracious, the Most Merciful.

37.1.. By those who arrange themselves in ranks (or rows, to serve and to worship Allah,)

37.2. And by those who raise the clouds in a holy way, (to keep away the fears from the mind of humans,)

37.3. And those who recite the Message (of Allah)!

37.4. Surely! (And assuredly,) your Allah is One!

37.5. Lord of the heavens and of the earth, and all (that is) between them, and Lord of every point of the sun-rising, (that keeps changing every day of the year)

37.6.. Verily, We have truly stored the lower heaven with beauty (of) the stars-

37.7. (For beauty) and for protection against every tough (unwilling and) revolting Satan,

37.8. (So that) they (the Satans') should not try to hear from the direction of the Exalted Assembly (of men and angels in Allah's service and worship) but (they) be thrown out from every side,

37.9. Outcast (and unwelcome), they are under an everlasting penalty,

37.10. Except such who may snatch something by stealing: And they are being followed by a flaming Fire of stabbing brightness.

37.11.. Then just ask (the disbelievers) what they think: Are they the more difficult to create, or the (other) creations whom We have created surely, We have created them (the disbelievers) out of a sticky clay!

37.12. Nay! Do you wonder while they mock (and make fun of you and the Quran)?

37.13. And when they are reminded, they pay no attention-

37.14. And when they see a Sign (*Ayâh* from Allah), they mock at it,

37.15. And they say: "This is nothing but evident magic!"

37.16. "What!" (they ask), "When we are dead, and become dust and bones, shall we (then) be resurrected (raised up again)?

37.17. "And also our fathers from the old (days)?"

37.18. You say: "Yes, then you shall (also) be put to shame (because of your evil)."

37.19. Then it will be a single (harsh) cry; And look, they will begin to see!

37.20. They will say: "Woe (misery) to us! This is the Day of Judgment!"

37.21. (A voice will say:) "This is the Day of Sorting Out, whose Truth you denied (once)!

37.22.. (The angels will be told): "Bring (all of) you up (for Judgment); The wrongdoers and their companions; And the things they worshipped-

37.23. "Besides Allah, and lead them to the way to the (burning) Fire!

37.24. "But stop them, verily, they must be asked:

37.25. " 'What is the matter with you, why do you not help each other (now)?' "

37.26.. No! But on that Day they shall submit themselves, (to the Judgment)

37.27. And they will turn to one another, and question one another.

37.28. They will say: "It was you who used to come to us from the right hand (of power and authority)!"

37.29. They will reply: "No, you, yourselves were not believers!

37.30. "Also we did not have any authority over you. No, it was you who were a transgressing people!

37.31. "So now (this moment) has come true against us, the Word of our Lord that we shall really taste (the penalty of our sins).

37.32. "We led you astray: Because, truly we were ourselves astray."

37.33.. Then truly, (on) that Day, they will (all) share in the Penalty.

37.34. Surely, that is how We shall deal with the criminals.

37.35. Truly, when they were told that there is no god except Allah, they would fill themselves up with (false) pride,

37.36. And they said: "What! Shall we give up our gods for the sake of a poet possessed?" (Referring to Prophet)

37.37. No, he (the Messenger) has come with the Truth, and he restates (the Message of) the messengers (before him).

37.38. Verily, you shall really taste the painful Penalty-

37.39. But it will be no more than the penalty for (the evil) that you have done -

37.40. Except the true (and loving) servants of Allah-

37.41. For them, their food (and provision) is known;

37.42. Fruits (and Joys); And they (shall have) honor and dignity,

37.43. In Gardens of (supreme) happiness

37.44. Facing each other on thrones (of dignity):

37.45. Around to them will be passed a Cup from a clear-flowing fountain,

37.46. Crystal-white (and) of a delicious taste for those who drink (from it),

37.47. Free from all pains; They will not suffer intoxication (from it).

37.48. And beside them will be noble (and pure) women, holding back their looks, with big eyes (filled wonder and beauty).

37.49. As if they were (delicate) eggs closely guarded (from evil).

37.50.. Then they will turn to one another and question one another.

37.51. One of them will start the speak and say: "Verily, I had a close companion (on the earth),

37.52. "Who used to say: 'What! Are you from those (people) who confirms the Truth (of the Message)?

37.53. " 'That when we die and become dust and bones, shall we really receive the rewards and punishments?' "

37.54. (The speaker) said: "Would you like to look down?"

37.55. So he looked down and saw him (the questioner) in the middle of the Fire.

37.56. He (the speaker) said: "By Allah! You brought me very close to ruin (in this Hell)!

37.57. "Had it not been for the Grace of my Lord, I would surely be among those brought (to Hell)!"

37.58. (The people of Paradise will say:) "Is it (true) that we will not die (again),

37.59. "Except our first death, and that we shall not be punished?"

37.60. Surely, this is the supreme success (to be in the Paradise of joy)!

37.61. For those who like (the state) this (joy) let (them) all work hard, (those) who wish to strive.

37.62.. Is that (the Paradise), the better place (of joy) or the (evil and wicked) tree of *Zaqqum* (in the Pit of Hell, see 37.64-65)?

37.63. Truly, We have made it (the tree of *Zaqqum*) a trial for the wrongdoers.

37.64. Verily, it is a tree that comes out from the bottom of Hell-Fire:

37.65. The buds of its fruit-stalk, come out of the stems; (They are) like the heads of Satans':

37.66. Truly, they (the wrongdoers) will eat from there and fill their stomachs with it.

37.67. Then on top of that they will be given a mixture made of boiling water.

37.68. Then, thereafter, verily their return will be to the burning Fire of Hell.

37.69. Truly, they found their fathers on the wrong path;

37.70. So they (also) were rushed down after them (in their fathers evil footsteps)!

37.71. And indeed, before them, many (people) from the olden days went astray-

37.72. And indeed, We sent (messengers) among them, to warn them-

37.73. Then see what was the end of those who were warned (but did not pay attention)-

37.74. Except the devoted (and loving) servants of Allah.

37.75.. And indeed, (in the old days), Nuh (Noah) cried to Us, and We are the best of those to answer him.

37.76. And We rescued him, and his family from the great destruction (of the Flood),

37.77. And made his children (and descendants) to live (and stay on this earth);

37.78. And We left for him (this noble blessing) in the generations to follow in later times:

37.79. "*Salaam*, (Peace and greetings) to Nuh (Noah) among the (Our) Creation!"

37.80. Truly, like this do We reward those who do good.

37.81. Verily, he (Nuh) was one of Our believing servants.

37.82. Then We drowned the others (in the Flood).

37.83.. And surely, among those who followed his (Nuh's) way was Ibrahim (Abraham).

37.84. When he came to his Lord with a pure heart.

37.85. When he said to his father and to his people, "What is it that, which you worship?

37.86. "Is it a lie, false gods other than Allah, that you want?

37.87. "Then what do you know about the Lord of the Worlds?"

37.88. Then he took a look at the stars,

37.89. And he said, "I am truly sick (at my heart)!"

37.90. So they (his people) turned away from him, and left (him).

37.91.. Then he turned to their gods and said: "Will you not eat (from what is offered to you)?...

37.92. "What is the matter with you that you do not speak (and make sense)?"

37.93. Then he turned upon them (their gods), striking (them) with the right hand.

37.94. Then (the worshippers) came with quick steps, and faced (him).

37.95. He said: "Do you worship what you have carved (yourselves)?

37.96. "While (it is) Allah (Who) has created you and (also) what you have made!"

37.97. They said: "Build for him a house (burning like a furnace), and throw him into the blazing fire!"

37.98. So (after having failed; See 21.69), they then took a way (to hurt) against him, but We made them the ones most ashamed!

37.99.. And he said: "Verily, I am going to my Lord! He will surely guide me!

37.100. "O my Lord! Grant me (a progeny) of the righteous!"

37.101. So, We gave him the good news of a boy ready (to be born) to suffer and be patient.

37.102. And when (his son, Ismail) became (the age to) work with him, he (Ibrahim) said: "O my son! I see in a dream (vision) that I offer you in sacrifice (to Allah): Now see what is your (own) thought!" (The son) said: "O my father! Do like you are commanded: You will find me, if Allah so wills one who has (great) patience (and constancy!)"

37.103. Then, when they both had submitted their wills (to Allah's Wish), and he (Ibrahim) had laid him (his son, Ismail) prostrate on his forehead (for sacrifice),

37.104. We called out to him, "O Ibrahim (Abraham)!

37.105. "You have already fulfilled your vision!"- Verily, thus We do reward those who do good.

37.106. Indeed, it was clearly a trial (for Ibrahim)-

37.107. And We ransomed him with a great sacrifice (with that of a ram):

37.108. And We left for him (this blessing) in the generations to follow in later times:

37.109. "*Salaam*, (Peace) be upon to Ibrahim (Abraham)!"

37.110. Verily, thus do We reward those who do good.

37.111. Indeed, he was one of Our believing servants.

37.112. And We gave him the good news of Isháq (Isaac)- A prophet- One of the righteous.

37.113. We blessed him and Isháq (Isaac): And of their children (and descendants) are (some) who do right, and (some) who clearly do wrong to their own souls.

37.114.. And again, (from the past) We bestowed Our favor on Musa (Moses) and Haroon (Aaron),

37.115. And We saved them and their people from (their) great misfortune;

37.116. And We helped them, so that they overcame (their troubles);

37.117. And We gave them the Book and Clear Scripture (*Taurát*, which helps to make things clear);

37.118. And We guided them to the Straight Path.

37.119. And We left for them (this blessing) in the generations to follow in later times:

37.120. "*Salaam*, (Peace) be upon Musa (Moses) and to Haroon (Aaron)!"

37.121. Verily, thus do We reward those who do good.

37.122. Indeed, they were two of Our believing servants.

37.123.. And verily, Ilyas (Elias) was one of Our messengers.

37.124. When he said to his people: "Will you fear (Allah)?

37.125. "Will you call upon the false god (Baal) and give up the Best of Creators-

37.126. "Allah- Your Lord and (Cherisher and) the Lord (and Cherisher) of your fathers from the earlier days?"

37.127. But they denied him, so they will be truly brought up (for punishment)-

37.128. Except the sincere and the devoted servants of Allah (among them).

37.129. And We left for him (this blessing) in the generations to follow in later times:

37.130. "*Salaam*, (Peace) be upon those like Ilyas (Elias)!"

37.131. Verily, thus do We reward those who do good.

37.132. Indeed, he was one of Our believing servants!

37.133.. And verily, Lut (Lot) was one of the messengers.

37.134. Truly, We saved him and all his people (with him)

37.135. Except an old woman (his wife) who was with those who fell behind:

37.136. Then We destroyed the rest.

37.137. Surely, you pass by their (sites) by the morning-

37.138. And by night: Will you not reflect and understand?

37.139.. And verily, Yunus (Jonah) was one of the messengers.

37.140. When he ran away (like a slave runs from captivity) to the ship (fully) loaded (with men and cargo),

37.141. Then he (agreed to foretell fortunes and) cast lots, (and he was blamed for the ships bad weather) and he was a loser, punished (and thrown in the sea):

37.142. Then the (big) fish swallowed him, and he had done actions worthy of blame (by running away from his mission).

37.143. If it was that he had not (repented and) glorified Allah,

37.144. He would surely have remained inside the fish till the Day of Resurrection (to be raised from the dead).

37.145. But We cast (threw) him on the open shore while he was (still) sick,

37.146. And We made a vine (of hard shelled fruit) to grow over him for shade.

37.147. And We sent him to (teach Allah's Message to) a hundred thousand (men) or more.

37.148. And they believed; So We let them enjoy (their lives) for a while.

37.149.. Now ask them (the unbelievers) what they think: Is it that your Lord has (only) daughters, and they have sons?

37.150. Or that We created the angels female, and they have seen (it)? (see Note 1 at the end of Sura).

37.151. Verily, is it not they who say (in their disbelief and), from their own lies and sayings:

37.152. "Allah has had children?" And verily, they are liars!

37.153. Did He (then) choose daughters rather than sons?

37.154. What is the matter with you? How do you decide?

37.155. Then will you not remember (receive the warning)?

37.156. Or do you have a clear authority?

37.157. (If so), then you bring your Book (of authority) if you are truthful!

37.158.. And they have invented a blood-relationship between Him and the jinns', but the jinns' know (very well) that they (also) have to appear (for Judgment)! (see Note 2 at the end of the Sura.-)

37.159. Glorified be Allah! (He is) Free from the things that they relate (to Him)!

37.160. Except those slaves of Allah, whom He chooses.

37.161. So surely, neither you nor those you worship-

37.162. Can lead (any of Allah's servants) into temptation (and lies) about Allah,

37.163. Except those who are (by themselves) going to the blazing Fire (of Hell)!

37.164.. (Those angels arranged in ranks to serve Allah say): "Not even one of us does not have a place appointed;

37.165. "And, verily we are surely arranged in ranks (for Allah's Service);

37.166. "And surely we are those who speak out (Allah's Supreme) Glory!"

37.167.. And indeed they (the pagan Arabs) used to say,

37.168. "If only we have had a Message before us from those (Books) of old,

37.169. "We would truly have been the Servants of Allah, sincere (and loving)!"

37.170. But (now that the Quran has come), they (still) reject it: But soon will they know (the penalty)!

37.171. And surely, Our Word, already has been given before (this) to Our servants and messengers sent.

37.172. That they would certainly be made victorious,

37.173. And that Our forces- Surely, they would the be victors

37.174. So you (O Prophet!) turn away from them for a little while,

37.175. And watch them (how they will do), and they shall soon see (how you do)!

37.176.. Do they really want to hurry Our punishment?

37.177. Then when it (the punishment) falls into the open space before them; Painful will be (see Note 3 at the end of the Sura.-) the morning for those who were warned (but did not pay attention)!

37.178. So you turn away from them for a little while,

37.179. And watch them (how they will do), and they shall soon see (how you do)!

37.180. Glorified be your Lord, the Lord of Honor and Power! (He is free) from the things that they relate (to Him)!

37.181. And Peace (be) on the messengers (of Allah)!

37.182. And all the Praises (and thanks) to Allah, the Lord (and Cherisher) of the Worlds.

Sura 37 Notes

Note 37.1. In *Ayâh* 150 this challenge is made to the false belief of the pagan Arabs that the angels are Allah's daughters.

Note 37.2. In *Ayâh* 158 this challenge is made to the false belief of the pagan Arabs that some evil spirits and jinns' are intertwined with the Supremacy of Allah.

Note 37.3. In *Ayâh* 177 this implies the battleground, but in a metaphorical sense, it means when evil is brought in the open.

****

Sura 38. Sád,

(The Quranic letter Sád): (Makkah, 88 Verses)
In the Name of Allah, the Most Gracious, the Most Merciful.

38.1. **Sád:** And the Quran, full of Guidance and Reminding (and Warning, this is the Truth).

38.2. No! Those who disbelieve are in arrogance and opposition (and think only about self-glory and separatism).

38.3. How many generations before them did We destroy? In the end, they cried but there was no more time (for them) to be saved!

38.4.. And they (pagans) are surprised that a Warner (the Prophet) has come to them from themselves! And the unbelievers say: "This is a magician (with unusual powers and) telling lies!

38.5. "Has he (the Warner) made (all) the gods into one god? Truly, this is a wonderful thing!"

38.6. And their leaders (the unbelievers) hurry away, (saying:) "You (also) walk away, and remain with your gods! Truly, this is a thing meant to be (against you)!

38.7. "We have never heard (anything like this) from the people of these latter days: This is nothing but an invention (made up story)!"

38.8. "What!" (they say in anger), "Has a Message been sent to him (of all the persons) from us?"... But they are in doubt about Me (and My Message); No, but they have not yet tasted My punishment!

38.9. Or do they have the wealth of the Mercy of your Lord- The Supreme in Power , the Bestower of Bounties without measure?

38.10. Or have they the kingdom of the heavens and the earth and all between? If so, let them reach up with the ropes and means (to get there)!

38.11. But there- Even a large number of (their) allies will be defeated.

38.12. Before them (there were many who rejected messengers of Allah)- The people of Nuh (Noah), and Ad, and Firon (Pharaoh), the lord of (wooden) poles, (to mark his empire.)

38.13. And Samood (Thamud), and the people of Lut (Lot), and the companions of the Wood- Like this were the Confederates (*Al-Ahzâb,* the allies of unbelievers)

38.14. Not one (of them did anything) but denied the messengers, but My punishment came justly and surely (to them).

38.15.. And these (people) only wait for a single Blast, which (is blown by Angel Israfil) will tolerate no delay.

38.16. They (the unbelievers will) say: "Our Lord! Hasten our sentence (of punishment, even) before the Day of Reckoning (and account)!"

38.17. Have patience at what they say, and remember Our servant Dawood (David), the man of (great) strength; Verily, he always came back in repentance (to Allah) .

38.18. Verily, We made the hills recite Our Praises together with him, in evening and at break of day,

38.19. And all the birds gathered (in flocks), did turn (to Allah) with him (Dawood).

38.20. We made his kingdom strong and gave him wisdom, and good judgment in what he talked and what he decided.

38.21.. And, has the story of the (two) who disagreed reached you? When they climbed over the wall of the private room (where he prayed);

38.22. When they entered in presence of Dawood (David), and he was frightened of them, they said: "Fear not: We are two litigant (who disagree), one of us has wronged the other: Therefore, decide between us now with truth, and do not treat us with injustice, and guide us to the Right way.

38.23. "Verily, this man is my brother (in religion): He has ninety and nine ewes (female sheep), and I have (only) one: Yet he says; 'Leave her (the one sheep) to me,' and (also he) is rude to me when he talks."

38.24. (Dawood) said: "Without a doubt he has done wrong to you by asking you for (the single) sheep to add to his (flock of) sheep: And truly, there are many partners (in business) who do wrong to each other, except those who believe and work deeds of righteousness do not act like that, and how few are they?"... And Dawood (David) gathered that We had tried him, and he asked forgiveness from his Lord, and he fell down, bowing (in prostration), and turned (to Allah in repentance).

{A Muslim generally prostrates to Allah after reciting this verse}

38.25. So, We forgave him (for) this: And he really enjoyed an extreme closeness to Us, and a Beautiful Place of (final) Return.

38.26. Oh Dawood (David)! Verily, We truly made you a successor and leader on earth: So you judge between men in truth (and justice): And do not follow the (idle) desires (of your heart), for they will take you away from the Path of Allah: Verily, those who go away from the Path of Allah, (there) is a painful penalty, because they forget the Day of Reckoning (and Account).

38.27.. And We did not create the heavens and the earth and all that is between (them) without purpose. That is what the unbelievers thought. But warning (and sorrow) to the unbelievers because of the Fire (of Hell)!

38.28. Shall We treat those who believe and do righteous good deeds in the same (way) as those who make (evil) mischief on earth? Or shall We treat those who are the pious and righteous, in the same (way) as those who turn away from right?

38.29. (This is the Quran) a Book that We have sent to you full of blessings, so that they may (carefully) think about its Signs, and so that men of understanding may be remember.

38.30.. And to Dawood (David), We gave (his son) Sulaiman (Solomon)- Verily, he always turned (to Us) very well in Our service!

38.31. When, in the evening, horses of the finest breeding, and quick in running, were brought before him;

38.32. And he (Sulaiman) said: "Truly, I love the good things, in order to see the Glory of my Lord," until (the sun) was hidden behind the curtain of (dusk). (During this late *Asr–Maghrib* time, Sulaiman used to pray to Allah.)

38.33. (Then, he said:) "Bring them (the horses) back to me." Then he began to pass his hand over (their) legs and their necks.

38.34.. And, indeed We did try Sulaiman (Solomon): We placed a body (without life) on his throne: (Like giving him power without giving him a soul) but he turned (to Us in true devotion):

38.35. He said: "O my Lord! Forgive me, and grant me a kingdom which may not suit another (king) after me: Verily, You are the Bestower of good things (without measure)."

38.36. So, We made the Wind obey his power, to flow gently by his order, where ever he wanted-

38.37. And like this did (others obey his order); The Evil ones of every kind of builder and diver-

38.38. As also others (obeyed his order those) tied together in chains

38.39. (Allah addressed Sulaiman and said:) "These are Our many gifts (of good things): Whether you (O Sulaiman!) give them (to others) or do not give them, no account will be asked."

38.40. And truly, he enjoyed, an extreme closeness to Us, and (it is) a Beautiful Place of (final) Return.

38.41.. And remember (with honor) Our Servant Ayub (Job). When he cried to his Lord and said: "The Satan has hurt me with pain and suffering!"

38.42. (An order from Us was given:) "Strike your foot: This is where (water) is to wash, to cool, to refresh, and to drink."

38.43. And We gave him (back) his people and doubled their number- As a Favor from Ourselves, and a thing to remember for all who have understanding.

38.44. "And take in your hand a little (bunch of thin) grass, and strike (your wife with) it: And do not break your promise." Truly, We found him (Ayub or Job) full of patience and constancy. How well in Our service did he ever return (to Us)!

38.45.. And remember (with honor) Our Servants Ibrahim (Abraham), Isháq (Isaac), and Yàqoub (Jacob), those who had power and vision.

38.46. Surely, We did choose them for a special (purpose)- Restating the Message of the Hereafter.

38.47. And (in Our sight,) they truly were of the company of the chosen and of the Good.

38.48.. And remember (with honor) Ismail (Ishmael), Al-Yasa (Elisha), and Zul-kifl: Each of them was of the company of the Good.

38.49.. This is a Remainder (with guidance and warning): And surely, for the Righteous, is a Beautiful Place of (final) Return-

38.50. Paradise, (Gardens of Eternity), whose doors will (forever) be open to them;

38.51. In there they will rest (in comfort) in there they can call for fruit in plenty, and (for delicious) drink;

38.52. And beside them will be modest (and noble) women withholding their looks, (and companions) of equal age.

38.53. This is the Promise made to you for the Day of Reckoning (and Account)!

38.54. Truly like this will be Our Rewards (to you,) it (the Promise) will never fail-

38.55.. Yes like this! And for those who do wrong the place of (their final) Return will be evil!

38.56. Hell, is where they will burn in there, an evil bed (to lie on)!

38.57. Yes like this! (And) then they shall taste it- A boiling fluid, and the murky discharge of dirty wounds!

38.58. And other similar penalties of the same kind!

38.59. (When they are taken to Hell)- Here is a group going straight with you! (There will be) no welcome (even in the Hell) for them! Truly, they shall burn in the Fire!

38.60. (The followers of evil will cry out to their leaders:) No, you (too)! (There is) no welcome for you! It is you who have made this happen to us! Now, (this) place to stay-in is evil!

38.61. They (the followers) will say: "Our Lord! Whoever has made this happen to us- Add a double penalty of Fire upon him!"

38.62. And they will (also) say: "What has happened to us that we see not men whom we used to count among the bad ones?

38.63. "Did we treat them with mockery, or have (our) eyes failed to see them?"

38.64. Truly, that is just and fitting- The charges made upon each other by the people of the Fire!

38.65.. (O Prophet) Say: "Truly, I am a Warner: There is no god except Allah, the One and Only, the Irresistible-

38.66. The Lord of the heavens and of the earth, and all that is between, - The Exalted in Might, , the Often Forgiving."

38.67. Say: "That is a Message Supreme (above all),

38.68. "From which you turn away!

38.69. "I have no knowledge about the high chiefs (angels), of the Exalted Assembly when they discuss (things) by themselves.

38.70. "Only this has been revealed to me: That I am to give (this) warning plainly and publicly."

38.71.. (Remember), your Lord said to the angels: "I am about to create man from clay:

38.72. "So, when I have fashioned him and breathed into him, his soul, from My Spirit, then you (angels should) fall down (and prostrate) in respect for him."

38.73. So, the angels prostrated themselves, all of them together:

38.74. Except the Chief Satan (*Iblis*): He was haughty, and became one of those who reject Faith.

38.75. (Allah) said: "O *Iblis*! What prevents you from prostrating yourself to the one whom I have created with Both My Hands? Are you proud (and haughty)? Or are you one of the high (and mighty) ones?"

38.76. (*Iblis*) said: "I am better than him (Adam): You created me from fire, and You created him from clay."

38.77. (Allah) said: "Then get yourself out from here: For verily, you are an outcast, rejected and accursed.

38.78. "And surely, My Curse shall be on you till the Day of Recompense (Judgment)."

38.79. (*Iblis*) said: "O my Lord! Then give me time (of relief) till the Day when the (dead) are Resurrected."

38.80. (Allah) said: "Surely, then time is given to you-

38.81. "Till the Day of the Time (which has been) appointed."

38.82. (*Iblis*) said: "Then by Your Power (and Permission) I will mislead them (men) all in the wrong (path)-

38.83. "Except (those of) Your Servants amongst them (the men who are) sincere and purified (by Your Grace)."

38.84. (Allah) said: "Then it is just and fitting- And I say what is just and fitting-

38.85. "That I will surely fill Hell with you and those (men) who follow you, together."

38.86.. (O Prophet) say: "I do not want any reward from you for this (Quran), and I am not a pretender.

38.87. "This (Quran) is not less than a Remainder to (all) the Worlds.

38.88. "And you will surely know the truth of it (all) after a while."

****

Sura 39. Az-Zumar,

(The crowds): (Makkah, 75 Verses)

In the Name of Allah, the Most Gracious, the Most Merciful.

39.1. the Revelation of this Book is from Allah; The Almighty, (the One Exalted in Power), the All Wise .

39.2. Surely, it is We Who have revealed (and made known) the Book to you in Truth: So, worship Allah, giving Him (your) sincere love and prayer.

39.3. Surely, for Allah Alone is the truest religion (of love, worship and sincerity). But those who take for protectors other than Allah, (say): "We only worship them so that they may bring us closer to Allah." Truly Allah will judge between them where they differ. But Allah does not guide him who is a liar and ungrateful.

39.4.. If Allah had wished to take to Himself a son, He could have chosen whomever He pleased from those He creates: But Glory be to Him! (He is above such things.) He is Allah, the (Single) One, the Compelling, (Overpowering)

39.5. He has created the heavens and the earth in truth (and in proper proportions): He makes the night reach into the day, and makes the day reach into the night: He has subjected the sun and the moon follow (His law): Each one follows a path for a certain (preset) time. Verily, is He not the (One) Exalted in Power - The Often Forgiving?

39.6. He created (all of) you from a single person, then created, his mate of a similar nature; And He has sent down for you eight heads of cattle in (four) pairs (of sheep, goats, oxen and camels); He makes you in the wombs of your mothers, creation after creation (in stages one after another), in three covers (trimesters) of darkness. Such is Allah, your Lord (and Cherisher). To Him belongs (all) kingdom. There is no god but He: Why, then are you turned away (from Him)?

39.7.. If you reject, Allah, surely (He) does not have any need of you; But He does not like the thankless from His servants. And if you are thankful, He is pleased with you. No (human being who is a) bearer of burdens can bear the burden of another (human being). Then to your Lord is your Return, in the end, when He will tell you the truth of all that you did (in this life). Verily, He knows well all that is in (everyone's) hearts.

39.8. And when some trouble comes to man; He cries to his Lord, turning to Him (the Lord) by feeling sorry for what he has done: But when He gives him (the man, a gift) of Mercy from Himself, (man) forgets what he cried and prayed for before, and he sets up rivals to Allah, so as to mislead others from His (Allah's) Path. Say (to such people): "Enjoy your disbelief for some time: Surely, you are from the companions of the Fire!"

39.9.. Is one who is obedient (to Allah) with love and sincerity in the hours of the night prostrating himself or standing (up in love and admiration), who pays attention to the Hereafter, and who places his hope in the Mercy of his Lord, (like one who does not)? Say: "Are those equal, those who know and those who do not know?" It is those who have understanding that receive guidance.

39.10.. Say: "O you my (people!) Servants who believe! Fear your Lord, for those who do good in this world, (the Reward) is good. Spacious is Allah's earth! Those who patiently work hard will truly receive a reward without measure!"

39.11. Say: "Surely, I am commanded to worship Allah with all my sincere love, servitude and prayer (to Him);

39.12. "And I am commanded to be the first of those who bow to Allah in Islam."

39.13. Say: "If I disobeyed my Lord, I would truly have fear of the penalty of a Mighty Day."

39.14. Say: "It is Allah Alone (Whom) I worship, with all my sincere love, servitude and payer (to Him):

39.15. "So you worship whatever you will besides Him." Say: "Truly, those in loss (now) are those who (will) lose their own souls and their people on the Day of Judgment: Verily! That is truly the (greatest and) real Loss!"

39.16. They shall have layers of Fire over them, and layers (of Fire) below them: With this, Allah does warn His servants: "Oh My Servants! Then you fear Me!"

39.17.. Those who avoid evil- And do not fall into its worship- And turn to Allah (in repentance), for them are the glad tidings and good news so announce the good news to My servants-

39.18. Those who listen to the Word, and follow the best (meaning) in it: Those are the ones whom Allah has guided, and those are the ones blessed with understanding.

39.19. Then, is the one against whom the judgment of punishment is justly due (equal to one who avoids evil)? Then, would you save one who is in the Fire?

39.20. But the high palaces (to live in) have been built one above another, for those who fear their Lord; Beneath them rivers (of joy) flow: (This is) the Promise of Allah, and He never fails in (His) Promise.

39.21. Do you not see that Allah sends down rain from the sky, and leads it (the rain water) through springs in the earth? Then from it, He makes produce of various colors to grow: Then it fades (due to lack of water): (And) you will see it grow yellow; Then He makes it dry up and fall down. Truly, in this, there is a Message to remember for men of understanding.

39.22.. Is one whose breast Allah has opened to Islam, so that he has received the Light from his Lord, (not better than one whose heart is in disbelief)? (There is) grief for those whose hearts are hardened against saying the Praises of Allah! They are clearly walking about in error!

39.23. Allah has sent down (from time to time) the Most Beautiful Message, in the form of a Book, (the Scripture, this Quran) true within (and to) itself, (always) repeating (its teaching): The skins of those who fear their Lord shiver and tremble by (reading and hearing) it; Then their skins and their hearts soften by to the remembrance of Allah. Like this is the Guidance of Allah. He guides like this whom He pleases, but no one can guide those whom Allah leaves to wander about.

39.24. Then, is the one who has to fear the hurt of the penalty on the Day of Judgment (and receive it) on his face, (like one who is safe from it)? And it will be said to the wrongdoers: "You taste (the fruits of) what you earned!"

39.25. (There were) those who rejected (the Message) before them and so (for them) the punishment came to them from directions they did not expect.

39.26. So, Allah gave them a taste of hurt (and disgrace) in the present life, but the punishment of the Hereafter is greater, if they only knew!

39.27.. And indeed, in this Quran, We have put forth every kind of similar (and meaningful) story for men in order that they may be informed (and warned).

39.28. (It is purely) a Quran in Arabic, without any (dishonesty or) crookedness in it: In order that they (those who read) may protect (themselves) against evil.

39.29. Allah puts forth a parable (the story with meaning and guidance in it)- A slave belonging to many different partners, (false gods) disputing with one another and a slave belonging only to one master : Are those two equal in comparison? All the Praises (and thanks) be to Allah! But most of them do not know.

39.30. Truly, you will die (one day), and truly they will also die (one day).

39.31. Then in the End, you will (all) on the Day of Judgment, settle your disagreements in the Presence of your Lord.

39.32.. Then, who does more wrong than one who talks a lie about Allah, and rejects the Truth when it comes to him! Is Hell not the home for disbelievers (and blasphemous)?

39.33. And he (the man) who says the Truth and he who restates (and supports) it- Such men are those who do right.

39.34. They shall have all that they wish for, in the Presence of their Lord: That is the reward for those who do good:

39.35. So that Allah will remove from them the evil of (the worst of) their deeds and give them their reward to suit the best of what they have done.

39.36.. Is not Allah enough for His servant? But they (the wrongdoers) try to frighten you with other (gods) besides Him! And whom Allah leaves to wander, for him, there can be no guide

39.37. And those whom Allah guides, for him there can be no one who can take them away (from the Straight Path). Is not Allah Supreme in Power, Imposer of Retribution?

39.38. And truly, if you are to ask them: "Who created the heavens and the earth?" Surely, they would say, "Allah." Say: "Do you see then? The things that you invoke besides Allah- If Allah gives me some penalty, can they remove His penalty? Or if He gives some mercy for me, can they keep back His mercy from?" Say: "Sufficient is Allah for me! In Him trust those who put their trust."

39.39. Say: "O my people! Do whatever you can: I will do (my part): But soon will you know-

39.40. "To whom comes a penalty of dishonor, and upon whom will fall a penalty that stays forever."

39.41.. Surely, We have revealed the Book to you in Truth, for (teaching the whole) mankind. Then, he who receives guidance helps his own soul: But he who wanders away hurts his own soul. You (O Prophet!) are not set over them as a trustee over them (for their affairs).

39.42.. It is Allah, Who takes the souls at their death; And from those who do not die during their sleep (He takes as they sleep): Those for whom He has ordered death, He does not let (them to return to life), but He sends the others (to their bodies) for a length of time. Surely, in this, are (His) Signs for those who think.

39.43. What! Do they take intercessors other than Allah? Say: "Even if they do not have any power whatever and (have) no intelligence?"

39.44. Say: "To Allah Only belongs every (right to grant) any intercession: To Him belongs the kingdom of the heavens and the earth: In the end, it is to Him that you shall be brought back."

39.45. And when (the Name of) Allah, the One and Only is mentioned, the hearts of those who do not believe in the hereafter are filled with disgust (and hate), and when (the false-gods) other than He are said, look, they are filled with joy!

39.46. Say: "O Allah! Creator of the heavens and the earth! Knower of all that is hidden, and all that is seen! It is You, Who will judge between Your Servants in those matters about which they have differed."

39.47.. And those who did wrong had all that there is on earth, and as much more, (for no use) they would offer it to save (themselves) from the pain of the penalty on the Day of Judgment: But something will confront them from Allah, over which they could never have counted upon!

39.48. And for the evils of their actions will confront them, and they will be (completely) surrounded by that which they used to mock at!

39.49. When trouble comes to man, then he cries (and calls) to Us for help: When We give him a favor all by Ourselves, he says: "This has been given to me because of a certain knowledge (I have)!" No, but this is only a trial, but most of them do not understand!

39.50. Verily, the (people) before them talked like this! But everything they did was of no use to them.

39.51. So, the evil results of their actions overtook them. And for the wrongdoers of this (generation)- The evil results of their actions will (also) soon overtake them, and they will never be able to stop or escape (Our Plan)!

39.52. Do they not know that Allah increases the things (He gives) or reduces them, for anybody whom He pleases? Surely, in this are Signs for those who believe!

39.53.. Say: "O servants (slaves of Allah, those) who have transgressed against their souls! Do not feel sad about the Mercy of Allah: For Allah forgives all sins: Truly, He is Often Forgiving, Most Merciful .

39.54. "And you turn to your Lord (in repentance) now and submit to His (Will), before the Penalty comes on you: And after that you shall not be helped.

39.55. "And follow the best (of the paths) revealed to you from your Lord, before the penalty comes upon you- All of a sudden, when you are not aware!"-

39.56. In case the soul should say: "Ah! I am in (deepest) sorrow because I neglected (my duty) to Allah, and (I) was among those who made fun!"-

39.57. Or (in case) he should say: "If Allah had only guided me, then I should really have been with the righteous!"

39.58. Or when it sees the penalty (in case) it should say: "If only I had another chance, I should really be with those who do good!"

39.59. Yes verily, (the reply will be:) "But there came to you My Signs (*Ayât*), and you did reject them: You were proud (and haughty) and became one of those who rejected Faith!"

39.60.. And on the Day of Judgment, you will see those who told lies against Allah their faces will be turned dark because of their lies and fabrication; Is it not in Hell, a home (shall be) for the arrogant and haughty?

39.61. And Allah will deliver the righteous to their place of joy and success (and to peace): Evil shall touch them not, and they shall not grieve (or be sad).

39.62. Allah is Creator of all things, and He is Guardian and the Trustee of all things.

39.63. To Him, belong the keys of the heavens and of the earth: And those who reject the Signs of Allah- It is they who will be in loss.

39.64.. Say: "Is it that you order me to worship someone other than Allah?, O you! (Foolish ones) who do not know."

39.65. And indeed, it has already been revealed to you- Like it was (made known) to those before you- "If you were to join (gods with Allah), truly useless (and meaningless) will be your work (in life), and surely you will be with those who lose (every good)."

39.66. No! But Allah (Alone, you) worship, and be among those who give thanks.

39.67. They have not made just estimate of Allah, like that which is due to Him: And on the Day of Judgment the whole of the earth will be held firmly by His hand, and the heavens will be rolled up in His right hand: Glory to Him! And He is high above the partners that they make up for Him!

39.68. And the Trumpet will be blown (by Angel Israfil, and sounded loudly), when all that are in the heavens and on earth will be dizzy (and faint), except what will please Allah. Then will a second (Trumpet) one be sounded, when, look, they will be standing and looking!

39.69. And the earth will shine with the Glory of its Lord: And the Record (of deeds) will be placed (open); And the prophets and the witnesses will be brought forward, and a fair decision made between them with truth and they will not be wronged (in the least).

39.70. And (the reward) of the actions of every soul will be paid in full; And (Allah) is All Aware of all that they do.

39.71.. And the unbelievers will be driven to Hell in groups; Till they arrive there, its gates will be opened. And the Keepers (of Hell, see 74.30) will say, "Did not the messengers come to you from yourselves telling you the Signs of your Lord, and warning you of your meeting (Allah) on this Day?" The answers will be: "Yes! But the Order of Punishment has been proved true against the unbelievers!"

39.72. It will be said (to them): "Enter you the gates of Hell, to live in there: And evil is (this) home of the haughty!"

39.73.. And those who feared their Lord will be led to the Paradise (Garden) in groups: When they arrive there, and its gates will be opened; And the Keepers (of Paradise) will say: "Peace be upon you! Well have you done! You enter here to live in there forever."

39.74. And they will say: "All Praises (and thanks) be to Allah, Who has truly fulfilled His Promise to us, and has given us (this) land in return: We can live in the Garden like we will: How excellent a reward for those who work (righteously)!"

39.75. And you will see the angels surrounding the (Divine) Throne on all sides, glorifying the Praises to their Lord. (At Judgment) the Decision between them will be in (perfect) justice, and it will be said (from all sides), "All Praises (and thanks) be to Allah, the Lord of the Worlds!" (see *Ayâh* 1.1)

****

Sura 40. Gháfer or Al-Mu'min,
(The Most forgiving or the believer): (Makkah, 85 Verses)
In the Name of Allah, the Most Gracious, the Most Merciful.

40.1. Ha Mim:

40.2. The Revelation of the Book (the Quran) is from Allah, the Almighty (Supreme in Power), the All Knowing (Full of Knowledge)-

40.3. The Forgiver of sin, the Acceptor of repentance, the Severe in punishment, the Bestower (of Mercy). There is no god but He: To Him is the Final Return.

40.4.. No one can dispute about the Signs of Allah (*Ayât*), except the unbelievers. Then, do not let their (useless and) broken words through the land deceive you!

40.5. But (there were people) before them, who rejected (the Signs)- The People of Nuh (Noah), and those who joined together (in evil) after them; And every (one of those) people who plotted against their messenger, to seize him, and disputed by means of pride (and falsehood) just to bring down and therefore to knock down the Truth: But it was I Who seized them! And how (terrible) was My punishment (for them)!

40.6. Thus the Judgment of your Lord against the unbelievers was proved to be true that really they are companions of the Fire!

40.7.. Those (angels) who bear the Throne (of Allah) and those around it recite the Glory and Praise of their Lord; And believe in Him; And pray for Forgiveness for those who believe: (Saying:) "Our Lord! Your reach is in all the things, in Mercy and Knowledge. Then forgive, those who turn in repentance, and follow Your Path; And save them from the punishment of Hell!

40.8. "And our Lord! Permit (them), that they enter the Gardens of Eternity, which You have promised to them, and to the righteous among their fathers, their wives, and their children! Verily, You are Almighty , the All Wise .

40.9. "And save them from (all) evils; And any (people) whom You do save from evils; That (Last) Day- You will have blessed them with Mercy indeed: And (for them) will be truly a great success."

40.10.. The unbelievers will be told: "Indeed, to you the dislike of Allah was greater than the dislike of yourselves, (by) seeing that you were called to the Faith and you used to refuse."

40.11. They will say: "Our Lord! Twice have You made us (when we were) without life, and twice You have given us Life! Now we have recognized our sins: Then, is there any way to get out (of this)?"

40.12. (The answer will be:) "This is because, when (you were told that) Allah was to be the Only (One for worship), you did reject Faith, and when partners were joined with Him, you believed (it)! The Command is with Allah, the Most High, the Most Great!"

40.13.. He, it is Who shows you His Signs (*Ayât*), and sends down the (rain and) provision for you from the sky; But only those who receive guidance will turn (to Allah).

40.14. Then, you call upon Allah, with sincere devotion to Him, even though the unbelievers, may not like it.

40.15. Raised high above ranks (or limits, He is Allah), the Lord of the Throne (of Authority): By His Command, He does send the spirit (of inspiration) to any of His servants He pleases, that it may warn (men) of the Day of Mutual Meeting-

40.16. The Day on which they will (all) come forward: Not a single thing concerning them is hidden from Allah. Whose will be the Kingdom that Day? It is Allah, the One, the Irresistible!

40.17. That Day will every soul be given back what it earned; There will be no injustice on that Day, truly, Allah is Swift in taking account.

40.18.. And warn them of the Day, which is (always) coming closer, when the hearts will (come) right up to the throats to choke (the unbelievers): No close friend, nor anybody will the wrongdoers have to plead, who could be listened from.

40.19. (Allah) knows (the tricks) that deceive the eyes and (He knows) all that the hearts (of men) hide.

40.20. And Allah will judge with (Justice and) Truth: But those whom (men) call upon besides Him (Allah), will not (be in a position) to judge at all. Surely, He is Allah, the All Hearing , the All Seeing.

40.21.. Do they not travel through the earth and see what was the end of those before them? Those (people) were even superior to them in strength, and (see) in the little (that they have left) in the land: But Allah did call them to account (and explain) for their sins, and they had nobody to help them against Allah.

40.22. That was because their (own) messengers (from Allah) came to them with clear proof, (evidence and signs), but they rejected them: So Allah called them to account (and punish them for their sins): Verily, He is All Strong, Strict in Punishment.

40.23.. And indeed (earlier), We sent Musa (Moses), with Our Signs (*Ayât*) and a clear Authority,

40.24. (And) to Firon (Pharaoh), Haman, and Qârûn (Qaroon); But they called (him) "A magician telling lies!"...

40.25. Then, when he came to them in Truth, from Us, they said: "Kill the sons of those who believe with him, and keep alive their females," but the plans of the unbelievers (end) in nothing but mistakes (and delusions)!

40.26. Said Firon (Pharaoh): "Leave me to kill Musa (Moses); And let him call on his Lord! What I fear is that he may change your religion, or that he may cause mischief to appear in the land!"

40.27. Musa (Moses) said; "I have really called upon my Lord and your Lord (for protection) from everyone (who is) proud (and) who does not believe in the Day of Account!"

40.28.. And a believing man from the people of Firon (Pharaoh), who had hidden his faith, said: "Will you kill a man because he says, 'My Lord is Allah?'- When he has indeed come to you with Clear (Signs) from your Lord? And if he is a liar, (the sin of) his lie is on him: But, if he is telling the Truth, then something of the (great misfortune) about which he warns you, will fall upon you: Truly, Allah does not guide the one who sins against (Him) and lies!

40.29. "O my people! The power this day is yours: You have the upper hand in the land: But who will help us from the Punishment of Allah, should it come upon us?" Firon (Pharaoh) said: "I point out to you only what I see (myself); Nor do I guide you to (any path) but to the path of right!"

40.30.. Then the man who believed said: "O my people! I do truly fear for you something like the Day (of great suffering) for those who join together (in sin)!

40.31. "Something like the fate of the people of Nuh (Noah), and 'Ad, and the Samood (Thamud), and those who came after them: And Allah never wishes injustice to His servants.

40.32. "And, O my people! Verily, I fear for you a Day when there will be calling one another (in sorrow)-

40.33. "A Day when you shall turn your backs and run away: No defender shall you have from Allah: And anyone whom Allah leaves to become lost, for him there is none to guide...

40.34. "And indeed, Yusuf (Joseph) came to you in earlier times, with Clear Signs, but you did not stop doubting about the (purpose) for which he had come: In the end, when he died, you said: 'No messenger will Allah send after him.' Thus does Allah leave (them) to be lost as those who act in sin and live in doubt-

40.35. "(Such as those) who dispute about the Signs of Allah, without any authority that has reached them. Serious (painful) and disliked (is such conduct) in the Sight of Allah and of the believers. Thus Allah closes every heart of proud and stubborn sinners."

40.36.. Firon (Pharaoh) said: "O Haman! Build me a lofty tower (high palace), that I may find the ways and means-

40.37. "The ways and means of (reaching) the heavens, and that I may climb up to God of Musa (Moses): But as far as I think, I think (Musa) is a liar!" Thus in Firon's (Pharaohs) eyes, the evil of his deeds, was made pleasant (and easy for him), and he was kept away from the (right) Path; And the plan of Firon (Pharaoh) led to nothing but destruction (for him).

40.38.. In addition, the man who believed said: "O my people! Follow me: I will lead you to the right Path;

40.39. "O my people! This life of the present is nothing but (temporary) comfort, it is the Hereafter that is the Home that will stay.

40.40. "He who works evil will not be repaid except by its own kind: And he who works a righteous deed- Whether male or female -and is a true believer- Such (a person) will enter the Garden (of happiness): In there they will have plenty without measure.

40.41. "And, O my people! How (strange) it is for me to call you to peace (and happiness) when you call me to the Fire!

40.42. "You do call upon me to lie against Allah and to join with Him partners of whom I have no knowledge: And I call you to the Supreme in Power , the Often-Forgiving!

40.43. "Without a lie! You do call me to one (the false god), who is not fit to be called to, either in this world, or in the Hereafter; And our Return will be to Allah; And those who exceed the limits will be companions of the Fire!

40.44. "And soon will you remember what I say to you (now). My (own) actions (and future) I leave to Allah: Verily, Allah (always) watches over His servants."

40.45.. So Allah saved him (the believer) from the evils that they planned (against him), while the evil of the penalty surrounded the people of Firon (Pharaoh) on all sides.

40.46. The Fire, they will be brought in front of it, morning and evening: And (the sentence will be) on the Day that Judgment will be established: "You throw the people of Firon (Pharaoh) into the severest Penalty!"

40.47.. And they will fight with one another in the Fire! The weak ones (who followed) will say to those who had been proud (and arrogant),

"Verily, we only followed you: Can you then take (upon yourselves) from us some share of the Fire?"

40.48. Those who had been proud (and arrogant) will say: "We are all in this (Fire)! Truly, Allah has judged between (His) servants!"

40.49. And those in the Fire will say to the keepers of Hell: "Pray to your Lord to lighten us the punishment (even) for a Day!"

40.50. They will say: "Did your messengers not come to you with clear evidences and signs?" They will say, "Yes." They will reply: "Then pray (as you like)! And the prayer of those without Faith is nothing but (useless wandering) in error!"

40.51.. Without doubt, We will make victors, Our messengers and those who believe, (both) in the life of the world and in the Day when the witnesses will stand forth-

40.52. The Day when it will be of no use for the wrongdoers to bring up their excuses, but they will (only) have the Curse, and the Home of Misery.

40.53. And indeed before now, We did give Musa (Moses) the Guidance, and We gave the Book (*Taurát*) to inherit the Scripture for the Children of Israel-

40.54. A Guide and a Message to men of understanding.

40.55. Patiently await, (O Prophet!): The Promise of Allah is true: And ask forgiveness for your fault, and celebrate the Praises of your Lord in the evening (*'Asr* prayer), and in the morning (*Faj'r* prayer)

40.56. Verily, those who disagree (and dispute) about the Signs of Allah without any authority given to them- In their hearts there is nothing but (the search for) greatness which they shall never get then, find (help and) shelter in Allah, Verily, it is He is the All Hearing , the All Seeing.

40.57.. Surely, the creation of the heavens and the earth is indeed a greater (matter) than the creation of mankind: Yet most men do not understand.

40.58. The blind and those who see are not equal: Those who believe and work the righteous deeds and those who do evil are (also) not equal. Little do you remember!

40.59. Verily, the Hour will certainly come: About this (there) is no doubt: Yet, most men do not believe.

40.60. And your Lord says: "Call upon Me; I shall answer your (prayer): Verily, those who are too proud to worship Me they will surely find themselves in Hell, in shame and in humiliation."-

40.61.. It is Allah Who has made the night for you that you may rest in it and (it is Allah Who has made) the day for you, as that which helps (you) to see surely, Allah is Full of Grace and Bounty to mankind: Yet, most men do not offer thanks.

40.62. Like this is Allah (in His Mercy), your Lord, the Creator of all things. There is no god but He: Then, why you are turned away from the Truth!

40.63. Like so are turned (away from Truth) those who are used to rejecting the Signs (*Ayât*) of Allah.

40.64.. It is Allah Who has made for you the earth as a resting place, and the sky as a canopy (and a cover): And (He) has given you shape- And made your shapes beautiful- And (He) has provided for your living, from things pure and good- Like this is Allah (in His Mercy), your Lord. Therefore Glory (be) to Allah, the Lord of the Worlds.

40.65. He is the Ever-Living: There is no god but He: Turn to Him, offering Him sincere love with gratitude. All the Praises (and thanks) be to Allah, Lord of the Worlds!

40.66.. Say: "I have been forbidden to worship those whom you worship besides Allah- Since that the clear evidences have come to me from my Lord; And I have been ordered to bow (down in Islam) to the Lord of the Worlds."

40.67. It is He Who has created you from dust, then from a sperm-ovary drop, then from a leach like clot, then He does get you out (into the light) as a child, then lets you (grow and) reach your age of full strength, then lets you become old, though there are some of you who die before, and lets some of you reach a term appointed; In order that you may understand (and learn wisdom).

40.68. It is He Who gives life and causes death; And when He decides upon a thing, He says to it only: "Be," and it is.

40.69.. Do you not see those who dispute about the Signs (*Ayât*) of Allah? How they are turned away (from reality)?

40.70. Those who do not accept the Book (this Quran), and the (Revelations) with which We sent Our messengers: But they shall soon know-

40.71. When the clamps of iron (shall be) round their necks, and the chains: They shall be dragged along-

40.72. In the boiling (foul smelling) water; Then they shall be burned in the Fire.

40.73. Then it shall be said to them: "Where are the (false gods) to which you gave part (of your) worship-

40.74. "Besides (and in offense to) Allah?" They will reply: "They have vanished and left us; No, we did not call upon anything before, anything (that had real existence) from the old." Thus Allah leaves the unbelievers to stray.

40.75. (It will be said to them,) "That was because you were used to being happy on the earth in things which were not the Truth, and that you were used to being haughty (and disrespectful).

40.76. "You enter the gates of Hell, to live therein," and evil is (this) home of the haughty (and disrespectful)!

40.77.. So keep (working, O Prophet!) with patience; Verily, the Promise of Allah is True: And whether We show you (in this life) some part of what We promise them- Or We cause you to die (in Our Mercy, in any case), it is to Us that they shall (all) return.

40.78. And indeed, We did send messengers before you: Of them there are some whose story We have told you and some whose story We have not told you, and it was not (possible) for any messenger to bring a Sign except by the Permission of Allah: But when the Order of Allah was given, the matter was decided in truth and justice, and those who stood on falsehoods were destroyed to be lost.

40.79.. Allah! It is He Who has made cattle for you, that you may ride on some of them, and some of them for food:

40.80. And, for you there are many other benefits in them (the cattle) and that you may use them for any need that (there may be) in your hearts; And on them and on ships (that) you are carried.

40.81. And He (always) shows you His Signs: Which, then of the Signs (*Ayât*) of Allah will you reject?

40.82. Do they not travel through the earth and see what was the end of those before them? They were more in number than them and (even) stronger in might and in the traces (they have left behind) in the land: Yet all that they did was of no use to them.

40.83. Then when their messengers came to them with clear proofs and evidences, they were only happy (and proud) with the knowledge (and worldly things) that they had; And that very (suffering) at which they used to mock surrounded them.

40.84. So when they saw Our Punishment, they said: "We believe in Allah-the One Allah- And we reject all the partners we used to enjoin with Him."

40.85. Then their accepting the Faith after they (actually) saw Our Punishment was not going to help them. (Such has been) Allah's Way of dealing with His servants, (from the oldest of times). And the rejecters of Allah were (totally) destroyed (in the Punishment)!

****

Sura 41. Ha-Mim or Ha-Mim Sajda,
[Fussilat (The detailed explanation)]: (Makkah, 54 Verses)
In the Name of Allah, the Most Gracious, the Most Merciful.

41.1. Ha Mim:

41.2. A Revelation from (Allah), the Most Gracious, the Most Merciful :

41.3. (This is Quran) a Book, in which the verses are explained in detail; A Quran in Arabic, for (those) people who understand;

41.4. Giving glad tidings (good news) and warning: But yet, most of them turn away, and so they do not hear.

41.5.. And they (those who do not hear) say: "Our hearts are (hidden) behind veils, from that to which you invite us; And in our ears is a deafness, and between us and you is a screen: So you do (whatever you wish); As for us, we shall do (whatever we wish!)"

41.6. (O Prophet!) You say: "I am only a human like you: By Revelation, it is made known to me that your God is One Allah: So take the true Path to Him, and be in obedience (to Him) and ask for forgiveness," and (as) a warning to those who join gods with Allah-

41.7. (And to) those who do not give regular charity, and (to those) who even deny the Hereafter.

41.8. Truly, those who believe and do righteous good deeds, for them is an eternal reward that will never fail.

41.9.. Say: "Is it that you deny Him (the One), Who created the earth in two Days? And do you join (others) equal with Him? That is the Lord of (all) the Worlds."

41.10. He set upon the (earth) mountains standing firm, high above it (the earth), and He gave blessings upon the earth, and measured all the things, to give them nourishment in proper proportions; In four Days, in accordance with (the needs of) those who search (for the nourishment).

41.11. Then, He rose over the high heavens when it was (like) smoke: And He said to it and to the earth:

"You (both) come together, willingly or unwillingly." They both said: "We do come (together), in willing obedience."

41.12. Then, He completed them like seven arches (of the sky) in two Days, and He assigned to each heaven its duty and affair (as a command). And We brightened the lower heaven with lights and (provided) it with guard. Such is the Decree (Command from Him the One) the Almighty (Exalted in Might), All Knower.

41.13.. But if they turn away, then you say (to them): "I have warned you of a sudden punishment (as of thunder and lightning) like that which (overtook) the 'Ad and the Samood (Thamud people)!"

41.14. When the messengers came to them, from before them and (from) behind them, (teaching) "Worship no one but Allah." They said, "If our Lord had so pleased, He would surely have sent down angels (to teach us): So, indeed we disbelieve in that with which you are sent. "

41.15. Now the 'Ad behaved haughtily through the land against all truth and reason, and said: "Who is superior to us in strength?" What! Did they not see that Allah, Who created them, was superior to them in strength? And they continued to reject Our Signs!

41.16. So, We sent against them a furious wind through days of misfortune so that We might give them a taste of a penalty of humiliation in this Life: But surely, the penalty of the Hereafter will be still more humiliating: And they will not find any help.

41.17. And as for the Samood (Thamud people), We gave them the guidance, but they preferred blindness (of heart) to Guidance: So the sudden punishment of humiliation got them, because of what they had earned.

41.18. And We saved those who believed and practiced righteousness (and those who had *Taq'wa*).

41.19.. And (remember) the Day when the enemies of Allah will be gathered together to the Fire, they will be marched in ranks.

41.20. At length, when they reach the (Fire), their hearing, their sight, and their skins will speak up against them, as to (all) their actions.

41.21. And they will say to their skins: "Why do you bear witness against us?" They will say: "Allah has made us to speak, (He) Who gives speech to everything: And He created you for the first time, and to Him were you to return.

41.22. "And you did not try to hide yourselves, because your hearing, your sight and your skins may bear witness against you! But you thought that Allah did not know many of the things that you used to do!

41.23. "And this thought of yours which you used to have about your Lord, has brought you to (your) destruction, and (now) you have become of those who are totally lost!"

41.24. Then, let them have patience, then (later) the Fire will be a Home for them! And if they beg to be received to please (Allah); They will not be among those who will ever please (Him).

41.25. And We have given to them close companions (of the same nature, those) who made it pleasing to them what was before them and behind them; And the sentence (of Judgment) among the earlier generation of jinns' and men, who have passed away before them, is clearly against them; For they are totally lost.

41.26.. And the unbelievers say: "Do not listen to the Quran; But (instead) talk randomly (to disturb) in the middle of its (reading), so that you may gain the upper hand!"

41.27. But surely, We will certainly give the unbelievers a taste of a severe penalty, and certainly, We will punish them for the worst of their deeds.

41.28. Such is the punishment of the enemies of Allah, the Fire: The eternal Home for them will in there: A (fit) punishment, because they used to reject Our Signs (*Ayât*).

41.29. And the unbelievers will say; "Our Lord! Show us those, among jinns' and men, who misled us: That we shall crush them beneath our feet, so that they become the most shameful (before all)."

41.30.. Verily, in the case of those (men) who say: "Our Lord is Allah," and further, (those who) stand straight and steadfast, the angels will descend upon them (from time to time and suggest) "You do not fear! And do not feel sad! But receive to the glad tidings (good news) of the paradise (of joy), about which you were promised!

41.31. "We are your protectors in this life and in the Hereafter: Therein, you shall have all that your souls shall desire: And therein shall you have all that you ask for!

41.32. "A welcome gift from (Allah) Often Forgiving, Most Merciful !"

41.33.. And who is better in speech than the one who calls (men) to Allah, and works righteousness, and says, "I am one of the Muslims (who bows to Allah in Islam)?"

41.34. And good deeds and evil deeds cannot be equal. (So) give up (evil) with what is better: Then verily, he (the one) between whom and you, was hatred, will become like your friend and close companion (to you as a Muslim brother)!

41.35. And no one will be granted such goodness except those who use patience and self-control, (such people are) the only persons of the greatest good fortune.

41.36. And if (at any time) a whisper is made to you by the Satan, seek refuge in Allah. Verily, He is the All Hearing, the All Knowing .

41.37.. And among His Signs (*Ayât*) are the night and the day, and the sun and the moon. Do not prostrate yourselves to the sun nor to the moon, but prostrate yourselves to Allah, Who created them, if it is Him that you wish to serve.

41.38. But if the (unbelievers) are proud, (it does not matter): Because, in the Presence of your Lord are those who celebrate His Praises by night and by day. And they are never tired of it (nor feel themselves above it).

{A Muslim generally prostrates to Allah after reciting this verse}

41.39. And among His Signs is this: You see the earth with nothing growing and wasted, but when We send down rain to it, it is (gently) brought to life and (the plants) regrow. Truly, He Who gives life to it (the earth which is dead) can surely give life to the dead. Indeed, over all things, He is most Powerful (Able to do all things).

41.40.. Verily, those who distort (and change) the Truth in Our Signs (*Ayât*) are not hidden from Us. Who is better? He who is thrown into the Fire, or he that comes safely through, on the Day of Judgment? Do what you want to do: (But be) sure, He is All Seeing of everything that you do.

41.41. Verily, those who reject the Message when it comes to them (are not hidden from Us). And indeed it (the Quran) is a Book protected by supreme power.

41.42. No falsehood can approach it (the Quran) from before or behind: It is sent down by (Allah, the One) full of Wisdom, Worthy of all Praise.

41.43. Nothing is said to you that was not (already) said to the messengers before you: Surely, that your Lord has, at His Command, (all the) Forgiveness and also the most painful penalty.

41.44. If We had sent this as a Quran (in a language) other than Arabic, they would have said: "Why are not its verses explained in details? What! (A Book) not in Arabic and (a Messenger) an Arab?" Say: "It is a guide and a healing (cure) for those who believe; And for those who do not believe, there is no hearing in their ears, and there is a blindness in their (eyes): They are (like those) being called from a far distant place!"

41.45.. And (indeed), We certainly gave Musa (Moses) the Book (*Taurát*) before: But differences came about in there. And if it was not for a Word that went out before from your Lord, (their differences) would have been settled between them. But truly, they remained in suspicious and discomforting doubt upon it.

41.46. Anyone who acts righteous good deeds helps his own soul; Anyone who works evil, it is against his own soul. And your Lord is never unjust (in the least) to his servants.

41.47. To Him (Allah) is left the Knowledge of the Hour (of Judgment:) No date-fruit comes out of its sheath, nor does a female conceive (in her womb) or bring forth (the young), without His Knowledge. And on the Day that (Allah) will ask them (the question), "Where are the partners (that you gave) to Me?" They will say: "We do assure You, not one of us can affirm now!"

41.48. And the (other gods) that they used to call for before will leave them in the anxiety (and pain), and they will see that they have no way to escape.

41.49.. Man does not get tired of asking for good (things); But if something bad touches him, then he gives up all hope (and he) is lost in sorrow.

41.50. And truly, if We give him a little bit of mercy from Ourselves, after some pain (and anxiety) has come to him, he is sure to say, "This is due to my (deserving it the most): I do not think that the Hour (of Judgment) will (ever) be established; But if I am brought back to my Lord, surely, I have (enough) good (stored) in His Sight!" But We will show the unbelievers the truth of all that they did, and We shall give them the taste of a severe penalty.

41.51.. And when We grant favor to man, he turns away (arrogantly), and pulls himself to his side (instead of coming to Us); But when evil comes to him, (then he comes) full of long prayer (and supplications)!

41.52.. Say: "See yourself that the (Message) is really from Allah, and yet do you reject it? Who is more misled than one who is divided (and is separated) far (from any purpose)?"

41.53. Soon We will show them Our Signs in the (very far) regions (of the earth, and also deep) in their own souls, till it becomes clear to them that this is the Truth. Is it not enough that your Lord Who Witnesses all things?

41.54. Listen, indeed! They are in doubt about the Meeting with their Lord: Yes indeed! He, it is Who Surrounds (and commands) all things!

****

Sura 42. Ash-Shu'ra,
(Consultation): (Makkah, 53 Verses)
In the Name of Allah, the Most Gracious, the Most Merciful.

42.1.. Ha Mim:

42.2. Ain Sin Káf:

42.3. This way does Allah, the Almighty , the All Wise , send Revelation to you (O Prophet!) as (Allah did) to those before you-

42.4. To Him (Allah) belongs all that is in the heavens and all that is in the earth: And He is the Most High, the Most Great.

42.5. The heavens (skies) are almost torn apart from their top (by His Glory): And the angels glorify (and perform) the Praises of their Lord, and ask pray for forgiveness for (all) beings on earth: Look! Surely, He is Allah, Often Forgiving, Most Merciful .

42.6. And those who take as protectors others besides Him- Allah does watch over them, and you are not the one to decide their affairs.

42.7. And, like this We have sent by Revelation to you an Arabic Quran; That you may warn the Mother of Cities (Makkah) and all around it (the City of Makkah)- And warn (them) of the Day of the Assembling, about which there is no doubt: (When) a party (some) will be in the Paradise (Gardens), and a party (some) in the blazing Fire.

42.8. And if Allah had so willed, He could have made them all one people (and one nation); But He admits those He wills to His Mercy; And the wrongdoers will have no protector nor helper.

42.9. Or, have they taken (for worship) protectors beside Him? But it is Allah- He is Alone, the Protector and it is He Who gives life to the dead: And it is He Who has Power over all things.

42.10.. And, in whatever (matters) which you differ, the decision about them is with Allah, (and) so is Allah, my Lord: In Him, I trust and to Him, I turn (in repentance).

42.11. (He is) the Originator of the heavens and the earth. He has made for you pairs (male and female), from (people) among yourselves, and (He has made) pairs among cattle: Also by this means does He create you: There is nothing whatever like Him, and He is the All Hearing and sees All Seeing.

42.12. To Him belong the keys of the heavens and of the earth: He increases and reduces the livelihood of anyone He wills: Surely, He is the All Knowing of every thing.

42.13. The same religion has He established for you as the one which He brought to Nuh (Noah)- And that which We have revealed to you- And that which We brought to Ibrahim (Abraham), to Musa (Moses), and to Isa (Jesus): And that is, that you should remain steadfast in religion, and make no division within it: For those (people) who worship things other than

Allah, the (Straight Way) to which you call them, is hard. Allah chooses to Himself those whom He pleases, and guides to Himself those who turn (to Him) in repentance.

42.14. And they (to whom you call) became divided only after knowledge came to them- Through selfish transgression and envy between themselves. If it was not for a Word that reached them before from your Lord, (regarding) a period (for repentance) appointed, the matter would have been settled between them. And truly, those (the Jews and Christians) who have inherited the Book (of Message, *Taurát* and *Injeel*) after them are in (uneasy and) suspicious doubt about it (the Quran).

42.15.. Now then, for that (reason), call (them to the Faith), and stand firm, as you are commanded, nor you follow their vain desires; But say: "I believe in the Book which Allah has sent down; And I am commanded to judge justly between you. Allah is our Lord and your Lord: For us (is the responsibility for) our deeds, and for you (is the responsibility for) your deeds. There is no dispute between us and you. Allah will bring us together and to Him is (our) final return."

42.16. And those who dispute about Allah after He has been accepted- Their dispute is useless in the sight of their Lord: And upon them is Anger (from Allah), and for them will be a terrible penalty.

42.17. It is Allah Who has sent down the Book in truth, and the Balance (to weigh human conduct). And what will make you realize that possibly the Hour (of Judgment) is close at hand?

42.18. Only those who wish to hasten it do not believe in it: While, those who believe hold it in fear, and know that it is the very (eternal) Truth. Surely those who dispute concerning the Hour are far astray.

42.19. Allah is Most Kind to His servants: He gives livelihood to whom He pleases: And He has All Powerful and Ever-Almighty .

42.20. To any who desires the reward of the Hereafter, We give increase in his reward; And to any who desires the reward of this world, We grant a part of it, and he has no share in the Hereafter.

42.21.. Or, have they 'partners' (the false gods) who have established for them some religion without permission of Allah? If it had not been for the Word of Judgment, (permitting them some freedom of action) the matter would have been decided between them (at once). And surely, the wrongdoers will have a grievous penalty.

42.22. You will see the wrongdoers in fear because of what they have earned, and of whatever (penalty) that must fall on them. But those who believe and work righteous deeds (will be) in the luxurious shadows in the Gardens. They shall have, before their Lord, all that they wished for. That will truly be the greatest reward (from Allah).

42.23. That is (the reward) about which Allah gives glad tidings (and good news) to His servants who believe and do righteous good deeds. Say: "No reward do I ask of you for this except to be kind to me in the love and kinship." And if anyone earns any good and righteous deeds, We shall give him an increase in the good (that he has earned in proper measure): Verily, Allah is Often Forgiving, Most Appreciative (of the service from His servants).

42.24. Or, do they say: "He has made up lies against Allah?" If Allah so willed, He could close up your heart. And Allah removes (false) pride, and proves the Truth by His Words. Verily, He knows well the secrets in all human breasts (hearts).

42.25. And He is the One Who accepts repentance from His servants, and forgives sins, and He knows all that you do.

42.26. And He hears those who believe and act righteously, and gives them increase of His Bounty: And as for the unbelievers there is a terrible penalty.

42.27. If Allah increases what is given to His servants, they would indeed rebel and cross all bounds in the earth; But He sends (it) down in right measure as He pleases. Verily, He is All Aware of His servants, All Seer (of what they do).

42.28. And He is the One Who sends down the rain (even) after (men) have despaired and given up any hope, and scatters His Mercy (far and wide). And He is the protector, Worthy of all Praise.

42.29. And among His Signs is the Creation of the heavens and the earth, and the living creatures that He has spread in them: And He can gather them together when He wills.

42.30.. And whatever misfortune comes to you, it is because of the things your hands have done, and for many (of them) He pardons generously.

42.31. And you cannot hinder (anything even a little bit while you are passing) through the earth; And you have none besides Allah- (Not) anyone to protect or to help.

42.32. And among His Signs are the ships, running smoothly through the oceans, (tall) as mountains.

42.33. If He so wills, He can stop the wind: Then would they become motionless on the back of the (seas). Surely, in this are Signs for everyone who patiently perseveres and is grateful.

42.34. Or He can cause them (the winds) to perish because of the (evil) which (the men) have earned; And He does forgive much.

42.35. And those who dispute about Our Signs (*Ayât*), know that there is for them no way to escape.

42.36.. So, whatever you are given (here) is (only) a mere convenience of this life: But that which is with Allah is better and more lasting: (It is) for those who believe and put their trust in their Lord;

42.37. And those who avoid the greater sins (crimes against humanity), and shameful (sexual) deeds and when they are angry, even then forgive;

42.38. And those who answer the call of their Lord, and establish regular prayer; And who (conduct) their affairs by mutual consultation; Who spend out of what We bestow on them for living;

42.39. And those who, when grave wrong is inflicted on them, (are not afraid but) help and defend themselves.

42.40.. The recompense for an injury (or evil) is an injury (or evil) equal to it (in degree): But if a person forgives and makes reconciliation, his reward is due from Allah: Verily He, (Allah) does not love those who do wrong.

42.41. And indeed, if any do help and defend themselves after a wrong is (done) to them, against such (men) there is no cause of blame.

42.42. The blame is only against those who hold back men with wrong-doing and haughtily cross bounds through land, defying right and justice:

For such there will be a grievous penalty.

42.43. And indeed whoever shows patience and forgiveness, that would truly be an act of bold will, (and resolution in the conduct of affairs) is truly recommended by Allah.

42.44. For any (of those) whom Allah leaves astray, there is no protector after Him. You will see the wrongdoers, when the penalty is close; Saying: "Is there any way to come back?"

42.45. And you will see them being brought up for the (penalty) in a humble frame of mind because of (their) disgrace, (and) looking with a unsteady glance. And the believers will say: Verily, those (wrongdoers) are indeed in loss, (those) who have given to ruin themselves and those belonging to them on the Day of Judgment. Truly, the wrongdoers are in a lasting penalty!

42.46. And no protectors have they to help them, other than Allah. And for any (of those) whom Allah leaves to stray, there is no way (towards the Goal).

42.47.. (You!) Answer the Call of your Lord, (O Mankind and jinns'), before there comes a Day on which there will be no putting back, because of (the command of) Allah! On that Day there will be no place of safety for you and there will be for you no way for denial (of your sins)!

42.48. But if they (those who stray) then turn away, We have not sent you (O Prophet,) as a guard over them. Your duty is only to convey (the Message to them). And truly, when We give man a taste of a Mercy from Ourselves, he does feel very happy with it, but when some ill happens to him, on account of the deeds which his hands have sent forth, (or because of what he himself has done) then truly, is man ungrateful!

42.49.. To Allah belongs the Kingdom of the heavens and the earth. He creates what He wants (and what He wills). He bestows female (children) upon whom He wills and bestows male (children) upon whom He wills according to His Will (and His plan),

42.50. Or He gives both males and females, and He leaves some whomever He wills, barren (without any children): Verily, He is full of knowledge and power.

42.51.. It is not fitting for a man that Allah should speak to him except by Revelation, or from behind a veil (or a curtain), or by sending of a messenger to reveal, with Allah's permission, what Allah wills: For He is most High, Most Wise.

42.52. And thus have We by Our Command, sent Revelation to you (O Prophet): You did not know (before) what was Revelation, and what was Faith; But We have made the (Quran), a (Divine) Light, with this We guide such of Our servants as We will; And surely, you (O Prophet) do guide (men) to the Straight Path-

42.53. The (Straight) Way of Allah, to Whom belongs all that is in the heavens and all that is in the earth. Verily! (How) all things (and events) return back to Allah (for Judgment)!

****

Sura 43. Az-Zukhruf,
(The gold ornaments): (Makkah, 89 Verses)
In the Name of Allah, the Most Gracious, the Most Merciful.

43.1.. **Ha Mim:**

43.2. And the clear Book (the Quran that makes things clearly visible)-

43.3. Verily, We have made it a Quran in Arabic that you may be able to understand (and learn).

43.4. And surely, it is (from within) the Mother of the Book (see *Ayâh* 13.39) with Us, indeed, in Our Presence, high (in dignity), full of wisdom.

43.5.. Shall We then take away the Remainder (this Quran) from you and keep (you) away, because you are people who exceed (your) limits?

43.6. And how many prophets We sent among the peoples of the old?

43.7. And there was never a prophet who came to them at whom they did not mock.

43.8. Then We destroyed (them)- (Even) stronger in power than these (people)- The stories of the olden peoples have been passed (to you to learn from them).

43.9.. And indeed, if you were to ask them, "Who created the heavens and the earth?" They would be sure to reply; "They were created by (Him), the Exalted in Power , the All Knowing ;"-

43.10. (Allah,) Who has made for you, the earth spread out (like a carpet), and has made for you roads (and channels) in there, that you may find guidance (on the way);

43.11. And (Allah,) Who sends down rain from the sky (from time to time) in correct amounts- And with it We raise to life a land that is dead; And in the same way you will be raised (from the dead);

43.12. That (He) has created pairs (male and female) in all (living) things, and (He) has made for you ships and cattle on which you ride,

43.13. In order that you may sit firm and square on their backs; And when are seated, you may think (and feel) the kindness of your Lord, and say, "Glory to Him Who has subjected this to our (use), and we could never have done this (for ourselves),

43.14. "And surely, to our Lord, we must return back!"

43.15. Yet, they give to some of His servants a share with Him (in His Supremacy)! Truly, man is known as being unjust and ungrateful.

43.16.. Or has He (Allah) chosen daughters from what He Himself creates, and given to you sons of choice?

43.17. And when news about (the birth of a baby-girl) that one sets up with a likeness to (Allah) Most Gracious, is brought back to (any) one of them (as his own baby), then his face darkens, and he is filled with inward grief!

43.18. Then, is one brought up in pettiness, and unable to give clear account in a dispute (to have the likeness to Allah)?

43.19. And they make into females angels who serve Allah. Did they witness their (the angel's) creation? Their evidence will be recorded, and they will be questioned (about it)!

43.20.. And they said: "If it was the Will of (Allah), Most Gracious, we should not have worshipped such (petty gods)!" About that they have no knowledge! They do nothing but lie!

43.21. Or have We give them a Book before this, (the Quran) to which they are holding fast?

43.22. No, they say: "We found our fathers following a certain way and religion, and we follow their footsteps."

43.23. And just the same way, whenever We sent a Warner before you to any people, the wealthy ones among them said: "We found our fathers following a certain way and religion, and we will certainly follow their footsteps."

43.24. He (the Warner) said: "Even if I brought you better guidance than that which you found your fathers following?" They said: "Verily, for us, we deny that you (prophets) are sent (for any purpose at all)."

43.25. So We took the toll from them: Now see what was the end of those who rejected (the Word of Allah)!

43.26.. And (remember) when Ibrahim (Abraham) said to his father and his people: "Verily, I am innocent of what you worship:

43.27. "Except Him (Allah) Who created me, and He will certainly guide me."

43.28. And he left it as a Word to remain for those who came after him, that they may turn back (to Allah).

43.29. Nay (in reality)! I (reference to Allah), have given the good things of this life. To these (men) and their fathers, until the Truth has come to them and a messenger who makes things clear.

43.30. And when the Truth came to them, they said: "This is magic, and we reject it."

43.31.. And they also say: "Why is this Quran not sent down to some leading man in either of the two (main) cities? (Makkah and Taif.) "

43.32. Is it they who would give out the Mercy of your Lord? It is We (reference to Allah) Who distribute their living between them. And in the life of this world, We (reference to Allah) raise some of them above others in position, so that some may ask (and order) others to work. But the Mercy of your Lord is better than the (wealth) that they gather

43.33. And could it not be possible that (all) men may become used to one (evil) way of life, We would give, for everyone who lies against (Allah) Most Gracious, silver roofs for their houses, and (silver) stair-ways on which to go up,

43.34. And (silver) doors to their houses, and (silver) thrones on which they could lean back,

43.35. And also adornments (ornaments made) of gold. But all this were nothing but good things for the present life: And in the Sight of your Lord, the Hereafter, is for the righteous.

43.36.. If anyone withdraws himself from remembering (Allah) Most Gracious, for him, We appoint an Evil one (Satan) to be a close friend to him.

43.37. And verily, such (Evil ones) really keep them (the misguided) away from the (Straight) Path but they think that they are being guided right!

43.38. Till, at the end, when (the misguided) comes to Us, he (the misguided) says (to his evil companion): "(I) wish that between me and you, there was the distance of the two Easts (East to far, far East or the West)!"

Ah! Evil is the companion (indeed).

43.39. When you have done wrong, it will be of no use to you: that Day, then you shall be partners in punishment!

43.40.. Can you then make the deaf to hear, or give direction to the blind or to such as (those who are) in open error?

43.41. And even if We take you (O Prophet!) away, We shall be sure to punish them,

43.42. Or if We show you that what We have promised to them (will become true): For surely We shall overcome them.

43.43. So, you hold fast to the Revelation sent down to you: Surely, you are on the Straight Path.

43.44. And verily, the (Quran) is indeed the Message, for you and for your people; And soon (all of) you shall be questioned (about it).

43.45. And you (O Prophet) question Our messengers whom We sent before you; Did We appoint any gods other than (Allah) the Most Gracious, to be worshipped?

43.46.. And We did send Musa (Moses) before this time, with Our Signs (*Ayât*), to Firon (Pharaoh) and his Chiefs: He (Moses) said: "Verily, I am a messenger of the Lord of the Worlds."

43.47. But when he came to them with Our Signs, look! They made fun of them (the Signs).

43.48. And We showed them Sign after Sign, (see *Ayâh* 7.133, and Note 28.4) each greater than the other, and (then) We gave them the punishment, in order that they might turn (to Us).

43.49. And they said (to Musa): "O you magician! Pray to your Lord for us according to His promise to you; Verily, we shall truly accept guidance."

43.50. But when We removed the penalty from them, look! They broke their promise.

43.51. And Firon (Pharaoh) announced to his people, saying: "O my people! Does not the kingdom of Egypt belong to me, (do you see) these streams flowing beneath my (palace)? What! Do you not see then?

43.52. "Am I not better than this (Musa), who is an undignified (and) miserable person and (who) cannot even speak (see *Ayâh* 28.34) clearly?

43.53. "Then why are not gold bracelets given to him, or (why do the) angels (not) come with him in procession (and groups)?"

43.54. Thus he made fools of his people, and they obeyed him: Truly, they were a people who turned rebellious (against Allah).

43.55. So, when at the end, they acted to Anger Us (Allah), We (grievously) punished them and We drowned them all.

43.56. And We made them (a people) of the past and an example for the ages to come.

43.57.. And when (Isa), the son of Maryam (Mary) is held up as an example, look! Your people raise an uproar at it (to pull it down)!

43.58. And (they) say: "Are our gods best or he (Isa)?" This they put in front of you, only by the way of dispute: Yes! They are a challenging (and opposing) people.

43.59. He (Isa) was no more than a servant: We granted Our favor to him, and We made him an example to the Children of Israel.

43.60. And if it was Our Will, We could make angels from (those) within you, to follow each other on the earth.

43.61. And (Isa) shall be a sign chosen (for the coming of) the Hour (of Judgment): Therefore have no doubt about the (Hour), but, you follow Me (Allah): This is the Straight Way.

43.62. Let not the Satan make it difficult for you: Verily, he is an open and declared enemy to you.

43.63.. And when Isa (Jesus) came with clear proofs, he said: "Now have I come to you with Wisdom, and in order to make clear to you some of the (points) about which you dispute: Therefore fear Allah and obey me.

43.64. "Verily Allah, He is my Lord and your Lord: So you worship Him: This is the Straight Path."

43.65. But groups from among themselves fell into disagreement: Then misery to the wrong doers, from the penalty of a painful Day!

43.66. Do they only wait for the Hour- That it should come on them all of a sudden, while they do not expect it?

43.67. Friends on that Day will be enemies, one against another- Except the righteous.

43.68.. My (Allah's) servants (and devotees)! There shall be no fear for you on that Day, and you shall not suffer-

43.69. (You are) those who have believed in Our Signs (*Ayât* of the Quran), and bowed (your wills) in Islam.

43.70. You will enter the Paradise, you and your wives, in (honor and) happiness.

43.71. To them will be passed round dishes and cups of gold: In there will be all that the souls could ever want, and all that the eyes could delight in: And you shall live in there (for ever).

43.72. Like this will be the Paradise to which you are made inheritors because of your (good) deeds (in life).

43.73. You shall have plenty of fruit in there, from which you shall have satisfaction.

43.74.. Verily, the sinners will be in the punishment of Hell, to live in there (for ever):

43.75. In no way will the (punishment) be lowered for them, and they will be thrown in destruction, despair and sorrow.

43.76. In no way shall We (Allah) be unjust to them: But it is they who have been unjust to themselves.

43.77. And they will cry: "O keeper, (of Hell)! If only your Lord put an end to us!" He will say, "Verily, you shall live on forever!"

43.78.. Surely, We (Allah) have brought the truth to you: But most of you hate the Truth.

43.79. Or have they settled some plan (among themselves)? But (in reality) it is We Who settle all things.

43.80. Or do they think that We do not hear their secrets and their private conversations? Indeed (We do), and Our (angels) messengers are beside them to record.

43.81.. Say: "If (Allah) Most Gracious had a son, then, I would be the first to worship."

43.82. Glory to the Lord of the heavens and the earth, the Lord of the

Throne! Exalted is He, (He is free) from the things they associate (with Him)!

43.83. So leave them (alone) to talk aimlessly and play (with petty things) until they meet that Day of theirs, which they have been promised.

43.84. It is He (Allah) Who is the Only God in the heaven and the Only God (Allah) on earth; And He is All Wise , All Knowing .

43.85. And blessed is He to Whom belongs the dominion of the heavens and the earth, and all between them: And with Him is the knowledge of the Hour (of Judgment): And to Himself shall you be returned.

43.86. And those whom they pray besides Allah, (they) have no power of act (for anyone); - Except he who bears witness to the Truth (Allah), and they know (him).

43.87. And if you ask them; Who created them? they will certainly say, "Allah": How then are they moved away (from the Truth)?

43.88. (Allah hears) the (Prophet's) cry, "O my Lord! Truly, these are a people who will not believe!"

43.89. So (O Prophet!) turn away from them, and say: "Peace!" But soon they shall know!

****

Sura 44. Ad-Dukhán,
(The smoke or mist): (Makkah, 59 Verses)
In the Name of Allah, the Most Gracious, the Most Merciful.

44.1.. Ha Mim:

44.2. And the Book that makes things clear-

44.3. We have sent it down during a blessed night: Verily, We (always) wish to warn (against evil)

44.4. In that (night) is set out (decreed) every item of wisdom,

44.5. By Command from Us (Allah), verily, We (always) send (revelations),

44.6. As a Mercy from your Lord: Verily, He is the All Hearing, the All Knowing ;

44.7. The Lord of the heavens and the earth, and all that is between them, if you have firm faith and certainty.

44.8. There is no god but He: It is He Who gives life and causes death, your Lord and Sustainer and the Lord and Sustainer of your (earliest) ancestors.

44.9.. Yet, they amuse themselves in doubt.

44.10. Then you watch for the Day on which the sky will bring out a kind of clearly visible smoke (or mist),

44.11. Surrounding the people: This will be a painful penalty.

44.12. (They will say:) "Our Lord! Remove the penalty from us, really, we are believers!"

44.13. How shall the Message be (meaningful) for them, seeing that a Messenger (the Prophet) has (already) come to them- (And is) explaining things clearly,

44.14. Yet they turned away from him and said: "Taught (by others), he is a madman (possessed by evil)!"

44.15. Indeed, We shall remove the penalty for a while, (but) truly, you will go back (to your ways).

44.16. One day We shall get to you with a mighty disaster that will come: (And then) We will truly make (you) suffer the real punishment.

44.17.. And indeed, We did try the people of Firon (Pharaoh), before them (those who reject the Message); To them came a most honorable messenger (Musa),

44.18. (Saying:) "Give me the servants of Allah verily, I am to you a messenger worthy of all trust:

44.19. "And do not be proud (especially) against Allah: Truly, I have come to you with clear authority.

44.20. "As for me, I have prayed to my Lord and your Lord, for safety against your injuring (stoning) me.

44.21. "But if you do not believe, keep yourselves away from me and leave me alone."

44.22. (But they were angry and haughty) then he cried to his Lord: "Truly, these are a criminal people used to sin."

44.23. (The reply came:) "March forth with My servants by night, surely, you will be followed.

44.24. "And leave the sea at the gap (across the ocean bed divided): Verily, they are a group to be drowned."

44.25. How many of the gardens and springs did they leave behind.

44.26. And green crops (and corn fields) and noble places,

44.27. And wealth (and things of life), in which they had taken such delight!

44.28. Like this (was their end)! And We made other people take over (those things they left behind)!

44.29. And neither heaven nor earth shed a tear for them: And they were not given any relief (again).

44.30.. And indeed, (before this), We did save the Children of Israel from disgraceful punishment,

44.31. Caused by Firon (Pharaoh), indeed he was proud (haughty and arrogant, even) among unruly transgressors.

44.32. And We chose them before above the nations, with knowledge

44.33. And granted them Signs in which there was an open trial.

44.34.. Verily, these (People of the Quraish), they openly say:

44.35. "There is nothing beyond our first death, and we shall not be resurrected.

44.36. Then bring (back) our forefathers, if you say the truth!"

44.37. Are they better than the people of Tubba' (see Note 1 at the end of Sura.-) and those who were before them? We destroyed them because they were criminals (guilty of sin).

44.38.. And We did not create the heavens and the earth, and all between them, just as (an idle) play:

44.39. We did not create them except for true (and noble) ends: But most of them do not understand.

44.40. Surely, the Day of Sorting Out is the time appointed for all of them-

44.41. The Day when the nearest of kin can be of no use to the related one, even the least, and no help can they receive,

44.42. Except such as those who receive Allah's Mercy: Verily, He is Exalted in Might , Most Merciful .

44.43.. Surely, the (evil) tree of *Zaqqum* (see Note 2 at the end of Sura.-)

44.44. Will be the food of the sinful-

44.45. Like molten brass; It will boil in their bellies,

44.46. Like the boiling of very hot water.

44.47. (A voice will cry:) "You seize him and drag him into the middle of the blazing Fire!

44.48. "Then pour over his head the penalty of boiling water.

44.49. "You taste (this)! Truly were you (all that) mighty, full of honor!

44.50. "Surely, this is what you used to doubt!"

44.51.. Verily, as to the righteous, (they will be) in a position of security,

44.52. Among Gardens and Springs;

44.53. Dressed in fine silk and in rich lace, they will face each other;

44.54. Like this, (it will be!) We shall enjoin them the companions with beautiful, big and lovely eyes.

44.55. There they can call for every fruit in peace and security:

44.56. There, they will not undergo death, except the first death; And He will preserve them from the penalty of the blazing Fire-

44.57. As a Gift from your Lord! That will be the supreme achievement!

44.58.. Surely, We have made this (Quran) easy, in your tongue, in order that they may remember.

44.59. So you wait and watch, verily, they (too) are waiting.

Sura 44 Notes

Note 44.1. The reference is to the Ancient and powerful people from Arabia and Africa who followed the Judaic and Christian religions.

Note 44.2. The reference is to the dreaded tree that grows at the pit of Hell. (Also see 37.62 to 37.66 and 56.52).

****

Sura 45. Al-Játhiya,
(Bowing the knee): (Makkah, 37 Verses)
In the Name of Allah, the Most Gracious, the Most Merciful.

45.1.. Ha Mim:

45.2. The Revelation of the Book is from Allah, the Almighty (Supreme in Power), All Wise (Full of Wisdom).

45.3. Surely, in the heavens and the earth, are Signs for the believers (those who believe).

45.4. And in the creation (of yourselves) and the moving creatures that are spread (through the earth), are Signs for those of firm Faith.

45.5. And in the alteration of night and day, and in the rain that Allah sends down from the sky, and with it, (He) rebuilds the earth after its death, and in the change of the winds (from the fair winds to the violent storms) - Are Signs for those who are wise.

45.6. These are the Signs of Allah (*Ayât*), which We read (and recite) to you

in truth: Then in what form will they believe after (rejecting) Allah and His Signs?

45.7.. Shame (and misery) for each sinful person who deals with lies:

45.8. (To him) who hears the Signs (Verses) of Allah recited to him yet, is unchanging (stubborn, haughty) and alone, as if he had not heard them: So tell him about a painful penalty!

45.9. And when he learns something of Our Signs (the Verses), he takes them as a joke: For such there will be a demeaning penalty.

45.10. In front of them, there is Hell: And anything they have worked for is of no use to them, and of no use any protectors they may have taken to themselves besides Allah: And for them is a very severe penalty.

45.11.. This is (Quran, the true) Guidance. And for those who reject the Signs of their Lord, for them is a grievous penalty of utmost pain.

45.12.. It is Allah Who has made the sea for you, so that ships may sail through it, by His command for you to seek from His bounty, (His wealth and His creation) and that you may be grateful.

45.13. And He has made for you, as (gifts) from Him, all that is in heavens and on earth: Verily, in that are Signs, for those who think deeply.

45.14. Say to those who believe, to forgive those who do not look forward to the Days of Allah: It is for Him to repay (for the good or the bad) each People according to what they have earned.

45.15. Whosoever does a rightful deed, it works to help his own soul; Whosoever does evil, it works against (his own soul). In the end will you (all) be brought back to your Lord.

45.16.. And indeed, We gave the Children of Israel the Book (*Taurát*, the Scripture, its Jewish Laws) and understanding and prophet hood; And We gave them good and pure things for living; And We chose them above the nations,

45.17. And We gave them clear Signs in matters dealing (with religion): And it was after knowledge had been given to them that they split into groups, through deep envy among themselves; Surely, your Lord will judge between them on the Day of Resurrection (and Judgment) as to those matters in which they made up differences (among themselves).

45.18. Then We have put you on the (true) Path of religion: So you follow that (Path), and do not follow the desires of those who do not know.

45.19. Verily, they will be of no use to you in the Sight of Allah: Surely, it is only people who do wrong (who stand as) protectors of one another: But Allah is the Protector of the righteous.

45.20. These (Verses) are clear proofs and evidence to mankind, guidance and a Mercy to people of firm faith and certainty.

45.21. Or do those who go after evil ways think that We shall consider them equal with those who believe and do righteous deeds, - In their present life and after their death will be equal? They make a wrong judgment.

45.22.. And Allah has created the heavens and the earth with truth and for noble ends, and for each soul to find the reward of what it has earned, and none of them be wronged.

45.23. Then do you see such (a person), the one who takes as his god his own foolish desire? Allah has, knowing (him as such), left him astray, and closed off his hearing and his heart (and understanding), and put a cover on his sight. Then, who will guide him after Allah (has taken away the Guidance)? Will you not then receive the warning?

45.24. And they say: "What is there other than our life in this world? We shall die and we live, and nothing except time can destroy us." And they have no knowledge of that: They only presume (and imagine):

45.25. And when Our Clear Signs are recited to them, their reasoning is nothing but this: They say: "Bring (back) our dead forefathers, if what you say is true!"

45.26. Say to them: "It is Allah Who gives you the life, then causes you the death: Then He will gather you together for the Day of Resurrection (and Judgment) about which there is no doubt:" But most men do not understand.

45.27.. To Allah belongs the dominion of the heavens and of the earth, and the Day and the Hour of Judgment is fixed- That Day those who deal with lies will perish!

45.28. And you will see every group (of people) bowing the knee in humility, (prayer and fear): Every group will be given its Record: "This Day you shall you be paid back for all that you did!

45.29. "This is Our record (written) with truth (and it) speaks about you: Verily, We used to write on record all that you did."

45.30.. Then, for those who believed and did the rightful good deeds, their Lord will admit them to His Mercy: That will be the reward of success to be seen.

45.31. But for those who rejected Allah, (it will be said to them): "Were not Our Signs recited to you? But you were too arrogant (haughty and proud) and you were criminals, a people used to sin!

45.32. "And when it was said: 'Verily, that the Promise of Allah was true, and the Hour- There was no doubt about its (coming:)' You used to say: 'We do not know what is the Hour: We only think it is conjecture (merely an idea), and we have no assurance (about it). ' "

45.33. And then the evil (returns) of what they did will appear before them, and they will be completely surrounded by that which they used to laugh at!

45.34.. And it will be said: "This Day We will forget you like you forgot your meeting on this Day! And your home is Fire, and you have no helpers!

45.35. "This is because you used to treat the Signs of Allah as joke, and the life of the world deceived you:" Therefore, (from) that Day, they shall not be taken out from there (the Fire), and they shall not be taken into (Allah's) Grace nor shall they be returned to this worldly life.

45.36.. So all the Praises (and thanks) be to Allah, Lord of the heavens and the Lord of the earth, Lord and Cherisher of all the (many) worlds !

45.37. To Him be Glory everywhere in the heavens and the earth: And He is exalted in Power, Full of Wisdom!

****

Sura 46. Al-Ahqáf,
(Winding sand-tracts): (Makkah, 35 Verses)
In the Name of Allah, the Most Gracious, the Most Merciful.

46.1. Ha Mim:

46.2. The Revelation of the Book is from Allah the Almighty, (Supreme in Power), the All Wise (Perfect in Wisdom).

46.3. We did not create the heavens and the earth and all between them except for (their) true ends, and for a (their) given time. But those who reject Faith turn away from that (the Faith); About this, they are warned!

46.4. Say: "Do you see what it is you call upon besides Allah? Show me what it is that they (whom you call upon) have created on earth, or have they a part in the heavens? Bring me a Book (revealed) before this, or any remaining knowledge (that you may have), if you are telling the truth!"

46.5. And who is more lost than the one who calls upon (others) besides Allah, they (others) will not answer him until the Day of Judgment, and who (in fact) are not aware of their call (to them)?

46.6. And when mankind is gathered together (on the Day of Judgment), they (who were called besides Allah) will be enemies (and denying) to (the unbelievers) and reject their worship (altogether)!

46.7.. And when Our Clear Signs are recited to them, the unbelievers say about the Truth, when it comes to them: "This is clearly magic!"

46.8. Or do they say: "He has forged it?" Say: "Had I forged it, then you can obtain not even one (blessing) from Allah for me. He knows best of what you talk among yourselves about it (Quran)! Enough is He for witness between me and you! And He is Often Forgiving, Most Merciful ."

46.9. Say: "I am not the one who brings newly made up faith among the messengers, nor do I know what will be done with me or with you. I only follow that which is made known to me by Revelation; I am only a Warner, open and clear."

46.10. Say: "Do you see? If (this teaching) be from Allah, and if you reject it, and a witness from among the Children of Israel says (with due surety) of its similarity (with the earlier Scripture; the *Taurát*), and has (himself) believed while you are proud and rejecting, (you are truly the unjust and) truly, Allah does not guide people who are unjust."

46.11. And the unbelievers say about those who believe: "If (this Message) were a good thing, (the believers) would not have gone to it first, before us!" And by seeing that they do not guide themselves, they will say: "This is an old lie!"

46.12. And before this, was the Book of Musa (Moses) as a guide and as a mercy and this Book confirms (it) in the Arabic tongue: To warn those who do wrong, and as good news to those who do right.

46.13. Surely, those who say: "Our Lord is Allah," and remain firm (on that Path)- On them shall be no fear, and they shall not remain unhappy.

46.14. Such shall be the companions of the Paradise, living in there (forever): A repayment for their (good) deeds.

46.15. And We have commanded that it is essential for man to be kind to his parents: In pain did his mother bear him, and in pain did she give him birth.

The carrying of the (child) to get him to eat food (away from the mothers milk) is (a period of) thirty months. At length when he reaches the age of full strength and attains forty years, he says: "O my Lord! Grant me (the gratitude) that I may be thankful for Your favor which You have given to me, and upon both my parents, and that I may work rightful deeds such as those that You may approve; And be gracious to me in my offspring. Truly, I have turned to You in repentance and truly I from those (who submit to You) as Muslims."

46.16. They are such (people) from whom We shall accept the best of their deeds and overlook their bad deeds: (They shall be) among the companions of the Paradise: A promise of truth, which was made to them (in this life).

46.17.. But (there is such a person) who says to his parents, "Shame (*Uff*) upon you! Do you hold out the promise to me that I shall be raised up (for Judgment), even though generations have passed before me (without rising again)?" And they too seek Allah's help, (and talk back to the son): "Misery to you! Have Faith! Verily, the Promise of Allah is true." But he says: "This is nothing but stories from the distant past!"

46.18. They are those (persons) against whom is given the sentence among the earlier generations of jinns' and men, that have passed away; Surely, they will be (totally) lost.

46.19. And to all are (given) grades according to the actions which they (have done), and in order that (Allah) may pay back for their actions, and no injustice may be done to them.

46.20. And on the Day when the unbelievers will be placed before the Fire, (it will be said to them): "You received your good things in the life of the world, and you took your pleasure out of them: But this Day shall you be paid back with a penalty of disgrace because you were proud on earth without a just cause, and that you (forever) crossed all bounds."

46.21.. And (remember, Hud) one of 'Ad's (own) brothers: When he warned his people about the winding sand-tracts: But there have been warners before him and after him: (He warned:) "You worship no one but Allah: Truly, I fear for you the penalty of a Mighty Day."

46.22. They said: "Have you come to turn us away from our gods? Then bring upon us the (penalty) with which you threaten us, if you are telling the truth!"

46.23. He said: "The knowledge (of when it will come) is only with Allah: And I declare to you the reason for which I have been sent: But I see that you are a people who do not know!"

46.24. Then, when they saw the (penalty as) a cloud moving in the sky coming to meet their valleys, they said: "This cloud will give us rain!" No! It was (really the penalty) you were asking to be sent without delay! A wind in which is a painful penalty!

46.25. It will destroy everything by the command of his Lord! Then by the morning, they (found nothing)- Nothing was to be seen except (the ruins of) their houses! Thus do We pay back those who act in sin!

46.26. And indeed, We had firmly established them (the 'Ad people) in (prosperity and) power which We have not given to you (the People of Quraish!) and We had endowed them with (ability of) hearings (many sounds), seeing(s) (many visions and sights), hearts (many emotions), and intellect: But no use to them were their (abilities of) hearings, sights, hearts and intellect, when they kept rejecting the Signs of Allah; And they were completely surrounded by that which they used to laugh at (in contempt)!

46.27.. And indeed, We have destroyed before, populations round about you; And We have shown the Signs in various ways, so that they may turn (to Us).

46.28. As for those whom they worshipped as gods, besides Allah, as a means to reach (to Allah) why then was no help coming to them (from false gods)? No! They (the false gods) left them helpless: But that was their falsehood and their invention.

46.29.. And remember when We turned towards you a company of jinns' (to be quietly) listening to the Quran: When they stood in the presence thereof they said: "Listen in silence!" When the (reading) was finished, they returned to their people, to warn (them of their sins).

46.30. They (the jinns') said: "O our people! Verily, we have heard a Book revealed after Musa (Moses), confirming what came before it: It guides (men) to the Truth and to the Straight Path.

46.31. "O our people! Pay attention to the one who calls to Allah, and believe in Him: He (Allah) will forgive you for your faults, and deliver you from a painful penalty.

46.32. "And if anyone does not pay attention to the one who invites (us) to Allah, he cannot frustrate (Allah's Plan) on earth, and no protectors can he have besides Allah: Such men (only wander) in open error."

46.33.. Do they not see that Allah, Who created the heavens and the earth, and never got tired with their creation, is able to give life to the dead? Yes! He indeed, is All Able to do all things.

46.34. And on the Day that the unbelievers will be placed before the Fire, (they will be asked:) "Is this not the Truth?" They will say: "Yes, by our Lord!" (One will say:) "Then you taste the penalty, for that you were used to denying (the Truth)!"

46.35.. Therefore patiently work hard, as did (all) messengers with unchanging purpose; And do not be in haste about the (unbelievers). On the Day that they see the (punishment) promised to them, (it will be) as if they had not spent more than an hour of a single day. (O Prophet! Your duty is only) to state and repeat the Message: But will any be destroyed except those who transgress (and exceed their limits)?

****

Sura 47. Muhammad,
(The Prophet): (Medinah, 38 Verses)
In the Name of Allah, the Most Gracious, the Most Merciful.

47.1.. Those who disbelieve (and reject Allah) and obstruct (others) from the Path of Allah- He (Allah) will make their deeds useless.

47.2. But those who believe and do righteous good deeds, and believe in the (Revelation) sent down to Muhammad- For it is the Truth from their Lord- He will remove from them, their sins (and their ills) and improve their condition.

47.3. This is because those who disbelieve follow falsehood, while those who believe follow the Truth from their Lord: This way does Allah bring out for men their lessons by similarity.

47.4. Therefore, when you meet the unbelievers [in battle], strike (hard) at their necks; Till you have fully defeated (and finally felled) them. Place a bond firmly (on them): Thereafter (is the time for) either kindness or negotiation (with ransom): Until, the war lays down its burdens, (and it ends). Like this (are you commanded); But if it had been Allah's Will, He (Himself) could certainly have ordered punishment for them; But (He lets you fight) in order to test you, some (to fight) with others. But those who are killed in the way of Allah- He will never let their deeds be lost.

47.5. Soon, He will guide them and improve their condition,

47.6. And (He will) admit them to the Paradise that He has declared (especially) for them.

47.7.. O you who believe! If you will help (the Cause of) Allah, He will help you and plant your feet firmly (to make you strong).

47.8. But those who disbelieve and (reject Allah)- For them awaits misery and destruction, and (Allah) will make their deeds useless.

47.9. That is because they hate the Revelation of Allah so He has made their actions fruitless.

47.10. Have they not traveled through the earth, and see what happened in the end of those before them (who did evil)? Allah brought total destruction on them, and similar (fate awaits) the disbelievers.

47.11. That is because Allah is the Protector of those who believe, and verily the disbelievers have no protector.

47.12.. Surely, Allah will admit those who believe and do righteous good deeds, to Paradise beneath which rivers flow; While the disbelievers will enjoy (this world) and eat as cattle eat: And Fire will be their home.

47.13. And how many cities, with more power than your city (Makkah) that has driven you out, have We destroyed (for the sins of their people)? And there was none to help them.

47.14. Then, can he who is on a clear (Path) from his Lord, no better than one to whom the evil of his conduct seems pleasing, and those who follow their own desires?

47.15.. (Here is) a story (of similarity) about the Paradise which the righteous (the pious) are promised: In it are rivers of water made pure and clean; Rivers of milk whose taste never changes; Rivers of wine, a joy to those who drink; And rivers of honey, pure and clear. In it, there are for them all kinds of fruits; And forgiveness (and grace) from their Lord. (Can those in these Gardens) be compared to those who shall live, forever in the Fire, and be given, to drink, boiling water, so that it cuts up their stomachs (to pieces)?

47.16.. And among them are men who listen to you, but in the end, when they go away from you, they say to those who have received knowledge, "What is it he said just then?" Such are men whose hearts Allah has sealed, because they follow their own (evil) wishes.

47.17. And as for those who receive (Allah's) guidance, He increases the (light of) guidance, and places on them their (true) Faith and (pure) control (away from evil).

47.18. Then, do they (the unbelievers) only wait for the Hour- That it should come on them of a sudden? But already have come some tokens of it, and when it is (actually) on them, then, how can they benefit by their warnings?

47.19. (O Prophet), therefore know, that there is no god but Allah, and ask forgiveness for your sin, and for the men and women who believe: For Allah knows how you move about and (Allah knows) how you live in your homes.

47.20.. Those who believe say, "Why is a (specific) Sura not sent down (for us)?" But when a Sura of basic or clear meaning is revealed, and fighting is said in it, you will see those (hypocrites) in whose heart is a disease looking at you with a look of one with great fear at the approach of death, but it is better (more fitting) for them-

47.21. Were they to obey (Allah) and say good word what are just, when a matter (of *Jihad*) is resolved (by Allah's Will), it would be best for them, if they were true to Allah.

47.22. Then, is it to be expected of you, if you were put in authority, that you will do mischief in the land, and break your ties with (people and) relatives?

47.23.. Such (unbelievers) are the men whom Allah has cursed for He has made them deaf and blinded their sight.

47.24. Then, do they not, honestly try to understand the Quran, or are their hearts locked up by them?

47.25. Verily, those who turn their back like the rejecters after guidance was clearly shown to them- The Satan has misguided them and built them up with false hopes.

47.26. That is because they said to those who hate what Allah has revealed: "We will obey (you) in part of (this) matter;" But Allah knows their (inner) secrets.

47.27. Then how (will it be) when the angels take their souls at death, and strike their faces and their backs?

47.28. That is because they acted upon that which brought about the Anger of Allah, and they hated Allah's good pleasure, so He made their deeds of no effect.

47.29.. Or do those in whose hearts is a disease, think that Allah will not bring to light all their evil intentions?

47.30. Had We so willed, We could have shown them to you, and you should have known them by their marks: But surely you will know them by the way they talk! And Allah knows all that you do.

47.31. And We shall try you until We test those among you who do their very best and continue to work very hard in patience; And We shall try your stated (and true character).

47.32. Verily, those who disbelieve and, obstruct (other men) from the Path of Allah, and resist the Messenger (the Prophet), after guidance has been clearly shown to them, they will not hurt Allah in the least, but He (Allah) will make their actions fruitless.

47.33. O you who believe! Obey Allah, and obey the Messenger (the Prophet Muhammad) and do not make your deeds useless!

47.34. Verily, those who disbelieve, and obstruct (other men) from the Path of Allah, and then die rejecting Allah, Allah will not forgive them.

47.35.. Be not tired (and timid), and faint-hearted, crying for peace, when you should be at the very top: Allah is with you, and (He) will never put you in loss for your (good) deeds.

47.36. The worldly life is nothing except a mere diversion (like play and amusement): And if you believe and guard against evil, He (Allah) will grant you your due rewards, and (He) will not ask you (for) your possessions.

47.37. If He were to ask you for all of them, (your possessions) and press you, you would carefully withhold, and He would bring out all your ill-feeling.

47.38. Behold! You are those invited to spend (of your wealth) in the Way of Allah: But among you are some who are miserly (and stingy). But those who are stingy are (miserly) at the expense of their own souls. But Allah is free of all wants, and it is you who are needy. If you turn back (from the Path), He will replace for you another people; Then they would not be like you!

****

Sura 48. Al-Fath,
(The victory): (Medinah, 29 Verses)
In the Name of Allah, the Most Gracious, the Most Merciful.

48.1.. Surely, We have granted you a clear Victory;

48.2. That Allah may forgive you your sins of the past and of the future; Fulfill His Favor to you; And guide you onto the Straight Path;

48.3. And that Allah may help you with powerful help.

48.4. It is He Who sent down the peace and calmness into the hearts of the believers, that they may add faith to their Faith- And to Allah belong the forces of the heavens and of the earth; And Allah is always All Knowing, , All Wise-

48.5. That He may admit the men and women who believe to the Gardens beneath which rivers flow to live in there for ever, and He may remove their evil deeds from them- And that is in the sight of Allah, the highest achievement-

48.6. And that He may punish the hypocrites, men and women, and also those who worship many gods, men and women, who keep an evil opinion of Allah, on them is a round of evil: And the Anger of Allah is on them: And He has cursed them and made Hell ready for them: And most evil is it, for a place to reach.

48.7. And to Allah belong the forces of the heavens and the earth; And Allah is Almighty (Supreme in Power), All Wise (Full of Wisdom).

48.8.. Verily, We have truly sent you as a witness, as one who brings good news, and as one who warns:

48.9. In order that you (O people!) may believe in Allah and His Messenger and that you may help and honor Him, and celebrate His Praises morning and evening.

48.10. Surely, for those who promise their pledge to you do no less than promise their pledge to Allah: The Hand of Allah is over their hands: Then anyone who breaks his pledge, does so to the harm of his own soul, and anyone who fulfills what he has promised to Allah- Allah will soon grant him a great reward.

48.11.. The desert Arabs (the Bedouins) who fell behind (to avoid fighting) will say to you: "We were engaged in (looking after) our flocks and herds, and our families: Do you then ask forgiveness for us." They say with their tongues what is not in their hearts. Say (to them): "Who then has any power at all (to intervene) on your behalf with Allah, if His Will is to give you some loss or to give you some profit? No! Allah is always All Aware with all that you do.

48.12. "No, you thought that the Messenger (the Prophet) and the believers would never return to their families; And this seemed pleasing in your hearts, and you thought an evil thought, and you are people lost."

48.13. And if any (of you) do not believe in Allah and His Messenger, then verily, We have prepared for those disbelievers a fierce Fire!

48.14. And to Allah belongs the Sovereignty (the kingdom and the ownership) of the heavens and the earth. He forgives whom He wills, and He punishes whom He wills. And Allah is Often Forgiving, Most Merciful .

48.15.. Those who lagged behind will say, when you (are free to) march and take the spoils (in war): "Permit us to follow you." They wish to change Allah's Word: Say: "You will not follow us like that: Allah has already declared (this) earlier:" Then they will say: "But you envy (are jealous of) us." No, but little do they understand.

48.16. Say to the desert Arabs (Bedouins) who fell behind: "You shall be called (to fight) against a people given to violent (and angry) war: Then shall you fight, or they shall surrender. Then if you shall show obedience, Allah will grant you a fair reward, but if you turn back as you did before, He will punish you with a painful penalty."

48.17. No blame or sin is there on the blind, nor is there blame on the lame, nor on one ill (if he does not join the war): And he who obeys Allah and His Messenger- (Allah) will admit him to gardens beneath which rivers flow; And he who turns back, (Allah) will punish him with a painful penalty.

48.18.. Indeed, Allah's good pleasure was on the believers when they made (their sincere) promise to you under the Tree: He knew what was in their hearts, and He sent down the peace and calmness upon them; And He rewarded them with a speedy Victory;

48.19. And many gains will they have (in addition): And Allah is Ever Almighty (Supreme in Power), All Wise (Full of Wisdom).

48.20. Allah has promised you many gains that you have captured, and He has given to you these earlier, and He has withheld the hands of men from you; That it may be a Sign for the believers, and that He may guide you to the Straight Path;

48.21. And (there are) other victorious (gains) that are not within your power, indeed Allah has foreseen them: And Allah is Always Able to do all things.

48.22.. And if the unbelievers should fight you, they would certainly turn their back; Then would they find no protector and no helper.

48.23. That has been the Way of Allah, already with those (peoples) of the past: No change will you find in the Way of Allah.

48.24. And it is He Who has blocked their hands from you and your hands from them in the middle of Makkah, after that He gave you the Victory over them. And Allah sees well all that you do.

48.25. They are the ones who disbelieved the Message and stopped you from the Sacred Mosque (at Makkah) and detained the sacrificial animals from reaching their place of sacrifice. If there were no believing men and believing women whom you did not know, that you were pushing aside and killed, and on whose account a crime would have resulted from you without (your) knowledge, (Allah would have allowed you to force your way, but He withheld your hands) that He may admit to His Mercy whom He will. If they were identified, We, certainly would have punished the unbelievers among them with a painful punishment.

48.26. When the unbelievers had heat (anger) and urge in their hearts - The heat and urge of ignorance, - Allah sent down His calm and tranquility to His Messenger and to the believers, and made them follow closely the command of self-restraint; And they were well entitled to it and worthy of it. And Allah is Ever All Knowing of all things.

48.27.. Indeed, Allah shall fulfill the true vision for His Messenger in reality. Certainly, if Allah (so) wills, you shall enter the Sacred Mosque (at Makkah), with minds full of protection, heads shaved, hair cut short, and without fear. He knew what you did not know, and besides this, He granted a fast Victory.

48.28. It is He Who has sent His Messenger with the Guidance and the Religion of Truth, that he may proclaim it (Islam) over all religions: And All Sufficient is Allah as a Witness.

48.29. Muhammad is the Messenger of Allah. And those who are with him are strong against the unbelievers, (but) compassionate within themselves. You will see them bowing and prostrating themselves seeking Grace from Allah and (His) good pleasure. On their faces are their marks, the traces of their (prayerful) prostration. This is their trait (semblance) in the *Taurát* (the Torah); And their trait (semblance) in the *Injeel* (the Gospel, which) is: Like a seed that sends forth its blade, it then becomes strong (and thick), and it stands on its own stem, (filling) the sowers (corns of the seed) with wonder and delight. As a result it fills the unbelievers with anger at them. Allah has promised those from them who believe and do righteous good deeds forgiveness, and a great reward.

****

Sura 49. Al-Hujurat,
[The inner apartments (of the Prophet)]:
(Medinah, 18 Verses)
In the Name of Allah, the Most Gracious, the Most Merciful.

49.1.. O you who believe! Do not make your decisions (and yourselves) ahead of Allah and His Messenger but fear Allah: Verily, Allah is All Hearing, All Knowing .

49.2.. O you who believe! Raise not your voices above the voice of the Prophet; Do not speak loudly to him in talk, as you may speak loudly to one another, else, your deeds may become useless while you perceive not.

49.3. Verily, those who lower their voice in the presence of Allah's Messenger- They are the ones whose hearts Allah has indeed tested for true dedication (to Himself): For them is forgiveness and a great reward.

49.4.. Verily, those who call unto you from behind the houses (their inner apartments) - Most of them do not have any sense.

49.5. And if only they had patience until you could come out to them, it would be better for them: And Allah is Often Forgiving, Most Merciful .

49.6.. O you who believe! If an ungodly person comes to you with any news, (first), verify the truth, in case that you may harm people unwittingly (unwillingly or unknowingly), and afterward have to be regretful for what you have done.

49.7.. And know that among you there is Allah's Messenger: If he were to obey or follow your wishes, in many matters, you would surely fall into misfortune: But Allah has made the endeared Faith for you, and has made it beautiful in your hearts, and He has made hateful for you unbelief, wickedness, and rebellion: Such (people who believe) indeed are those who walk in righteousness-

49.8. A Grace and Favor from Allah; And Allah is All Knowing , All Wise.

49.9.. If two parties among the believers fall into a quarrel, then you make peace between them both: But if one of them exceeds the bounds against the other, then (all of) you fight against the one who exceeds until it (the one) complies with the Command of Allah. Then if it (the one) complies, then make peace between them with justice, and be equitable and fair: Verily, Allah loves those who are fair (and just).

49.10. The believers are a single brotherhood. So make reconciliation (offering peace and agreement) between your two (contending) brothers: And fear Allah, that you may receive (His) Mercy.

49.11.. O you who believe! Let not some men among you laugh (and scoff) at others: It may be that they (the latter) are better than the former: Let not some women laugh at other women: It may be that the latter are better than the former: Nor defame nor be nasty to each other, nor call each other by (offensive) nicknames: Ill-seeming is a nickname: That implies wickedness, (if it is used by anyone) after he has believed: And those who do not repent (this practice) are (indeed) doing wrong.

49.12.. O you who believe! Avoid much suspicion (as much as possible): Indeed some (types of) suspicion are sins: And do not spy on each other, do not speak ill of each other, behind their backs. Would any of you like to eat the flesh of his dead brother? No! You would hate it... But fear Allah: Verily, Allah is One Who accepts repentance, Most Merciful .

49.13.. O mankind! We have created you from a single (pair) of male and female, and made you into nations and tribes, that you may know one another (not that you may hate each other). Surely, the most honorable of you, in the Sight of Allah is (he, who is) the most righteous of you. Verily, Allah is All Knowing and is Well-Aware (of all things).

49.14.. The desert Arabs (Bedouins) say: "We believe." Say: "You have no faith: But you (only) say, 'We have submitted our wills to Allah,' because Faith has not yet come into your hearts. But if you obey Allah and His Messenger, He will not ignore the smallest of your deeds: Verily, Allah is Often Forgiving, Most Merciful ."

49.15. Only those believers who have believed in Allah and His Messenger, and have never since doubted, but have worked hard with their belongings and their persons in the Cause of Allah. Those (believers)! They are the sincere ones.

49.16. Say: "Will you instruct Allah about your Religion, while Allah knows all that is in heavens and all that is on earth? And Allah is All Knowing of all things."

49.17. They impress on you as a favor that they have joined Islam. Say: "Count not your Islam as a favor upon me: No! Allah has handed down a favor upon you that He has guided you to the Faith, if you be true and sincere.

49.18. "Surely, Allah knows the unseen secrets of the heavens and the earth: And Allah is the All Seeing of whatever you do."

****

Sura 50. Qáf,

(The Quranic letter Qáf): (Makkah, 45 Verses)
In the Name of Allah, the Most Gracious, the Most Merciful.

50.1.. Qáf: By the Glorious **Quran**: (A Book, Pure and Holy).

50.2. But they wonder that a Warner (the Prophet,) has come to them from among themselves. So the unbelievers say: "This is a strange thing!

50.3. "When we die and become dust, (shall we live again?) that is a (sort of) return far (from our understanding)."

50.4.. We already know how much of them the earth takes away: And with Us is a Record guarding (the full account).

50.5. No! But they deny the truth when it comes to them: So they are in a confused state.

50.6. Do they not look at the sky above them, how We have made it and decorated it, and there are no flaws in it?

50.7. And the earth! We have spread it out, and set on it mountains standing firm, and produced in there every kind of beautiful growth (in pairs)-

50.8. To be observed and remembered by every servant turning (to Allah and seeking forgiveness).

50.9. And We send down from the sky rain filled with blessing, and We produce with it, gardens and grain for harvest;

50.10. And tall (and stately) palm-trees, with shoots of fruit-stalks, placed one over another-

50.11. As sustenance for (Allah's) servants- And We give (new) life with it to land that is dead. Thus the New Life (resurrection) begins.

50.12.. Before them (the Hereafter) was denied by the People of Nuh (Noah), and the companions of the Rass, and the Samood (Thamud),

50.13. And 'Ad, and Firon (Pharaoh), and the brothers of Lut (Lot),

50.14. And the companions of the Wood, and the People of Tubba'; each one (of them) rejected (their) messengers, so My warning was truly fulfilled (for them).

50.15. Were We then tired with the first Creation? Nay! They are in a confused (state of) doubt about a new Creation.

50.16.. And indeed, We have created man, and We know what (evil) temptation his innermost self may bring to him: And We are nearer to him than (his) jugular vein.

50.17. (Remember) that two (guardian angels) appointed to learn (his deeds) learn (and note them), one sitting on the right and one on the left.

50.18. Not a word does he (each angel) say, but there is a guard by him, ready (to note the deeds).

50.19. And the agony of death will bring truth (before his eyes, and he says): "This was the thing you were attempting to escape!"

50.20.. And the Trumpet shall be blown:- That will be the Day (of Resurrection) about which warning (had been given).

50.21. And every soul will come forward; With each soul will be an (angel) to drive, and an (angel) to bear witness.

50.22. (It will be said to the sinners:) "Indeed, you were careless about this; Now We have removed from you, your veil, and sharp is your sight this Day!"

50.23. And his companion (angel) will say: "Here is (his record) ready with me!"

50.24. (The sentence from Allah will be:) "Both of you (angels) throw, into Hell every miserable rejecter (of Allah)!

50.25. "Who prevented what was good, exceeded all bounds, created doubts and suspicions;

50.26. "Who set up another god besides Allah: Both of you (angels), throw him into a severe penalty."

50.27. His companion, (the Satan in the Hell) will say: "Our Lord! I did not make him transgress, but he was (himself) far away (from good)."

50.28. He (Allah) will say: "Dispute not with each other in front of Me: I had already in advance sent you the Threat and Warning.

50.29. "The sentence that comes from Me shall not be changed, and I do not do the least injustice to My servants."

50.30.. On that Day, We will ask Hell, "Are you filled to the full?" It will say: "Are there any more (to come)?"

50.31.. And the Garden will be taken near the righteous- It will not be a far away thing.

50.32. (A voice will say:) "This is what was promised for you- For every one who turned (to Allah) with true repentance, (those) who kept (His Command),

50.33. "(Those) who feared (Allah), Most Gracious, Unseen, and brought a heart turned in repentance (and love for Him):

50.34. "Therein, you enter in peace and security; This is a Day of Eternal Life!"

50.35. For them, there will be all that they wish for- And more besides in Our Presence.

50.36.. And how many generations before them did We destroy (for their sins)- (Though) they were stronger in power than them? And they wandered through the land: Was there any place of escape (for them)?

50.37. Surely in this there is a Reminder and a Message for anyone who has a heart and understanding or who gives ear and truly sees (the truth).

50.38.. And indeed, We created the heavens and the earth and all between them in six Days, and no sense of tiredness touches Us.

50.39. Then bear with patience, all that they say, and celebrate the Praises of your Lord, before the rising of the sun (*Faj'r*) and before (its) setting (*Zuh'r* and *'Asr*),

50.40. And during part of the night (*Maghrib* and *Isha*), (also) celebrate His praises and (glorify Him) after the prayers (of *Sunnah* and *Nawafil* in His adoration).

50.41. And listen on the Day when the Caller will call out from a place close by-

50.42. The Day when they will hear a (mighty) Blast in truth (for awakening): That will be the Day of Resurrection.

50.43. Surely, it is We Who give life and cause death; And to Us is the Final Return-

50.44. On the Day when the earth will be torn apart, from (men) quickly getting out: That will be a gathering together- (It is) quite easy for Us.

50.45.. We know best what they say, and you (O Prophet) are not the one to bring Faith in them by force. But warn (him, the weary and confused) with the Quran such as (he, who) fears My Warning!

****

Sura 51. Adh-Dháriyat,
(The winds that scatter): (Makkah, 60 Verses)
In the Name of Allah, the Most Gracious, the Most Merciful.

51.1.. By (the winds) that scatter (around) the dust;

51.2. And those (winds) that lift and carry away heavy weights;

51.3. And those that flow with ease, (joy) and gentleness;

51.4. And those that distribute and rearrange by (His) Order-

51.5. Surely, that which you have been promised is indeed true;

51.6. And surely, Judgment and Recompense must indeed become established.

51.7.. By the sky with (its) numerous paths (through it),

51.8. Truly, you are in a disagreeing opinion (about Faith and Islam)

51.9. Through (such opinions) which (people are) misled (away from the Truth) such as those who would be misled.

51.10. Misery to the liars and falsehood-mongers-

51.11. Those who (are) carelessly (blundering) in a state of confusion (about the Faith of Islam):

51.12. They ask: "When will be the Day of Judgment and Recompense?"

51.13. (It will be) a Day when they will be tried (and burned) over the Fire!

51.14. "Taste you your trial! This is what you asked to be hastened!"

51.15.. Verily, as to the righteous (with firm Faith), they will be within the Gardens and Springs,

51.16. Taking joy in the things that their Lord has given them, verily, they were the doers of good deeds.

51.17. They were in the habit of sleeping but little by night,

51.18. And in the hours of early dawn, they (were found) praying for Forgiveness;

51.19. And in their wealth and possessions (were remembered) the right of the (needy) he who asked and he who was prevented (from asking).

51.20.. On the earth are Signs for those with certainty in Faith,

51.21. As also in your selves: Will you not then see?

51.22. And in the heavens is (beautiful) provision, and (all) that which (you) are promised.

51.23. Then by the Lord of heaven and earth, this is the very Truth, as much as the fact that you can speak intelligently to each other.

51.24.. Has the story of the honored guests (three angels) of Ibrahim (Abraham) reached you?

51.25. When they entered his presence, and said: "Peace!" He said, "Peace!" And said: "You are a people unknown to me."

51.26. Then he turned quickly, to his household, brought out a fatted calf,

51.27. And placed it before them... He said, "Will you not eat?"

51.28. (When they did not eat), he became afraid of them. They said, "Fear not," and they gave him glad tidings of a son endowed with knowledge.

51.29. Then his wife came forward (laughing) aloud: She touched her face (in wonder) and said: "A barren old woman!"

51.30. They said, "Even so, your Lord has spoken: Verily, He is All Wise and All Knowing ."

51.31.. (Ibrahim) said: "Then for what purpose have you have come, O messengers?"

51.32. They said, "We have been sent to a people who are criminals in (deep sin)-

51.33. "To bring on, on them, (a shower of) stones of clay (brimstones).

51.34. "Marked as from the Lord for those who trespass beyond bounds."

51.35. Then We safely removed those of the believers who were there,

51.36. But We did not find there any just (believing) persons except in one house:

51.37. And We have left there a Sign for those who may fear the painful penalty.

51.38.. And in (Musa was another Sign) when We sent him to Firon (Pharaoh), with clear authority

51.39. But (Firon) turned back with his Chiefs, and said, "An (evil) magician, or a madman!"

51.40. So We took him and his forces, and threw them into the sea; And the blame was his.

51.41.. And in the 'Ad (people, is another Sign): We sent against them the devastating Wind:

51.42. It left nothing whatever that it came up against. But reduced it to ruin and decay.

51.43.. And in the Samood (Thamud) people (was another sign): They were told, "Enjoy (your brief day) for a little while!"

51.44. But they angrily defied the Command of their Lord: So the stunning and destructive noise (of an earthquake) caught them, even while they were looking on.

51.45. Then they could not even stand (on their feet), nor could they help themselves.

51.46.. So were the people of Nuh (Noah) before them: Verily, they wickedly exceeded all limits.

51.47.. With Power (and Skill) did We construct the (mighty Arch of the) heaven : Verily, We are Who create the vastness of space with it.

51.48. And We have spread out the (spacious) earth: How excellently We do spread out!

51.49. And of everything We have created pairs: That you may remember and receive guidance.

51.50. So hasten you then (at once) to Allah: Verily, from Him, I am a Warner to you, clear and open!

51.51. And make no other object of worship with (Almighty) Allah: Verily, from Him, I am a Warner to you, clear and open!

51.52.. Like this, no messenger came to the peoples before them, but they said (of him) in like manner, an (evil) magician, or a madman!

51.53. Is this the teaching they have transmitted, one to another? No! They are themselves a people breaking beyond (their) bounds!

51.54. So turn away from them: Yours is not the blame.

51.55. And remind (the message) truly teaching the benefits (of the Quran) to the believers.

51.56.. And I (Allah) have only created jinns' and men, that they may worship (and serve) Me.

51.57. No sustenance do I require from them, nor do I require that they should feed Me.

51.58. Verily, Allah is the All Providing of the provision- Lord of Power-Supreme, the Almighty -

51.59. And verily, for the wrongdoers, their portion (of punishment) is like the portion of their fellows (of earlier generations): Then let them not ask Me to hasten (that portion)!

51.60. Misery, then, to the unbelievers, on account of that Day of theirs which they have been promised!

****

Sura 52. At-Túr,

(The mount): (Makkah, 49 Verses)

In the Name of Allah, the Most Gracious, the Most Merciful.

52.1. By (the Mountain of) Túr;

52.2. And by the Book inscribed (and is carved out),

52.3. In a scroll (that is left open) unfolded;

52.4. And by the frequently visited Place of Worship (the mosque for angels above *Ka'bah*);

52.5. And by the sky raised high;

52.6. And by the ocean that fills with waves-

52.7. Surely, the (severe) penalty from your Lord will really come true-

52.8. There is no one who can change it-

52.9. On the Day when the sky will swing in terrible fear.

52.10. And the mountains will fly here and there.

52.11.. Then woe (fear and misery), that Day to those (people) who treat (Truth) as falsehood;

52.12. Those (people) who play (and indulge) in small and silly talk.

52.13. That Day when they shall be pushed down to the Fire of Hell, without any questions (being asked).

52.14. "This," (it will be said:) "Is the Fire- Which you habitually deny!

52.15. "Is this a fake, or is it you who do not see?

52.16. "So you burn in there, it is the same to you whether you can bear it with patience, or not: You only receive the penalty for your (own) deeds."

52.17.. Verily, as to the righteous (people), they will be in the Gardens, and

in happiness-

52.18. Enjoying the (true joy) which their Lord has given to them, and their Lord shall save them from the penalty of Fire.

52.19. (It will be said to them:) "You eat and drink, with blessings and health, because of your (good) deeds."

52.20. They will rest (in comfort) on Thrones (of dignity) arranged in ranks; And We shall join them to companions, with beautiful, wide and lovely eyes.

52.21. And those who believe and whose families follow them in Faith- To them We shall join their families: And We shall not take away from them (the reward) of their works: (Still) each person is accountable for his deeds.

52.22. And We shall provide them fruit and meat, anything that they want (to have).

52.23. There they shall exchange, one with another, a (loving) cup, free of pettiness, free of all signs of impurity.

52.24. And there will go around (devoted) to them, youths (handsome) as pearls, well-guarded.

52.25. They will approach one another, engaging in mutual inquiry and questioning.

52.26. They will say: "Before now we were not without fear for the sake of our people.

52.27. "So Allah has been gracious to us, and has delivered us from the penalty of the Burning Wind.

52.28. "Truly, we did pray to Him from of old; Truly, it is He, the Beneficent, the Most Merciful !"

52.29.. Therefore remind (mankind to celebrate the Praise of Allah). By the Grace of your Lord, you are not (any) petty-talker, and you are not a madman (nor one possessed).

52.30. Or do they say:- "A Poet! We will wait for him that some misfortune (will come) in time!"

52.31. You say (to them): "You wait! I will also wait among those who wait!"

52.32. Or do they in their capacity to understand take themselves to this (way of lying), or are they only people exceeding beyond (their) bounds?

52.33. Or do they say: "He made up (the Message);" No, they have no faith!

52.34. (If they can,) let them produce words (of the Message) like it, if they are telling the truth.

52.35.. Or were they created out of nothing? Or were they themselves the creators?

52.36. Or did they create the heavens and the earth? No! They have no firm belief.

52.37. Or are the treasures of your Lord with them? Or are they the tyrants to do anything they wish?

52.38. Or do they have a ladder, by which they can (climb up to the heaven and) listen (to the secrets)? Then let (such a) listener of theirs come up with a clear proof.

52.39. Or has He only daughters and you have sons?

52.40. Or is it that you ask for a reward, so that they will be burdened with a load of debt?

52.41. Or that the Unseen is in their hands, and they write it (the Suras) down?

52.42. Or do they intend a plot (against you)? But those who act in disbelief (in Allah) are themselves involved in a (sinful) plot!

52.43. Or have they a god other than Allah? Glorified is Allah, far above the things they associate with Him!

52.44.. And if they were to see a piece of the sky falling (on them), they would only say: "Clouds gathered in heaps!"

52.45. So leave them alone until they face their Day (of Judgment), when they shall be taken over (with fear)-

52.46. The Day when their plotting will become useless for them and no help shall be given to them.

52.47. And surely, for those who do wrong, there is another punishment (in the life) before this (Day), but most of them do not understand.

52.48. Now wait for the Decision of your Lord, with patience for surely, you are in Our eyes: And celebrate the Praises of your Lord the while you stand forth.

52.49. And also for part of the night you praise Him- And at the setting of the stars (during the dawn)!

****

Sura 53. An-Najm,
(The star): (Makkah, 62 Verses)
In the Name of Allah, the Most Gracious, the Most Merciful.

53.1. By the Star when it goes down (and sets)-

53.2. Your Companion (the Prophet) is not in evil ways and (he is) not being misled.

53.3. And he does not say (anything) from (his own) desire.

53.4. It is nothing less than Revelation sent down to him:

53.5. He was taught by one (Angel *Jibrael* (Gabriel), who is) mighty in power,

53.6. Gifted with wisdom, because he came clearly (in a noble way from *Dhu-Mirrah* to *Heistawâ*)

53.7. While he was in the highest place of the horizon (in the distant skies):

53.8. Then he approached (nearer) and came closer,

53.9. And was at a distance of only two bow-lengths (of spiritual union) or even nearer;

53.10. Like this (Allah) brought the Revelation (and the Message) to His servant (the Prophet)- (made known) what He (wanted) to reveal.

53.11. The (mind and) heart (of the Prophet) in no way lied about what he saw.

53.12.. Then will you disagree with him about what he saw?

53.13. And indeed, he (the Prophet) truly saw him (*Jibrael*) as (he) came down second (time),

53.14. Near the lote-tree (a thorny but a fruit bearing tree in Middle East beyond which none may pass: Symbolically, it is the limit of human understanding):

53.15. Near it is the Garden of Abode (Allah's Divine Presence and His Paradise.)

53.16. When the lote-tree was covered (in mystic wisdom that cannot be spoken!)

53.17. The (Prophet's) vision (of Angel Gabriel) was never broken and it did not go wrong!

53.18. Indeed he (the Prophet) saw, from the Signs of his Lord, the Greatest!

53.19.. Have you seen Al-Lat and Al-Uzza, (two forms of pagan Arabs goddesses in human forms)

53.20. And another, the third (goddess), Manât?

53.21. What (silliness)! For you (yourselves) the male sex, and for Him, the female?

53.22. That indeed, such a division will truly be most unjust!

53.23. These are nothing (at all) except names that you have made up- You and your fathers- For which Allah has not sent down any authority (whatever). They follow nothing but their own guesswork and what their own souls wish! Even though, already there has come to them guidance from their Lord!

53.24. No! Shall man have anything (just because) he wishes for it?

53.25. But it is Allah to Whom the end and the beginning (of everything) belong.

53.26.. And there are many angels in the heavens, their pleading will be of no use except after Allah has given permission for whom He pleases and that he is acceptable to Him.

53.27. Verily, those who do not believe in the Hereafter, give names to the angels that are female names

53.28. But they do not have knowledge about it. They follow nothing except (their) guesswork; And, surely, guesswork is of no use against Truth.

53.29. Therefore keep away from those who turn away from Our Message and (those who) want nothing except the life of this world.

53.30. That is as far as knowledge will reach them. Surely, your Lord knows best those who wander away from His Path, and He knows best those who receive guidance.

53.31. And, to Allah belongs all there is in the heavens and on earth: So He rewards those who do evil, according to their actions, and He rewards those who do good, with what is best.

53.32. Those who keep away from great sins and shameful deeds, only (being caught up in) small faults- Surely, your Lord is plentiful in forgiveness. He knows you well when he creates you out of the earth (your chromosomes), and when you are hidden in your mothers' wombs. Therefore do not justify yourselves: He knows best who it is who keeps away evil.

53.33.. Do you see the one who turns back (from Faith),

53.34. Gives (in) a little then hardens his heart (and his feelings)?

53.35. Does he have knowledge about the unseen so that he can see?

53.36. No! Is he not familiar with what is in the books of Musa (Moses)-

53.37. And of Ibrahim (Abraham) who filled his promises?

53.38. Namely, that no bearer of burdens can carry the burden of another;

53.39. And that man can have nothing except what he works (hard) for;

53.40. That (the fruit of) his work will soon come in sight;

53.41. Then will he be rewarded with a complete reward;

53.42. And that the final Goal is to your Lord;

53.43. That it is He Who gives laughter and tears;

53.44. That it is He Who causes death and gives life (again);

53.45. And that He created in pairs- Male and female,

53.46. From a seed when placed (finally in the womb);

53.47. And that He has promised a second Creation (by raising the dead at Resurrection);

53.48. And that it is He Who gives wealth and satisfaction;

53.49. That He is the Lord of Sirius (*Shi'ra*, the Mighty Star in the constellation of Canis Major)

53.50. And that it is He Who destroyed the (powerful) 'Ad (people) of the old,

53.51. And the Samood (Thamud), and (He) did not grant them an eternal life.

53.52. And before them, the people of Nuh (Noah) because they were (all) most unjust and most arrogant (people) exceeding their limits,

53.53.. And He destroyed the defeated Cities (of Sodom and Gomorrah),

53.54. So that (soil and debris) have covered them up.

53.55. Then which of the gifts of your Lord (O man) will you question?

53.56. This is a Warner (the Prophet), from the (number of) warners of old!

53.57. The (Judgment) ever approaching comes nearer:

53.58. None besides Allah, can alter (the timing of) it.

53.59. Then, do you wonder at (the recitation of) this message?

53.60. And will you laugh and not weep-

53.61. Wasting your time in useless things?

53.62. But you fall down in prostration to Allah, and (adoringly) worship (Him)!

{A Muslim generally prostrates to Allah after reciting this verse}
****

Sura 54. Al-Qamar,
(The moon): (Makkah, 55 Verses)
In the Name of Allah, the Most Gracious, the Most Merciful.

54.1.. The Hour (of Judgment) has drawn nearer, and the moon has been torn apart (cleft asunder.)

54.2. And if they see a Sign they turn away, and say: "This is persistent magic."

54.3. They reject (the warning) and follow their (own) desires and every matter has its appointed time.

54.4. And indeed there have already come to them, recitations in which there is (enough) warning

54.5. Perfect wisdom (in this Quran)- But (the preaching of) warners does not profit them.

54.6.. Therefore, (O Prophet,) turn away from them. The Day when the Caller will call (them) to a terrible affair.

54.7. They will come forth- Their eyes humbled-. From (their) graves, (dazed) like locusts scattered aboard.

54.8. Hastening, with eyes transfixed, towards the Caller! The unbelievers will say: "Hard is this Day!"

54.9.. Before them, the people of Nuh (Noah) rejected (their prophet): They rejected Our servant, and said, "Here is one possessed!," and he was driven out.

54.10. Then he called on his Lord: "I am the one overcome: Then You help (me)!"

54.11. So, We opened the gates of heaven, with water pouring forth.

54.12. And We caused the earth to gush forth with spring so, the waters met (and rose) to the decreed level.

54.13. And We bore him on an (Ark) made of broad planks held together with palm-fiber:

54.14. She (the Ark) floated under Our eyes (and care): A reward to the one who had been rejected (with contempt by his own people)!

54.15. And indeed, We have left this as a Sign (for all time): Then is there any who will receive the teachings?

54.16.. Then! How (terrible) was my Penalty and My Warning?

54.17. And We have indeed made the Quran easy to understand and remember: Then is there any who will receive the teachings?

54.18.. The 'Ad (people also) rejected (the Truth): Then! How terrible was my Penalty and My Warning?

54.19. Verily, We sent against them a furious wind, on a Day of violent disaster,

54.20. Plucking out men as if they were roots of palm-trees torn up (from the ground).

54.21. Then! How (terrible) was my Penalty and My Warning!

54.22. And We have indeed made the Quran easy to understand and remember: Then is there any who will receive the teachings?

54.23.. The (people of) Samood (Thamud), also rejected (their) Warners.

54.24. And they said: "A man! A solitary one from among ourselves! Shall we follow him? Truly, should we then be straying in mind, and mad!

54.25. "Is it that the Message sent to him of all people amongst us? No! He is a liar, a disrespectful one!"

54.26. They will know the next day, who is the liar, the disrespectful one!

54.27. Verily, We will send the she-camel by the way of trial for them. So watch them, (O Sálih) and keep yourself in patience!

54.28. And tell them that the water is to be divided between them: Each ones right to drink being brought forward (by suitable turns).

54.29. But they called to their companion (in evil) and he took a sword in hand, and killed (the she-camel cutting her hamstrings).

54.30. Then! How (terrible) was My Penalty and My Warning!

54.31. Verily, We sent against them a single Mighty Blast, and they became like the dry stubble used by one that keeps the cattle.

54.32. And We have indeed made the Quran easy to understand and remember: Then is there any who will receive the teachings?

54.33.. The People of Lut (Lot) rejected (his) warning.

54.34. Verily, We sent against them a violent tornado with showers of stones, (which destroyed them), except (Lut's) household: (And) We delivered them by early part of the morning-

54.35. As a Grace from Us: Thus do We reward those who give thanks.

54.36. And (Lut) did warn them of Our punishment, but they disputed about the Warning.

54.37. And they even sought to snatch away his guests from him, so, We blinded their eyes. (And they heard:) "Now you taste My Wrath and My Warning."

54.38. And Verily, early on the next day an abiding punishment seized them:

54.39. "So you taste My Wrath and My Warning."

54.40. And We have indeed made the Quran easy to understand and remember: Then is there any who will receive the teachings?

54.41.. Also to the People of Firon (Pharaoh), before have, came Warners (from Allah).

54.42. They (the people) rejected all Our Signs; So, We seized them with such penalty (that comes) from Almighty (Exalted in Power), Able and Powerful to enforce His Will.

54.43. Are your unbelievers, (O Quraish), better than they were or have you an immunity in the Sacred Books?

54.44. Or do they say: "We acting together can defend ourselves?"

54.45. Soon will their multitude be put to flight and they will show their backs.

54.46. No! But the Hour (of Judgment) is the time promised them (for their full recompense): And that Hour will be most painful and most bitter.

54.47. Truly, those in sin are the ones straying in mind, and mad.

54.48. The Day they will be dragged through the Fire on their faces, (it will be said:) "You taste the touch of Hell!"

54.49. Surely, all things We have created in proportion and measure.

54.50. And Our Command is but a single (Act)- Like the twinkle of an eye.

54.51. And indeed (often) in the past, We have destroyed groups like you: Then is there any who will receive the teachings?

54.52.. And all that they do is noted in (their) books (of deeds):

54.53. And every matter, small and large, is on record.

54.54.. Verily, as to those who act right, they will be in the in the midst of gardens and streams,

54.55. In an Assembly of Truth, in the Presence of a Sovereign Almighty (Omnipotent Allah).

****

Sura 55. Ar-Rahmán,

(Allah, Most Gracious): (Medinah, 78 Verses)

In the Name of Allah, the Most Gracious, the Most Merciful.

55.1. (Allah;) The Most Gracious

55.2. It is He Who has taught the Quran.

55.3.. He has Created man;

55.4. He has taught him to talk (and understand).

55.5. The sun and the moon that follow (their) calculated courses;

55.6. And the herbs (also the Galaxy of stars) and the trees -Both prostrate (bow) themselves in respect (to Allah);

55.7. And the Arch of the Sky - He has raised high (above), and He has set up the balance (of Justice);

55.8. So that you may not willfully overstep (the fine) balance.

55.9. So establish (accurate) weight with justice and do not fall short in the balance.

55.10. It is He Who has spread out the earth for (His) Creatures:

55.11. In there is fruit and date-palms, producing the long leaves (enclosing dates):

55.12. Also corn, with (its) leaves and stalks for feeding the cattle and the sweet smelling plants.

55.13. Then which of the miracles from your Lord will you both (men and jinns') renounce?

55.14.. He created man from sounding clay like the clay of pottery,

55.15. And He created jinns' from a smokeless flame of fire:

55.16. Then which of the miracles from your Lord will you both renounce?

55.17.. (He is the) Lord of the two easts (east and the far, far east) and the Lord of the two wests (west and the far, far west):

55.18. Then which of the miracles from your Lord will you both renounce?

55.19.. (He has created) the two free streams of flowing (salt and sweet) water, meeting together:

55.20. Between them is a barrier that they do not willfully overstep;

55.21. Then which of the miracles from your Lord will you both renounce?

55.22.. Out of them come pearls and coral:

55.23. Then which of the miracles from your Lord will you both renounce?

55.24.. And His are the ships sailing through the seas, high (and majestic) as mountains:

55.25. Then which of the miracles from your Lord will you both renounce?

55.26.. All that is on earth will perish:

55.27. But will remain (Alive for ever), the Face of your Lord- Full of Majesty, Bounty and Honor.

55.28. Then which of the miracles from your Lord will you both renounce?

55.29.. To Him begs (for its need) every creature in the heavens and on the earth: Every day in (new) splendor does He (shine)!

55.30. Then which of the miracles from your Lord will you both renounce?

55.31.. We shall soon settle your affairs- O both of you (jinns' and men)!

55.32. Then which of the miracles from your Lord will you both (jinns' and men) renounce?

55.33.. O you assembly of jinns' and men! If you can cross the zones of the heavens and the earth, then you cross (them)! (But) you shall not be able to cross, except with the authority (from Allah!)

55.34. Then which of the miracles from your Lord will you both (jinns' and men) renounce?

55.35.. On you both (the evil ones from jinns' and men)! Will be sent (both) a flame of fire (to burn) and a smoke (to choke); No defense will you have:

55.36. Then which of the miracles from your Lord will you both renounce?

55.37. When the sky is split open, and it becomes red like (molten) ointment:

55.38. Then which of the miracles from your Lord will you both renounce?

55.39. On that Day no question will be asked of man or jinn as to his sin,

55.40. Then which of the miracles from your Lord will you both renounce?

55.41. The sinners will be known by their Marks: And they will be caught by their hair and their feet.

55.42. Then which of the miracles from your Lord will you both renounce?

55.43. This is the Hell that the sinners (of this world) ignore:

55.44. In the middle, and (yes) in the middle of boiling hot water will they float around!

55.45. Then which of the miracles from your Lord will you both renounce?

55.46.. But for him who fears the time when they (the jinns' and men) will stand before (the Throne of Judgment of) their Lord, there will be two Gardens-

55.47. Then which of the miracles from your Lord will you both renounce?

55.48. Containing many kinds (of trees and delights)-

55.49. Then which of the miracles from your Lord will you both renounce?

55.50. In them (each) will be two Springs (of water) flowing (free);

55.51. Then which of the miracles from your Lord will you both renounce?

55.52. In them will be Fruits of every kind, two and two (for sufficiency and completeness).

55.53. Then which of the miracles from your Lord will you both renounce?

55.54. They will recline (and rest) on carpets whose inner lining will be of rich embroidery: The fruit of the Garden will be near, (and easy to reach).

55.55. Then which of the miracles from your Lord will you both renounce?

55.56. In them will be (maidens), chaste, restricting their glances, whom no man or jinn has ever before touched-

55.57. Then which of the miracles from your Lord will you both renounce?

55.58. They are like Rubies and Coral.

55.59. Then which of the miracles from your Lord will you both renounce?

55.60. Is there any Reward for good - Other than good?

55.61. Then which of the miracles from your Lord will you both renounce?

55.62.. And below these two, there are two other Gardens-

55.63. Then which of the miracles from your Lord will you both renounce?

55.64. Dark-green in color (and lush with water).

55.65. Then which of the miracles from your Lord will you both renounce?

55.66. In them (each) will be two Springs with plenty of flowing water:

55.67. Then which of the miracles from your Lord will you both renounce?

55.68. In them both will be fruits and dates and pomegranates:

55.69. Then which of the miracles from your Lord will you both renounce?

55.70. In them will be fair (companions), good and beautiful-

55.71. Then which of the miracles from your Lord will you both renounce?

55.72. Fair companions restricting (their glances), in (beautiful and decorated) homes-

55.73. Then which of the miracles from your Lord will you both renounce?

55.74. (Companions) whom no man or jinn has ever before touched-

55.75. Then which of the miracles from your Lord will you both renounce?

55.76. Reclining (and resting) on green cushions and rich carpets of beauty.

55.77. Then which of the miracles from your Lord will you both (jinns' and men) renounce?

55.78.. Blessed be the Name of your Lord, Full of Majesty and Honor.

****

Sura 56. Al-Wáqi'ah,

(The inevitable event): (Makkah, 96 Verses)

In the Name of Allah, the Most Gracious, the Most Merciful.

56.1. When the Event that must occur will become a reality,

56.2. Then no (soul) will have denial regarding its happening.

56.3. It will bring down (many) it will raise (many others);

56.4. When the earth shall be shaken to its depths.

56.5. And the mountains shall be crushed to atoms,

56.6. So that they will become dust scattered around,

56.7. And you shall be sorted out into three classes.

56.8.. Then (there will be) the companions of the right hand- What will be the companions of the right hand?

56.9. And (there will be) the companions of the left hand- What will be the companions of the left hand?

56.10. And those foremost (in Faith) will be foremost (in the Hereafter).

56.11.. These will be those nearest to Allah:

56.12. In Garden of (true) joy:

56.13. A number of people from those of the old,

56.14. And a few ones from those of later times.

56.15. (They will be) on thrones inlaid (with gold and precious stones),

56.16. Reclining on them, face to face,

56.17. Around them will (serve) youths of ever lasting (freshness),

56.18. With little glasses, (shining) tumblers, and cups (filled) from clear-flowing fountains:

56.19. No ill effects will they suffer from them, and they will not be dazed;

56.20. And with fruits, any that they may select;

56.21. And the flesh of fowls, any that they desire.

56.22. And (there will be) companions with beautiful, big and lustrous eyes-

56.23. Like (they are) pearls, well-guarded.

56.24. A reward for the deeds of their past (life).

56.25. No pettiness will they hear in there, and not even a little of sinful speech (or idle talk)-

56.26. But only the saying; "_Salaam, Salaam,_ (Peace! Peace)."

56.27.. And those on the right (hand)- What will be the companions of the right hand?

56.28. (They will be joyful) among the (heavenly) lote-tree without thorns,

56.29. Among _Talh_ (beautifully flowering) trees with flowers (or fruits) piled one above another-

56.30. In (the) long-extended shade;

56.31. By water flowing constantly;

56.32. And fruit in abundance.

56.33. Whose season is not limited, and (whose supply is not) stopped,

56.34. And on thrones (of dignity) raised high.

56.35. Verily, We have created (their companions) of special creation.

56.36. And made them virgin, pure (and untouched)-

56.37. Loving (by nature), equal in age-

56.38. For the companions of the right hand.

56.39.. A (good) number from the first generation (in Islam),

56.40. And a (good) number from those of later generations.

56.41.. The companions of the left hand- What will be the companions of the left hand?

56.42. (They will be) in the middle of a brutal blast of Fire and in boiling water,

56.43. And in the shades of black smoke:

56.44. (There will be) nothing to refresh, nothing to please:

56.45. Verily, they used to indulge, before that, in wealth (and luxury).

56.46. And willfully continued in the worst wickedness!

56.47. And they used to say, "When we die and become dust and bones, shall we then indeed be Resurrected again?

56.48. "We and our fathers of old?"

56.49. Say: "Yes, verily, those of old and those of later times,

56.50. "All will certainly be gathered together for the meeting appointed for a well-known Day

56.51. "Then surely, will you truly- O you who go wrong, and treat (Truth) as falsehood!

56.52. "You will surely taste of the (Evil) tree of *Zaqqum.*

56.53. "Then will you fill your insides with it,

56.54. "And drink boiling water on top of it:

56.55. "Indeed you shall drink like diseased camels raging with thirst!"

56.56. This will be their entertainment on the Day of Judgment!

56.57.. It is We Who have created you: Why will you not see (and accept) the Truth?

56.58. Do you see it? The (human) seed, (the chromosomes in the sperm and ovum) that you throw out-

56.59. Is it you who created it? - Or are We, the Creator?

56.60. We have ordered death to be your common ending, and We are not to be frustrated-

56.61. In changing your shapes and recreating you (again) in (shapes) that you have not known.

56.62. And indeed, you certainly know already the first form of creation: Why then do you not celebrate His praises?

56.63.. Do you see the seed that you sow in the ground?

56.64. Is it you that cause it to grow, or are We the cause?

56.65. If it was Our Will, We could crumble it to dry powder, and you would be left in wondering,

56.66. (Saying), "We are indeed left in debts (for no reason):

56.67. "Nay! Certainly we are denied (of the fruits of our labor)."

56.68.. Do you not see the water that you drink?

56.69. Do you bring it down (as rain) from the cloud or do We send it?

56.70. If it was Our Will We verily, could make it salt (and bitter) then why do you not give thanks (to Allah)?

56.71.. Do you not see the Fire that you kindle?

56.72. Is it you who grow the tree which feeds the fire, or do We grow it?

56.73. We have made it (the fire) a monument and an article of comfort and convenience for those who live in the desert (this world).

56.74. Then celebrate with Praises the Name of your Lord, the Greatest!

56.75.. Next, I swear by the setting of the Stars-

56.76. And surely, that is indeed a mighty and holy oath if you only knew-

56.77. That, this is indeed a Quran most honorable,

56.78. In a Book well-guarded (with Allah),

56.79. Which none shall touch except those who are clean:

56.80. A Revelation from the Lord of the Worlds.

56.81.. Is it that such a Message that you would hold in light regard?

56.82. And have you made it your livelihood that you should renounce it?

56.83. Then why do you not (intervene) when (the soul of the dying man) reaches the throat

56.84. And you (sit) looking on-

56.85. But We are nearer to him than you, and you see not-

56.86. Then why do you not- If you are excused from (future) account.-

56.87. Return the soul, if you are truthful, (in your claim of independence)?

56.88.. Therefore, if he be among those nearest to Allah,

56.89. (For him there is) rest and satisfaction, and a Garden of (heavenly) delights.

56.90. And if he be of the companions of the right hand,

56.91. (For him is the salutation); "Peace be upon you," for the companions of the right hand.

56.92. And if he be of those who treat (truth) as falsehood, who go wrong,

56.93. Then for him, the entertainment is with boiling water,

56.94. And burning in Hell-Fire.

56.95. Surely this! This is the very Truth and Certainty.

56.96.. So, celebrate with Praises the Name of your Lord, the Greatest.

****

Sura 57. Al-Hadid,

(The iron): (Medinah, 29 Verses)

In the Name of Allah, the Most Gracious, the Most Merciful.

57.1.. All that is in the heaven and on the earth- Glorifies Allah, and He is Almighty, (Exalted in Might), All Wise.

57.2. To Him belongs the kingdom of the heavens and the earth: It is He Who gives life and causes death: And He is Able to do all things.

57.3. He is the First and (He is) the Last, and the All Present, (Omnipresent, the All Evident): And (He is) the Hidden, and He is the All Knower of all the (minutest) things.

57.4. He it is Who created the heavens and the earth in six Days, and then He rose over the Throne (of Authority). He knows what enters within the earth and what comes out of it: And what comes down from heaven and what rises up to it. And He is with you where ever you may be. And Allah sees well all that you do.

57.5. To Him belongs the kingdom of the heavens and the earth: And to Allah, all affairs return (for the final decision).

57.6. He merges night into day and He merges day into night; And He has complete knowledge of the secrets in the breasts (in the hearts of humans).

57.7.. Believe in Allah and His Messenger and spend (in charity) out of the (sustenance) for which He has made you the inheritors. And (for those) who believe and spend (in charity), for them is a great reward.

57.8. And what reason do you have? Why you should not believe in Allah? While the Messenger invites you to believe in your Lord; And (He) has indeed taken your truest promise, (your covenant), if you are real believers.

57.9. It is He, the One Who sends to His servant (the Prophet,) clear Signs, that He (Almighty Allah) may lead you from the depths of darkness into the Light. And surely, Allah is full of Kindness , Most Merciful .

57.10. And what reason do you have? Why you should not spend in the cause of Allah? And it is to Allah that belongs the heritage of the heavens and the earth. Not equal among you are those who spent (freely) and fought (the wars) before the Victory (of Makkah, with those who did so later). Those are higher in rank than those who spent (freely) and fought after (the Victory). But to all has Allah promised a best (reward). And Allah is familiar with all that you do.

57.11.. Who is he who will lend to Allah a goodly and handsome loan? Then, He (Allah) will increase it many times to his credit, and he will (also) receive a generous reward.

57.12. On the Day you shall see the believing men and the believing women- How their Light runs forward before them and by their right hands: (Their greeting will be): "Good News for you this Day! Gardens (of Paradise) beneath which flow rivers! To live in there for ever! This is indeed the highest success!"

57.13. On the Day the hypocrites- Men and women, will say to the believers: "Wait for us! Let us get something (a light) from your Light!" It will be said: "(You) go back to the rear! Then seek a light (where you can)!" So, a wall will be put between them, with a gate in it. Within it (the wall) will be mercy throughout, and outside and all alongside of it, will be (anger and) punishment!

57.14. (Those hypocrites outside) will call the believers, "Were we not with you?" (The others) will reply, "True! But you led yourselves into temptation; You looked forward (to our destruction); And you doubted (Allah's Promise); And (your false) desires deceived you; Until the Command of Allah became true. And the Deceiver (Satan) deceived you in respect to (Almighty) Allah.

57.15. "So, this Day shall no ransom be taken from you, or from those who disbelieved. Your home is Fire: That is the proper place to claim you: And it is an evil place to rest!"

57.16.. Has not the time yet arrived for the believers, with their hearts, in all humility, should engage in the remembrance of Allah and of the Truth which has been made known (to them); And that they should not become like those to whom was given the Message before, and during long ages (that) passed over them and their hearts grew hard? And many of them are rebellious transgressors.

57.17. You (who believe!) know that Allah gives life to the earth after its death! Already We have shown the Signs plainly to you. If you would only understand.

57.18. Verily, those who give in charity, men and women, and loan to Allah, a beautiful loan, it shall be increased manifold (to their credit). And they shall have (besides) a generous reward.

57.19. And those who believe in Allah and His messengers- They are the sincere (caretakers of Truth), and the witnesses (who testify), in the eyes of their Lord: They shall have their reward and their light. But those who reject Allah and deny Our Signs (*Ayât*), they are the companions of Hell-Fire.

57.20. You (who believe!) know that the life of this world is but a play and amusement, self-praising and boasting (within yourselves), and multiplying, (in rivalry) among yourselves, riches and children. Here is a similarity - Like a rain and the growth which it brings forth, give happiness (to the hearts of) the tillers; (But) soon it withers; You will see it grow yellow; Then it becomes dry and it crumbles away. But in the Hereafter is a penalty severe (for those who follow wrong), and a Forgiveness from Allah and (His) Good Pleasure, (for those who love and worship Him). And what is the life of the world, but goods and possessions (objects) of deception!

57.21. Race with one another (to be the foremost in seeking) forgiveness from your Lord, and a Garden (Paradise of Bliss), whose width is the width of heaven and earth, prepared for those who believe in Allah and His messengers. That is the Grace of Allah that He bestows on whom He is pleased with: And Allah is the Owner of Gifts, great, (plentiful) and abounding.

57.22.. No misfortune can happen on earth or in your souls except that which is recorded in a command (written) before which We bring into existence: That is truly easy for Allah:

57.23. In order that you may not be sorry over matters that pass you by, nor become overjoyed by mercies bestowed upon you; Allah does not love any petty and showy boasters- (With praise for themselves).

57.24. Such persons are stingy (with a selfish desire to own) and (they) suggest stinginess to men. And if any turn back (from Allah's way), surely, Allah is free of all needs, worthy of all praise.

57.25.. Indeed, We have sent Our messengers before with clear proofs and sent down with them the Book (the Scripture) and the balance (between right and wrong), that men may stand together in justice: And We sent down iron, in which is (material for) power and might (in war), as well as many benefits for mankind, that Allah may test who are those who will help Him (and His Religion), the Unseen and His messengers: Surely, Allah is Full of Strength, exalted in Might (and able to enforce His Will).

57.26.. And indeed, We sent Nuh (Noah) and Ibrahim (Abraham) and established in their line prophethood and revelation: And some of them (their people) were on right guidance but many of them became rebellious transgressors.

57.27. Then, afterwards, We followed them with (others of) Our messengers; And We sent after them Isa (Jesus) the son of Maryam (Mary), and gifted him the *Injeel* (Gospel): And We placed compassion and mercy in the hearts of those who followed him. But the self isolation and self-denial (practiced by monks in monasteries) which they made up for themselves, We did not place it upon them: (We commanded) only the seeking for the good Pleasure of Allah: But that they did not continue it as they should have done. So, We blessed, on those among them who believed, their (due) reward, but many of them are rebellious transgressors.

57.28.. O you who believe! Fear Allah, and believe in His Messenger, and He will bless on you with twice the portion of His Mercy: And He will provide for you a light by which you shall walk (straight in your path), and

He will forgive you (for your past): And Allah is Often Forgiving, Most Merciful :

57.29. That the People of the Book may know that they do not have any power over the Grace of Allah, that (His) Grace is (entirely) in His Hand, to (grant) it on anyone He wills. For Allah is the Owner of Gifts, great, (plentiful) and abounding.

****

Sura 58. Al-Mujadila,
[The woman who cries (for justice)]: (Medinah, 22 Verses)
In the Name of Allah, the Most Gracious, the Most Merciful.

58.1.. Indeed, Allah has heard (and accepted) the cries of the woman (Khaulah bint Thalabah) who pleads with you about her husband (Aus bin As-Samit) and brings her complaint (in prayer) to Allah; And Allah (always) hears the arguments between both sides among you: For Allah is All Hearing, All Seeing (of all things).

58.2. Those men among you who make their wives unlawful to them (the men) by *Zihar* (a primitive and pagan custom of calling them mothers, see 33.4, these men know that) they (the wives) cannot be their mothers (of the men): None can be their mothers (of the men) except those who gave them birth. And in fact they (the men) use words (that are) unjust and false: But truly, Allah is All Pardoning (the sins), Often-Forgiving

58.3. But those who make unlawful their wives by *Zihar*, and wish to go back on the words they said- (It is necessary that such a man) should set a slave free before they (man and estranged wife) touch each other: This you are warned to do: And Allah is Well-Acquainted with (all) that you do.

58.4. And if any (man) does not have (the means to free a slave), he should fast for two successive months (every day) continuously before they touch each other. And if anyone is unable to do so, he should feed sixty persons in need. This is (commanded to be) so, that you may show your faith in Allah and His Messenger. And these are the limits (set by) Allah. For those who disbelieve (in Him), there is a painful penalty.

58.5. Verily, those who oppose Allah and His Messenger will be disgraced down to dust, like those who were disgraced before them: For We have already sent down clear Signs (*Ayât*). And the unbelievers (will suffer) a shameful penalty-

58.6. On the Day when Allah will raise (resurrect) them all up (again) and show them the truth (and record) of their deed (and conduct). Allah has kept an account of it, while they may have forgotten it, and Allah is Witness to all things.

58.7.. Do you not see that Allah does know (all) that is in the heavens and on earth? There is not a secret talk between three (persons), but He makes the fourth among them (with his knowledge)- Nor between (any) five but He makes the sixth- Nor between fewer nor more but He is with them, wherever they may be: And in the end, He will tell them the truth of their conduct, on the Day Of Judgment. Verily, Allah is All Knowing of all things.

58.8. Do you not see those who were advised against secret discussions: Yet (they) go back to that which they were asked not to do, and they hold secret discussions among themselves for injustice and hostility, and disobedience to the Messenger. And when they come to you, they greet and salute you, not as Allah salutes you, (but in crooked ways): And they say to themselves: "Why does Allah not punish us for our words?" Enough for them is Hell: In it they burn, and evil is that place to go!

58.9.. O you who believe! When you hold secret discussions, do it not for injustice and hostility, and disobedience to the Messenger; But do it for good reasons and self-control; And fear Allah, to Whom you shall be brought back.

58.10. Secret discussions are for only (those inspired) by Satan, in order that he may cause unhappiness to the believers; But he cannot harm them in the least, except as Allah permits; And on Allah let the believers put their trust.

58.11.. O you who believe! When you are told to make room in the gatherings, (spread out and) make room: (Ample) room will Allah provide for you. And when you are told to rise up, then rise up: Allah will raise up, to (suitable) ranks (and levels), those of you who believe and who have been granted (mystic) knowledge. And Allah is Well Acquainted with all you do.

58.12.. O you who believe! When you speak with the Messenger in private, spend something in charity before the consultation. That will be best for you, and most helpful towards purity (of conduct). But if you do not find, (the means to spend in charity), then verily, Allah is Often Forgiving, Most Merciful .

58.13. Is it that you are afraid of spending sums in charity before your private consultation (with the Prophet)? If (that is the case), then, you do not do so, and Allah forgives you, but, establish regular prayer; Practice regular charity; And obey Allah and His Messenger. And Allah is Well-Acquainted with all that you do.

58.14.. Do you not turn your attention to those who seek (friendship) of such (people) that have the anger of Allah upon them? They are neither of you nor of them, and they swear to falsehood knowingly.

58.15. Allah has prepared for them a severe Penalty: Evil indeed are their deeds.

58.16. They have made their oaths a screen (to hide their misdeeds): Thus they obstruct (men) from the Path of Allah. Therefore they shall have a shameful penalty.

58.17. Their wealth and their sons will not be of any profit to them, against Allah; They will be companions of the Fire, to live in there (for ever)!

58.18. On the Day, when Allah will raise all of them up (for Judgment): Then they will swear to Him as they swear to you: And they think that they have something (to stand upon). No indeed! They are liars!

58.19. The Satan has taken the better of them. So he has made them forget the remembrance of Allah. They are the party of the Satan. Truly, it is the party of the Satan that will perish!

58.20.. Verily, those who oppose Allah and His Messenger they will be among those most humiliated.

58.21. Allah has affirmed (and decreed): "Verily, it is I and My messengers who must win (prevail):" Verily, Allah is One full of Strength, Almighty (Able to make His Will become reality).

58.22. You will not find any people who believe in Allah and the Last Day, loving those who oppose Allah and His Messenger, even though they were their fathers, or their sons, or their brothers, or their kindred (by blood relationship). For such (people who believe) He (Allah) has written Faith in their hearts, and (He has) strengthened them with a spirit from Himself. And He will admit them to Gardens beneath which rivers flow, to live in there (for ever). Allah will be well pleased with them, and they (will be well pleased) with Him. They are the party of Allah. Truly, it is the party of Allah who will be successful (and the ultimate happiness).

****

Sura 59. Al-Hashr,
[About the gathering (banishment)]: (Medinah, 24 Verses)
In the Name of Allah, the Most Gracious, the Most Merciful.

59.1.. Whatever is in heavens and whatever is on earth, glorifies and Praises Allah: And He is the Exalted in Might (and) the All Wise .

59.2.. It is He, Who got out the unbelievers among the People of the Book (Scripture) from their homes at the first gathering (of the forces). You did not think that they would get out: And they thought that their fortresses would defend them from Allah! But the (anger of) Allah came to them from sources that they had not expected, and He cast fear into their hearts, so that they demolished their houses by their own hands, and by the hands of the believers. Take warning, then, O you (people) with eyes (to see)!

59.3. And, if Allah had not decided exile (and banishment) for them, He would certainly have punished them in this world: And in the Hereafter they shall have the punishment of the Fire.

59.4. That is because they opposed Allah and His Messenger: And if anyone opposes Allah, then surely, Allah is severe in punishment.

59.5. Whether you (O Muslims!), cut down the tender palm-trees, or you left them standing on the roots, it was the willingness of Allah, and (it was) because He might cover with shame those who exceed their limits.

59.6.. And what (booty) Allah has (taken) from them and granted to His Messenger, - Towards this (cause) you provided neither horses nor camels: But Allah gives power to His messengers over anybody He pleases; Verily, Allah is Able to do all things.

59.7. What Allah has granted (as booty) to His Messenger (and taken away) from the people of the townships, - Belongs to Allah, to His Messenger, - And to relatives and the orphans, the needy and the wayfarer; In order that it may not (merely) be circulated between the wealthy among you. So take what the Messenger gives to you, and deny yourselves that which he withholds from you. And fear Allah; For Allah is Strict in punishment.

59.8.. (Some part of the booty is due) to the needy *Mahajirs* (those emigrants who came from Makkah), those who were expelled from their homes and their property, while seeking Grace from Allah, and (His) Good Pleasure, and helping Allah and His Messenger (the Prophet): Such are indeed the sincere ones:-

59.9. And (it is also for) those who before them, had homes (in Medinah) and had adopted faith (in Islam)- Show their affection to those who came to them for refuge, and entertain no desire for things in their hearts, (and had) given to the (refugees), and give them preference over themselves, even though poverty was their (own lot), and those saved from the selfishness of their own souls- Such are they, the ones who are successful.

59.10. And those who came after them say: "Our Lord! Forgive us, and our brethren who came before us into the Faith (of Islam), and leave not in our hearts, hate (or sense of injury) against those who believed. Our Lord! You are indeed Full of Kindness , Most Merciful ."

59.11. Have you not seen the hypocrites say to the disbelieving brethren among the People of the Book (Scripture)? "If you are forced out, we will also go out with you, and we will never listen to anyone about your affair; And if you are attacked (in fight) we will help you." But Allah sees that they are indeed liars.

59.12. Surely, if they are forced out, never will they go out with them; And if they are attacked (in fight) they will never help them; And if they do help them, they will turn their backs; And they will not be victorious.

59.13. (Verily), you are stronger in their breasts (and hearts of hypocrites of *Banu An-Nadîr*) than Allah (because of victories won by you). That is because they are men without understanding (for the Supreme Power of Allah).

59.14. They will not fight you (even) together, except in fortified townships, or from behind walls. Their fighting (spirit) is strong among themselves: You would think they are united, but their hearts are divided. That is because they are a people who understand not.

59.15.. They are like those who recently came before them, they have tasted the evil result of what they did; And (in the Hereafter there is) a painful penalty for them;

59.16. (Their friends deceive them), like the Satan, when he says to man, "Deny Allah," but when (man) denies Allah, (the Satan secretively) says, "I am free of you, I do fear Allah, the Lord of the Worlds!"

59.17. So the end of both will be that (both) go into the Fire, to live in there, for ever. Such is the reward for the wrongdoers.

59.18.. O you who believe! Fear Allah, and let every soul look to what it has put forward for the future. Yes, fear Allah! Verily, Allah knows well (all) that you do.

59.19. And you do not be like those who forget Allah; And He caused them forget their own souls! Such are those who are rebellious!

59.20. The companions of the Fire are not equal to the companions of the Garden; They will achieve the true happiness.

59.21.. If We sent down this Quran on a mountain, surely, you would have seen it humble itself and split open with the fear of Allah. Such are the examples that We offer men that they may (deeply) think.

59.22.. Allah is He, other than Whom, there is no other god:- The All Knowing, of the hidden and open, He, (is) the Most Gracious, the Most Merciful .

59.23. Allah is He, Other than Whom there is no other god:- The Sovereign Ruler, the Holy One, the Source of Perfection (and Peace), the Guardian of

Faith, the Preserver of Safety, the Exalted in Might , the Compeller, the Supreme and Majestic. Glory to Allah! (High is He) above the partners they give to Him.

59.24. He is Allah, the Creator, the Evolver, the Grantor of Forms to Him belong the Most Beautiful Names. Whatever is in the heavens and on earth, declares His Praises and Glory, and He is the Exalted in Might , the All Wise .

****

Sura 60. Al-Mumtahana,
(The woman to be examined): (Medinah, 13 Verses)
In the Name of Allah, the Most Gracious, the Most Merciful.

60.1.. O you who believe! Do not take My enemies, and yours, as protecting friends (or protectors by) offering them (your) love, even though they disbelieve the Truth that has come to you: And have (on the contrary) driven the Messenger (the Prophet) and yourselves (from your homes), (simply) because you believe in Allah, your Lord. If you have come out to strive in My Way (Cause) and to seek My Good Pleasure, (take them not as protectors); Holding secret conversation of love with them: For I (Allah) completely know what you hide, and all that you reveal. And any of you who does this has strayed from the Straight Way.

60.2. Should they gain an upper hand over you, they would treat you as enemies, and stretch forth their hands and their tongues against you with evil, and they desire that you should be disbelievers (and reject the Truth).

60.3. Neither your relative, nor your children will benefit you on the Day of Judgment; He will judge between you: And Allah is All Seeing of all that you do.

60.4.. Indeed for you, there is, an excellent example in Ibrahim (Abraham) and those with him, when they said to their people: "Verily, we have rejected you, and whatever you worship besides Allah. We have disbelieved you, and there has arisen, between us and you, a hostility and hatred for ever- Unless you believe in Allah and Him Alone." But (it was) not so when Ibrahim (Abraham) said to his father: "Verily, I will pray for forgiveness for you, though I have no power (to get) anything on your behalf from Allah." (They prayed) "Our Lord! In You do we trust, and to You do we turn in repentance, and to You is (our) final return.

60.5. "Our Lord! Do not make us a (test and) trial for the unbelievers, but forgive us, our Lord! Verily, You are the Exalted in Might , the Wise ."

60.6. Certainly, there is indeed, in them an excellent example for you to follow- (And) for those who await the meeting with Allah and believe in the Last Day. And if any turn away, then truly, Allah is free of all wants, worthy of all Praise.

60.7.. It may be that Allah will grant love and friendship between you and those whom you (now) hold as enemies, and Allah has the Power (over all things): And Allah is Often Forgiving, Most Merciful .

60.8. Allah does not forbid you to act justly and kindly with those (for friendship) who do not fight with you regarding (your) faith (of Islam), and do not drive you out of your homes. Verily, Allah loves those who practice equity and justice.

60.9. Allah only forbids you, those (for friendship) who fight against you regarding (your) faith (of Islam), and drive you out of your homes, and (those who) support (others) in driving you out, from turning to them (for friendship and protection). It is those who turn towards them (for friendship) that do wrong.

60.10.. O you who believe! When believing women come to you as refugees (and emigrants) examine (and verify) them (for their faith): Allah knows best as to their faith: Then if you ascertain that they are believers, then do not send them back to the unbelievers. They are not lawful (wives) for the unbelievers, nor are the (unbelievers) lawful (husbands) for them.

But pay the unbelievers what they have spent (on their dowry). And there will be no sin (or blame) on you, if you marry them on payment of their dowry to them. But do not hold the guardianship of unbelieving women: Ask for what you have spent for their dowry, and let the (unbelievers) ask for what they have spent (on their dowers of women who have come to you). Such is the Judgment (the Command) of Allah: He judges (with justice) between you. And Allah is All Knowing , All Wise.

60.11. And if any of your wives have gone (fallen in) to go to the disbelievers, then you succeed over them (by gaining victory over the disbelievers), then pay (from the booty) to those whose wives have gone, the equivalent of what they had spent (on their dowry). And fear Allah, in Whom you believe.

60.12.. O Prophet! When believing women come to you with an oath of their loyalty to you, (with a promise, pledging), that they will not associate in worship any other thing whatever with Allah, and that they will not steal, and that they will not commit adultery and that they will not kill their children, that they will not utter slander, fabricating falsehood from their hands and feet, and that they will not disobey you in any goodly just matter- Then, you accept their pledge (oath) of loyalty, and pray to Allah for the forgiveness (of their sins): Verily, Allah is Often Forgiving, Most Merciful .

60.13.. O you who believe! Turn not (for protection) to people on whom is the Anger of Allah. About the Hereafter they are already in pain and suffering, just as the unbelievers are in pain and suffering, about those (buried) in graves.

****

Sura 61. As-Saff,
(The battle array): (Medinah, 14 Verses)
In the Name of Allah, the Most Gracious, the Most Merciful.

61.1.. Whatsoever that is in the heaven and on earth, Glory Allah, and He is Almighty , the All Wise .

61.2. O you who believe! Why do you say that which you do not do?

61.3. Surely, it is most unpleasant, in Allah's sight that you say that which you do not do.

61.4. Truly Allah loves those who fight in His Cause in the battle array (rows), as if they were solid walls.

61.5.. And (remember), when Musa (Moses) said to his people: "O my people! Why do you hurt and insult me? Certainly, you know that I am a messenger of Allah (sent) to you?" So when they turned away (from the right path), Allah let their heart go wrong. And Allah does not guide those who are rebellious and disobedient.

61.6.. And (remember) when, Isa (Jesus), the son of Maryam (Mary), said: "O Children of Israel! I am a messenger of Allah (sent) to you, reaffirming *Taurát* (the Torah, that came) before me, and giving the good news of a Messenger (reference to the Prophet Muhammad) to come after me, whose name shall be Ahmad." But when he (the Prophet) came to them with clear proofs, they said, "This is clearly magic (aimed at deception)!"

61.7.. And who does greater wrong than the one who invents lies against Allah, while he is being invited to Islam? And Allah does not guide the wrongdoers.

61.8. Their intention is to darken Allah's Light (by bellowing) with their mouths: But Allah will complete (brightening) His Light. Even though the unbelievers may dislike (it).

61.9. It is He Who has sent His Messenger with Guidance and the Religion of Truth, that he may proclaim it over all religions even though the idolaters may dislike (it).

61.10.. O you who believe! Shall I guide you to a trade (situation) that will save you from a painful penalty,

61.11. That you believe in Allah and His Messenger (the Prophet), and that you strive very hard (to your best) in the Cause of Allah, with your property and your persons: That will be best for you, if you only knew!

61.12. (If you do that), He will forgive you (for) your sins, and admit you to Gardens beneath which rivers flow, and to beautiful palaces in the *'Adn* (Eden or Paradise) of eternity: That is indeed the highest Achievement.

61.13. And another (favor) which you will love, -Help from Allah and a near (and quick) victory. So give glad tidings (and good news) to the believers.

61.14.. O you who believe!– Be(come) you, the helpers (in the Cause) of Allah: As Isa (Jesus), the son of Maryam (Mary), said to the followers (disciples); "Who will be my helpers to (the work of) Allah?" Said the followers (disciples), "We are Allah's helpers!" Then a portion of the Children of Israel believed, and a portion disbelieved: So, We gave power to those who believed, against their enemies, and they became the ones who won.

****

Sura 62. Al-Jumuah,

(The assembly, (Friday) prayer): (Medinah, 11 Verses)
In the Name of Allah, the Most Gracious, the Most Merciful.

62.1.. Whatever is in the heavens and on earth, glorifies of Allah, - The Sovereign King, the Holy and Pristine, the Almighty , the All Wise .

62.2. It is He Who has sent amongst the unlettered ones a messenger from among themselves to rehearse to them His Verses, to purify them, and to instruct them in (Book, Quran) Scripture and Wisdom- Verily, they had been openly in error before.

62.3. And (He has sent the Prophet to) others among them (the Muslims ready to accept the Faith), who have not already joined them (the Muslims);

And He is the Almighty , the All Wise .

62.4. That is the Grace of Allah that He grants on whom He wills; And Allah is the Lord of the highest grace.

62.5.. The similarity of those who were entrusted and charged with the (obligations of the Judaic Law) *Taurát*, but did not carry it (the trust) out, is (like) that of a donkey which carries voluminous scriptures (without understanding it). Evil is the likeness of people who falsify the Signs of Allah: And Allah guides not the wrongdoers.

62.6. Say: "O you (Jewish people) who profess Judaism! If you think that you are friends to Allah, to the exclusion of (other believing) men, then express your desire for death, if you are truthful!"

62.7. But they will not express their desire (for death), because of the (deeds) their hands have sent on before them! And Allah knows well the wrongdoers!

62.8. Say: "Verily, the death from which you run away will really overtake you: Then will you be sent back to the All-Knower of things that are unseen and seen: And He will tell you the things that you did!"

62.9.. O you who believe! When the call is recited for prayer on Friday (the day of assembly), hurry sincerely to the Remembrance of Allah, and leave behind the business (and traffic): That is best for you if you only knew!

62.10. Then when the (Friday) prayer is finished, then may you may disperse through the land, and seek of the Grace and Bounty of Allah: And celebrate the Praises of Allah much and often (and without restriction): That you may be successful.

62.11.. And when they see some bargain or some amusement, they leave to run to it, and leave you standing. Say: "The (blessing) from the Presence of Allah is better than any amusement or bargain! And Allah is the Best to Provide (for all needs)."

****

Sura 63. Al-Munafiqún,
(The hypocrites):   (Medinah, 11 Verses)
In the Name of Allah, the Most Gracious, the Most Merciful.

63.1.. When the hypocrites come to you, they say, "We bear witness that you are indeed the Messenger of Allah." Allah knows that you are indeed His Messenger, and Allah bears witness that the hypocrites are indeed liars.

63.2. They have made their oaths a way (to hide what they really are and) like this they stop (men) from the Path of Allah: Truly, their deeds are evil.

63.3. That is because they had believed, and then they disbelieved; So a seal was set on their hearts; Therefore, they do not understand.

63.4.. And when you look at them, their bodies (that they show) please you; And when they speak, you listen to their words. They are like blocks of wood propped up, (unable to stand by themselves). They think that every cry is against them. They are the enemies, so (keep yourselves) beware of them. May the curse of Allah be on them! How are they deluded (away from the right truth).

63.5. And when it is said to them, "Come, that the Messenger of Allah may pray for your forgiveness (from Allah) for you," they turn aside their heads, and you could see them turning away their faces in arrogance.

63.6.. It is equal (all the same) for them whether you (O Prophet!) pray for their forgiveness or pray not for their forgiveness; Allah will not forgive them. Truly Allah guides not those who rebel and transgress.

63.7. They are the ones who say: "Spend nothing on those who are with Allah's Messenger, until they may disperse (and quit Medinah)." And to Allah belong the treasures of the heavens and the earth; But the hypocrites do not understand.

63.8. They say: "If we return to Medinah, surely, the more honorable (element) will expel from there the weaker." But honor belongs to Allah and to His Messenger, and to the believers; But the hypocrites do not know.

63.9.. O you who believe! Let not your properties nor your children distract you from remembering Allah. If any act like this, the loss is their own.

63.10. And spend something (in charity) out of the sustenance that We have bestowed on you, before death should come to any of you and he should say, "My Lord! Why did You not give me relief for a little while? I should then have given (largely) in charity, and I should have been one of those who do good (deeds)."

63.11. And Allah grants relief to none when the appointed time (for it) has come; And Allah knows well of (all) that you do.

****

Sura 64. At-Taghabun,
(The mutual loss and gain): (Medinah, 18 Verses)
In the Name of Allah, the Most Gracious, the Most Merciful.

64.1.. Whatever is in the heavens and whatever is on earth, glorifies of Allah: His is the (entire) Dominion, and to Him belongs all the Praise (and thanks) and He is Able to do all things.

64.2. It is He, Who has created you; Some of you are unbelievers, and some of you are believers: And Allah is All Seeing of all that you do.

64.3. He has created the heavens and the earth in proper proportions, and has given you shape, and made your shapes beautiful: And to Him is the final return.

64.4. He knows what is in the heavens and (what is) on earth; And He knows what you hide and what you reveal: And Allah is All Knower of what (secret) lies in the breasts (and hearts of men).

64.5.. Has the story not reached you, of the disbelievers before you? And so they tasted the evil result of their conduct; And they had a painful penalty.

64.6. That was because messengers came to them with clear proofs, but they said: "Shall (mere) human beings direct us?" So they rejected (the Message) and turned away. But Allah is Free of all Needs, worthy of all Praise.

64.7.. The unbelievers think that they will not be raised up (for Judgment), say: "O Yes! By my Lord, you shall surely be raised up: Then shall you be told (the truth) of all that you did, and that is easy for Allah."

64.8. Therefore, believe in Allah and His Messenger, and in the Light that We have sent down. And Allah is All Aware of all that you do.

64.9. The Day when He assembles you (all) for a Day of Assembly- That will be a day of mutual loss and gain (among you), and (for) those who believe in Allah and do righteous deeds- He will remove from them their sorrows, and He will admit them to Gardens beneath rivers flow, to live in there forever: That will be the supreme achievement.

64.10. But those who reject Faith and treat Our Signs as lies, they will be companions of the Fire to live in there forever: And evil is that goal.

64.11.. No type of misfortune can occur, except by the permission of Allah: And if anyone believes in Allah, (Allah) guides his heart (towards right): And Allah is All Knowing of all things.

64.12. And obey Allah, and obey His Messenger: But if you turn away, the duty of Our Messenger is only to announce (the Message) clearly and openly.

64.13. Allah! There is no god but He: And in Allah (Alone), therefore, let the believers put their trust.

64.14.. O you who believe! Truly, among your wives and your children are (some that are) enemies to yourselves: So be aware of them! But if you forgive them and overlook, and cover up (their faults), Surely Allah is Often Forgiving, Most Merciful .

64.15. Your wealth and your children may be a trial: But in the Presence of Allah is the Highest Reward.

64.16.. So fear Allah as much as you can; Listen and obey; And spend in charity for the benefit of your own souls! And those saved from the selfishness for themselves- Then they are the ones who achieve abundance (and wealth).

64.17. If you loan to Allah a beautiful loan, He will double it to your (credit), and He will grant you Forgiveness: And Allah is Most ready to appreciate and reward, Most Forbearing.

64.18. (Allah is the) All Knower of what is hidden and of what is open, the Almighty , the All Wise

****

Sura 65. At-Talaq,
(The divorce): (Medinah, 12 Verses)
In the Name of Allah, the Most Gracious, the Most Merciful.

65.1.. O Prophet! When you (Muslims) divorce women, divorce them at their prescribed periods, and count their prescribed periods (accurately). (The Prophet himself never divorced any of his wives.) And fear Allah, your Lord: And turn them not out of their houses, nor shall they (themselves) leave except in case they are guilty of some clear and serious (sexual) misconduct. And these are the set-limits by Allah. And whosoever transgresses the set-limits of Allah, does indeed wrong his (own) soul: You do not know if by chance, Allah will bring about some new situation (later on).

65.2. When they fulfill their appointed term, either take them back in a good (and honorable) manner or part with them in a good (and honorable) manner. And take for witness two persons from among you, blessed with (a sense of) justice, and establish the evidence (as if you are) before Allah. Such is the guidance given to him who believes in Allah and the Last Day. And for those who fear Allah, He (always) prepares a way out.

65.3. And He provides for him by (means that) he could never imagine. And if anyone puts his trust in Allah, then (Allah) is sufficient for him. Surely, Allah will accomplish His Purpose. Truly, for all things Allah has appointed proper proportions.

65.4.. Such of your women who have passed the age of monthly courses, for them the prescribed period, if you have any doubts, (the period) is three months, and for those who have no courses (it is the same). And for those who carry (life within their wombs) their period is until they deliver their burden, and for he who fears Allah, He will make their path easy for him.

65.5. That is the Command of Allah, which He has sent down to you: And if anyone fears Allah, He will remove his sorrows from him, and will increase his reward.

65.6.. Let the women live (during waiting) in the same style as you live, according to your means: Do not annoy them, so as to restrict them. And if they carry (life in their wombs), then spend (your sustenance) on them until they deliver their burden: And if they suckle your (offspring) for you, give them their recompense: And mutually consult together, according to what is just and reasonable. And if you find yourselves in difficulties for one another, let another woman suckle (the child) on the (fathers) behalf.

65.7. Let the man of means spend according to his means: And the man whose resources are restricted, let him spend according to what Allah has given him. Allah puts no burden on any person beyond what He has given him. After a difficulty, Allah will soon grant relief.

65.8.. And how many towns (populations) that proudly opposed the command of their Lord and of His messengers; And have We called (them) to account- To severe account? And We imposed on them a strict punishment.

65.9. Then they tasted the evil result of their conduct, and the end of their action was (their) total loss.

65.10. Allah has prepared a severe punishment for them (in the Hereafter). Therefore fear Allah, O men of understanding- Those who have believed! Allah has indeed sent down to you a Reminder (and a Message; The Quran)-

65.11. A Messenger, who rehearses to you the Signs of Allah containing clear explanations, that he (the Prophet) may lead forth those who believe and do righteous deeds from the depths of darkness into light. And whosoever believe in Allah and do righteous good deeds, He (Allah) will admit him to Gardens beneath which rivers flow, to live in there forever; Allah has indeed granted for them a most excellent provision.

65.12. Allah is He Who has created seven Orbits (of heavenly planets) and of the earth a similar number. His Command descends between and through them: That you may know that Allah has power over all things, and that Allah comprehends all things in (His) Knowledge.

****

Sura 66. At-Tahrim,
(Holding (something) to be forbidden): (Medinah, 12 Verses)
In the Name of Allah, the Most Gracious, the Most Merciful.

66.1. O Prophet! Why do you forbid what Allah has made lawful to you? You seek to please your wives. And Allah is Often Forgiving, Most Merciful .

66.2. Allah has already made possible for you, (O men), to absolve your oaths (in some cases): And Allah is your Protector, and He is All Knowing , All Wise.

66.3.. And (remember) when the Prophet told in privacy a matter to one of his wives (Hafsah), and she then says it (to another, 'Âishah), and Allah made it known to him, he (the Prophet,) informed a part of it and questioned a part. Then when he (the Prophet) told her about it, she said, "Who told you this?" He said, "He (Allah) told me; (He) Who knows and is Well-Acquainted (with all things.)"

66.4. If you two turn in repentance to Him (Allah), with sincerity in your hearts; But if you support each other against him, truly Allah is his Protector, and *Jibrael* (Gabriel), and every righteous one among those who believe- And after that the angels -will support him.

66.5.. It may be, if he (the Prophet) divorced you (all) that Allah will give him in exchange wives better than you- Who submit (their wills), who believe, who are (devoutly) obedient, who turn to Allah in repentance, who sincerely worship (in humility) who travel (for their faith in Islam) and who fast- Previously married or virgins.

66.6. O you who believe! Save yourselves and your families from a Fire whose fuel is men and stones, over which are (appointed) angels strong and severe, who do not hesitate (from executing) the commands they receive from Allah, but do (precisely) what they are commanded.

66.7. (They will say) "O you unbelievers! Make no excuses this Day! You are only being punished for all that you did!"

66.8.. O you who believe! Turn to Allah with sincere repentance: In the hope that your Lord will remove from you your sorrows and admit you to Gardens beneath which rivers flow- The Day that Allah will not disgrace the Prophet and those who believe with him, their light will run before them and on their right hands, while they say, "Our Lord! Perfect our light for us, and grant us forgiveness: Verily, You are Able to do all things."

66.9.. O Prophet! Strive (work) hard against the unbelievers and the hypocrites, and be firm against them. Their home is Hell- And (it is) an evil refuge (indeed).

66.10.. Allah has set forth, for an example to the unbelievers, the wife of Nuh (Noah), and the wife of Lut (Lot); They were each under two of Our righteous servants, but they were untrue to their (husbands), and they gained nothing before Allah on their account, but they were told: "You enter the Fire along with (others) who enter!"

66.11. And Allah has set forth, as an example to those who believe the wife of Firon (Pharaoh): When she said: "My Lord! Build for me, in nearness to You, a mansion in the Garden, and save me from Firon (Pharaoh) and his (evil) actions, and save me from those who do wrong;"

66.12. And Maryam (Mary), the daughter of Imran, she guarded her chastity; And We breathed into (her body) of Our Spirit and she testified to the truth of the words of her Lord and the Books (of Revelation) and was one of the devout (servants).

****

Sura 67. Al-Mulk,

(The Dominion): (Makkah, 30 Verses)

In the Name of Allah, the Most Gracious, the Most Merciful.

67.1.. Blessed be He in Whose hands is the Dominion; And He is All Powerful, Able to do all things;

67.2. He Who created Death and Life, that He may test which of you is best in deed: And He is the Almighty , the Often Forgiving -

67.3. He Who created the seven heavens one above the other: You will see no want of proportion in the Creation of (Allah) Most Gracious. So look again, do you see any flaw?

67.4. Then look again and once again: (And) your vision will come back to you dull and disjointed, in a worn out condition.

67.5. And indeed, We have decorated the lowest heaven with lamps, and We have made them (like) missiles to drive away the Satans, and have prepared for them the penalty of the blazing Fire.

67.6.. And for those who disbelieve in their Lord (and Cherisher) is the Penalty of Hell: And evil is (their) destination.

67.7. When they are cast therein, they will hear the (terrible) sighing of its breath even as it blazes forth,

67.8. It almost flares up in fury: Every time a group is cast therein, its keepers will ask, "Did no Warner come to you?"

67.9. And they will say: "Yes, indeed a Warner did come to us but we rejected him and said (to him), Allah did not send down any (Message): You are making a serious error!"

67.10. And they will also say: "Had we only listened or used our understanding, we should not (now) be among the companions of the blazing Fire!"

67.11. Then they will confess their sins: (But forgiveness will be far), so away with the dwellers of the blazing Fire!

67.12.. Verily, those who fear their Lord Unseen, for them is forgiveness and a great reward.

67.13. And whether you hide your word in secret or make it known, He is the All Knowing , of what is in the breasts (men's hearts).

67.14. Would He not know- He Who has created? And He is the Most Generous (to His servants and He is) the All Aware.

67.15.. It is He Who has made the earth manageable (and amenable) for you, so you may travel through its open lands and enjoy the gifts which He furnishes: And to Him is the Resurrection.

67.16. Do you feel secure that He Who is in Heaven will not cause you to be swallowed up by the earth when it rumbles (as if it is an earthquake)?

67.17. Or do you feel secure that He Who is in Heaven will not send against you a violent tornado (with gravel and stones) so that you shall know how (terrible) was My warning (to them)?

67.18. And indeed men before them rejected (My warning): Then how (terrible) was My rejection (of them)?

67.19.. Do they not watch the birds above them, spreading their wings and folding them in? None can uphold them except (Allah) Most Gracious. Truly, it is He who is All Seeing all things.

67.20. Who is there besides (Allah) Most Gracious who can help you, (even if it was) an army? But the unbelievers are in nothing but a delusion (and serious mistake).

67.21. Or who is there who can give you sustenance if He were to withhold His provision? But, they (the unbelievers) knowingly continue in willful disbelief and escape (from the Truth).

67.22.. Is then (the man) who walks headlong, with his face bitter and marred, better guided- Or the one who walks evenly on the Straight Path?

67.23. Say: "It is He, Who has created you (and made you grow), and made for you the faculties of hearing, (and) seeing, (feeling with your) heart (and its kindness): Little thanks it is you give."

67.24. Say: "It is He, Who has created you on the earth, and to Him shall you be gathered together."

67.25.. They ask: "When will this promise be (fulfilled)? If you are telling the truth."

67.26. Say: "As to the knowledge of the time, it is with Allah Alone: I am (sent) only to warn plainly in public."

67.27. At length, when they see it (the time) close at hand, painful will be the faces of the unbelievers, and it will be said (to them): This is (the Promise fulfilled), which you were asking for!

67.28.. Say: "Do you see? If Allah were to destroy me, and those with me, or if He bestows His Mercy on us- Yet who can deliver the unbelievers from a grievous Penalty?"

67.29. Say: "He is (Allah), Most Gracious: We have believed in Him, and on Him have we put our trust: So, soon will you know which (of us) who is in serious error."

67.30. Say: "Do you see? - That if your streams (in the underground earth), on some morning become lost, then who can supply you with clear-flowing water?"

****

Sura 68. Al-Qalam,
(The pen or Nu'n): (Medinah, 52 Verses)
In the Name of Allah, the Most Gracious, the Most Merciful.

68.1. Nu'n, (the Pen): By the Pen and by the (Record) which (men) write-

68.2. You (O Prophet!) are not, by the grace of your Lord, mad, insane or possessed.

68.3. No (in reality), and surely, for you is a reward unfailing:

68.4. And verily, you (are placed) on an exalted standard of character.

68.5. Soon will you see, and they will see,

68.6. Which of you is affected with madness.

68.7. Surely, it is your Lord Who knows best, which (among men) has strayed from His Path: And He Knows best those who receive (true) Guidance.

68.8.. So listen not to those who deny (the Truth).

68.9. Their desire is that you should be suffering: So they would be suffering.

68.10.. Do not pay attention to the type of lowly man- Ready with (false) words,

68.11. A slanderer, going about with hurtful falsehoods,

68.12. (By habit) stopping (all) good, exceeding all bounds (and) deep in sin.

68.13. Violent (and cruel) and in addition a shrewd manipulator-

68.14. Because he possesses wealth and numerous sons.

68.15. When Our Signs are rehearsed to him, he cries; "Tales of the men of old (ancient peoples),"

68.16. Soon shall We brand (the beast) on the nose!

68.17.. Surely, We have tried them as We tried the People of the Garden, when they swore to pluck the fruits of the (garden) in the morning,

68.18. But made no reservation, (by saying: "Inshâ-Allah", or "If Allah Wills it.")

68.19. Then there came on the (garden) a visitation from your Lord, (which swept away) all around while they were asleep.

68.20. So the (garden) became, by the morning, like a dark desolate spot (whose fruit had been gathered).

68.21. As the morning broke, they called out, one to another-

68.22. Saying: "You go to your garden early in the morning, if you were to gather the fruits."

68.23. And so they departed, conversing in secret low tones, (saying)

68.24. "Let not a single needy person break in upon you into the (garden) this day."

68.25.. And they opened the morning, strong in an (unjust) claim.

68.26. But when they saw the (garden) they said: "We have surely lost our way:

68.27. "Nay! Indeed we are denied (of the fruits of our labor)!"

68.28. Said one (person) more just than the rest of them: "Did I not say to you; Why not Glorify [Allah by saying, if Allah so Wills, (or Insha Allah)]?"

68.29. They said: "Glory to our Lord! Surely, we have been doing wrong!"

68.30. Then they turned, one against another, in blame.

68.31. They said: "Woe be unto us! We have indeed exceeded our limits;

68.32. "It may be that our Lord will give us in exchange a better (garden) than this: Truly, we do turn to Him (in repentance)!"

68.33. Such is the punishment (in this life); But surely, greater is the Punishment in the Hereafter- If only they knew!

68.34.. Surely, for the righteous, are the Gardens of Delight, in the Presence of their Lord.

68.35. Shall We then treat the people of faith like (We treat) the criminals (and the peoples of sin)?

68.36. What is the matter with you? How can you judge?

68.37. Or do you have a Book through which you learn-

68.38. That you shall have, through it whatever you choose?

68.39. Or have you promises with Us on oath reaching to the Day of Judgment, (providing) that you shall have whatever you shall demand?

68.40. You ask of them, which of them will stand guarantee for that!

68.41. Or have they some (false) 'partners' (in godhead referring the Nasrani's idle notion of trinity)? Then let them produce their 'partners', if they are truthful!

68.42.. The Day that when the Shin shall be laid bare, and they shall be summoned to prostrate themselves but they (the hypocrites) shall not be able to do so.-

68.43. Their eyes will be cast down- Intense shame will cover them: Seeing that they had been summoned before to prostrate themselves (in love and prayer to Allah and His admiration) while they were whole, (human beings in this world and they had refused).

68.44. Then leave Me Alone with those who falsify this Message: By degrees shall We punish them from directions they perceive not.

68.45. A (long) time will I give for them: (But) truly Powerful is My plan.

68.46. Or is it that you do ask them for a reward, so that they are not burdened with a load of debt?

68.47. Or that the unseen is in their hands, so that they can write it down?

68.48.. So wait with patience for the Decision of your Lord, and be not like the companion of the Fish when he cried out (to his Lord) in grief (see 21.87)

68.49. Had not the Grace from His Lord reached him, he would indeed, have remained (within the fish and not) cast off on the naked shore, while he was to be blamed.

68.50. Thus did his Lord choose him and grant him the company of the righteous.

68.51.. And verily, the unbelievers would almost deceive with their eyes when they hear the Reminder (the Quran); And they say: "Surely, he is possessed!"

68.52. But it is nothing other than a Message to all creatures (men jinns' and all creations of) the worlds.

****

Sura 69. Al-Háqqa,
(The sure reality): (Makkah, 52 Verses)
In the Name of Allah, the Most Gracious, the Most Merciful.

69.1. The Sure Reality! (The Word and Retribution of Allah.)

69.2. What is the Sure Reality?

69.3. And what will make you realize what the Sure Reality is?

69.4.. The Samood (Thamud) and the 'Ad people (treated) the stunning calamity as false!

69.5. But the Samood (Thamud)- They were destroyed by a terrible storm of thunder and lightning!

69.6. And the 'Ad- They were destroyed by a furious wind extremely fierce;

69.7. Which (wind) He (Allah) made it rage against them for seven nights and eight days continuously so that you could see all the people lying on their faces in its (path), as if they had been roots of hollow palm-trees tumbled down!

69.8. Then do you see any of them left (still) living?

69.9.. And Firon (Pharaoh), and those before him and the cities overthrown, committed the same habitual sin,

69.10. And (each) disobeyed the messenger of their Lord: So He punished them with a severe penalty.

69.11. Verily, when the water (of Nuh's Flood) overflowed beyond its limits, We carried you (mankind) in the floating Ark,

69.12. That We might make it a Message for you, that (your) ears (may listen) and retain (its extraordinary lessons) in memory

69.13.. Then, when the blast is sounded on the Trumpet once,

69.14. And the earth and its mountains shall be dislodged from their places and are crushed to powder at one stroke-

69.15. On that Day shall the Event (and Reality) become true,

69.16. And the sky will be split apart, for that Day will be flimsy and torn apart,

69.17. And the angels will be on its (the sky) sides, and on that Day eight (angels) will bear the Throne of your Lord above them.

69.18.. That Day shall you be brought to Judgment: Not (even) one act of yours that you hide will be hidden.

69.19. Then he who will be given his record in his right hand will say: "Here! Read my record!

69.20. "Surely, I did really know that my account would (One Day) reach me!"

69.21. So, he will be in a life of (ultimate) joy,

69.22. In a Garden placed high,

69.23. The fruits in bunches there, will be low and near at hand.

69.24. (The greeting will be:) "You eat and drink, with full satisfaction; Because of the good that you sent before you, in the days that are gone!"

69.25.. And he who will be given his record in his left hand, will say: "I wish my record was not been given to me!

69.26. "And that I had never known what my account (contained)!

69.27. "Would that (death) had made an end of me!

69.28. "My wealth has been of no profit to me!

69.29. "My power has departed from me!"...

69.30.. (The command will be:) "Seize him and bind (shackle) him,

69.31. "And throw him in the blazing Fire.

69.32. "Further, make him march in a chain, whose length is seventy cubits (≈112 ft)!

69.33. "He was one, who would not believe in Allah, the Most Great,

69.34. "And would not encourage the feeding of those in need!

69.35. "So, no friend does he have here this Day.

69.36. "Nor does he have any food (here) except the corruption from the washing of wound,

69.37. "Which none do eat except those who have sinned."

69.38.. So, I swear by what you see

69.39. And what you see not,

69.40. That this is truly the word of an honorable Messenger (of Allah, the Prophet Muhammad);

69.41. It is not the word of a poet: Little it is you believe!

69.42. Nor is it the word of a soothsayer (or a fortune teller): Little warning (and advice) it is, that you receive.

69.43. (This is) a Message sent down from the Lord of the Worlds .

69.44.. And if he (the Messenger) were to invent any saying in Our Name,

69.45. We should certainly have seized him by his right hand,

69.46. And then We certainly would have cut off the artery of his heart

69.47. Nor could any of you withhold him (from Our Anger).

69.48.. But truly this is a Reminder (the Quran) for those who fear Allah.

69.49. And We certainly, know that there are among you those who reject (it).

69.50. But truly, it (the Reminder, this Quran) is a cause of sorrow for the unbelievers.

69.51. And verily, it (the Quran) is the Truth of total certainty.

69.52. So glorify the Name of your Lord the Most Great.

****

Sura 70. Al-Ma'árij,
(The way of ascent): (Makkah, 44 Verses)
In the Name of Allah, the Most Gracious, the Most Merciful.

70.1. A questioner asked about the penalty to befall (yet to happen)-

70.2. Upon the unbelievers- There is none that can avert (the penalty)-

70.3. (A penalty) from Allah, Lord of the Ways of Ascent.

70.4. The angels and the Spirit [*Jibrael* (Gabriel)] rise up to Him in a Day whose measure is fifty thousand years:

70.5. Therefore you stay patient- With a good Patience (of beautiful contentment).

70.6. They see the (Day) indeed as a far-off (event):

70.7. But We see it (quite) near.

70.8.. The Day that the sky will be like molten brass,

70.9. And the mountains will be like wool,

70.10. And no friend will ask about a friend,

70.11. Though they will be put in sight of each other- The sinners (only) wish will be that he could save himself from the penalty of that Day by (even offering) his children.

70.12. His wife and his brother,

70.13. And his relatives who sheltered him,

70.14. And all, all that is on earth- So that it could save him -

70.15. By no means! Verily, it would be the Fire of Hell!

70.16. Tearing out (his existence) right out of his skull!

70.17. Inviting (all) those who turn their backs and turn away their faces (from the right),

70.18. And collect (wealth) and hide it (from use for Allah)!

70.19. Truly, man was created very impatient-

70.20. Anxious and angry when evil touches him;

70.21. And miserly when good reaches him-

70.22. Not so (are) those devoted to prayer-

70.23. Those who remain steadfast to their prayer;

70.24. And those in whose wealth, is a recognized right (of Allah);

70.25. For the (needy) who ask and him who is prevented (for some reason from asking);

70.26. And those who hold to the Truth of the Day of Judgment;

70.27. And those who fear the displeasure of their Lord-

70.28. Verily, their Lord's displeasure is the opposite of peace and serenity:-

70.29. And those who guard their chastity (and sexuality),

70.30. Except from their wives and the (captive) whom their right hand possess- For (them), they are not to be blameworthy,

70.31. But those who go beyond this are transgressors-

70.32. And those who respect their trusts and covenants;

70.33. And those who stand firm in their testimonies;

70.34. And those who safeguard (the sacredness) of their worship-

70.35. Such will be the honored ones in the Gardens (of Joy).

70.36.. So, what is the matter with the unbelievers that they rush madly before you-

70.37. From the right and from the left in crowds?

70.38. Does every man from them wish to enter the Paradise (and the Garden of Joy)?

70.39. Definitely no! Verily, We have created them out of the (base matter) they know!

70.40.. But now, I swear by the Lord of (every point in) the Easts' and the Wests' that We can certainly-

70.41. Substitute them by others better (men) than them; And We are not to be defeated (in Our Plan).

70.42. So, leave them to sink in idle talk and play about- Until they encounter that Day of theirs that they have been promised!

70.43. The Day when they will come out of from their graves in sudden haste as if they were rushing to a goal-post (fixed for them)-

70.44. With their eyes lowered in sadness- Fear and shame covering them (all over)! That is the Day that they were promised!

****

Sura 71. Nuh,

(The prophet Noah): (Makkah, 28 Verses)
In the Name of Allah, the Most Gracious, the Most Merciful.

71.1. Verily, We sent Nuh (Noah) to his people (with the command, saying): "Warn your people before there comes to them a painful penalty."

71.2. He said: "O my people! Verily, I am an open Warner to you:

71.3. "That you should worship Allah, fear Him and obey me:

71.4. "So He will forgive you your sins and give you relief for a fixed (and written) time: Verily, when the time is finished by Allah it cannot be put forward (changed or altered): If you only knew:"

71.5.. He said: "O my Lord! Verily, I have called to my people night and day:

71.6. "But my calling them only increases (their) flight (from the right).

71.7. "And verily, every time I have called to them, that You may forgive them, they have (only) pushed their fingers into their ears, covered themselves up with their clothes, grown firmer (against faith), and given themselves up to false pride.

71.8. "Then verily, I have called them loudly;

71.9. "Then verily, I have spoken to them in public and secretly in private,

71.10. "Saying to them, 'Ask forgiveness from your Lord; Verily, He is Often Forgiving;

71.11. " 'He will send rain to you in plenty;

71.12. " 'Give you increase in wealth and children; And grant to you gardens and grant to you rivers (of flowing water),

71.13. " 'What is the matter with you, that you do not place your hope for kindness and long-suffering in Allah-

71.14. " 'Seeing that it is He Who has created you in many different stages?

71.15. " 'Do you not see how Allah has created the seven heavens, one above another,

71.16. " 'And made the moon a light in the middle, and made the sun as a (glorious) lamp,

71.17. " 'And Allah has produced you from the earth, growing (you gradually),

71.18. " 'And in the end, He will return you into the (earth) and raise you up (again at the Resurrection),

71.19. " 'And Allah has made the earth for you as a carpet (a wide expanse, spread out),

71.20. " 'That you may go about in there on broad and spacious roads?' "

71.21.. Nuh (Noah) said: "My Lord! They have disobeyed me, and they follow one whose wealth and children give them no increase but only loss.

71.22. "And they have planned a huge (and evil) plot.

71.23. "And they have said (to each other); 'do not give up your gods: And do not give up Wadd, nor Suwa, neither Yaguth, nor Ya'uq, nor Nasr'-" (These are the false gods of the people of Nuh)

71.24. "And indeed, they have already misled many; And (Allah,) You grant no increase to the wrongdoers but in wandering (aimlessly in their goal)."

71.25. Because of their sins they were drowned (in the Flood), and they were made to enter the Fire (of punishment) and they found- Other than Allah, none to help them.

71.26.. And Nuh (Noah) said: "My Lord! Do not leave of the unbelievers, (even) a single one on earth!

71.27. "For, if You do leave (any of) them, they will only mislead Your servants and they will breed only the wicked ungrateful ones.

71.28. "My Lord! Forgive me, and my parents, and all who enter my house in Faith, and (all) believing men and believing women. And to the wrongdoers, You grant them no increase except in their loss!"

****

Sura 72. Al-Jinn,
(The spirits): (Makkah, 28 Verses)
In the Name of Allah, the Most Gracious, the Most Merciful.

72.1.. Say: "It has been revealed to me that an assembly of jinns' listened (to the Quran). They said, 'Verily, we have really heard a Wonderful Recitation (this Quran)!

72.2. " 'It gives guidance to the Right (Path,) and we have believed in it (what is read, i.e., the Quran): We shall not join (in worship) any (gods) with our Lord.

72.3. " 'And unequaled is the Majesty of our Lord: He has taken neither a wife nor a son.

72.4. " 'And that the foolish ones among us, who used to say terrible and worst lies against Allah;

72.5. " 'And verily, we do think that no man or spirit (among jinns') should say anything that is untrue against Allah.

72.6.. " '(It is) true, there were persons among mankind who took shelter with persons (other personifications) among the jinns', but they (only) increased them in their mistakes.

72.7. " 'And they (used to) think as you thought, that Allah would not raise up anyone (to Judgment).

72.8. " 'And we have wanted to reach the (secrets of) heavens; But we found it filled with strong (and unfailing) guards and flaming fires (and shooting stars).

72.9. " 'And verily, we used indeed, to sit there in (the hidden) places, to listen in but anyone who listens now will find a flaming fire (and shooting stars) watching him in hiding (to drive him away).

72.10. " 'And we do not understand whether suffering is intended for those on earth, or whether their Lord intends to guide them to the right conduct.

72.11.. " 'There are some among us who are righteous, and some (that are) the opposite:- We are assemblies (of jinns') having different ways.

72.12. " 'But we think that we cannot resist Allah all through the earth, nor can we resist Him by flight.

72.13. " 'And indeed for us, since we have listened to the Guidance, (from the Quran), we have believed therein: And anyone who believes in his Lord (he or she) has no fear, neither of a decrease in reward for the good deeds, nor an increase in punishment for the sins.

72.14. " 'And among us are some who submit their wills (to Allah as Muslims), and some who wander away from justice. Now those who submit their wills (as Muslims)- They have sought the right Path:

72.15. " 'And those who wander away (from the right Path)- They are (only) fuel for fire of Hell ' "-

72.16.. (And Allah's Message is): "If they (the pagan) had (only) believed in Allah and walked on the (right) Path, we should certainly have granted (in kindness) to them (the) bountiful rain.

72.17. "That We might try them by that (means), and if anyone turns away from remembering his Lord, he will cause (for himself) to undergo a severe penalty.

72.18. "And the places of worship are for Allah (Alone): So do not pray to anyone along with Allah;

72.19. "And when the one devoted (the Prophet) to Allah stands forward to pray to Him, they (the jinns') just make around him a dense crowd as if sticking to one over the other (to listen)."

72.20. Say: "I do no more than call upon my Lord, and I do not join any (false gods) with Him."

72.21. Say: "It is not in my power to cause you harm, nor to bring you to right conduct."

72.22. Say: "No one can save me from Allah's punishment, (if I were to disobey Him) nor should I find protection except in Him,

72.23. "Unless I proclaim what I receive from Allah and His Messages; For whoever that disobeyed Allah and His Messenger- Then verily, for him (the one who disobeys) is Hell:- He shall live in there forever."

72.24.. At length, when they see (with their own eyes) that which they are promised- Then will they know who is the one weakest as (their) helper and least important in point of numbers.

72.25. Say: "I do not know whether the (punishment) which you are promised is near or whether my Lord will appoint for it a long time (later).

72.26. "He (Allah, Alone) is All Knowledgeable of the Unseen, nor does He make anyone familiar with His Unseen mysteries-

72.27. "Except a messenger whom He has chosen, and then He makes a band of watchers (angels) march before him and behind him.

72.28. "That he (the messenger) may know that they have (truly) brought and delivered the Messages of their Lord. And He surrounds (all with mysteries) that are with them, and takes account of every single thing."

****

Sura 73. Al-Muzzammil,
(The one folded in garments): (Makkah, 20 Verses)
In the Name of Allah, the Most Gracious, the Most Merciful.

73.1.. O you (Prophet! Clothed and) folded up in garments!

73.2. Stand up (in prayer) by night, except a little (less)-

73.3. Half of it (the night), or less than that by a little,

73.4. Or a little more; And recite the Quran in slow, stately (and) rhythmic tones.

73.5.. Verily, soon We shall send down upon you a weighty message.

73.6. Truly, the rising by night is most powerful for governing (the soul) and most suitable for (understanding) the Word (of Prayer and Praise)

73.7. Verily, for you by the day, there is long (and hard) work with ordinary duties:

73.8. And keep remembering the Name of your Lord and devote yourself to Him entirely.

73.9. (He is) Lord of the east and the west: There is no god but He: Therefore take Him to be the disposer of (your) affairs.

73.10. And have patience with what they say, and leave them with noble (dignity).

73.11. And leave Me Alone to deal with those in possession of the good things of life, who (still) reject the Truth; And (patiently) give them respite for a little while.

73.12. With Us are shackles (to bind them), and a Fire (to burn them),

73.13. And a food that chokes, and a penalty that is painful.

73.14. On the Day when the earth and the mountains will be in violent bang and the mountains will be like a heap of sand poured out and flowing down.

73.15.. Verily, We have sent to you (O men!) a Messenger, (the Prophet) to be a witness about yourselves, like We had sent a messenger (Musa) to Firon (Pharaoh).

73.16. But Firon (Pharaoh) did not obey the messenger; So We seized him with a stiff punishment.

73.17. Then how shall you, if you deny (Allah) save yourselves against the punishment of Allah on a Day that will change children into gray-headed (old men)-

73.18. When the sky will be torn apart- His Promise certainly will come true!

73.19. Surely, this is a (stern) warning and a guidance! Therefore, whoever wishes, let him take a (straight) Path to his Lord!

73.20.. Verily, (O Prophet), your Lord knows that you stand up (to prayer) a little less than two-thirds of the night, or half the night, or a third of the night, and so do some of those with you. And Allah measures the night and day in proper parts. He knows that you are not able to keep praying the whole night. So He has turned to you (in His Mercy), therefore you read the Quran as much as it may be easy for you. He knows that there may be (some) among you that are sick; Others traveling through the land, seeking of Allah's Bounty; Yet others fighting in Allah's Cause. You recite, therefore, as much of the Quran as may be easy (for you); And establish regular prayer and give regular charity; And loan to Allah a beautiful loan. And whatever good you send forward for your souls, you shall find it in Allah's Presence: Yes, better and greater, in reward. And you seek the Forgiveness of Allah: Verily, Allah is Often Forgiving, Most Merciful .

****

Sura 74. Al-Muddaththir,
(The one wrapped up): (Makkah, 56 Verses)
In the Name of Allah, the Most Gracious, the Most Merciful.

74.1.. O you (Prophet) wrapped up (in garments, blanket)!

74.2. Get up and announce your warning!

74.3. And you praise your Lord!

74.4. And keep your clothes cleansed!

74.5. And stay away from all pollution!

74.6. And do not expect, in giving (the warning), any gain (for yourself)!

74.7. And for (the duties) to your Lord be patient and unchanging!

74.8.. Then, when the trumpet is sounded,

74.9. Truly, that will be - That Day, - A Day of suffering-

74.10. Far from being easy for the disbelievers.

74.11.. Leave Me Alone, to deal with the (creature) whom I created (bare and) alone!

74.12. And then to whom I (reference to Allah, have) granted resources in plenty,

74.13. And children to be by his side! -

74.14. And made (life) smooth and comfortable for him!

74.15. Yet is he greedy that I should add (more and more), -

74.16. Nay! Truly, he has been opposing Our Signs (*Ayât*)!

74.17. Soon will I visit him with a mountain of miseries!

74.18.. Verily, he thought and he plotted-

74.19. So, let him be the cursed (one)! How he plotted!

74.20. And again let him be the cursed (one)! How he plotted!

74.21. Then he thought (a little);

74.22. Then he and frowned (in anger) and glowered (with rage);

74.23. Then he turned back and was haughty;

74.24. Then he said: "This is nothing but magic taken from the old;

74.25. "This is nothing but the word of a (mere) human being!"

74.26.. Soon will I throw him into the Fire of Hell!

74.27. And what will explain to you what is the Fire of Hell?

74.28. Neither will it permit to tolerate, nor does it leave alone!

74.29. Darkening and changing (and burning away) the color of man!

74.30.. Over it are nineteen (angels as the keepers).

74.31. And We have set none but angels as guardians of the Fire: And We have fixed their number (at 19 and it is so written in other Books) confirming it only as a trial for unbelievers- So that the People of the Book (Scripture) may become certain, and the believers may become convinced of their Faith- And that no doubts may be left for the People(s) of the Book (Scripture), and the believers; And that those in whose hearts is a disease (of hypocrisy) and the unbelievers may say, "What does Allah mean by this (symbol of 19 angels)?" Thus does Allah leave to wander those whom He pleases, and guide those whom He pleases. And none can know the forces of your Lord, except He. And this is no other than a warning to mankind.

74.32.. No, surely, by the moon,

74.33. And by the night, as it leaves,

74.34. And by the morning, as it shines forward-

74.35. Verily, this is but one of the mighty (events unfortunate to the disbelievers),

74.36. A warning to mankind-

74.37. To any one of you who chooses to move forward, or to those that fall behind-

74.38.. Every soul will be (held) to account for its deeds.

74.39. Except the companions of the right hand,

74.40. (They will be) in Gardens (of happiness): They will question each other,

74.41. And (ask) of the sinners:

74.42. "What led you into the Fire of Hell?"

74.43. They will say: "We were not from those who prayed;

74.44. "Nor were we from those who fed the poor;

74.45. "And we used to speak idle-talk with those who spoke against Truth,

74.46. "And we used to reject the Day of Judgment,

74.47. "Until there came upon us (the Hour) that is certain."

74.48. There will be no pleading or intercession from (any) pleaders (to) profit them.

74.49.. Then what is the matter with them that they turn away from plain warning-

74.50. As if they were frightened wild donkeys,

74.51. Running away from a lion!

74.52. No doubt, each one of them wants to be given scrolls (of Revelation from Allah) spread out!

74.53. By no means! But they fear not the Hereafter.

74.54. Nay! Verily, this surely is a (stern) warning:

74.55. Let any who will keep it (the warning) in memory!

74.56. And they will not keep it in memory (mind) except as Allah wills: He is the One Who deserving the righteousness (with prayer and supplication to Him) and He is the One Who grants forgiveness (of the sins).

****

Sura 75. Al-Qiyámah,
(The Resurrection): (Makkah, 40 Verses)
In the Name of Allah, the Most Gracious, the Most Merciful.

75.1.. I swear by the day of Resurrection (when the dead shall be awakened).

75.2. And I swear by the spirit that blames itself:

75.3.. Does man think that We cannot assemble his bones together?

75.4. Yes! We are able to put together the very tips of his fingers perfectly.

75.5. But man wishes to do wrong (even) in the time (now) for the time that is to come.

75.6. He asks: "When is the Day (of Resurrection)on which the dead shall be awakened?"

75.7.. (Say:) "Soon, when the sight is bewildered,

75.8. "And the moon is buried in darkness.

75.9. "And the sun and moon are joined together,"-

75.10. On that Day man will say: "Where is the place to flee?"

75.11. By no means! (There will be) no place of safety!

75.12. Before your Lord, that Day will be the place of rest.

75.13. On the Day will man be told (all) that he put in front of him and all that he put behind.

75.14. No! Man will be (a true) evidence against himself,

75.15. Even though he may give his excuses.

75.16.. Move not your tongue (O Prophet!) about the (Quran) to hurry on with it (in its reading).

75.17. It is for Us to put it together and to make it known and be recited.

75.18. And when We have it (known to you), then you follow its recitation (and form):

75.19. Then, it is for Us to explain it (and to make it clear):

75.20.. But no, (you men!) you love the present life of this world.

75.21. And neglect (and put aside) the Hereafter.

75.22. Some faces that Day, will glow (in brightness and beauty):-

75.23. Looking towards their Lord:

75.24. And some faces that Day, will be sad and sorry.

75.25. In the fear that some back-breaking unhappy action was about to be started upon them:

75.26. Yes, when (the soul) reaches the collar-bone (as it leaves the body)

75.27. And when there will be a cry (saying:), "Who is a magician (to put him together)?"

75.28. And he will conclude that it was (the time) of leaving (this world):

75.29. And one leg will be joined with another leg:

75.30. (All) the drive (movement) on that Day will be to your Lord!

75.31. But he disregarded (the truth), and he did not pray!

75.32. And even more, he lied (against the truth) and turned away!

75.33. Then he went back to his family with false pride!

75.34. Suffering and sorrow to you (woe unto you, O man!), and a great suffering to you!

75.35. Again, suffering and sorrow to you (woe unto you, O man!), and a great suffering to you!

75.36.. Does man think that he will be neglected (and left alone), (without purpose for which he was created)?

75.37. Was he not a drop of sperm emitted (without any form)?

75.38. Then did he become a leech-like clot; Then (Allah) made and gave (him) the right size and shape.

75.39. He made two sexes, male and female of him.

75.40. Does He not have, the Power to give life to the dead?

****

Sura 76. Ad-Dahr,

[Time also known as Al-Insan, (man)]: (Medinah, 31 Verses)
In the Name of Allah, the Most Gracious, the Most Merciful.

76.1.. Has there not been a long period of time, when man was nothing- (Not even) mentioned?

76.2. Surely We have created man from a drop of mixed sperm and ovary fluids, in order to try him, so, We gave him (the gifts) of hearing and of sight.

76.3. Verily, We showed him the Way: Whether he be thankful or not (rests upon his own will).

76.4. Verily, We have prepared for the disbelievers: Chains, shackles, and a blazing Fire.

76.5. As to the righteous: They shall drink of a cup blended with Kafur-

76.6. A fountain where the devoted servants of Allah drink, making it flow in plenty.

76.7. They make (their) vows, and they fear a Day whose sorrow spreads far and wide.

76.8. And they feed for the love of Allah the needy, the orphan, and the captive and the needy,-

76.9. (Saying), "We feed you for the sake of Allah Alone, no reward do we want from you, nor thanks.

76.10. "Verily, We only fear a Day of painful suffering (that may arrive) from the side of our Lord."

76.11. So, Allah will save them from the sorrow of that Day, and will spread over them a Light of beauty and a (cheerful) joy.

76.12. And because they were patient and steady, He will reward them with a Garden and (clothes of) silk.

76.13. Reclining in the (Garden) on raised couches (thrones), they will see there neither the sun's (extreme heat) nor the moon's (extreme cold).

76.14. And the shades of the (Garden) will come low over them, and the bunches (of fruit), there will hang low in (their) easy reach.

76.15. And among them will be passed round containers of silver and glasses of crystal-

76.16. Crystal-clear, made of silver: They will determine the amount in there (according to their wishes).

76.17. And they will be given to drink from a Cup (of drink) mixed with *Zanjabil* (ginger)-

76.18. A fountain there called *Salsabil.*

76.19. And round about them will (serve) youths of perpetual (freshness): If you were to see them you would think them as pearls scattered about.

76.20. And when you look, it is there that you will see a joy and a magnificent kingdom (an immense constellation of beauty).

76.21. Upon them will be green garments of fine silk and heavy ornaments and they will be decorated with bracelets of silver; And their Lord will give to them to drink a cleansing drink, pure and holy.

76.22. (It will be said to them:) "Surely, this is a reward for you, and your struggle (in life) is accepted and recognized."

76.23. Verily, it is We Who have sent down the Quran to you by stages.

76.24. Therefore be patient with uniformity to the Command of your Lord, and do not listen to the sinner or the thankless among them.

76.25. And praise (with joy) the Name of your Lord every morning (*Faj'r*) and afternoon (*Zuh'r* and *'Asr*).

76.26. And part of the night prostrate yourself to Him (*Maghrib* and *Isha* prayers) and glorify Him (in *Tahajjud* prayer) the long night through.

76.27. Verily, as to these (thankless), they love the present life of this world, and put away behind them a heavy Day (that will be) hard.

76.28. It is We Who created them, and We have made their joints strong; And when We (so) wish, We can replace them bringing others like them in their place.

76.29. Verily, this (Verse of the Quran) is a warning: So whoever wishes, let him take a (straight) Path to his Lord.

76.30. But you will not except as Allah wishes; Verily, Allah is Ever All Knowing , All Wise .

76.31. He will admit to His Mercy whomever He wishes; But the wrongdoers- For them, He has prepared a painful penalty.

76.27. Verily, as to these (thankless), they love the present life of this world, and put away behind them a heavy Day (that will be) hard.

76.28. It is We Who created them, and We have made their joints strong; And when We (so) wish, We can replace them bringing others like them in their place.

76.29. Verily, this [*Ayâh* (verse) of the Quran] is a warning: So whomever wishes let him come to his Lord on a (straight) Path.

76.30. But you will not, except as Allah wishes; Verily, Allah is Ever All Knowing , All Wise .

76.31. He will admit to His Mercy whomever He wishes; But the wrongdoers- For them, He has prepared a painful penalty.

****

Sura 77. Al-Mursalat,

(Those sent forth): (Makkah: 50 Verses)

In the Name of Allah, the Most Gracious, the Most Merciful.

77.1.. By the (winds) sent one after another,

77.2. Which then blow very hard in violent storms,

77.3. And drive (things and the clouds) far and wide;

77.4. Then separate them, one from another,

77.5. Then spread a Message,

77.6. Whether of justification or of warning

77.7. Surely, what has been promised to you (shall) really happen.

77.8.. Then when the stars lose their light (and glow);

77.9. And when the heaven is torn apart;

77.10. And when the mountains are blown (to the winds) as dust;

77.11. And when (all) the messengers are appointed a time (to gather)-

77.12. For what Day are these Signs (of Allah) deferred?

77.13. For the Day of Sorting out (those destined to paradise from those destined to Hell).

77.14. And what will explain to you what is the Day of Sorting out?

77.15. And, woe (sorrow and suffering), that Day for those (people) who reject the Truth.

77.16.. Did We not destroy the people before (for their evil ways)?

77.17. So shall We make later generations to follow them.

77.18. We deal with men of sin in this way.

77.19. And, woe (sorrow and suffering), that Day for those (people) who reject the Truth.

77.20.. Have We not created you from a fluid (held) in low esteem?

77.21. Then We placed in a place of rest (the womb), securely placed,

77.22. For a period (of growth) depending (upon the need of the infant)?

77.23. (And) We decide (the need); For We are the Best to decide (things).

77.24. And, woe (sorrow and suffering), that Day for those (people) who reject the Truth.

77.25.. Have We not made the earth (as a place) to bring together

77.26. For the living and the dead,

77.27. And made mountains in there standing firm, high (in stature) and provided for you water that is sweet (to drink)?

77.28. And, woe (sorrow and suffering), that Day for those (people) who reject the Truth.

77.29.. (It will be said to the disbelievers:) "You go to that which you used to reject (the Fire) as false!

77.30. "You go away to a shadow (of smoke climbing) in three columns,

77.31. "(Which gives) no shade with coolness, and is of no use against the fierce Fire.

77.32. "Verily, it (Hell) throws sparks (of fire huge) as Forts,

77.33. "As if there were (a string of) yellow camels (marching swiftly)."

77.34. And, woe (sorrow and suffering), that Day for those (people) who reject the Truth.

77.35.. That will be a Day when they shall not be able to speak (for parts of the Day), **77.36.** And they will not be allowed to bring out any excuse (begging for mercy).

77.37. And, woe (sorrow and suffering), that Day for those (people) who reject the Truth.

77.38.. That will be a Day of Judgment! We shall gather you and those before you together!

77.39. Now, if you have a trick (or plot), use it against Me!

77.40. And, woe (sorrow and suffering), that Day for those (people) who reject the Truth.

77.41.. Verily, as to the righteous (people) they shall be in (cool) shades and springs (of water).

77.42. And (they shall have) the fruits- All that they wish.

77.43. (It will be said to the righteous:) "Eat you and drink you to your hearts content: Because you (have) worked (towards righteousness).

77.44. Verily, We certainly reward the doers of good deeds, in this way.

77.45. And, woe (sorrow and suffering), that Day for those (people) who reject the Truth.

77.46.. (O you rejecters of the Truth,) you eat and enjoy yourselves (but) a little while, verily, you are the criminals (and sinners).

77.47. And, woe (sorrow and suffering), that Day for those (people) who reject the Truth.

77.48. And when it is said to them, "Bow yourselves (in Islam)!" They do not do so.

77.49. And, woe (sorrow and suffering), that Day for those (people) who reject the Truth.

77.50. Then, in what Message, after that (warning) will they believe?

****

Sura 78. An-Naba',

[The (great) news]: (Makkah: 40 Verses)

In the Name of Allah, the Most Gracious, the Most Merciful.

78.1. Concerning what are they asking?

78.2. Concerning the great news,

78.3. About which they cannot agree.

78.4. Surely, they shall soon know!

78.5. Surely, (but) surely, they shall soon know!

78.6. Have We not made the earth as a wide expanse (as a bed),

78.7. And the mountains as pegs?

78.8. And (have We not) created you in pairs,

78.9. And made your sleep for rest,

78.10. And made the night as an umbrella of peace,

78.11. And made the day for finding livelihood

78.12. And (have We not) built over you the seven strong arches of the heavens?

78.13. And placed (in there) a Light of brilliance?

78.14. And do We not send down from the clouds water, in plenty?

78.15. That We may produce with it, corn and vegetables,

78.16. And gardens of rich growth?

78.17. Surely, the Day of Judgment is an event appointed-

78.18. The Day that the Trumpet shall be sounded and you shall come forward in crowds;

78.19. And the heavens shall be opened as if there were doors,

78.20. And the mountains shall vanish, as if they were a mirage.

78.21. Truly, Hell is like a place of ambush-

78.22. For those who fought (against Faith); (Their) place of eternal stay:

78.23. They will live in there for ages.

78.24. Nothing cool shall they taste there, nor any drink,

78.25. Save a boiling fluid and a fluid, dark, grim, bitterly cold-

78.26. A fitting return (for their actions and for them).

78.27. Because, they did not fear any accounting (of their deeds),

78.28. But they (grimly) treated Our Signs as false.

78.29. And all things, We have preserved on record.

78.30. So taste you (the reward), because We shall not grant you any increase except in (your) punishment.

78.31. Surely, For the righteous there will be a fulfillment of (their hearts) desires;

78.32. Gardens enclosed, and grapevines;

78.33. Companions of equal age;

78.34. And a Cup full (to the very top).

78.35. In there, they shall not hear useless talk, vanity (and they shall not hear) anything false-

78.36. Reward from your Lord a gift, (large and) sufficient,

78.37. (From) the Lord of the heavens and the earth, and all between- (Allah) Most Gracious: None shall have power to argue with Him.

78.38. The Day that the Spirit (*Jibrael* or Gabriel) and the angels will stand forth in ranks, none shall speak, except anyone who is permitted by (Allah): Most Gracious, and he (the speaker) will say (only) what is correct.

78.39. Surely, that Day will be the Reality: Therefore, let anyone who wishes, let him take a (straight) path returning to his Lord!

78.40. Surely, We have warned you of a penalty near- The Day when man will see (the very acts) which his hands have sent forward, and the unbelievers will say, "Misery upon me! I may as well be (mere) dust!"

****

Sura 79. An-Nazi'at,
(Those who tear): (Makkah: 46 Verses)
In the Name of Allah, the Most Gracious, the Most Merciful.

79.1. By the (angels) who tear out (the soul of the wicked, from its depths) with great force:

79.2. By those who gently draw out (the soul of the blessed):

79.3. And by those who move along (the path of mercy),

79.4. Then move swiftly as if they were in a race,

79.5. Then arrange (themselves) to complete (the Commands of Allah)-

79.6. One Day, when everything that can be improper will be in violent

shock,

79.7. Followed by often repeated (shocks):

79.8. That Day, hearts will be trembling with fear:

79.9. The eyes (of men) will be looking down.

79.10.. (Now) they say: "What! Shall we really be returned to (our) former state?

79.11. "What! When we shall have become rotten bones?"

79.12. They say: "In that case, it will be a return with loss!"

79.13.. But surely, there will be a single (far reaching) cry,

79.14. And then watch! They will be (completely) awake (to receive Judgment).

79.15.. Has the story of Musa (Moses) reached you?

79.16. Listen, your Lord called out to him in the sacred valley of Tuwa:-

79.17. "You go to Firon (Pharaoh), because he has indeed exceeded all limits:

79.18. "And say to him: 'Would you (wish) that you should be purified (from sin)?

79.19. " 'And that I guide you to your Lord, so you should fear Him?' "

79.20. Then (Musa, Moses) showed him the great Sign,

79.21. But (Firon) rejected it and disobeyed (the guidance);

79.22. Also, he turned his back, working hard (against Allah).

79.23. Then he collected (his men) and made a (false) claim,

79.24. Saying, "I am your lord, most high,"

79.25. But Allah punished him, (and made) him an example- In the Hereafter, and in this life.

79.26. Surely, in this (instance) is a warning with guidance for those who fear (Allah).

79.27.. What! Are you (men) more difficult to make than the heaven (that Allah) has created:

79.28. High above has He raised its cover, and He has given it order and perfection.

79.29. At night He grants its darkness and its brightness He brings out (with light):

79.30. And more, He has extended the earth (far and wide also in the shape of an egg):

79.31. He draws out its moisture from there and its grazing lands;

79.32. And the mountains He has firmly fixed-

79.33. For use and benefit to you and your cattle.

79.34.. Therefore, when the great and fearful (event) comes!

79.35. The Day when man shall remember all what he struggled for.

79.36. And the Fire of Hell shall be placed in full sight for (everyone) to see-

79.37. Then for those that had exceeded all limits,

79.38. And (those who) had liked the life of this world,

79.39. The home will be the Fire of Hell;

79.40. And for those who had felt the fear of standing before their (Almighty) Lord and had restrained (their) souls from lowly desires,

79.41. Their home will be the Garden.

79.42.. They will ask you (O Prophet) about the Hour- "When will be its appointed time?"

79.43. How are you (even included) in the announcement of its time?

79.44. Your Lord (Alone) knows the limit fixed for it.

79.45. You are only a Warner for those who fear it.

79.46. The Day when they see it, (it will be) as if they had waited for it a single evening, or the following morning!

****

Sura 80. 'Abasa,

(He frowned): (Makkah: 42 Verses)

In the Name of Allah, the Most Gracious, the Most Merciful.

80.1.. (The Prophet) frowned and turned away,

80.2. Because there came to him the blind man (breaking into the discussion).

80.3. But what could tell you but that he (the blind man) might by chance grow (in his understanding)?

80.4. Or that he may receive guidance and the teachings that might profit him?

80.5. About the one who considers himself independent,

80.6. You attend to him;

80.7. Even though there is no blame on you if he did not grow (in understanding).

80.8. But to him (the blind man) who came to you with effort and sincerity,

80.9. And with fear (in his heart),

80.10. Were you (O Prophet!) unmindful in shifting your attention to another.

80.11.. By no means (should it be so), because it is indeed a Message of Instruction:

80.12. Therefore let anyone who makes up the mind, remember (and accept) it.

80.13.. (It is) in Books held in (great) honor,

80.14. Supreme (in dignity) kept pure and holy,

80.15. (Written) by the hands of holy scribes (writers) -

80.16. Blessed and just.

80.17.. Warning to man! What has made him reject Allah?

80.18. From what stuff has He (Allah) created him?

80.19. From a sperm-drop has He (Allah) created him, and then (He) makes him in proper size and shape;

80.20. Then He (Allah) makes the path smooth for him;

80.21. Then He (Allah) causes him to die and puts him in his grave;

80.22. Then, when it is His (Allah's) Will, He will raise him up (again).

80.23. By no means has he (man) fulfilled what Allah has commanded him to do.

80.24.. Then let man look at his food, (how We provide it):

80.25. For that We pour forth water in plenty,

80.26. And We split the earth into pieces,

80.27. And produce from there corn,

80.28. And grapes and plants to eat,

80.29. And olives and dates,

80.30. And enclosed gardens thick with tall trees,

80.31. And fruits and herbage (and the grasses)-

80.32. For you to use and (for your) help and for your cattle.

80.33.. At last! When there comes the deafening noise-

80.34. That Day man will run away from his own brother,

80.35. And from his mother and his father,

80.36. And from his wife and his children.

80.37.. On that Day each of the men, will have enough worry (of his own) to make him not mindful of the others.

80.38.. Some faces that Day will be shining,

80.39. Laughing, being happy.

80.40. And other faces that Day will be soiled with dust;

80.41. Blackness will cover them:

80.42. Such will be the rejecters of Allah, the unrighteous.

****

Sura 81. At-Takwir,
(The folding up): (Makkah: 29 Verses)
In the Name of Allah, the Most Gracious, the Most Merciful.

81.1. When the sun (with its spacious light) is folded up;

81.2. When the stars fall, losing their glitter;

81.3. When the mountains vanish (like a dream);

81.4. When the she camels, ten months with young are left untended;

81.5. When the wild beasts are herded together (in human habitations);

81.6. When the oceans boil over with a swell;

81.7. When the souls are sorted out, (Put together, righteous with righteous and unrighteous with unrighteous)

81.8. When the female (infant) buried alive, is questioned

81.9. For what crime she was killed;

81.10. When the books of deeds are laid open;

81.11. When the world on High (heavens) is made visible;

81.12. When the fire of Hell is set to a fierce burn;

81.13. And when the Garden (of the heavens) is brought near;

81.14. (Then) shall each soul know what it has brought (forward for this Day).

81.15.. So truly I call to witness the receding stars that hide away

81.16. Go straight, or hide;

81.17. And the night as it comes to an end;

81.18. And the (glorious) morning as it moves away the darkness;

81.19. Surely this is the Word of a most honorable Messenger, [The Angel *Jibrael* (Gabriel)]

81.20. Given the power with rank before the Lord of the Throne,

81.21. With authority there, (and) faithful to his trust.

81.22.. And (O people!), your companion (the Prophet) is not one who is possessed;

81.23. And without doubt he (the Prophet) saw him (the messenger from Allah) in the clear horizon.

81.24. And he does not withhold purposely any knowledge of the unseen.

81.25. And it is not the word of an evil spirit (Satan) that is outcast.

81.26.. Where, then are you going?

81.27. Surely, this is the Message to (all jinns and men, all the) creations of the worlds.

81.28. (With guidance) to each one among you who is willing to walk straight:

81.29. But you shall not make up your mind except as Allah, the Lord of the worlds, wishes.

****

Sura 82. Al-Infitár,

(The splitting apart): (Makkah: 19 Verses)
In the Name of Allah, the Most Gracious, the Most Merciful.

82.1.. When the sky is split apart;

82.2. When the stars fall thrown around;

82.3. When the oceans are made to burst apart; (into one big ocean covering the earth)

82.4. And when the graves are turned upside down;

82.5. (Then) each soul shall know what it has sent forward and (what it has) kept back.

82.6.. O man! What has misled you (away) from your Lord, Most Generous?

82.7. He, Who created you, given you the proper size and shape, and gave you a just basis (for thinking);

82.8. In whatever form He wishes, He puts you together.

82.9.. No! But you (men) reject the (Final) Judgment!

82.10. But surely, over you (are angels) to protect you,

82.11. Kind and honorable writing down (your deeds and works):

82.12. They know (and understand) all that you do.

82.13. As for the righteous, they will be in Joy;

82.14. And the wicked, they will be in Fire,

82.15. Which they will enter on the Day of Judgment,

82.16. And they will not be able to keep away from there,

82.17.. And what will explain to you what the Day of Judgment is?

82.18. Again, what will explain to you what the Day of Judgment is?

82.19. (It will be) the Day when no soul shall have power (to do) anything for another: Because on that Day, the Command will be wholly with Allah.

****

Sura 83. Al-Mutaffifin,

(Dealing in fraud): (Makkah: 36 Verses)

In the Name of Allah, the Most Gracious, the Most Merciful.

83.1.. Misery to those who deal in fraud, (woe be unto those who cheat)-

83.2. Those who demand full measure, when they have to receive by measure from men,

83.3. But when they have to give by measure or weight to men give less than due.

83.4. Do they not think that they will be called to account?

83.5. On a Mighty Day,

83.6. A day when (all) mankind will stand before the Lord of the worlds ?

83.7.. But! Surely the record of the wicked is (saved) in prison register.

83.8. And what will explain to you what the prison register is?

83.9. (There is) a register (fully) written.

83.10. Misery, on that Day, to those who deny-

83.11. Those who do not accept the Day of Judgment.

83.12. And none can deny it except the transgressor beyond limits, the sinner!

83.13. When Our Signs are read (and repeated) to him, he says, "Tales of old!"

83.14.. By no means! But on their hearts is the stain of (the evil,) whatever they do!

83.15. Surely, from the Light (of) their Lord, on that Day will they be blocked.

83.16. Further, they will enter the Fire of Hell.

83.17. Further, it will be said to them: This is the (reality), which you rejected as false!

83.18.. But no! Surely the record of the righteous is (saved) in register of the Supreme.

83.19. And What will explain to you what the register of the Supreme is?

83.20. There is a register (fully) written,

83.21. To which bear witness those nearest (to Allah).

83.22.. Truly the righteous will be in happiness:

83.23. On Thrones (of dignity) they will be able to see a view (of all things):

83.24. You will recognize in their faces the beaming brightness of joy.

83.25. Their thirst will be quenched with pure wine sealed:

83.26. The seal will be musk: And for this let them desire, those who have true desires:

83.27. With it will be (given) a mixture of *Tasnim*: (The nectar from the pure heavenly fountain)

83.28. A spring, from (which) drink those nearest to Allah.

83.29.. Those in sin used to laugh at those who believed,

83.30. And whenever they passed by them, used to wink at each other (in mockery);

83.31. And when they returned to their own people, they would return mocking;

83.32. And whenever they saw them (those who believed), they would say,

"Look! These are the people truly astray!"

83.33. But they (the unbelievers) had not been sent as keepers over them (those who believed)!

83.34. But on this Day the believers will laugh at the unbelievers:

83.35. On Thrones (of dignity) they will be able to see a view (of all things).

83.36. Will not the unbelievers have been paid back for what they did?

****

Sura 84. Al-Inshiqáq,
(The rending asunder): (Makkah: 25 Verses)
In the Name of Allah, the Most Gracious, the Most Merciful.

84.1.. When the sky is split apart

84.2. And obeys the command of its Lord, and it must do so;

84.3. And when the earth is flattened out,

84.4. And spills over what is within it and becomes empty,

84.5. And obeys the command of its Lord, and it must do so;

84.6.. O you man! You are surely always moving towards your Lord painfully moving but you shall meet Him.

84.7. Then he who is given his record (of deeds) in his right hand,

84.8. Soon his account will be taken by an easy settlement

84.9. And he will be together with his people, happy!

84.10. But he who is given his record behind his back,

84.11. Soon will he cry for his lost soul,

84.12. And, he will enter a blazing Fire.

84.13. Truly, (on this earth) did he go about among his people, happy!

84.14. Truly, did he think that he would not have to return (to Us)!

84.15. But, for sure! His Lord was (always) watchful of him!

84.16.. So, I swear by the deep (red) glow of sunset;

84.17. The night and its gathering (of nightly creatures);

84.18. And the moon in her fullness:

84.19. You shall surely travel from one stage to the next (life to Hereafter).

84.20.. What then, is the matter with them that they do not believe?

84.21. And when the Quran is read to them, they do not fall prostrate,

{A Muslim generally prostrates to Allah after reciting this verse}

84.22. But being the opposite the unbelievers reject (Islam and the Message).

84.23. But Allah has full knowledge of what they do and think,

84.24. So announce to them a painful penalty,

84.25. Except to those who believe and work righteous good deeds: For them is a reward that will never be the end.

****

Sura 85. Al-Burúj,
(The zodiacal signs): (Makkah: 22 Verses)
In the Name of Allah, the Most Gracious, the Most Merciful.

85.1.. By the sky, (displaying) the Zodiacal Signs;

85.2. By the promised Day (of Judgment);

85.3. By the one who sees and that which is seen-

85.4. Accursed are (unbelievers, who become) the makers of the pit (of Fire)

85.5. Fire, (amply) supplied with fuel:

85.6. Look! They sat by the (fire),

85.7. And they saw (all) that they were doing against the believers.

85.8. And they ill-treated them (the believers) for no reason other than that they believed in Allah, exalted in Power, Worthy of all Praise!

85.9. (It is) to Him that belongs the dominion of the heavens and the earth! And Allah is the One to Witness all things.

85.10.. Those who are cruel or unkind to (or draw into evil) the believing men and women, and do not turn in repentance, will have the penalty of Hell: They will have the penalty of the burning Fire.

85.11. For those who believe and do righteous deeds, will be Gardens, beneath which rivers flow; That is the great success, (the fulfillment of all desires).

85.12.. The Grip (and Power) of your Lord is truly Strong!

85.13. It is He Who creates from the very beginning, and He can restore (life).

85.14. And He is the Often Forgiving and full of loving Kindness,

85.15. (The Supreme) Owner of the Throne of Glory,

85.16. (He) does everything (without an exception) that He intends to do.

85.17. Has the story reached you (O Prophet,) of the forces-

85.18. Of Firon (Pharaoh) and of Samood (Thamud)

85.19. No! Yet the unbelievers reject (the Truth)!

85.20. And Allah does overtake them from behind!

85.21.. No! (But) this is a Glorious Quran,

85.22. (Written) within a tablet preserved (to last forever)!

****

Sura 86. At-Táriq,
(The divine visitor by the night): (Makkah: 17 Verses)
In the Name of Allah, the Most Gracious, the Most Merciful.

86.1.. By the sky (the heaven) and by the Visitor by the night,

86.2. And what will explain to you what is the Visitor by the night -

86.3. The shinning Star of intense brightness-

86.4. There is no soul without a Protector over it.

86.5. Now, let man only think from what he is created!

86.6. He is created from a drop emitted-

86.7. Proceeding from between the backbone and the ribs:

86.8. Surely (Allah) is able to bring him back (to life)!

86.9.. The Day that (all) things secret will be tested.

86.10. (Man) will have no power and no helper.

86.11. By the sky that returns (with rains again and again),

86.12. And by the earth which opens out (for the gushing springs or the budding plants)-

86.13. Watch! This is the Word that separates out (Good from evil):

86.14. It is not a thing for amusement.

86.15.. As for them (the disbelievers), they are only plotting a scheme,

86.16. And I am planning a Scheme.

86.17. Therefore (O Prophet!) give a little time for the disbelievers: Bear with them gently (for a while).

****

Sura 87. Al-Alá,
(The Most High): (Makkah: 19 Verses)
In the Name of Allah, the Most Gracious, the Most Merciful.

87.1.. Praise (and Glorify) the Name of your Lord, the Most High,

87.2. Who has created, and given form and proper size;

87.3. Who has prescribed laws (to live by) and given you guidance (in His Books);

87.4. And Who grows the (green and rich) pasture.

87.5. And then makes it dry and stalky (with grain).

87.6.. By small amounts We shall teach you (O Prophet!) To declare (the Message), so that you shall not forget,

87.7. Except as Allah wills for He knows what is openly known and what is hidden.

87.8.. And We will make it easy for you (to follow) the simple (Path).

87.9. Therefore give guidance in case the guidance will profit (the listener).

87.10. The guidance will be received by those who fear (Allah)

87.11. But it will be avoided by those most unfortunate ones,

87.12. Who will enter the great Fire,

87.13. In which they will neither die nor live.

87.14.. But those will prosper, who purify themselves,

87.15. And praise the Name of their Guardian-Lord and (purify their hearts) in prayer.

87.16.. But no! You prefer the life of this world;

87.17. But the Hereafter is better and (it) lasts longer.

87.18.. And this is in the pages (of Books) of the very early (Revelations)-

87.19. The pages (of Books) of Ibrahim (Abraham) and Musa (Moses).

****

Sura 88. Al-Gháshiya,
(The overwhelming event): (Makkah: 26 Verses)
In the Name of Allah, the Most Gracious, the Most Merciful.

88.1.. Has the story of The Overwhelming (Event) reached you?

88.2. On that Day, some faces will suffer humiliation,

88.3. Working (hard in) weariness-

88.4. While they enter the blazing Fire-

88.5. While they are given, from a boiling hot spring (fluid), to drink,

88.6. No food will there be for them but a bitter *Dhari'* (a dry, bitter and thorny fruit)

88.7. Which will neither nourish nor satisfy hunger.

88.8.. On that Day (other) faces will be joyful,

88.9. Pleased with their struggle (of this life)-

88.10. In a Garden raised high,

88.11. Where they shall not hear (empty words);

88.12. In there will be a bubbling spring;

88.13. In there will be Thrones (of dignity), raised high,

88.14. Cups placed (ready),

88.15. And cushions set in rows,

88.16. And rich carpets spread out.

88.17.. Do they (the unbelievers) not look at the Camels, how they are made?

88.18. And at the sky, how it is raised high?

88.19. And at the mountains, how they are fixed firm?

88.20. And at the earth, how it is spread out?

88.21.. Therefore you (O Prophet) give Guidance: For you are the one to guide.

88.22. You are not the one to manage (men's) affairs.

88.23. But if any (one) turns away and rejects Allah-

88.24. Allah will punish him with a severe punishment,

88.25. For to Us will be their return;

88.26. Then it will be for Us to call them to account.

****

Sura 89. Al-Fajr,

(The break of day): (Makkah: 30 Verses)

In the Name of Allah, the Most Gracious, the Most Merciful.

89.1.. By the break of Day; (Allah swears by the Dawn of the Day)

89.2. And by the ten nights:

89.3. And by the even and odd (contrasted);

89.4. And by the night when it passes away; -

89.5. Is there (not) in these a Sign for those who understand?

89.6. Do you not see how your Mighty Lord dealt with the people of 'Ad -

89.7. (And with the people) of the (city of) Iram, with lofty pillars,

89.8. Which have not been reproduced in (all) the land?

89.9. And with the people of Samood (Thamud) who cut out (huge) rocks in the valley? -

89.10. And with Firon (Pharaoh), the lord of stakes?

89.11. These (people) exceeded beyond limits in the lands.

89.12. And here (they) piled mischief (upon mischief).

89.13. Therefore did your Mighty Lord send upon them very lowly punishments:

89.14. Because your (Mighty) Lord is (like a Guardian) on a watch tower.

89.15.. Now, as for man, when his Mighty Lord tries him (by) giving him honor and gifts then he (proudly) says, "My Mighty Lord has honored me."

89.16. But when He tries him, (by) restricting his livelihood for him, then he says (in despair), "My Mighty Lord has put me to shame!"

89.17.. No, no! But you do not honor the orphans!

89.18. Nor do you encourage one another to feed the poor! -

89.19. And you (wrongly) consume inheritance - With all (the) greed,

89.20. And you love wealth with passion!

89.21.. No! When the earth is pounded to powder,

89.22. And your Mighty Lord arrives and His angels, rank upon rank,

89.23. And on that Day, (when) Hell is brought (face to face), - On that Day will man remember, but (alas!) how will that remembrance profit him?

89.24. He (the man) will say: "Ah! Had I sent forward (good deeds) for my (future) Life!"

89.25. Because, that Day, his punishment will be such like no one (else) can inflict,

89.26. And His bonds will be such as none (else) can bind.

89.27.. (To the righteous person will be said:) "O, (you) soul, with (complete) rest and satisfaction!

89.28. "Come back you to your Lord, - Well pleased (yourself), and well-pleasing to Him!

89.29. "Enter you, among My devotees!

89.30. "Yes, enter you My heaven!"

****

Sura 90. Al-Balad,

(The city): (Makkah: 20 Verses)

In the Name of Allah, the Most Gracious, the Most Merciful.

90.1.. I (reference is to Allah) do swear by this City (of Makkah);

90.2. That you (O Prophet!) are a free-man of this City;

90.3. And (with the ties of) parent and child;

90.4. Surely, We have created man into hard work and struggle.

90.5.. Does he think, that no one has power over him?

90.6. He may (wrongly) say: "I have wasted away a lot of wealth!"

90.7. Does he think that no one oversees him?

90.8.. Have We not made a pair of eyes for him?

90.9. And a tongue and a pair of lips?

90.10. And shown him the two highways? (The right and the wrong)

90.11. But he has made no haste for the path that is hard,

90.12. And what will explain to you the path that is hard?

90.13. (It is) freeing the slave;

90.14. Or the giving of food in a day of want (and suffering),

90.15. To the orphan with claims of relationship,

90.16. Or to the needy one (down) in the dust.

90.17.. Then will he be (one) of those who believe and practices patience, (constancy, and self-restraint), and practices acts of kindness and compassion.

90.18. Such are the companions of the right hand.

90.19.. But those who reject Our Signs, they are the (unhappy) companions of the left hand.

90.20. On them will be the Fire covering over (all around).

****

Sura 91. Ash-Shams,

(The sun): (Makkah: 15 Verses)

In the Name of Allah, the Most Gracious, the Most Merciful.

91.1.. By the sun and its glory,

91.2. And by the moon as follows it;

91.3. And by the Day as it reveals (the sun's) glory;

91.4. And by the night as it conceals it

91.5. And by the sky and its (wonderful) structure;

91.6. And by the earth and its (vast) territory;

91.7. And by the soul and the proportion and order given to it;

91.8. And its enlightenment and to its wrong and to its right-

91.9. Truly, he succeeds who purifies it,

91.10. And he fails who corrupts it!

91.11. The people of Samood (Thamud) rejected (their messenger) by their excessive wrong-doing.

91.12. Look, the most wicked man among them was chosen (for the crime)

91.13. But the messenger of Allah said to them: "It is a she-camel of Allah! And (let her) have her drink!"

91.14. Then they rejected him (as a false prophet) and they injured her (by cutting her hamstrings, See 54.29). So their Lord, on account of their crime, removed their traces and made them equal (in destruction).

91.15. And for Him, there is no fear of its consequences.

****

Sura 92. Al-Layl,

(The night): (Makkah: 21 Verses)

In the Name of Allah, the Most Gracious, the Most Merciful.

92.1.. By the night when it becomes dark;

92.2. By the day as it appears in glory;

92.3. By (the mystery of) the creation of male and female-

92.4. Surely, you seek diverse (goals)

92.5.. So, he who gives (in charity) and fears (Allah),

92.6. And (in all sincerity) accepts and follows the best-

92.7. We will indeed make smooth for him the path to happiness.

92.8. But he who is a greedy miser and thinks himself to be self-sufficient,

92.9. And gives the lie to the best-

92.10. We will indeed make smooth for him the path to misery;

92.11. (All of) his wealth will not profit him when he falls headlong (into the pit of Fire).

92.12.. Surely, We take upon Ourselves to guide,

92.13. And surely to Us (belong both) the end and the beginning.

92.14.. Therefore do I warn you of a Fire flaming fiercely;

92.15. None shall reach it except the most unfortunate ones,

92.16. Who give the lie to truth and turn their backs.

92.17.. But those most devoted to Allah shall be removed far from it-

92.18. Those who spend their wealth for increase in self-purification,

92.19. And have in their minds no favor from anyone for which a reward is expected in return,

92.20. But only the desire to seek the Approval of their Lord Most High;

92.21. And soon will they attain (complete) satisfaction.

****

Sura 93. Ad-Duhá,

(The glorious morning light): (Makkah: 11 Verses)

In the Name of Allah, the Most Gracious, the Most Merciful.

93.1.. By the Glorious Morning Light,

93.2. And by the night when it is still-

93.3. Your Guardian-Lord has not forsaken you (O Prophet), nor is He displeased.

93.4. And surely the Hereafter will be better for you than the present.

93.5. And soon your Guardian-Lord will give you that with which you shall be well pleased.

93.6.. Did He not find you an orphan and give you shelter (and care)?

93.7. And He found you wandering, and He gave you guidance.

93.8. And He found you in need, and made you independent.

93.9. Therefore, do not treat the orphan with harshness,

93.10. Do not shut off the beggar (without listening gently);

93.11. But the Bounty of your Lord- Rehearse and proclaim!

****

Sura 94. Ash-Sharh or Al-Inshiráh,

[The expansion (of the chest)]: (Makkah: 8 Verses)

In the Name of Allah, the Most Gracious, the Most Merciful.

94.1.. Have We not expanded for you (O Prophet), your chest?

94.2. And removed from you your burden,

94.3. The (burden) that did strained your back?

94.4. And elevated your fame (in the eyes of the people?)

94.5.. So, surely with every difficulty there is relief:

94.6. Surely, with every difficulty there is relief.

94.7. Therefore, when you are free (from your immediate duties), continue in your hard work

94.8. And to your Lord, turn (all) your attention.

****

Sura 95. At-Tin,

(The fig): (Makkah: 8 Verses)

In the Name of Allah, the Most Gracious, the Most Merciful.

95.1.. By the Fig and the Olive,

95.2. And the Mount of Sinai,

95.3. And the City (Makkah) of security -

95.4. We have truly created man in the best of forms,

95.5. Then We bring him down (to be) the lowest of the low -

95.6. Except those who believe and do righteous deeds: For they shall have an unfailing reward!

95.7. Then what can be against you (O Prophet!), after this regarding the

Judgment (to come)?

95.8. Is Allah not the Wisest of judges?

****

Sura 96. Al-'Alaq,
(The clot of congealed blood): (Makkah: 19 Verses)
In the Name of Allah, the Most Gracious, the Most Merciful.

96.1.. Proclaim! (And read aloud!) in the Name of the Lord and Cherisher, Who created -

96.2. Created man, out of a (mere) clot of thickened blood:

96.3. Proclaim! And your Lord is Most Bountiful -

96.4. He, Who taught (the use of) the pen-

96.5. Taught man that which he did not know.

96.6.. Alas! But man oversteps all bounds,

96.7. And he considers himself as self-sufficient.

96.8. Surely, to your Lord is the return (of all).

96.9.. Do you see the one who forbids -

96.10. A true believer when he (turns) to pray?

96.11. Do you see if he (Our servant) is on (the path towards) Guidance? -

96.12. Or enjoins the right deeds?

96.13. Do you see if he stands against (the Truth) and turns away?

96.14.. Does he not know that Allah sees?

96.15. Let him become aware! If he does not stop, We will drag him by the hair (upon his forehead) -

96.16. A lying, sinful hair!

96.17. Then, let him call (for help) to his own group (of friends):

96.18. We will call the angels of punishment (to deal with him)!

96.19.. But no! Do not pay any attention to him: But prostrate and bring yourself closer (to Allah)!

{A Muslim generally prostrates to Allah after reciting this verse}
****

Sura 97. Al-Qadr,
(The night of power or glory or honor): (Makkah: 5 Verses)
In the Name of Allah, the Most Gracious, the Most Merciful.

97.1.. We have indeed revealed this (Message, Quran) in the Night of Power (Honor):

97.2. And what will explain to you (O Prophet) what the Night of Power is?

97.3. The Night of Power is better than a thousand Months,

97.4. In it come down the angels and the Spirit [*Jibrael* (Gabriel)] by Allah's permission, to perform every task:

97.5. Peace! (Be in) this (Night) until the rise of dawn!
****

Sura 98. Al-Baiyina,
(The clear evidence): (Medinah: 8 Verses)
In the Name of Allah, the Most Gracious, the Most Merciful.

98.1.. Those who reject (truth), among the People of the Book and among the polytheists, who were not going to depart (from their ways) until there should come to them Clear Evidence-

98.2. A Messenger (the Prophet) from Allah (is) rehearsing Scriptures, kept pure and holy:

98.3. In which the laws (or decrees) are explained right and straight.

98.4.. The People of the Book did not make religious split until after there came to them Clear Evidence,

98.5. And they have been commanded no more than this: To worship Allah, offering Him sincere devotion, being true (in faith); To establish regular prayer; And to practice regular charity: And that is the religion right and straight.

98.6.. Those who reject (truth), among the (Jewish and Christian) People of the Book and among the polytheists, will be in the Fire of the Hell, to live in there (for ever)- They are the worst of creatures.

98.7. Those who have faith and do righteous deeds- They are the best of creatures.

98.8. Their reward is with Allah: Gardens of Eternity, beneath which rivers flow; They will live in there for ever; Allah well pleased with them, and they (well pleased) with Him: All this (is) for such as (those who) fear their Lord and Cherisher.

****

Sura 99. Az-Zalzalah,
[The (convulsive) earthquake]: (Medinah: 8 Verses)
In the Name of Allah, the Most Gracious, the Most Merciful.

99.1.. When the earth is shaken to her (deepest) Convulsion,

99.2. And the earth throws up her burdens (from within),

99.3. And man cries (out in great pain): "What is the matter with her?"

99.4. On that Day will she (the earth) declare her news:

99.5. For that (Day), your (Mighty) Lord will have given her (the earth) His (Allah's) Order.

99.6. On that Day will men proceed in groups sorted out, to be shown the deeds that they (had done).

99.7. Then anyone who has done an atoms weight of good,
Shall see it!

99.8. And anyone who has done an atom's weight of evil,
Shall see it!

****

Sura 100. Al-'Adiyát,
(Those that run): (Makkah: 11 Verses)
In the Name of Allah, the Most Gracious, the Most Merciful.

100.1.. By the (majestic horses) that run with panting (breath),

100.2. And strike sparks of fire,

100.3. And raid (the enemy camp) with force in the morning,

100.4. And raise the dust in clouds (for) the while,

100.5. And penetrate straight in the middle (of enemies) in formation-

100.6. Truly, man is ungrateful to his (Almighty) Lord

100.7. And to that (fact), he bears witness (by his deeds);

100.8. And violent is he in his love for wealth.

100.9.. Does he not know- That when whatever is in the graves is thrown about,

100.10. And whatever (locked up) in (human) breasts is made (clearly) evident-

100.11. That their Lord had been well aware of them, (even to) that Day?

****

Sura 101. Al-Qári'ah,

(The Day of noise and chaos): (Makkah: 11 Verses)

In the Name of Allah, the Most Gracious, the Most Merciful.

101.1.. The (Day) of Noise and Chaos (of the Calamity):

101.2. What is the (Day) of Noise and Chaos?

101.3. And what will explain to you what is the (Day) of Noise and Chaos?

101.4. (It is) a Day when men will be like moths thrown about,

101.5. And the mountains will be like torn wool.

101.6. Then, he whose balance (of good deeds) will be (found) heavy-

101.7. Will be in a life of good pleasure and satisfaction.

101.8. But he whose balance (of good deeds) will be (found) light-

101.9. Will have his home in a pit (of Fire).

101.10. And what will explain to you what this is?

101.11. (It is) a Fire flaming fiercely!

****

Sura 102. At-Takáthur,

(The piling up; The greed for more): (Makkah: 8 Verses)

In the Name of Allah, the Most Gracious, the Most Merciful.

102.1.. The rivalry among yourselves for piling up diverts you (from your duties),

102.2. Until you visit the graves,

102.3. But no, you soon shall know (the reality).

102.4. Again, you soon shall know!

102.5. No, if you were to certainly know within the mind (You would be aware!)

102.6. You shall certainly see the Fire of Hell!

102.7. Again you shall see it with the certainty of sight!

102.8. Then, shall you be questioned that Day about the joy (that you indulged in!)

****

Sura 103. Al-'Asr,

(The Time through the ages): (Makkah: 3 Verses)

In the Name of Allah, the Most Gracious, the Most Merciful.

103.1.. By (the Promise of) time (infinite), (*'Asr* also refers to afternoon prayer, or later part in life)

103.2. Surely, man is in loss,

103.3. Except such as (those who) have Faith and do righteous deeds and (join together) in the mutual teaching of truth, and of patience and perseverance.

****

Sura 104. Al-Humazah,

(The Slanderer): (Makkah: 9 Verses)

(Hamazah: Slander by speech, Lumazah: Slander by action):

In the Name of Allah, the Most Gracious, the Most Merciful.

104.1.. Grief (and warning) to every Scandal-monger and backbiter,

104.2. Who piles up wealth and lays it by,

104.3. Thinking that his wealth would make him last for ever!

104.4.. By no means! He will be sure to be thrown into that which breaks to pieces.

104.5. And what will explain to you that which breaks to Pieces?

104.6. (It is) the Fire of Allah lighted up (to a flame),

104.7. The (Fire) which rises to the heart:

104.8. It shall be made to cover over them,

104.9. In pillars stretched out.

****

Sura 105. Al-Fil,

(The elephant): (Makkah: 5 Verses)

In the Name of Allah, the Most Gracious, the Most Merciful.

105.1.. Did you not see how your Lord dealt with the companions of the elephant?

105.2. Did He not make their evil plan go astray?

105.3. And He sent against them flights of birds,

105.4. Striking them (the companions of the elephant) with stones of baked clay,

105.5. Then did He make them like an empty field of stalks and straw, (of which the corn) has been eaten up.

****

Sura 106. Quraish,

(Custodians of the Ka'bah): (Makkah: 4 Verses)

In the Name of Allah, the Most Gracious, the Most Merciful.

106.1.. For the agreements (promises) of security and safeguard (enjoyed) by Quraish,

106.2. Their agreements (covering) journeys by winter and summer-

106.3. Let them adore the Lord of this House,

106.4. (The One) Who provides them with food against hunger, and with security against fear (of danger).

****

Sura 107. Al-Má'ún,

(The neighborly needs): (Makkah: 7 Verses)

In the Name of Allah, the Most Gracious, the Most Merciful.

107.1.. Do you see the one who denies the Judgment (to come)?

107.2. Then, it is such a (man) who repels (and discards) the orphan (with harshness),

107.3. And does not encourage the feeding of the needy.

107.4.. So, (this is a) warning to the worshippers

107.5. Who are neglectful of their prayers,

107.6. Those who (only want) to be seen (by men),

107.7. But refuse (to offer even) the neighborly needs.

****

Sura 108. Al-Kawthar,
[The (fountain of) abundance]: (Makkah: 3 Verses)
In the Name of Allah, the Most Gracious, the Most Merciful.

108.1.. To you (O Prophet!) We have granted the Fountain (of Abundance),

108.2. Therefore turn to your Lord in prayer and sacrifice,

108.3. Because he who hates you- He will be cut off (from the hope of the future).

****

Sura 109. Al-Káfirún,
(Those who reject faith): (Makkah: 6 Verses)
In the Name of Allah, the Most Gracious, the Most Merciful.

109.1.. Say: "O you people who reject Faith!

109.2. "I do not worship what you worship,

109.3. "Nor will you worship what I worship,

109.4. "And I will not worship what you have been used to worship,

109.5. "Nor will you worship what I worship,

109.6. "To you be your religion, and to me (be) my religion."

****

Sura 110. An-Nasr,
(The help): (Medinah: 3 Verses)
In the Name of Allah, the Most Gracious, the Most Merciful.

110.1.. When the Help of Allah and victory (of Makkah) comes,

110.2. And you (O Prophet!) see the people enter Allah's Religion in crowds,

110.3. Then celebrate the Praises of your Lord, and pray for forgiveness from Him: Surely, He is One Who accepts repentance, returning (in grace and kindness) with forgiveness.

****

Sura 111. Al-Masad,
[The palm fiber, Also known as **Abú-Lahab,**
(The father of flame)]: (Makkah: 5 Verses)
In the Name of Allah, the Most Gracious, the Most Merciful.

111.1.. Perish the hands of the Father of Flame (Abu'-Lahab)! Perish he!

111.2. (There is) no benefit to him (in the Hereafter) from all his wealth, and from all his gains!

111.3. Soon he will be burnt in a Fire of burning Flame!

111.4. And his wife shall carry the (crackling) wood, as fuel!

111.5. A twisted rope of palm-leaf fiber around her (own) neck!

****

Sura 112. Al-Ikhlás,
(The (absolute) purity): (Makkah: 4 Verses)
In the Name of Allah, the Most Gracious, the Most Merciful.

112.1.. Say: "He is Allah, The One (and Only One).

112.2. "Allah the Eternal (the Ever Enduring), the Absolute (and Alone);

112.3. "He begets not (has no descendents, no children, none), nor was He (ever) begotten;

112.4. "And there is none like (or comparable) unto Him."

****

Sura 113. Al-Falaq,
(The dawn): (Makkah: 5 Verses)
In the Name of Allah, the Most Gracious, the Most Merciful.

113.1.. Say: "I seek shelter (and security) with the Lord of the dawn

113.2. "From the mischief of the created things;

113.3. "From the mischief of darkness as it spreads over;

113.4. "From the mischief of those who practice secret (and evil) arts as they blow into knots (riddles);

113.5. "And from the mischief of the envious one as he practices envy."

****

Sura 114. An-Nás,
(The mankind): (Makkah: 6 Verses)
In the Name of Allah, the Most Gracious, the Most Merciful.

114.1.. Say: "I seek shelter (and security) with the Lord (the Cherisher) of mankind,

114.2. "King (and Ruler) of mankind,

114.3. "God (Almighty) of mankind-

114.4. "From the mischief of the Whisperer (of evil, the Satan, or the Evil one), who hides away (after his whisper)-

114.5. "(The same Evil one) who whispers into the breasts (hearts) of mankind-

114.6. "Among the jinns' and among the men."

****

A Brief Index of the Quranic words and their Reference in The Holy Quran

Names of the Suras and
Quranic Words (*Italicized*)

A

Aaron (*Haroon*), 2.248;
4.163; 6.84; 7.122,142;
10.75; 19.28, 53; 20.30,
70, 90, 92; 21.48; 23.45;
25.35; 26.13, 48; 28.34;
37.114, 120.

Abasa, Sura 80;
frowned 74.22

Ablutions, (*Wadu*), 4 .43;
5.6

Abraham (*Ibrahim*) Sura
14,

Abraham 2.124-127, 130,
132, 133, 135, 136, 148,
258, 260; 3.33, 65, 67, 68,
84, 95, 97; 4.54, 125,
163; 6.74, 75, 83, 114;
161; 9.70, 11.69, 74-76;
12.6, 38; 14.35; 15.51;
16.120, 123; 19.41, 46,
58; 21.51, 60, 62, 69;
22.26, 43, 78; 26.69;
29.16, 31; 33.7; 37.83,
104, 109; 38.45; 42.13;
43.26; 51.24; 53.37;
57,26; 60.4; 87.19

Abu Lahab (Father of
Flame) 111.1-5

'Ad people, 7.65-74; 9.70;
11.59; 14.9; 22.42; 25.38;
26.123; 29.38; 38.12;
40.31; 41.13, 15; 46.21;
50.13; 51.41; 53.50;
54.18; 69.4-6; 89.6

Adam, 2.31, 33-35, 37;
3.33, 59; 5.27; 7.11, 19,
26, 27, 31, 35, 172; 17.61,
70; 18.50; 19.58; 20.116-
117, 120, 121; 36.60

Adiyat, Sura 100

Ahmad, 61.6

Ahqaf, Sura 46; 46: 21,

Ahzab, Sura 33; 11.17;
13.36; 19.37; 38.113;
40.5, 30; 43.65

Amish, dwellers of, People
of the Woods, 15.78;
26.176; 38.13; 50.14, also
see Note 8, Sura 26.

A'ala, Sura 87, 87.1; 92.20

'Alaq, Sura 96

Al-Imran, Sura 3

Allah appears more than
3250 times in the text of
this Quran.

Angel or Angels, Either
word occurs 117 times in
the text.

'Ankabut, Sura 29

A'raf, Sura 7; 7:266, 48:

Arafat, 2.198

Ayât-Al-Kursi, 2:255

B

Backbiter, 49.12; 104.1

Badr, battle of, 3.13
lessons from, 8.5-19, 42-
48

Bakkah (Makkah), 3.96

Balad, Sura 90

Balance, 7.8, 9; 17.35;
21.47; 55.7-9; 57.25;
101.6-9

Baqara, Sura 2

Barzakh, (Barrier), 23.100;
25.53; 55.20; See 18.94-
97; 34.54; 36.9 for barrier

Baiyina, Sura 98

Beast, 27.82

Bedouins, 9.90, 97-99,
101, 120; 48.11,16; 49.14

Bee, 16.68-69

Bequest, 2.180, 240; 4.7,
12; 36.50;

Betray (deceive or fraud),
2.187; 4.107; 5.13; 8.27,
58, 71; 12.52; 22.38;
66.10

Birds, 2.260; 3, 49; 5.110;
6.38; 12.36, 41; 16.79;
21.79; 22.31; 24.41;
27.16, 17, 20; 34.10;

38.19; 56.21; 67.19;
105.3.

Blood repayment (*Diya*),
2:178, 179, 4:92; 17.33

Booty of wars, 3.161, 4:94.
8:41; 59.6-8;
illegal 3.162

Bribe 2.188

Burden
of another, no bearer of
burdens shall bear than,
35.18; 39.7; 53.38
the burdens of others,
16.25; 29.13
evil burdens that they will
bear 6.3 I, 164
Allah burdens not a person
beyond his capacity,
2.286; 7.42; 23.62

Burúj (Stars), Sura 85;
85.1; 15.16; 25.6

C

Calmness and tranquility,
2.248; 9.26, 40; 48.4, 18,
26

Camel, 6.144; 7, 40; 77.33;
88.17

Captives, 4.25; S.67, 70,
71; 9.60, 33.26, 27; 76.8

Cattle, 3.14; 4.119; 5.1;
6.136, 138, 139, 142; 7.,
79; 10.24; 16.5, 6, 7, 8,
10, 66, 80; 20.54; 22.28,
30, 34; 23.21, 25.44, 49;
26.133; 32.27; 35.28;
36.71-73; 39.6; 40.79;
42.11; 43.12, 13; 47.12;
79.33; 80.32.

Cave 9.40

Cave, people 18.9-22, 25,
26

Certainty with truth, 56.95;
69.51

Charity, (*Sadaqah,*)
2.196, 263, 264, 270, 271,
273; 4.114; 9.58, 75, 76,

confronted with all he has done, 3.30

Good deed, 4.149; 5.48

Gospel (*Injeel*), 3.3, 48, 65; 5.46, 47, 66, 68, 110; 7.157; 9.111; 48.29; 57.27.

Great News, 78.1-5

H

Hadid, Sura 57

Hady (offering for sacrifice), 2.196

Hajj, Sura 22

Hajj (Pilgrimage), 2.158, 196-203; 3.97; 22.30

Haman, 28.6, 38; 29.39; 40.24,36,37

Hands and feet will verify, 36.65

Háqqa, Sura 69

Hardship, and its relief every, 94.56

Haroon, (see Aaron).

Harut, 2.102

Hashr, Sura 59

Hearts,

made up, 2.74; 22.53; 39.22; 57.16

sealed, 7.100, 101; 40.35; 47.16; 63.3

covered, 17.46; 41.5

locked up, 47.24

divided, 59.14

in fear, 22.35

in sickness, disease, 2.10; 5.52; 8.49; 9.125; 22.53;

fools and mockers, 2.13-15

purchased error for guidance, 2.16

deaf, dumb and blind, 2.17, 18

in fear 2.19, 20

worldly talk, 2.204-206

refuse to fight, 3.167,168

what is in their hearts, 2.204, 3.167; 4.63

when a catastrophe befalls, 4.60-62

in misfortune and in success, 4.72, 73

24.50; 33.12, 32, 60; 47.20, 29; 74.31

Heavens,

belong to Allah, 16.77

not created for a play, 21.16

and earth joined together, 21.30

nothing hidden in the, 27.75

without any pillars, 31.10

will be rolled up in His Right Hand, 39.67

creation of the heavens in two days, 41.12

decorated nearest heaven with lamps, 41.12

to Allah belong all that is in the, 45.27; 53.31

seven heavens, one above another, 67.3

Hereafter,

better, 6.32; 7.169

end in the, 6.135

home of the evil, 12.109; 16.30; 28.83; 29.64

who do not believe in the, 17.10

reward of the, 42.20 43.33-35

only for the righteous 43.35

punishment of, 68.33

better and more lasting, 87.17; 93.4

Highways,(wide roads), 21.31

Allah has cast them back, 2.206; 4.88

not to be taken as friends, 4.89; 58.14-19

seek to deceive Allah, 4.142-145

afraid of being found out, 9.64, 65

not to pray for, 9.84

wherever found, they shall be seized and killed, 33.61

Allah will punish the, 33.73

liars are divided, 59.11-14

Hijr, (Rocky Tract), 15.80-85

Hijr, Sura 15

Horses, 16.8

Hour,

the knowledge of 7.187; 33.63; 41.47; 68.26

all of a sudden 6.31; 7.187; 12.107; 43.66

comes upon you, 6.40; 12.107; 20.15; 34.3

has drawn near, 54.1-5

nearer, 16.77

earthquake of the, 22.1 will be established, on the Day, 30.12,14

surely coming, there is no doubt, 40.59; 45.32; 51.5,6

Houses, manners about entering, 24.27-29

Hu'd, Sura 11

Hu'd, 7.65-72; 11.50-60; 26.123-140; 46.21 -26

Hujurat, Sura 49

Humazah, Sura104

Hunain (battle), 9.25

Hu'r (female companions in Paradise), 44.54; 52.20

Hypocrites,

do not believe 2.8

deceive themselves, 2.9

disease in their hearts, 2.10; 8.49; 22.53; 33.12; 47.29

making mischief, 2.11, 12

hearts are closed; 63.1-4

do not understand or know 63.7,8

to strive hard against, 66.9

I

Iblis (Satan, the Evil one), 2.34; 7.11-18; 15.31-44; 17.61-65; 18.50; 20.116-120; 34.20, 21; 38.71-85 (see also Satan)

Ibrahim, (see Abraham)

Ibrahim, Sura 14

'Iddah (divorce prescribed period of women), 2.228, 231, 232, 234, 235;

33.49; 65.1-7

Idris, 19.56, 57; 21.85; 96.4

I'hram, 2.197; 5.2,95

Ikhlás, Sura 112

Iláh, (only One), 2.163; 6.19; 16.22, 51; 23.91; 37.4; 38.65

Illegal sexual conduct; evidence of witnesses, 4.15-18; 24.2719

'Iliyin, Register of the Supreme, 83.18-21

'Imran, wife of, 3.35; daughter of, 66.12

Infitár, Sura82

Inheritance, 2.180, 240; 4.7-9, 11, 12, 19, 33, 176; 5.106-108

Injustice, done, 4.30,

Insan (also *Dahr*), Sura 76

Inshiqáq, Sura 84

Inshirah, Sura 94

Inspiration (Revelation), 6.93; 10.2, 109; 12.102; 17.86; 40.15; 42.3, 7, 51, 52; 53.4, 10

Intercession/intercessor, 6.51, 70, 93, 94; 10.3; 19.87; 20.106, 109; 30.13; 34.23; 39.44; 40.18; 43.86; 53.26; 74.48

Intoxicants, 5.90; 2.219

Iqr'a' (see *'Alaq*), Sura 96

Isa, Jesus *'Isa* son of Mary, 3.45-47; 19.22, 23 Messenger to the Children of Israel, 3.49-51 disciples, 3.52, 53; 5.111 - 115; 3.52; 61.14 raised up, 3.55-58; 4.157-159 likeness of Adam, 3.59 not crucified, 4.157 inspired 4.163 only a messenger of Allah, 4.171; 5.75; 43.63, 64 disbelief in, 5.17, 72; 9.30 the Prophet has come, 5.19 giving the Gospel, 5.46 disciples saying we are

Muslims, 5.111

Table spread with food, 5.114

taught no false worship, 5.116-118

as a prophet, 6.85

as a Sign, 23.50; 43.61

an example to the Children of Israel, 43.59

Reference to the Prophet whose name shall be Ahmad, 61.6

Isaac, (*Isháq*) 2.133; 4.163; 6.84; 19.49; 21.72; 29.27; 37.112, 113

Ishmael (*Ismail*),2.125-129, 133; 4.163; 6.86; 19.54, 55; 21.85; 38.48

Islam, 3.19, 85; 5.3; 6.125; 39.22; 61.7

first Muslims, 6.14, 163; 39.12

First to embrace, 9.100; 39.22

as a favor, 49.17

Isra, Sura 17

Israel, Children of, 2.40-86

favor bestowed, 2.47-53, 60, 122; 45.16, 17

rebel Allah's obedience, 2.54-59, 61, 63-74; 5.71; 7.138-141

arrogance, 2.80, 88, 91; 2.75-79; 2.86

covenants, 2; 80, 83-86, 93, 100; 5.12, 13, 70

promised twice, 17.4-8

delivered from enemy, 20.80-82

given Scripture 32.23-25; 40.53, 54

scholars of, knew the Quran as true, 26.197

J

Jacob, (*Yàqoub*) 2.132, 133; 4.163; 6.84; 12.18; 19.49; 21.72; 29.27

sons of Jacob, 2.140; 3.84, 4.163

Jalut, see Goliath.

Játhiya, Sura 45

Jews, and Christians,

2.140; 4.153-161, 171; 5.18; 5.41, 42

accursed 5.64

enmity to the believers 5.82

in Islam, 26.197; 28.53; 29.47

Jibrael, (see Gabriel)

Jinn, Sura 72

jinn, 6.100, 112; 15.27; 34.41; 38.37; 46.18, 29; 55.15, 33, 39; 72.1-15

Job, 4.163; 6.84; 21.83, 84; 38.41-44

John, (*Yahya*), 3.39; 21.90; 6.85; 19.12-15

Jonah (Jonas or *Yunus*), 4.163; 6.86; 10.98; 21.87; 37.139-148; 21.87; 68.48-50

Joseph (*Yusuf*), 6.84; 12.4-101

Judi, Mount, 11 .44

Jumu'ah, Sura 62

Justice 2.282; 4.58, 135; 7.29; 16.90; 57.25; 4.65, 105

K

Ka'bah,

built 2.125-127

no killing, 5.94-96

asylum of security, 5.97; 7.28

round, 2.200; 7.29, 31

Káfirún, Sura 109

Kafur, cup mixed with, 76.5

Kahf, Sura18

Kawthar, Sura108

Kawthar (Fountain) 108.1

Keys, 39.63; 42.12; 6.59

Killing,

a person, 5.32

not to kill anyone, 17.33

Kind words

better than charity, 2.263

Kindred (children's), rights of, 2.83, 177, 215; 4.7 9, 36; 8.41; 16.90; 17.26; 24.22; 29.8; 30.38; 42.23

Knowledge,

He knows it, 6.59 without,

6.140
five things, with Allah
  Alone, 31 .34
certainty, 102.5-7
Korun (*Qaroon*), 28.76-82;
  29.39; 40.24

L

Lahab, Sura 111
Layl, Sura 92
Lamp, 25.61; 67.5; 71.16;
  78.13
Languages,
difference in, and colors of
  men, 30.22
Lat 53.19Law, prescribed,
  5.48
Laws from Allah, 2.219;
  98.3
Liars, 26.221-223
Life, saved 5.32
Life of this world, 2.86
enjoyment of deception,
  3.185
for the Hereafter, 4.74;
  9.38; 13.26; 28.60
amusement and play, 6.32;
  29.64; 47.36; 57.20
deceives, 6.130
as the rain, 10.24
glad tidings in the, 10.64
  11.15, 16; 17.18; 42.20;
  75.20, 21; 76.27; 87.16
Light, 4.174 ; 6.1; 24.35;
  57.12-15; 66.8
Believers 57.2
Limits by Allah, 2.173,
  187, 190, 230; 9.112;
  58.4; 65.1; 78.22
set forth 2.187; 229, 230;
  4.13; 58.4; 65.1
transgress not 2.190, 229;
  4.14; 78.22
but forced by necessity,
  2.173; 6.145 do not
  exceed the, in your
  religion, 4.171; 5.77
when they exceeded
  7.166
who observe the, 9.112
Lion, 74.51
Loan, lend to Allah 2.245;
  73.20

doubled, 64.17
increased manifold, 57.11,
  18
Loss, 39.15
Lot, (*Lut*) 6.86; 7.80;
  11.70, 74, 77, 81, 89;
  15.59, 61; 21.71, 74;
  22.43; 26.160, 161, 167;
  27.54-56; 29.26, 28, 32,
  33; 37.133; 38.13; 50.13;
  54.33, 34; 66.10
his wife, 11.81; 15.60;
  66.10
Lote tree, 34.16; 53.14-16;
  56.28
Luqman, Sura 31
Luqman, the Wise one
  31.12-14

M

Ma'árij, Sura 70
Medinah (*Yathrib*),
  9.120; 33.13, 60; 63.8
Madyan,
  7.85-93; 11.84-95; 20.40;
  22.44; 28.22, 23; 29.36,
  37
Mahr (bridal-money),
  2.229, 236, 237; 4.4, 19-
  21, 24, 25; 5.5; 33.50;
  60.10, 11
Ma'ida, Sura 5
Makkah (*Bakkah*), 3.96,
  90.1, 2; City of Security,
  95.3
Man,
  2.30; 6.165; 35.39; 2.83,
  84, 88, 177; 4.1-36; 8.41;
  16.90; 17.23-39; 24.22;
  29.8, 9; 30.38; 33.33;
  42.23; 64.14; 70.22-35;
  2.155; 3.186; 47.31;
  57.25; 3.14 (for more,
  also see) 4.1; 6.2; 15.26,
  28, 33; 16.4; 21.30; 22.5;
  23.12-14; 25.54; 30.20;
  32.7-9; 35.11; 36.77, 78;
  37.11; 39.6; 40.67; 49.13;
  55.14; 56.57-59; 75.37-
  40; 76.1, 2; 77.20, 23;
  80.18, 19; 86.5-8; 96.2
stated term for, 6.2; 15.26
and wife, 4.35

return, 6.60, 72, 164;
  10.45, 46
the burden of another,
  6.164
ungratefulness, 7.10; 11.9;
  30.34; 32.9; 80.17; 100.6
warned, 7.27
wife and children, 7.189,
  190
in face of harm or evil,
  10.12; 11.9, 10; 16.53-55;
  17.67; 29.10; 30.33;
  31.32; 39.8, 49; 41.49-51;
  42.48; 70.19-21; 89.16
returning to the Lord,
  10.23; 84; 6; 96.8
wronging himself, 10.44
boastful, I 1.10
is hasty, 17.11
deeds fastened to his neck,
  17.13; 17.15
not be dealt unjustly, 17.71
death and resurrection,
  23.15, 16; 23.53
witness against, 24.24;
  75.14
his own desire, 25.43
by blood and marriage,
  25.54
in the heaven and earth,
  31.20
worship Allah, 39.64-66
has earned, 42.30, 48
angels recording his
  doings, 50.17, 18, 23;
  85.11
angels to guard him, 13.11;
  86.4
into three classes, 56.7-56
those nearest to Allah,
  56.10, 11
companions of Right
  Hand, 56.27-40
companions of Left Hand,
  56.41-56
transfigured unknown,
  56.60-62
made shapes good, 64.3
wealth and children 64.15
endowed with, 67.23, 24;
  74.12-15; 90.8-10
impatient, 70.19-21

Moses (*Musa*), 2.51-61; 5.20-29; 7.138-141, 159-162; 14.5-8;

Pharaoh, 2.49, 50; 7.103-137; 10.75-92; 11.96-99; 17.101-103; 20.17-53, 56-79; 23.45-49; 25.35, 36; 26.10-69; 28.4-21, 31-42; 40.23-46; 43.46-56; 51.38-40; 73.16; 79.15-26

guidance from Allah, 6.84

mountain and Lord's appearance, 7.142, 145

calf-worship, 7.148, 156; 20.86-98

his Book, and differences 11.110

the Scripture, 17.2

nine Clear Signs, 7.133; 17.101

the two seas, 18.60, 82

called and given Messenger's position, 19.51-53; 20.9-56; 28.29-

his work, 3.164; 7.157; 36.6; 52.29; 74.1-7

sent as a favor 3.164

sent with truth, 4.170

not made a watcher, 6.107

unlettered, 7.157; 62.2

sent as the Messenger of Allah, 7.158; 48.9, 29

a plain warner, 7.184, 188; 11.2;15.89; 53.56

not a madman, 7.184; 68.2; 81.22

who accuse you, 9.58

men who hurt the Prophet, 9.61

a mercy to the Believers, 9.61

that which is revealed, 10.15, 16; 11.12-14; 46.9

his sayings, 11.2-4; 12.108; 34.46-50

Allah is Witness over him, 13.43; 29.52; 46.8

sent as a bearer of good news and a warner, 11.2; 15.89; 26.194; 33.45; 34.28; 48.8

35 his childhood, mother and sister, 20.38-40; 28.7-13

magicians converted, 20.70-73; 26.46, 52

in Madyan, 20.40; 28.22-28 granted the Criterion, 21.48 the mystic fire, 27.7-12; 28.29-35

his mishap in the city, 28.15-21

came with clear *Ayât*, 29.39

guided to the Right Path, 37.114-122

Scripture of, 53.36; 87.19

Mosque (of Jerusalem), 17.7

Mosque (of *Quba*) 9.107, 108

Mosques, 2.187; 9.17-19 to maintain, of Allah, 9.17, 18

Mosquito, a parable, 2.26

not to be distressed, 15.97; 16.127; 18.6

sent to be a witness, 16.89; 22.78; 73.15

to invite with wisdom and fair preaching, 16.125

inspired, 18.110

mercy for the Believers 21.107

asks no reward, 25.57; 38.86; 42.23

has been commanded to, 27.91-93; 30.30; 66.9

mercy from Allah, 28.46, 47

to the believers, 33.6

example to follow, 33.21

Last of the Prophets, 33.40

send *Salat* on, 33.56

sent to all mankind, 34.28

wage is from Allah only, 34.47

only a human being, 41.6

sent as a protector, 42.48

not a new in messengers, 46.9

witness from among the Children of Israel, 46.10

Mountains, 15.19; 16.15; 20.105-107; 21.31; 22.18; 31.10; 42.32, 33; 59.21; 73.14; 77.10, 27; 81.3; 101.5

Muddaththir, Sura 74

Muhajir (Emigrants), 4.100; 9.100, 107, 117; 22.58, 59; 24.22; 33.6; 59.8, 9

women, 60.10-12

Muhammad, Sura 47

Muhammad

mocked, 2.104; 4.46; 25.41, 42; 34.78

respect the Messenger, 2.104; 4.46; 49.1-5

covenant to believe in, 3.81

a witnesses over believers, 2.143

no more than a Messenger, 3.144

dealing gently, 3.159

pledge to him is pledge to Allah, 48.10, 18

saw Gabriel, 53.4-18; 81.22-25

oppose him not, 58.20-22

foretold by Jesus, 61.6

victorious overall religions, 61.9

from the darkness to the light, 65.11

strive hard against hypocrites, 66.9

exalted standard of character, 68.4

not a poet or soothsayer, 69.41,42

devoted to prayer, 3.1-8, 20; 74.3

and the blind man, 80.1-12

prostrate and draw near to Allah, 96.19

reciting pure, 98.2

Ayât regarding family of, 24.11-17; 33.28-34, 50-53, 55, 59; 66.1, 3-6; 108.3

Muhsinûn (Good-doers), 2.117, 195; 4.125, 128;

snatched by birds, 22.31

a fly, 22.73

Light, 4.35, 36

mirage, 24.39

darkness in a sea, 24.40

spider, 29.41

partners, 30.28

dwellers of the town,
36.13-32

a man and many partners,
39.29

seed growing, 48.29

vegetation after rain, 57.20

mountain humbling itself
59.21

donkey, 62.5

water taken away, 67.30

people of the garden,
68.17-33

Paradise, *Firdaus* 53.15
Paradise, 18.107;23.11
Gardens under which
rivers flow, 3.15, 198;
4.57; 5.119; 7.43; 9.72;
18.31.22.23; 39.20;
57.12; 64.9; 98.8

Gardens, Everlasting 9.72;
13.23; 18.31; 19.61;
20.76

Gardens of Eternity 16.31;
35.33; 98.8

Gardens of delight, 37.43;
56.12, 89

Gardens with everlasting
delights, 9.21

Gardens and Grapes, 78.32

fruits of two gardens,
55.54,62

fruits of all kinds 36.57;
37.42; 43.73; 44.55;
47.15; 55.52, 68; 56.20,
29, 32; 77.42

fruits will be near at hand,
55.54; 69.23

fruit and meat, 52.22

flesh, 56.21

thorn less lote trees and
Talh (banana trees),

Hu'rs, chaste females with
wide and beautiful eyes,
as if preserved eggs,

56.28, 29

spring, running, 88.12

spring called Salsabil
76.18

a spring called Kafur 76.5

a spring Tasnim, 83.27, 28

a river in Paradise,
Kawthar 108.1

rivers of wine, milk
clarified honey, 47.15

pure wine, white,
delicious, 37.45, 46;
56.18; 76.21; 83.25

cup, mixed with, Zanjabil
76.17; 78.34;

water, 76.5

trays of gold and cups,
43.71

vessels of silver and cups
of crystal, 76.15, 16

green garments of fine and
thick silk,
18.31; 22.23; 35.33; 44.53;
76.12, 21

adorned with bracelets of
gold and pearls, 18.31;
22.23; 35.33; 76.21

coaches lined with silk
brocade, 55.54

green cushions and rich
beautiful mattresses, set
in row, 55.76; 88.15

thrones woven with gold
and precious stones,
raised high 56.15;88.13

rich carpets spread out,
88.16

beautiful mansions, lofty
rooms, 9.72; 39.20

abiding therein forever,
3.198; 4.57; 5.119; 9.22,
72; 11.108; 43.71; 57.12;
98.8

eternal home, 3.15; 35.35

facing one another on
thrones, 15.47; 37.44;
44.53; 56.16

never taste death therein,
37.48, 49; 44.54; 52.20;
55.58, 70; 56.22, 23

pure wives, 3.15

wives in pleasant shade,

44.56

nor they (ever) be asked to
leave it, 15.48

hatred or injury removed
from their hearts, 7.43;
15.41

all grief removed, 35.34

no sense of fatigue,
15.48.35.35

neither will be any hurt,
37.47; 56.19

no vain talk nor sinful
speech, 19.62; 56.25

neither harmful speech nor
falsehood, 78.35; 88.11

free from sin, 37.47; 52.23

neither excessive heat nor
biter cold, 76.13

there will be a known
provision, 37.41; 56.89

in peace and security,
15.46; 44.51, 55; 50.34

home of peace, 6.127

greetings in, 7.46; 10.10;
13.24; 14.23; 16.32;
19.62; 36.58; 39.73;
56.26

righteous will enter, 4.124;
42.22; 44.51, 39.73

been made to inherit 43.72

pleased with them and they
with Him, 5.119

My (Allah's) Paradise,
89.30

the greatest bliss, 9.72

the great success, 57.12;
64.9; 9.72; 44.57

for believers are Gardens
32.19

busy in joyful things that
Day, 36.35

water springs, 15.45;
19.63; 44.52; 52.17;
54.54; 55.46

see the angels surrounding
the Throne, 39.75; 54.55

all that they desire, 50.35

reclining on thrones,
36.55

of equal age, 78.33

Immortal boy-servants to

serve them, as pearls, 52.24; 56.17; 76.19

Parents, kindness to, 2.83, 215; 4.36; 16.90; 17.23; 29.8; 31.14; 46.15-17

'partners' of Allah, a falsehood, 4.116; 10.34, 35, 66; 16.86; 28.62-64, 71-75; 30.40; 42.21

Path (or way), 5.77; 16.94; 42.52, 53; 43.43; 90.11, 12

Patience, 3.186, 200; 10.109; 11.115; 16.126, 127; 20.130; 40.55, 77; 42.43; 46.35; 70.5; 73.10

seek help in, and prayer, 2.45, 153; 20.132; 50.39

Patient, will receive reward in full, 39.10

Allah is with those who are, 8.46 end tee, 11.115

in performing duties to Allah, 16.90 to be,

at the time of anger, 41.34

Peace, incline to, 8.61

Pearl and coral, preserved, 52.24; 55.-22; 56.23

Pen, 68.1; 96.4

Person, Allah burdens not a, beyond his scope, 2.286; 7.42

Allah tax not any, except according to his capacity, 23.62

and in what land he will die, 31.34

everyone confronted with all the good and evil done 3.30

pleading for himself, 16.111

every, is a pledge for what he has earned, 74.38

Allah swears by the self-reproaching, 75.2

Pharaoh, 28.6; 40.24

people of, 2.49; 3.11, 7.141; 44.17-33

drowned, 2.50

dealings with Moses, 7.103-137; 10.75-92

transgressed beyond bounds; 20.24; 69.9; 73.16; 85.17-20; 89.10-14

righteous wife, 28.8, 9

claims to be god, 28.38; 79.24

destroyed, 29.39

a believing man from Pharaoh's family, 40.28-44

building of a tower, 40.36, 37

Piling up of the worldly things, 102.1-4

Pledge, for Islam, 16.91

to the Messenger is a (pledge) to Allah, 48.10

of the Believers, 48.18; 60.12

Pledge, let there be a, 2.283

every person is a, for that which he has earned, 52.21; 74.38

Poetry, 36.69

Poets, 26.224-227; 69.41

Pomegranates, 6.141

Poor, 2.88, 177, 215, 273; 4.8, 36; 8.41; 9.60; 17.26; 24.22, 32; 30.38; 47.38; 51.19; 59.7, 8; 69.34; 74.44; 76.8; 89.18; 90.16; 93.8; 107.3

Prayer, 1.1-7; 3.8, 26, 27, 147, 191-194; 4.103; 17.80; 23.118

neither aloud nor in a low voice, 17.110

invocation for disbelievers, 9.113, 114

invocation of disbelievers, 13.14

He answers (the invocation of) those, 42.26

Prayers, five obligatory, seek help in patience and, 2.45, 153; 20.132; 50.39

facing towards Qibla, 2.142-145, 149, 150

guard strictly the, 2.238

in travel and attack, 2.239;

4.101, 102

approach not when in a drunken state, 4.43

nor in a state of Janabah, 4.43

purifying for, 4.43; 5.6

when finished the, 4.103

times of, 11.114; 17.78, 79; 20.130; 30.17, 18; 50.39, 40; 52.48, 49; 73.16, 20

prostration for Allah Alone, 13.15

Prayers, Friday, 62.9-11

Precautions in danger, 4.71

Prisoners of war, 8.67-71

Promise of Truth, 46.16,17

Property, 2.188;3.186;4.5,7,29;51.1 9;59.7-9;70.25

Prophets, 3.33, 34, 146; 4.163; 5.20; 6.8490; 23.23-50; 57.26

promises of the, 3.81; 33.7-8 illegal for, 3.161

an enemy for every, 6.112; 25.31

Prostration, to Allah falls in, whoever in the heavens and the earth and so do their shadows, 13.15

Provision, 10.59; 13.26; 14.32; 16.73, 34.36, 39; 42.12; 51.57; 67.21; 79.33

Psalms, 4.163

Punishment, postponing of, 3.178

cutting of hands or feet, 5.33

punish them with the like of that with which you were afflicted, 16.126

of this life and Hereafter, 24.19; 68.33

Purifying, bodily, 4.43; 5.6;

spiritually 87.14; 91.9

Q

Qadr, Sura97
Qáf, Sura 50
Qalam, Sura 68
Qamar, Sura 54
Qári'ah, Sura 101.
Qaroon (*Korah*), 28.76-82;
29.39

a manifest light, 4.174;
42.52
revealed, 6.19
Allah is Witness to it, 6.19
clear proof, 6.157
falsehood about verses of,
6.68
Reminder, 7.63; 12.104;
18.101; 20.3, 99,124;
25.29; 36.11, 69; 43.44;
50.8; 65.10; 72.17
when recited, 7.204
Dhikr, 7.205; 15.6, 9
Book of Wisdom, 10.1;
31.2; 36.2
inspired Message, 10.2,
109; 42.52
those reject it, 11.17
in Arabic, 12.2; 13.37;
16.103; 20.113; 26.195;
39.28; 41.3, 44; 42.7;
43.3; 44.58; 46.12
revealed in stages,
15.91; 17.106; 25.32;
76.23
change of verse, 16.10
recite the, 16.98, 17.78
guides, 17.9
good news and warning,
17.9, 10.
and the disbelievers,
17.45-47
healing and mercy, 17.82
similitude and example,
17.89; 18.54; 39.27
easy, 19.97; 44.58; 54.17,
22, 32, 40
confirmed by the
Scriptures, 26.196
narrates to the Children of

Qasas, Sura28.
Qibla, 2.142-145, 149
Qisas (Law of equality in
punishment), 2.178, 179,
194; 5.45; 16.126; 17.33;
22.60; 42.40
Quran, described, 13.31,
36, 37; 14.1; 56.77-80
is not such as could ever
Israel, 27.76
recite and pray, 29.45
Truth from Allah, 32.3;
35.31
on blessed Night, 44.3
think deeply in the, 47.24
warn by the, 50.45
taught by Allah, 55.1
honorable recital, well-
guarded, 56.77, 78
non can touch but who are
pure, 56.79
if sent down on a
mountain, 59.21
an anguish for the
disbelievers, 69.50
an absolute truth with
certainty, 69.51
recite in a slow style, 73.4
in Records held in honor,
kept pure and holy,
80.13-16
disbelievers belie, 84.22
Tablet preserved, 85.22
Word that separates the
truth from falsehood,
86.13
reciting pure pages, 98.2
Quraish, Sura 106
Quraish,
disbelievers of, 54.43-46,
51
faming of, 106.1-4

R

Rabbis, 9.31,34
Race, strive as in a, in
good deeds, 5.48
Raid, Sura 13
Rahmán, Sura 55
Raiment of righteousness

be produced by other than
Allah, 2.23; 10.38; 11.13;
17.88
had it been from other than
Allah, 4.82

is better, 7.26
Rain,
Allah's Gift, 56.68-70
of stones, 27.58
Ramadan, 2.185
Ransom,
none, shall be taken, 57.15
offered by disbelievers,
3.91; 10.54; 13.18
Fidyah (Compensation), of
fast, 2.196;
for freeing the captives,
8.67
Rass, dwellers of the,
25.38; 50.12
Reality, 69.1 -3
Recompense, the Day of,
1.4; 37.20; 51.12; 56.56;
82.17, 18; 96.7
deniers of, 107.1 -7
of an evil is an evil like
thereof, 42.40
Reconciliation, whoever
forgives and makes, 42.40
between man and wife,
4.35
between believers, 49.9, 10
Record,
a Register inscribed, 83.7-
9, 18-21
each nation will be called
to its, 45.28, 29
written pages of deeds of
every person, 81.10
which speaks the truth,
23.62
in right hand, 69.19; 84.7-9
in left hand, 69.25
behind the back, 84.10-15
Recording angels, 50.17;
18, 23; 85.11

Notes

Notes

Notes

Notes

Notes